Lecture Notes in Computer Science 8340

Commenced Publication in 1973
Founding and Former Series Editors:
Gerhard Goos, Juris Hartmanis, and Jan van Leeuwen

Artiom Alhazov   Svetlana Cojocaru
Marian Gheorghe   Yurii Rogozhin
Grzegorz Rozenberg   Arto Salomaa (Eds.)

Membrane Computing

14th International Conference, CMC 2013
Chişinău, Republic of Moldova, August 20-23, 2013
Revised Selected Papers

 Springer

Volume Editors

Artiom Alhazov
Svetlana Cojocaru
Yurii Rogozhin
Academy of Sciences of Moldova, Institute of Mathematics and Computer Science
5, Academiei Str, Chişinău, MD-2028, Republic of Moldova
E-mail: {artiom, svetlana.cojocaru, rogozhin}@math.md

Marian Gheorghe
University of Sheffield, Department of Computer Science
211 Portobello Street, Sheffield S1 4DP, UK
E-mail: m.gheorghe@sheffield.ac.uk

Grzegorz Rozenberg
Leiden University, Leiden Center of Advanced Computer Science (LIACS)
Niels Bohrweg 1, 2333 CA Leiden, The Netherlands
E-mail: rozenber@liacs.nl

Arto Salomaa
Turku Centre for Computer Science (TUCS)
Leminkaisenkatu 14, 20520 Turku, Finland
E-mail: asalomaa@cs.utu.fi

ISSN 0302-9743   e-ISSN 1611-3349
ISBN 978-3-642-54238-1   e-ISBN 978-3-642-54239-8
DOI 10.1007/978-3-642-54239-8
Springer Heidelberg New York Dordrecht London

Library of Congress Control Number: 2014930331

CR Subject Classification (1998): F.1.1-2, F.2.1-2, D.2.2, D.3

LNCS Sublibrary: SL 1 – Theoretical Computer Science and General Issues

Typesetting: Camera-ready by author, data conversion by Scientific Publishing Services, Chennai, India

Printed on acid-free paper

Springer is part of Springer Science+Business Media (www.springer.com)

Preface

This volume contains a selection of papers presented at CMC 14, the 14th International Conference on Membrane Computing, held in Chişinău, Republic of Moldova, during August 20-23, 2013 (*http://www.math.md/cmc14/*).

The CMC series was initiated by Gheorghe Păun as the Workshop on Multiset Processing in the year 2000. Then two workshops on Membrane Computing were organized in Curtea de Argeş, Romania, in 2001 and 2002. A selection of papers from these three meetings were published as volume 2235 of the *Lecture Notes in Computer Science* series, as a special issue of *Fundamenta Informaticae* (volume 49, numbers 1–3, 2002), and as volume 2597 of *Lecture Notes in Computer Science*. The next six workshops were organized in Tarragona, Spain (in July 2003), Milan, Italy (in June 2004), Vienna, Austria (in July 2005), Leiden, The Netherlands (in July 2006), Thessaloniki, Greece (in June 2007), and Edinburgh, UK (in July 2008), with the proceedings published in *Lecture Notes in Computer Science* as volumes 2933, 3365, 3850, 4361, 4860, and 5391, respectively. The 10th workshop returned to Curtea de Argeş in August 2009 (LNCS volume 5957).

From the year 2010, the series of meetings on membrane computing continued as the Conference on Membrane Computing with the 2010, 2011, and 2012 editions held in Jena, Germany (LNCS volume 6501), Fontainebleau, France (LNCS volume 7184) and Budapest, Hungary (LNCS volume 7762). Today a Steering Committee takes care of the continuation of the CMC series, which is organized under the auspices of the European Molecular Computing Consortium (EMCC). A regional version of CMC, the Asian Conference on Membrane Computing, ACMC, started with the 2012 edition in Wuhan, China, and continued with the 2013 edition in Chengdu, China.

CMC 14 was organized by the Institute of Mathematics and Computer Science (IMCS) of the Academy of Sciences of Moldova Republic in conjunction with the International Conference on Intelligent Information Systems, IIS 2013. These two conferences represent the starting point of a series of events dedicated to the 50th anniversary of IMCS, celebrated in April 2014. A special session organized in connection with IIS was dedicated to the memory of Prof. Yuri Pechersky, the founder of artificial intelligence research at IMCS. These two conferences obtained extensive media coverage in the Republic of Moldova. On August 20 the major news program of the national broadcasting television station started with comprehensive reportage on the opening session of CMC 14 and IIS 2013. Other radio and television stations also provided news and presented interviews with organizers and participants of the conferences. On August 22, "Literatura şi Arta" (Literature and Art), the weekly main cultural newspaper in Moldova, published an article about these conferences as well as about Artiom Alhazov's Doctor habilitation defence.

On the first day a special session with invited speakers from both CMC 14 and IIS 2013 was organized for the participants. In the afternoon, Dr. Artiom Alhazov defended his Doctoral habilitation thesis, "Small Abstract Machines" (*http://www.cnaa.md/en/thesis/24558/*), in front of a panel with scientists from six countries.

The Program Committee of CMC 14 invited lectures from Jozef Gruska (Brno, Czech Republic), Gheorghe Păun (Bucharest, Romania/Seville, Spain), Marian Gheorghe (Sheffield, UK), Alberto Leporati (Milan, Italy), Petr Sosík (Opava, Czech Republic), and Sergey Verlan (Paris, France). Based on the votes of the CMC 14 participants, the Best Paper Award of this year's CMC conference was given to Alberto Leporati, Giancarlo Mauri, Antonio E. Porreca, and Claudio Zandron for their paper "Enzymatic Numerical P Systems Using Elementary Arithmetic Operations".

In addition to the texts of the invited talks, this volume contains 16 papers out of 26 presented at the conference. Each paper was subject to at least two referee reports for the conference and of an additional one for this volume.

The editors warmly thank the Program Committee, the invited speakers, the authors of the papers, the reviewers, and all the participants for their contributions to the success of CMC 14.

November 2013

Artiom Alhazov
Svetlana Cojocaru
Marian Gheorghe
Yurii Rogozhin
Grzegorz Rozenberg
Arto Salomaa

Organization

Steering Committee

Gabriel Ciobanu	Iaşi, Romania
Erzsébet Csuhaj-Varjú	Budapest, Hungary
Rudolf Freund	Vienna, Austria
Marian Gheorghe	Sheffield, UK - Chair
Vincenzo Manca	Verona, Italy
Maurice Margenstern	Metz, France
Giancarlo Mauri	Milan, Italy
Linqiang Pan	Wuhan, China
Gheorghe Păun	Bucharest, Romania/Seville, Spain
Mario J. Pérez-Jiménez	Seville, Spain
Petr Sosík	Opava, Czech Republic
Sergey Verlan	Paris, France

Organizing Committee

Artiom Alhazov	Chişinău, Moldova
Lyudmila Burtseva	Chişinău, Moldova
Svetlana Cojocaru	Chişinău, Moldova
Alexandru Colesnicov	Chişinău, Moldova
Ludmila Malahov	Chişinău, Moldova
Olga Popcova	Chişinău, Moldova
Yurii Rogozhin	Chişinău, Moldova

Program Committee

Artiom Alhazov	Chişinău, Moldova – Co-chair
Gabriel Ciobanu	Iaşi, Romania
Alexandru Colesnicov	Chişinău, Moldova
Erzsébet Csuhaj-Varjú	Budapest, Hungary
Giuditta Franco	Verona, Italy
Rudolf Freund	Vienna, Austria
Marian Gheorghe	Sheffield, UK – Co-chair
Thomas Hinze	Cottbus, Germany
Florentin Ipate	Bucharest, Romania
Alberto Leporati	Milan, Italy
Vincenzo Manca	Verona, Italy

Table of Contents

A Kernel P Systems Survey

Marian Gheorghe[1] and Florentin Ipate[2]

[1] Department of Computer Science
University of Sheffield
Portobello Street, Regent Court, Sheffield, S1 4DP, UK
m.gheorghe@sheffield.ac.uk
[2] Department of Computer Science
University of Bucarest
Str Academiei, 14, Bucarest, Romania
florentin.ipate@ifsoft.ro

Abstract. In this short paper one overviews the two years development of kernel P systems (kP systems for short), a basic class of P systems combining features of different variants of such systems. The definition of kP systems is given, some examples illustrate various features of the model and the most significant results are presented.

1 Introduction

Membrane computing, a branch of natural computing, is a well-established body of research and many models have been introduced and studied [5,6]. Such models are called P systems and many variants have been considered. The concept of *kernel P system (kP system)* has ben introduced in [2] in order to include the most used concepts from P systems into a single, coherent setting which allows various solutions to a certain problem to be specified, compared and formally verified.

Kernel P systems use a graph-like structure (like the so called, *tissue P systems*) of the model, with a set of symbols, labels of membranes, and rules of various types. The rules selected against the multiset of objects available in each compartment are executed in accordance with well-defined execution strategies. These rules are responsible for either transforming and moving objects between compartments or for changing the structure of the model.

The model has been revised in [3] and is now equipped with a specification language, called kP-lingua, allowing a problem to be specified and then automatically translated into a model-checker that helps verifying its correctness. A software platform, called kPWorkbench, supports the kP-lingua verification process [8].

We first introduce some preliminary definitions, then present some examples and results, and end this paper with a brief description of the kP-lingua specification language.

A. Alhazov et al. (Eds.): CMC 2013, LNCS 8340, pp. 1–9, 2014.

2   Definitions, Examples and Main Results

We consider that standard concepts like strings, multisets, rewriting rules, and computation are well-known and point to [6] as a reference in this respect. First we introduce the key concept of a compartment.

Definition 1. *T is a set of compartment types, $T = \{t_1, \ldots, t_s\}$, where $t_i = (R_i, \sigma_i)$, $1 \leq i \leq s$, consists of a set of rules, R_i, and an execution strategy, σ_i, defined over $Lab(R_i)$, the labels of the rules of R_i.*

The compartments introduced by the definition of the kP systems will be instantiated from the compartment types defined above.

Definition 2. *A kernel P (kP) system of degree n is a tuple*

$$k\Pi = (A, \mu, C_1, \ldots, C_n, i_0),$$

where A is a finite set of elements called objects; *μ defines the* membrane structure, *which is a graph, (V, E), where V are vertices indicating components, and E edges; $C_i = (t_i, w_i)$, $1 \leq i \leq n$, is a* compartment *of the system consisting of a compartment type from T and an* initial multiset, *w_i over A; i_0 is the* output compartment *where the result is obtained.*

The inner part of each compartment is called *region*, which is delimited by a *membrane*.

Each rule r may have a **guard** g, its generic form is $r \{g\}$. The rule r is applicable to a multiset w when its left hand side is contained into w and g is true for w. In the sequel we will analyse how the guards are specified and evaluated. The guards are constructed using multisets over A and relational and Boolean operators – like Boolean expressions. Before presenting the definition we introduce some notations.

For a multiset w over A and an element $a \in A$, we denote by $\#_a(w)$ the number of a's occurring in w. Let $Rel = \{<, \leq, =, \neq, \geq, >\}$ be the set of relational operators, $\gamma \in Rel$, a relational operator, a^n a multiset and $r \{g\}$ a rule with guard g.

Definition 3. *If g is the* abstract relational expression γa^n *and the current multiset is w, then the guard denotes the* relational expression $\#_a(w)\gamma n$. *The guard g is true for the multiset w if $\#_a(w)\gamma n$ is true.*

Let us consider the Boolean operators ¬ (negation), ∧ (conjunction) and ∨ (disjunction), listed w.r.t. decreasing precedence order. Abstract relational expressions can be connected by Boolean operators generating *abstract Boolean expressions*.

Definition 4. *If g is the* abstract Boolean expression *and the current multiset is w, then the guard denotes the* Boolean expression for w, *obtained by replacing abstract relational expressions with relational expressions for w. The guard g is true for the multiset w when the Boolean expression for w is true.*

Definition 5. *A guard is: (i) one of the Boolean constants* true *or* false*; (ii) an abstract relational expression; or (iii) an abstract Boolean expression.*

Example 1. *If the rule is* $r : ab \to c \ \{\geq a^5 \wedge \ \geq b^5 \vee \neg \ > c\}$, *then this can be applied iff the current multiset, w, includes the left hand side of r, i.e., ab and the guard is true for w - it has at least 5 a's and 5 b's or no more than a c.*

Definition 6. *A rule from a compartment $C_{l_i} = (t_{l_i}, w_{l_i})$ can have one of the following types:*

- *(a)* **rewriting and communication** *rule: $x \to y \ \{g\}$,*
  where $x \in A^+$ and y has the form $y = (a_1, t_1) \ldots (a_h, t_h)$, $h \geq 0$, $a_j \in A$ and t_j indicates a compartment type from T – see Definition 2 – with instance compartments linked to the current compartment; t_j might indicate the type of the current compartment, i.e., t_{l_i} – in this case it is ignored; if a link does not exist (the two compartments are not in E) then the rule is not applied; if a target, t_j, refers to a compartment type that has more than one instance connected to l_i, then one of them will be non-deterministically chosen;
- *(b)* **structure changing rules**; *the following types are considered:*
  - *(b1)* **membrane division** *rule: $[x]_{t_{l_i}} \to [y_1]_{t_{i_1}} \ldots [y_p]_{t_{i_p}} \ \{g\}$,*
    where $x \in A^+$ and y_j has the form $y_j = (a_{j,1}, t_{j,1}) \ldots (a_{j,h_j}, t_{j,h_j})$ like in rewriting and communication rules; the compartment l_i will be replaced by p compartments; the j-th compartment, instantiated from the compartment type t_{i_j} contains the same objects as l_i, but x, which will be replaced by y_j; all the links of l_i are inherited by each of the newly created compartments;
  - *(b2)* **membrane dissolution** *rule: $[]_{t_{l_i}} \to \lambda \ \{g\}$;*
    the compartment l_i will be destroyed together with its links;
  - *(b3)* **link creation** *rule: $[x]_{t_{l_i}} ; []_{t_{l_j}} \to [y]_{t_{l_i}} - []_{t_{l_j}} \ \{g\}$;*
    the current compartment is linked to a compartment of type t_{l_j} and x is transformed into y; if more than one instance of the compartment type t_{l_j} exists then one of them will be non-deterministically picked up; g is a guard that refers to the compartment instantiated from the compartment type t_{l_1};
  - *(b4)* **link destruction** *rule: $[x]_{t_{l_i}} - []_{t_{l_j}} \to [y]_{t_{l_i}} ; []_{t_{l_j}} \ \{g\}$;*
    is the opposite of link creation and means that the compartments are disconnected.

Input-output rules considered in [2] will be expressed as rewriting and communication rules.

2.1 kP System Execution Strategy

In kP systems the way in which rules are executed is defined for each compartment type t from T – see Definition 1. As in Definition 1, $Lab(R)$ is the set of labels of the rules R.

Definition 7. *For a compartment type* $t = (R, \sigma)$ *from* T *and* $r \in Lab(R)$, $r_1, \ldots, r_s \in Lab(R)$, *the execution strategy,* σ, *is defined by the following:*

- *$\sigma = \lambda$, means no rule from the current compartment will be executed;*
- *$\sigma = \{r\}$ – the rule r is executed;*
- *$\sigma = \{r_1, \ldots, r_s\}$ – one of the rules labelled $r_1, \ldots, r_s$ will be chosen non-deterministically and executed; if none is applicable then none is executed; this is called* alternative *or* choice;
- *$\sigma = \{r_1, \ldots, r_s\}^*$ – the rules are applied an arbitrary number of times (arbitrary parallelism);*
- *$\sigma = \{r_1, \ldots, r_s\}^\top$ – the rules are executed according to* maximal parallelism *strategy [6];*
- *$\sigma = \sigma_1 \& \ldots \& \sigma_s$, means executing sequentially $\sigma_1, \ldots, \sigma_s$, where σ_i, $1 \leq i \leq s$, describes any of the above cases, namely λ, one rule, a choice, arbitrary parallelism or maximal parallelism; if one of σ_i fails to be executed then the rest is no longer executed;*
- *for any of the above σ strategy only one single structure changing rule is allowed.*

The result of a computation will be the number of objects collected in the output compartment. For a kP systems $k\Pi$, the set of all these numbers will be denoted by $M(k\Pi)$.

2.2   kP System Examples

In this section we illustrate the newly introduced P system model with some examples.

Example 2. Let us consider the set of component types
$T = \{t_1, t_2, t_3\}$, where $t_1 = (R_1, \sigma_1)$, $t_2 = (R_2, \sigma_2)$, $t_3 = (R_3, \sigma_3)$, with
$R_1 = \{r_1 : a \to a(b, 2)(c, 3) \{\geq p\}; r_2 : p \to p; r_3 : p \to \lambda\}$, and $\sigma_1 = Lab(R_1)^\top$,
$R_2 = \{r_1 : b \to (b, 0)c \{\geq p\}; r_2 : p \to p; r_3 : p \to \lambda\}$, and $\sigma_2 = Lab(R_2)^\top$,
$R_3 = \emptyset$ and $\sigma_3 = Lab(R_3)^\top$.
A kP system with $n = 4$ compartments is $k\Pi_1 = (A, \mu, C_1, \ldots, C_4, 1)$, where
$A = \{a, b, c, p\}$, $C_1 = (t_1, w_{1,0})$, $C_2 = (t_2, w_{2,0})$, $C_3 = (t_2, w_{3,0})$, $C_4 = (t_3, w_{4,0})$;
with $w_{1,0} = a^3 p$, $w_{2,0} = w_{3,0} = p$, $w_{4,0} = \lambda$;
μ is given by the graph with nodes $\{C_1, C_2, C_3, C_4\}$ and edges $\{C_1, C_2\}, \{C_1, C_3\}$, $\{C_1, C_4\}$.

One can note that we do not use targets for objects meant to stay in the current compartment (i.e., we have $r_1 : a \to a(b, 2)(c, 3) \{\geq p\}$ instead of $r_1 : a \to (a, 1)(b, 2)(c, 3) \{\geq p\}$). The rule r_1 in R_2 simulates an input/output rule [2] which is meant to bring a c from the environment (0) and to send out a b instead.

In this example there are only rewriting and communication rules; some rules have a guard, $\geq p$, others do not have any and in each compartment the rules are applied in maximal parallel way in every step, as indicated by σ_j, $1 \leq j \leq 3$. As two instances of the compartment type t_2, C_2, C_3, appear in the system, when the rule r_1 from the compartment C_1 is applied, the object b goes non-deterministically to one of the two compartments labelled 2 (from t_2) as long as p remains in compartment C_1; object c goes always to the compartment C_4, of type t_3.

The initial configuration of $k\Pi_1$ is $M_0 = (a^3 p, p, p, \lambda)$. The only applicable rules are r_1, r_2 and r_3 from C_1 and r_2, r_3 from C_2, C_3. If r_1, r_2 are chosen in C_1 and r_2 in C_2, C_3, then $a^3 p$ is rewritten by r_1, r_2 in C_1 and p in C_2, C_3 by r_2; then three a's stay in C_1, three b's go non-deterministically to C_2, C_3, three c's go to compartment C_4, and each p in C_2, C_3 stays in its compartment. Let us assume that two of them go to C_2 and one to C_3. Hence, the next configuration is $M_1 = (a^3 p, b^2 p, bp, c^3)$. If in the next step the same rules are applied identically in the first compartment, C_1, and rules r_1, r_2 are used in C_2 and r_1, r_3 in C_3, then the next configuration is $M_2 = (a^3 p, b^2 c^2 p, bc, c^6)$. If now r_1, r_3 are used in C_1, with r_1 used in the same way and r_1, r_3 in C_2 (no rule is available in C_3) then $M_3 = (a^3, b^2 c^4, b^2 c, c^9)$; this is a final configuration as there is no p to trigger a further step.

Example 3. Let us reconsider the example above enriched with rules dealing with the system's structure. First the set T will be replaced by $T' = \{t_1, t_2', t_3\}$, where $t_2' = (R_2', \sigma_2')$, with $R_2' = R_2 \cup R_2^{str}$ and $\sigma_2' = Lab(R_2)^\top \& Lab(R_2^{str})$. We can notice that σ_2' tells us that first the rewriting and communication rules are applied in a maximal parallel manner and then one of system's structure rules is chosen to be executed. The set R_2^{str} denotes the set of membrane division rules for t_2', i.e., $R_2^{str} = \{r_4 : []_2 \to []_2[]_2 \{\geq b^2 \wedge \geq p\}\}$. The new kP system, denoted $k\Pi_2$, will have the following four compartments:
$C_1 = (t_1, w_{1,0}), C_2' = (t_2', w_{2,0}), C_3' = (t_2', w_{3,0}), C_4 = (t_3, w_{4,0})$.

If the system follows the same pathway as $k\Pi_1$ then M_2 shows a different configuration given that in C_2' after applying R_2 in a maximal parallel manner, R_2^{str} is applied as indicated by σ_2', when the guard of r_4 is true. The compartment C_2' is divided into two compartments, $C_{2,1}, C_{2,2}$, instantiated from the same compartment type t_2, with the content of C_2' and appearing on positions 2 and 3 in the new configuration, $M_2' = (a^3 p, b^2 c^2 p, b^2 c^2 p, bc, c^6)$; the new compartments, $C_{2,1}, C_{2,2}$, are linked to compartment C_1. Compartment C_3' is not divided as the guard of r_4 is not true for its current multiset. In the next step both $C_{2,1}, C_{2,2}$ are divided as they contain the guard triggering the membrane division rule r_4. The process will stop when either p will be rewritten to λ or b^2 stops coming to these compartments.

Remark 1. If we aim to dissolve one of the compartments instantiated from t_2, once a certain condition is true, for instance $\{\geq b^2 \wedge \geq c^2 \wedge \geq p\}$, then one more rule will be added to R_2^{str}, namely $r_5 : []_2 \to \lambda \{\geq b^2 \wedge \geq c^2 \wedge \geq p\}$. The expression σ_2' remains the same, but in this case R_2^{str} contains two elements and at most one is applied at each step, in every compartment with label 2. For this reason σ_2' can also be written as $Lab(R_2)^\top \& Lab(R_2^{str})$.

2.3 Neural-Like P Systems and P Systems with Active Membranes versus kP Systems

In order to prove how powerful and expressive kP systems are, we will show how two of the most used variants of P systems are simulated by kP systems. More precisely, we will show how neural-like P systems and P systems with active membranes are simulated by some reduced versions of kP systems. These results below are from [3].

Definition 8. *A neural-like P system (tissue P system with states) of degree n is a construct* $\Pi = (O, \sigma_1, \ldots \sigma_n, syn, i_0)$ *([5], p. 249), where:*

- *O is a finite, non-empty set of objects, the* alphabet;
- *$\sigma_i = (Q_i, s_{i,0}, w_{i,0}, R_i)$, $1 \le i \le n$, represents a* cell *and*
  - *Q_i is the finite set of* states *of cell σ_i;*
  - *$s_{i,0} \in Q_i$ is the* initial state;
  - *$w_{i,0} \in O^*$ is the* initial multiset *of objects contained in cell σ_i;*
  - *R_i is a finite set of* rewriting and communication rules, *of the form $sw \to s'xy_{go}z_{out}$; when such a rule is applied, x will replace w in cell σ_i, the objects from y will be sent to neighbouring cells, according to the transmission mode (see Remark 2) and the objects from z will be sent out into the environment; cell σ_i will move from state s to s';*
- *$syn \subseteq \{1, ..., n\} \times \{1, ..., n\}$, the connections between cells,* synapses;
- *i_0 is the output cell.*

Remark 2. We discuss here a special class of P systems introduced in Definition 8 that will help us to prove a first result.

1. For neural-like P systems, three processing modes are considered, called "max", "min", "par", and three transmission modes, namely "one", "repl", "spread". For formal definitions and other details we refer to [5].
2. We denote by *simple neural-like P systems* the class of P systems given by Definition 8, where the rewriting and communication rules have the form $sw \to s'x(a_1, t_1) \cdots (a_p, t_p)$, where t_h, $1 \le h \le p$, denotes the target cell (σ_h), and processing mode "max", transmission mode defined by the target indications mentioned in each rule.

Notation. For a given P system, Π, the set of numbers computed by Π will be denoted by $M(\Pi)$.

Theorem 1. *If Π is neural-like P system of degree n, then there is a kP system, Π', of degree n and using only rules of type (a), rewriting and communication rules, simulating Π and such that $M(\Pi') \subseteq M(\Pi) \cup \{2\}$.*

We study now how P systems with active membranes are simulated by kP systems. In this case we are dealing with a cell-like system, so the underlying structure is a tree and a set of labels (types) for the compartments of the system. The system will start with a number of compartments and its structure will evolve. In the study below it will be assumed that the number of compartments simultaneously present in the system is bounded.

Definition 9. *A P system with active membranes of initial degree n is a tuple (see [6], Chapter 11) $\Pi = (O, H, \mu, w_{1,0}, \ldots, w_{n,0}, R, i_0)$ where:*

- *O, $w_{1,0}, \ldots, w_{n,0}$ and i_0 are as in Definition 8;*
- *H is the set of labels for compartments;*
- *μ defines the tree structure associated with the system;*
- *R consists of rules of the following types*
  - *(a) rewriting rules: $[u \to v]_h^e$, for $h \in H$, $e \in \{+, -, 0\}$ (set of electrical charges), $u \in O^+$, $v \in O^*$;*
  - *(b) in communication rules: $u[]_h^{e_1} \to [v]_h^{e_2}$, for $h \in H$, $e_1, e_2 \in \{+, -, 0\}$, $u \in O^+$, $v \in O^*$;*
  - *(c) out communication rules: $[u]_h^{e_1} \to []_h^{e_2} v$, for $h \in H$, $e_1, e_2 \in \{+, -, 0\}$, $u \in O^+$, $v \in O^*$;*
  - *(d) dissolution rules: $[u]_h^e \to v$, for $h \in H \setminus \{s\}$, s denotes the skin membrane (the outmost one), $e \in \{+, -, 0\}$, $u \in O^+$, $v \in O^*$;*
  - *(e) division rules for elementary membranes: $[u]_h^{e_1} \to [v]_h^{e_2}[w]_h^{e_3}$, for $h \in H$, $e_1, e_2, e_3 \in \{+, -, 0\}$, $u \in O^+$, $v, w \in O^*$;*

The following result shows how a P system with active membranes starting with n_1 compartments and having no more than n_2 simultaneously present ones can be simulated by a kP system using only rules of type (a).

Theorem 2. *If Π is a P system with active membrane having n_1 initial compartments and utilising no more than n_2 compartments at any time, then there is a kP system, Π', of degree 1 and using only rules of type (a), rewriting and communication rules, such that Π' simulates Π.*

2.4 Solving 3-Col Problem

Many variants of P systems have been considered for solving NP-complete problems in an efficient way. We show now how one such problem, the 3-colouring (3-Col) problem, can be solved using kP systems. Another NP-complete problem, the partition problem, has been already solved using kP systems [3,7]. The 3-Col problem has been already solved in linear time by recogniser tissue P systems with cell division and symport/antiport rules [1]. A solution for the 3-Col problem by using kP systems has been provided in [4]. Here we just reproduce this solution.

Theorem 3. *The 3-Col problem for a graph with n, $n \geq 2$, nodes can be solved by a kP system with two types of compartments, two initial compartments, $n(n-1)/2 + 7n + 10$ objects, $2n$ division rules and $2n + 7$ rewriting and communication rules. An answer to whether a solution exists or not is obtained in at most $2n + 3$ steps using maximum $3^n + 1$ compartments.*

3   Specification Language for kP Systems

The specification language allows to describe problems and then, by using kp-Workbench, one can simulate and verify them. The language uses two key concepts:

1. Type definitions - encompassing the instruction set, organised in accordance with the type's associated execution strategy.
2. Instance definitions and interlinking - establish the set of compartments and related connections, assembling the graph-like structure of comprtments.

A type is declared using the keyword **type** followed by the name of the type. The body of a type declaration consists of a succession of guarded rules or rule ensembles (choice, arbitrary execution and maximal parallel execution blocks) as specified in the type's execution strategy. A rule is represented as a guarded transition, symbolised by an arrow, between two terms. We illustrate the syntax of a type definition and its constituents with a simple example:

Example 4. A type definition in kP–Lingua.

```
type C1 {
    2a, 3b -> c .
    >= 2c & > 2b : b, c -> a .

    choice {
        b -> 2b .
        < 3b : b ->  3b .
    }

    max {
      a -> a, a(C2), {a, 2b}(C3) .
    }

    = 5a : a -> [3a, 3b](C1) [3b](C2) [3a](C3) .
}
```

In this example we define type C1 with the following sequence of rules: a rewriting rule which takes two a objects and three b objects and produces a c; a guarded rewriting rule which yields an object a if and only if there are at least two c's and more than two b's in the compartment the rule is applied on; next we have a **choice** block with two rewriting rules of which one is guarded, followed by a maximally parallel block where the rewrite communication rule is exhaustively executed, producing an object a inside the membrane and sending an object a to compartments of type C2, one a and two b's to membranes of type C3 respectively; finally, a guarded membrane division rule takes one object a and divides the compartment into three distinct compartments of types C1, C2, C3 respectively, if the number of a's in the membrane is precisely five.

Acknowledgement. The work of MG and FI was partially supported by the MuVet project, Romanian National Authority for Scientific Research (CNCS – UEFISCDI), grant number PN-II-ID-PCE-2011-3-0688.

References

1. Díaz-Pernil, D., Gutiérrez-Naranjo, M.A., Pérez-Jiménez, M.J.: A Uniform Family of Tissue P Systems with Cell Division Solving 3-COL in a Linear Time. Theoretical Computer Science 404, 76–87 (2008)
2. Gheorghe, M., Ipate, F., Dragomir, C.: Kernel P Systems. In: Martínez-del-Amor, M.A., Păun, G.H., Romero-Campero, F. (eds.) Membrane Computing, Tenth Brainstorming Week, BWMC 2012, Sevilla, Spain, pp. 153–170. Universidad de Sevilla (February 2012)
3. Gheorghe, M., Ipate, F., Dragomir, C., Mierlă, L., Valencia-Cabrera, L., García-Quismondo, M., Pérez-Jiménez, M.J.: Kernel P Systems – Version I. In: Valencia-Cabrera, L., García-Quismondo, M., Macías-Ramos, L.F. (eds.) Membrane Computing, Eleventh Brainstorming Week, BWMC 2013, Sevilla, Spain, pp. 97–124. Universidad de Sevilla (February 2013)
4. Gheorghe, M., Ipate, F., Lefticaru, R., Pérez-Jiménez, M.J., Turcanu, A., Valencia, L., García-Quismondo, M., Mierlă, L.: 3-COL Problem Modelling Using Simple Kernel P Systems. International Journal of Computer Mathematics 90(4), 816–830 (2013)
5. Păun, Gh.: Membrane Computing: An Introduction. Springer (2002)
6. Gh. Păun, G., Rozenberg, A., Salomaa, A.: The Oxford Handbook of Membrane Computing. Oxford University Press (2010)
7. http://www.p-lingua.org/mecosim/doc/case_studies/partition.html – Partition case study at MeCoSim web page
8. http://muvet.ifsoft.ro/kpworkbench/ – kPWorkbench webpage

Roads to New Grand Challenges of Informatics
(Extended Abstract)

Jozef Gruska

Faculty of Informatics
Masaryk University
Brno, Czech Republic
gruska@fi.muni.cz

1 A Birth of Modern Informatics

Currently dominating perception of computer science has its origin in in a very cleverly written, and much influential, paper of *Newel, Simon and Perlis*, published in Science in 1967, that well captured the perception of the field at that time.

The basic ideas presented in their paper were:

"*Whenever there are phenomena there can be a science dealing with these phenomena. Phenomena breed sciences. Since there are computers, there is computer science. The phenomena surrounding computers are varied, complex and rich.*"

There are nowadays a variety of reasons why such a computer-centric view of the field should be seen as very obsolete, not broad and not deep enough, and actually damaging the development of the field. They will be discussed only briefly in this paper, for details see [2]. Here are some of them.

– An understanding starts to be developed that information processing plays the key role both in physical and biological nature. For example, quantum, DNA and molecular information processing do that. In particular, an understanding has developed that information processing is of such an importance for life as breathing and eating and that even very primitive live being can perform exceptionally well exceptionally complex information processing surprisingly efficiently.

– All natural sciences, and not only these sciences, are starting be be increasingly seen as being, to a large extend at least, information processing driven. Actually, it starts to be understood that all sciences start to converge, in an important way, to informatics once they are seen in a proper broadness and deepness.

– On a more practical level, it starts to be clear that in the coming future any very significant innovation will have to use advanced informatics tools, methods and paradigms.

All that requires that a much broader and deeper view of the field should be taken and developed, see [1] for details.

A. Alhazov et al. (Eds.): CMC 2013, LNCS 8340, pp. 10–18, 2014.

2   Informatics and Information Processing in Nature

Two big discoveries led to an understanding that natural sciences are information processing driven.

The first one was the discovery, by Francis Crick and James Watson, in 1953, of the twin-corkscrew structure of DNA and how genetic information is encoded into DNA - followed by a demonstration, due to Adleman, how DNA computing could be performed and that it has a potential for remarkable efficiency.

The second one was the discovery of quantum teleportation and of the unconditionally secure quantum generation of shared random classical key, by Charles Bennett et al. during years 1984-1993 - followed by the demonstration due to Shor, in 1994-1996, that quantum information processing can be, inspite of damaging impacts of environments, performed and has also a potential for remarkable efficiency.

These discoveries changed views on physics and biology that started to be seen and explored as being, to a significant extent, information processing driven sciences.

From that it has been only a natural and logical step to see other natural sciences in this way, as being to an important degree information processing driven - and a new revolution in the study of natural and also other sciences has emerged.

Of importance has been also an observation that there are primitive one cell organisms, like paramecium (from 50 to 350 μm in length), that do information processing par excellence in order to find foods, to avoid predators, to find a mate and to have sex - without having any synapses.

All that converged to a view that information processing is for life of key importance in many way, and led, step by step, to an intensive development and exploration of various by living nature inspired models of information processing. Membrane computing has been one of them and one of the more deeply explored one with a variety of interesting outcomes and as the one behind new computation paradigms.

These discoveries also started to bring new views on the goals and relations between such fundamental sciences as physics, biology an informatics.

Let us first go to look to the relation between physics and informatics. One can surely say that:

The main goal of *Physics* can be seen as to study laws, limitations and phenomena of the *physical worlds*.

Physics has been extremely successful in pursuing its goal and one of the key role by that played an understanding that it is useful to consider many physical worlds and to take quite broad, deep and also futuristic/mathematical approach in doing that.

The main goal of *Informatics* can be seen, in an analogous way, as to study laws, limitations and phenomena of the *information worlds*.

It started to be also clear that also informatics needs to concentrate on the study of various natural, real and virtual information processing worlds.

Physics and Informatics can therefore be seen as representing two windows through which we could and should try to perceive and understand the worlds around us.

In a similar way we can see life-sciences and Informatics as providing two windows and tools with which we try to understand, imitate and outperform the biological world and its highlights - human (physical) brain, mind, consciousness, and cognitive capabilities.

Concerning Physics, information started to be considered also as a very important physical concept, especially in the connection with the *Black hole paradox*.[1]

John Archibald Wheeler, a famous physicists, and one that coined the term *black hole*, expressed his view on the role of information in physics in the following way:

I think of my lifetime in physics as divided into three periods. In the first period ...I was in the grip of the idea that everything is particle. I see my second period as believing that everything is field. Now I am in the grip of a new vision. Namely, that that everything is *information*.

In particular he said: *"I have been led to think of analogies between the way a computer works and the way the universe works. The computer is built on yes-no logic. So, perhaps is the universe ... The universe and all that it contains ("it") may arose from the myriad yes-no choices of measurements (the "bits").*

By Wheeler, *Information has some connection to existence, a view he advertised with the slogan "It from bit"* - or, in other words, that *"Everything is information"*.

A similar position was actually taken by another famous physicist, W. Heisenberg, quite long time ago:

I think that modern physics has definitely decided in favour of Plato. In fact the smallest units of matter are not physical objects in the ordinary sense: they are forms, ideas which can be expressed unambiguously only in mathematical language.

3   A New Perception of Informatics

A new perception of the informatics here presented see the field as consisting of four much interleaved components:

- scientific informatics;
- technological informatics;
- new methodology;
- applied informatics.

---

[1] It is known that black holes evaporate. It is known that information that gets into black holes cannot get out. All that means that information can disappear. However, quantum mechanics says that information cannot be lost. Quantum gravity theory therefore says that information can get lost - quantum mechanics that it cannot. Both theories has already turned out as being excellent in describing universe or microworld.

As a scientific discipline of a very broad scope and deep nature, Informatics has many goals. Its main task is to discover, explore and exploit in depth, the laws, limitations, paradigms, concepts, models, theories, phenomena, structures and processes of both natural and virtual information processing worlds.

To achieve its tasks, scientific Informatics concentrates on new, information processing based, understanding of the universe, evolution, nature, life (both natural and artificial), brain and mind processes, intelligence, creativity, information storing, processing and transmission systems and tools, complexity, security, and other basic phenomena of information processing worlds.

Development and analysis of a variety of formal, descriptional, computation, interaction and communication models and modes, development and analysis of (deterministic, randomized, genetic, evolutionary, quantum, ...) algorithms, protocols and games are some of the main tools of Informatics.

Data, information, knowledge, formal systems, logics, algorithms, protocols, games, resources, models and modes of information processing, communication and interactions are the key concepts behind.

In order to meet its goals, informatics develops close relations with other sciences and technology fields, especially with physics and biology, on one hand, and with electronics and nanotechnologies on the other hand.

The basis of the relationship between informatics and the natural sciences rests on the fact that information carriers are always elements of the physical, biological or chemical worlds, and consequently information processing is governed and constrained by their laws and limitations.

Informatics as a science includes also numerous theories much needed for its development to depth and in broadness. Some theories are very abstract, others quite specific, and some theories are oriented on making better use of the outcomes of the scientific informatics to create a scientific basis of informatics as of an engineering/technology discipline.

One way to illustrate such a broad and deep perception of scientific informatics will be in this paper through a presentation and analysis of its grand challenges. They will be discussed briefly below. In the same way one can illustrate main tasks of technological and applied informatics, but this is beyond the scope of this paper, see [1] for details.

3.1   Grand Challenges of Scientific Informatics

New main grand challenges of scientific informatics can be briefly summarized as follows:

- To explore our world as a point in the space of potential information processing worlds.
- To explore laws and limitations of information processing that governs universe, evolution and life.
- To develop theoretical foundations for design, analysis, verification, security, simulation and modeling of huge information processing systems

- To understand intelligence, creativity, mind and consciousness.
- To make foundations for science and engineering of the science making activities.
- To understand and manage all aspects of computation, communication and structural complexity.

4   Informatics-Driven Methodology

Of a key importance for a new perception of informatics is also an understanding that informatics, as a symbiosis of a scientific and a technology discipline, develops also basic ingredients of a new, in addition to theory and experiments, the third basic methodology for all sciences, technologies and society in general.

This new, informatics-based or informatics-driven, methodology provides a new way of thinking and a new language for sciences and technologies, extending the Galilean mathematics-based approach to new heights.

Main components of this new methodology can be briefly summarized as follows:

- Modeling - design and study of information processing models of phenomena and processes.
- Simulation methods and systems.
- Visualisation and animation.
- Searching (sophisticated search as an alternative to deep knowledge based reasoning)
- Design and exploration of systems with human and even superhuman intelligence.
- Design of systems for mechanized problem solving and reasoning.
- Development of methods to specify, design, analyse, verify and reliably run complex (information processing) systems.
- Design of algorithms, study of their performances and study of inherent complexities of computational, communication and description systems as a way to get deep understanding of various phenomena and of their interrelations.
- Design, analysis and comparison of descriptional languages and systems and of the relations between objects and their specifications.
- Transformation of the study of problems of the real world to the study of problems of information processing worlds.

Informatics-driven methodology subsumes and extends the role and improves tools mathematics used to play in advising, guiding and serving other scientific and technology disciplines and society in general.

Power of new methodology is discussed in details in [1]. Here are only few of the reasoning:

- Informatics-driven methodology brings new dimension to both old methodologies;

- It brings into new heights an enormous power of modeling, simulations and visualisation for knowledge acquisition and utilisation;
- It utilises an enormous exploratory and discovery power of automata, algorithms and complexity considerations.
- It utilizes enormous discovery and exploratory power of the correctness and truth searching considerations, systems and tools.
- It utilizes an enormous potential that the study of virtual worlds brings for an understanding of the real worlds.
- It seems to have a big chance to make hard sciences from (at least some) soft sciences.

5 Life, Brain and Informatics

Our optimism that science starts to be in the position to understand life and especially brain processes and that technology starts to be in the position to simulate them using different, more efficient and more reliable substrates is bases on some belief, on the advances of the GNR-revolution and on successes in the genome engineering, in the reverse engineering of the human brain, and in our understanding that we are to have soon information processing technology available to outperform information processing potential of all human brains - see [3].

Some of the basic beliefs/assumptions behind these developments are: (a) We are able to use our own thinking to understanding our own thinking; (b) Our intelligence is just above the critical threshold necessary to for us to scale our own ability to unrestricted heights of creative power.

Science's understanding of life is based on the Darwinian evolution by natural selection, and selection is, in its essence, information processing. Virtually all forms of life, including humans, are descendants from their ancestors, by the transmission of DNA. DNA information storage function alone is the reason enough to regard the life, as in essence, an information processing process. Therefore, in a deep biological sense, computing is as much a part of the life as eating and breathing.

Concerning the developments in technology, so called GNR-revolution is seen as the key factor. Here "G' stands for genetics, "N" for nanotechnology and "R" for robotics (actually for the whole artificial intelligence).

Genetics tries to harvest information processing features of the biological nature. *Nanotechnology* gives us tools to play with atoms and molecules and therefore our possibilities to create new materials and things, and even to print many of them, appear as unlimited. Nanotechnology paves also roads to the increasing performance and decreasing miniaturization of processors. *Robotics*, or better all artificial intelligence, tries to design superintendent systems robots/humans.[2]

---

[2] Nanobots, robots of nanoscale, are seen as very important tools to brows in human bodies to collect information and to deliver drugs and in this way to contribute much to our attempts to reach longevity and to beat natural death - see [3].

Another foundation of the conviction that reverse engineering of the brain and simulation of the brain is based on the progress in these areas and in the belief/understanding that needed information processing potential is likely to be soon available.

For example, by the neuroscientist Lloyd Watts, "*At about the turn of the 21-st century, we passed a detectable turning point in both neuroscience knowledge and computing power. For the first time in the history, we collectively know enough about our own brains, and have developed such advanced computing technology, that we can now seriously undertake the construction of a verifiable, real-time, high-resolution models of significant parts of our brains.*"

Concerning the information processing potential needed to outperform ingenious, but very slow (comparing to the speed of electronic circuits) and not much reliable, biological brains, they are based on two estimations - of information processing of brains and of the expected information processing technologies.

A number of estimations have already been made concerning the information processing potential of brains - see, for example, [4,5]. They are reasonably similar with respect to the order-of-magnitude estimations. Estimations are based on replications of the functionality of brain regions that have already been reverse engineered (that is their functionality understood) at human levels of performance. Estimation of the computational capacity of a region is then multiplied by the number of regions. Estimations are based on the functional simulations of a region and not on simulations of each neuron and interneural connection in the region. These estimation put the total number of elementary computations in the brain to $10^{14} - 10^{16}$ per second.

These estimations, as well as estimations concerning the development of information rocessing technology based on the Moore law, and on the developments in new information processing technologies, shows that around 2040-50 we could have not only supercomputers, but actually even laptops with information processing potential outperforming all human brains - see [3].[3]

6   Informatics and New Megachallenges of Science and Technology

Because of its enormous guiding power for practically all areas of science, technology and and many other components of society as well as enormously powerful tools Informatics offers, we can see Informatics as a new queen and at the same time a new powerful servant for all sciences, technologies and for all society.[4]

---

[3] Performance of top supercomputers, in the November lists and in petaflops: 1.7 in 2009, 2.6 in 2010, 10.5 in 2011, 17.6 in 2012, 33.8 in 2013 - 20 times increase in 3.5 years.

[4] There has ever been a "queen of science" with very broad impacts, also on all education. Some examples: (a) Medicine in Padua and at the same time theology in Paris in 17th century; (b) Philology at the Renaissance; (c) Mathematics after the Galileo time due to its methodological impacts and physics in the 20th century during its impacts on industrial revolution and other areas of science and technology. This view was well captured by Ernest Rutherford (1912), who said *In Science there is only Physics: all the rest is stamps collecting.*

In particular Informatics is expected to play the key role in dealing with two main megachallenges of the current science, technology and society. Namely:

- **To beat natural human intelligence.** More exactly, to create super-powerful non-biological intelligence and its merge with biological intelligence.
- **To beat natural human death**. More exactly, to increase much longevity for human bodies and to achieve uploading for human minds. In more details, to fight natural death as another disease and to find ways to upload human mind to a non-biological substrate.

We start to have enough reasons to see the above megachallenges as being currently realistic enough to pursue them. Here are some of them.

- Since computers performance keeps developing not only very fast, exponentially fast, and actually faster faster, there are good reasons to assume that we can have soon (around 2045?) information processing power and capacity larger than of all human brains - see [3].
- Exponential scaling up concerns not only of the development in computers, but actually of all main information processing technologies, especially genetic and nanotechnologies as well as artificial intelligence. This creates another basis for seeing both of the above mentioned megachallenges as already feasible ones.
- Exponential developments of all information processing related technologies are believed to lead also to enormous speed ups in developments of all sciences and technologies to such an extend that what is nowadays seen as needed several hundred years to come will actually happen in several tenth of years.
- Of special importance is that tools to reverse engineering brains keep also developing exponentially, concerning their potential, precision, speed and cost, and so we can assume to have quite soon ways to simulate well functionality of human brains.
- Society keep putting enormous effort, actually more and more human and money resources, to develop and apply genome engineering, to model human brains and minds as well as to vastly extend human longevity. Such huge project as that of *Human brain* of EU, supported by 1.2 milliards of EUR, is one of them.
- A vision starts to be accepted to see the development of superintelligent machines as the next stage of evolution and to prepare society for handling and accepting such developments.

To deal with new megachallenges practically all areas of sciences and technologies have to be involved. However, informatics is expected to play by that a very important role for several reasons. here is one of them;

- It starts to be clear that in order to understand more deeply functionality of living systems, on all levels - from cells to brains - and to design, using other, non-biological, substrates, systems to outperform them, information processing models of such systems are needed. Chemistry and biology has been able to gather enormous number of data about the composition and isolated behaviour of basic elements of particular living systems, but informatics tools are needed to model their functionality as complex, concurrent systems, in such a way that we can then model their functionality using non-biological substrates. It starts to be understood that modeling of elements and their behaviour through differential equations can hardly lead to the design of efficient models and that modeling using informatics tools to model concurrent and parallel systems may be much needed.

7   Conclusions - Food for Thoughts

Some observation of famous scientists inspired also developments suggested in this paper

- There is nothing in biology found yet that indicates the inevitability of death. *Richard Feynman*
- It seems probable that once the machine thinking method had started, it will not take long to outstrip our feeble power. They would be able to converse with each other to sharpen their wits. At some stage therefore, we should have to expect machine to take control.   *Alan M. Turing*
- Let an ultraintelligent machine be defined as a machine that can far surpass all intellectual activities of any man, however clever. Since the design of machines is one of intellectual activities, an ultraintelligent machine could design even better machines; there would then unquestionably be and "intelligent explosion" and the intelligence of man would be left far behind. Thus the first ultraintelligent machine is the last invention that man needs ever make.   *I. J. Good, 1965, a British mathematician*
- Since there is a real danger that computers will develop intelligence and take over we urgently need to develop direct connections to brains so that computers can add to human intelligence rather than be in opposition. *Stephen Hawking*
- When you reach for stars you may not quite get one, but you won't come with a handful of mud either *Leo Burnett.*

References

1. Gruska, J.: A perception of Informatics, web page of Academia Europaea, 55 pages, http://www.AE-Info.org/ae/user/Gruska.Jozef
2. Gruska, J.: Impulses and roads to a new perception of informatics. In: Calude, C., Salomaa, A., Rozenberg, G. (eds.) Rainbow of Computer Science, pp. 183–199. Springer Verlag (2011)
3. Kurzweil, R.: The singularity is near. Penguin Books (2006)
4. Moravec, H.: When will computer hardware match the human brain? Journal of Evolution and Technology V1 (1998), http://www.jetpress.org/volume1/moravec.pdf
5. Watts, L.: Event-driven simulation of networks of spiking neurons. In: Seventh Neural Information Processing Systems Foundation Conference (1993)

Computational Complexity of P Systems
with Active Membranes

Alberto Leporati

Dipartimento di Informatica, Sistemistica e Comunicazione
Università degli Studi di Milano-Bicocca
Viale Sarca 336/14, 20126 Milano, Italy
alberto.leporati@unimib.it

Abstract. P systems with active membranes constitute a very interesting model of computation, defined in the framework of Membrane
Computing. Since their appeareance, they have been used to solve computationally difficult problems (usually in the classes **NP** and **PSPACE**),
due to their ability to generate an exponential size workspace in a polynomial number of time steps. Several computational complexity techniques
have thus been applied to study their computing power and efficiency.
In this extended abstract I will briefly survey some of these techniques
and the main results which have been obtained in the last few years by
the group of Membrane Computing at the University of Milano-Bicocca
(also known as the "Milano Team"), sometimes in collaboration with
collegues from the international Membrane Computing community.

1 Introduction

P systems with *active membranes* are a very interesting and stimulating model
of computation, defined in the framework of *membrane systems* [9]. They were
first introduced in [10] to attack **NP**-complete problems. Since then, they have
generated several variants; a general survey of these can be found in chapters 11
and 12 of [11].

In this model of P systems, also the membranes play an active role in the computations: they possess an electrical charge that can inhibit or activate the rules
that govern the evolution of the system, and they can also increase exponentially
in number via division rules. This latter feature makes them extremely efficient
from a computational complexity standpoint: using exponentially many membranes that evolve in parallel, they can be used to solve **NP**-complete and even
PSPACE-complete problems [23,1] in polynomial time. Surprisingly, polarizations are not even needed (provided that division rules are powerful enough)
to solve these kinds of problems, as shown in [29,4]. On the other hand, when
the ability of dividing membranes is limited the efficiency apparently decreases:
the so-called Milano theorem [28] tells us that no **NP**-complete problem can be
solved in polynomial time without using division rules, unless **P** = **NP** holds.

Needless to say, several computational complexity techniques have been applied to investigate the computational power and efficiency of P systems with

A. Alhazov et al. (Eds.): CMC 2013, LNCS 8340, pp. 19–32, 2014.

active membranes. In what follows, I will briefly recall the main results which
have been obtained using such techniques by the group of Membrane Computing
at the University of Milano-Bicocca (the so-called "Milano team"), sometimes
in collaboration with collegues from the international Membrane Computing
community.

This extended abstract is organized as follows. In Section 2 I recall the formal
definition and operation of P systems with active membranes, as well as the
definition of *time* and *space* complexity. Section 3 summarizes the results on the
complexity of P systems with active membranes we have obtained in the last few
years; it also proposes directions for further research, to attack some problems
which are still open.

2   P Systems with Active Membranes

We start by recalling the definition of P systems with active membranes that
will be used in the rest of this paper. For a more formal definition we refer the
reader to chapter 12 of [11].

Definition 1. *A P system with active membranes of the initial degree $d \geq 1$ is
a tuple $\Pi = (\Gamma, \Lambda, \mu, w_1, \ldots, w_d, R)$, where:*

- *Γ is a finite alphabet of symbols (the objects);*
- *Λ is a finite set of labels for the membranes;*
- *μ is a membrane structure (i.e., a rooted unordered tree) consisting of d
  membranes, enumerated by $1, \ldots, d$; furthermore, each membrane is labeled
  by an element of Λ, not necessarily in a one-to-one way;*
- *$w_1, \ldots, w_d$ are strings over Γ, describing the initial multisets of objects placed
  in the d regions of μ;*
- *R is a finite set of rules.*

As usual in Membrane Computing, the membrane structure of a P system
is represented symbolically as a string of balanced nested brackets, where each
pair of corresponding open/close ones represents an individual membrane. The
nesting of brackets corresponds to the ancestor-descendant relation of nodes in
the tree; brackets at the same nesting levels can be listed in any order.

Each membrane possesses, besides its label and position in μ, another attribute called *electrical charge* (or polarization), which can be either neutral (0),
positive (+) or negative (−) and is always neutral before the beginning of the
computation.

The rules are of the following kinds:

- *Object evolution rules*, of the form $[a \rightarrow w]_h^\alpha$
  They can be applied inside a membrane labeled by h, having charge α and
  containing an occurrence of the object a; the object a is rewritten into the
  multiset w (i.e., a is removed from the multiset in h and replaced by every
  object in w).

- *Send-in communication rules*, of the form $a\,[\ ]_h^\alpha \to [b]_h^\beta$

  They can be applied to a membrane labeled by h, having charge α and such that the external region contains an occurrence of the object a; the object a is sent into h becoming b and, simultaneously, the charge of h is changed to β.

- *Send-out communication rules*, of the form $[a]_h^\alpha \to [\ ]_h^\beta\,b$

  They can be applied to a membrane labeled by h, having charge α and containing an occurrence of the object a; the object a is sent out from h to the outside region becoming b and, simultaneously, the charge of h is changed to β.

- *Dissolution rules*, of the form $[a]_h^\alpha \to b$

  They can be applied to a membrane labeled by h, having charge α and containing an occurrence of the object a; the membrane h is dissolved and its contents are left in the surrounding region unaltered, except that an occurrence of a becomes b.

- *Elementary division rules*, of the form $[a]_h^\alpha \to [b]_h^\beta\,[c]_h^\gamma$

  They can be applied to a membrane labeled by h, having charge α, containing an occurrence of the object a but having no other membrane inside (an *elementary membrane*); the membrane is divided into two membranes having label h and charges β and γ; the object a is replaced, respectively, by b and c while the other objects in the initial multiset are copied to both membranes.

- *Nonelementary division rules*, of the form

$$[[\ ]_{h_1}^+ \cdots [\ ]_{h_k}^+ [\ ]_{h_{k+1}}^- \cdots [\ ]_{h_n}^-]_h^\alpha \to [[\ ]_{h_1}^\delta \cdots [\ ]_{h_k}^\delta]_h^\beta [[\ ]_{h_{k+1}}^\epsilon \cdots [\ ]_{h_n}^\epsilon]_h^\gamma$$

  They can be applied to a membrane labeled by h, having charge α, containing the positively charged membranes $h_1,\ldots,h_k$, the negatively charged membranes $h_{k+1},\ldots,h_n$, and possibly some neutral membranes. The membrane h is divided into two copies having charge β and γ, respectively; the positive children are placed inside the former, their charge changed to δ, while the negative ones are placed inside the latter, their charges changed to ϵ. Any neutral membrane inside h is duplicated and placed inside both copies.

Each instantaneous configuration of a P system with active membranes is described by the current membrane structure, including the electrical charges, together with the multisets located in the corresponding regions. A computation step changes the current configuration according to the following set of principles:

- Each object and membrane can be subject to at most one rule per step, except for object evolution rules (inside each membrane any number of evolution rules can be applied simultaneously).
- The application of rules is *maximally parallel*: each object appearing on the left-hand side of evolution, communication, dissolution or elementary division must be subject to exactly one of them (unless the current charge of the membrane prohibits it). The same reasoning applies to each membrane

that can be involved to communication, dissolution, elementary or nonelementary division rules. In other words, the only objects and membranes that do not evolve are those associated with no rule, or only to rules that are not applicable due to the electrical charges.

- When several conflicting rules can be applied at the same time, a nondeterministic choice is performed; this implies that, in general, multiple possible configurations can be reached after a computation step.
- While all the chosen rules are considered to be applied simultaneously during each computation step, they are logically applied in a bottom-up fashion: first, all evolution rules are applied to the elementary membranes, then all communication, dissolution and division rules; then we proceed towards the root of the membrane structure. In other words, each membrane evolves only after its internal configuration has been updated.
- The outermost membrane cannot be divided or dissolved, and any object sent out from it cannot re-enter the system again.

A *halting computation* of a P system is a finite sequence of configurations $\mathcal{C} = (\mathcal{C}_0, \ldots, \mathcal{C}_k)$, where $\mathcal{C}_0$ is the initial configuration, every $\mathcal{C}_{i+1}$ is reachable by $\mathcal{C}_i$ via a single computation step, and no rules can be applied anymore in $\mathcal{C}_k$. A *non-halting* computation consists of infinitely many successive configurations $\mathcal{C} = (\mathcal{C}_i : i \in \mathbb{N})$.

P systems can be used as *recognisers* by employing two specified objects YES and NO; exactly one of these must be sent out from the outermost membrane during each computation, in order to signal acceptance or rejection respectively; we also assume that all computations are halting. If all computations starting from the same initial configuration are accepting, or all are rejecting, the P system is said to be *confluent*. If this is not necessarily the case, we have a *non-confluent* P system, and the overall result is established as for nondeterministic Turing machines: it is acceptance iff an accepting computation exists.

In order to solve decision problems (i.e., decide languages), we use *families* of recogniser P systems $\boldsymbol{\Pi} = \{\Pi_x : x \in \Sigma^\star\}$ for some finite alphabet Σ. Each input x is associated with a P system Π_x that decides the membership of x in the language $L \subseteq \Sigma^\star$ by accepting or rejecting. The mapping $x \mapsto \Pi_x$ is restricted, in order to be computable efficiently; usually one of the following *uniformity conditions* is imposed.

Definition 2. *A family of P systems* $\boldsymbol{\Pi} = \{\Pi_x : x \in \Sigma^\star\}$ *is said to be semi-uniform if the mapping* $x \mapsto \Pi_x$ *can be computed in polynomial time by a deterministic Turing machine.*

The Turing machine can encode its output Π_x by describing the membrane structure with brackets, the multisets as strings of symbols (in unary notation) and listing the rules one by one. However, any explicit encoding of Π_x is allowed as output, as long as the number of membranes and objects represented by it does not exceed the length of the whole description, and the rules are listed one by one. We pose this restriction in order to enforce the initial membranes, initial objects and rules to be at most polynomial in number, as they can be super-polynomial if more compact representations (e.g., binary numbers) are used; this mimics a (hypothetical) realistic process of construction of the P systems, where membranes and objects are presumably placed one by one, and require actual physical space in proportion to their number (see also how the size of a configuration is defined in the following, and [7]).

Definition 3. *A family of P systems* $\boldsymbol{\Pi} = \{\Pi_x : x \in \Sigma^\star\}$ *is said to be* uniform *if the mapping* $x \mapsto \Pi_x$ *can be computed by two deterministic polynomial-time Turing machines* M_1 *and* M_2 *as follows:*

- *The machine* M_1, *taking as input the length* n *of* x *in unary notation, constructs a P system* Π_n *with a distinguished input membrane (the P system* Π_n *is common for all inputs of length* n).
- *The machine* M_2, *on input* x, *outputs a multiset* w_x *(an encoding of the specific input* x).
- *Finally,* Π_x *is simply* Π_n *with* w_x *added to the multiset placed inside its input membrane.*

Notice how the uniform construction is just a restricted case of semi-uniform construction. The relations between the two kinds of uniformity have not completely been clarified yet; see [11,7] for further details on uniformity conditions (including even weaker constructions).

Finally, we describe how time and space complexities for families of recogniser P systems are measured.

Definition 4. *A* uniform *or* semi-uniform *family of P systems* $\boldsymbol{\Pi} = \{\Pi_x : x \in \Sigma^\star\}$ *is said to decide the language* $L \subseteq \Sigma^\star$ *in time* $f : \mathbb{N} \to \mathbb{N}$ *iff, for each* $x \in \Sigma^\star$,

- *the system* Π_x *accepts if* $x \in L$, *and rejects if* $x \notin L$;
- *each computation of* Π_x *halts within* $f(|x|)$ *computation steps.*

The notion of space complexity has been formally introduced in the Membrane Computing setting in [14], in order to analyse the time/space trade-off that is common when solving computationally hard problems via P systems. The size $|\mathcal{C}|$ of a configuration $\mathcal{C}$ of a P system is given by the sum of the number of objects and the number of membranes; this definition assumes that every component of the system requires some fixed amount of physical space, thus approximating (up to a polynomial) the size of a real cell. The space required by a halting computation $\mathcal{C} = (\mathcal{C}_0, \ldots, \mathcal{C}_k)$ is then given by $|\mathcal{C}| = \max\{|\mathcal{C}_0|, \ldots, |\mathcal{C}_k|\}$, and the space required by a P system Π is

$$|\Pi| = \max\{|\mathcal{C}| : \mathcal{C} \text{ is a computation of } \Pi\}.$$

We can finally give the following definition.

Definition 5. *A* uniform *or* semi-uniform *family of P systems* $\boldsymbol{\Pi} = \{\Pi_x : x \in \Sigma^\star\}$ *operates in space* $f : \mathbb{N} \to \mathbb{N}$ *if* $|\Pi_x| \leq f(|x|)$ *for all* $x \in \Sigma^\star$.

Several complexity classes can be defined referring to the languages recognized by P systems with active membranes (possibly with restrictions on their rules), when a polynomial, exponential, logarithmic (or other) bound is fixed on the amount of time or space allowed in computations. Here we do not recall them, so as not to burden the exposition. For precise definitions, we refer the reader to the cited papers.

3   The Complexity of P Systems with Active Membranes

We now recall the main results we have obtained in the last few years on the time and space complexity of P systems with active membranes, that is, the amount of time and/or space needed to solve a given problem (equivalently, recognize a given language) by a uniform or semi-uniform family of P systems with active membranes. The leading question is: "When we bound the amount of time and/or space by a given quantity, what is the class of decision problems (resp., languages) we can solve (resp., recognize)?".

We start with the simulation of deterministic single-tape Turing machines, operating in polynomial space with respect to the input length, by semi-uniform families of P systems with active membranes and three polarizations, presented in [27]. The simulation is efficient both in terms of time and space, and what is particularly remarkable is that it only uses communication rules. Basing upon this simulation, a result similar to the *space hierarchy theorem* [22] can be obtained for P systems with active membranes: the larger the amount of space we can use during the computations, the harder the problems we are able to solve.

We then continue by considering the case in which only communication rules and nonelementary division rules (which apply to membranes containing other membranes) are allowed. It turns out that the resulting P systems are not computationally universal, neither in the uniform nor in the semi-uniform setting; nonetheless, they are very powerful, as they characterize the class of languages decidable by Turing machines using time (or, equivalently, space) bounded by an exponential function, known as *tetration*, iterated polynomially many times [13].

The computing power of polynomial-time P systems with division rules operating only on *elementary* membranes (that is, membranes not containing other membranes) is possibly the most interesting case. It is a known fact that elementary division rules suffice to efficiently solve **NP**-complete problems (and, due to closure under complement, also **coNP**-complete ones). This result dates back to 2000 in the semi-uniform case [28], and to 2003 in the uniform case [12]. Since these results do not require membrane dissolution rules, they hold also for the so-called *P systems with restricted elementary active membranes* [1], where dissolution is avoided. Although a **PSPACE** upper bound was proved in 2007 [24], no significant improvement on the **NP ∪ coNP** lower bound for these P systems has been found until 2010. In [16] we have shown that there exists a uniform family of P systems with restricted elementary active membranes that solves the **PP**-complete problem SQRT-3SAT, which can be stated as follows: given a Boolean formula of m variables in 3CNF, do at least $\sqrt{2^m}$ among the 2^m

possible truth assignments satisfy it? The solution is a variation of the classical scheme introduced in [10] to attack **NP**-complete problems: given the input formula $\phi(x_1, \ldots, x_m)$, the P system first generates 2^m membranes using elementary division, each one containing a different truth assignment to the variables occurring in ϕ; then, it evaluates ϕ under the 2^m assignments, in parallel, and sends out from each membrane an object t whenever the formula is satisfied by the corresponding assignment; subsequently it erases $\lceil \sqrt{2^m} \rceil - 1$ copies of t (or all of them, if less than $\lceil \sqrt{2^m} \rceil - 1$ occur); finally, it outputs YES if at least one copy of t remains, otherwise it outputs NO. The construction is made uniform by providing an encoding of m-variable Boolean formulae as binary strings of length $8\binom{m}{3}$, where the i-th bit of a string is 1 if and only if the i-th clause (under a fixed ordering of all possible 3-clauses in m variables) occurs in the corresponding Boolean formula. Such Boolean strings can then be represented as multisets of objects (one object for each clause occurring in the formula, that is, for each 1 in the corresponding bit string — since each binary string is at most polynomially long, a polynomial number of different objects suffices) and fed as input to a P system that solves all possible instances of SQRT-3SAT in m variables. Unfortunately, the fact that the **PP**-complete problem SQRT-3SAT can be efficiently solved by P systems with restricted elementary active membranes does not allow one to immediately conclude that the entire class **PP** of problems can be solved by the same families of P systems, as incorrectly stated in [16], at least under the uniformity condition expressed in Definition 3. This is due to the fact that closure under polynomial-time reductions is not given for free under our uniformity condition, as it happens with the stronger notion of polynomial-time uniformity usually employed in the literature [12]. The ability to solve all decision problems in the complexity class **PP** has then been proved in [17], and follows from a solution of the **PP**-hard problem THRESHOLD-3SAT, similar to the one given for SQRT-3SAT in [16]. The THRESHOLD-3SAT problem is more general than SQRT-3SAT, and is defined as follows: Given a Boolean formula of m variables in 3CNF, and a non-negative integer $k < 2^m$, do more than k assignments (out of 2^m) satisfy it? In this case, the solution scheme has been modified so that k copies of object t (instead of $\lceil \sqrt{2^m} \rceil - 1$) are erased from the system, in order to check whether the number of assignments that satisfy the input Boolean formula ϕ is greater than k. Once again, to make the solution uniform the formula is encoded as an appropriate multiset of clause-objects, plus a multiset of objects representing the binary encoding of k. Note that the complexity class **PP** appears to be larger than **NP**, since it contains **NP** as a subset and it is closed under complement: thus $\mathbf{NP} \cup \mathbf{coNP} \subseteq \mathbf{PP}$. However, neither the upper bound proved in [24] nor the lower bound proved in [16] are known to be strict.

The existence of the uniform family of P systems with restricted elementary active membranes shown in [17] has an interesting consequence. As shown in [19], it is possible to use the P systems that solve THRESHOLD-3SAT presented in [17] as modules inside larger P systems; this means that we can simulate computations using (appropriately crafted) subroutines or *oracles*. In this way, all problems in the class $\mathbf{P}^{\mathbf{PP}}$ turn out to be solvable in polynomial time by P systems with active membranes, without requiring nonelementary division or dissolution rules. This result, together with Toda's theorem [26], allows us to conclude that P systems with restricted elementary active membranes are able to solve all the decision problems residing in the *polynomial hierarchy* **PH** [25].

Another interesting line of research is the characterization of P systems with active membranes performing computations within *polynomial, exponential* and *logarithmic* space bounds.

Concerning polynomial space, our attention goes to recognizer P systems with active membranes in which three polarizations are associated to each membrane, and for which division and dissolution rules are forbidden. In [15] it has been proved that these P systems are able to efficiently simulate deterministic register machines, using only communication and evolution rules. Such a simulation can then be used to illustrate the following result: recognizer P systems with active membranes are able to solve, in a uniform way, the **PSPACE**-complete problem QUANTIFIED-3SAT, using a polynomial amount of space (and an arbitrary amount of time — in a sense, we are here trading time for space). This means that the complexity class **PSPACE** is contained into the class of decision problems which can be solved in polynomial space by the above kind of recognizer P systems; furthermore, such P systems can solve in arbitrary time (and polynomial space) problems which cannot be solved in polynomial time unless **P** = **PSPACE**. On the contrary, in [18] it has been proved that P systems with active membranes can be simulated by Turing machines with only a polynomial increase in space complexity. By combining this result with the above stated ability of P systems to solve **PSPACE**-complete problems in polynomial space, we obtain a *characterization* of **PSPACE** in terms of membrane systems. An interesting aspect of this result is that it holds for both confluent and non-confluent systems, and even when strong features such as division rules are used.

An analogous characterization of the complexity class **EXPSPACE** can be obtained by P systems with active membranes working in *exponential* space, as shown in [2]. This result is proved by simulating Turing machines working in exponential space via uniform families of P systems with restricted elementary active membranes; the simulation is efficient, in the sense that the time and space required are at most polynomial with respect to the resources employed by the simulated Turing machine. Indeed, the most interesting aspect of this result is the technique used to represent the configurations and simulate the computation steps of Turing machines by P systems with restricted elementary active membranes. In fact, it should be noted that the simulation technique used in [18] does not seem to be applicable when the space bound is exponential (or even super-exponential): we would need to use P systems with an exponential number of membranes with distinct labels, and such systems cannot be built in a polynomial number of steps by a deterministic Turing machine — as required by the uniformity condition expressed in Definition 3, or even in the stronger notion of polynomial-time uniformity usually employed in the literature [12].

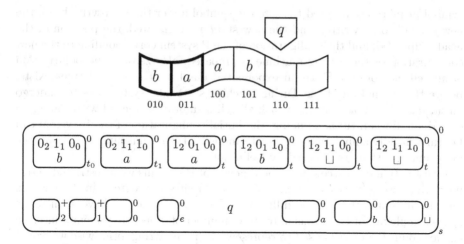

Fig. 1. A generic configuration of a single-tape Turing machine, and its representation by a P system with restricted elementary active membranes

To overcome this difficulty we represented the configurations of a single-tape Turing machine by means of P systems configurations, as illustrated in Figure 1. In the figure, the first two tape cells (corresponding to membranes t_0 and t_1) contain the input string ba, whereas the other cells (corresponding to the membranes labelled by t) contain the symbols written up to now in the rest of the tape. The positions (addresses) of tape cells are written in binary, and are encoded as appropriate multisets of 0 and 1 objects contained into the so-called *cell membranes*; since at most an exponential number of cells exist, at most a polynomial number of different 0 and 1 objects suffice to write their position. Apart from cell membranes, our P systems contain so-called *position membranes*, labelled with 2, 1 and 0 in Figure 1, that encode in their polarizations the current position of the Turing machine's read-write head. The *symbol membranes*, one for each symbol of the alphabet of the Turing machine (a, b and ⊔ in Figure 1), are used to store the symbol read from the head during the simulation of a computation step, whereas the state of the machine is stored in the only symbol occurring in the region determined by the skin membrane. To simulate a computation step performed by the Turing machine, say $\delta(q, \sqcup) = (r, b, \lhd)$, the P system has to *guess* what is the cell membrane corresponding to the tape cell currently addressed by the read-write head. It does so by letting the state symbol enter one of the cell membranes having a neutral polarization; the polarization of the chosen membrane is set to positive, and a comparison between the address of this membrane and the position stored in the polarizations of the position membranes is performed; if the comparison fails, the polarization of the chosen membrane is set to negative, so that it will not be chosen again in the future; then, the membrane labelled by e is used to signal that an error occurred, and to restore the configuration of the system so that a new cell membrane can be chosen at random. If, on the other hand, the comparison was successful, then the symbol membranes are used to store the symbol under the read-write head; the new symbol to be written and the new state are generated, the position of the head is updated, and the configuration of the P system corresponding to the new configuration of the Turing machine is prepared, also zeroing the polarization of all cell membranes. Since an exponential number of cell membranes exists, before the simulation of the Turing machine starts the system has to undergo an *initialization phase*, during which all cell membranes labelled with t are generated via division rules. So doing, the initial configuration of the P system can be built in polynomial time by a deterministic Turing machine, satisfying the uniformity constraints imposed by Definition 3.

Investigation on the computational power of P systems with restricted active membranes working in *logarithmic* space is currently in progress. In this case we have to overcome at least two difficulties. First of all, since we have defined the space complexity of P systems in terms of number of objects and membranes, we cannot count the objects used to represent the input string, otherwise we would exceed the logarithmic bound. A natural solution to this problem is to split the alphabet of the P systems in two parts: input symbols and work symbols. Input symbols do not contribute to the size of configurations, but on the other hand the rules of the systems have to be designed in such a way that no input symbol is ever created or rewritten during the computations.

Another problem is related to the uniformity condition: since the Turing machine that builds the P system Π_x (or Π_n, in the uniform case) can perform computations in polynomial time, we do not want to cheat by letting it solve the problem and produce a trivial P system that just outputs a YES or NO object in one step, corresponding to the correct solution. Hence a new notion of uniformity is needed, which is weaker than the P systems themselves. Inspired by Boolean circuits complexity [6] we have introduced **DLOGTIME**-uniformity [20], which is obtained by substituting in Definition 3 polynomial-time deterministic Turing machines with *deterministic logarithmic-time* (**DLOGTIME**, for short) Turing machines. A **DLOGTIME** Turing machine [6] is a Turing machine having a read-only input tape of length n, a constant number of read-write work tapes of length $O(\log n)$, and a read-write address tape, also of length $O(\log n)$. The input tape is not accessed by using a sequential tape head (as the other tapes are); instead, during each step the machine has access to the i-th symbol on the input tape, where i is the number written in binary on the address tape (if $i \geq |n|$ the machine reads an appropriate end-of-input symbol, such as a blank symbol). The machine is also required to operate in time $O(\log n)$, hence only $O(\log n)$ bits of information of the input may be read during a **DLOGTIME** computation. Despite their seemingly weak computational power, **DLOGTIME** Turing machines are able to perform many interesting computations, such as determining the length of their input, compute sums, differences and logarithms of numbers of $O(\log n)$ bits, decode simple pairing functions on strings of length $O(\log n)$ and extract portions of the input of size $O(\log n)$ [6]. They are also used in the uniformity construction of several classes of Boolean circuits [21]. As P systems are more complicated devices than Boolean circuits, in [20] we have defined a

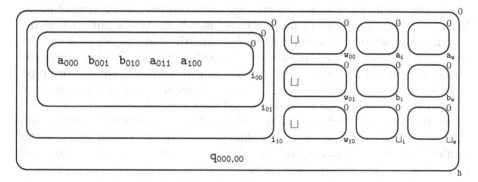

Fig. 2. A P system with active membranes representing a generic configuration of a logarithmic-space Turing machine

series of predicates describing their various features: number of symbols in the alphabet, number and type of rules, membrane hierarchy, etc. All together, these predicates define a **DLOGTIME**-computable function $1^n \mapsto \Pi_n$ for $n \in \mathbb{N}$.

We have then proved that **DLOGTIME**-uniform families of P systems with active membranes working in logarithmic space (not counting their input) can simulate logarithmic-space deterministic Turing machines. Also in this case, the interesting part of the construction is the representation of Turing machines configurations by P systems configurations, and the simulation of Turing machines computation steps by sequences of P systems computation steps. Figure 2 shows how Turing machine configurations are represented as P systems configurations. The *state object* has now two subscripts, indicating the current position on the input tape and on the work tape, respectively; the object itself represents the current state of the machine. The membrane hierarchy on the left (membranes labelled with i_{00}, i_{01} and i_{10} in the figure) has a logarithmic depth, and represents the input tape; membranes w_{00}, w_{01} and w_{10} represent the work tape, whereas the other membranes are associated with the symbols of the input and of the work alphabet, and play the same role of the *symbol membranes* in exponential-space simulations. The input tape of the machine represented in Figure 2 contains the string **abbaa**; all the input objects are normally contained in the innermost membrane of the hierarchy associated with the input tape, and the positions of the symbols on the input tape are encoded in binary. To simulate a computation step of the Turing machine, say $\delta(r, b, a) = (s, b, \rhd, \lhd)$ — meaning that the machine, being in state r and having symbols b and a respectively under the input read head and under the work read-write head, goes into state s, writes b on the work tape and moves the input head and the work head to the right and to the left, respectively — the P system operates as follows. First the state object crosses the membrane hierarchy associated with the input tape, setting the polarizations according to the position of the tape cell to be read. All the objects contained in the innermost membrane then start to leave, crossing the membranes in the hierarchy according to their position subscript; only one object, corresponding to the tape cell read, reaches the region enclosed by the skin membrane. Such object stores its presence in the corresponding symbol membrane, and then goes back to the innermost membrane of the input hierarchy, together with all the other input symbols, while the state object goes back to the region enclosed by the skin membrane, resetting to zero all the polarizations in the hierarchy. The state object is then used to read the current work tape cell, and to store the symbol read in the corresponding symbol membrane. By means of the polarizations of the input and work symbol membranes, the state object has now all the information needed to generate the new state (comprising the two modified subscripts corresponding to the new heads positions) and the symbol to be written on the work tape. In the meanwhile all polarizations are resetted to neutral, and so the P system correctly represents the new state of the Turing machine, ready to simulate the next computation step.

Unfortunately, the possibility to perform the opposite simulation (that is, simulating **DLOGTIME**-uniform families of P systems by Turing machines operating in logarithmic space) remains open. It thus remains to be established whether these P systems may or not characterize the class **L** of problems solvable in logarithmic space by deterministic Turing machines, or maybe solve harder problems like, for instance, those in **NL**.

Acknowledgements. I warmly thank the organizers of the 14th International Conference on Membrane Computing for inviting me. The research here described was partially supported by Università degli Studi di Milano-Bicocca, Fondo di Ateneo (FA) 2011.

References

1. Alhazov, A., Martín-Vide, C., Pan, L.: Solving a PSPACE-complete problem by recognizing P systems with restricted active membranes. Fundamenta Informaticae 58(2), 67–77 (2003)
2. Alhazov, A., Leporati, A., Mauri, G., Porreca, A.E., Zandron, C.: The computational power of exponential-space P systems with active membranes. In: Martínez-del-Amor, M.A., et al. (eds.) Proceedings of the Tenth Brainstorming Week on Membrane Computing, January 30-February 3, vol. I, pp. 35–60. Research Group on Natural Computing, Seville (2012)
3. Garey, M.R., Johnson, D.S.: Computers and intractability: a guide to the theory of NP-completeness. W.H. Freeman & Co. (1979)
4. Leporati, A., Ferretti, C., Mauri, G., Pérez-Jiménez, M.J., Zandron, C.: Complexity aspects of polarizationless membrane systems. Natural Computing 8, 703–717 (2009)
5. Mauri, G., Leporati, A., Porreca, A.E., Zandron, C.: Recent complexity-theoretic results on P systems with active membranes. Journal of Logic and Computation, online first (2013), doi:10.1093/logcom/exs077
6. Mix Barrington, D.A., Immerman, N., Straubing, H.: On uniformity within NC[1]. Journal of Computer and System Sciences 41(3), 274–306 (1990)
7. Murphy, N., Woods, D.: The computational power of membrane systems under tight uniformity conditions. Natural Computing 10(1), 613–632 (2011)
8. Papadimitriou, C.H.: Computational complexity. Addison-Wesley (1993)

9. Păun, G.: Computing with membranes. Journal of Computer and System Sciences 1(61), 108–143 (2000)
10. Păun, G.: P systems with active membranes: attacking NP-complete problems. Journal of Automata, Languages and Combinatorics 6(1), 75–90 (2001)
11. Păun, G., Rozenberg, G., Salomaa, A. (eds.): The Oxford handbook of membrane computing. Oxford University Press (2010)
12. Pérez-Jiménez, M.J., Romero Jiménez, A., Sancho Caparrini, F.: Complexity classes in models of cellular computing with membranes. Natural Computing 2(3), 265–285 (2003)
13. Porreca, A.E., Leporati, A., Zandron, C.: On a powerful class of non-universal P systems with active membranes. In: Gao, Y., Lu, H., Seki, S., Yu, S. (eds.) DLT 2010. LNCS, vol. 6224, pp. 364–375. Springer, Heidelberg (2010)
14. Porreca, A.E., Leporati, A., Mauri, G., Zandron, C.: Introducing a space complexity measure for P systems. International Journal of Computers, Communications & Control 4(3), 301–310 (2009)
15. Porreca, A.E., Leporati, A., Mauri, G., Zandron, C.: P systems with active membranes: trading time for space. Natural Computing 10(1), 167–182 (2011)
16. Porreca, A.E., Leporati, A., Mauri, G., Zandron, C.: P systems with elementary active membranes: beyond NP and coNP. In: Gheorghe, M., Hinze, T., Păun, G., Rozenberg, G., Salomaa, A. (eds.) CMC 2010. LNCS, vol. 6501, pp. 338–347. Springer, Heidelberg (2010)
17. Porreca, A.E., Leporati, A., Mauri, G., Zandron, C.: Elementary active membranes have the power of counting. International Journal of Natural Computing Research 2(3), 35–48 (2011)
18. Porreca, A.E., Leporati, A., Mauri, G., Zandron, C.: P systems with active membranes working in polynomial space. International Journal of Foundations of Computer Science 2(1), 65–73 (2011)
19. Porreca, A.E., Leporati, A., Mauri, G., Zandron, C.: P systems simulating oracle computations. In: Gheorghe, M., Păun, G., Rozenberg, G., Salomaa, A., Verlan, S. (eds.) CMC 2011. LNCS, vol. 7184, pp. 346–358. Springer, Heidelberg (2012)
20. Porreca, A.E., Leporati, A., Mauri, G., Zandron, C.: Sublinear-space P systems with active membranes. In: Csuhaj-Varjú, E., Gheorghe, M., Rozenberg, G., Salomaa, A., Vaszil, G. (eds.) CMC 2012. LNCS, vol. 7762, pp. 342–357. Springer, Heidelberg (2013)
21. Ruzzo, W.L.: On uniform circuit complexity. Journal of Computer and System Sciences 22(3), 365–383 (1981)
22. Sipser, M.: Introduction to the theory of computation, 3rd edn. Cengage Learning (2012)
23. Sosík, P.: The computational power of cell division in P systems: beating down parallel computers? Natural Computing 2(3), 287–298 (2003)
24. Sosík, P., Rodríguez-Patón, A.: Membrane computing and complexity theory: a characterization of PSPACE. Journal of Computer and System Sciences 73(1), 137–152 (2007)
25. Stockmeyer, L.J.: The polynomial hierarchy. Theoretical Computer Science 3, 1–22 (1976)
26. Toda, S.: PP is as hard as the polynomial–time hierarchy. SIAM Journal on Computing 20(5), 865–877 (1991)
27. Valsecchi, A., Porreca, A.E., Leporati, A., Mauri, G., Zandron, C.: An efficient simulation of polynomial-space Turing machines by P systems with active membranes. In: Păun, G., Pérez-Jiménez, M.J., Riscos-Núñez, A., Rozenberg, G., Salomaa, A. (eds.) WMC 2009. LNCS, vol. 5957, pp. 461–478. Springer, Heidelberg (2010)

28. Zandron, C., Ferretti, C., Mauri, G.: Solving NP-complete problems using P systems with active membranes. In: Antoniou, I., et al. (eds.) Unconventional Models of Computation, UMC2K: Proceedings of the Second International Conference. Discrete Mathematics and Theoretical Computer Science, pp. 289–301. Springer (2001)
29. Zandron, C., Leporati, A., Ferretti, C., Mauri, G., Pérez-Jiménez, M.J.: On the Computational Efficiency of Polarizationless Recognizer P Systems with Strong Division and Dissolution. Fundamenta Informaticae 87(1), 79–91 (2008)

Some Open Problems about Catalytic, Numerical, and Spiking Neural P Systems
(Extended Abstract)

Gheorghe Păun

Institute of Mathematics of the Romanian Academy
PO Box 1-764, 014700 Bucureşti, Romania, and
Department of Computer Science and Artificial Intelligence
University of Sevilla
Avda. Reina Mercedes s/n, 41012 Sevilla, Spain
gpaun@us.es, ghpaun@gmail.com

Abstract. Some open problems and research topics are pointed, about three classes of P systems: catalytic, numerical, and spiking neural P systems. In each case, several issues are briefly discussed, in general, related to questions already formulated as open problems in the literature and also related to recent results dealing with these questions.

1 Introduction

In spite of the large bibliography accumulated in the fifteen years since this research area was initiated, [26], membrane computing still exhibits a lot of open problems and research topics, some of them "going back to basics", others being related to more recent branches of the theory. We recall here three sets of such problems, from both categories mentioned above.

First, we start from the already "classic" question whether or not catalytic P systems with one catalyst, or purely catalytic P systems with two catalysts are computationally universal, and we add to this basic issue three related research topics: (i) give an example of a P system with two catalysts computing a non-trivial (e.g., non-semi-linear) set of numbers, find additional features to be added to (ii) P systems with one catalyst or to (iii) purely catalytic P systems with two catalysts in order to get universality. Recent results in this respect were reported – see, e.g., [11], [8].

Then, we consider the numerical P systems. Besides the basic question, of constructing a complexity theory for these systems, especially related to and important for applications, open problems related to a recent important progress concerning the power of enzymatic numerical P systems ([20]) are formulated. In particular, an interesting question concerns of the computing power of numerical P systems with a small number of enzymes.

Finally, with respect to the spiking neural (SN) P systems, we mention two problems already mentioned elsewhere (e.g., in [15]) and with respect to a new

A. Alhazov et al. (Eds.): CMC 2013, LNCS 8340, pp. 33–39, 2014.

class of SN P systems, recently introduced in [35], where the spiking and the forgetting rules are associated with the synapses, not with the neurons.

In view of the assumed non-Turing computing power/behavior of the brain, an interesting issue would be to find SN P systems able to compute beyond Turing barrier; suggestions from the hypercomputation area could be useful.

The reader is assumed to be familiar with membrane computing (e.g., from [28], [33], [42]), hence we recall no prerequisites. Instead, for the use of the reader, we indicate a series of primary references, without being complete from this point of view; further references can be found in the above mentioned comprehensive sources of information in membrane computing.

2   Catalytic P Systems

P systems with catalytic rules were already introduced in [26], with their computing power left open.

We denote by $NP_m(cat_r)$ the family of sets of numbers computed (generated) by P systems with at most m membranes, using catalytic or non-cooperative rules, containing at most r catalysts. When all the rules of a system are catalytic, we say that the system is *purely catalytic*, and the corresponding families of sets of numbers are denoted by $NP_m(pcat_r)$. When the number of membranes is not bounded by a specified m (it can be arbitrarily large), then the subscript m is replaced with $*$.

The following fundamental results are known:

Theorem 1. (i) $NP_2(cat_2) = NRE$, [10];
(ii) $NREG = NP_*(pcat_1) \subseteq NP_*(pcat_2) \subseteq NP_2(pcat_3) = NRE$, [13], [14].

Two intriguing open problems appear here, related to the borderline between universality and non-universality: (1) are catalytic P systems with only one catalyst universal? (2) are purely catalytic P systems with two catalysts universal? The conjecture is that both these questions have a negative answer, but it is also felt that "one catalyst is almost universal": many features which look "innocent" at the first sight are enough to lead P systems with one catalyst to universality (see [11]) – and similar results were obtained also for purely catalytic P systems with two catalysts (see [8]).

Here we briefly recall the universality results for one catalyst P systems with additional ingredients:

- Introducing a *priority* relation among rules, [26].
- Using *promoters* and *inhibitors* associated with the rules.
- Controlling the computation by means of controlling the *membrane permeability*, by actions δ (decreasing the permeability) and τ (increasing the permeability), [27].
- Besides catalytic and non-cooperating rules, also using rules for *membrane creation*, [22].
- Considering, instead of usual catalysts, *bi-stable catalysts*, [34], or *mobile catalysts*, [18].

- Imposing *target restrictions* on the used rules, [11]; the universality was obtained for P systems with 7 membranes, and it is an open problem whether or not the number of membranes can be diminished).
- Imposing to P systems the idea from *time-varying* grammars and splicing systems, [11]; the universality of time-varying P systems is obtained for one catalyst P systems with only one membrane, having the period equal to 6, and it is open the question whether the period can be decreased.
- Using in a transition only (labeled) rules with the same label – so-called *label restricted* P systems, [19].

Several of these results were extended in [8] to purely catalytic P systems with two catalysts. It remains open to do this for all the previous results, as well as to look for further ingredients which, added to one catalyst P systems or to purely catalytic P systems with two catalysts, can lead to universality. It would be interesting to find such ingredients which work for one catalyst systems and not for purely catalytic systems with two catalysts, and conversely. Suggestions from the regulated rewriting area [6] or the grammar systems area [3] in formal language theory can be useful.

We end this section with a somewhat surprising issue: we know that $NP_2(cat_2) = NRE$, but no example of a P system with two catalysts which generates a non-trivial set of numbers (for instance, $\{2^n \mid n \geq 1\}, \{n^2 \mid n \geq 1\}$) is known. In fact, the problem is to find a system of this kind as simple as possible (otherwise, just repeating the construction in the proof from [10], starting from a register machine computing a set as above, we get an example, but of a large size). A first answer to this question is given in [36], where a catalytic P system with 54 rules is produced, but it is expected that this number could be reduced.

3   Numerical P Systems

Numerical P systems form an "eccentric" class of P systems, because of their "non-syntactic" character, far from language and automata theory, but closer to numerical analysis. This is probably one of the reasons for which only a few papers were accumulated in this area. However, because of the economic motivations, [31], and of the recent applications in robot control, [24], [25], [40], [39], the subject started to call the attention. There are many questions to be investigated in this framework (see a list of such questions in [30]).

Two recent papers, making important steps ahead in the study of numerical P systems are [20] and [21]. The first paper considerably improves the universality results for enzymatic numerical P systems. We do not recall here the definitions, but we only mention that one deals with enzymatic numerical P systems working in the so-called *all-parallel* or *one-parallel* modes introduced in [41].

Thus, two immediate questions are to consider also the case of (i) numerical P systems without enzymes and (ii) of sequential numerical P systems (with or without enzymes).

Then, let us remember that the enzyme variables behave like catalysts (actually, they are closer to promoters) in catalytic P systems. This suggests the problem of considering numerical P systems with a small number of enzymes. Which is the smallest number of enzyme variables for which enzymatic numerical P systems (working in a specified manner: sequential, all-parallel, or one-parallel) is universal?

4   Spiking Neural P Systems

The SN P systems area contains many open problems and research topics. We have mentioned in the Introduction the paper [15]. Three main problems are recalled there:

- To further investigate the power and the properties of SN dP systems, that is, to combine the idea of distributed P systems introduced in [32] with that of spiking neural P systems from [17]. SN dP systems were introduced in [16], but only briefly investigated.
- To investigate the possibility of using SN P systems as pattern recognition devices, in general, in handling 2D patterns. One of the ideas is to consider a layer of input neurons which can read an array line by line and the array is recognized if and only if the computation halts.
- In some sense, the SN P systems is the only class of P systems which have only a few and somewhat metaphoric applications in the study of the "real" brain, of interest for biologists, and this is an important issue: should we change the definition of an SN P system in order to have such applications, or we simply failed to find them in the present setup?

Actually, several modifications in the initial definition of SN P systems were considered already. We only mention the SN P systems with astrocytes ([29], [1]), the SN P systems with *request rules* ([5]), the SN P systems with anti-spikes ([23]), and the axon computing systems ([4]).

One further modification in the initial definition was recently introduced in [35], namely, one moves the firing rules (they can be both spiking and forgetting rules, of the standard forms in SN P systems) on the synapses. The neurons contain spikes; when the number of spikes in a given neuron is "recognized" by a rule on a synapse leaving from that neuron, then the rule is fired, a number of spikes are consumed and a number of spikes are sent to the neuron at the end of the synapse. Precise details can be found in [35]. Using one rule per synapse, with all synapses firing in parallel, we get computations, in the usual style of SN P systems.

In [35], the universality of SN P systems with rules on synapses (with the result of a computation being the number of spikes stored in a designated neuron, the output one, in the end of the computation) is proved, and small universal SN P systems with the rules on synapses are produced.

We end this section with one further research idea: changing the definition of SN P systems in such a way to obtain hypercomputations, going beyond the

Turing barrier. In membrane computing there are are, as far as we know, only two papers dealing with this subject (but not with SN P systems), the accelerated P systems with membrane creation from [2], and the lineages of P systems from [37]. Suggestions from the general hypercomputation area could be useful – see, e.g., the survey from [38].

5   Final Remarks

We end this note by recalling the attention about the "mega-paper" [12], where a lot of open problems and research topics in membrane computing can be found.

Acknowledgements. Work supported by Proyecto de Excelencia con Investigador de Reconocida Valía, de la Junta de Andalucía, grant P08 – TIC 04200.

References

1. Binder, A., Freund, R., Oswald, M., Vock, L.: Extended spiking neural P systems with excitatory and inhibitory astrocytes. In: Proc. Eighth WSEAS Intern. Conf. on Evolutionary Computing, pp. 320–325. Vancouver, Canada (2007)
2. Calude, C., Păun, G.: Bio-steps beyond Turing. BioSystems 77, 175–194 (2004)
3. Csuhaj-Varjú, E., Dassow, J., Kelemen, J., Păun, G.: Grammar Systems. In: A Grammatical Approach to Distribution and Cooperation, Gordon and Breach, London (1994)
4. Chen, H., Ishdorj, T.-O., Păun, G.: Computing along the axon. Progress in Natural Science 17(4), 418–423 (2007)
5. Chen, H., Ishdorj, T.-O., Păun, G., Pérez-Jiménez, M.J.: Spiking neural P systems with extended rules. In: Proc. Fourth Brainstorming Week on Membrane Computing, Sevilla, RGNC Report 02/2006, pp. 241–265 (2006)
6. Dassow, J., Păun, G.: Regulated Rewriting in Formal Language Theory. Springer, Berlin (1989)
7. Freund, R.: Particular results for variants of P systems with one catalyst in one membrane. In: Proc. Fourth Brainstorming Week on Membrane Computing, vol. II, pp. 41–50. Fénix Editora, Sevilla (2006)
8. Freund, R.: Purely catalytic P systems: Two catalysts can be sufficient for computational completeness. In the present volume
9. Freund, R., Ibarra, O.H., Păun, A., Sosík, P., Yen, H.-C.: Catalytic P systems. In: [33], ch. 4
10. Freund, R., Kari, L., Oswald, M., Sosík, P.: Computationally universal P systems without priorities: two catalysts are sufficient. Theoretical Computer Science 330, 251–266 (2005)
11. Freund, R., Păun, G.: Universal P systems: One catalyst can be sufficient. In: Proc. 11th Brainstorming Week on Membrane Computing, February 4-8, Fénix Editora, Sevilla (2013)
12. Gheorghe, M., Păun, G., Pérez-Jiménez, M.J., Rozenberg, G.: Frontiers of membrane computing: Open problems and research topics. Intern. J. Found. Computer Sci. (2013) (first version in Proc. Tenth Brainstorming Week on Membrane Computing, vol. I, Sevilla, January 30-February 3, pp. 171–249 (2012))

13. Ibarra, O.H., Dang, Z., Egecioglu, O.: Catalytic P systems, semilinear sets, and vector addition systems. Th. Computer Sci. 312, 379–399 (2004)
14. Ibarra, O.H., Dang, Z., Egecioglu, O., Saxena, G.: Characterizations of catalytic membrane computing systems. In: Rovan, B., Vojtáš, P. (eds.) MFCS 2003. LNCS, vol. 2747, pp. 480–489. Springer, Heidelberg (2003)
15. Ionescu, M., Păun, G.: Notes about spiking neural P systems. In: Proc. Ninth Brainstorming Week on Membrane Computing, January 31-February 4, pp. 169–182. Fénix Editora, Sevilla (2011)
16. Ionescu, M., Păun, G., Pérez-Jiménez, M.J., Yokomori, T.: Spiking neural dP systems. Fundamenta Informaticae 11(4), 423–436 (2011)
17. Ionescu, M., Păun, G., Yokomori, T.: Spiking neural P systems. Fundamenta Informaticae 71(2-3), 279–308 (2006)
18. Krishna, S.N., Păun, A.: Results on catalytic and evolution-communication P systems. New Generation Computing 22, 377–394 (2004)
19. Krithivasan, K., Păun, G., Ramanujan, A.: On controlled P systems. In: Fundamenta Informaticae (to appear)
20. Leporati, A., Porreca, A.E., Zandron, C., Mauri, G.: Improving universality results on parallel enzymatic numerical P systems. In: Proc. 11th Brainstorming Week on Membrane Computing, February 4-8, Fénix Editora, Sevilla (2013)
21. Leporati, A., Mauri, G., Porreca, A.E., Zandron, C.: Enzymatic numerical P systems using elementary arithmetic operations. In: Alhazov, A., Cojocaru, S., Gheorghe, M., Rogozhin, Y., Rozenberg, G., Salomaa, A. (eds.) CMC 2013, vol. 8340, pp. 249–264. Springer, Heidelberg (2014)
22. Mutyam, M., Krithivasan, K.: P systems with membrane creation: Universality and efficiency. In: Margenstern, M., Rogozhin, Y. (eds.) MCU 2001. LNCS, vol. 2055, pp. 276–287. Springer, Heidelberg (2001)
23. Pan, L., Păun, G.: Spiking neural P systems with anti-spikes. Intern. J. Computers, Comm. Control 4(3), 273–282 (2009)
24. Pavel, A.B., Arsene, O., Buiu, C.: Enzymatic numerical P systems – a new class of membrane computing systems. In: The IEEE Fifth Intern. Conf. on Bio-Inspired Computing. Theory and applications. BIC-TA 2010, Liverpool, pp. 1331–1336 (September 2010)
25. Pavel, A.B., Vasile, C.I., Dumitrache, I.: Robot localization implemented with enzymatic numerical P systems. In: Prescott, T.J., Lepora, N.F., Mura, A., Verschure, P.F.M.J. (eds.) Living Machines 2012. LNCS, vol. 7375, pp. 204–215. Springer, Heidelberg (2012)
26. Păun, G.: Computing with membranes. J. Comput. Syst. Sci. 61, 108–143 (2000) (see also TUCS Report 208, November 1998, www.tucs.fi)
27. Păun, G: Computing with membranes – A variant. Intern. J. Found. Computer Sci. 11(1), 167–182 (2000)
28. Păun, G.: Membrane Computing. An Introduction. Springer, Berlin (2002)
29. Păun, G.: Spiking neural P systems with astrocyte-like control. JUCS 13(11), 1707–1721 (2007)
30. Păun, G.: Some open problems about numerical P systems. In: Proc. 11th Brainstorming Week on Membrane Computing, February 4-8, Fénix Editora, Sevilla (2013)
31. Păun, G., Păun, R.: Membrane computing and economics: Numerical P systems. Fundamenta Informaticae 73, 213–227 (2006)
32. Păun, G., Pérez-Jiménez, M.J.: Solving problems in a distributed way in membrane computing: dP systems. Int. J. of Computers, Communication and Control 5(2), 238–252 (2010)

33. Păun, G., Rozenberg, G., Salomaa, A. (eds.): The Oxford Handbook of Membrane Computing. Oxford University Press (2010)
34. Păun, G., Yu, S.: On synchronization in P systems. Fundamenta Informaticae 38(4), 397–410 (1999)
35. Song, T., Pan, L., Păun, G.: Spiking neural P systems with rules on synapses. Submitted (2013)
36. Sosí, P.: k: A catalytic P system with two catalysts generating a non-semilinear set. Romanian J. Inf. Sci. Technology (in press)
37. Sosík, P., Valík, O.: On evolutionary lineages of membrane systems. In: Freund, R., Păun, G., Rozenberg, G., Salomaa, A. (eds.) WMC 2005. LNCS, vol. 3850, pp. 67–78. Springer, Heidelberg (2006)
38. Syropoulos, A.: Hypercomputation: Computing Beyond the Church-Turing Barrier. Springer, Berlin (2008)
39. Vasile, C.I., Pavel, A.B., Kelemen, J.: Implementing obstacle avoidance and follower behaviors on Koala robots using numerical P systems. In: Tenth Brainstorming Week on Membrane Computing, Sevilla, vol. II, pp. 215–227 (2012)
40. Vasile, C.I., Pavel, A.B., Dumitrache, I.: Universality of enzymatic numerical P systems. In: Intern. J. Computer Math (in press)
41. Vasile, C.I., Pavel, A.B., Dumitrache, I., Păun, G.: On the power of enzymatic numerical P systems. Acta Informatica 49(6), 395–412 (2012)
42. The P Systems Website, http://ppage.psystems.eu

Active Membranes, Proteins on Membranes, Tissue P Systems: Complexity-Related Issues and Challenges

Petr Sosík

Research Institute of the IT4Innovations Centre of Excellence,
Faculty of Philosophy and Science, Silesian University in Opava
74601 Opava, Czech Republic
petr.sosik@fpf.slu.cz

Abstract. We resume computational complexity aspects of several models of membrane systems, namely P systems with active membranes, P systems with proteins on membranes and tissue P systems both with membrane separation and membrane division. A sequence of common issues is studied in relation to these P system models, and 16 open problems are stated in the text.

We question the role of families of P systems and their necessity to solve computationally hard problems in polynomial time. For each P system model we focus on conditions guaranteeing the polynomial equivalence of families of P systems and Turing machines. The ability of P systems to solve NP/co-NP-complete problems in polynomial time (trading space for time) is a very popular issue. Interesting characterizations of the borderline between tractability and intractability, i.e., **P/NP**, have been recently shown. Similarly important, although less popular, is the relation between **NP/co-NP** and further classes as **PP**, the polynomial hierarchy **PH** and **PSPACE**. Several models of P systems has been shown to characterize the class **PSPACE** which itself characterizes parallel computations with an unlimited number of processors but a limited propagation of data between them.

1 Introduction

The key ingredient of P system is an abstract membrane which lets pass only certain objects, only in certain directions or only under some conditions. The membranes can be embedded, hence the name "membrane system." Objects can also react and produce other objects. Gradually, many variants of membrane system have been proposed, enriched with further operations as membrane division, membrane dissolution, membrane polarization, tissue P systems, membrane with regulating proteins etc.

In the remaining sections we shall study the mutual relation of several abstract operations in membrane systems: membrane division, membrane dissolution, membrane polarization, symport/antiport of objects, regulation by proteins on membranes etc. Various combinations of these operations yield various levels of

A. Alhazov et al. (Eds.): CMC 2013, LNCS 8340, pp. 40–55, 2014.
© Springer-Verlag Berlin Heidelberg 2014

computational power of the system. Our aim is to give a survey of the known results arranged in a comparative way. Where possible, we omit technical details and refer the reader to more technical papers. We also omit explanation of definitions and we limit the number of examples which can be also found in the sources referred to.

2 Preliminaries

A *multiset* M over an underlying set A is a pair (A, f) where $f : A \to \mathbb{N}$ is a mapping. If $M = (A, f)$ is a multiset then its *support* is defined as $supp(M) = \{x \in A \mid f(x) > 0\}$. The total number of elements in a multiset, including repeated memberships, is the *cardinality* of the multiset. A multiset is empty (resp. finite) if its support is the empty set (resp. a finite set). If $M = (A, f)$ is a finite multiset over A, and $supp(M) = \{a_1, \ldots, a_k\}$ then it can also be represented by the string $a_1^{f(a_1)} \ldots a_k^{f(a_k)}$ over the alphabet $\{a_1, \ldots, a_k\}$. Nevertheless, all permutations of this string precisely identify the same multiset M. Throughout this paper, we speak about "the finite multiset M" where M is a string, and meaning "the finite multiset represented by the string M".

If $M_1 = (A, f_1)$, $M_2 = (A, f_2)$ are multisets over A, then we define the union of M_1 and M_2 as $M_1 + M_2 = (A, g)$, where $g = f_1 + f_2$.

In the rest of the paper we use extensively the computational complexity classes **P**, **NP**, **co-NP** and **PSPACE**. We also denote by $\mathbf{AC}^0$ the class of problems solvable by uniform families of acyclic logic circuits with constant depth and a polynomial size, and by **PP** the class of decision problems solvable by a probabilistic Turing machine in polynomial time, with an error probability of less than $1/2$ for all instances. We refer the reader to, e.g., [15] for more details.

Definition 1. *A P system of degree $m \geq 1$ is a construct*

$$\Pi = (O, H, \mu, w_1, \ldots, w_m, R, i_{out}) \ \text{where:}$$

1. *O is the alphabet of objects;*
2. *H is the set of labels of membranes;*
3. *μ is a membrane structure of degree m with membranes labeled with elements of H;*
4. *$w_1, \ldots, w_m \in O^*$ are the multisets of objects initially present in the m regions of μ;*
5. *R is a finite sets of evolution rules (associated with labels) which can change contents of membranes and eventually also structure of the system; types of rules are specified in further sections;*
6. *$i_{out} \in H$ indicates the output region of Π.*

The membrane structure and the multisets represented by w_i, $1 \leq i \leq m$, in Π constitute the *initial configuration* of the system. A transition between configurations means applying a maximal multiset of evolution rules in parallel. Other execution modes as sequential or minimal parallelism are possible.

The computation stops when there is no rule which can be applied to objects and membranes in the last configuration. The result of computation is then defined by the content of the output membrane.

In this paper we study the accepting (or recognizer) variant of P systems. A *recognizer P system* solving a decision problem has a specific *input membrane* i_{in} which initially contains a multiset of objects encoding an instance of the problem. Alternatively, if the system solves only one instance, the instance may be encoded within the structure of the system; then we speak about P systems *without input membrane*.

A recognizer P system must furthermore comply with the following requirements: (a) the alphabet O contains two distinguished elements *yes* and *no*; (b) all computations halt; and (c) exactly one of the object *yes* (accepting computation) or *no* (rejecting computation) must be sent to the output membrane of the system, and only at the last step of each computation.

3   Complexity Classes of P Systems

Consider a decision problem $X = (I_X, \theta_X)$ where elements of I_X are called instances and θ_X is a total boolean function over I_X. In a family of recognizer systems *without input membrane*, denoted by $\mathbf{\Pi} = \{\Pi(w) : w \in I_X\}$, an instance w of a problem X is encoded into the structure of a P system $\Pi(w)$. The system $\Pi(w)$ is supposed to solve the instance w. If we use recognizer P systems *with input membrane*, then such a family is denoted by $\mathbf{\Pi} = \{\Pi(n) : n \in \mathbb{N}\}$. A member $\Pi(n)$ of the family solves all the instances of the problem X of size n, properly encoded as its input. (Let us denote by $|w|$ the size of an instance $w \in I_X$.)

Definition 2 ([28]). *A family of recognizer membrane systems is polynomially uniform by Turing machines if there exists a deterministic Turing machine which constructs each member Π of the family in polynomial time with respect to the size of the instance(s) solved by Π.*

In the sequel we will for short denote such a family just as *uniform*. Formally, [28] defines the conditions of *soundness* and *completeness* of $\mathbf{\Pi}$ with respect to X. A conjunction of these two conditions ensures that for every $w \in I_X$, if $\theta_X(w) = 1$, then every computation of $\Pi(w)$ is accepting, and if $\theta_X(w) = 0$, then every computation of $\Pi(w)$ is rejecting.

Note that the P system $\Pi(w)$ can be generally nondeterministic, i.e, it may have different possible computations, but with the same result. Such a P system is also called *confluent*.

Definition 3 ([28]). *A decision problem X is solvable in polynomial time by a family $\mathbf{\Pi} = \{\Pi(w) : w \in I_X\}$ of recognizer P systems without input membrane if the following holds:*

- *The family $\mathbf{\Pi}$ is polynomially uniform by Turing machines.*

– *The family* **Π** *is polynomially bounded; that is, there exists a polynomial* p
  such that for each instance $w \in I_X$, *every computation of* $\Pi(w)$ *performs at*
  most $p(|w|)$ *steps.*
– *The family* **Π** *is sound and complete with respect to* X.

The family **Π** is said to provide a *semi-uniform solution* to the problem X.
Analogously one could define a family **Π** = $\{\Pi(n) : n \in \mathbb{N}\}$ of recognizer P
systems with input membrane which provide a *uniform solution* to the problem
X. We refer to [28] for more details.

Let **R** be a class of recognizer P systems. We denote by **PMC$_\mathbf{R}$** the set of all
decision problems which can be solved in a uniform way and polynomial time
by means of families of systems from **R**. We denote by **PMC$_\mathbf{R}^*$** the set of all
decision problems which can be solved by such families in a semi-uniform way.
By the definition, for any family **R** we obtain **PMC$_\mathbf{R}$** $\subseteq$ **PMC$_\mathbf{R}^*$**.

3.1   The Need for Families?

It became usual to express the computational power of various kinds of membrane systems in terms of families just described in the previous section. It is
long known, however, that most of the studied types of P systems are computationally universal and, by the Church-Turing thesis, there exists a universal P
system of each such type, capable to solve all instances of any decidable problem.

The need for families is therefore given by the *efficiency* of computation. It is
easy to simulate the Minsky register (or counter) machine [21] by virtually any
transition P system in linear time. The content of any register can be represented
by a multiset of specific object in a specific membrane, see Fig. 1. Most types
of P systems are capable to decrement or increment a given multiset of objects
in a membrane. However, the register machine is *exponentially slower* than the
Turing machine.

One could turn to other models as the RAM machine which are known to
be polynomially equivalent with Turing machine (TM). The simulation of TM
by RAM in polynomial time, however, typically uses an unbounded number of
individually addressable registers which cannot be achieved with common models
of P systems (unless some special extension is used). If one tries to simulate a
TM by P system directly, the same problem arises. However, there still might be
a way how to avoid its obstacle: many models of P systems are able to perform
the multiplication and division by a constant in one step. Could this capability
be used to encode the whole content of tape of a TM into one multiset and to
manipulate it effectively?

Finally, if one wanted to construct a P system solving all instances of an NP-
complete problem in polynomial time, it seems inevitable to have an unbounded
number of individually accessible cells. Known models of P systems, however,
use a fixed set of cell labels or a fixed diameter of a communication graph with
a bounded number of distinguishable cells. Although an unlimited number of
cells can be produced by cell division, separation or creation, they cannot be accessed individually unless nondeterminism is involved as in [1]. Which extension

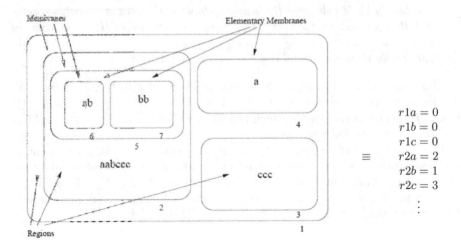

Fig. 1. An example of contents of membranes representing registers

(e.g., a dynamically growing communication graph) would be nature inspired and not much artificial, on one hand, and powerful enough to overcome this obstacle, on the other hand?

Open Problem 1. *Is there any known standard model of P system capable of solving a P-complete problem in polynomial time without the use of families, i.e., all instances are solved by the same P systems? Alternatively, such a P system must simulate any Turing machine in polynomial time.*

Open Problem 2. *How to design a natural (not much "extraordinary") model of P system capable of solving an NP-complete problem in polynomial time without the use of families?*

4   P Systems with Active Membranes

The term "active membranes" denotes the fact that, in this model, an operation inspired by division of live cells is introduced: membranes can divide into two, copying their contents (including eventual embedded membranes) into both descendants. Some objects, however, can be modified, imitating mutations. Besides, the membranes contain objects which can evolve and pass between membranes under pre-defined conditions.

The following definition is given without any broad explanation and examples; for further details please see, e.g., [38] or [37]. *A P system with active membranes* [38], abbreviated here as *AM system*, is a construct

$$\Pi = (O, H, \mu, w_1, \ldots, w_m, R, i_{out}),$$

where $O, H, w_1, \ldots, w_m$ and i_{out} are as in Definition 1, μ is a *membrane structure* of m membranes with possible polarizations $\{+, -, 0\}$, and R is a finite set of *developmental rules* of the following forms:

- $[_h a \to v]_h^\alpha$, for $h \in H, \alpha \in \{+, -, 0\}, a \in V, v \in V^*$
  (object evolution rules);
- $a[_h \ ]_h^{\alpha_1} \to [_h b]_h^{\alpha_2}$, for $h \in H, \alpha_1, \alpha_2 \in \{+, -, 0\}, a, b \in V$
  (communication rules);
- $[_h a \ ]_h^{\alpha_1} \to [_h \ ]_h^{\alpha_2} b$, for $h \in H, \alpha_1, \alpha_2 \in \{+, -, 0\}, a, b \in V$
  (communication rules);
- $[_h a \ ]_h^\alpha \to b$, for $h \in H, \alpha \in \{+, -, 0\}, a, b \in V$
  (dissolving rules);
- $[_h a \ ]_h^{\alpha_1} \to [_h b \ ]_h^{\alpha_2} [_h c \ ]_h^{\alpha_3}$,
  for $h \in H, \alpha_1, \alpha_2, \alpha_3 \in \{+, -, 0\}, a, b, c \in V$
  (division rules for elementary membranes);
- $[_{h_0} [_{h_1} \ ]_{h_1}^{+} \cdots [_{h_k} \ ]_{h_k}^{+} [_{h_{k+1}} \ ]_{h_{k+1}}^{-} \cdots [_{h_n} \ ]_{h_n}^{-}]_{h_0}^{\alpha_2}$
  $\to [_{h_0} [_{h_1} \ ]_{h_1}^{\alpha_3} \cdots [_{h_k} \ ]_{h_k}^{\alpha_3}]_{h_0}^{\alpha_5} [_{h_0} [_{h_{k+1}} \ ]_{h_{k+1}}^{\alpha_4} \cdots [_{h_n} \ ]_{h_n}^{\alpha_4}]_{h_0}^{\alpha_6}$,
  for $n > k \geq 1, h_i \in H, 0 \leq i \leq n$, and $\alpha_2, \ldots, \alpha_6 \in \{+, -, 0\}$;
  (division of non-elementary membranes).

All the above rules are applied in parallel, but at one step, an object a can be subject to only one rule of type (a)–(e) and a membrane h can be subject to only one rule of type (b)–(f). In the case of type (f) rules, this means that none of the membranes $h_0, \ldots, h_n$ listed in the rule can be simultaneously subject to another rule of type (b)–(f). However, this restriction do not apply to membranes with neutral charge contained in h_0.

The system Π starts its computation in the *initial configuration* $(\mu, w_1, \ldots, w_m)$ when all the membranes are neutral (polarization 0), and it continues the computation until no rule can be applied.

Since another paper [16] in this volume is devoted solely to the complexity issues in P systems with active membranes, we skip many details and we summarize basic known results in Table 1, describing the influence of various combinations of operations on the computational power of AM systems. Each column in the table corresponds to a specific combination of operations described in the above definition of AM systems. The last row compares the computational power of polynomially uniform families of AM systems using these operations with known computational complexity classes. Most of these characterizations hold for both families with and without input; some, however, are known to hold for only one of these variants. See, e.g., [28,42] for more details. Table 1 summarizes results reported in [2,44,45,29,41,31].

Open Problem 3. *Is the lower bound* **PP** *or the upper bound* **PSPACE** *for the power of families of AM systems without non-elementary membrane division optimal? If not, how to improve it?*

Table 1. The computational power of uniform families of recognizer AM systems with polarization. X denotes used operations, ? denotes operations not affecting the computational power.

Polarization	X	X	X
Evolution rules (a)	?	X	X
Communication rules (b),(c)	X	X	X
Membrane dissolution (d)	?	?	?
Division of elementary membranes (e)		X	?
Division of non-elementary membranes (f)			X
Class of problems solved	=	$\supseteq$	=
in polynomial time	**P**	**PP**	**PSPACE**

4.1   AM Systems without Polarization

In AM systems without polarization, denoted by AM^0 systems, all membranes are always polarized neutrally. In such a case the condition that the membranes $h_1, \ldots, h_k$ and $h_{k+1}, \ldots, h_n$ in rules of type (f) have opposite polarization is relaxed. We start with rather surprising result: if, in addition to polarizations, we remove also the rules (d) of membrane dissolution, the system looses almost all its computational power [22]. Actually, such a system can be replaced by a computationally equivalent AM^0 system with a single membrane and with evolution rules only, which immediately transform certain input objects to *yes* and others to *no*. In other words, the behavior of such a system is trivial. It is interesting that even the non-elementary membrane division does not increase the power of these systems.

Whenever the the membrane dissolution is allowed, the resulting computational power corresponds to that of conventional computers, even only with object evolution rules (a). The power of these families remains unchanged if we add communication rules of type (b) a (c), and also division rules (e) restricted to the form $[_h a]_h \to [_h b]_h [_h b]_h$ (symmetric division of elementary membranes).

Interestingly, if unrestricted elementary membrane division is allowed, the resulting computational power is not known (marked by ??? in Table 2. The so-called Păun's conjecture claims that the computational power is still **P**. With non-elementary membrane division and only the rules of types (d), (e), (f) are allowed, then semi-uniform families of AM^0 systems solve in polynomial time problems in $\mathbf{NP} \cup \mathbf{co\text{-}NP}$[46].

Finally, with all possible operations (a)–(f) including the non-elementary membrane division we again get the power of the second class computers, i.e., the capability to solve PSPACE-complete problems in polynomial time. The results based on publications [3,22,23,46,17,41] are summarized in Table 2.

Open Problem 4. *Find a relevant example(s) of AM or AM^0 systems so that the computational power of polynomially uniform families with and without input would be different.*

Table 2. The computational power of uniform families of recognizer AM systems without polarization. X denotes used operations, the symbol ? denotes operations which do not affect the computational power.

Evolution rules (a)	X	X	X		X
Communication rules (b),(c)	X	?	X		X
Membrane dissolution (d)		X	X	X	X
Division of elementary membranes (e)	X		X	X	X
Div. of non-elementary membranes (f)	X			X	X
Class of problems solved	$\subseteq$	$=$		$\supseteq$ **NP**	$=$
in polynomial time	$\mathbf{AC^0}$	**P**	**???**	$\cup$ **co-NP**	**PSPACE**

Open Problem 5. *How to characterize the computational power of AM^0 systems without non-elementary membrane division (Păun's conjecture)?*

Open Problem 6. *Is the lower bound **NP** $\cup$ **co-NP** or the upper bound* **PSPACE** *for the power of families of AM^0 systems with rules of types (d), (e), (f) optimal? What is their relation to the class **PP**?*

5   P Systems with Proteins on Membranes

The research of P systems with proteins on membranes in the form presented here started in [33] and [34] where insoluble membrane proteins have been modeled in the broad area of membrane computing. P systems with proteins on membranes can be viewed as a model combining membrane systems and brane calculi as introduced in [6]. Besides the crucial role of membrane proteins in cells, further research motivation is the fact that maximally parallel processing of different species of molecules in membrane systems was not realistic. Here we limit the parallelism through the modeling of a limited number of trans-membrane proteins (protein channels).

Definition 4. *A P system with proteins on membranes and membrane division is a tuple $\Pi = (O, P, \mu, w_1/z_1, \ldots, w_m/z_m, E, R_1, \ldots, R_m, i_o)$, where*

m is the degree of the system (the number of membranes),
O is the set of objects, P is the set of proteins (with $O \cap P = \emptyset$),
μ is the membrane structure (a rooted tree) with membranes labelled uniquely
    $1, \ldots, m$
$w_1, \ldots, w_m$ are (strings representing the) multisets of objects present in the m
    regions of the membrane structure μ,
$z_1, \ldots, z_m$ are multisets of proteins present on the m membranes of μ,
$E \subseteq O$ is the set of objects present in the environment (in an arbitrarily large
    number of copies each),
$R_1, \ldots, R_m$ are finite sets of rules associated with the m membranes of μ, and
i_o is the label of the output membrane.

Both proteins and objects can be manipulated via rules associated with membranes. In all of these rules, a, b, c, d are objects, p is a protein, and i is a label ("res" stands for "restricted"):

Type	Rule	Effect
1res	$[{}_ip\|a]_i \to [{}_ip\|b]_i$ $a[{}_ip\|\ ]_i \to b[{}_ip\|\ ]_i$	modify an object, but not move
2res	$[{}_ip\|a]_i \to a[{}_ip\|\ ]_i$ $a[{}_ip\|\ ]_i \to [{}_ip\|a]_i$	move an object, but not modify
3res	$[{}_ip\|a]_i \to b[{}_ip\|\ ]_i$ $a[{}_ip\|\ ]_i \to [{}_ip\|b]_i$	modify and move one object
4res	$a[{}_ip\|b]_i \to b[{}_ip\|a]_i$	interchange two objects
5res	$a[{}_ip\|b]_i \to c[{}_ip\|d]_i$	interchange and modify two objects

In all the cases above, the protein is not changed, it plays the role of a catalyst. A generalization is to allow rules of the forms below ("cp" means "change protein"):

Type	Rule	Effect (besides changing also the protein)
1cp	$[{}_ip\|a]_i \to [{}_ip'\|b]_i$ $a[{}_ip\|\ ]_i \to b[{}_ip'\|\ ]_i$	modify an object, but not move
2cp	$[{}_ip\|a]_i \to a[{}_ip'\|\ ]_i$ $a[{}_ip\|\ ]_i \to [{}_ip'\|a]_i$	move an object, but not modify
3cp	$[{}_ip\|a]_i \to b[{}_ip'\|\ ]_i$ $a[{}_ip\|\ ]_i \to [{}_ip'\|b]_i$	modify and move one object
4cp	$a[{}_ip\|b]_i \to b[{}_ip'\|a]_i$	interchange two objects
5cp	$a[{}_ip\|b]_i \to c[{}_ip'\|d]_i$	interchange and modify two objects

where p, p' are two proteins. If $p \neq p'$ at each rule, then we denote them $ncpp$, $n = 1, 2, 3, 4, 5$ (pure change-protein rules).

An intermediate case is to allow at most two states for each protein, $p, \bar{p}$, and each rule must change from p to $\bar{p}$ and back (like in the case of bistable catalysts). Rules with such flip-flop proteins are denoted by $nffp$, $n = 1, 2, 3, 4, 5$.

The rules are used in the non-deterministic maximally parallel way. However, at each step each object and each protein can be involved in application of at most one rule. The membranes are not considered as involved in the rule applications hence the same membrane can appear in any number of rules at the same time.

We denote by $NOP_m(pro_r; list\text{-}of\text{-}types\text{-}of\text{-}rules)$ the family of sets of numbers generated by P systems with proteins on membranes, with at most m membranes, using rules as specified in the list-of-types-of-rules, and with at most r proteins present on a membrane. The following results were proven in [33], [27], [13]. Let NRE denote the class of all recursively enumerable sets of non-negative integers.

Theorem 1.
$NOP_1(pro_2; 2cpp) = NOP_1(pro_2; 2res; 4cpp) = NOP_1(pro_2; 2res; 1cpp) =$
$= NOP_1(pro_6; 3ffp) = NOP_1(pro_6; 2ffp; 4ffp) = NOP_1(pro_6; 2ffp; 5ffp) =$
$= NOP_1(pro_9; 1res; 2ffp) = NOP_1(pro_6; 1ffp; 2ffp) = NOP_1(pro_8; 1ffp; 2res) =$
$= NOP_1(pro_8; 2ffp; 3res) = NOP_1(pro_7; 1ffp; 3res) = NOP_1(pro_8; 3res; 4ffp) =$
$= NOP_1(pro_7; 2ffp; 5res) = NRE.$

5.1   Introducing Membrane Division

To *divide a membrane*, we use the following type of rule (referred to as *type 6*), where p, p', p'' are proteins (possibly equal):

$$[_i p| \ ]_i \rightarrow [_i p'| \ ]_i [_i p''| \ ]_i$$

Membrane i can be non-elementary. The rule doesn't change the membrane label i and instead of one membrane, at next step, we will have two membranes with the same label i and the same contents (except for p' and p'') replicated from the original membrane. Let us denote by $\mathcal{MP}(+n)$ the class of recognizer P systems with proteins on membranes and membrane division (with no restrictions on the types of rules described above). The strongest recently known result [43] is the following:

Theorem 2. $\mathbf{PMC}^*_{\mathcal{MP}(+n)} = \mathbf{PSPACE}.$

Open Problem 7. *What is the computational power of polynomially uniform families of $\mathcal{MP}$ systems without membrane division? Do they characterize the class* **P**, *and what happens under restrictions on the form of rules used in Theorem 1?*

Open Problem 8. *Does a result analogous to Theorem 2 hold true for the class* $\mathbf{PMC}_{\mathcal{MP}(+n)}$ *(i.e., families of P systems with input solving problems in a uniform way)?*

Open Problem 9. *Which restrictions on the form of rules (as in Theorem 1) can be applied so that the Theorem 2 remains valid?*

Open Problem 10. *What is the computational power of polynomially uniform families of $\mathcal{MP}$ systems using only restricted rules? Is there an analogy with polarizationless AM systems?*

Open Problem 11. *What is the computational power of polynomially uniform families of $\mathcal{MP}$ systems with elementary membrane division?*

6   Tissue P Systems

The basic idea of tissue P systems is the principle of symport and antiport [35]. Symport rules move objects across a membrane together in one direction, whereas antiport rules move objects across a membrane in opposite directions. In tissue P systems these two variants were unified as a unique type of rule manipulating a certain number of objects. From the original definitions of tissue P systems [19,20], several research lines have been developed and other variants have arisen (see, for example, [4,5,10,12,14]).

Definition 5. *A tissue P system of degree $q \geq 1$ is a tuple*

$$\Pi = (\Gamma, \mathcal{E}, \mathcal{M}_1, \ldots, \mathcal{M}_q, \mathcal{R}, i_{out}),$$

where:

1. *Γ is a finite alphabet whose elements are called objects;*
2. *$\mathcal{E} \subseteq \Gamma$ is a finite alphabet of objects initially in the environment of the system in inexhaustibly many copies each, and 0 is the label of the environment;*
3. *$\mathcal{M}_1, \ldots, \mathcal{M}_q$ are strings over Γ, representing the finite multisets of objects placed in the q cells of the system at the beginning of the computation;*
4. *$\mathcal{R}$ is a finite set of communication rules of the form $(i, u/v, j)$, for $i, j \in \{0, 1, 2, \ldots, q\}, i \neq j, u, v \in \Gamma^*$, and the length of the rule is $|uv| > 0$;*
5. *$i_{out} \in \{0, 1, 2, \ldots, q\}$ is the output cell.*

When applying a rule $(i, u/v, j)$, the objects of the multiset represented by u are sent from region i to region j and, simultaneously, the objects of the multiset v are sent from region j to region i. A communication rule $(i, u/v, j)$ is called a *symport rule* if $u = \lambda$ or $v = \lambda$. A symport rule $(i, u/\lambda, j)$, with $i \neq 0, j \neq 0$, provides a virtual arc from cell i to cell j. A communication rule $(i, u/v, j)$ is called an *antiport rule* if $u \neq \lambda$ and $v \neq \lambda$. An antiport rule $(i, u/v, j)$, with $i \neq 0, j \neq 0$, provides two arcs: one from cell i to cell j and another one from cell j to cell i. Thus, every tissue P systems has an underlying directed graph whose nodes are the cells of the system and the arcs are obtained from communication rules.

Recognizer variant of tissue P system is defined analogously as in the previous sections. We denote the class of recognizer tissue P systems by TC. The following result was shown by simulation of basic transitional P systems in [8]:

$$\mathbf{P} = \mathbf{PMC}_{TC}.$$

6.1   Tissue P Systems with Cell Division

Tissue P system with cell division is based on the cell-like model of P systems with active membranes [38]. The biological inspiration is the following: alive tissues are not static network of cells but new cells are produced by membrane division in a natural way. In these models, the cells are not polarized; the two cells obtained by division have the same labels as the original cell, and if a cell is divided, its interaction with other cells or with the environment is blocked during the division process.

Division Rules: $[a]_i \rightarrow [b]_i[c]_i$, where $i \in \{1, 2, \ldots, q\}$ and $a, b, c \in \Gamma$, and $i \neq i_{out}$. In reaction with an object a, the cell i is divided into two cells with the same label; in the first cell the object a is replaced by b; in the second cell the object a is replaced by c; the output cell i_{out} cannot be divided;

For each natural number $k \geq 1$, we denote by $TDC(k)$ the class of recognizer tissue P systems with cell division and communication rules of length at most k. We denote by TDC the class of recognizer tissue P systems with cell division and without restriction on the length of communication rules. Obviously, $TDC(k) \subseteq TDC$ for all $k \geq 1$.

The following result in [11] states that only problems in **P** can be solved by families of recognizer tissue P systems with the rules of length 1, on one hand:

$$\mathbf{P} = \mathbf{PMC}_{TDC(1)}. \tag{1}$$

On the other hand, [32] places a tight borderline between efficiency and non-efficiency in the sense of the length of rules:

$$\mathbf{NP} \cup \mathbf{co\text{-}NP} \subseteq \mathbf{PMC}_{TDC(2)}. \tag{2}$$

Finally, the upper bound on the power of these P systems is given in [39]:

$$\mathbf{PMC}_{TDC} \subseteq \mathbf{PSPACE}. \tag{3}$$

Open Problem 12. *Is the lower bound on* $\mathbf{PMC}_{TDC(k)}$*,* $k \geq 2$ *tight? If not, improve it. Particularly, which is the relation of* **PP** *and* $\mathbf{PMC}_{TDC(k)}$*?*

Open Problem 13. *Is* $\mathbf{PSPACE} \subseteq \mathbf{PMC}_{TDC}$ *? (This might resolve also the previous problem.)*

6.2 Tissue P Systems with Cell Separation

The operation of membrane separation was introduced in [24]. It is motivated by the fact that during a cell division, its content is split between the two descendants.

Definition 6 ([25]). *A tissue P system with cell separation of degree* $q \geq 1$ *is a tuple*

$$\Pi = (\Gamma, \Gamma_1, \Gamma_2, \mathcal{E}, \mathcal{M}_1, \ldots, \mathcal{M}_q, \mathcal{R}, i_{out}),$$

where:

1. *$\Gamma, \mathcal{E}, \mathcal{M}_1, \ldots, \mathcal{M}_q$, i_{out} are as in Definition 5;*
2. *$\{\Gamma_1, \Gamma_2\}$ is a partition of Γ, that is, $\Gamma = \Gamma_1 \cup \Gamma_2$, $\Gamma_1, \Gamma_2 \neq \emptyset$, $\Gamma_1 \cap \Gamma_2 = \emptyset$;*
3. *$\mathcal{R}$ is a finite set of rules of the following forms:*
   (a) Communication rules: $(i, u/v, j)$, for $i, j \in \{0, 1, 2, \ldots, q\}, i \neq j, u, v \in \Gamma^*, |uv| > 0$;

(b) Separation rules: $[a]_i \to [\Gamma_1]_i[\Gamma_2]_i$, where $i \in \{1, 2, \ldots, q\}$ and $a \in \Gamma$, and $i \neq i_{out}$. *In reaction with an object a, the cell i is separated into two cells with the same label; at the same time, object a is consumed; the objects from Γ_1 are placed in the first cell, those from Γ_2 are placed in the second cell; the output cell i_{out} cannot be separated.*

As in the previous section, we introduce the notation $TSC(k)$ or TSC for the class of recognizer tissue P systems with cell separation and communication rules of length at most k, or without restriction, respectively. The known results are summarized as follows:

$$\mathbf{P} = \mathbf{PMC}_{TSC(2)} \qquad \text{(Characterization of } \mathbf{P}, \text{ [26]);}$$
$$\mathbf{NP} \cup \mathbf{co\text{-}NP} \subseteq \mathbf{PMC}_{TSC(3)} \qquad \text{((In)Tractability borderline, [30]);}$$
$$\mathbf{PMC}_{TSC} \subseteq \mathbf{PSPACE} \qquad \text{(Upper bound on the computing power, [40]).}$$

It is interesting that, although the frameworks of tissue P systems with cell division and cell separation is rather similar, the borderline between tractability and intractability is placed differently. Further variants of tissue P systems with cell division/separation and their computational power were studied, e.g., in [18].

Open Problem 14. *Is the lower bound on $\mathbf{PMC}_{TSC(k)}$, $k \geq 3$ tight? If not, improve it. Particularly, which is the relation of $\mathbf{PP}$ and $\mathbf{PMC}_{TSC(k)}$?*

Open Problem 15. *Is $\mathbf{PSPACE} \subseteq \mathbf{PMC}_{TSC}$? (This might resolve also the previous problem.)*

Open Problem 16. *What happens if only symport (respectively, only antiport) rules are allowed in tissue P systems with cell division or cell separation?*

7 Conclusion

We have addressed a sequence of open problems and challenges in the computational complexity theory of P systems with active membranes, P systems with proteins on membranes, and tissue P systems. We focused on polynomially uniform families of recognizer P systems working in polynomial time and often using the strategy of trading space for time. We questioned also some very basic concepts commonly used in the computational complexity of membrane computing, namely the construction of uniform families. Due to limited space we did not present many details of the cited results but rather their synopsis which would allow to compare the power of various operations used in the P system models mentioned above. We presented a sequence of the most important recent open problems in these fields, related mostly to basic variants of these P systems. For further details on computational complexity in P systems with active membranes and tissue P systems, the reader is referred to [28,16]. However, as the progress in the research of tissue P systems is recently very fast, some open problems mentioned in [28] are already resolved. Also new variants of P systems continuously emerge, the reader can find many of them under the cited references.

Acknowledgements. This work was supported by the European Regional Development Fund in the IT4Innovations Centre of Excellence project (CZ.1.05/1.1.00/02.0070), by the European Social Fund under the project OPVK No. CZ.1.07/2.2.00/28.0014, and by the Silesian University in Opava under the Student Funding Scheme, project SGS/7/2011.

References

1. Alhazov, A., Leporati, A., Mauri, G., Porreca, A., Zandron, C.: The computational power of exponential-space P systems with active membranes. In: Martínez-del-Amor, M., Păun, G., Pérez-Hurtado, I., Romero-Campero, F. (eds.) Proceedings of the Tenth Brainstorming Week on Membrane Computing, pp. 35–60. Fénix Editora, Sevilla (2012)
2. Alhazov, A., Martín-Vide, C., Pan, L.: Solving a PSPACE-complete problem by P systems with restricted active membranes. Fundamenta Informaticae 58(2), 67–77 (2003)
3. Alhazov, A., Pérez-Jiménez, M.J.: Uniform solution of QSAT using polarizationless active membranes. In: Durand-Lose, J., Margenstern, M. (eds.) MCU 2007. LNCS, vol. 4664, pp. 122–133. Springer, Heidelberg (2007)
4. Alhazov, A., Freund, R., Oswald, M.: Tissue P systems with antiport rules and small numbers of symbols and cells. In: De Felice, C., Restivo, A. (eds.) DLT 2005. LNCS, vol. 3572, pp. 100–111. Springer, Heidelberg (2005)
5. Bernardini, F., Gheorghe, M.: Cell communication in tissue P systems and cell division in population P systems. Soft Computing 9(9), 640–649 (2005)
6. Cardelli, L.: Brane calculi. In: Danos, V., Schachter, V. (eds.) CMSB 2004. LNCS, vol. 3082, pp. 257–278. Springer, Heidelberg (2005)
7. Csuhaj-Varjú, E., Gheorghe, M., Rozenberg, G., Salomaa, A., Vaszil, G. (eds.): CMC 2012. LNCS, vol. 7762. Springer, Heidelberg (2013)
8. Díaz-Pernil, D., Pérez-Jiménez, M.J., Romero-Jiménez, Á.: Efficient simulation of tissue-like p systems by transition cell-like p systems. Natural Computing 8(4), 797–806 (2009)
9. Eleftherakis, G., Kefalas, P., Păun, G., Rozenberg, G., Salomaa, A. (eds.): WMC 2007. LNCS, vol. 4860. Springer, Heidelberg (2007)
10. Freund, R., Păun, G., Pérez-Jiménez, M.: Tissue P systems with channel states. Theoretical Computer Science 330, 101–116 (2005)
11. Gutiérrez-Escudero, R., Pérez-Jiménez, M., Rius-Font, M.: Characterizing tractability by tissue-like P systems. In: Păun, et al. (eds.) [36], pp. 289–300
12. Krishna, S., Lakshmanan, K., Rama, R.: Tissue P systems with contextual and rewriting rules. In: Păun, G., Rozenberg, G., Salomaa, A., Zandron, C. (eds.) WMC 2002. LNCS, vol. 2597, pp. 339–351. Springer, Heidelberg (2003)
13. Krishna, S.N.: On the computational power of flip-flop proteins on membranes. In: Cooper, S.B., Löwe, B., Sorbi, A. (eds.) CiE 2007. LNCS, vol. 4497, pp. 695–704. Springer, Heidelberg (2007)
14. Lakshmanan, K., Rama, R.: The computational efficiency of insertion deletion tissue P systems. In: Subramanian, K., Rangarajan, K., Mukund, M. (eds.) Formal Models, Languages and Applications, pp. 235–245. World Scientific (2006)
15. van Leeuwen, J. (ed.): Handbook of Theoretical Computer Science, vol. A: Algorithms and Complexity. Elsevier, Amsterdam (1990)

16. Leporati, A.: Computational complexity of P systems with active membranes. In: Alhazov, A., Cojocaru, S., Gheorghe, M., Rogozhin, Y., Rozenberg, G., Salomaa, A. (eds.) CMC 2013, vol. 8340, pp. 19–32. Springer, Heidelberg (2014)

17. Leporati, A., Ferretti, C., Mauri, G., Pérez-Jiménez, M., Zandron, C.: Complexity aspects of polarizationless membrane systems. Natural Computing 8(4), 703–717 (2009)

18. Macías-Ramos, L.F., Pérez-Jiménez, M.J., Riscos-Núñez, A., Rius-Font, M., Valencia-Cabrera, L.: The efficiency of tissue P systems with cell separation relies on the environment. In: Csuhaj-Varjú, et al. (eds.) [7], pp. 243–256

19. Martín-Vide, C., Pazos, J., Păun, G., Rodríguez-Patón, A.: A new class of symbolic abstract neural nets: Tissue P systems. In: Ibarra, O.H., Zhang, L. (eds.) COCOON 2002. LNCS, vol. 2387, pp. 573–679. Springer, Heidelberg (2002)

20. Martín Vide, C., Pazos, J., Păun, G., Rodríguez Patón, A.: Tissue P systems. Theoretical Computer Science 296, 295–326 (2003)

21. Minsky, M.: Computation – Finite and Infinite Machines. Prentice Hall, Englewood Cliffs (1967)

22. Murphy, N.: Uniformity Conditions for Membrane Systems: Uncovering Complexity Below P. National University of Ireland, Maynooth, PhD thesis (2010)

23. Murphy, N., Woods, D.: Active membrane systems without charges and using only symmetric elementary division characterise P. In: Eleftherakis, et al. (eds.) [9], pp. 367–384

24. Pan, L., Ishdorj, T.O.: P systems with active membranes and separation rules. Journal of Universal Computer Science 10(5), 630–649 (2004)

25. Pan, L., Pérez-Jiménez, M.: Computational complexity of tissue–like P systems. Journal of Complexity 26(3), 296–315 (2010)

26. Pan, L., Pérez-Jiménez, M.J., Riscos, A., Rius, M.: New frontiers of the efficiency in tissue P systems. In: Pan, L., Paun, G., Song, T. (eds.) Preproceedings of Asian Conference on Membrane Computing, pp. 61–73. Huazhong University of Science and Technology, Wuhan, China (2012)

27. Păun, A., Rodríguez-Patón, A.: On flip-flop membrane systems with proteins. In: Eleftherakis, et al. (eds.) [9], pp. 414–427

28. Pérez-Jiménez, M.: A computational complexity theory in membrane computing. In: Păun, et al. (eds.) [36], pp. 125–148

29. Pérez-Jiménez, M., Romero-Jiménez, A., Sancho-Caparrini, F.: Complexity classes in models of cellular computing with membranes. Natural Computing 2, 265–285 (2003)

30. Pérez-Jiménez, M., Sosík, P.: Improving the efficiency of tissue P systems with cell separation. In: Martínez-del-Amor, M., Păun, G., Pérez-Hurtado, I., Romero-Campero, F. (eds.) Proceedings of the Tenth Brainstorming Week on Membrane Computing, pp. 105–140. Fénix Editora, Sevilla (2012)

31. Porreca, A.E., Leporati, A., Mauri, G., Zandron, C.: P systems with elementary active membranes: Beyond NP and coNP. In: Gheorghe, M., Hinze, T., Păun, G., Rozenberg, G., Salomaa, A. (eds.) CMC 2010. LNCS, vol. 6501, pp. 338–347. Springer, Heidelberg (2010)

32. Porreca, A.E., Murphy, N., Pérez-Jiménez, M.J.: An optimal frontier of the efficiency of tissue P systems with cell division. In: García-Quismondo, M., et al. (eds.) Proceedings of the Tenth Brainstorming Week on Membrane Computing, vol. II, pp. 141–166. Fénix Editora, Sevilla (2012)

33. Păun, A., Popa, B.: P systems with proteins on membranes. Fundamenta Informaticae 72(4), 467–483 (2006)

34. Păun, A., Popa, B.: P systems with proteins on membranes and membrane division. In: Ibarra, O.H., Dang, Z. (eds.) DLT 2006. LNCS, vol. 4036, pp. 292–303. Springer, Heidelberg (2006)

35. Păun, A., Păun, G.: The power of communication: P systems with symport/antiport. New Generation Comput. 20(3), 295–306 (2002)

36. Păun, G., Pérez-Jiménez, M.J., Riscos-Núñez, A., Rozenberg, G., Salomaa, A. (eds.): WMC 2009. LNCS, vol. 5957. Springer, Heidelberg (2010)

37. Păun, G., Rozenberg, G., Salomaa, A. (eds.): The Oxford Handbook of Membrane Computing. Oxford University Press, Oxford (2010)

38. Păun, G.: P systems with active membranes: attacking NP-complete problems. J. Automata, Languages and Combinatorics 6(1), 75–90 (2001)

39. Sosík, P.: Limits of the power of tissue P systems with cell division. In: Csuhaj-Varjú, et al. (eds.) [7], pp. 390–403

40. Sosík, P., Cienciala, L.: Tissue P systems with cell separation: Upper bound by PSPACE. In: Dediu, A.-H., Martín-Vide, C., Truthe, B. (eds.) TPNC 2012. LNCS, vol. 7505, pp. 201–215. Springer, Heidelberg (2012)

41. Sosík, P., Rodríguez-Patón, A.: Membrane computing and complexity theory: A characterization of PSPACE. J. Comput. System Sci. 73(1), 137–152 (2007)

42. Sosík, P.: Selected topics in computational complexity of membrane systems. In: Kelemen, J., Kelemenová, A. (eds.) Păun Festschrift. LNCS, vol. 6610, pp. 125–137. Springer, Heidelberg (2011)

43. Sosík, P., Păun, A., Rodríguez-Patón, A.: P systems with proteins on membranes characterize pspace. Theoretical Computer Science 488, 78–95 (2013)

44. Valsecchi, A., Porreca, A., Leporati, A., Mauri, G., Zandron, C.: An efficient simulation of polynomial-space turing machines by P systems with active membranes. In: Păun, et al. (eds.) [36], pp. 461–478

45. Zandron, C., Ferretti, C., Mauri, G.: Solving NP-complete problems using P systems with active membranes. In: Antoniou, I., Calude, C., Dinneen, M. (eds.) UMC, pp. 289–301. Springer, Heidelberg (2001)

46. Zandron, C., Leporati, A., Ferretti, C., Mauri, G., Pérez-Jiménez, M.: On the computational efficiency of polarizationless recognizer P systems with strong division and dissolution. Fundam. Inform. 87(1), 79–91 (2008)

Using the Formal Framework for P Systems

Sergey Verlan

1 Laboratoire d'Algorithmique, Complexité et Logique,
Université Paris Est – Créteil Val de Marne,
61, av. gén. de Gaulle, 94010 Créteil, France
2 Institute of Mathematics and Computer Science,
Academy of Sciences of Moldova,
Academiei 5, Chisinau, MD-2028, Moldova
verlan@u-pec.fr

Abstract. In this article we focus on the model called the *formal framework for P systems*. This model provides a descriptional language powerful enough to represent in a simple way, via a strong bisimulation, most of the variants of P systems. The article presents a series of concrete examples of the application of the formal framework in order to understand, extend, compare and explain different models of P systems leading to new research ideas and open problems.

1 Introduction

The model called *the formal framework for P systems* (FF) was introduced in [4] and later developed in [3]. It aims to provide a concrete variant of P systems that can act as descriptional language powerful enough to represent in a simple way most of the variants of P systems with the goal of better understanding and comparison of different models of P systems.

The formal framework permits to simulate most of variants of P systems. Moreover, in most cases it is a strong bisimulation, i.e. one step in the original system is done by one step in the formal framework. This becomes possible because the form of configurations and rules is close to multiset rewriting and generalizes most common configuration changes in P systems. Hence, most of existing models of P systems could be obtained by a restriction (eventually using a simple encoding) of FF with respect to different parameters. The strong bisimulation property also permits a discussion about the semantics of the target P system, although this is not the primary goal of FF.

Using FF mainly benefits for the following cases (a) understand the functioning of some variant of P systems; (b) compare variants of P systems; (c) explain points of the definition and semantics that can have different interpretations; (d) extend variants of P systems with new features.

The aim of this paper is not to present the framework itself, but rather several examples of its application for the description and the comparison of different variants of P systems with static structure, with probabilities and with dynamic structure. We also show how these investigations give a uniform view on P systems and lead to new research ideas and open problems.

A. Alhazov et al. (Eds.): CMC 2013, LNCS 8340, pp. 56–79, 2014.

2   A Short Presentation of the Formal Framework

We assume that the reader is familiar with basic notions on formal languages and on P systems and we refer to [9] and [8] for missing details. We will use a string notation to denote multisets and we denote the set of finite multisets over an alphabet V as V°. For a multiset M we denote by $|M|$ its size and by $card(M)$ its cardinal (i.e. the number of different occurring symbols in M). By $|M|_x$ we denote the number of occurrences of symbol x in M.

Before giving the definition of the formal framework we would like to make some remarks about the definition of different variants of P systems. Informally speaking, a definition of a P system consists of:

- a description of the initial structure (indicating the graph relation between the compartments and any additional information like labels, charges, etc),
- a list of the initial multisets of objects present in each compartment at the beginning of the computation,
- a set of rules, acting over objects and / or over the structure.

The configuration of a P system is generally representing the contents of each compartment and the current structure (if it can be modified).

A computation of a P system can be defined as a sequence of transitions between configurations ending in some halting configuration. To give a more precise description of the semantics we must define the following 4 notions (functions):

- $Applicable(\Pi, \mathcal{C}, \delta)$ – the set of multisets of rules of Π applicable to the configuration $\mathcal{C}$, according to the derivation mode δ.
- $Apply(\Pi, \mathcal{C}, R)$ – the configuration obtained by the (parallel) application of the multiset of rules R to the configuration $\mathcal{C}$.
- $Halt(\Pi, \mathcal{C}, \delta)$ – a predicate that yields true if $\mathcal{C}$ is a halting configuration of the system Π evolving in the derivation mode δ.
- $Result(\Pi, \mathcal{C})$ – a function giving the result of the computation of the P system Π, when the halting configuration $\mathcal{C}$ has been reached. Generally this is an integer function, however it is possible to generalize it, allowing, for example, Boolean or vector functions.

The transition of a P system Π according to the derivation mode δ (generally this is the maximally parallel mode) is defined as follows: we pass from a configuration $\mathcal{C}$ to $\mathcal{C}'$ (written as $\mathcal{C} \Rightarrow \mathcal{C}'$) iff

$$\mathcal{C}' = Apply(\Pi, \mathcal{C}, R), \text{ for some } R \in Applicable(\Pi, \mathcal{C}, \delta)$$

In general, the result of the computation of a P system is interpreted as the union of the results of all possible computations (in the same way as the language generated by a grammar is defined in formal language theory, gathering all possible derivations). Note that this is a theoretical (non-constructive) definition, since there may exist an infinite number of halting configurations reachable from a single initial configuration $\mathcal{C}_0$.

The precise definition of the four functions above depends on the selected model of P systems. The goal of works [3,4,12] is to provide a concrete class of P systems (hence with concrete definitions of these functions), called the *formal framework*, such that most of existing models of P systems could be obtained by a strong bisimulation of a restriction (eventually using a simple encoding) of this formal framework with respect to different parameters.

In the remainder of this section we give a summarized version of the definition of a *network of cells*, the class containing all networks of cells being the formal framework. We base the definitions on those given in [4] and we will call the obtained model *FF1*. This version takes into account only P systems where the membrane structure does not evolve in time (is static). In paper [3], an extension of the formal framework to the case of P systems with dynamically evolving structure is proposed (we will call this version of the definition *FF2*). However, in order to have a more simple presentation, in this paper we will only consider the FF1 variant, except for Section 6 which is devoted to the dynamical extension of FF and therefore uses the FF2. We remark that in the case of static structures FF1 and FF2 variants coincide, although the notation is slightly different.

Definition 1 ([4]). *A network of cells of degree $n \geq 1$ is a construct*

$$\Pi = (n, V, w, Inf, R)$$

where

1. *n is the number of cells;*
2. *V a finite alphabet;*
3. *$w = (w_1, \ldots, w_n)$ where $w_i \in V^\circ$, for all $1 \leq i \leq n$, is the finite multiset initially associated to cell i;*
4. *$Inf = (Inf_1, \ldots, Inf_n)$ where $Inf_i \subseteq V$, for all $1 \leq i \leq n$, is the set of symbols occurring infinitely often in cell i (in most of the cases, only one cell, called the environment, will contain symbols occurring with infinite multiplicity);*
5. *R is a finite set of rules of the form*

$$(X \to Y; P, Q)$$

where $X = (x_1, \ldots, x_n)$, $Y = (y_1, \ldots, y_n)$, $x_i, y_i \in V^\circ$, $1 \leq i \leq n$, are vectors of multisets over V and $P = (p_1, \ldots, p_n)$, $Q = (q_1, \ldots, q_n)$, p_i, q_i, $1 \leq i \leq n$ are finite sets of multisets over V. We will also use the notation

$$(x_1, 1) \ldots (x_n, n) \to (y_1, 1) \ldots (y_n, n) ; [(p_1, 1) \ldots (p_n, n)]; [(q_1, 1) \ldots (q_n, n)]$$

for a rule $(X \to Y; P, Q)$; moreover, if some p_i or q_i is an empty set or some x_i or y_i is equal to the empty multiset, $1 \leq i \leq n$, then we may omit it from the specification of the rule.

The semantics of the above rule is to rewrite objects x_i from cells i into objects y_j in cells j, $1 \leq i, j \leq n$, if every cell k, $1 \leq k \leq n$, contains all multisets from

p_k and does not contain any multiset from q_k. In other words, the first part of the rule specifies the rewriting of symbols, the second part of the rule specifies permitting conditions and the third part of the rule specifies the forbidding conditions.

For a rule r of the form above, the set

$$\{i \mid x_i \neq \lambda \text{ or } y_i \neq \lambda \text{ or } p_i \neq \emptyset \text{ or } q_i \neq \emptyset\}$$

induces a (hypergraph) relation between the interacting cells. However, this relation need not give rise to a *structure* relation like a tree as in P systems or a graph as in tissue P systems.

A *configuration* C of Π is an n-tuple of multisets over V $(u_1, \ldots, u_n)$ satisfying $u_i \cap Inf_i = \emptyset$, $1 \leq i \leq n$.

Example 1. Consider the network of cells $\mathfrak{C}$ having 5 cells and the configuration $C = (ba, c, a, \lambda, \lambda)$. Suppose that $\mathfrak{C}$ has the following rule:
$r = (1, a)(2, c) \rightarrow (1, c)(4, a)(5, b); [(1, b)]; [(3, d)]$.
Then $C \Longrightarrow^r C'$, where $C' = (bc, \lambda, a, a, b)$.

The semantics of network of cells is defined as follows (see [4] for more details):

Applicable(Π, C, δ): An algorithm is used to compute *Applicable*$(\Pi, C, asyn)$, the set of multisets of all possible (parallel) applications of rules, which correspond to the set of multisets applicable in the asynchronous mode $(asyn)$. Then this set is (set-)restricted according to δ. As well known examples of δ we can cite max, seq, min, min_k.

Apply(Π, C, R): The application is performed using an algorithm. In the dynamical case (in FF2 definition) there are several variants.

Halt(Π, C, δ): This function is not specified in the definition and is defined separately. Several examples include total halting (no rule is applicable), signal halting (the configuration has some properties) and adult halting (no changes in the configuration occur).

Result(Π, C): This function is not specified in the definition and is defined separately. Generally it is the contents of some cell.

2.1 Comparison with Multiset Rewriting

It is known that any variant of static P systems can be seen as multiset rewriting: an object x in membrane i corresponds to a symbol x_i and each rule moving or rewriting x in membrane i, can be rewritten as corresponding multiset rewriting involving x_i. For example an antiport P system with 3 membranes arranged in the structure $[_1[_2]_2[_3]_3]_1$, the initial configuration (bc, λ, a) and a rule $(a, out; b, in)$ in membrane 3 can be rewritten as the following multiset rewriting: starting multiset $b_1 c_1 a_3$ and a rule $a_3 b_1 \rightarrow a_1 b_3$.

However, considering a P system like a multiset rewriting loses the important structural information. For example, try to figure out what happens in the system defined as follows.

Example 2. Consider the multiset rewriting system with the starting multiset $a_1b_2c_3$ and the rules $a_1b_2 \rightarrow a_2b_1$, $a_1c_2 \rightarrow a_2c_1$, $a_2c_3 \rightarrow a_3c_2$, $a_2b_3 \rightarrow a_3b_2$, $a_3c_1 \rightarrow a_1c_3$, $a_3b_1 \rightarrow a_1b_3$.

The formal framework groups the information in cells/membranes, does a group rewriting and represents the structure of the P system separately. So it is extremely close to the multiset rewriting, it just reorders objects and rules. This permits to keep the information about the static structure: rules induce a hypergraph. The communication graph can be deduced from this hypergraph. A similar approach is used in Petri nets, for example a multiset rewriting rule $aabc \rightarrow cde$ is represented as shown in Figure 1.

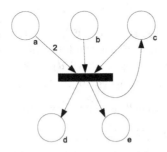

Fig. 1. A Petri net representation of the rule $aabc \rightarrow cde$

Example 3. Consider the system from Example 2. By rewriting the rules in terms of network of cells we obtain the following rules:

$$(1,a)(2,b) \rightarrow (2,a)(1,b) \qquad (1,a)(2,c) \rightarrow (2,a)(1,c)$$
$$(2,a)(3,c) \rightarrow (3,a)(2,c) \qquad (2,a)(3,b) \rightarrow (3,a)(2,b)$$
$$(3,a)(1,c) \rightarrow (1,a)(3,c) \qquad (3,a)(1,b) \rightarrow (1,a)(3,b)$$

Consider the hyperedge induced by the first rule: it goes from the cells 1 and 2 to cells 1 and 2. So we can make a supposition that we could have a communication graph that would contain an edge $1 - 2$. By looking at what the rule is doing we remark that it exchanges symbols a and b located in cells 1 and 2 respectively. Hence it corresponds to an antiport rule a/b on the edge $1 - 2$. By repeating this process for all above rules we obtain the antiport tissue P system shown in Figure 2. Hence it is clear that the system is moving symbol a in clockwise direction and symbols b and c in anticlockwise direction.

3 Implementing Different Features of P Systems

In this section we discuss the implementation of some features of P systems that are not present by default in the framework.

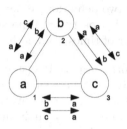

Fig. 2. The antiport system obtained in Example 3. The arc $a \leftrightarrow b$ corresponds to the antiport rule a/b.

3.1 New Derivation Modes

In order to define a new derivation mode for a P system it is sufficient to consider the network of cells equivalent to that system and to provide a set restriction for asynchronous (asyn) mode. Then, because of the bisimulation, the definition can immediately be interpreted in the corresponding P system.

Example 4. In this example we define two derivation modes: *minimally parallel mode restricted to partitions of size 1 (min_1)* and *mixed set minimally parallel mode restricted to partitions of size 1 ($msmin_1$)*. In order to do this we assume that the ruleset R is divided into several sets $R_1, \ldots, R_m$, $m > 0$, such that $R = \bigcup_{1 \le i \le m} R_i$. Due to historical reasons we will call these sets *partitions* although this term is not accurate because the sets $R_1, \ldots, R_m$ are not necessarily disjoint.

The min_1 mode is defined as follows (see also [5]):

$$Applicable(\Pi, C, min_1) = \{S \in Applicable(\Pi, C, asyn) : |S \cap R_i| \le 1, 1 \le i \le m$$
$$\text{and } \nexists S' \in Applicable(\Pi, C, asyn),$$
$$\text{with } |S' \cap R_i| \le 1 \text{ such that } S' \supsetneq S\}$$

Hence, the min_1 mode is in some sense requiring to take at most one rule from each partition, when possible. It coincides with the definition of the minimally applicable multiset of rules from Section 1.9 of [9].

For the $msmin_1$ mode we additionally classify the partitions into two categories: *-partitions and 1-partitions. In order to simplify the definition we suppose that R is divided into m partitions $R_1, \ldots, R_m$ and that the first k partitions are 1-partitions and the partitions from $k+1$ until m are *-partitions. Then the mode is defined as follows:

$$Applicable(\Pi, C, msmin_1) = \{S \in Applicable(\Pi, C, asyn) :$$
$$\text{such that for all } i, j \text{ where } 1 \le i \le k < j \le m,$$
$$|S \cap R_i| \le 1 \text{ and } card(S \cap R_j) \le 1,$$
$$\text{and } \nexists S' \in Applicable(\Pi, C, asyn),$$
$$\text{with } |S \cap R_i| \le |S' \cap R_i| \le 1,$$
$$card(S \cap R_j) \le card(S' \cap R_j) \le 1 \text{ and } S' \supsetneq S\}$$

The difference between the two definitions is that in $msmin_1$ mode one rule is chosen and applied from each 1-partition, if possible, and one rule is chosen and applied a maximal number of times from each *-partition, if possible.

Example 5. Consider a symport/antiport P system with a mode that ensures that a cell is used sequentially, only in a single operation. This can be done by using a partition of rules such that a rule involving cell i, will be a part of partition i. Hence, each rule will be in two partitions. The desired result is then obtained by applying the min_1 mode with the obtained partitions.

3.2   Membrane Thinkness/Polarization/Labels

We remark that the notions of membrane thickness, polarization and label are related to each other and designate the property of a membrane to be in some finite state. In order to be able to simulate efficiently these concepts we introduce into each membrane a special object coding the state of the membrane. All rules involving a membrane will additionally have a permitting context (promoter) checking this state object.

Example 6. Consider following active membranes rules (1) $[a \to bc]_h$ and (2) $a[]_h \to [b]_{h'}$ in membrane k. They are simulated in the formal framework by the following rules: $(k, a) \to (k, bc); [(k, h)]$ and $(k', a)(k, h) \to (k, bh')$, where k' is the parent of k.

As we can see the change of the state is done directly by the rule (case (2)). However, it should be noted that in the above implementation only one state change per membrane can occur in one step which is consistent with actual definitions used in P systems.

We remark that in the example above the rules (1) and (2) become cooperative after translation. This translates the intuitive idea that the object that is communicated/rewritten is cooperating with membrane state at the level of the rule.

We would like to remark that in FF2 the membrane state is an explicit part of the configuration, so no special object is needed for its representation. This is done because in P systems with dynamic structure the membrane labels are always used, so considering them as a part of configuration permits to save space in the description of the rule. However, it shall be noted that like in the case above there is an implicit cooperation between the membrane state and the objects used in the rule.

3.3   Priorities

Already in the first models of P systems a priority relation on the rules of the system was considered. The underlying relation is a strict partial order (i.e. an irreflexive, asymmetric, and transitive). We consider here two notions of priority following [6], the *strong* priority and the *weak* priority. Under the semantics of strong priority, if a rule with higher priority is used, then no rule of a lower priority can be used even if the two rules do not compete for objects. For weakly prioritized systems, a rule is applicable if it cannot be replaced by a higher priority one. In the original definition of transitional P systems from [7] the strong priority is used.

Example 7. Consider a transitional P system which has following three rules: $r_1 : ab \rightarrow cd$, $r_2 : ac \rightarrow bd$ and $r_3 : bc \rightarrow aa$. Let the priority relation be $r_3 > r_1$. Suppose that the current configuration contains the multiset $aabbc$ in the corresponding membrane. Then in the case of the strong priority only rules r_2 or r_3 are applicable. In the case of the weak priority it is possible to apply additionally rule r_1, yielding the following applicable sets: $\{r_1, r_2\}$ and $\{r_1, r_2\}$.

It is not difficult to see that the strong priority corresponds directly to forbidding conditions: indeed $r_1 > r_2$ corresponds to two rules (1) r_1 and (2) r_2 enriched with forbidding sets containing the left-hand sides of all rules $r > r_2$.

Example 8. Consider the system from Example 7. We can translate the first rule to the formal framework as follows: $r_1' : (k, ab) \rightarrow (k, cd); []; [(k, bc)]$.

The case of weak priorities can be handled using a special derivation mode that keeps track of the relation between rules. It will choose those multisets where a rule of higher priority cannot be applied anymore even if all rules of a lower priority are not taken:

$$Applicable(\Pi, C, Pri_w \delta) = \{R \in Applicable(\Pi, C, \delta) \mid \nexists R' \in Applicable(\Pi, C, \delta),$$
$$\text{such that } r \in R' \setminus R \text{ and } R'' \notin Applicable(\Pi, C, \delta),$$
$$\text{where } R'' \supseteq R \cup \{r\} \setminus \{r' \in R \mid r > r'\}\}$$

3.4   Dissolution

We recall that the dissolution operation (denoted by δ) removes the membrane in which it occurred as well as all rules involving the dissolved membrane. All objects present in that membrane are transferred to its parent. In a general case this operation is handled in FF2 as a special operation acting on the structure like the creation or the division of membranes. However, if we consider the class of P systems where only dissolution is used (no creation/division of membranes) then it is obvious that such systems have a finite number of possible membrane structures (the dissolution operation can only decrease the number of membranes already present at the beginning of the computation). Hence, it is possible to mimic the effect of the dissolution by assigning a marker to each membrane in order to indicate if the membrane is dissolved or not, by using permitting and/or forbidding context in order to check this marker and by using a subset construction at the level of rules in order to capture all possible structure changes.

Example 9. Consider the following transitional P system (see Figure 3)
$\Pi = (\{a, b, c, d, \#\}, [_0[_1]_1[_2]_2]_0, \{ac\}, \{c\}, \{a\}, R_0, R_1, R_2)$, where

$$R_0 = \{r_{01} : ac \to \lambda, r_{02} : da \to \#, r_{03} : bc \to \#, r_{04} : \# \to \#\},$$
$$R_1 = \{r_{11} : c \to cc, r_{12} : c \to d\delta\},$$
$$R_2 = \{r_{21} : a \to aa, r_{22} : a \to b\delta\}.$$

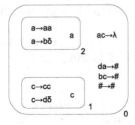

Fig. 3. The P system from Example 9

In order to translate it to the formal framework we shall use 3 objects s_0, s_1 and s_2 indicating that corresponding membranes are not yet dissolved. We place these objects in corresponding cells, although they all can be placed in a particular cell, e.g. cell 0. There are 4 possible membrane structures and they are encoded by the following combinations of objects s_i: $\{(0, s_0)(1, s_1)(2, s_2)\}$, $\{(0, s_0)(1, s_1)\}$, $\{(0, s_0)(2, s_2)\}$ and $\{(0, s_0)\}$. Now in order to finalize the translation we shall do a subset construction for all rules in membrane 0 in order to take into account that corresponding objects can originate from a dissolved membrane:

Rules from R_1 are translated as follows:

$(1, c) \to (1, cc); [(1, s_1)]$ $\qquad\qquad$ $(1, s_1)(1, c) \to (0, d)$

Rules from R_2 are translated as follows:

$(2, a) \to (2, aa); [(2, s_2)]$ $\qquad\qquad$ $(2, s_2)(2, a) \to (0, b)$

Rules from R_0 are translated as follows:

$(0, ac) \to \lambda; [(2, s_0)]$ $\qquad\qquad$ $(0, a)(1, c) \to \lambda; [(0, s_0)]; [(2, s_2)]$

$(0, c)(2, a) \to \lambda; [(0, s_0)]; [(1, s_1)]$ $\quad$ $(1, c)(2, a) \to \lambda; [(0, s_0)]; [(1, s_1)(2, s_2)]$

$(0, da) \to (0, \#); [(0, s_0)]$ $\qquad\qquad$ $(0, d)(2, a) \to (0, \#); [(0, s_0)]; [(2, s_2)]$

$(0, bc) \to (0, \#); [(0, s_0)]$ $\qquad\qquad$ $(0, b)(1, c) \to (0, \#); [(0, s_0)]; [(1, s_1)]$

$(0, \#) \to (0, \#); [(0, s_0)]$

We observe that for the translation of rule r_{01} we had to consider 4 cases depending on the possible origin of symbols a and c. The difference between cases is done by corresponding permitting and forbidding conditions.

We also remark that is is possible to avoid forbidding conditions by considering that a state of the membrane i is defined by one of two (dual) objects s_i or $\bar{s}_i$, where the first one indicates that the membrane exists and the second one indicates that the membrane is dissolved. In this case the rule dissolving the membrane will rewrite s_i to $\bar{s}_i$ and the forbidding contexts for s_i are replaced by permitting for $\bar{s}_i$. For example, in the case above the second rule from R_1 becomes $(0, s_1)(1, c) \rightarrow (0, d)(1, \bar{s}_1)$ and the second rule from R_0 becomes $(0, a)(1, c) \rightarrow \lambda; [(0, s_0)(2, \bar{s}_2)]$.

In some particular cases it is possible to simplify the above construction by assigning a number (hence a special object) to each of possible membrane structures and checking by permitting context the current structure. The drawback of this method is the difficulty to perform several dissolutions in parallel, as several rules should modify the same object at the same step. In some cases (e.g. if the maximally parallel or sequential derivation mode is used) it is possible to overcome this difficulty by using additional rules that perform all required dissolutions in one step.

Example 10. Consider system Π from Example 9. We encode by objects s_i, $1 \leq i \leq 4$, placed in cell 0, the four possible variants of the membrane structure (initial, membrane 2 dissolved, membrane 1 dissolved, membrane 1 and 2 are dissolved). In order to handle the parallel dissolution of membranes 1 and 2 a special rule is introduced.

Rules from R_1 are translated as follows:

$$(1, c) \rightarrow (1, cc); [(0, s_1)] \qquad\qquad (1, c) \rightarrow (1, cc); [(0, s_2)]$$
$$(0, s_1)(1, c) \rightarrow (0, ds_3) \qquad\qquad (0, s_2)(1, c) \rightarrow (0, ds_4)$$

Rules from R_2 are translated as follows:

$$(2, a) \rightarrow (2, aa); [(0, s_1)] \qquad\qquad (2, a) \rightarrow (2, aa); [(0, s_3)]$$
$$(0, s_1)(2, a) \rightarrow (0, bs_2) \qquad\qquad (0, s_3)(2, a) \rightarrow (0, bs_4)$$

Rules from R_0 are translated as follows:

$$(0, ac) \rightarrow \lambda \qquad\qquad (0, a)(1, c) \rightarrow \lambda; [(0, s_3)]$$
$$(0, c)(2, a) \rightarrow \lambda; [(0, s_2)] \qquad\qquad (1, c)(2, a) \rightarrow \lambda; [(0, s_4)]$$

$$(0, da) \rightarrow (0, \#) \qquad\qquad (0, d)(2, a) \rightarrow (0, \#); [(0, s_1)]$$

$$(0, bc) \rightarrow (0, \#) \qquad\qquad (0, b)(1, c) \rightarrow (0, \#); [(0, s_3)]$$

$$(0, \#) \rightarrow (0, \#)$$

Additional rule for parallel dissolution:

$$(0, s1)(1, c)(2, a) \rightarrow (0, bds_4)$$

We remark that the above construction cannot be generalized to any case. For example, consider a P system evolving in a special derivation mode that requires to use exactly one rule from every membrane at each step. In this case the above construction would fail as the two dissolutions were replaced by a single rule performing both of them.

3.5   Flattening

We call a *flattening* of a P system Π the process of construction of a new P system Π' having only one cell such that $N(\Pi) = N(\Pi')$. We remark that system Π' need not belong to the same class of P systems as Π. A *strong* flattening requires that Π and Π' belong to the same class.

In the case of P systems with static structure (that does not change in time) it can easily be seen that the flattening is very simple, because of the one-to-one relation with multiset rewriting grammars. If the dissolution is present, then it is possible to simulate it as described in previous subsection, hence the flattening procedure will require the use of permitting and eventually forbidding contexts. In the case of systems with dynamically evolving structure (with creation and/or dissolution of membranes) the flattening is not trivial as one should deal with an unbounded number of membranes. A trivial translation yields an unbounded alphabet and an unbounded number of rules, so encodings are necessary to represent the flattening correctly and it is a challenge to provide an algorithm that performs this task.

For the strong flattening it can easily be seen that it is not always possible. For example, any P system that does not allow rules corresponding directly to the multiset rewriting (e.g. symport P systems or minimal symport/antiport P systems) cannot be strongly flattened.

Another example of systems that do not admit strong flattening are systems that have dissolution and do not allow permitting and forbidding contexts, e.g. transitional P systems with dissolution. Because the algorithms eliminating the dissolution require at least a permitting context, it is clear that the flattening cannot be done if remaining inside the same model.

A longer discussion on flattening can be found in [2].

4   Examples of Application of FF

In this section we consider three applications of the formal framework. The first one is the comparison of (purely) catalytic P systems with context-free transitional P systems. The second application consists in extending symport/antiport P systems with variable membrane thickness. The third application studies the model of P colonies and helps in understanding this model and allows to easily obtain some new results.

4.1   Catalytic P Systems

The translation of (purely) catalytic P systems to FF can be done in a quite straightforward manner as follows: every rule $ca \to c(a_1, tar_1) \dots (a_k, tar_k)$ of cell i becomes $(i, ca) \to (F(i, tar_1), a_1) \dots (F(i, tar_k), a_k)$, where $F(i, here) = i$, $F(i, in_j) = j$ and $F(i, out) = m$, where m is the parent of i.

Now we remark that the inherent property of catalytic P systems is that at each step only one rule can be chosen among all rules involving the same catalyst. This property can be deduced from the form of rules of such systems. At the same time it is clear that this property relates more to the way the rules are used together, i.e. to the derivation mode, than to rules' action itself. In FF it is possible to consider a derivation mode that obeys the above restriction. It is not difficult to see that in the case of catalytic (resp. purely catalytic) P systems the above requirements are satisfied by the $msmin_1$ (resp. min_1) derivation mode. The (1-)partitions used for the definition of corresponding modes correspond to each catalyst. In the case of non-purely systems the *-partitions consist of single rules, those that are used in a context-free manner. From the above analysis we can also deduce that catalytic P systems having several membranes and one catalyst are a restricted variant of catalytic P systems with one membrane and using several catalysts.

Hence, we obtain that catalytic P systems evolving in the maximally parallel mode are equal to context-free transitional P systems working in the $msmin_1$ mode, where the 1-partitions correspond to catalysts and *-partitions to each context-free rule. The systems corresponding to purely catalytic P systems have the number of 1-partitions equal to the number of catalysts and no *-partitions, so they evolve in the min_1 mode. It immediately follows that the model of purely catalytic P systems is weaker than the general variant, as context-free rules add more complexity, that can be quantified by the increase of the number of partitions and by the increase of the degree of parallelism.

The usage of the $msmin_1$ mode may look a little bit artificial, so we remark that it is also possible to consider a special mixed mode derived in a straightforward way from the real semantics of catalytic P systems with k catalysts: using $k + 1$ partitions with k partitions working in the min_1 mode (corresponding to catalysts) and one special partition working in the maximally parallel mode.

Example 11. Consider the following catalytic P system
$$\Pi = (O, \{c\}, [_0[_1[_3]_3[_4]_4]_1[_2]_2]_0, \{abc\}, \{aac\}, \{c\}, \{a\}, \emptyset, R_0, R_1, R_2, R_3, R_4),$$
where $O = \{a, b, c, d, e\}$, $R_0 = \{cb \to ca_{in_2}\}$, $R_1 = \{ca \to cb_{in}d_{in_4}b_{out}e_{out}e_{here}\}$, $R_3 = \{b \to aa, a \to bc\}$, $R_2 = R_4 = \emptyset$.

The straightforward translation of this system gives the following rules:

$$(0, cb) \to (0, c)(2, a)$$
$$(1, ca) \to (0, be)(1, ce)(4, bd) \qquad (1, ca) \to (0, be)(1, ce)(3, b)(4, d)$$
$$(3, a) \to (3, bc) \qquad\qquad\qquad (3, b) \to (3, aa)$$

We remark that the translation of the in target is done as in_k, for all k.

Now we construct the context-free network of cells Π' equivalent to Π. Consider following sets of rules:

$$P_1 = \{(1, a) \to (0, be)(1, e)(4, bd), (1, a) \to (0, be)(1, e)(3, b)(4, d)\},$$
$$P_2 = \{(0, b) \to (0, c)(2, a)\},$$
$$P_3 = \{(3, a) \to (3, bc)\},$$
$$P_4 = \{(3, b) \to (3, aa)\}.$$

Let P_1 and P_2 form 1-partitions and let P_3 and P_4 form *-partitions. Then from the discussion above it is clear that Π' working in the $msmin_1$ mode is equivalent to Π. We remark that the obtained network of cells can easily be translated to a context-free transitional P system working in the $msmin_1$ mode.

4.2   Symport/Antiport

In this subsection we discuss how it is possible to use the formal framework in order to extend an existing class of P systems.

Consider the class of symport/antiport P systems. We will extend it with two features: (1) membrane permeability – a symport rule can modify the membrane permeability (with δ or τ). If the membrane is in state 2, then no antiport rule involving this membrane can be used. At each step only one permeability changing rule per membrane can be applied; (2) maximal objects: at each step if there are several maximally parallel evolutions choose the one having the maximal number of objects involved.

In order to define the semantics for both features we will translate symport/antiport P systems to the formal framework, then we will do the necessary transformations in order to accommodate the desired behavior. Then due to the strong bisimulation we can recover the desired semantics in symport/antiport P systems.

The translation of symport and antiport rules can be done in a quite simple way: each antiport rule $(a, in; b, out)$ (resp. symport rule (a, out)) of membrane i is translated as $(i, b)(j, a) \to (i, a)(j, b)$ (resp. $(i, a) \to (j, a)$), where j is the parent membrane of i; each symport rule (a, in) is translated as $(i, a) \to (j, a)$, for all child membranes j of i.

Now in order to implement the first proposed extension, for each membrane i we consider an object in cell i taken from the triple (D, N, C) indicating the state of the membrane (dissolved, normal, closed). Each symport rule having δ or τ will modify this object (going to the left or right in the above sequence) and each antiport rule will check the permitting context if it is in state N. For example: the rule $(ab, out); \tau$ in membrane i will correspond to rules $(i, abN) \to (i, C)(j, ab)$ and $(i, abC) \to (i, C)(j, ab)$.

Now in order to satisfy the second requirement we consider the following derivation mode $max_{obj}max$:

$$Applicable(\Pi, C, max_{obj}max) = \Big\{ R \in Applicable(\Pi, C, max) \mid$$
$$\nexists R' \in Applicable(\Pi, C, max) :$$
$$\sum_{r' \in R'} |lhs(r')| > \sum_{r \in R} |lhs(r)| \Big\}$$

It should be clear that the network of cells obtained using the transformations above will be a strong bisimulation of the initial P system.

4.3 P Colonies

We recall the definition of P colonies taken from [9].

A P colony consists of n cells (agents) C_i, $1 \leq i \leq n$, each of them containing a multiset of exactly k symbols and an environment containing initially a distinguished symbol e in an unbounded number of copies. Each cell C_i has a set of programs $\{p_{i,1}, \ldots, p_{i,k_i}\}$, where each program $p_{i,j}$ consists of exactly k rules of the forms $a \rightarrow b$ (*internal point mutation*), $c \leftrightarrow d$ (*one object exchange with the environment*), or r_1/r_2 (*priority rule*, where r_1 and r_2 are arbitrary combinations of point mutation and/or exchange rules). The computation can be performed in the maximally parallel or in the sequential mode with respect to the programs of cells. If no more programs are applicable, the system halts and the result is collected as the number of distinguished symbols f in the environment. The number of cells, the maximal number of programs in a cell, and the maximal number of rules in each program in a given P colony Π are called the degree, the height, and the capacity of Π, respectively. The family of sets of numbers computed in the derivation mode x for $x \in \{par, seq\}$ by P colonies of capacity k, degree at most $n \geq 1$ and height at most $h \geq 1$, without (resp. with) using priority rules in their programs, is denoted by $NPCol_x(k, n, h)$ (resp. $NPCol_x K(k, n, h)$).

We will construct a strong bisimulation of the P colony model in the formal framework:

- each rule $a \rightarrow b$ in p_{ij} becomes $r_{ij} : (i, a) \rightarrow (i, b)$;
- each rule $a \leftrightarrow b$ in p_{ij} becomes $r_{ij} : (i, a)(0, b) \rightarrow (i, b)(0, a)$;
- each rule r_1/r_2 in p_{ij} is replaced by two rules: r_1, and $r2; [\emptyset]; [\{(i, a)\}]$ if r_1 is $a \rightarrow b$ and $r2; [\emptyset]; [\{(i, a)(0, b)\}]$ if r_1 is $a \leftrightarrow b$.

For the derivation mode each program becomes a rule partition and then the derivation mode requires to be maximal, but using exactly k rules from each partition (or using all rules from a partition). In the sequential case, the derivation mode implies to use only one partition (but all rules from that partition).

Example 12. Consider the following P colony Π having 3 cells.

- C_1 contains the initial multiset aa and the following programs: $p_{11} : a \rightarrow b, a \leftrightarrow e$, $p_{12} : a \rightarrow c, a \leftrightarrow e$, $p_{13} : b \rightarrow a, e \rightarrow a$.

- C_2 contains the initial multiset be and the following program: $p_{21} : b \leftrightarrow e, e \rightarrow b$.
- C_3 contains the initial multiset ee and the following programs: $p_{31} : e \leftrightarrow a, e \leftrightarrow b$, $p_{32} : b \rightarrow f, a \rightarrow b$, $p_{33} : f \leftrightarrow a, b \rightarrow b$.

Figure 4 shows a graphical representation of this system.

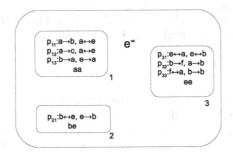

Fig. 4. The P colony from Example 12

We translate this system to a network of cells Π' having 4 cells (numbered from 0 to 3), corresponding to the cells of Π, and having same initial contents as corresponding agents and $Inf_0 = \{e\}$. System Π' contains the following rules:

Rules simulating programs from the first cell:

$$r_{111} : (1, a) \rightarrow (1, b) \qquad\qquad r_{112} : (1, a)(0, e) \rightarrow (1, e)(0, a)$$
$$r_{121} : (1, a) \rightarrow (1, c) \qquad\qquad r_{122} : (1, a)(0, e) \rightarrow (1, e)(0, a)$$
$$r_{131} : (1, b) \rightarrow (1, a) \qquad\qquad r_{132} : (1, e) \rightarrow (1, a)$$

Rules simulating programs from the second cell:

$$r_{211} : (2, b)(0, e) \rightarrow (2, e)(0, b) \qquad\qquad r_{212} : (2, e) \rightarrow (2, b)$$

Rules simulating programs from the third cell:

$$r_{311} : (3, e)(0, a) \rightarrow (3, a)(0, e) \qquad\qquad r_{312} : (3, e)(0, b) \rightarrow (3, b)(0, e)$$
$$r_{321} : (3, b) \rightarrow (3, f) \qquad\qquad r_{322} : (3, a) \rightarrow (3, b)$$
$$r_{331} : (3, f)(0, a) \rightarrow (3, a)(0, f) \qquad\qquad r_{332} : (3, b) \rightarrow (3, b)$$

We remark that the derivation mode of P colonies groups rules corresponding to programs, uses maximal parallelism or sequentiality, and requires that all rules from a group shall be used. Since working with one symbol, the group r_{111} and r_{112} from example above is equivalent to the application of a single rule

$r_{11} : (1, aa)(0, e) \rightarrow (1, be)(0, a)$. Hence we obtain that a program corresponds to a more complicated rule, and k is the size of the LHS of this rule (and equal to RHS). By considering such rules, the evolution of a P colony becomes just maximally parallel or sequential.

Example 13. Consider the system Π from Example 12. Using the above remark it can be translated to the following network of cells Π'':

$$r_{11} : (1, aa)(0, e) \rightarrow (1, be)(0, a) \qquad r_{12} : (1, aa)(0, e) \rightarrow (1, ce)(0, a)$$
$$r_{13} : (1, be) \rightarrow (1, aa)$$
$$r_{21} : (2, be)(0, e) \rightarrow (2, be)(0, b)$$
$$r_{31} : (3, ee)(0, ab) \rightarrow (3, ab)(0, ee) \qquad r_{32} : (3, ab) \rightarrow (3, fb)$$
$$r_{33} : (3, bf)(0, a) \rightarrow (3, ab)(0, f)$$

We can go further by remarking that the number of combinations of objects in an agent is finite, so it can be represented by a single symbol, the state. Symbol e from cell 0 can be ignored as it carries no information. This permits to deduce that a P colony corresponds to a cooperative rewriting with the size of LHS or RHS at most $k + 1$ and forbidding conditions (if checking rules are present). It can be also possible to consider it as a catalytic P system with catalysts having n-states.

Example 14. Consider system Π from Example 12. Consider the array of multisets $A = (aa, be, ce, ee, ab, bf)$ and the following encoding $f(A[i]) = s_i$. Then the rules from Example 13 can be rewritten as follows:

$$r_{11} : (1, s_1) \rightarrow (1, s_2)(0, a) \qquad r_{12} : (1, s_1) \rightarrow (1, s_3)(0, a) \quad r_{13} : (1, s_2) \rightarrow (1, s_1)$$
$$r_{21} : (2, s_2) \rightarrow (2, s_2)(0, b)$$
$$r_{31} : (3, s_4)(0, ab) \rightarrow (3, s_5) \qquad r_{32} : (3, s_5) \rightarrow (3, s_6)$$
$$r_{33} : (3, s_6)(0, a) \rightarrow (3, s_5)(0, f)$$

In order to highlight the original semantics (that only one program per cell can be executed), we can use catalysts: the rule $r_{11} : (1, s_1) \rightarrow (1, s_2)(0, a)$ becomes $c_1 s_1 \rightarrow c_1 s_2 a$. Although using catalysts is not necessary as the state is unique, this permits to consider a restricted variant of the model of P colonies that uses only rules of the above type and therefore corresponds to specific purely catalytic P systems. This remark permits us to transpose results from P colonies to purely catalytic P systems and conversely. For example, from the results for P colonies (Remark after Theorem 23.1.1 and Theorem 23.1.2 from [9]) we immediately obtain that:

Proposition 1. *The following results hold:*

- *Purely catalytic P systems with one catalyst and the size of the rule equal to 3 are not computationally complete.*
- *Purely catalytic P systems of with rules of size 2, an unbounded number of catalysts and using at most 6 rules for each catalyst are computationally complete.*

In the other direction we can also immeadiately obtain (Theorem 4.1 from [9]) that:

Proposition 2. $NPCol_{par}(3, 3, *) = RE$.

Our representation of P colonies permits to answer the open question raised in Section 23.1.3 from [9]:

Proposition 3. $NPCol_{seq}(*, 1, *) \subsetneq RE$.

This follows from the fact that the corresponding model is identical to purely sequential multiset rewriting which is known to not be computationally complete.

5   Probabilistic P Systems

In this section we extend the formal framework in order to take into account probabilities and thus become able to represent via bisimulation different variants of probabilistic P systems. This section closely follows [11]. To achieve the proposed goal we recall that in order to perform a computational step in a P system a set of multisets of applicable rules, denoted by $Applicable(\Pi, C, \delta)$, is computed according to the type of the system and the derivation mode δ, for any configuration of the system C. After that, one of the elements from this set is chosen, non-deterministically, for the further evolution of the system.

We remark that from the point of view of the computer simulation of P systems the non-deterministic choice can be considered equivalent to a probabilistic choice where each multiset of rules has an equal probability to be chosen. Permitting these multisets to have a *different probability* is the main idea of the extension that we discuss in this section. More precisely, for each multiset of rules $R \in Applicable(\Pi, C, \delta)$ we compute the probability $p(R, C)$ based on the propensity function $f : \mathcal{R}^\circ \times (\mathbb{N} \times O^\circ)^* \to \mathbb{R}$, where $\mathcal{R}$ and O are the set of rules and objects of Π respectively. This function associates a real value for a multiset of rules with respect to a configuration. Hence the value $f(R, C)$ depends not only on the multiset of rules R, but also on the configuration C.

The probability to choose a multiset $R \in Applicable(\Pi, C, \delta)$ is defined as the normalization of corresponding probabilities:

$$p(R, C) = \frac{f(R, C)}{\sum_{R' \in Applicable(\Pi, C, \delta)} f(R', C)} \tag{1}$$

5.1   Discussion

So far we did not indicate the propensity function f, which is the main ingredient of the model. Below we will give examples of simple propensity functions each leading to different execution strategies.

Constant strategy: each rule r from $\mathcal{R}$ has a constant contribution to f and equal to c_r:

$$f(R, C) = \prod_{r \in R} c_r \tag{2}$$

Multiplicity-dependent strategy: each rule r from $\mathcal{R}$ has a contribution to f proportional to the number of times this rule can be applied and to a stochastic constant c_r that only depends on r:

$$N_r(C) = \min_{x \in lhs(r)} \left\lfloor \frac{|C|_x}{|lhs(r)|_x} \right\rfloor \tag{3}$$

$$f(R, C) = \prod_{r \in R} c_r N_r(C) \tag{4}$$

Concentration-dependent strategy: each rule r from $\mathcal{R}$ has a contribution to f proportional to $h_r(C)$, the number of distinct combinations of objects from C that activate r, and to a stochastic constant c_r that only depends on r (by $\binom{a}{b}$ we denote the binomial function):

$$h_r(C) = \prod_{x \in lhs(r)} \binom{|C|_x}{|lhs(r)|_x} \tag{5}$$

$$h_R(C) = \prod_{r \in R} c_r h_r(C) \tag{6}$$

$$f(R, C) = h_R(C) \tag{7}$$

Gillespie strategy: each rule r from $\mathcal{R}$ has a contribution to f that depends on the order in which it was chosen and it is equal to $c_r \cdot h_r(C')$, where C' is the configuration obtained by applying all rules that were chosen before r.

We remark that the concentration-dependent strategy is not equal to Gillespie strategy. More precisely, in a Gillespie run the probability to choose a new rule depends on the objects consumed and produced by previously chosen rules. We can consider a Gillespie run as a sequence of sequential (single-rule) applications using the concentration-dependent strategy.

We also remark that the Gillespie algorithm uses the notion of time that we do not consider in this paper. However, the definitions can easily be adapted for to handle this case.

5.2   Examples

Dynamical Probabilistic P Systems Dynamical probabilistic P (DPP) systems were introduced in [10]. Below, we present the definition of the evolution step. For the sake of the simplicity we will consider only one compartment, however the discussion below can easily be generalized to several compartments.

Let C be the current configuration and $\mathcal{R}$ be the set of all rules. Then the system evolves from C to C' as follows.

1. For each rule $r \in \mathcal{R}$, the propensity of $a_r(C) = c_r * h_r(C)$ (h_r being defined as in Equation (5)) is computed.

2. The propensities are normalized giving a probability for a rule r to be chosen:
$p_r(C) = \frac{a_r(c)}{\sum_{r' \in \mathcal{R}} a_{r'}(C)}$.
3. The rules to be applied are chosen according to their probabilities. If a non-applicable rule is chosen, the choice is repeated.
4. The process stops when a maximal (parallel) multiset of rules R is obtained.
5. The multiset of rules obtained at the previous step is applied and yields a new configuration C'.

It can be easily seen that, since the probabilities to apply a rule (p_r) are computed only at the beginning of each step, the maximal multiset of rules R then is composed from independent rules (the order in which the rules were chosen has no influence). Hence the probability to choose a multiset of rules R is equal to the product of the probabilities of each rule: $p_R(C) = \prod_{r \in R} p_r$. Now if we normalize this value with respect to all possible maximally parallel multisets of rules we obtain:

$$\frac{\prod_{r \in R} p_r(C)}{\sum_{R' \in Appl(\Pi, C, max)} \prod_{z \in R'} p_z(C)} = \frac{\prod_{r \in R} \frac{a_r(C)}{\sum_{r' \in \mathcal{R}} a_{r'}(C)}}{\sum_{R' \in Appl(\Pi, C, max)} \prod_{z \in R'} \frac{p_z(C)}{\sum_{r' \in \mathcal{R}} a_{r'}(C)}}$$

$$= \frac{\prod_{r \in R} a_r(C)}{\sum_{R' \in Appl(\Pi, C, max)} \prod_{z \in R'} a_z(C)} \quad (8)$$

Since in the case of the concentration-dependent strategy we have that $f(R, C) = \prod_{r \in R} a_r(C)$, it follows that (8) equals (1). Hence we just showed that DPP systems can be translated to probabilistic P systems with a concentration-dependent strategy.

Probabilistic Functional Extended P Systems Probabilistic functional extended P (PFEP) systems where introduced in [1] as a part of a framework used to model eco-systems. In order to simplify the presentation we consider a flattening of the structure of the P system, thus using only multiset rewriting rules. We also consider that the rules having the same left-hand side form a partition of the set of rules $\mathcal{R}$ into n subsets $\mathcal{R} = \mathcal{R}_1 \ldots \mathcal{R}_n$, where $r_1, r_2 \in \mathcal{R}_i \Rightarrow lhs(r_1) = lhs(r_2)$, $1 \le i \le n$.

The evolution of a PFEP system is done as follows:

1. A maximally parallel multiset of rules R is chosen.
2. R is partitioned into submultisets based on the left-hand side of rules: $R_i = \{r \in R \mid r \in \mathcal{R}_i\}$.
3. For each non-empty partition R_i, $|R_i|$ rules from $\mathcal{R}_i$ are chosen according to the given probability $f_r(a)$, where $r \in \mathcal{R}_i$ and a is a moment of time.
4. The resulting multiset of rules is applied yielding a new configuration.

From the description of the strategy it is clear that it corresponds to the multiplicity-dependent strategy for the maximally parallel derivation mode (and where the constant c_r is replaced by $f_r(a)$).

6   Active Membranes

In this section we consider the FF2 model described in [3]. The first change with respect to FF1 is the definition of the configuration, which now shall take into account the labels and the membrane structure. Hence, a configuration becomes a couple (L, ρ), where L is a list of "labeled cells" $(i_1, l_1, w_1) \ldots (i_n, l_n, w_n)$, with the id $i_j \in \mathbb{N}$, the label $l_j \in Lab$ (the set of labels) and the contents $w_j \in O^*$ (O being the alphabet of the system), for $1 \leq j \leq n$, such that all the cells' id's (the first element of each triple) are different from each other. The second component $\rho \subseteq \mathbb{N} \times \mathbb{N}$ is a relation that represents the connections between cells (it can be seen as a graph where the nodes are the cells id's).

Note that in a configuration each cell has an id which is unique and a label which is not necessarily unique.

The interpretation of relation ρ may differ depending on the selected P system model, but its goal is to capture how cells (or membranes) are organized in the "membrane structure". In cell-like P systems this corresponds to the parent relation, while in tissue P systems this corresponds to the communication graph of the system.

The simulation of most existing variants of active membranes can be done by rules that use following actions:

1. Rewriting of objects (in several cells simultaneously as it is done for the static case).
2. Label change.
3. Creation of a new cell.
4. Creation of a new cell having a contents of some existing cell (and also some additional object rewriting).
5. Deletion of a cell (loosing its contents).
6. Deletion of a cell and moving its contents to some other cell.
7. Arbitrary rewriting of the structure ρ using a graph transducer.

A rule of the network of cells is defined in terms of pattern-matching. First a pattern subgraph structure is given and all actions like rewriting, membrane deletion etc. are given in terms of the pattern structure. During the applicability check the pattern is matched to the actual structure given by the relation ρ. This procedure can yield several matches (instances), so all of them are considered. For each match the preconditions given by the rule (presence or absence of some objects in some cells) are checked and if all of them are satisfied then the rule is applicable. The applicability check is extended to a multiset of rules in a way that is consistent with individual instances of rules. The resulting set of all applicable rules ($Applicable(\Pi, C, asyn)$) is computed as the multisets of couples rule/instance that are applicable to C. Based on this set it is possible to define derivation modes as in the static case. However, additional possibilities related to instances of rules may be investigated, e.g. accepting only particular instances during the derivation (e.g. mandatory including cell number 1).

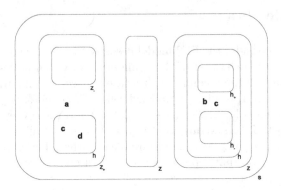

Fig. 5. The P system with active membranes from Example 15. The bold symbols represent the objects.

Example 15. Consider a P system with active membranes having the configuration shown on Figure 5. Let r be the following rule (according to FF2):

$$r : Labels(r) = (z_+, h); \quad \rho(r) = \{(1,2)\}; \quad Rewrite(r) = (1,a)(2,c) \rightarrow (1,c)(2,a).$$

In order to apply r we first should find a combination of two membranes having the labels z_+ and h. There are two such combinations. After that we check the relation $\rho(r)$ which states that membrane 1 (the one identified by the label z_+) is the parent of membrane 2 (the one identified by h). Hence, only the couple at the left remains. We now can identify the numbers 1 and 2 with corresponding cells. Next, the rewriting part of the rule can be applied. It will exchange the symbols a and c, which are located in cells 1 and 2 respectively.

It can easily be seen that the "maximally parallel" derivation mode for active membranes is not really maximally parallel. More precisely it is min_1 for rules involving membranes and max otherwise, so it can be seen as $msmin_1$. This fact makes the active membrane model similar to catalytic P systems, so interesting links can be done. We also remark that even if it is not mentioned explicitly, membrane labels induce cooperation to all rules, thus they have a hidden promoter/permitting context. In the case of the minimally parallel derivation mode for active membranes (min), see Section 11.5 from [9], there could be several interpretations of this concept depending on whether rewriting and membrane rules for a cell are considered to be in the same partition or not.

We would like to emphasize that the current definition of the derivation mode for active membranes allows only one rule per membrane (except rewriting). Using the formal framework it is possible to define in a consistent non-ambiguous way the application of several creation, communication and deletion rules involving the same membrane/cell.

The application $Apply(\Pi, C, R)$ is defined using an algorithm that first applies the rewriting, then creation and then deletion parts of R. At the end, the structure can be modified in an arbitrary way by a graph transducer. We remark that we used the order rewrite, create, delete (RCD), which is consistent with actual definitions of active membranes. However, it is possible to define the application using other orders like RDC or DCR, yielding slightly different semantics. For example, in RDC order deleted membranes cannot be copied to newly created ones and in CDR order the newly duplicated membranes get the "old" contents, before rewriting. The application of rules in some sense is "global", because the applicability imposes the order of their application to be irrelevant. It is possible to relax this condition and to obtain new application strategies that will differ depending on whether the rules are applied from inside-out or not.

Example 16. Consider a P system with active membranes Π having the configuration shown in Figure 5. Suppose that Π has the following rules:

$$r_1 : a[\,]_h \rightarrow [b]_{h_+} \quad r_2 : [b]_h \rightarrow c[\,]_{h_-} \quad r_3 : [c \rightarrow da]_h \quad r_4 : [d]_h \rightarrow [e]_{h_+}[f]_h$$

These rules are translated according to FF2 as follows (see [3]). We suppose that h' is an arbitrary membrane label from the set Lab. We also use the following shorthand notation Ls for $Labels$, RW for $Rewrite$, LR for $Label - Rename$, GC for $Generate - and - Copy$ and CR for $Change - Relation$.

$Ls(r_1) = (h', h);$ $\rho(r_1) = \{(1, 2)\};$ $RW(r_1) = (1, a) \rightarrow (2, b);$ $LR(r_1) = \{(2, h_+)\};$

$Ls(r_2) = (h', h);$ $\rho(r_2) = \{(1, 2)\};$ $RW(r_2) = (2, b) \rightarrow (1, c);$ $LR(r_2) = \{(2, h_-)\};$

$Ls(r_3) = (h);$ $\rho(r_3) = \emptyset;$ $RW(r_3) = (1, c) \rightarrow (1, da);$ $LR(r_3) = \emptyset;$

$Ls(r_4) = (h', h);$ $\rho(r_4) = \{(1, 2)\};$ $RW(r_4) = (2, d) \rightarrow (2, e);$ $LR(r_4) = \{(2, h_+)\};$

$GC(r_4) = \{(1', h, 2, d \rightarrow f)\};$ $CR(r_4) = \{INSERT - EDGE(1, 1')\}.$

It can easily be seen that to the leftmost membrane labeled by h rules r_1, r_3, and r_4 are applicable, while to the rightmost membrane labeled by h only rules r_2 and r_3 are applicable. The result of the maximally parallel evolution can be seen in Figure 6.

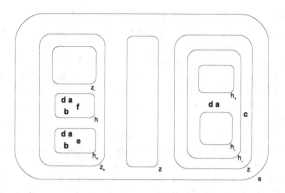

Fig. 6. The result of the application of rules given in Example 16 on the configuration from Figure 5

We remark that this evolution does not correspond to a standard active membranes derivation, because, as it was mentioned above, P systems with active membranes evolve in the $msmin_1$ mode and therefore it is not possible to apply in parallel rules r_1 and r_4 to the leftmost membrane h.

7   Conclusion

In this article we described the model of P systems called the formal framework and we showed how it can be useful when dealing with the following questions: (1) understanding an existing model of P systems; (2) extending a model of P systems with new features or using a different derivation mode; (3) compare two different models of P systems; and (4) explaining details of the semantics that can have several interpretations and raising questions related to these interpretations.

The presented formalism permits to have a powerful language for the description of the features of P systems and is especially useful for making links and transposing results between different models of P systems like it is exemplified in Sections 4.3. Another advantage of the formalism is the ability to treat in a uniform way P systems with static structure, with dynamically evolving structure, and with priorities. This permits to share some basic concepts like derivation modes and may be useful in order to create new formalisms like P systems with active membranes and probabilities.

Acknowledgements. The author would like to thank Rudi Freund for many interesting remarks and suggestions that permitted to improve this paper as well as the support of ANR project SynBioTIC.

References

1. Cardona, M., Colomer, M.A., Margalida, A., Palau, A., Pérez-Hurtado, I., Pérez-Jiménez, M.J., Sanuy, D.: A computational modeling for real ecosystems based on P systems. Natural Computing 10(1), 39–53 (2011)
2. Freund, R., Leporati, A., Mauri, G., Porreca, A.E., Verlan, S., Zandron, C.: Flattening in (Tissue) P systems. In: Alhazov, A., Cojocaru, S., Gheorghe, M., Rogozhin, Y., Rozenberg, G., Salomaa, A. (eds.) CMC 2013, vol. 8340, pp. 173–188. Springer, Heidelberg (2014)
3. Freund, R., Pérez-Hurtado, I., Riscos-Núñez, A., Verlan, S.: A formalization of membrane systems with dynamically evolving structures. International Journal of Computer Mathematics 90(4), 801–815 (2013)
4. Freund, R., Verlan, S.: A formal framework for static (Tissue) P systems. In: Eleftherakis, G., Kefalas, P., Păun, G., Rozenberg, G., Salomaa, A. (eds.) WMC 2007. LNCS, vol. 4860, pp. 271–284. Springer, Heidelberg (2007)
5. Freund, R., Verlan, S.: P systems working in the k-restricted minimally parallel mode. In: International Workshop on Computing with Biomolecules, vol. 244, Wien, Austria. Oesterreichische Computer Gesellschaft, pp. 43–52 (2008)

6. Ibarra, O., Yen, H.: Deterministic catalytic systems are not universal. Theor. Comput. Sci. 363(2), 149–161 (2006)
7. Păun, G.: Membrane Computing. An Introduction. Springer, Berlin (2002)
8. Rozenberg, G., Salomaa, A. (eds.): Handbook of Formal Languages. Springer (1997)
9. Păun, G., Rozenberg, G., Salomaa, A. (eds.): The Oxford Handbook Of Membrane Computing. Oxford University Press (2010)
10. Pescini, D., Besozzi, D., Mauri, G., Zandron, C.: Dynamical probabilistic P systems. International Journal of Foundations of Computer Science 17, 183–204 (2006)
11. Verlan, S.: A note on the probabilistic evolution for P systems. In: Proc. of Tenth Brainstorming Week on Membrane Computing Sevilla, vol. II, pp. 229–234 (2012)
12. Verlan, S.: Study of language-theoretic computational paradigms inspired by biology. Habilitation thesis, University of Paris Est (2010)

A P System for Annotation of Romanian Affixes

Artiom Alhazov, Svetlana Cojocaru, Alexandru Colesnicov,
Ludmila Malahov, and Mircea Petic

Institute of Mathematics and Computer Science,
Academy of Sciences of Moldova
Academiei 5, Chișinău, MD-2028, Moldova
{artiom,Svetlana.Cojocaru,kae,mal,mirsha}@math.md

Abstract. This paper describes membrane computational models parsing affixed Romanian words with prefixes, suffixes, terminations, alterations in the root, and continues previous works on word derivation
modeling. An algorithm for Romanian affixes extraction is given, and
several models of P systems are proposed.

Keywords: affixation, morphemes, parsing, P system models, membrane computing, linguistic resources.

1   Introduction

Linguistic resources are necessary to solve different problems in natural language processing (NLP). They can exist as text collections, corpora, or dictionaries containing a lot of information. Processing of big volume of information
takes the corresponding computer resources. Many problems in computer linguistics could be solved more effectively using parallel computations. Formal
models based on principles of bio-molecular computations have inherent parallelism. Therefore, we found it natural to use these models to solve such problems.
Models of membrane systems [10] for Romanian word derivation were proposed
in [5,4,2,1].

This paper discusses construction of membrane, or P systems to parse Romanian words with affixes. This is important because it permits to solve the
inverse problem of creation of affixed linguistic. This contributes to replenish-
ment of corpora and dictionaries, and to formation of morphological word nest
for derivation.

Affixation is the most productive technique to form new Romanian words as
the Romanian language possesses 86 prefixes and approximately 600 suffixes [8].
Nevertheless, this process has its peculiarities. Using inflexion, we get a priori
correct words and know their morphological categories. Affixation as a mechanism of new word production cannot guarantee their correctness and does not
permit to preview their semantic and morphological categories. This characterizes affixation as a totally non-regular process that complicates word generation.
That is why automated affixation is a difficult task as compared with other
methods of word derivation.

A. Alhazov et al. (Eds.): CMC 2013, LNCS 8340, pp. 80–87, 2014.

Using data extracted from accessible lexicographical resources, we developed methods to check affixed words [6,9]. We found their quantitative and qualitative characteristics. We developed a technique to produce affixed words, and got a set of restrictions that permits to filter inappropriate words.

We proposed in [1] several models of P systems to select affixed Romanian words based on these results. This is a continuation of that work, where we allow a derivation step to have more than one root alternation, addition of a prefix and a suffix, replacement of a termination with another one, as well as all of the above.

The paper consists of introduction, two sections, and conclusion. Sec. 2 gives main definitions of membrane systems and word derivation model. Sec. 3 of this paper discusses automated affix selection inside a word. An algorithm to solve this problem is given. A model of P system with replication is constructed to automatically analyze derived words with affixes. The model uses the matrix of rules taking into account alterations in the root in dependence of fixed prefixes and suffixes that we proposed. Sec. 4 gives examples of the constructed model work at affixed Romanian words parsing.

2 Definitions

2.1 Word Derivation Model

Consider a finite alphabet V. We assume that we are given a finite set of word pairs A of root alternations and finite languages Pref of prefixes, RR of roots, Suf of suffixes and T of terminations (T may include the empty word), all over V. We also write elements of A in the form $x \rightarrow y$. We use $\overline{\text{Pref}}$, $\widehat{\text{Suf}}$ to denote the sets Pref, Suf, where all symbols of each word have lines or hats over them. These two cases correspond to operations of adding a prefix and adding a suffix. We denote the marked terminations by $\boxed{T} = \{\boxed{t} \mid t \in T\}$, and the termination rewriting rules by $\overset{\square}{T} = \{\boxed{t_1} \rightarrow \boxed{t_2} \mid t_1, t_2 \in T\}$. Let $Op = \overline{\text{Pref}} \cup \widehat{\text{Suf}} \cup \overset{\square}{T} \cup A$. The fourth case ($A$) corresponds to an operation of performing an alternation.

Moreover, we assume we are given a finite language M over Op. A derivation step corresponding to a control word $s = o_{i_1} \cdots o_{i_k} \in M$ consists of k operations from a set described above. We now define them more formally, using the syntax $o(w)$ to denote the result of operation o over a word w (note that the result of some operations may be undefined on some words, the corresponding choice not leading to any result):

- $\overline{p}(w) = \overline{p}w$,
- $\widehat{s}(w\boxed{t}) = w\widehat{s}\boxed{t}$,
- $(\boxed{x} \rightarrow \boxed{y})(w\boxed{x}) = w\boxed{y}$,
- $(x \rightarrow y)(w_1 x w_2) = w_1 y w_2$,
- $(o_{i_1} \cdots o_{i_m})(w) = o_{i_1}(\cdots (o_{i_m}(w)) \cdots)$.

We will speak about the problem of **accepting** a language obtained by removing the prefix, suffix and termination marks from the words of the minimal language L, such that

- if $wt \in$ RR, then $w\boxed{t} \in L$, and
- if $w \in L$ and $s \in M$ then $s(w) \in L$ is defined.

Moreover, we would like the acceptor to also produce the lexical decomposition of the input.

2.2 Computing by P Systems

Membrane computing is a recent domain of natural computing started by Gh. Păun in 1998. The components of a membrane system are a cell-like membrane structure, in the regions of which one places multisets of objects which evolve in a synchronous maximally parallel manner according to given evolution rules associated with the membranes. The necessary definitions are given in the following subsection, see also [11] for an overview of the domain and to [12] for the comprehensive bibliography.

Let O be a finite set of elements called symbols, then the set of words over O is denoted by O^*, and the empty word is denoted by λ.

Definition 1. *A P system with string-objects and input is a tuple*

$$\Pi = \left(O, \Sigma, \mu, M_1, \cdots, M_p, R_1, \cdots, R_p, i_0\right), \text{ where:}$$
- *O is the working alphabet of the system whose elements are called objects,*
- *$\Sigma \subset O$ is an input alphabet,*
- *μ is a membrane structure (a rooted tree) consisting of p membranes,*
- *M_i is an initial multiset of strings over O in region i, $1 \le i \le p$,*
- *R_i is a finite set of rules defining the behavior of objects from O^* in region i, $1 \le i \le p$, as described below,*
- *i_0 identifies the input region.*

In this paper we consider string rewriting with target indications. A rule $x \to (y, tar) \in R_i$ can be applied to a string uxv in region i, resulting in a string uyv in region specified by $tar \in \{in_j \mid 1 \le j \le p\} \cup \{here, out\}$. The target $here$ may be omitted, together with a comma and parentheses.

We assume the following **computation mode**: whenever there are multiple ways to apply different rules (or the same rule) to a string, all possible results are produced (each possible result is performed on a different copy of the string; the string is either replicated, or assumed to be present in sufficient number of copies to allow this).

In our model of P systems, the membrane structure does not change. A configuration of a P system is its "snapshot", i.e., the multisets of strings of objects present in regions of the system. While initial configuration is $C_0 = (M_1, \cdots, M_p)$, each subsequent configuration C' is obtained from the previous configuration C by maximally parallel application of rules to objects, denoted by $C \Rightarrow C'$ (no further rules are applicable together with the rules that transform C into C'). A computation is thus a sequence of configurations starting from C_0, respecting relation $\Rightarrow$ and ending in a halting configuration (no rule is applicable).

If S is a multiset of strings over the input alphabet $\Sigma \subseteq O$, then the *initial configuration* of a P system Π with an input S over alphabet Σ and input region i_0 is

$$(M_1, \cdots, M_{i_0-1}, M_{i_0} \cup S, M_{i_0+1} \cdots, M_p).$$

We consider the strings sent out of the skin membrane into the environment as the result of the computation.

3   Main Construction

We proceed with parsing as the reverse process of the generation. For each possible decomposition of the string, the system sends outside a string, obtained from the input by erasing the endmarkers and inserting hyphens (for technical reasons, letters in prefixes and suffixes are marked, the reverse alternations are performed in both the termination and the rest of the word, and the termination is moved to the left of suffixes). In the notation below, we use $'$ as a morphism: u' is a string obtained from u by priming all its letters.

We construct the following P system for accepting words x given in form $\$_1 x \$_2$. We use an enumeration of elements of Op and T: $Op = \{o_1, \cdots, o_k\}$ and $T = \{t_1, \cdots, t_n\}$. We recall that elements o_j, $1 \leq j \leq k$ are of the following forms: $\overline{p}$, $\widehat{s}$, $\boxed{t_1} \to \boxed{t_2}$, and $x \to y$, where $p \in \mathrm{Pref}$, $s \in \mathrm{Suf}$, $t_1, t_2 \in T$ and $x, y \in V^*$. We also define a set $W = Suf(M^r)$ of suffixes of the mirror language of M; words from W may appear in angular brackets. This corresponds to operations remaining to be undone at possible points of the parsing process.

$$\Pi = (O, \mu, \Sigma, w_1, w_2, w_{o_1}, \cdots, w_{o_k}, w_{t_1}, \cdots, w_{t_n},$$
$$R_1, R_2, R_{o_1}, \cdots, R_{o_k}, R_{t_1}, \cdots, R_{t_n}, i_0 = 2),$$
$$O = V \cup \overline{V} \cup \widehat{V} \cup \boxed{T} \cup Op \cup \{\$_1, \$_2, -, \langle, \rangle\}, \quad V = \{a, \cdots, z\},$$
$$\Sigma = V \cup \{\$_1, \$_2\}, \quad \overline{V} = \{\overline{a}, \cdots, \overline{z}\}, \quad \widehat{V} = \{\widehat{a}, \cdots, \widehat{z}\},$$
$$\mu = [\ [\ ]_2[\ ]_{o_1} \cdots [\ ]_{o_k}[\ ]_{t_1} \cdots [\ ]_{t_n}\ ]_1,$$
$$w_i = \lambda, \ i \in \{1, 2\} \cup Op \cup T,$$
$$R_1 = \{\langle\rangle \to \langle w\rangle \mid w \in M^r\} \cup \{\langle o \to (\langle, in_o) \mid o \in Op\},$$
$$\cup \{\langle\rangle \boxed{t} \to (\lambda, in_t) \mid t \in T\},$$
$$\cup \{\$_1 q - t\$_2 \to (q - t, out) \mid qt \in \mathrm{RR}, \ t \in T\},$$
$$R_2 = \{t\$_2 \to (\$_2\langle\rangle\boxed{t}, out) \mid t \in T\},$$
$$R_{\overline{p}} = \{\$_1 p \to (\overline{p} - \$_1, out)\}, \ p \in \mathrm{Pref},$$
$$R_{\widehat{s}} = \{s\$_2 \to (\$_2 - \widehat{s}, out)\}, \ s \in \mathrm{Suf},$$

$$R_q = \{ \boxed{t_2} \to (\boxed{t_1}, out)\}, \ q = \boxed{t_1} \to \boxed{t_2}, \ t_1, t_2 \in T.$$
$$R_a = \{(y \to x, out)\}, \ a = (x \to y) \in A,$$
$$R_t = \{\$_2 \to (-t\$_2, out)\}, \ t \in T.$$

Indeed, the work of Π consists of the reverse application of operations of adding affixes and alternations in terminations and the rest of the word, according to the control words from M. The role of endmarkers $\$_1$ and $\$_2$ consists of ensuring that prefixes from Pref and suffixes from Suf are only removed from the appropriate ends of the word.

The first step consists in marking of a termination in the word, sending the string out to region 1. The subsequent evolution is reduced to selecting and performing reverse derivation steps in regions corresponding to the operations; region 1 serves to control the substeps of the process. At any time, the system sends a copy of the word into a region corresponding to its termination, and back to region 1, effectively unmarking the termination and moving it to the left of all suffixes, separated by a hyphen from the root, in case the control word was emptied to $\langle\rangle$. If the word between the markers (the root and the termination) matches some word in RR, the resulting word is sent out.

Besides accepting words, the system also produces the decomposition of the word. In order to do so, instead of removing prefixes and suffixes, they are moved outside of the interval between $\$_1$ and $\$_2$.

3.1 A Finer Algorithm

We propose a variation of the algorithm above, fulfilling the following goal: the alternations are only allowed in the root of the word, not in the prefixes or suffixes to be removed. We proceed as follows: all reverse alternations are replaced with the prime version of the letters. Once the choice is made to stop performing the operations (the string is in a region corresponding to its termination and the control symbol is removed), every letter can be unprimed, and then the result is sent out if some word from RR is obtained between the markers. We present the resulting P system.

$$\Pi = (O, \mu, \Sigma, w_1, w_2, w_{o_1}, \cdots, w_{o_k}, w_{t_1}, \cdots, w_{t_n},$$
$$R_1, R_2, R_{o_1}, \cdots, R_{o_k}, R_{t_1}, \cdots, R_{t_n}, i_0 = 2),$$
$$O = V \cup V' \cup \overline{V} \cup \widehat{V} \cup \boxed{T} \cup Op \cup \{\$_1, \$_2, -\}, \ V = \{a, \cdots, z\},$$
$$V' = \{a', \cdots, z'\}, \ \overline{V} = \{\overline{a}, \cdots, \overline{z}\}, \ \widehat{V} = \{\widehat{a}, \cdots, \widehat{z}\}, \ \Sigma = V \cup \{\$_1, \$_2\},$$
$$\mu = [\ [\ ]_2 [\ ]_{o_1} \cdots [\ ]_{o_k} [\ ]_{t_1} \cdots [\ ]_{t_n}\ ]_1,$$
$$w_i = \lambda, \ i \in \{1, 2\} \cup Op \cup T,$$
$$R_1 = \{\langle\rangle \to \langle w\rangle \mid w \in M^r\} \cup \{\langle o \to (\langle\rangle, in_o) \mid o \in Op\},$$
$$\cup \{\langle\rangle\boxed{t} \to (\lambda, in_t) \mid t \in T\},$$
$$\cup \{\$_1 q - t\$_2 \to (q - t, out) \mid qt \in RR, \ t \in T\},$$

$R_2 = \{t\$_2 \to (\$_2 \langle \rangle \boxed{t}, out) \mid t \in T\},$

$R_{\bar{p}} = \{\$_1 p \to (\bar{p} - \$_1, out)\},\ p \in \text{Pref},$

$R_{\hat{s}} = \{s\$_2 \to (\$_2 - \hat{s}, out)\},\ s \in \text{Suf},$

$R_q = \{\boxed{t_2} \to (\boxed{t_1}, out)\},\ q = \boxed{t_1} \to \boxed{t_2},\ t_1, t_2 \in T.$

$R_a = \{(z \to x', out) \mid '^{-1}(z) = y\},\ a = (x \to y) \in A,$

$R_t = \{a' \to a \mid a \in V\} \cup \{\$_2 \to (-t\$_2, out)\},\ t \in T.$

The notation $'^{-1}$ means removing all primes from the letters of the argument. Although it assumes an exponential number of rules with respect to the size of a root alternation, this size is never too long.

4   Parsing in the Romanian Language

We start by illustrating the work of the last P system by an example of a fragment of a computation where Pref = {des}, RR = {praf}, Suf = {ui,re}, $T = \{\lambda\}$ and $M = \{(\bar{d}\,\bar{e}\,\bar{s}), (a \to \breve{a})(\widehat{ui}), (\widehat{re})\}$, and the system processes input $\$_1$desprăfuire$\$_2$. For conciseness, we only list the first evolution of the copies of the string leading to the output, using the notation (string,region). (The other two are obtained if the prefix des is marked before both suffixes or after one of them, yielding the same results, while for technical reasons some strings remain blocked in the system, not contributing to the result).

$(\$_1\text{desprăfuire}\$_2, 2) \Rightarrow (\$_1\text{desprăfuire}\$_2\langle\rangle\boxed{\lambda}, 1) \Rightarrow$

$(\$_1\text{desprăfuire}\$_2\langle(\widehat{re})\rangle\boxed{\lambda}, 1) \Rightarrow (\$_1\text{desprăfuire}\$_2\langle\rangle\boxed{\lambda}, (\widehat{re})) \Rightarrow$

$(\$_1\text{desprăfui}\$_2 - \widehat{re}\langle\rangle\boxed{\lambda}, 1) \Rightarrow (\$_1\text{desprăfui}\$_2 - \widehat{re}\langle(\widehat{ui})(a \to \breve{a})\rangle\boxed{\lambda}, 1) \Rightarrow$

$(\$_1\text{desprăfui}\$_2 - \widehat{re}\langle(a \to \breve{a})\rangle\boxed{\lambda}, (\widehat{ui}) \Rightarrow (\$_1\text{desprăf}\$_2 - \widehat{ui} - \widehat{re}\langle(a \to \breve{a})\rangle\boxed{\lambda}, 1)$

$\Rightarrow (\$_1\text{desprăf}\$_2 - \widehat{ui} - \widehat{re}\langle\rangle\boxed{\lambda}, (a \to \breve{a})) \Rightarrow (\$_1\text{despra}'\text{f}\$_2 - \widehat{ui} - \widehat{re}\langle\rangle\boxed{\lambda}, 1)$

$\Rightarrow (\$_1\text{despra}'\text{f}\$_2 - \widehat{ui} - \widehat{re}\langle(\bar{d}\,\bar{e}\,\bar{s})\rangle\boxed{\lambda}, 1) \Rightarrow$

$(\$_1\text{despra}'\text{f}\$_2 - \widehat{ui} - \widehat{re}\langle\rangle\boxed{\lambda}, (\bar{d}\,\bar{e}\,\bar{s})) \Rightarrow (\bar{d}\,\bar{e}\,\bar{s} - \$_1\text{pra}'\text{f}\$_2 - \widehat{ui} - \widehat{re}\langle\rangle\boxed{\lambda}, 1)$

$\Rightarrow (\bar{d}\,\bar{e}\,\bar{s} - \$_1\text{pra}'\text{f}\$_2 - \widehat{ui} - \widehat{re}, \lambda) \Rightarrow (\bar{d}\,\bar{e}\,\bar{s} - \$_1\text{praf}\$_2 - \widehat{ui} - \widehat{re}, \lambda) \Rightarrow$

$(\bar{d}\,\bar{e}\,\bar{s} - \$_1\text{praf-}\$_2 - \widehat{ui} - \widehat{re}, 1) \Rightarrow (\bar{d}\,\bar{e}\,\bar{s}-\text{praf- -}\widehat{ui} - \widehat{re}, 0).$

By inspecting the examples, we have come to the conclusion that a derivation step can include, in the worst case, a prefix, a suffix, two root alternations and replacing a termination with another one. Some of the above mentioned operations may be absent.

We should note that the division of a word into morphemes may sometimes differ from the one commonly accepted in linguistics. However, this should not restrict the generality of the approach, and we did so in order to simplify the explanation.

In the parsing process described above, we accounted for the prefixes, suffixes, root alternations and the terminations. As we have already stated, Romanian language has 86 prefixes and about 600 suffixes, see, e.g., [8]. Processing the dictionary [7] (not claiming its comprehensiveness) let us distinguish the following types of root alternations during the word derivation:

- of vowels: a→ ă, a→ e, e→ ă, o→ u, î→ i, ă→ e,
  ea→ e, e→ ea, oa→ o, oa→ u, ia→ ie
- of consonants: t→ ţ, d→ z, h→ ş, z→ j, d→ j, t→ c, t→ ci

Note that, if desired, we can use the context information to refine the scope of the the root alternation rules, e.g., if we only wanted to perform the alternation a→ ă between letters t and r, we could write this as a rule tar→ tăr, which does not affect the model at all.

The set of terminations that we use in our algorithm (set T) consists of terminations for nouns and adjectives (ă, e, ea, a, i, ică, the empty termination λ, u, o, a, l, iu, ui, iu, ie, uie) and those for verbs (a, ea, e, i, î).

We now proceed with some more examples of input and output, so let us agree that

$$\text{Pref} \supseteq \{\text{im,în,de,re,des}\},$$
$$\text{RR} \supseteq \{\text{pune,flori,flex,scrie,cicl,fac,tânăr,fată,mult,deştept,brad,praf}\},$$
$$\text{Suf} \supseteq \{\text{ere, are, ibil, re, ire, i, iţ, im, uţ, ui}\},$$
$$T \supseteq \{\lambda, \breve{a}, e\},$$
$$A \supseteq \{\hat{a} \to i, \breve{a} \to e, a \to e, t \to \textcommabelow{t}, e \to ea, a \to \breve{a}\},$$
$$M \supseteq \{(\widehat{\hat{\imath}\ \overline{m}}), (\widehat{\overline{\imath}\ \overline{n}}), (\widehat{\overline{d}\ \overline{e}}), (\widehat{\overline{r}\ \overline{e}}), (\widehat{\overline{d}\ \overline{e}\ \overline{s}}), (\widetilde{\widehat{ere}}), (\widehat{are}), (\widehat{ibil}), (\widehat{re}), (\widehat{ire}),$$
$$(\hat{a} \to i)(\breve{a} \to e)(\widehat{\overline{\imath}n})(\hat{\imath}), \ (a \to e)(\widehat{\imath\textcommabelow{t}}), \ (t \to \textcommabelow{t})(\widehat{\imath m}), (\boxed{\lambda} \to \boxed{e})$$
$$(e \to ea)(\boxed{\lambda} \to \boxed{\breve{a}}), \ (a \to \breve{a})(\widehat{u\textcommabelow{t}}), \ (a \to \breve{a})(\widehat{ui})\}.$$

Examples without root alternations: words
$\$_1$înflorire$\$_2$, $\$_1$flexibil$\$_2$, $\$_1$descriere$\$_2$, $\$_1$reciclare$\$_2$, $\$_1$desfacere$\$_2$ (burst into blossom, flexible, description, recycling, disassembling) will yield output $\hat{\imath}\ \overline{n}$-flori--$\widetilde{\widehat{re}}$, flex--$\widehat{ibil}$, $\overline{d}\ \overline{e}$-scrie--$\widehat{re}$, $\overline{r}\ \overline{e}$-cicl--$\widehat{are}$, and $\overline{d}\ \overline{e}\ \overline{s}$-fac-$\widehat{ere}$, respectively.

Examples with root alternations: words $\$_1$întineri$\$_2$, $\$_1$fetiţă$\$_2$, $\$_1$mulţime$\$_2$, $\$_1$deşteaptă$\$_2$, $\$_1$brăduţ$\$_2$ and $\$_1$desprăfuire$\$_2$ (youthen, little girl, multitude, dignified (fem.), small spruce, undusting) will yield output $\overline{\imath n}$-tânăr--$\hat{\imath}$, fat-ă-$\widehat{\imath\textcommabelow{t}}$, mulţ--$\widehat{\imath m}$, deştept-, brad-$\widehat{u\textcommabelow{t}}$, and $\overline{d}\ \overline{e}\ \overline{s}$-praf--$\widehat{ui} - \widehat{re}$, respectively.

5   Conclusions

The paper discussed P systems used to word derivation in Romanian, namely, affixation of nouns, adjectives, and verbs as most productive parts of speech at lemmas affixation. We proposed variants of membrane parsing model taking into account alternations in the root dependent of fixed prefixes and suffixes. We may deduce that these models can be used not only for Romanian but for other languages with analogous type of word derivation. These models can also be integrated into another NLP applications to solve more complicated problems in computer linguistics.

Acknowledgements. This work was supported by project STCU-5384 "Models of high performance computations based on biological and quantum approaches", and project ref. nr. 12.819.18.09A "Development of IT support for interoperability of electronic linguistic resources" from Supreme Council for Science and Technological Development of the Republic of Moldova.

References

1. Alhazov, A., Boian, E., Cojocaru, S., Colesnicov, A., Malahov, L., Petic, M., Ciubotaru, C.: Membrane Models of Romanian Word Affixation. In: Applied Linguistics and Linguistic Technologies, MegaLing 2012, Kyiv (2013) (in print) (in Russian)
2. Alhazov, A., Boian, E., Cojocaru, S., Rogozhin, Y.: Modelling Inflections in Romanian Language by P Systems with String Replication. Computer Science Journal of Moldova 2(50), 160–178 (2009)
3. Alhazov, A., Cojocaru, S., Malahova, L., Rogozhin, Y.: Dictionary Search and Update by P Systems with String-Objects and Active Membranes. International Journal of Computers, Communications & Control IV(3), 206–213 (2009)
4. Boian, E., Cojocaru, C., Colesnicov, A., Malahov, L., Ciubotaru, C.: Modeling of Romanian Word Derivation by Membrane Computations. In: Applied linguistics and linguistic technologies, MegaLing 2011, Kyiv, pp. 57–72 (2012) (in Russian)
5. Boian, E., Cojocaru, C., Colesnicov, A., Malahov, L., Ciubotaru, C.: P Systems in Computer Linguistics. In: Applied Linguistics and Linguistic Technologies, MegaLing 2009, pp. 62–70 (2009) (in Russian)
6. Cojocaru, S., Boian, E., Petic, M.: Stages in Automatic Derivational Morphology Processing. In: Knowledge Engineering, Principles and Techniques, KEPT 2009, pp. 97–104. Cluj-Napoca University Press (2009)
7. Constantinescu, S.: Dictionary of Derived Words, HERRA, Bucharest, p. 288 (2008) (in Romanian)
8. Graur, A., Avram, M.: Word formation in Romanian, vol. II, p. 310. Romanian Academy Press, Bucharest (1978) (in Romanian)
9. Petic, M.: Automatic Derivational Morphology Contribution to Romanian Lexical Acquisition. Natural Language Processing and its Application. Research in Computing Science 46, 67–78 (2010)
10. Păun, G.: Membrane Computing. An Introduction, p. 420. Springer (2002)
11. Păun, G., Rozenberg, G., Salomaa, A.: The Oxford Handbook of Membrane Computing, pp. 118–143. Oxford University Press (2010)
12. P systems webpage, http://ppage.psystems.eu

Behavioural Equivalences
in Real-Time P Systems

Bogdan Aman and Gabriel Ciobanu

Romanian Academy, Institute of Computer Science
Blvd. Carol I no.8, 700506 Iași, Romania
baman@iit.tuiasi.ro, gabriel@info.uaic.ro

Abstract. We present a real-time extension of P systems in which each membrane and each object has a lifetime attached to it, and we use these lifetimes to define and study various behavioural equivalences. We also establish sufficient conditions for guaranteeing progression over time.

1 Introduction

Biologists are becoming increasingly aware that formal methods can help to avoid resources consumption in lab experiments [3]. The field of "computational methods in system biology" provides formal frameworks that are able to faithfully describe the behaviour of complex systems, to provide qualitative and quantitative reasoning, as well as to compare the similar behaviour of two related systems. During the last years, membrane computing [9,14] has been applied to biology and could have an important impact in understanding how biological systems work, giving at the same time a way to describe, manipulate, analyse and verify them.

In this paper we define and study a real-time extension of P systems, inspired by the P systems with lifetimes [1] and from biology where cells and intracellular proteins have a well-defined lifetime. We assign real-time lifetimes to each membrane and to each object and in order to simulate the passage of time, we use rules of the form $(a, t) \overset{d}{\rightsquigarrow} (a, t - d)$ for objects, and $[\ ]_{(i,t)} \overset{d}{\rightsquigarrow} [\ ]_{(i,t-d)}$ for membranes, where $d \in \mathbb{R}$ and $d \leq t$. If the lifetime of an object a reaches 0 then the object is used to create a new multiset of objects u by applying a rule of the form $(a, 0) \rightarrow u$, while if the lifetime of a membrane i reaches 0 then the membrane is marked for dissolution by applying a rule of the form $[\ ]_{(i,0)} \rightarrow [\delta]_{(i,0)}$. After dissolving a membrane, all objects and membranes previously contained in it become elements of the immediately upper membrane. A similar idea has been considered for spiking P systems, where a life duration was added for spikes, but not for cells [11]. If a spike has a lifetime equal to zero, it is removed.

A time-independent P system is a P system that always produces the same result, independently of the execution times of the rules [6]. If one assumes the existence of two time scales (an external time for the user, and an internal time for the device), then it is possible to construct accelerated P systems [5].

A. Alhazov et al. (Eds.): CMC 2013, LNCS 8340, pp. 88–100, 2014.
© Springer-Verlag Berlin Heidelberg 2014

Behavioural equivalence is an important concept in biology, necessary for comparing the behaviour of various (sub)systems. For example, an artificial organ should be the functional equivalent of a natural organ, meaning that both behave in a similar manner up to a given time; e.g. the artificial kidney has the same functional characteristics as an "in vivo" kidney. Recently, it was shown in [12] that the vas deferens' of the human, canine and bull are equivalent in many ways, including histological similarities. In [10], different methods are presented for comparing protein structures in order to discover common patterns.

When choosing which equivalence relation to adopt for a given model, we need to decide what properties are to be preserved by the equivalence relation. In membrane computing, two P systems (also called membrane systems) are considered to be equivalent whenever they have the same input/output behaviour [14]. Such an equivalence does not consider the temporal evolution of the two systems. Behavioural equivalences (bisimulations) for membrane systems were defined in [2,4,8]. As a novelty, we are looking for systems with equivalent timed behaviour. By defining several equivalences, we offer flexibility in selecting the right one when verifying biological systems and comparing them.

In computer science, theoretical methods are used to implement software tools able to verify the properties of complex concurrent systems. It is reasonable to expect that, for real-time P systems, we can create or adapt some tools based on verification techniques using temporal logics. What we do in this paper represents a first step in this direction, namely establishing the formal framework used in software verifications for biological systems sensitive to timeouts.

2   Real-Time P Systems

Membrane systems are essentially parallel and non-deterministic computing models inspired by the compartments of eukaryotic cells and their biochemical reactions. The structure of the cell is represented by a set of hierarchically embedded membranes that are all contained inside a skin membrane. The molecular species (ions, proteins, etc.) floating inside cellular compartments are represented by multisets of objects described by means of symbols over a given alphabet. The objects can be modified or communicated between adjacent compartments. Chemical reactions are represented by evolution rules that operate on the objects, as well as on the compartmentalised structure (by dissolving, dividing, creating, or moving membranes).

A membrane system can perform computations in the following way: starting from an initial configuration (the initial membrane structure and the initial multisets of objects placed inside the membranes), the system evolves by applying the evolution rules of each membrane in a non-deterministic manner. A rule is applicable when all the objects that appear in its left hand side are available in the membrane where the rule is placed.

Several variants of membrane systems are inspired by different aspects of living cells (communication through membranes, membrane mobility, etc.). Their computing power and efficiency have been investigated using the approaches of formal languages, grammars, register machines and complexity theory. Membrane systems are presented together with many variants and examples in [13]. Several applications of these systems are presented in [9]. An updated bibliography can be found at the P systems web page http://ppage.psystems.eu.

For an alphabet $V = \{a_1, \ldots, a_n\}$, we denote by V^* the set of all strings over V; λ denotes the empty string and $V^+ = V^* \backslash \{\lambda\}$. We use the string representation of multisets that is widely used in the field of membrane systems. An example of such a representation is the multiset $u = aba$, where $u(a) = 2$, $u(b) = 1$. Given two multisets u, v over V, for any $a \in V$, we have $(u \uplus v)(a) = u(a) + v(a)$ as the multiset union, and $(u \backslash v)(a) = max\{0, u(a) - v(a)\}$ as the multiset difference. We use $\mathbb{R}_+$ to denote the non-negative reals.

Next we define real-time P systems, a variant of P systems with lifetimes [1].

Definition 1. *A* **real-time P system** *of degree* $n \geq 1$ *is a construct*
$$\Pi = (V_t, H_t, \mu_t, w_1, \ldots, w_n, \mathcal{L}, (R_1, \rho_1), \ldots, (R_n, \rho_n)), \ where:$$

1. $V_t \subseteq V \times (\mathbb{R} \cup \infty)$ *is a set of pairs of the form* (a, t_a), *where* $a \in V$ *is an object and* $t_a \in (\mathbb{R} \cup \infty)$ *is the lifetime of the object* a;
2. $H_t \subseteq H \times (\mathbb{R} \cup \infty)$ *is a set of pairs of the form* (h, t_h), *where* $h \in H$ *is a membrane label and* $t_h \in (\mathbb{R} \cup \infty)$ *is the lifetime of the membrane* h;
3. $\mu_t \subseteq H_t \times H_t$ *is a tree that describes the* membrane structure, *such that* $((i, t_i), (j, t_j)) \in \mu_t$ *denotes that the membrane labelled by* j *with lifetime* t_j *is contained in the membrane labelled by* i *with lifetime* t_i; *this structure does not depend on the lifetimes of the involved membranes*;
4. $w_i \subseteq (V_t)^*$ *is a multiset of pairs from* V_t *assigned initially to membrane* i;
5. $\mathcal{L}$ *is a set of labels that attaches a unique label to each rule from* $R_1, \ldots, R_n$;
6. R_i, $1 \leq i \leq n$, *is a finite set of* evolution rules *from membrane* i *of the following forms:*
   (a) $r : u \to v$, *with* $u \in V_t^+$, *either* $v = v'$ *or* $v = v'\delta$, $v' \in ((V_t \times \{here, out\}) \cup (V_t \times \{in_j \mid 1 \leq j \leq n\}))^*$, $r \in \mathcal{L}$; δ *is a special symbol not appearing in* V;
   Considering that the multiset of objects u *was placed inside membrane* i, *the targets indicate where, in the membrane structure, the multiset of objects* v *obtained from* u *should be placed:*
   - *here - it remains in* i;
   - *out - is placed in the parent membrane of* i;
   - in_j - *is moved in a child of* i *labelled by* j.
   (b) $r : (a, 0) \to u$, *for all* $a \in V$, $u \in V_t^+$, $r \in \mathcal{L}$
   If an object a *has the lifetime* 0 *then the object is replaced with the multiset* u, *thus simulating the degradation of proteins and the fact that new compounds are obtained.*
   (c) $r : [\ ]_{(i,0)} \to [\delta]_{(i,0)}$, *for all* $1 \leq i \leq n$, $r \in \mathcal{L}$
   If the lifetime of a membrane i *reaches* 0 *the membrane is dissolved.*
7. ρ_i, *for all* $1 \leq i \leq n$, *is a partial order relationship defined over the rules in* R_i *specifying a* priority relation *between these rules.*

Therefore, a real-time P systems consists of a membrane structure μ containing $n \geq 1$ membranes, where each membrane i gets assigned a finite multiset of objects w_i and a finite set of evolution rules R_i. The sets V_t and H_t are potentially uncountable, but at any moment a real-time P system contains just a finite number of objects and membranes. An evolution rule can produce the special object δ to specify that, after the application of the rule, the membrane containing δ has to be dissolved. After dissolving a membrane, all objects and membranes previously present in it become elements of the immediately upper membrane, while the rules of the dissolved membrane are removed. When no rule from R_i, $1 \leq i \leq n$, is applicable, all clocks of a real-time P system are decreased with the same value (the minimum value of the present delays), such that a new rule from R_i, $1 \leq i \leq n$, is applicable.

Definition 2. *For a real-time P system Π the initial configuration is defined as $C_0 = (\mu_t, w_1, \ldots, w_n)$. The set of all configurations over a real-time P system Π is denoted by $\mathcal{C}_\Pi$.*

Example 1. Consider the following real-time P system of degree 2:

$\Pi_1 = (a \times (\mathbb{R} \cup \infty), \{1 \times \infty, 2 \times (\mathbb{R} \cup \infty)\}, \{(1, \infty), (2, 5)\}, \emptyset, (a, 2), \{r\}, \emptyset,$
$(\{r : (a, 0) \to (a, 6)\}))$. Graphically this looks like this:

$$
\begin{array}{c}
\boxed{\begin{array}{l}
\boxed{\begin{array}{l}
(a, 2) \\
r : (a, 0) \to (a, 6) \\
(2, 5)
\end{array}}
\end{array}} \\
(1, \infty)
\end{array}
$$

The initial configuration for Π_1 is $C_1^0 = (\{(1, \infty), (2, 5)\}, \emptyset, (a, 2))$. Starting from this initial configuration, Π has the following evolution:

$C_1^0 \overset{2}{\rightsquigarrow} (\{(1, \infty), (2, 3)\}, \emptyset, (a, 0)) \overset{r}{\rightarrow} (\{(1, \infty), (2, 3)\}, \emptyset, (a, 6)) \overset{3}{\rightsquigarrow} \ldots$

Graphically these steps of evolution are represented as

$$
\boxed{\begin{array}{l}
\boxed{\begin{array}{l}
(a, 2) \\
r : (a, 0) \to (a, 6) \\
(2, 5)
\end{array}}
\end{array}} \overset{2}{\rightsquigarrow}
\boxed{\begin{array}{l}
\boxed{\begin{array}{l}
(a, 0) \\
r : (a, 0) \to (a, 6) \\
(2, 3)
\end{array}}
\end{array}} \overset{r}{\rightarrow}
\boxed{\begin{array}{l}
\boxed{\begin{array}{l}
(a, 6) \\
r : (a, 0) \to (a, 6) \\
(2, 3)
\end{array}}
\end{array}} \overset{3}{\rightsquigarrow} \ldots
$$
$(1, \infty) \qquad\qquad (1, \infty) \qquad\qquad (1, \infty)$

The label of $\overset{2}{\rightsquigarrow}$ is determined by comparing the lifetime of object a (namely 2) with the lifetime of membrane 2 (namely 5), and then taking the minimum value (namely 2). Similar for the label of $\overset{3}{\rightsquigarrow}$, that is the minimum between 6 and 3.

3   Timed Labelled Transition Systems

The operational semantics of a formalism is typically defined by using labelled transition systems. For formalisms involving time, modelling the passage of time may be encoded in timed labelled transition systems that distinguish between transitions due to rules and those due to passage of time.

A *timed labelled transition system (shortly TLTS)* is a tuple $(\mathcal{C}, C_0, \mathcal{L}, \rightarrow, \rightsquigarrow)$ where $\mathcal{C}$ is a set of configurations, C_0 is the initial configuration, $\mathcal{L}$ is a set of labels, $\rightarrow \subseteq \mathcal{C} \times \mathcal{L} \times \mathcal{C}$ is a *rule transition relation* and $\rightsquigarrow \subseteq \mathcal{C} \times \mathbb{R}_+ \times \mathcal{C}$ is a *timed transition relation*. We write $C \xrightarrow{r} C'$ for $(C, r, C') \in \rightarrow$ and $C \xrightarrow{d} C'$ for $(C, d, C') \in \rightsquigarrow$. If there is no $C' \in \mathcal{C}$ such that either $C \xrightarrow{r} C'$ or $C \xrightarrow{d} C'$, then we write either $C \not\xrightarrow{r}$ or $C \not\xrightarrow{d}$, respectively.

The timed labelled transition system defined above is general and can be applied to any formalism involving time. A particular system for real-time P systems is given by Table 1 and Definition 3.

Table 1. Rule Transitions (left column) and Timed Transitions (right column)

(OBJ) $\dfrac{\begin{array}{c} r : (a,0) \rightarrow u \in R_i,\ (a,0) \in w_i, \\ C = (\mu_t, w_1, \ldots, w_n) \end{array}}{\begin{array}{c} C \xrightarrow{r} C' = (\mu_t', w_1', \ldots, w_n'),\ \text{with } \mu_t' = \mu_t, \\ w_i' = (w_i \backslash (a,0)) \uplus \{u_t \mid (u_t, here) \in u\} \\ w_j' = w_j \uplus \{u_t \mid (u_t, out) \in u, ((j,t_j),(i,t_i)) \in \mu_t\} \\ w_k' = w_k \uplus \{u_t \mid (u_t, in_k) \in u, ((i,t_i),(k,t_k)) \in \mu_t\} \\ w_m' = w_m, m \neq i,j,k \end{array}}$	**(TOBJ)** $\dfrac{\begin{array}{c}(a,t) \in V_t, \\ 0 \leq d \leq t\end{array}}{(a,t) \xrightarrow{d} (a, t-d)}$
	(TMULT) $\dfrac{\begin{array}{c} 0 \leq d \leq t \\ \forall (a,t) \in w_i,\ (a,t) \xrightarrow{d} (a,t-d) \end{array}}{w_i \xrightarrow{d} w_i',\ \text{with } w_i' = \{(a,t-d) \mid (a,t) \in w_i\}}$
(MEM) $\dfrac{\begin{array}{c} r : [\,]_{(i,0)} \rightarrow [\delta]_{(i,0)}, \\ ((j,t_j),(i,0)) \in \mu_t\ \ C = (\mu_t, w_1, \ldots, w_n) \end{array}}{\begin{array}{c} C \xrightarrow{r} C' = (\mu_t', w_1', \ldots, w_n') \\ \text{with } w_i' = \emptyset,\ w_j' = w_i \uplus w_j \\ w_k' = w_k,\ \text{for } k \neq i,\ k \neq j \\ \text{and } \mu_t' = ((\mu_t \backslash ((i,t_i),(j,t_j))) \\ \backslash \{(i,0),(k,t_k)\}) \uplus \{(j,t_j),(k,t_k)\} \end{array}}$	**(TMEM)** $\dfrac{(i,t) \in H_t,\ 0 \leq d \leq t}{(i,t) \xrightarrow{d} (i, t-d)}$
	(TSTRUCT) $\dfrac{\begin{array}{cc} 0 \leq d \leq t_i, 0 \leq d \leq t_j & \forall ((i,t_i),(j,t_j)) \in \mu_t, \\ (i,t_i) \xrightarrow{d} (i,t_i - d) & (j,t_j) \xrightarrow{d} (j,t_j - d) \end{array}}{\begin{array}{c} \mu_t \xrightarrow{d} \mu_t' \\ \text{with } \mu_t' = \{((i,t_i - d),(j,t_j - d)) \mid ((i,t_i),(j,t_j)) \in \mu_t\} \end{array}}$
(EVOL) $\dfrac{\begin{array}{c} r : u \rightarrow v \in R_i, u \in w_i, \\ C = (\mu_t, w_1, \ldots, w_n) \end{array}}{\begin{array}{c} C \xrightarrow{r} C' = (\mu_t', w_1', \ldots, w_n') \\ \text{with } w_j' = w_j,\ \text{for } j \neq i \\ \text{and } w_i' = (w_i \backslash u) \uplus v \end{array}}$	**(TEVOL)** $\dfrac{\begin{array}{c} d \in \mathbb{R}_+, \mu_t \xrightarrow{d} \mu_t', \\ \forall 1 \leq i \leq n, w_i \xrightarrow{d} w_i' \\ C = (\mu_t, w_1, \ldots, w_n) \end{array}}{C \xrightarrow{d} C' = (\mu_t', w_1', \ldots, w_n')}$

The transition relation $\rightarrow$ describes rule application and a sequence of such transitions describes an execution within the same instant of real-time, whereas the timed transition relation $\rightsquigarrow$ describes the passage of real-time. The operational semantics of a real-time P system Π is:

Definition 3. *A **TLTS** for a **P** system Π is a tuple $(\mathcal{C}_\Pi, C_0, \mathcal{L}, \rightarrow, \rightsquigarrow)$ where the relations $\rightarrow$ and $\rightsquigarrow$ are the smallest relations satisfying the inference rules from Table 1, the priority relations ρ_i of Π, and the following constraint expressing that $\rightarrow$ has a higher priority than $\rightsquigarrow$ and guaranteeing maximal progress:*

$$\text{if there exists } C' \text{ such that } C \xrightarrow{r} C', \text{ then } C \overset{d}{\not\rightsquigarrow} \text{ for all } d > 0.$$

According to Table 1, in rule **(OBJ)** an object $(a, 0) \in w_i$ is replaced by a multiset u and the membrane structure remains unchanged, thus the configuration $C = (\mu_t, w_1, \ldots, w_n)$ is transformed into configuration $C' = (\mu'_t, w'_1, \ldots, w'_n)$ with $\mu'_t = \mu_t$, and the objects distributed among membranes according to the structure μ_t and the targets from u. Rules **(EVOL)** and **(TEVOL)** are similar to **(OBJ)**. In rule **(MEM)** a membrane i is dissolved (i is placed inside j) and thus w_i, w_j and μ_t are modified to $w'_i = \emptyset$, $w'_j = w_i \uplus w_j$ and μ'_t, respectively; μ'_t is identical to μ_t excepting that the pair $((i, t_i), (j, t_j))$ is removed and all (i, i_t) are replaced by (j, j_t).

Proposition 1. *For any $C, C', C'' \in \mathcal{C}_\Pi$, and any $d, d' \in \mathbb{R}_+$,*

1. **(Time determinacy)** *If $C \overset{d}{\rightsquigarrow} C'$ and $C \overset{d}{\rightsquigarrow} C''$, then $C' = C''$.*
2. **(Time continuity)** *$C \overset{d+d'}{\rightsquigarrow} C''$ if and only if*

$$\text{there is a } C' \text{ such that } C \overset{d}{\rightsquigarrow} C' \text{ and } C' \overset{d'}{\rightsquigarrow} C''.$$

4 Timed Equivalences

Behavioural equivalence should be used to compare systems behaviour; whenever two systems are shown to be identical, no observer or context can distinguish between them. A good behavioural equivalence guarantees that, in any context, a system can be safely replaced by an equivalent system, thus allowing compositional reasoning. A suitable notion of equivalence between timed systems is obtained by extending the standard notion of bisimilarity to take into account timed transitions [7].

The notions defined in this section are generally applicable to all formalisms involving time than can be encoded in a TLTS. Since in the previous section we defined a specific TLTS for real-time P systems, we use their corresponding behavioural equivalences to compare membrane systems (e.g., as in Example 1).

Definition 4. *Let $(\mathcal{C}_{\Pi 1}, C_{01}, \mathcal{L}_1, \rightarrow, \rightsquigarrow)$ and $(\mathcal{C}_{\Pi 2}, C_{02}, \mathcal{L}_2, \rightarrow, \rightsquigarrow)$ be two TLTSs. A binary relation $\mathcal{R} \subseteq \mathcal{C}_{\Pi 1} \times \mathcal{C}_{\Pi 2}$ is called a **strong timed simulation** (ST simulation) if whenever $(C, D) \in \mathcal{R}$, then:*

1. *for any $r \in \mathcal{L}$, $C' \in \mathcal{C}_{\Pi 1}$, if $C \xrightarrow{r} C'$, then there exists some $D' \in \mathcal{C}_{\Pi 2}$ such that $D \xrightarrow{r} D'$ and $(C', D') \in \mathcal{R}$;*

2. *for any $d \in \mathbb{R}_+$, $C' \in \mathcal{C}_{\Pi 1}$, if $C \xrightarrow{d} C'$, then there exists some $D' \in \mathcal{C}_{\Pi 2}$ such that $D \xrightarrow{d} D'$ and $(C', D') \in \mathcal{R}$.*

If $\mathcal{R}$ and $\mathcal{R}^{-1}$ are strong timed simulations, then $\mathcal{R}$ is called a **strong timed bisimulation** *(ST bisimulation). We define* **strong timed bisimilarity** *by*
$$\sim \stackrel{def}{=} \{(C, D) \in \mathcal{C}_{\Pi 1} \times \mathcal{C}_{\Pi 2} \mid there \ exists \ an \ ST \ bisimulation \ \mathcal{R} \ and \ (C, D) \in \mathcal{R}\}.$$

Definition 4 treats timed transitions as rule transitions and thus strong timed bisimilarity coincides with the original notion of bisimilarity over two labelled transition systems $(\mathcal{C}_{\Pi 1}, C_{01}, \mathcal{L}_1 \cup \mathbb{R}_+, \to \cup \rightsquigarrow)$, and $(\mathcal{C}_{\Pi 2}, C_{02}, \mathcal{L}_2 \cup \mathbb{R}_+, \to \cup \rightsquigarrow)$.

Remark 1. $\sim$ is the largest ST bisimulation; moreover, $\sim$ is an equivalence.

4.1   Bounded Timed Equivalence

Strong timed bisimilarity is too strong since all behaviours that violate time constraints are considered failures. An alternative is to weaken comparison criteria to behaviours up to a given deadline, ignoring the behaviours after the deadline.

Example 2. Consider the following systems:
$\Pi_1 = (a \times (\mathbb{R} \cup \infty), \{1 \times \infty, 2 \times (\mathbb{R} \cup \infty)\}, \{(1, \infty), (2, 5)\}, \emptyset, (a, 2), \{r\}, \emptyset, (\{r : (a, 0) \to (a, 6)\}))$ and
$\Pi_2 = (a \times (\mathbb{R} \cup \infty), \{1 \times \infty, 2 \times (\mathbb{R} \cup \infty)\}, \{(1, \infty), (2, 7)\}, \emptyset, (a, 4), \{r\}, \emptyset, (\{r : (a, 0) \to (a, 6)\}))$.
The initial configuration for Π_1 is $C_1^0 = (\{(1, \infty), (2, 5)\}, \emptyset, (a, 2))$, while for Π_2 is $C_2^0 = (\{(1, \infty), (2, 7)\}, \emptyset, (a, 4))$. Before time 2, both Π_1 and Π_2 have exactly the same evolutions. If we do not care about the behaviour of the systems beyond time 2, it makes sense to identify the two systems up to time 2. Nevertheless, these systems cannot be identified by strong timed bisimulation. We can see that Π_1 has the following evolution:
$C_1^0 \xrightarrow{2} (\{(1, \infty), (2, 3)\}, \emptyset, (a, 0)) \xrightarrow{r} (\{(1, \infty), (2, 3)\}, \emptyset, (a, 6))$;
however this cannot be matched by the evolution of Π_2:
$C_2^0 \xrightarrow{2} (\{(1, \infty), (2, 5)\}, \emptyset, (a, 2)) \xrightarrow{2} (\{(1, \infty), (2, 3)\}, \emptyset, (a, 0)) \xrightarrow{r} (\{(1, \infty), (2, 3)\}, \emptyset, (a, 6))$.
Hence, Π_1 and Π_2 cannot be identified by strong timed bisimulation. We need a notion of equivalence that allows us to identify systems whose behaviours match up to a given deadline.

A notion of *timed bisimilarity up to time t* is introduced in [18] to compare the behaviour of timed CSP processes. This notion can be applied to any pair of TLTSs, and also to our formalism. In order to define an *equivalence up to time t* we need the following terminology.

A *binary relation* over $\mathcal{C}_{\Pi 1}$ and $\mathcal{C}_{\Pi 2}$ is a relation $\mathcal{R} \subseteq \mathcal{C}_{\Pi 1} \times \mathcal{C}_{\Pi 2}$, where $\mathcal{C}_{\Pi 1}$ and $\mathcal{C}_{\Pi 2}$ can be equal. The *identity relation* is $id \stackrel{def}{=} \{(C, C) \mid C \in \mathcal{C}_{\Pi 1} \cap \mathcal{C}_{\Pi 2}\}$. The *inverse of a relation* $\mathcal{R}$ is $\mathcal{R}^{-1} \stackrel{def}{=} \{(D, C) \mid (C, D) \in \mathcal{R}\}$. The *composition of relations* $\mathcal{R}_1$ and $\mathcal{R}_2$ is $\mathcal{R}_1 \mathcal{R}_2 \stackrel{def}{=} \{(C, C'') \mid \exists C' \in \mathcal{C}_{\Pi 1} \cap \mathcal{C}_{\Pi 2} \text{ s.t. } (C, C') \in \mathcal{R}_1 \text{ and } (C', C'') \in \mathcal{R}_2\}$.

Definition 5. *The binary relation* $\mathcal{R}_t$, $t \in \mathbb{R}_+$, *over* $\mathcal{C}_{\Pi 1}$ *and* $\mathcal{C}_{\Pi 2}$ *is called a* **strong time-bounded simulation** *(STB simulation) if whenever* $(C, D) \in \mathcal{R}_t$, *then:*

1. *for any rule* $r \in \mathcal{L}$, $C' \in \mathcal{C}_{\Pi 1}$, *if* $C \xrightarrow{r} C'$, *then there exists* $D' \in \mathcal{C}_{\Pi 2}$ *such that* $D \xrightarrow{r} D'$ *and* $(C', D') \in \mathcal{R}_t$;
2. *for any* $d \in \mathbb{R}_+$, $d < t$ *and* $C' \in \mathcal{C}_{\Pi 1}$, *if* $C \overset{d}{\rightsquigarrow} C'$, *then there exists* $D' \in \mathcal{C}_{\Pi 2}$ *such that* $D \overset{d}{\rightsquigarrow} D'$ *and* $(C', D') \in \mathcal{R}_{t-d}$.

If $\mathcal{R}_t$ *and* $\mathcal{R}_t^{-1}$, $t \in \mathbb{R}_+$ *are STB simulations, then* $\mathcal{R}_t$ *is called a* **strong time-bounded bisimulation** *(STB bisimulation). We define* **STB bisimilarity** *by*

$$\simeq_t \overset{def}{=} \{(C, D) \in \mathcal{C}_{\Pi 1} \times \mathcal{C}_{\Pi 2} \mid \text{ for } t \in \mathbb{R}_+ \text{ there exists an STB bisimulation } \mathcal{R}_t \\ \text{and } (C, D) \in \mathcal{R}_t\}.$$

We also define the union of all STB bisimilarities $\simeq_t$, as

$$\simeq = \bigcup_{t \in \mathbb{R}_+} \simeq_t.$$

The first clause of Definition 5 states that the derived configurations are matched up to *the same time* t. The second clause states that the derived configurations are matched up to time $t - d$, namely when they advance in time (by d time units), the bound is reduced accordingly.

Now let us come back to Example 1.

Example 3. We have that $C_1^0 \simeq_2 C_2^0$, as the two configurations C_1^0 and C_2^0 have a timed transition at any time $d < 2$, namely $C_1^0 \overset{d}{\rightsquigarrow} C_1^d$ and $C_2^0 \overset{d}{\rightsquigarrow} C_2^d$. Note that bisimilarity up to time 2 does not include bisimilarity at time 2 since $C_1^0 \overset{2}{\rightsquigarrow} C_1^2$ and $C_1^2 \xrightarrow{r} C_1'$; however $C_2^0 \overset{2}{\rightsquigarrow} C_2^2$ and $C_2^2 \overset{r}{\nrightarrow} C_2'$.

This bisimilarity "up to time t" satisfies the following property that states how equivalence up to a deadline t includes equivalence up to any bound $u \leq t$.

Proposition 2. *For any TLTSs* $(\mathcal{C}_{\Pi 1}, C_{01}, \mathcal{L}_1, \rightarrow, \rightsquigarrow)$ *and* $(\mathcal{C}_{\Pi 2}, C_{02}, \mathcal{L}_2, \rightarrow, \rightsquigarrow)$, $t, u \in \mathbb{R}_+$, $C \in \mathcal{C}_{\Pi 1}$, $C' \in \mathcal{C}_{\Pi 1} \cap \mathcal{C}_{\Pi 2}$ *and* $C'' \in \mathcal{C}_{\Pi 2}$:

1. *If* $C \simeq_t C''$, *then for any* $u \leq t$, $C \simeq_u C''$.
2. *If* $C \simeq_t C'$ *and* $C' \simeq_u C''$, *then* $C \simeq_{\min\{t,u\}} C''$.

Furthermore, we also have the following properties.

Proposition 3. *For any TLTSs* $(\mathcal{C}_{\Pi 1}, C_{01}, \mathcal{L}_1, \rightarrow, \rightsquigarrow)$ *and* $(\mathcal{C}_{\Pi 2}, C_{02}, \mathcal{L}_2, \rightarrow, \rightsquigarrow)$,

1. $\simeq$ *is an STB bisimulation.*
2. $\simeq$ *is closed to identity, inverse, composition and union.*
3. $\simeq$ *is the largest STB bisimulation.*
4. $\simeq$ *is an equivalence.*

Proof (Sketch).

1. Assume that $C \simeq D$. By definition of $\simeq$, there must be an STB bisimulation $\simeq_t$ such that $(C, D) \in \simeq_t$. We need to check that $\simeq$ and $\simeq^{-1}$ satisfy the conditions of STB simulations.

2. (a) The identity timed relation id is an STB bisimulation because any C can match its own transitions up to any time t.

   (b) Since $\simeq$ is an STB bisimulation, the inverse $\simeq^{-1}$ is also an STB bisimulation, by definition.

   (c) If $\mathcal{R}_1$ and $\mathcal{R}_2$ are STB bisimulations $\simeq$, then their composition $\mathcal{R}_1\mathcal{R}_2$ is an STB bisimulation as well.

   (d) Finally, we obtain that the union $\cup_{i\in I}\mathcal{R}_i$ of STB bisimulations $\mathcal{R}_i$ is an STB bisimulation, as follows. Let $(C,D) \in \cup_{i\in I}\mathcal{R}_i\cap \simeq_t$. For some $i \in I$, $(C,D) \in \mathcal{R}_i\cap \simeq_t$. If $C \xrightarrow{r} C'$, then $D \xrightarrow{r} D'$ and $(C',D') \in \mathcal{R}_i\cap \simeq_t$ and therefore, $(C',D') \in \cup_{i\in I}\mathcal{R}_i\cap \simeq_t \subseteq \cup_{i\in I}\mathcal{R}_i$. Similarly, if $C \overset{d}{\rightsquigarrow} C'$ for some $d < t$, then $D \overset{d}{\rightsquigarrow} D'$ with $(C',D') \in \mathcal{R}_i\cap \simeq_t$, and so $(C',D') \in \cup_{i\in I}\mathcal{R}_i\cap \simeq_t \subseteq \cup_{i\in I}\mathcal{R}_i$, as required.

3. Suppose that there is an STB bisimulation $\mathcal{R} = \cup_{t\in\mathbb{R}_+}\mathcal{R}_t$ larger than $\simeq$, i.e. $\simeq \subsetneq \mathcal{R}$. This means that there are C, D and t such that $(C,D) \in \mathcal{R}_t$, while $C \not\simeq_t D$. However, $C \not\simeq_t D$ is possible only if there is no STB bisimulation $\mathcal{R}_t$ that contains (C,D), contradicting the assumption.

4. To show that $\simeq$ is an equivalence, it is proved that $\simeq$ is reflexive, symmetric and transitive. $\qquad\qquad\square$

4.2   Bounded Timed Bisimulation "up to" Techniques

In what follows we provide some techniques that extend the "up to" techniques from [17] to the context of bounded timed bisimulations. The standard proof technique to establish that C_1 and C_2 are bisimilar is to find a bisimulation $\mathcal{R}$ such that $(C_1,C_2) \in \mathcal{R}$, and $\mathcal{R}$ is closed under transitions, namely the derivatives (C_1',C_2') of (C_1,C_2) are also in $\mathcal{R}$. Since such derivatives are added to $\mathcal{R}$ without the possibility of manipulating them, a bisimulation relation often contains many strongly related pairs. As an example, a bisimulation relation might contain pairs of configurations obtainable from other pairs through the application of several algebraic laws. These redundancies can make both the definition and the verification of a bisimulation relation annoyingly heavy and tedious. This means that sometimes is difficult to find directly such a relation $\mathcal{R}$.

A property that we naturally expect to hold is that symbols appearing in the left-hand side of the evolution rules do not influence the evolution of real-time P systems. Let us consider a configuration $C_0 = (\mu_t, w_0, w_1)$, and two objects $(b,3)$ and $(c,3)$ appearing only in time passing rules. To prove that $C_{01} = (\mu_t, w_0(b,3), w_1)$ and $C_{012} = (\mu_t, w_0(c,3), w_1)$ are bisimilar, we would like to use the binary relation $\mathcal{R} \overset{def}{=} \{(C_{01}, C_{02})\}$.

However, according to Definition 5, $\mathcal{R}$ is not a bisimulation relation. If we add pairs of configurations to $\mathcal{R}$ in order to turn it into a bisimulation relation, then we might find that the simplest solution is to take the relation

$$\mathcal{R}' \overset{def}{=} \{(C,D) \mid C \simeq C_{01},\ D \simeq C_{02}\}.$$

The size of R' is rather discouraging. However, this extension is unnecessary because the bisimilarity between the two configurations in $\mathcal{R}$ already implies the bisimilarity between the configurations of all pairs of $\mathcal{R}'$. The notions defined in the current section aim to simplify the bisimulation proof method. The new technique would allow for the above example to prove that C_{01} and C_{02} are bisimilar simply using the relation $\mathcal{R}$. In this sense, we generalise the bisimulation proof method by relaxing Definition 5 by using an useful alternative technique, the so-called bisimulation "up to" some relation $\mathcal{R}'$: for a non-bisimulation relation $\mathcal{R}$, if $(C_1, C_2) \in \mathcal{R}$, then the derivatives (C_1', C_2') are in $\mathcal{R}'$. Under certain conditions we can establish that C_1 and C_2 are bisimilar. For this technique, a general framework that works on untimed labelled transition systems is presented in [16]. We cannot use directly that framework; however the framework can be extended to timed labelled transition systems.

Definition 6. *Let $(\mathcal{C}_{\Pi 1}, C_{01}, \mathcal{L}_1, \rightarrow, \rightsquigarrow)$ and $(\mathcal{C}_{\Pi 2}, C_{02}, \mathcal{L}_2, \rightarrow, \rightsquigarrow)$ be two TLTSs, and let $\mathcal{R}_t$, $\mathcal{R}_t'$, $t \in \mathbb{R}_+$ be any timed relations. We say that $\mathcal{R}_t$ **strongly progresses** to $\mathcal{R}_t'$, written $\mathcal{R}_t \mapsto \mathcal{R}_t'$, if for any $C, D \in \mathcal{C}_\Pi$, whenever $(C, D) \in \mathcal{R}_t$, then:*

1. *for any rule $r \in \mathcal{L}$, $C' \in \mathcal{C}_{\Pi 1}$, $C \xrightarrow{r} C'$, then there exists $D' \in \mathcal{C}_{\Pi 2}$ such that $D \xrightarrow{r} D'$ and $(C', D') \in \mathcal{R}_t'$;*

2. *for any $d \in \mathbb{R}_+$, $d < t$ and $C' \in \mathcal{C}_{\Pi 1}$, if $C \xrightarrow{d} C'$, then there exists $D' \in \mathcal{C}_{\Pi 2}$ such that $D \xrightarrow{d} D'$ and $(C', D') \in \mathcal{R}_{t-d}'$.*

The definition is similar to that of STB bisimulation, except that the derivatives (C', D') must be in $\mathcal{R}_t'$ rather than in $\mathcal{R}_t$. In fact, STB bisimulation can be seen as a specific case:

Remark 2. $\mathcal{R}_t$ is an STB bisimulation if and only if $\mathcal{R}_t \mapsto \mathcal{R}_t$.

Proposition 4. *If $\mathcal{R}_t \mapsto \mathcal{R}_t'$ and $\mathcal{R}_t'$ is an STB bisimulation, then $\mathcal{R}_t \subseteq \simeq$.*

Hence, to establish that $C \simeq_t D$ it is enough to find a relation $\mathcal{R}_t$ with $(C, D) \in \mathcal{R}_t$ that strongly progresses to a known STB bisimulation $\mathcal{R}_t'$. The choice of $\mathcal{R}_t'$ depends on the particular equivalence we are trying to establish. One of the most common cases is when $\mathcal{R}_t' = \simeq_t$. However, in general we may not have at hand a relation $\mathcal{R}_t'$ known to be a bisimulation. Nevertheless, we may find that $\mathcal{R}_t$ progresses to a relation $\mathcal{R}_t' = \mathcal{F}(\mathcal{R}_t)$ for some function $\mathcal{F}$ over relations. The idea is that if $\mathcal{R}_t$ progresses to $\mathcal{F}(\mathcal{R}_t)$ and $\mathcal{F}$ satisfies certain conditions, then $\mathcal{R}_t$ is included in $\simeq_t$. Thus, to establish $C \simeq_t D$ we need to find such $\mathcal{F}$ and $\mathcal{R}_t$ containing (C, D).

In order to characterise the functions $\mathcal{F}$, we use the following results:

Proposition 5. *Let $\mathcal{R}_t, \mathcal{R}_t', \mathcal{R}_t'', \mathcal{R}_t''' \subseteq \mathcal{C}_\Pi \times \mathcal{C}_\Pi$, $t \in \mathbb{R}_+$ be some timed relations.*

1. *If $\mathcal{R}_t \subseteq \mathcal{R}_t'$ and $\mathcal{R}_t' \mapsto \mathcal{R}_t''$, then $\mathcal{R}_t \mapsto \mathcal{R}_t''$.*
2. *If $\mathcal{R}_t \mapsto \mathcal{R}_t'$ and $\mathcal{R}_t' \subseteq \mathcal{R}_t''$, then $\mathcal{R}_t \mapsto \mathcal{R}_t''$.*
3. *If $\mathcal{R}_t \mapsto \mathcal{R}_t''$ and $\mathcal{R}_t' \mapsto \mathcal{R}_t'''$, then $\mathcal{R}_t \mathcal{R}_t' \mapsto \mathcal{R}_t'' \mathcal{R}_t'''$.*

Proof (Sketch).

1. Assume $\mathcal{R}_t \subseteq \mathcal{R}'_t$ and $\mathcal{R}'_t \mapsto \mathcal{R}''_t$. Let $(C, D) \in \mathcal{R}_t$. Then $(C, D) \in \mathcal{R}'_t$ and since $\mathcal{R}'_t \mapsto \mathcal{R}''_t$, we have that

   (a) $C \xrightarrow{r} C'$ implies $D \xrightarrow{r} D'$ with $(C', D') \in \mathcal{R}''_t$ (and vice-versa);

   (b) $C \xrightarrow{d} C'$ for $d < t$ implies $D \xrightarrow{d} D'$ with $(C', D') \in \mathcal{R}''_{t-d}$ (and vice-versa). This shows that $\mathcal{R}_t \mapsto \mathcal{R}''_t$.

The other two cases are treated in a similar manner.   □

Proposition 6. *Let $\{\mathcal{R}_i\}_{i \in I}$ and $\{\mathcal{R}'_j\}_{j \in J}$ be two sets of timed relations, and define the relations $\mathcal{R} \overset{def}{=} \bigcup_{i \in I} \mathcal{R}_i$ and $\mathcal{R}' \overset{def}{=} \bigcup_{j \in J} \mathcal{R}'_j$. Then*

1. *If for each $i \in I$ there is a $j \in J$ such that $\mathcal{R}_i \mapsto \mathcal{R}'_j$, then $\mathcal{R} \mapsto \mathcal{R}'$.*
2. *If for each $i \in I$ there is an $i' \in I$ such that $\mathcal{R}_i \mapsto \mathcal{R}_{i'}$, then $\mathcal{R}$ is an STB bisimulation.*

Definition 7 (Safe functions). *A function $\mathcal{F}$ on timed relations is safe if for any timed relations $\mathcal{R}$, whenever $\mathcal{R} \mapsto \mathcal{F}(\mathcal{R})$ then $\mathcal{R} \subseteq \simeq$.*

Using this definition, it is hard to check whether a function is safe. An example of a function that is not safe is the function that maps every relation to the relation $C_\Pi \times C_\Pi$. In what follows we define a class of safe functions for which membership is easy to check. We define strongly safe functions:

Definition 8 (Strongly safe functions). *A function $\mathcal{F}$ on timed relations is strongly safe if for any timed relations $\mathcal{R}, \mathcal{R}'$, whenever $\mathcal{R} \subseteq \mathcal{R}'$ and $\mathcal{R} \mapsto \mathcal{R}'$ then $\mathcal{F}(\mathcal{R}) \subseteq \mathcal{F}(\mathcal{R}')$ and $\mathcal{F}(\mathcal{R}) \mapsto \mathcal{F}(\mathcal{R}')$.*

Proposition 7. *The following functions are strongly safe:*

1. $\mathcal{F}_{id}(\mathcal{R}) \overset{def}{=} \mathcal{R}$;
2. $\mathcal{F}_\simeq(\mathcal{R}) \overset{def}{=} \simeq$.

The main property, the core of the technique, is the following:

Lemma 1. *If $\mathcal{R} \mapsto \mathcal{F}(\mathcal{R})$ for some strongly safe function $\mathcal{F}$, then $\mathcal{R} \subseteq \simeq$ and $\mathcal{F}(\mathcal{R}) \subseteq \simeq$.*

This technique relies on providing a safe function $\mathcal{F}$ on timed relations. We have given two basic strongly safe functions ($\mathcal{F}_{id}$ and $\mathcal{F}_\simeq$), but often they are not enough. As shown in [16,17], it is possible to start from basic strongly safe functions and build more complex ones. The following result provides basic operators on these functions that preserve the safety property.

Proposition 8. *If $\mathcal{F}_i$, $\mathcal{F}$ and $\mathcal{G}$ are strongly safe, so are $\cup_{i \in I} \mathcal{F}_i$, $\mathcal{F} \circ \mathcal{G}$ and $\mathcal{F}\mathcal{G}$, where:*

- $(\cup_{i \in I} \mathcal{F}_i)(\mathcal{R}) \overset{def}{=} \cup_{i \in I} \mathcal{F}_i(\mathcal{R})$;

- $(\mathcal{F} \circ \mathcal{G})(\mathcal{R}) \overset{def}{=} \mathcal{F}(\mathcal{G}(\mathcal{R}))$;
- $(\mathcal{F}\mathcal{G})(\mathcal{R}) \overset{def}{=} \mathcal{F}(\mathcal{R})\mathcal{G}(\mathcal{R})$.

Lemma 2. *The following functions are strongly safe:*

1. $\mathcal{F}_{\mathrm{ius}} \overset{def}{=} \mathcal{F}_{\mathrm{id}} \cup \mathcal{F}_{\simeq}$;
2. $\mathcal{F}_{\mathrm{sis}} \overset{def}{=} \mathcal{F}_{\simeq}\mathcal{F}_{\mathrm{id}}\mathcal{F}_{\simeq}$.

For example, using $\mathcal{F}_{\mathrm{ius}}$ we can prove $C \simeq_t D$ by finding a relation $\mathcal{R}_t$ containing (C, D) that progresses to $\mathcal{F}_{\mathrm{ius}}(\mathcal{R}_t) = \mathcal{R}_t \cup \simeq$, namely its derivatives (C', D') are in either $\mathcal{R}_t$ or in $\simeq$. Another common example is given by $\mathcal{F}_{\mathrm{sis}}(\mathcal{R}_t) = \simeq \mathcal{R}_t \simeq$. In this case, proving $C \simeq_t D$ requires finding an $\mathcal{R}_t$ containing (C, D) that progresses to $\simeq \mathcal{R}_t \simeq$, namely for its derivatives (C', D') there are C_1 and C_2 such that $C' \simeq C_1$, $(C_1, C_2) \in \mathcal{R}_t$ and $C_2 \simeq D'$.

5   Conclusion

In this paper we proposed a real-time extension of P systems in which we assigned lifetimes to each membrane and to each object. The semantics is given by two types of transitions: the rule relation $\to$ and the timed relation $\rightsquigarrow$. If the lifetime of an object reaches 0 then the object is used to create a new (possible empty) multiset of objects, while if the lifetime of a membrane reaches 0 then the membrane is marked for dissolution.

Behavioural equivalence could represent an important concept in biology, necessary for comparing the behaviour of various (sub)systems. We established a formal framework for biological systems sensitive to timeouts. For real-time P systems we have defined timed bounded equivalences by using timed labelled transition systems, and presented an extended "up to" technique. An important goal of defining these bisimulations is to offer, depending on what properties should be preserved, flexibility in selecting the right equivalence when studying the timed behaviour of biological systems. An appropriate behavioural equivalence guarantees that, in any context, a real-time P system can be safely replaced by another equivalent real-time P system.

Acknowledgements. The work was supported by a grant of the Romanian National Authority for Scientific Research, project number PN-II-ID-PCE-2011-3-0919.

References

1. Aman, B., Ciobanu, G.: Adding Lifetime to Objects and Membranes in P Systems. In: International Journal of Computers, Communication & Control, vol. V, pp. 268–279 (2010)
2. Andrei, O., Ciobanu, G., Lucanu, D.: A Rewriting Logic Framework for Operational Semantics of Membrane Systems. Theoretical Computer Science 373, 163–181 (2007)

3. Bachman, J., Sorger, P.: New Approaches to Modelling Complex Biochemistry. Nature Methods 8, 130–131 (2011)
4. Barbuti, R., Maggiolo-Schettini, A., Milazzo, P., Tini, S.: Compositional Semantics and Behavioural Equivalences for P Systems. Theoretical Computer Science 395, 77–100 (2008)
5. Calude, C.S., Păun, G.: Bio-Steps Beyond Turing. Biosystems 77, 175–194 (2004)
6. Cavaliere, M., Sburlan, D.: Time and Synchronization in Membrane Systems. Fundamenta Informaticae 64, 65–77 (2005)
7. Ciobanu, G.: Behaviour equivalences in timed distributed π-calculus. In: Wirsing, M., Banâtre, J.-P., Hölzl, M., Rauschmayer, A. (eds.) Soft-Ware Intensive Systems. LNCS, vol. 5380, pp. 190–208. Springer, Heidelberg (2008)
8. Ciobanu, G.: Semantics of P Systems. In: The Oxford Handbook of Membrane Computing, pp. 413–436 (2010)
9. Ciobanu, G., Păun, G., Pérez-Jiménez, M.J. (eds.): Applications of Membrane Computing. Natural Computing Series. Springer (2006)
10. Eidhammer, I., Jonassen, I., Taylor, W.: Structure Comparison and Structure Patterns. Journal of Computational Biology 7, 685–716 (2000)
11. Freund, R., Ionescu, M., Oswald, M.: Extended Spiking Neural P Systems with Decaying Spikes and/or Total Spiking. International Journal of Foundations of Computer Science 19, 1223–1234 (2008)
12. Leocadio, D.E., Kunselman, A.R., Cooper, T., Barrantes, J.H., Trussell, J.C.: Anatomical and Histological Equivalence of the Human, Canine, and Bull Vas Deferens. The Canadian Journal of Urology 18, 5699–5704 (2011)
13. Păun, G.: Membrane Computing. An Introduction. Springer (2002)
14. Păun, G., Rozenberg, G., Salomaa, A. (eds.): The Oxford Handbook of Membrane Computing. Oxford University Press (2010)
15. Sangiorgi, D.: A Theory of Bisimulation for the π-Calculus. In: Best, E. (ed.) CONCUR 1993. LNCS, vol. 715, pp. 127–142. Springer, Heidelberg (1993)
16. Sangiorgi, D.: On the Bisimulation Proof Method. Journal of Mathematical Structures in Computer Science 8, 447–479 (1998)
17. Sangiorgi, D., Walker, D.: The π-calculus: A Theory of Mobile Processes. Cambridge University Press (2001)
18. Schneider, S.: An Operational Semantics for Timed CSP. Information and Computation 116, 193–213 (1995)

Modelling of Surface Runoff
Using 2D P Colonies

Luděk Cienciala, Lucie Ciencialová, and Miroslav Langer

Institute of Computer Science
and
Research Institute of the IT4 Innovations Centre of Excellence,
Silesian University in Opava, Czech Republic
{ludek.cienciala,lucie.ciencialova,miroslav.langer}@fpf.slu.cz

Abstract. We continue the investigation of 2D P colonies introduced as a class of abstract computing devices composed of independent agents, acting and evolving in a shared 2D environment where the agents are located. Agents have limited information about the contents of the environment where they can move in four directions. In this paper we continue the research of modelling surface runoff in 2D P colonies. We have added information about flow direction and amount of water in sinks (places without runoff, lakes,...) to the simulation environment. The data from the simulation is compared with the data generated by simulation model of water erosion SIMWE.

1 Introduction

P colonies were introduced in the paper [7] as formal models of computing devices belonging to membrane systems and similar to formal grammars called colonies. This model is inspired by the structure and the behaviour of communities of living organisms in a shared environment. The independent organisms living in a P colony are called agents. Each agent is represented by several objects embedded in a membrane. The number of objects inside each agent is the same and constant during computation. The environment is agents' communication channel and storage place for objects. At any moment all agents "know" about all the objects in the environment and they can access any object immediately. The reader can find more information about P colonies in [6,2]. P colonies are one of the types of P systems. They were introduced in 2000 in [9] by Gheorghe Păun as a formal model inspired by the structure and the behaviour of cells.

With each agent a set of programs is associated. The program, which determines the activity of an agent, is very simple and depends on the contents of agents and on types and number of objects placed in the environment. An agent can change the contents of the environment through programs and it can affect the behaviour of other agents through the environment. This influence between agents is the key factor in the functioning of the P colony. At any moment each object inside every agent is affected by the execution of the program.

For more information about P systems see [11,10] or [13].

A. Alhazov et al. (Eds.): CMC 2013, LNCS 8340, pp. 101–116, 2014.

In addition 2D P colony has the environment in a form of a 2D grid of square cells. The agents are located in this grid and their view is limited to the cells that immediately surround them [1]. Based on the contents of these cells, the agents decide their future locations.

Behaviour of each agent is based on its set of programs. The programs are formed from two rules of type rewriting, communication or movement. By using the rewriting rule one object within the agent is changed (evolved) to another object. When the communication rule is applied one object from the environment is consumed by the agent and one object from content of the agent is placed to the environment. The last type of rules is the movement rule. The condition for the movement of an agent is to find specific objects in specific locations in the environment. This is specified by a matrix with elements - objects. The agent is looking for at most one object in every surrounding cell. If the condition is fulfilled then the agent moves one cell up, down, left or right.

The program can contain one movement rule at most. To achieve the greatest simplicity in agent behaviour, we set another condition. If the agent moves, it cannot communicate with the environment. So if the program contains a movement rule, then the second rule is the rewriting rule.

Although the colony is a theoretical computing model through 2D, it is a suitable tool for modelling the behaviour of natural multi-agent systems - colonies of bacteria or ants, spreading substances in homogeneous and non-homogeneous medium.

In this paper we present hydrological modelling flow of liquid over the Earth's surface using 2D P colonies. Based on the entered data - the slope surface, a source of fluid and quantity - we simulate the fluid distribution in the environment.

To obtain the similarity of our model with the real situation of water overflow we compare the results obtained by the simulation using 2D P colonies with results that provide a hydrological simulation model SIMWE. SIMWE is implemetnation of process based water erosion simulation developed by Mitas et al. in 1996 in [8].

The first part of the paper is devoted to 2D P colonies. The rest is organised as follows: The issue of the flow of liquid over the surface, problem solution - maps preparation, definition of the agent, process simulation, comparison with results of the model SIMWE and future expansion.

2   Definitions

Throughout the paper we assume that the reader is familiar with the basics of the formal language theory.

We use NRE to denote the family of the recursively enumerable sets of natural numbers, N is the set of natural numbers. Let Σ be the alphabet. Let Σ^* be the set of all words over Σ (including the empty word ε). We denote the length of the word $w \in \Sigma^*$ by $|w|$ and the number of occurrences of the symbol $a \in \Sigma$ in w by $|w|_a$.

A multiset of objects M is a pair $M = (V, f)$, where V is an arbitrary (not necessarily finite) set of objects and f is a mapping $f : V \to N$; f assigns to each object in V its multiplicity in M. The set of all multisets with the set of objects V is denoted by V°. The set V' is called the support of M and is denoted by $supp(M)$ if for all $x \in V'$ $f(x) \neq 0$ holds. The cardinality of M, denoted by $|M|$, is defined by $|M| = \sum_{a \in V} f(a)$. Each multiset of objects M with the set of objects $V' = \{a_1, \ldots a_n\}$ can be represented as a string w over alphabet V', where $|w|_{a_i} = f(a_i)$; $1 \leq i \leq n$. Obviously, all words obtained from w by permuting the letters represent the same multiset M. The ε represents the empty multiset.

3   2D P Colonies

We briefly summarize the notion of 2D P colonies. A P colony consists of agents and an environment. Both the agents and the environment contain objects. With each agent a set of programs is associated. There are three types of rules in the programs.

The first rule type, called the evolution rule, is of the form $a \to b$. It means that the object a inside the agent is rewritten (evolved) to the object b. The second rule type, called the communication rule, is of the form $c \leftrightarrow d$. When the communication rule is performed, the object c inside the agent and the object d outside the agent swap their places. Thus, after the execution of the rule, the object d appears inside the agent and the object c is placed outside the agent. The third rule type, called the motion rule, is of the form matrix $3 \times 3 \to$ "move direction". Based on the contents of the neighbouring cells, an agent can move one step to the left, right, up or down.

A program can contain maximum one motion rule. When there is a motion rule inside a program, there cannot be a communication rule inside the same program.

Definition 1. *The 2D P colony is a construct*
$$\Pi = (A, e, Env, B_1, \ldots, B_k, f), k \geq 1, \text{ where}$$

- *A is an alphabet of the colony, its elements are called objects,*
- *$e \in A$ is the basic environmental object of the colony,*
- *Env is a pair $(m \times n, w_E)$, where $m \times n, m, n \in N$ is the size of the environment and w_E is the initial contents of environment, it is a matrix of size $m \times n$ of multisets of objects over $A - \{e\}$.*
- *B_i, $1 \leq i \leq k$, are agents, each agent is a construct $B_i = (O_i, P_i, [o, p])$, $0 \leq o \leq m$, $0 \leq p \leq n$, where*
  - *O_i is a multiset over A, it determines the initial state (contents) of the agent, $|O_i| = 2$,*
  - *$P_i = \{p_{i,1}, \ldots, p_{i,l_i}\}$, $l \geq 1, 1 \leq i \leq k$ is a finite set of programs, where each program contains exactly 2 rules, which are in one of the following forms each:*
    - *$\ast$ $a \to b$, called the evolution rule, $a, b \in A$;*

  * $c \leftrightarrow d$, called the communication rule, $c, d \in A$
  * $[a_{q,r}] \to s, 0 \le q, r \le 2, a_{q,r} \in A, s \in \{\Leftarrow, \Rightarrow, \Uparrow, \Downarrow\}$, called the motion rule;
  * The third part of program is natural number $h \in N$, which determine priority level of the program.
- $[o, p]$ are the coordinates of the initial placement agent in the environment.
- $f \in A$ is the final object of the colony.

The configuration of the 2D P colony is given by the state of the environment - matrix of type $m \times n$ with multisets of objects over $A - \{e\}$ as its elements, and by the state of all agents - pairs of objects from alphabet A and the coordinates of the agents. An initial configuration is given by the definition of the 2D P colony.

The computational step consists of three parts. The first part lies in determining the applicable set of programs according to the actual configuration of the P colony. In the second part we have to choose one program corresponding to each agent from the set of applicable programs with maximum priority level. The third part is the execution of the chosen programs.

A change of the configuration is triggered by the execution of programs and it involves changing the state of the environment, contents and placement of the agents.

The computation is nondeterministic and maximally parallel. The computation ends by halting when no agent has an applicable program.

The result of the computation is the number of copies of the final object placed in the environment at the end of the computation.

The reason for the introduction of 2D P colonies is not the study of their computational power but monitoring of their behaviour during computation. We can define measures to describe the dynamics of the computation:

- the number of moves of agents
- the number of agents inside a certain cell or a set of cells
- the number of visited cells (or non-visited cells)
- the number of copies of a certain object in the home cell or throughout the environment.

4 The Issue of Flow of Liquid over the Surface

The issue of the flow of liquid over the Earth's surface is studied by experts from two areas - hydrology and geoinformatics. Both of these disciplines work closely together on the issue of the so-called "surface runoff". Surface runoff is the water flow that occurs when the soil is saturated to full capacity and excess water from rain, meltwater, or other sources flows over the land.

Surface runoff can be generated in four scenarios: infiltration excess overland flow, saturation excess overland flow, antecedent soil moisture, subsurface return flow. Infiltration excess overland flow occurs when the rate of rainfall on a surface exceeds the rate at which water can infiltrate the ground, and any depression storage has already been filled. When the soil is saturated and the depression storage filled, and rain continues to fall, the rainfall will immediately produce surface runoff - saturation excess overland flow. Soil retains a degree of moisture after a rainfall. This residual water moisture (antecedent soil moisture) affects the soil's infiltration capacity. During the next rainfall event, the infiltration capacity will cause the soil to be saturated at a different rate. The higher the level of antecedent soil moisture, the more quickly the soil becomes saturated. Once the soil is saturated, runoff occurs. After water infiltrates the soil on an up-slope portion of a hill, the water may flow laterally through the soil, and exfiltrate (flow out of the soil) closer to a channel. This is called subsurface return flow or throughflow.

We can say that generation surface runoff depends on type of soil, temperature, humidity and rainfall. The task of our model is to determine which way the flow would run and which areas could be affected by flash floods. In the first phase of construction of the model, we focus on the issue of the influence of terrain slope to the direction of waterflow. The input will be two raster files: the first raster file with the slope of terrain and the second one with place and amount of rainfall.

4.1 SIMWE - Simulation of Water Erosion

SIMWE is a bivariate model of erosion, sediment transport and deposition by overland flow, designed for complex terrain, soil and cover conditions. It uses a Green's function Monte Carlo method to solve the underlying continuity equations. More can reader find in [8]. The model is implemented as two modules in software GRASS GIS. It is a Geographic Information System (GIS) used for data management, image processing, graphics production, spatial modelling, and visualization of many types of data (see [4]).

The first module is called r.sim.water and it is a landscape scale simulation model of overland flow designed for spatially variable terrain, soil, cover and rainfall excess conditions. A 2D shallow water flow is described by the bivariate form of Saint Venant equations (e.g. [5]). The numerical solution is based on the concept of duality between the field and particle representation of the modeled quantity. The key inputs of the model include elevation, flow gradient vector, rainfall excess rate and a surface roughness coefficient. Output includes a water depth raster map and a water discharge raster map.

The second module r.sim.sediment is simulation model of soil erosion, sediment transport and deposition caused by flowing water designed for spatially variable terrain, soil, cover and rainfall excess conditions. The function of this module is out of scope of this paper.

5 Applicationof 2D P Colonies in Solving the Problem of Surface Runoff

2D P colonies seem to be suitable tool for modeling surface runoff. The environment can contain objects representing slope of terrain, type of cover and soil.

Agents represent the units of water and their programs determine behaviour of water running over the surface. We can assume that the soil is already saturated thus the main factor of overland flow is the slope of the field. The type of terrain and soil is not implemented yet.

We divide solution of the problem into two parts - (1) preparation of maps (2D P colony's environment) and (2) definition of agents. We assume that the soil is already saturated thus the main factor of overland flow is the slope of the field.

5.1   Preparation of Maps

Map data is obtained from the geographic information system (GIS) and processing system GRASS. We use the map data for the Czech Republic obtained from dataset FreeGoedataCZ.

Raster graphics images are probably the most appropriate format for modelling real-world phenomena in the field of GIS. To process this format, many tools were created and can be used for performing various analyses. A raster image is composed of a regular network of cells, usually in a square shape, to which values of displayed properties can be assigned independently. More information about GIS and image processing the reader can find in [3] and about geosimulation in [12].

The first step to simulate the flow of liquid over relief was the determination of its runoff from individual pixels (cells). Gradient with respect to an adjacent cell is defined as the ratio of the height difference to the horizontal distance. Gradient is positive due to the lower neighbours, or negative due to higher and zero in relation to the neighbours of the same height. Lowest neighbour is neighbour with the largest positive gradient.

There are two basic algorithms to calculate the runoff:

- Single flow direction (SFD) - each pixel of the liquid flows in one direction only (toward neighbour in the direction of the largest gradient). Each pixel belongs to only one basin.
- Multiple flow direction (MFD) - fluid can flow out of each pixel in multiple directions, maximum of eight. In the case of MFD a unit volume flow is fairly distributed among all lower neighbours. The MFD may include the pixel to multiple basins.

There is implemented a tool for calculating the flow direction in GRASS software, called simply TerraFlow. TerraFlow tool works as a multiple flow (MFD) or simple flow direction (SFD). After its execution integer raster file is created that specifies the flow direction for each cell.

Eight basic directions of the flow are represented by the numbers 45, 90, 135, 180, 225, 270, 315 and 360 (see Table 1). If there is more than one direction (MFD), the number contained in the cell is generated as sum of values of the directions.

In 2D P colony model we can use the result of both algorithms. If the MFD is used to generate the directions the agent can only move in one of the directions specified in the cell.

Table 1. The eight basic directions

135	90	45
180	↖ ↑ ↗ ← → ↙ ↓ ↘	360
225	270	315

What we obtain from GRASS is a raster file with natural number in each cell corresponding to the runoff from this cell. Because 2D P colony works with discrete symbols and not with numbers, it is necessary to transcode numbers to symbols. A coding table is shown on Table 2

Table 2. The coding table

direction	→	←	↑	↓	↘	↙	↗	↖
symbol	a	E	i	m	q	u	y	2

5.2 Definition of the Agent

Agents in 2D P colonies have capacity of 2. It means that an agent contains two objects, and each program is composed by two rules.

Each of the objects inside the agent carries the information about the state of the agent. The first object has information about the activity of the agent. At this stage of the simulation it is the information that the agent "flows" down the terrain (object X) or it is still inactive (belonging to the rainfall that have not fall - objects $A, B, C, D, F, G, R, S, T, U, V, W$, it stops in sinks - configuration of agent is VS) . The second object stores information about the previous direction of flow. This information can further modify the way of the agent as inertia.

Objects and their association to the flow directions are given in the following table.

direction	→	←	↑	↓	↘	↙	↗	↖
the first set of symbols S_1	9	8	6	7	D	D	U	U
the second set of symbols S_2	L	K	H	I	I	I	H	H

One time step will take two steps of computation of the 2D P colony. This is the reason why we need two sets of object associted with flow directions.

All the programs can reader find in Apendix at the end of the paper.

The first subset of programs with priority 0 is defined for the first step of computation. The initial configuration of each "working" agent is Xe. The agents move in a direction that represent object in the cells - a one step right (program

(1)), E one step left (program(2)), i one step up (program (3)) and m one step down (program(4)).

In the case of cross direction (after applying the programs (5) and (6) resp. (7) and (8)) the agent moves one step left or right and it is neccessary to take one step down (resp. up). It uses program with priority 1 (9) (resp. (10)).

Programs (1) - (8) are of the form

$$\left\langle \begin{bmatrix} * & * & * \\ * & \text{direction} & * \\ * & * & * \end{bmatrix} \rightarrow \text{ move}; \ e \rightarrow s_1; 0 \right\rangle,$$

direction$\in \{a, E, i, m, q, u, y, 2\}$, move$\in \{\Rightarrow, \Leftarrow, \Uparrow, \Downarrow\}$, $s_1 \in S_1 \cup \{U, D\}$;

While agents apply programs (9) or (10), agents, that do not move in a cross direction, must stand for the next step. Therefore, they use programs ((11) to (14) with priority 2) composed of two rewriting rules. The programs are of the form

$$\langle X \rightarrow X; \ s_1 \rightarrow s_2; 2 \rangle, \text{ where}$$

$s_i \in S_i$ for $i = 1, 2$;

The programs (15)-(46) with priority 0 are used to guide the agent in the next steps, the agent may hold information about the movement in the previous step. The programs are in the form

$$\left\langle \begin{bmatrix} * & * & * \\ * & \text{direction} & * \\ * & * & * \end{bmatrix} \rightarrow \text{ move}; \ s_2 \rightarrow s_1; 0 \right\rangle,$$

direction$\in \{a, E, i, m, q, u, y, 2\}$, move$\in \{\Rightarrow, \Leftarrow, \Uparrow, \Downarrow\}$, $s_1 \in S_1 \cup \{U, D\}$ and $s_2 \in S_2$;

We need one more program for "resetting" inertia. This is for the case when the slope of the terrain changes extremely. (47) $\langle X \rightarrow X; \ N \rightarrow e; 0 \rangle$;

The next set of programs (47)-(51) with priority 7 is applied in the case that there are sinks in studied area. We add some number of copies of object V to every cell in the sink area. The number of the objects corresponds to the quantity of water which can be contained in the sink and the same number of agents have to be stopped here.

(48) $\langle X \leftrightarrow V; \ I \rightarrow S; 7 \rangle$;(49) $\langle X \leftrightarrow V; \ J \rightarrow S; 7 \rangle$; (50) $\langle X \leftrightarrow V; \ K \rightarrow S; 7 \rangle$; (51) $\langle X \leftrightarrow V; \ L \rightarrow S; 7 \rangle$;

If we run the obtained 2D P colony in the simulator, agents, which represent a unit volume of water, will begin to move around the environment. The number of agents located in one cell at one moment corresponds to the quantity of water that at once flowed through the territory in one unit of time.

The agents that "overflow" from the filled sinks move on the direction to the neighboring cell containing direction out of the sink. It is done by the programs (52)-(59) with the priority set to 6. The main condition for application of the program is set in matrix in movement rule. When agent is placed in the cell with object X and no object V (in this case because of higher priority one of the the programs (48)-(51) will be applied) the agent tries to find wat out from the sink and search for suitable direction object inside the neighbouring cells.

For example $\begin{bmatrix} * & E & * \\ * & X & * \\ * & * & * \end{bmatrix}$ means that in side the west cell agent find object E

corresponding with direction $\leftarrow$ and it is possible way out from the sink.

The initial configuration of the 2D P colony is given by the objects placed in the environment - processed map, by number of agents, by their contents and placement. The number of agents corresponds to amount of water falling down during whole examined time. The content of the agent corresponds to the time when the agent has to start working.

The computation is nondeterministic. Starting with the maps without sinks and with one direction per cell the computation runs deterministically.

6   The Example Simulation

The example visualization is based on data from FreeGoedataCZ. The final statistics is done over four different data sets - four different locations.

The processed map is map of area with sink and its size is 10×10 and its directions are shown in the Table 3. Transcoded symbols are shown in the Table 4.

Table 3. Processed map

	0	1	2	3	4	5	6	7	8	9
0	↑	↑	↑	↑	↑	↑	↑	↑	↑	↑
1	←	←	↘	↓	↙	↙	←	↘	↘	→
2	←	←	↘	↓	↙	←	←	→	→	→
3	←	←	↓	↓	←	←	↙	↓	→	→
4	←	↓	↙	↙	←	←	↙	↓	↙	→
5	←	↓	↓	↙	↙	↙	↙	↓	↙	→
6	←	→	↘	↓	↓	↙	↙	↙	←	→
7	←	↑	→	↘	↓	↙	↙	↙	↙	→
8	←	↗	↑	→	↓	←	↙	←	↙	→
9	↓	↓	↓	↓	↓	↓	↓	↓	↓	↓

Table 4. Transcoded symbols

	0	1	2	3	4	5	6	7	8	9
0	i	i	i	i	i	i	i	i	i	i
1	E	E	q	m	u	u	E	q	q	a
2	E	E	q	m	u	E	E	a	a	a
3	E	E	m	m	E	E	u	m	a	a
4	E	m	u	u	E	E	u	m	u	a
5	E	m	m	u	u	u	u	m	u	a
6	E	a	q	m	m	u	u	u	E	a
7	E	i	a	q	m	u	u	u	u	a
8	E	y	i	a	m	E	u	E	u	a
9	m	m	m	m	m	m	m	m	m	m

A source of water is placed into cells $[2,3]$, $[3,3]$, $[4,3]$, $[2,4]$, $[3,4]$, $[4,4]$, $[2,5]$, $[3,5]$, $[4,5]$. In every source cell there are 8 agents. To simulate rain all agents are inactive in the initial configuration. Only one agent has the configuration of Xe in each cell. The next nineteen become active always in two computational steps. The numbers of active agents in the environment are shown in the Tables 5(A) - 10(A) - the first column of tables (heatmaps). The tables (heatmaps) in the second column (Tables 5(B)-10(B) show corresponding results achieved from SIMWE algorithm.

0   1.5   4.5   7.5   10.5 13.5 16.5 19.5 22.5 25.5   28.5 ...

Legend for heatmaps - depth of water in mm

Table 5. (A)Active agents after 2nd step of computation, (B) raster data - depth of water after 4 minutes of rainfall (in mm)

	0	1	2	3	4	5	6	7	8	9
0	0	0	0	0	0	0	0	0	0	0
1	0	0	0	0	0	0	0	0	0	0
2	0	0	0	0	0	0	0	0	0	0
3	0	0	1	2	1	0	0	0	0	0
4	0	0	2	3	1	0	0	0	0	0
5	0	1	2	1	1	0	0	0	0	0
6	0	0	1	1	0	0	0	0	0	0
7	0	0	0	0	0	0	0	0	0	0
8	0	0	0	0	0	0	0	0	0	0
9	0	0	0	0	0	0	0	0	0	0

	0	1	2	3	4	5	6	7	8	9
0	*	*	*	*	*	*	*	*	*	*
1	*	0	0	0	0	0	0	0	0	*
2	*	0	0	0	0	0	0	0	0	*
3	*	0	3.3	4.1	3.7	0	0	0	0	*
4	*	0	8.0	9.2	4.8	0	0	0	0	*
5	*	3.4	7.1	5.1	4.8	0	0	0	0	*
6	*	0.7	4.7	4.1	0.8	0	0	0	0	*
7	*	0	0.5	0.9	0.5	0	0	0	0	*
8	*	0	0	0	0	0	0	0	0	*
9	*	*	*	*	*	*	*	*	*	*

Table 6. (A)Active agents after 4th step of computation, (B) raster data - depth of water after 8 minutes of rainfall (in mm)

	0	1	2	3	4	5	6	7	8	9
0	0	0	0	0	0	0	0	0	0	0
1	0	0	0	0	0	0	0	0	0	0
2	0	0	0	0	0	0	0	0	0	0
3	0	0	1	2	1	0	0	0	0	0
4	0	0	5	5	1	0	0	0	0	0
5	0	1	4	1	1	0	0	0	0	0
6	0	2	4	1	0	0	0	0	0	0
7	0	0	0	1	0	0	0	0	0	0
8	0	0	0	0	0	0	0	0	0	0
9	0	0	0	0	0	0	0	0	0	0

	0	1	2	3	4	5	6	7	8	9
0	*	*	*	*	*	*	*	*	*	*
1	*	0	0	0	0	0	0	0	0	*
2	*	0	0	0	0	0	0	0	0	*
3	*	0	3.3	4.1	3.7	0	0	0	0	*
4	*	0	14.8	15.3	4.3	0	0	0	0	*
5	*	1.7	12.1	5.6	4.8	0	0	0	0	*
6	*	6.2	13.7	4.2	1.8	0	0	0	0	*
7	*	0	0.7	4.7	0.5	0	0	0	0	*
8	*	0	0	0	0	0	0	0	0	*
9	*	*	*	*	*	*	*	*	*	*

We compare the simulation process using 2D P colonies and using SIMWE algorithm.

One agent corresponds to 3 mm of water and two steps of computation take 4 minutes. From the previous tables we can derive the following results: At the begining of simulation the agents move more slowly than water over the surface but during the second half of simulation the agents move more quickly than water. Area touched by water is larger in SIMWE simulation but depth of water in these cells is only about 1 mm. The graphical representation of the frequency of depth of water is shown on the Figure 1. The models give different results in 8.854 percent of cells in the whole simulation.

Table 7. (A)Active agents after 6th step of computation, (B) raster data - depth of water after 12 minutes of rainfall (in mm)

	0	1	2	3	4	5	6	7	8	9
0	0	0	0	0	0	0	0	0	0	0
1	0	0	0	0	0	0	0	0	0	0
2	0	0	0	0	0	0	0	0	0	0
3	0	0	1	1	1	0	0	0	0	0
4	0	0	4	3	1	0	0	0	0	0
5	0	1	4	1	1	0	0	0	0	0
6	0	3	5	2	0	0	0	0	0	0
7	0	0	0	1	0	0	0	0	0	0
8	0	0	0	0	3	0	0	0	0	0
9	0	0	0	0	0	0	0	0	0	0

	0	1	2	3	4	5	6	7	8	9
0	*	*	*	*	*	*	*	*	*	*
1	*	0	0	0	0	0	0	0	0	*
2	*	0	0	0	0	0	0	0	0	*
3	*	0	3.3	4.1	3.7	0	0	0	0	*
4	*	0	11.9	10.0	4.3	0	0	0	0	*
5	*	2.7	13.8	5.7	4.8	0	0	0	0	*
6	*	9.5	16.6	8.2	1.8	0	0	0	0	*
7	*	0.5	1.6	6.8	1.5	0	0	0	0	*
8	*	0	1.6	8.3	0	0	0	0	0	*
9	*	*	*	*	*	*	*	*	*	*

Table 8. (A)Active agents after 8th step of computation, (B) raster data - depth of water after 16 minutes of rainfall (in mm)

	0	1	2	3	4	5	6	7	8	9
0	0	0	0	0	0	0	0	0	0	0
1	0	0	0	0	0	0	0	0	0	0
2	0	0	0	0	0	0	0	0	0	0
3	0	0	1	1	1	0	0	0	0	0
4	0	0	3	3	1	0	0	0	0	0
5	0	1	3	1	1	0	0	0	0	0
6	0	1	10	2	0	0	0	0	0	0
7	0	0	0	4	3	0	0	0	0	0
8	0	0	0	0	4	0	0	0	0	0
9	0	0	0	0	3	0	0	0	0	0

	0	1	2	3	4	5	6	7	8	9
0	*	*	*	*	*	*	*	*	*	*
1	*	0	0	0	0	0	0	0	0	*
2	*	0	0	0	0	0	0	0	0	*
3	*	0	3.3	4.1	3.7	0	0	0	0	*
4	*	0	8.9	10.0	4.3	0	0	0	0	*
5	*	2.7	12.8	5.7	4.8	0	0	0	0	*
6	*	5.5	32.3	7.4	1.8	0	0	0	0	*
7	*	0.8	1.3	15.6	10.6	0	0	0	0	*
8	*	0	1.6	2.1	13.2	0	0	0	0	*
9	*	*	*	*	*	*	*	*	*	*

Table 9. (A)Active agents after 10th step of computation, (B) raster data - depth of water after 20 minutes of rainfall (in mm)

	0	1	2	3	4	5	6	7	8	9
0	0	0	0	0	0	0	0	0	0	0
1	0	0	0	0	0	0	0	0	0	0
2	0	0	0	0	0	0	0	0	0	0
3	0	0	1	2	1	0	0	0	0	0
4	0	0	2	4	1	0	0	0	0	0
5	0	2	4	1	1	0	0	0	0	0
6	0	2	6	4	0	0	0	0	0	0
7	0	0	0	8	1	0	0	0	0	0
8	0	0	0	0	4	0	0	0	0	0
9	0	0	0	0	10	0	0	0	0	0

	0	1	2	3	4	5	6	7	8	9
0	*	*	*	*	*	*	*	*	*	*
1	*	0	0	0	0	0	0	0	0	*
2	*	0	0	0	0	0	0	0	0	*
3	*	0	3.3	4.1	3.7	0	0	0	0	*
4	*	0	6.9	12.0	4.3	0	0	0	0	*
5	*	3.7	13.8	5.7	4.8	0	0	0	0	*
6	*	6.2	17.4	14.4	1.8	0	0	0	0	*
7	*	0.5	1.8	25.0	4.9	0	0	0	0	*
8	*	0	0.6	1.5	13.5	0	0	0	0	*
9	*	*	*	*	*	*	*	*	*	*

Table 10. (A)Active agents after 12th step of computation, (B) raster data - depth of water after 24 minutes of rainfall (in mm)

	0	1	2	3	4	5	6	7	8	9
0	0	0	0	0	0	0	0	0	0	0
1	0	0	0	0	0	0	0	0	0	0
2	0	0	0	0	0	0	0	0	0	0
3	0	0	1	2	1	0	0	0	0	0
4	0	0	2	4	1	0	0	0	0	0
5	0	2	5	1	1	0	0	0	0	0
6	0	2	7	2	0	0	0	0	0	0
7	0	0	0	6	3	0	0	0	0	0
8	0	0	0	0	8	0	0	0	0	0
9	0	0	0	0	15	0	0	0	0	0

	0	1	2	3	4	5	6	7	8	9
0	*	*	*	*	*	*	*	*	*	*
1	*	0	0	0	0	0	0	0	0	*
2	*	0	0	0	0	0	0	0	0	*
3	*	0	3.3	4.1	3.7	0	0	0	0	*
4	*	0	6.9	12.0	4.3	0	0	0	0	*
5	*	3.7	15.8	5.7	4.8	0	0	0	0	*
6	*	7.2	22.0	6.6	1.8	0	0	0	0	*
7	*	1.8	2.0	20.3	9.2	0	0	0	0	*
8	*	0	1.6	2.3	25.1	0	0	0	0	*
9	*	*	*	*	*	*	*	*	*	*

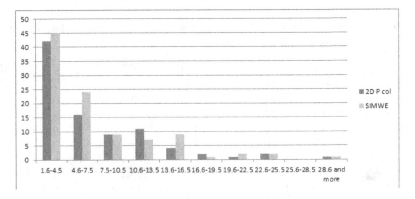

Fig. 1. Frequency of depth of water in 2D P colony and SIMWE

7 Comparison of Models

This work has been an initial attempt to model surface runoff using two different methods, namely algorithm SIMWE and 2D P colonies. The algorithm SIMWE is based on the description of water flow and sediment transport processes by first-principles equations. Inputs and outputs of the simulations are represented by multivariate functions (scalar or vector fields). The underlying continuity equations are solved by a Green's function Monte Carlo method to provide the robustness necessary for spatially variable conditions and high resolutions. In contrast, 2D P colonies provide a multiagent framework with agents performing simple instructions in a collaborative environment. Based on non-deterministic parallel execution of simple instructions agents to the behaviour of the entire system can be very similar to the real behaviour of natural systems.

The are some advantages and disadvantages of 2D P colonies for modelling surface runoff. The first disadvantage is the "calibration" of the model. This procedure gives us the answer to the questions: What amount of water one agent represents? What time corresponds to two computational steps? Answer to the first question is given by rainfall per unit of time. How long one time unit takes is given by the average speed of water - we must take into account resolution of map and roughness of terrain. The SIMWE algorithm is constructed to model surface runoff and it does not need such calibration - roughness is one of input parameters.

The requirements for the computations depend not only on algorithm but on simulation environment too. As we wrote before the SIMWE is integrated for example as a module of software GRASS GIS. We use simulation environment for 2D P colonies called simply "2D P colony" simulator already introduced in [1]. The computational space used for SIMWE in GRASS GIS (r.sim.water) depends mainly on the number of cells. In the whole computation it works with all the matrices on input. We can set in what time period we want to have outputs. In the 2D P colony simulator the whole matrix of input map is processed only once at the beginnig of computation. During the rest of the simulation only agents are active and local changes are made. To compare space requirements of computations we prepare maps in sizes 10×10 (15 random maps) and 100×100 (10 random maps). We run simulations with 10 and 100 agents in 2D P colony simulator without visualisation. On the table 11 the reader can find average values of space used in computation for 50 time units.

Table 11. Average values of used space

size of map	2D P colony simulator			r.sim.water		
	number of agents	min (in MB)	average (in MB)	max (in MB)	min (in MB)	average (in MB)	max (in MB)
10×10	10	6.2	7.9	10.1	296.0	296.2	296.3
	100	16.5	18.3	22.8			
100×100	10	9.6	10.3	11.8	296.7	296.9	328.8
	100	17.6	18.9	22.8			

If we compare results obtained from SIMWE and 2D P colony, we get the values similar to those of the representative example (graph in the figure 1) and the percentage of cell with different values becomes 8.795.

8   Conclusion

The aim of this paper was to analyse the situation and to create 2D model P colonies that would simulate the flow of liquid over the Earth's surface, a phenomenon called Surface runoff. This process is very common in nature and accumulation of water leads to flash flooding or floods in general. Flow of water over the surface is influenced by many factors: the surface slope, soil saturation, temperature, humidity, size of source and lots of others. We applied the slope of the terrain in the environment of 2D P colonies. Finally, we compared the process of the simulations with the results provided by the algorithm SIMWE, module of geographic information system software GRASS GIS. To achieve more realistic movement of agents through the environment (not only one average speed) and adjustment of the amount of water in the sinks we plan to extend 2D P colonies with parameters. It will help us to use more different states of agents and cells than use of object labelled by common symbols.

Remark 1.
This work was partially supported by the European Regional Development Fund in the IT4Innovations Centre of Excellence project (CZ.1.05/1.1.00/02.0070), by SGS/24/2013, SGS/7/2011 and by project OPVK no. CZ.1.07/2.2.00/28.0014.

References

1. Cienciala, L., Ciencialová, L., Perdek, M.: 2D P colonies. In: Csuhaj-Varjú, E., Gheorghe, M., Rozenberg, G., Salomaa, A., Vaszil, G. (eds.) CMC 2012. LNCS, vol. 7762, pp. 161–172. Springer, Heidelberg (2013)
2. Csuhaj-Varjú, E., Kelemen, J., Kelemenová, A., Păun, G., Vaszil, G.: Cells in environment: P colonies. Multiple-valued Logic and Soft Computing 12(3-4), 201–215 (2006)
3. Eastman, R.J.: IDRISI Andes Guide to GIS and Image Processing, Clerk Lab. Clerk University, Worcester, MA, USA (2006)
4. GRASS DEVELOPMENT TEAM. GRASS GIS: The world's leading Free GIS software (1998), http://grass.osgeo.org/ (May 25, 2013) (cit. July 01, 2013)
5. Julien, P.Y., Saghafian, B., Ogden, F.L.: Raster-based Hydrologic modeling of spatilly varied surface funoff. Water Resources Bulletin 31(3), 523–536 (1995)
6. Kelemen, J., Kelemenová, A.: On P colonies, a biochemically inspired model of computation. In: Proc. of the 6th International Symposium of Hungarian Researchers on Computational Intelligence, Budapest TECH, Hungary, pp. 40–56 (2005)
7. Kelemen, J., Kelemenová, A., Păun, G.: Preview of P colonies: A biochemically inspired computing model. In: Bedau, M., et al. (eds.) Workshop and Tutorial Proceedings, Ninth International Conference on the Simulation and Synthesis of Living Systems, ALIFE IX, Boston, Mass, pp. 82–86 (2004)
8. Mitas, L., Mitasova, H., Brown, W.M., Astley, M.: Interacting fields approach for evolving spatial phenomena: application to erosion simulationfor optimized land use. In: Goodchild, M.F., et al. (eds.) Proc. of the III. Int. Conf. On Integration of Environmental Modeling and GIS, Santa Barbara, USA (1996)
9. Păun, G.: Computing with membranes. Journal of Computer and System Sciences 61, 108–143 (2000)
10. Păun, G.: Membrane computing: An introduction. Springer, Berlin (2002)
11. Păun, G., Rozenberg, G., Salomaa, A.: The Oxford Handbook of Membrane Computing. Oxford University Press (2009)
12. Torrents, B.: Geosimulation. John Wiley & Sons (2004)
13. P systems web page, http://psystems.disco.unimib.it

A   Programs for 2D P Colony Π

$(1)\left\langle\begin{bmatrix}*&*&*\\ *&a&*\\ *&*&*\end{bmatrix}\to\Rightarrow;\ e\to 9;0\right\rangle;\ (2)\left\langle\begin{bmatrix}*&*&*\\ *&E&*\\ *&*&*\end{bmatrix}\to\Leftarrow;\ e\to 8;0\right\rangle;$

$(3)\left\langle\begin{bmatrix}*&*&*\\ *&i&*\\ *&*&*\end{bmatrix}\to\Uparrow;\ e\to 6;0\right\rangle;\ (4)\left\langle\begin{bmatrix}*&*&*\\ *&m&*\\ *&*&*\end{bmatrix}\to\Downarrow;\ e\to 7;0\right\rangle;$

$(5)\left\langle\begin{bmatrix}*&*&*\\ *&q&*\\ *&*&*\end{bmatrix}\to\Rightarrow;\ e\to D;0\right\rangle;\ (6)\left\langle\begin{bmatrix}*&*&*\\ *&u&*\\ *&*&*\end{bmatrix}\to\Leftarrow;\ e\to D;0\right\rangle;$

$(7)\left\langle\begin{bmatrix}*&*&*\\ *&y&*\\ *&*&*\end{bmatrix}\to\Rightarrow;\ e\to U;0\right\rangle;\ (8)\left\langle\begin{bmatrix}*&*&*\\ *&2&*\\ *&*&*\end{bmatrix}\to\Leftarrow;\ e\to U;0\right\rangle;$

$(9)\left\langle\begin{bmatrix}*&*&*\\ *&*&*\\ *&*&*\end{bmatrix}\to\Downarrow;\ D\to I;1\right\rangle;\ (10)\left\langle\begin{bmatrix}*&*&*\\ *&*&*\\ *&*&*\end{bmatrix}\to\Uparrow;\ U\to H;1\right\rangle;$

$(11)\ \langle X\to X;\ 6\to H;2\rangle;\ (12)\ \langle X\to X;\ 7\to I;2\rangle;\ (13)\ \langle X\to X;\ 8\to K;2\rangle;$
$(14)\ \langle X\to X;\ 9\to L;2\rangle;$

$(15)\left\langle\begin{bmatrix}*&*&*\\ *&a&*\\ *&*&*\end{bmatrix}\to\Rightarrow;\ H\to 9;0\right\rangle;\ (16)\left\langle\begin{bmatrix}*&*&*\\ *&E&*\\ *&*&*\end{bmatrix}\to\Leftarrow;\ H\to 8;0\right\rangle;$

$(17)\left\langle\begin{bmatrix}*&*&*\\ *&i&*\\ *&*&*\end{bmatrix}\to\Rightarrow;\ H\to\mathbf{U};0\right\rangle;\ (18)\left\langle\begin{bmatrix}*&*&*\\ *&m&*\\ *&*&*\end{bmatrix}\to\Downarrow;\ H\to 7;0\right\rangle;$

$(19)\left\langle\begin{bmatrix}*&*&*\\ *&q&*\\ *&*&*\end{bmatrix}\to\Rightarrow;\ H\to D;0\right\rangle;\ (20)\left\langle\begin{bmatrix}*&*&*\\ *&u&*\\ *&*&*\end{bmatrix}\to\Leftarrow;\ H\to D;0\right\rangle;$

$(21)\left\langle\begin{bmatrix}*&*&*\\ *&y&*\\ *&*&*\end{bmatrix}\to\Rightarrow;\ H\to U;0\right\rangle;\ (22)\left\langle\begin{bmatrix}*&*&*\\ *&2&*\\ *&*&*\end{bmatrix}\to\Leftarrow;\ H\to U;0\right\rangle;$

$(23)\left\langle\begin{bmatrix}*&*&*\\ *&a&*\\ *&*&*\end{bmatrix}\to\Rightarrow;\ I\to 9;0\right\rangle;\ (24)\left\langle\begin{bmatrix}*&*&*\\ *&E&*\\ *&*&*\end{bmatrix}\to\Leftarrow;\ I\to 8;0\right\rangle;$

$(25)\left\langle\begin{bmatrix}*&*&*\\ *&i&*\\ *&*&*\end{bmatrix}\to\Uparrow;\ I\to 6;0\right\rangle;\ (26)\left\langle\begin{bmatrix}*&*&*\\ *&m&*\\ *&*&*\end{bmatrix}\to\Downarrow;\ I\to 7;0\right\rangle;$

$(27)\left\langle\begin{bmatrix}*&*&*\\ *&q&*\\ *&*&*\end{bmatrix}\to\Rightarrow;\ I\to D;0\right\rangle;\ (28)\left\langle\begin{bmatrix}*&*&*\\ *&u&*\\ *&*&*\end{bmatrix}\to\Leftarrow;\ I\to D;0\right\rangle;$

$(29)\left\langle\begin{bmatrix}*&*&*\\ *&y&*\\ *&*&*\end{bmatrix}\to\Rightarrow;\ I\to U;0\right\rangle;\ (30)\left\langle\begin{bmatrix}*&*&*\\ *&2&*\\ *&*&*\end{bmatrix}\to\Leftarrow;\ I\to U;0\right\rangle;$

$(31)\left\langle\begin{bmatrix}*&*&*\\ *&a&*\\ *&*&*\end{bmatrix}\to\Rightarrow;\ J\to 9;0\right\rangle;\ (32)\left\langle\begin{bmatrix}*&*&*\\ *&E&*\\ *&*&*\end{bmatrix}\to\Leftarrow;\ J\to L;0\right\rangle;$

$(33)\left\langle\begin{bmatrix}*&*&*\\ *&i&*\\ *&*&*\end{bmatrix}\to\Uparrow;\ J\to 6;0\right\rangle;\ (34)\left\langle\begin{bmatrix}*&*&*\\ *&m&*\\ *&*&*\end{bmatrix}\to\Downarrow;\ J\to 7;0\right\rangle;$

$(35) \left\langle \begin{bmatrix} * & * & * \\ * & q & * \\ * & * & * \end{bmatrix} \rightarrow \Rightarrow; \ J \rightarrow 7; 0 \right\rangle;$ $(36) \left\langle \begin{bmatrix} * & * & * \\ * & u & * \\ * & * & * \end{bmatrix} \rightarrow \Leftarrow; \ J \rightarrow D; 0 \right\rangle;$

$(37) \left\langle \begin{bmatrix} * & * & * \\ * & y & * \\ * & * & * \end{bmatrix} \rightarrow \Rightarrow; \ J \rightarrow 6; 0 \right\rangle;$ $(38) \left\langle \begin{bmatrix} * & * & * \\ * & 2 & * \\ * & * & * \end{bmatrix} \rightarrow \Leftarrow; \ J \rightarrow U; 0 \right\rangle;$

$(39) \left\langle \begin{bmatrix} * & * & * \\ * & a & * \\ * & * & * \end{bmatrix} \rightarrow \Rightarrow; \ K \rightarrow N; 0 \right\rangle;$ $(40) \left\langle \begin{bmatrix} * & * & * \\ * & E & * \\ * & * & * \end{bmatrix} \rightarrow \Leftarrow; \ K \rightarrow 8; 0 \right\rangle;$

$(41) \left\langle \begin{bmatrix} * & * & * \\ * & i & * \\ * & * & * \end{bmatrix} \rightarrow \Uparrow; \ K \rightarrow 6; 0 \right\rangle;$ $(42) \left\langle \begin{bmatrix} * & * & * \\ * & m & * \\ * & * & * \end{bmatrix} \rightarrow \Downarrow; \ K \rightarrow 7; 0 \right\rangle;$

$(43) \left\langle \begin{bmatrix} * & * & * \\ * & q & * \\ * & * & * \end{bmatrix} \rightarrow \Rightarrow; \ K \rightarrow D; 0 \right\rangle;$ $(44) \left\langle \begin{bmatrix} * & * & * \\ * & u & * \\ * & * & * \end{bmatrix} \rightarrow \Leftarrow; \ K \rightarrow 7; 0 \right\rangle;$

$(45) \left\langle \begin{bmatrix} * & * & * \\ * & y & * \\ * & * & * \end{bmatrix} \rightarrow \Rightarrow; \ K \rightarrow U; 0 \right\rangle;$ $(46) \left\langle \begin{bmatrix} * & * & * \\ * & 2 & * \\ * & * & * \end{bmatrix} \rightarrow \Leftarrow; \ K \rightarrow 6; 0 \right\rangle;$

$(47) \langle X \rightarrow X; \ N \rightarrow e; 0 \rangle;$

$(48) \langle X \leftrightarrow V; \ I \rightarrow S; 7 \rangle;$ $(49) \langle X \leftrightarrow V; \ J \rightarrow S; 7 \rangle;$ $(50) \langle X \leftrightarrow V; \ K \rightarrow S; 7 \rangle;$

$(51) \langle X \leftrightarrow V; \ L \rightarrow S; 7 \rangle;$

$(52) \left\langle \begin{bmatrix} \alpha & * & * \\ * & X & * \\ * & * & * \end{bmatrix} \rightarrow \Leftarrow; \ \beta \rightarrow U; 6 \right\rangle; \alpha \in \{a, E, i, 2\}$

$(53) \left\langle \begin{bmatrix} * & \alpha & * \\ * & X & * \\ * & * & * \end{bmatrix} \rightarrow \Uparrow; \ \beta \rightarrow 6; 6 \right\rangle; \alpha \in \{i, E, a, y, 2\}$

$(54) \left\langle \begin{bmatrix} * & * & \alpha \\ * & X & * \\ * & * & * \end{bmatrix} \rightarrow \Rightarrow; \ \beta \rightarrow U; 6 \right\rangle; \ \alpha \in \{y, 2, i, a, E\}$

$(55) \left\langle \begin{bmatrix} * & * & * \\ \alpha & X & * \\ * & * & * \end{bmatrix} \rightarrow \Leftarrow; \ \beta \rightarrow 8; 6 \right\rangle; \alpha \in \{E, i, m, 2, u\}$

$(56) \left\langle \begin{bmatrix} * & * & * \\ * & X & \alpha \\ * & * & * \end{bmatrix} \rightarrow \Rightarrow; \ \beta \rightarrow 9; 6 \right\rangle \alpha \in \{a, i, m, y, q\};$

$(57) \left\langle \begin{bmatrix} * & * & * \\ * & X & * \\ \alpha & * & * \end{bmatrix} \rightarrow \Leftarrow; \ \beta \rightarrow D; 6 \right\rangle; \alpha \in \{E, i, m, 2, u\}$

$(58) \left\langle \begin{bmatrix} * & * & * \\ * & X & * \\ * & \alpha & * \end{bmatrix} \rightarrow \Downarrow; \ \beta \rightarrow 7; 6 \right\rangle; \alpha \in \{a, E, m, q, u\}$

$(59) \left\langle \begin{bmatrix} * & * & * \\ * & X & * \\ * & * & \alpha \end{bmatrix} \rightarrow \Rightarrow; \ \beta \rightarrow D; 6 \right\rangle; \ \alpha \in \{a, i, m, y, q\}; \ \beta \in \{I, J, K, L\}$

Implementation of P Systems by Using Big Data Technologies

Alex Ciobanu[1] and Florentin Ipate[2,1]

[1] Department of Computer Science, Faculty of Mathematics and Computer Science, University of Pitesti, Str. Targu din Vale 1, 110040 Pitesti, Romania
[2] Department of Computer Science, Faculty of Mathematics and Computer Science, University of Bucharest, Str. Academiei nr.14, sector 1, Bucharest, Romania
alex.ciobanu@gmail.com, florentin.ipate@ifsoft.ro

Abstract. Due to their inherent parallel and non-deterministic nature, P system implementations require vast computing and storage resources. This significantly limits their applications, even more so when the calculation of *all possible evolutions* of the P system is required. This article exposes the scalability possibilities available with the Big Data ecosystem for P systems implementations, using Map Reduce parallelism to build the P system computation tree. The Hadoop based implementation is then used for generating test suites for cell like P systems, in particular for context-dependent rule coverage testing. Our preliminary evaluations on a benchmark of automatically generated P systems confirm that the proposed approach scales well.

Keywords: P systems testing, Hadoop, P system computation tree, Map Reduce, Big Data, NoSQL.

1 Introduction

Membrane computing, a field of research which studies distributed and parallel computing models called *P systems*, is a rapidly growing research area. Initially coined by Gheorghe Păun in [1], P systems have been studied from a computational and modelling perspective. Many variants have been introduced [2] and investigated, further a set of applications has been identified and modelled with such systems. P systems offer the possibility of modelling natural phenomena using a very natural and logical syntax. Unfortunately natural phenomena are inherently extremely complex and the simulation of P systems which model such phenomena inherit the complexity, therefore requiring significant computational power to process. At a certain point the computational power and storage capacity of a single machine is simply insufficient for the simulations and testing of such P systems, at which point grid or clustered computing is considered. In an attempt to reuse established technologies for the computations of P systems we will show a method of using a Map Reduce framework and a NoSQL database in the simulation of P systems. These technologies (which at times fall under the

A. Alhazov et al. (Eds.): CMC 2013, LNCS 8340, pp. 117–137, 2014.

blanket term of Big Data) are designed to leverage large scale commodity hardware clusters as massively scalable environment for parallel computing. We will use Big Data technologies to compute a computation tree of a non-deterministic P system, and show a potential application of such computations. Some theoretical work has been done in using Hadoop with P systems in [7], but no implementation has been attempted.

There however have been many attempts to generate Psystem simulators which use parallel computing, with varying levels of success. These are all enumerated in: [8]. Possibly the most successful attempts have used speciality hardware to enable the simulation. These include GPU, FPGA, and Micro Controller implementations. These simulators usually run much faster (per server) then the one developed in this article, but they have two major drawbacks: they require speciality equipment and they are limited to the storage and processing capacity of a single device. Our solution is able to scale to multiple commodity machines extending the storage capacity to very large data sets. At the same time a possible integrated approach between Hadoop and GPU approach would be very interesting to attempt as it might enable a best of both worlds implementations were the drawbacks of both system can be counterbalanced.

There have also been attempts at using clustered computing, using either c++ and Message Passing Interface, or Java and remote method calls. Both methods showed great potential but were limited by the communication overhead of the implementations. Our approach uses a distributed database to enable our communication and a slightly different approach to simulation (given tour multi path approach). Although Hadoop is a more rigid infrastructure then the other used, its rigidity also mitigates some of the issues faced with bespoke clustering technologies.

2   Preliminaries

2.1   Map Reduce

MapReduce [3] is a framework developed circa 2004 at Google in an attempt to deal with their very large scale data warehousing needs. Although the Google implementation of the Map Reduce ecosystem is proprietary, Doug Cutting from within the Apache foundation developed an open source implementation under the project name Hadoop. We use this implementation for our experiments. The Hadoop ecosystem has many subcomponents including a file system, coordination applications, meta programming languages and many other components. For the purposes of our discussion we will focus on the core map reduce functionality developed as a basis for distributed computation within applications. Map Reduce is conceptually based on functional programming paradigms or to be more specific two primitives (higher order functions) called map and reduce.

Map (in functional programming) is defined as a higher order function with type signature: $map :: (\alpha \rightarrow \beta) \rightarrow [\alpha] \rightarrow [\beta]$. In other words a function that acts upon a vector of data in one data domain α and returns a vector of data in another data domain β having transformed from domain α to domain β by the given transformational function. In more familiar syntax if we have an input vector $A = [a_1, a_2...a_n]$ and a function f, then $map(A, f) = f(A) = A'$ *where* $A' = [f(a_1), f(a_2)...f(a_n)]$. The data type of the resulting vector does not have to match the data type of initial vector but the cardinality of the two vectors must be equal.

Reduce also referred to as fold, accumulate, compress, or inject (in functional programming) is defined as a higher order function with type signature $reduce ::$ $(\alpha \rightarrow \beta \rightarrow \beta) \rightarrow [\alpha] \rightarrow \beta \rightarrow \beta$. In other words a function that acts upon a vector and returns the aggregation of the elements within that vector, aggregating based on the provided function. If we had our vector $V = [v_1, v_2..v_n]$ and our reduce function g), then $reduce(V, g) = v'$ where $v' = g(v1, g(v2, (...g(v_(n - 1), v_n)))$ (assuming a right side evaluation). In this case the type of V and v' are the same but the cardinality of the input vector is n while the cardinality of the result is 1. At the same time the reduce function g must be associative, commutative, and distributive as to allow for random ordering in the reduce process. Although in this example the reduce is right evaluated, evaluation can happen in any direction and in any order.

Map-Reduce within the context of Hadoop deviates from this strict definition of functional programming in a couple of ways. Most notable is the format of the input and output of both the map and reduce function, which are defined as a tuple of order 2. These tuples also referred to as a Key Value pair $\langle K, V \rangle$ are the basis of all interactions within Hadoop. The Map task takes input of a $\langle K, V \rangle$ pair and produces i $\langle K, V \rangle$ pairs (where $0 \leq i \leq$ n). In the next step (reduce) all $\langle K, V \rangle$ pairs where the key is identical are passed to the reduce function. Basically the input of a Reduce function is a key with a list of values $\langle K, [V, V, V...] \rangle$. In the reducer (the execution of a reduce task) all of the values are reduced together and a series of j $\langle K, V \rangle$ pairs (where $0 \leq j \leq m$) are produced which are the output of the entire process. The output of one execution can now become the input of next run of the application in series of executions. The Map and Reduce processes are written in Java and the execution of a Map or Reduce task entails running the map or reduce function on a server in a cluster of machines. A Mapper is a server in the cluster which is running a map task at that particular instance in time. Upon initiation of the application all servers run map tasks until the entire input set has been exhausted. Afterwards all servers become reducers and run the reduce function until again all $\langle K, V \rangle$ pairs produced by the mappers are exhausted. The resultant $\langle K, V \rangle$ pairs produced by the reducers are written out to the file system. Since all of the processes run on independent servers with very little shared between processes, clusters can scale up to thousands of servers.

To give an example of MapReduce we can look at the canonical example, word count. Word count calculates the number of occurrences of each word within a

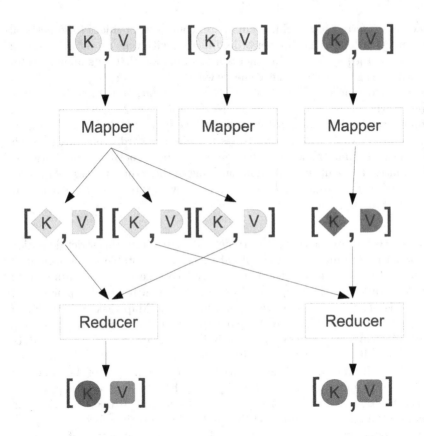

Fig. 1. Example of the flow of data with a Map-Reduce execution

text. The Map task takes as input a chunk of the file (the key being the byte offset of the file and the value is the actual test in the file). The map task tokenizes the test and creates $\langle K, V \rangle$ pairs where the key is the actual word and value is the number of occurrences of the word (1 initially). The reducer takes in each unique key (in our case word) and does a sum of the integer values associated with it, fundamentally doing a world count. Figure 2 exemplifies the case where we have two input files one with the text "hello world" and the other with the text "goodbye world"

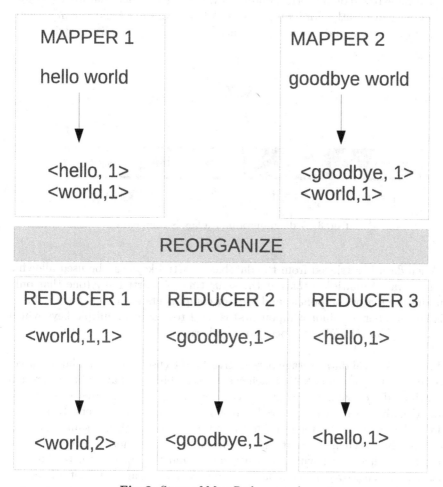

Fig. 2. Steps of Map-Reduce word count

2.2   NoSQL Database

NoSQL is actually a blanket term to describe a suite database technologies which are not compliant to standard relational paradigms. Most of the underlying concepts come from a Google article [4] which describes a technology for distributed databases. NoSQL comprises of many different database technologies including document orient databases, graph databases, columnar stores and the technology we used for our experiments Key-Value stores. Most NoSQL databases use a lightweight mechanism for storing and retrieving data in exchange for greater scalability and availability. Oracle NoSQL database (the implementation of NoSQL used for this article) has similar properties to a map or dictionary from computer science theory. The database is able to store a key value pair, and it's able to retrieve a value based on its corresponding key. In Oracle NoSQL database the keys are defined in a slightly more complex way. A key is composed of two components: a major component and a minor component, which are both a list of strings.

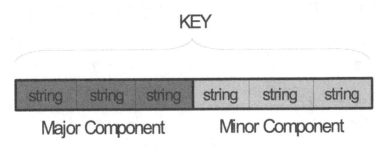

Fig. 3. A diagram of how a key is composed

When data is retrieved from the database, partial keys can be used allowing the retrieval of multiple values at the same time. A partial key (one that only contains the major component and i minor components where $0 \leq i < n - 1$ and n is the number of minor components) is used to retrieve multiple keys which are logically linked and are processed together.

From a physical data storage perspective NoSQL uses a very similar architecture to a Hadoop cluster. NoSQL achieves its scalability and availability through a distributed storage mechanism. Multiple parallel servers are used to store the data. Usually the data is mirrored across multiple distinct servers. If a server is lost, the data can be retrieved from another server with the same data. At the same time if client requests data from an overloaded server a jump can be made to another server with lower utilization and the same data. Hashing algorithms are employed to eliminate the need for a linear search of all servers when retrieving data. In Oracle's NoSQL Database the major component of the keys is used as the indicator for which server to use, as an effort is made to keep all keys with identical major components together on one server. This enables faster multi-retrieve executions.

There is an important side effect of distributed databases relating to the consistency of data, or better said the lack there of. NoSQL databases uses a term called eventual consistency which states given a long enough period in which

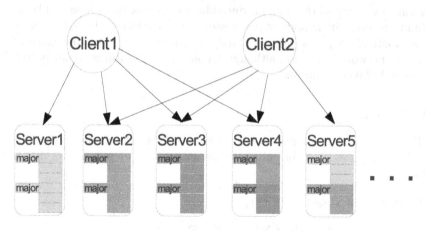

Fig. 4. A diagram of a NoSQL physical deployment

no updates occur, the system will reach a consistent state, but at a particular point in time there is no guarantee the system will be consistent. Given the distributed nature of the storage (usually triple mirroring) an update pushed to one sever is not guaranteed to propagate to all servers before a reading of the exact data point, hence a read might offer an old version of that data point. These limitations must be considered when designing an application against a NoSQL database. For more information see [9].

2.3 Parallelism

The subject of parallelism in computing can be split into many different categories including symmetric multiprocessing, grid computing massive parallel processing, grid computing and many more. The focus of this article will be exclusively grid computing, the distribution of work to multiple physical machines weakly linked through commodity networking, an architecture in which many of the worlds super computers share. This architecture allows for massive scaling (theoretically to unlimited number of processing units) while at the same time eliminating the need for exotic hardware which is both expensive and difficult to come by. An excellent overview and description of Parallelism in computing and the different can be found at [8]. Looking at the map and reduce function from a parallelism perspective it is quite natural that they distribute very nicely. Looking at the map function there is no link or sharing between the mapping of individual elements of a vector hence the map function can be executed on a different node of a cluster for each element of a vector with linear scaling and no performance impact as the number of nodes increases (baring data movement issues). The reduce function shares a similar parallelism capability (assuming associativity, commutativity, and distributivity) as little as two elements can be reduced (combined) on each node of the cluster and (given a set of n unique keys) we can theoretically scale to a n node cluster. It is to note there is some communications overheard as the data produced by a map task (with identical keys) needs to moved on a single node of the cluster to be able to run the reduce function. For practical purposes implementation is usually limited to thousands of nodes due to network limitation although larger implementations are suspected to exist at web 2.0 corporations.

2.4 P Systems

A (cell like) P system is a computational model inspired by the chemical reactions across cell membranes. The formal definition with which we will be working is as follows:

DEFINITION 2.41 *A P system is a tuple*

$$\Pi = (\mathcal{V}, \mu, \mathcal{W}_1, \ldots, \mathcal{W}_n, \mathcal{R}_1 \ldots \mathcal{R}_n)$$

where

- $\mathcal{V}$ *is the alphabet (a finite and nonempty) set of objects;*
- μ *is the membrane structure, a hierarchical arrangement of compartments named membranes identified by integer 1 to n;*
- $\mathcal{W}_i$, *where $0 \leq i \leq n$, are strings over $\mathcal{V}$, describing the multisets of objects initially placed in the i regions of μ;*
- $\mathcal{R}_i$, $0 \leq i \leq n$, *is a finite set of evolution rules for each region i where evolution rule r is of the form*

$$r : u \rightarrow (a_1, t_1) \ldots (a_n, t_n) \tag{1}$$

where u and a_i are multiset over $\mathcal{V}$, and t_i is an element from μ; t_i is limited to the current membrane, the region immediately outside the current region or any of the region immediately inside the current region.

Although many variations on P system exist, for the purposes of this article we will concern ourselves with only this very basic definition (above) to look at how Big Data technologies can help in handling the state explosion problem. Complications such as polarization can be added to the computations upon request. It is also important to note that although this definition can have P systems which can only have one possible evolution path, our focus will be on non-deterministic P system with multiple possible evolutions for every membrane, in every configuration.

2.5 Computation Tree

A computation tree is a directed acyclic graph representation of the evolutions of a P system. The graph has a single root node (which represents the initial multiset of the P system), and every edge represents a possible evolution of the P system. All subsequent nodes in the graph are possible evolutions of the P system where the edges leading to the node represent the rules which must be applied to reach that configuration. Our computation tree assumes maximally parallel execution. For example, if we have the following P system:

$$\Pi = (\mathcal{V}, \mu, \mathcal{W}_1, \mathcal{R}_1),$$

where

- $\mathcal{V} = \{a, b\}$
- $\mu = []'1$
- $\mathcal{W}_1 = a^2$
- $\mathcal{R}_1 = \{r_1 : a \rightarrow a, b; r_2 : a \rightarrow b\}$,

Then we would see the computation tree as shown in Figure 5:

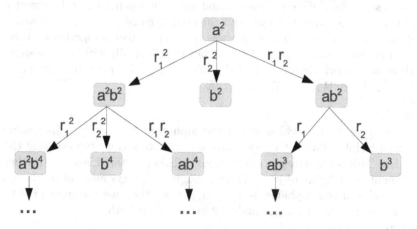

Fig. 5. A sample of a computation tree

3 Building a P System Computation Tree with Hadoop and NoSQL Database

In developing the computation three of a P system we will be using the Oracle NoSQL database and Hadoop to facilitate a massively parallel calculation of the computation tree. The use of these technologies bring several complications as to ensure all relevant steps are parallelizable, hence we have developed the following steps to calculate the computation tree.

1. Load the components $(\mathcal{V}, \mu, \mathcal{W}_n, \mathcal{R}_n)$ of the P system into the NoSQL database;
2. Calculate all possible rule combinations for each multiset at the current level of the computation tree;

3. Calculate the multisets which are produced by applying the rule sequences discovered in step 2;
4. Repeat Step 2 and 3 for subsequent levels of the computation tree;

It is important to note that we are creating the computation tree in a breath first manner, where all of the nodes for a level n are calculated before any of the nodes for level $n + 1$ are discovered.

3.1 Representing a P System as a Series of $\langle K, V \rangle$ Pairs

A $\langle K, V \rangle$ is a very simple model for storing data and there are theoretically many ways in which a P system can be represented as a series of pairs. For our implementation we focused on developing a model that is most conducive to the computation tree calculations we wanted to do. In that way there was an explicit effort in using integers to represent elements of the P system rather than strings, as integer operations are much more efficient than string operations. Further integer representations allow for matrix and vector mathematics to be directly applied during our computations without the need to consider how strings would be handled. The second design decision was to group elements together by their use within our calculations and not by how they fit in logically within a P system. Given these design principles we used the following $\langle K, V \rangle$ pairs to represent a P system $\Pi = (\mathcal{V}, \mu, \mathcal{W}_1, \ldots, \mathcal{W}_n, \mathcal{R}_1, \ldots, \mathcal{R}_n)$.

Alphabet $\mathcal{V}$

There is a single key which stores the alphabet. Its corresponding value is a Java serialized object which stores an array of strings representing the alphabet. This is the only place the actual alphabet is stored, and any further mention of an alphabet object is done through the integer index of this array. For example, if our alphabet is $\mathcal{V} = [\alpha, \beta, \gamma, \delta]$, then we use number 0 to reference α, number 1 for β, number 2 for γ and so forth.

Membrane Structure μ

The absolute membrane structure is not very interesting to our calculations, rather the children and parent membranes of each membrane is useful. In that way for each membrane there are two $\langle K, V \rangle$ pairs stored. A $\langle K, V \rangle$ to record all children of a membrane (materialized as s Java serialized array of strings) and a second $\langle K, V \rangle$ to record the parent membrane (as a simple string). Although storing both parents and children is redundant, the over-heard is minimal and it eliminates the need of searching relationship trees to discover ancestry. This is also a $\langle K, V \rangle$ pair which holds a list of all membranes IDs (without any semantic information) to enable iteration through all membranes.

Rules $\mathcal{R}$

The rules are the most performance critical element of our application as they are used in many of the calculations that are done. The rules are grouped by membrane and split by sides of the equation. The rules are stored as integer matrices where each row represents a rule and each column represents an alphabet object. For example, if we have

$$\mathcal{V} = \{a, b, c\}$$
$$\mathcal{R}_1 = a^1 c^2 \rightarrow a^2 b^1$$
$$\mathcal{R}_2 = b^2 \rightarrow a^2 c^1$$

then the first matrix will be an aggregation of the rules left sides. We call this the consumers

$$\text{consumers} = \begin{bmatrix} 1 & 0 & 2 \\ 0 & 2 & 0 \end{bmatrix}.$$

The second matrix will be an aggregation of the rules right sides. We call this the producers

$$\text{producers} = \begin{bmatrix} 2 & 1 & 0 \\ 2 & 0 & 1 \end{bmatrix}.$$

For each membrane there will be these two matrices stored as Java serialized objects of two dimensional arrays. The decision to split the rules into left side and right side was made out of the realization that these two elements will be used independently of each other. When dealing with rules which produces objects in multiple membranes we transform the matrix into a cube where the third dimension maintains a list of all relevant membranes.

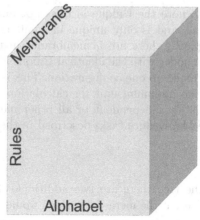

Fig. 6. Cube representation of the rules of a membrane

This storage schema assumes a dense coding of the objects and is very efficient if most of the alphabet objects are used in every rule. If there is a very sparse use of objects within rules then this coding mechanism may use excess storage.

Multisets

The multisets are stored as an array of integers, similar to the way rules are stored. The index of a multiset array corresponds to an object from the alphabet and the integers stored represents the multiplicity of that object.

3.2   Storing a Computation Tree as a Series of $\langle K, V \rangle$ Pairs

Nodes

To represent a tree as a series of $\langle K, V \rangle$ we use the smallest piece of information to store in each $\langle K, V \rangle$ pair, particularly we store the multiset of a membrane. For P systems which have multiple membranes each membrane has its own node, so a configuration of the P system is actually comprised of multiple $\langle K, V \rangle$ pairs. When storing a node of the computation tree the key under which it is stored contains a significant amount of meta-data. In defining the key we exploit the make-up of a key described in section 2.2. There are three different pieces of information stored in the key of a node.

1. The level of the computation tree this node corresponds to;
2. The membrane of the P system this node corresponds to;
3. An unique id for this particular configuration.

The first two make up the major component of the Key, while the third makes up the minor component.

Major Component: List (Level of tree , membrane number)
Minor Component: (Unique id)

It is important to note the Unique id does not uniquely identify a node in the computation tree, and is only unique in combination with the membrane number. For example, if there are 5 membranes in the P system then there should be 5 different nodes with the identical Unique id, one for each membrane, and combined they make up one configuration. This is done so each $\langle K, V \rangle$ pair in the database is the minimum unit for calculation, as the computation of a membrane is completely independent of all other membranes. This will fit in very nicely into the MapReduce tasks described in the next section.

Edges

For each node of the tree there are two additional data points stored in the database. These represent the meta-data which would normally be stored in the edges of the graph:

1. A list of all child configuration for each Unique ID,
2. A list of all rules applied on a particular evolution,

This information is stored separate to the tree nodes as it applies to multiple nodes simultaneously. Each node represents only one membrane from a configuration and it is trivial which membrane is the child of which membrane. This mapping can only be done at the configuration level as there is a directly link between the parent and child of a configuration. The same applies to storing which rules were applied to go from one configuration to another. It is very difficult to separate which rules produced all of the objects in a particular membrane given membrane communication as such, the rules applied are per configuration not per node. As described in the previous section the Unique ID identifies a configuration so it is quite easy to store a $\langle K, V \rangle$ where the key is the unique ID and the value is a Java serialized array of all the children or a list of rules applied. These two supplementary $\langle K, V \rangle$ enable the traversing of the tree in a logical way.

3.3   Determining All Possible Evolutions

One of the most critical and performance intensive aspects of developing the computation tree is discovering the possible evolutions of a configuration (particularly when dealing with a non deterministic P system). This calculation is non parallelizable and the performance of the entire system is gated on the algorithm used to discover all possible evolutions. The applicability of a rule is context dependent (dependent on the particular configuration) hence reuse of calculation is difficult, and brute force evaluation is a linear search to a potentially very large set of all possible rule combinations. In this section we have developed two algorithms, one for the general case, and one optimized for a specific case.

General Case Algorithm

To calculate all of the possible evolutions of a P system from a given configuration for the general case where there is not apriori information about the rules within a membrane we use a brute force algorithm. This algorithm goes through each of the rules and discovers the maximum number of time a particular rule can be applied in a context independent space (i.e. ignoring all other rules). Next we calculate all of the possible vectors of rules which could possibly be applied. For a Pystem where the maximum time $rule_i$ can be applied is $max(r_i)$, there should be at most $\Pi max(r_i)$ combinations. Once every possible combination is calculated each one of these vectors is tested for correctness and maximality. If they pass both criteria then they are stored in list of possible evolutions of the P system in that particular configuration. The algorithm for checking a possible vector is described next.

To describe our function we have the following definitions:

- $\mathcal{R}$ is the vector of rules in the membrane;
- $\mathcal{X}$ is the vector of rules under test;
- $\mathcal{M}$ is the configuration (multiset) of the membrane;
- $applyAllRules$ is a function which takes a vector of rules and returns the multiset resultant from applying those rules;
- $applicable$ check if rule r is applicable given the multiset s.

The algorithm is as follows:

$\mathcal{C} \leftarrow applyAllRules(\mathcal{R})$
if $\mathcal{C} = \mathcal{M}$ **then**
    return maximal

```
else
   for all  c ∈ C  do
      if |c_i| > |m_i| then
         return incorrect
      end if
   end for
   for all  r ∈ R  do
      if applicable(r, M − C) then
         return not maximal
      end if
   end for
   return maximal
end if
```

Once every possible combination of rules has been tested with this algorithm, the rules vectors (which return maximal) are the vectors which produce all possible evolutions of the P system from the specified configuration for that membrane.

Special Case Algorithm

If we impose certain restriction on the acceptable rule, new solving mechanisms for finding all possible maximal combinations of rules become available. Similar approaches have been tried by: [6].We offer the following explanation for our approach:

For M a given multiset and R a set of rules, where r_i is of the form $u \to (a_1, t_1) \dots (a_n, t_n)$ and $|r_i|$ represents the number of times a rule i is applied,

$$\forall m \in M, \Sigma |r_i| \leq |m| \tag{2}$$

where u of r_i contains m

But if

$$\forall v \in V \exists r \in R : r = v \to \alpha \tag{3}$$

where V is the alphabet of the P system and α is an arbitrary vector over V (in other words if every object in the multiset is consumed), then

$$\forall m \in M, \Sigma |r_i| = |m|. \tag{4}$$

Combine (4) with the fact that $|r_i| \in \mathbb{N}$, you get a system of linear equation which can be solved. The solutions to the system of equations represent all possible combinations of rules which satisfy the maximality requirements.

Numerical Example: If we have the following configuration:

$$V = \{a, b, c\}$$

$$\mathcal{M} = \{a^4, b^5, c^3\}$$

$$\mathcal{R} = \begin{cases} r_1 = a^1, b^1 \rightarrow \alpha \\ r_2 = a^1, c^1 \rightarrow \alpha \\ r_3 = a^1 \rightarrow \alpha \\ r_4 = b^1 \rightarrow \alpha \\ r_5 = c^1 \rightarrow \alpha \end{cases} \quad \text{where } \alpha \text{ is any arbitrary multiset over } \mathcal{V}$$

By expanding the equation (4) we get

$$\begin{cases} |r_1| + |r_2| + |r_3| = 4 \\ |r_1| + |r_4| = 5 \\ |r_2| + |r_5| = 3 \end{cases}$$

This now becomes a problem of n equations and m unknowns. In order to solve the problem we will rewrite the equations as an augmented matrix.

$$\begin{bmatrix} 1 & 1 & 1 & 0 & 0 & | & 4 \\ 1 & 0 & 0 & 1 & 0 & | & 5 \\ 0 & 1 & 0 & 0 & 1 & | & 3 \end{bmatrix}$$

If we perform Gaussian elimination on this matrix with the solution, we get

$$\begin{bmatrix} 1 & 0 & 0 & 1 & 0 & | & 5 \\ 0 & 1 & 0 & 0 & 1 & | & 3 \\ 0 & 0 & 1 & -1 & -1 & | & -4 \end{bmatrix}$$

From here we have two free variables, we will call them t_1 and t_2 and the solution is:

$$\begin{cases} r_1 = 5 - t_1 \\ r_2 = 3 - t_2 \\ r_3 = -t_1 - t_2 + 4 \\ r_4 = t_1 \\ r_5 = t_2 \end{cases}$$

which produces an infinite number of solution, but we know that $|r_i| \in \mathbb{N}$, so we can add the following restrictions on t_1 and t_2

$$\begin{cases} 0 \geq t_1 \geq 5 \\ 0 \geq t_2 \geq 3 \\ t_1 + t_2 \leq 4 \end{cases}$$

and if we plug in all acceptable values for t_1 and t_2 into the solution matrix, we get the 14 different possible evolutions of that particular configuration.

This algorithm is not exceptionally efficient as Gaussian elimination is $O(n^3)$ but as rules in a membrane do not change through the evolution of the P system we can solve the equation for a generic multiset and then simple plug in the values when calculating all possible evolutions. This will significantly reduce the amount of time required to calculate all possible evolutions.

3.4   Determining Next Level's Nodes

Once we have calculated all possible evolutions of a particular configuration of a P system, then the calculation of the next level of the computation tree is quite straight forward. We follow the steps:

1. Take one possible rule application sequence (calculated in section 4.3)
2. Given the particular input set apply the rule combination and get the output multiset
3. Take that multiset and do a cross product with the multisets of all of the other membranes available for the unique ID
4. Break up the resultant configuration and store each node in a unique key in the database
5. Repeat for all rule application sequences and possible cross products with different membranes

Following these steps we are able to compute all of the children nodes for a particular configuration of the P system.

3.5   The Map Reduce Implementation

Developing a computation tree for a P system requires the calculation of all possible evolutions of each node in the tree recursively. As each node's possible evolution is absolutely independent of another, its calculation can be performed independently and most importantly in parallel. To facilitate this parallelism we use the Map construct of the Hadoop infrastructure, as it allows us to parallelize very naturally this calculation. As the calculation of the next level's nodes requires the aggregation of multiple membrane's possible evolutions, the Reduce construct is used to perform this task. Each MapReduce cycle calculates one more level of the computation tree, and as multiple calls are made to the MapReduce infrastructure the output of one cycle becomes the input for the next cycle. In other words, the Map task implements one of the algorithms described in section 4.3 and stores the results under the Unique Id of the configuration.

The Reduce task receives all of the results from the MAP task for a particular configuration (a list who's cardinality is equal to the number of membranes in a configuration). In the Reduce task a cross product between the possible configurations of each membrane and stored the products as the nodes of the next level. For example, if we have 3 membranes and each membrane has 4 possible evolutions, then we would store 192 nodes in the computation tree (assuming all of the configurations produce objects in all of the membranes). The cross product of all of the possible evolutions is $4 \times 4 \times 4$ which is 64. Each of those configuration has objects in all three membranes, but in the computation tree a node only represents one membrane, hence for each configuration there will be 3 nodes stored in the database; therefore $64 \times 3 = 192$ nodes stored.

4   Experimental Results

We developed several P systems of varied size to determine the time required to generate a computation three of n levels for a particular P system. We also vary the number of servers in the cluster to be able to get an idea of scaling possibilities. The cluster was composed of 16 servers each with a single core 2 duo processor 4 GB of Ram and a single hard disk on a SATA bus. It is important to note a single server in a modern Hadoop cluster can be more power than the sum of the 16 machines we used, as such the following results need to be taken within that context. Most of the 16 nodes were configured identically with on server dedicated to administrating the Hadoop cluster and another for the NoSQL database. These two services (Haddop MapReduce server and NoSQL storage server) run concurrently on the same physical machines with on core for each process.

4.1   Testing Different Algorithms

We experimented with the different algorithms described in section 4.3 to notice the performance difference between the algorithms. The experiment tried to find all of the possible evolutions of a single membrane given a different number of rules. The multiset used for each experiment was a vector with one of each element in the alphabet ($\mathcal{V}$). This experiment was performed on a single machine. These are the results:

Number Of Rules	Time for General Case (ms)	Time for Equation Solving (ms)
10	15	86
20	1146	188
30	1915509	891
40	8hrs +	30444
50	???	7808309 (2.16 hrs)

To understand the results there are a couple of practical notes to consider for the Equation Solving algorithm.

1. The calculation of the reduced row echelon form matrix was not taken into consideration for the total execution time, since it is calculated only once at

the loading of the P system into the database, hence not relevant in repeated executions.

2. Although the example in section 3.3 showed lower and upper bounds for each free variable more complex execution usually only provide lower bounds for the free variables. As such it required the calculation of theoretical upper bounds, and then doing a linear search through all combinations of free variables to check if the comply with restrictions imposed by the equations in the reduced matrix.

3. The use of the Equation Solving algorithm has a static set-up time which is why for small search sets the General Case algorithm is more efficient as there is no set-up required for that algorithm.

4.2   Testing Number of Nodes

We used some P systems with varying number of rules to test how many nodes we could store in the database and how much space would be required. All experiments were performed with simple mirroring of data across the cluster.

Our first test used a simple P system with 4 membranes, 3 objects and 5 rules per membrane. This P system had a high number of possible evolutions per membrane. Our experiment of running this P system had:

Number Of Nodes	Storage Space	Execution time
65471486	84.9 GB	16.54 hrs

This experiment did not finished as Hadoop time-out start to disrupt the execution.

We did run the computation again without clearing the database to see if more nodes could be stored. The results were:

Number Of Nodes	Storage Space	Execution time
77186334	105.4 GB	5.52 hrs

This execution was exited by the system due to database issues. The Oracle NoSQL Database caches the keys in memory for single IO retrieval when accessed, and some of the servers running the database ran out of memory. This forced the keys to be cached on the hard disk, significantly reducing performance and timing out the database.

We also used a much larger P system with 5 membranes, 10 objects and 30 rules per membrane and the following results were achieved:

Number Of Nodes	Storage Space	Execution time
40445334	90 GB	10.52 hrs

This execution also timed out due to system resource limitations.

These experiments were designed to show the size of the computation trees which could be stored in the database. The number of nodes stored is not the total number of nodes which exist in the computation tree but the number of nodes store before system stability issues interfered. We can extract from those results we have about 770 thousand nodes per gigabyte, and 450 thousand nodes per gigabyte for the respective P systems. The storage requirements do not grow perfectly proportionally with the number of objects in the multiset as metadata describing the edges of the tree is also stored in the database which is not affected by the alphabet size.

4.3   Testing with Different Numbers of Servers

We will also vary the cluster size from 2 to 16 servers with the same P system to test the scaling factor use a P system of 3 membranes 10 objects and 25 rules per membrane. We observed the following results:

Tree Level	Number Of Nodes	2 Servers	4 Servers	8 Servers	16 Servers
1	18411	2m 51s	1m 22s	1m 43s	1m 18s
2	1438047	55m 34s	24m 12s	12m 44s	7m 56s

This experiment really demonstrates the scaling factor of Hadoop where doubling the number of nodes effectively doubles the performance of the application. The results of the experiments were significant despite the cluster being composed of low power machines. Hadoop clusters have scaled to thousands of servers where each server was significantly more powerful than the machines used for these tests. This experiment also shows the potential variance of the system. The first line of the table required to derivation of a single node (the root node) hence no parallelism was possible. All results for the first derivation should be the same as the number of servers does not matter for a non parallelisable task. The variance in the numbers is because of unpredictable elements in the Hadoop infrastructure.

4.4   Variance in Results

Hadoop (as an infrastructure) is designed for large scale deployment of a distributed system (100 - 1000 of servers), and there is a high potential for server failure, server slowdowns, and data loss, situations which Hadoop is designed to deal with. These include data replication across servers (to deal with server loss) and speculative execution to deal with individual server performance issues. As exact execution path are both unpredictable, the timing results provided in this article come with a potential error factor. Repeated experiments will produce the same results but with different execution times, although these deltas are usually within an acceptable margin.

5   Practical Uses

To demonstrate a practical use of this application we developed a tool which would perform (Context Dependent Rule Coverage) CDRC test oracle discovery using the computation tree stored on the database. CDRC is a testing strategy where all possible sequences of 2 rules which can sequentially occur during the simulation of a Psystem are tested. For more details on CDRC please see article [5] . The process of discovering tree walks, which cover context dependent rules, is as followed:

1. Go through all of the rules and discover the CDRC rule pairs. Store these inside the NoSQL database.
2. Run a Map task which take as input a unique configuration at a specific level of the computation, the goes through all children nodes of that configuration and tests the applied rules of the two steps.
3. Each evolution of the P system (which covers a CDRC rule pair) is stored and the CDRC pair is removed from the database as it is discovered.

6   Conclusion

In this article we have shown how big data technologies can be used to massively extend the reach of our P system simulators and calculators. The use of these technologies constituted several conceptual elements:

1. The use of a NoSQL database to store the computation tree of a P system.
2. The use of a Hadoop Map task to compute all possible evolutions of a membrane.
3. Two different algorithms which can be used to compute the possible evolutions of a membrane.
4. The use of a Hadoop Reduce task to simulate membrane communication with the context of developing a computation tree.
5. The implementation of this code which scale to computing and storing millions of nodes of a computation tree within a distributed storage to allow sub second access to the data even on low grade hardware.
6. The explanation and implementation of a possible use of the computation tree in Context Dependent Rule Coverage testing.

We can now extend the use of Hadoop and NoSQL to empower P system to simulate real world problems and possibly find solutions as we now have a viable strategy for potentially unlimited scaling.

Further work will now be performed to extend the application both from a technology perspective and a P system perspective. We will extend the technology to allow for other NoSQL database to underpin the system as to allow for the use of server rental services. We will also try the extend in the type of Psystem which can be simulated including conditional rules. We will also look at using this technology for different practical purposes including different testing strategies.

In working with the current code base we will try to extend the existing code in several ways. We will try to use theories from numerical computing to find better implementations for generating all possible evolutions, as well as try to implement that particular component using GPU or APU computation to accelerate execution time. As an extension of that idea, the Hadoop core libraries will be extended to allow for mixed software hardware simulators to function as a system. Lastly, to reduce the number of nodes in the tree we will use graph theory to find loops and use pointer references rather then expand those branches. That would aid in both reducing the number of nodes and the complexity of walking the tree. Potentially, we will also look at implementing algorithms which find patterns in the graph as to further reduce the number of nodes and the computation load.

For access to the source code for this application go to GitHub at URL: https://github.com/alexciobanu/psystem

Acknowledgments. We would like to thank Cristi Stefan of University of Pitesti who has enabled all of the experiments done in the development of this code. He worked tirelessly to maintain the equipment and ensure it was available for experimentation.

This work was partially supported by a grant of the Romanian National Authority for Scientific Research, CNCS–UEFISCDI, project number PN-II-ID-PCE-2011-3-0688. We are indebted to the anonymous reviewers for their valuable comments and suggestions

References

1. Păun, G.: Computing with membranes. Journal of Computer and System Sciences 61(1), 108–143 (2000)
2. Păun, G., Rozenberg, G., Salomaa, A.: The Oxford Handbook of Membrane Computing. Oxford University Press (2010)
3. Dean, J., Ghemawat, S.: MapReduce: Simplified Data Processing on Large Clusters. In: Sixth Symposium on Operating System Design and Implementation (2004)
4. Chang, F., Dean, J., Ghemawat, S., Hsieh, W.C., Wallach, D.A., Burrows, M., Chandra, T., Fikes, A., Bigtable, R.E.G.: A Distributed Storage System for Structured Data. In: Seventh Symposium on Operating System Design and Implementation (2006)
5. Lefticaru, R., Ipate, F., Gheorghe, M.: Model checking based test generation from P systems using P-lingua. Romanian Journal of Information Science and Technology 13(2), 153–168 (2010); special issue on membrane computing containing selected papers from BWMC (2010)
6. Juayong, R.A.B., Cabarle, F.G.C., Adorna, H.N., Martinez-del-Amor, M.A.: On the Simulations of Evolution-Communication P Systems with Energy without Antiport Rules for GPUs. In: 10th Brainstorming Week on Membrane Computing Proceeding, pp. 267–289 (2012)
7. Diez Dolinski, L., Núñez Hervás, R., Cruz Echeandía, M., Ortega, A.: Distributed Simulation of P Systems by Means of Map-Reduce: First Steps with Hadoop and P-Lingua. In: Cabestany, J., Rojas, I., Joya, G. (eds.) IWANN 2011, Part I. LNCS, vol. 6691, pp. 457–464. Springer, Heidelberg (2011)
8. Amor, M.A.M.: Accelerating Membrane Systems Simulators using High Performance Computing with GPU. PHD thesis University of Seville (2013)
9. http://docs.oracle.com/cd/NOSQL/html/index.html (visited May 10, 2013)
10. http://www.p-lingua.org (visited May 10, 2013)

On Counter Machines versus dP Automata[*]

Erzsébet Csuhaj-Varjú[1] and György Vaszil[2]

[1] Department of Algorithms and Their Applications, Faculty of Informatics
Eötvös Loránd University
Pázmány Péter sétány 1/c, 1117 Budapest, Hungary
csuhaj@inf.elte.hu
[2] Department of Computer Science, Faculty of Informatics
University of Debrecen
P.O. Box 12, 4010 Debrecen, Hungary
vaszil.gyorgy@inf.unideb.hu

Abstract. Continuing the study of connections between classical and P automata variants, we show that dP automata, i.e., distributed systems of P automata, where the input multiset is mapped to the set of strings consisting of all permutations of its elements, are as powerful as the class of distributed systems of special counter machine acceptors. These variants of counter machines read multisets (represented as sets of all permutations of their elements) and manipulate counters in a conventional manner.

1 Introduction

P automata are purely communicating P systems accepting strings in an automaton-like fashion. In the standard case they are based on antiport systems with promoters or inhibitors. The concept was introduced in [3,4]; for a summary on P automata the interested reader is referred to Chapter 6, [13]. Elements of the language (over some alphabet) of a P automaton are obtained by some mapping of the multiset sequences which enter the system through the skin membrane during an accepting computation.

Studying simple, non-erasing mappings, it was shown that if the rules of the P automaton are applied sequentially, then the accepted language class is strictly included in the class of languages accepted by one-way Turing machines with a logarithmically bounded workspace (1LOGSPACE), or if the rules are applied in the maximally parallel manner, then the class of context-sensitive languages is obtained [1].

If the input mapping is defined in such a way that it maps a multiset to the set of strings consisting of all permutations of its elements (we denote this mapping by f_{perm}), then a class of languages is obtained which is strictly included in the class of languages of so-called *restricted logarithmic space Turing machines*

---

[*] Supported in part by the Hungarian Scientific Research Fund, "OTKA", grant no. K75952, and by the European Union through the TÁMOP-4.2.2.C-11/1/KONV-2012-0001 project which is co-financed by the European Social Fund.

(r1LOGSPACE) [6]. (In the case of restricted logarithmic space Turing machines, the actual workspace available for a computation is dynamically changing: it is in logarithmic accordance with the length of the already consumed input, and not with the total input length.) To prove the statement, special variants of counter machines, called RCMA (restricted counter machine acceptors) and SRCMA (special restricted counter machine acceptors) were introduced in [6]. These counter machines manipulate their counters in a restricted, but more or less conventional manner, but unlike ordinary counter automata, they are able to read several input symbols in a single computational step.

Motivated by communication complexity questions, the notion of a distributed P automaton (a dP automaton, in short) was introduced in [12]. Such a system consists of a finite number of component P automata which have their separate inputs and which may communicate with each other by means of special antiport-like rules. A string accepted by a dP automaton is defined as the concatenation of the strings accepted by the individual components during a computation performed by the system [12]. The generic variant of dP automata uses the mapping f_{perm} to define its language, that is, a string accepted by a component P automaton is the concatenation of strings which are permutations of the objects of the multisets imported by the skin membrane during an accepting computation; all combinations are considered.

In the last few years, dP automata were studied in detail (see, for example [12], [8], [14], and [15,16]). It was shown that using the mapping f_{perm}, dP automata are strictly more powerful than P automata (with f_{perm}), but the language family accepted by them is strictly included in the family of context-sensitive languages. Investigations have also been made with the aim of comparing P and dP automata classes to classical or well-known classes of acceptors. Connections between dP automata and multi-head finite automata were studied in [5], based on the concepts of agreement languages of dP automata and the notion of a two-way dP automaton. In [5], it was shown how the languages of non-deterministic one-way and two-way multi-head finite automata can be obtained as the agreement languages of one-way and two-way finite dP automata. (A dP automaton is finite if the number of its configurations is a finite number.)

Continuing this line of research, in this paper we show that the classes of concatenated and agreement languages of dP automata with mapping f_{perm} and working in the nondeterministic maximally parallel mode, are equal to the classes of concatenated and agreement languages of distributed systems of special restricted counter machine acceptors.

2   Preliminaries and Definitions

We assume the reader to be familiar with the basics of formal language theory and membrane computing; for details consult [18] and [13].

An alphabet is a finite non-empty set of symbols. For an alphabet V, we denote by V^* the set of all strings over V; if the empty string, λ, is not included, then we use notation V^+. The length of a string $x \in V^*$ is denoted by $|x|$. For any symbol $a \in V$, $|x|_a$ denotes the number of occurrences of the symbol a in x; and for any set of symbols $A \subseteq V$, the number of occurrences of symbols from A in x is denoted by $|x|_A$.

A finite multiset over an alphabet V is a mapping $M : V \to \mathbb{N}$ where $\mathbb{N}$ denotes the set of non-negative integers; $M(a)$ is said to be the multiplicity of a in M. The set of all finite multisets over an alphabet V is denoted by V°, and we use the notation $V^\oplus$ for denoting the set of nonempty (finite) multisets. A multiset M can be represented by any permutation of the string $w = a_1^{M(a_1)} a_2^{M(a_2)} \ldots a_n^{M(a_n)} \in V^*$, where $V = \{a_1, \ldots, a_n\}$. The empty multiset is denoted by λ as in the case of the empty string. If confusion may arise, we make explicit whether we speak of a string or a multiset.

We denote by f_{perm} the mapping which maps a multiset M over V to the set of its string representations, that is, $f_{perm} : V^\circ \to 2^{V^*}$ where $V = \{a_1, \ldots, a_n\}$, and

$$f_{perm}(M) = \{w' \in V^* \mid w' \text{ is a permutation of the}$$
$$\text{string } a_1^{M(a_1)} a_2^{M(a_2)} \ldots a_n^{M(a_n)}\}.$$

A P system (or a membrane system) is a structure of hierarchically embedded membranes (a rooted tree), each membrane (node) having a unique label and enclosing a region containing a multiset of objects. The outermost membrane (the root of the tree), called the skin membrane, is unique and usually labeled with 1. Each region (membrane) is associated with a set of rules over multisets of objects which are used for changing the configuration of the P system.

An antiport rule is of the form $(u, in; v, out)$, $u, v \in V^\circ$ for a finite set of objects V. If such a rule is applied in a region, then the objects of u enter from the parent region and in the same step, objects of v leave to the parent region. If only (u, in) or (u, out) is indicated, then we speak of symport rules. (Note that the meaning of the "in" tag in these rules is different from the meaning of the target indicator "in" in the rules of type $u \to (v, in)$ used in other types of P systems.) Antiport rules can be associated with promoter or inhibitor multisets of objects, denoted by $(u, in; v, out)|_z$, or $(u, in; v, out)|_{\bar{z}}$, $z \in V^\circ$. In the first case the rule can only be applied if the objects of the promoter multiset z are all present in the given region, in the second case, the rule can be applied if no element of z is present. Analogously, promoters or inhibitors can be added to symport rules as well. The environment of the P system is supposed to contain an unlimited supply of objects, thus if an antiport rule (with promoters or inhibitors) is to be applied in the skin region, then the requested multiset is always available to enter the system.

A P automaton (of degree k) is a membrane system $\Pi = (V, \mu, w_1, \ldots, w_k, P_1, \ldots, P_k)$ with object alphabet V, membrane structure μ, initial contents (multisets) of the ith region $w_i \in V^\circ$, $1 \le i \le k$, and sets of antiport rules with promoters or inhibitors P_i, $1 \le i \le k$. Furthermore, P_1 must not contain any rule of the form (u, in) (neither $(u, in)|_z$ or $(u, in)|_{\bar{z}}$), $u \in V^\circ$.

The configurations of the P automaton (the actual k-tuple of multisets of objects over V in the regions) can be changed by transitions. The transition is performed by applying rules according to the working mode of the P automaton. For simplicity, we consider only the non-deterministic maximally parallel (working) mode, where as many rules are applied simultaneously in the regions at the same step as possible (this is why we exclude symport rules which only import objects to the skin region from the environment). Thus, a transition in the P automaton Π is $(v_1, \ldots, v_k) \in \delta_\Pi(u_0, u_1, \ldots, u_k)$, where δ_Π denotes the transition relation defined implicitly by the rules and the working mode of Π, $u_1, \ldots, u_k$ are the contents of the k regions, u_0 is the multiset entering the system from the environment, and $v_1, \ldots, v_k$, respectively, are the contents of the k regions after performing the transition. A sequence of transitions starting from the initial configuration $(w_1, \ldots, w_k)$ is a computation.

In this way, there is a sequence of multisets which enter the system from the environment during the steps of any computation. If the computation is accepting, that is, if it enters an accepting configuration, then this multiset sequence is called an accepted multiset sequence. Here we consider a configuration accepting, if and only if it is halting, that is, if no rule can be applied in any of the regions of the system.

From any accepted sequence of multisets over V, a string of the accepted language, that is, a string over some alphabet Σ is obtained by the application of a mapping $f : V^\circ \to 2^{\Sigma^*}$, mapping each multiset to a finite set of strings.

Let Π be a P automaton as above, and let f be a mapping $f : V^\circ \to 2^{\Sigma^*}$ for some finite alphabet Σ. The *language* over Σ accepted by Π with respect to f is defined as

$$L(\Pi, f, \Sigma) = \{f(v_1) \ldots f(v_s) \in \Sigma^* \mid v_1, \ldots, v_s \text{ is an accepted}$$
$$\text{multiset sequence of } \Pi\}.$$

In [8] the authors consider P automata with f_{perm}. Since in this case Σ does not differ from V, we denote the accepted language by $L(\Pi, f_{perm})$. The class of languages accepted by P automata defined by mapping f_{perm} is denoted by $\mathcal{L}(PA, f_{perm})$. We note that the first appearance of f_{perm} is in [7], where the so-called analyzing P system, a closely related concept to the P automaton was introduced, almost at the same time as [3].

A finite collection of P automata forms a distributed P automaton, a dP automaton, in short, introduced in [12]. A *dP automaton* (of degree $n \geq 1$) is a construct $\Delta = (V, \Pi_1, \ldots, \Pi_n, R)$, where V is the alphabet of objects; $\Pi_i = (V, \mu_i, w_{i,1}, \ldots, w_{i,k}, P_{i,1}, \ldots, P_{i,k_i})$ is a P automaton of degree $k_i \geq 1$, $1 \leq i \leq n$, called the ith component of the system; R is a finite set of rules of the form $z_i|(s_i, u/v, s_j)|_{z_j}$, $1 \leq i, j \leq n$, $i \neq j$, $uv \in V^\oplus$, called the set of inter-component communication (shortly, communication) rules of Δ; s_l, $1 \leq l \leq n$ denotes the skin membrane of Π_l. The multisets z_i, z_j are promoters (or inhibitors) associated to the rule which can be applied if region s_i and s_j contain (or do not contain) the elements of the multisets z_i, z_j, respectively.

We say that Δ accepts an n-tuple of multiset sequences over V, denoted by $(\alpha_1, \ldots, \alpha_n)$, if the component Π_i, starting from its initial configuration, using the symport/antiport rules (with promoters or inhibitors) as well as the inter-component communication rules in the non-deterministic maximally parallel way, takes from the environment the multiset sequence $\alpha_i = v_{i,1} \ldots v_{i,s_i}$, $v_{i,j} \in V^\circ$, $1 \leq j \leq s_i$, $1 \leq i \leq n$, and Δ eventually halts, i.e., enters an accepting configuration.

Analogously to standard (non-distributed) P automata, we may associate a language to a dP automaton by using a mapping from the object multisets to an alphabet of symbols. In this paper we study systems with the mapping f_{perm}, see above. We note that in [3] the mapping to define the alphabet of the language of the dP automaton was considered in a more general manner.

The *(concatenated) language* of Δ (introduced in [12]) with respect to the mapping f_{perm}, is defined as

$$L_{concat}(\Delta, f_{perm}) = \{w_1 \ldots w_n \in V^* \mid w_i \in f_{perm}(v_{i,1}) \ldots f_{perm}(v_{i,s_i}) \text{ and}$$
$$\alpha_i = v_{i,1} \ldots v_{i,s_i}, \ 1 \leq i \leq n, \text{ for an } n\text{-tuple of}$$
$$\text{accepted multiset sequences } (\alpha_1, \ldots, \alpha_n)\}.$$

In [5] two variants of languages based on agreement of the components were introduced, namely, the weak and strong agreement languages. The strong agreement language consists of all words which can be accepted in such a way that all components accept the same sequence of multisets. In weak agreement languages, however, the accepted multiset sequences can be different, only the equality of the images of all accepted multiset sequences is required. Note that in the special case of f_{perm}, the two types of agreement languages coincide, since in general (considering multisets from V° containing at least two different symbols $a, b \in V$), the sets of words obtained as the images of two multiset sequences under the permutation mapping are equal only if the multiset sequences themselves are also equal. Thus, to obtain a "weaker" requirement, similarly to the weak agreement languages for more general input mappings in [5], we will use here a variant of the notion defined as follows.

The *(weak) agreement language* with respect to the mapping f_{perm} is defined as

$$L_{agree}(\Delta, f_{perm}) = \{w \in V^* \mid w \in f_{perm}(v_{i,1}) \ldots f_{perm}(v_{i,s_i}) \text{ for all } 1 \leq i \leq n,$$
$$\text{where } \alpha_i = v_{i,1} \ldots v_{i,s_i}, \ 1 \leq i \leq n,$$
$$\text{and } (\alpha_1, \ldots, \alpha_n) \text{ is an } n\text{-tuple of accepted multiset}$$
$$\text{sequences of } \Delta\}.$$

In the case of $L_{concat}(\Delta, f_{perm})$, the words accepted by the components are concatenated to obtain the words of the language accepted by the dP automaton. In the case of the agreement language $L_{agree}(\Delta, f_{perm})$, those words are accepted by the dP automaton which can be obtained as the image of the accepted multiset sequence of all of the components.

The classes of concatenated and weak agreement languages accepted by dP automata using the mapping f_{perm} are denoted by $\mathcal{L}_{concat}(dPA, f_{perm})$ and $\mathcal{L}_{agree}(dPA, f_{perm})$.

Example 1. Let Δ be a dP automaton $\Delta = (\{a, b, c, d\}, \Pi_1, \Pi_2, \emptyset)$ with $\Pi_i = (\{a, b, c, d\}, [\,]_1, d, P_i)$, $1 \leq i \leq 2$, where $P_1 = \{(ab, in; d, out), (c, in; a, out)\}$, $P_2 = \{(a, in; d, out), (bc, in; a, out)\}$.

This simple example system Δ has only one computation where Π_1 and Π_2 accept the following sequences of two multisets: In the sequence accepted by Π_1, the first multiset contains a symbol a and a symbol b, the second contains a symbol c. In the sequence accepted by Π_2, the first multiset contains a symbol a, the second contains a symbol b and a symbol c. Thus, Δ accepts the pair of sequences of multisets $(\{a, b\}\{c\}, \{a\}\{b, c\})$. (We enumerated the elements between curly brackets, as in the usual set notation.)

Then, the concatenated language of Δ is $L_{concat}(\Delta, f_{perm}) = \{abcabc, bacabc, abcacb, bacacb\}$, while the agreement language is $L_{agree}(\Delta, f_{perm}) = \{abc\}$.

In the following we recall some notions concerning complexity classes used to characterize classes of languages accepted by P automata. We start with a notion from [1].

A nondeterministic Turing machine with a one-way input tape is *restricted logarithmic space bounded* if for every accepted input of length n, there is an accepting computation where the number of nonempty cells on the work-tape(s) is bounded by $O(\log d)$ where $d \leq n$ is the number of input tape cells already read, that is, the *distance* of the reading head from the left end of the one-way input tape. The class of languages accepted by such machines is denoted by r1LOGSPACE.

Motivated by restricted logarithmic space bounded Turing machines and P automata, the following two variants of counter machines were introduced in [6]: A *restricted k-counter machine acceptor* M, an RCMA in short, is a (nondeterministic) counter machine with k counters (holding non-negative integers) and a one-way read only input tape. Thus, $M = (Q, \Sigma, k, \delta, q_0, F)$ for some $k \geq 1$, where Q is the set of internal states, Σ is the input alphabet, $q_0 \in Q$ is the initial state, $F \subseteq Q$ is the set of final states, and $\delta : Q \times \Sigma^* \times C^k \to 2^{Q \times D^k}$ is the transition relation, where $C = \{zero, nonzero\}$, denoting the two types of observations the machine can make on its counters, $D = \{increment, decrement, none\}$ denoting the operations the machine can execute on its counters. Note that δ is finitely defined, that is, defined for a finite subset of Σ^*, and a counter can be incremented/decremented by one at any computational step. Moreover,

(a) the transition relation is defined in such a way that the reading head is able to read a finite multiset of symbols in one computational step in the following sense: $\delta(q, x, \alpha) = \delta(q, y, \alpha)$ for each $x, y \in \Sigma^*$ which represent the same multiset, that is, when $x, y \in f_{perm}(M)$ for some $M \in \Sigma^\circ$. Moreover,

(b) the sum of the values stored in the counters can only increase as much in one computational step as the number of symbols read in that same step, that is, for all $(q', \beta) \in \delta(q, x, \alpha)$ we have $|\beta|_{increment} - |\beta|_{decrement} \leq |x|$.

A *special restricted k-counter machine acceptor*, an SRCMA in short, is a restricted k-counter machine acceptor $M = (Q, \Sigma, k, \delta, q_0, F)$, but in addition, the transition relation δ is defined in such a way, that if the length of the string

x read in one computational step is l, then the sum of the values stored in the counters can only increase at most as much as $l - 1$ in the same computational step. Thus, instead of point (b) of the above definition, we have

(b') for all $(q', \beta) \in \delta(q, x, \alpha)$, we have $|\beta|_{increment} - |\beta|_{decrement} \le |x| - 1$.

The classes of languages accepted by RCMA and SRCMA are denoted by $\mathcal{L}(\text{RCMA})$ and $\mathcal{L}(\text{SRCMA})$, respectively.

3 Distributed Systems of Counter Machine Acceptors and dP Automata

A *distributed system of special restricted counter machine acceptors*, a dSRCMA in short, is a system $\mathcal{M} = (\Sigma, M_1, \ldots, M_n, \delta_\mathcal{M})$ for some $n \ge 1$, where Σ is an alphabet, $M_i = (Q_i, \Sigma, k, \delta_i, q_{i,0}, F_i)$ for $1 \le i \le n$ are SRCMA, the components of the system, and $\delta_\mathcal{M}$ is the communication relation, where if we denote $Q = \bigcup_{i=1}^n Q_i$, then $\delta_\mathcal{M} : (Q \times C^k)^2 \to 2^{(Q \times D^k)^2}$ and, as above, $C = \{zero, nonzero\}$, $D = \{increment, decrement, none\}$. The relation $\delta_\mathcal{M}$ is defined in such a way that the sum of the counter contents cannot increase during a communication step.

When a dSRCMA works, each component processes its own input in a parallel and synchronized manner. The components may use their own transition relations δ_i, $1 \le i \le n$, or when appropriate, they may communicate as described by $\delta_\mathcal{M}$. The relation $\delta_\mathcal{M}$ governs the communication of the components as follows. Let us assume that M_{i_1} and M_{i_2} for some $1 \le i_1, i_2 \le n$ are in the configurations (q_1, α_1) and (q_2, α_2), $q_1 \in Q_{i_1}, q_2 \in Q_{i_2}$, and $\alpha_i \in C^k, 1 \le i \le 2$, respectively. Now, if $(q_1', \beta_1, q_2', \beta_2) \in \delta_\mathcal{M}(q_1, \alpha_1, q_2, \alpha_2)$, then the components change their internal states to q_1' and q_2', and update their counter contents according to $\beta_i \in D^k$, $1 \le i \le 2$, respectively. Note that it is required that $|\beta_1\beta_2|_{increment} \le |\beta_1\beta_2|_{decrement}$.

Let $(w_1, \ldots, w_n)$ be the n-tuple of words accepted by the components of the dSRCMA system $\mathcal{M}$. The *concatenated language* and the *agreement language* of $\mathcal{M}$ are defined as

$$L_{concat}(\mathcal{M}) = \{w_1 \ldots w_n \in \Sigma^* \mid (w_1, \ldots, w_n) \text{ is an accepted}$$
$$n\text{-tuple of words of } \mathcal{M}\},$$

and

$$L_{agree}(\mathcal{M}) = \{w \in \Sigma^* \mid (w, \ldots, w) \text{ is an accepted}$$
$$n\text{-tuple of words of } \mathcal{M}\}.$$

The classes of concatenated languages and agreement languages accepted by dSRCMA systems are denoted by $\mathcal{L}_X(\text{dSRCMA})$ for $X \in \{concat, agree\}$.

Now we are going to show that dSRCMA systems and dP automata characterize the same class of languages.

Lemma 1. $\mathcal{L}_X(\text{dPA}, f_{perm}) \subseteq \mathcal{L}_X(\text{dSRCMA})$ *for any* $X \in \{concat, agree\}$.

Proof. Let $L = L_X(\Delta, f_{perm})$, for $X \in \{concat, agree\}$, and let Δ be the dP automaton $\Delta = (\Sigma, \Pi_1, \ldots, \Pi_n, R)$, $\Pi_i = (\Sigma, \mu_i, w_{i,1}, \ldots, w_{i,m_i}, P_{i,1}, \ldots, P_{i,m_i})$, for $1 \le i \le n$. We construct a dSRCMA system $\mathcal{M} = (\Sigma, M_1, \ldots, M_n, \delta_\mathcal{M})$ such that $L = L_X(\mathcal{M})$.

The components $M_i = (Q_i, \Sigma, k, \delta_i, q_{i,ini}, F_i)$ of $\mathcal{M}$ are able to simulate the computations of the components of Δ by keeping track of the number of different objects in the different regions of Π_i, $1 \le i \le n$. Each M_i has three counters for each symbol-region pair (a, j), $a \in \Sigma$, $1 \le j \le m_i$, these are called storage counters, temporary counters, and assistant counters; three additional counters for each symbol-component pair (a, j), $a \in \Sigma$, $1 \le i \le n$, plus three additional ones for each symbol and the environment, these are called output counters, input$_1$ counters, input$_2$ counters. In addition, M_i has d_i additional counters called input assistant counters where d_i is the maximal number of objects which can enter the skin membrane of Π_i from the environment or from another component by the application of one antiport rule, that is, $d_i = \max(\{|v| \mid (u, out; v, in)|_z \in P_{i,1}\} \cup \{|v| \mid z_i|((i,1), u/v, (j,1))|_{z_j} \in R, 1 \le j \le n\})$. Apart from these, the components may need a number of assistant counters in order to be able to perform basic arithmetic operations and to check the equality of counter values during the computation. In order to have an equal number of counters in each component, we can take the maximum of the sum of the values defined above as the number k of counters in any component. These counters are initially empty, so the numbers of different objects in different regions in the initial configuration of M_i must be stored in the internal states of the components given in Q_i. Such a state can be written as $q_{i,j} = (q'_{i,j}, c_{i,1}, \ldots, c_{i,k}) \in Q_i = Q'_i \times \mathbb{N}^k$ for some set of symbols denoted by Q'_i.

The simulation of a computational step $(v_1, \ldots, v_{m_i}) \in \delta_{\Pi_i}(u_0, u_1, \ldots, u_{m_i})$ of Π_i by M_i can be described as follows. First M_i nondeterministically chooses symport/antiport rules (with promoters or inhibitors) from the sets $P_{i,j}$, $1 \le j \le m_i$, of Π_i or from the communication rules in R, then updates the counters which keep track of the configuration of Π_i according to the chosen rules. The storage counters corresponding to the region and the objects which leave the region are decremented with the necessary amount of objects, and the number of objects entering the region are added to the corresponding temporary counters. If objects are exchanged between the skin regions of different components by the use of a communication rule of R, then the dSRCMA system also uses a communicating transition (described by $\delta_\mathcal{M}$) to increase the temporary counters corresponding to the exchanged symbols and the skin regions of the two components. If an object leaves to the environment from the skin region of Π_i, then the corresponding output counter of M_i is incremented.

(We would like to note that the "counter components" $(c_1, \ldots, c_k)$ of the internal states $(q, c_1, \ldots, c_k) \in Q = \bigcup_{i=1}^n Q_i$ are also taken into account: their value and the value of the corresponding "real" counter together represent the numbers of various objects in the regions of Δ. When such an "internal counter" is decremented, then the increment of the necessary temporary counter also takes place in the corresponding "internal" version of that counter. This way this nondeterministic rule choosing and configuration modifying phase of the computations of the components of the dSRCMA $\mathcal{M}$ do not increase the overall sum of the values stored in the different counters.)

When this phase is finished, $\mathcal{M}$ checks whether the configuration change implied by the rules chosen above corresponds to the maximally parallel mode of rule application. This means that each M_i, $1 \leq i \leq n$, must check the applicability of rules in each region, which can be done one by one, using the corresponding assistant counters to store the numbers which are subtracted from various counters during the process in order to be able to easily restore the original configuration when the checking of the applicability of a rule fails. The check also includes the skin regions, to make sure that the multisets leaving to the environment are also maximal.

After the checking of the maximality of the chosen rule set, $\mathcal{M}$ realizes the configuration change by updating the storage counters using the values from the temporary counters, and by simulating the entering of objects from the environment (corresponding to the ones that leave the skin region), which can be done as follows. The number and type of objects which are supposed to leave to the environment are recorded in the output counters of the component. First components M_i of $\mathcal{M}$, $1 \leq i \leq n$, choose antiport rules $(u, out; v, in)|_z \in P_{i,1}$ and decrement the output counters corresponding to the objects of u while incrementing their input assistant counters. Now M_i reads $|v|$ symbols from its input tape, and records them in the $input_1$ counters, and also records the symbols of v (from the chosen antiport rule) in the $input_2$ counters. This process can be repeated a number of times, and when it is finished, the component M_i simulated the entering of objects into the skin region of Π_i from the environment, if two conditions are satisfied: first, the output counters should be empty, and second, each $input_1$ and $input_2$ counter corresponding to the same symbol should hold the same value. The second requirement corresponds to the fact that the same multiset of objects was read from the tape of M_i (although, possibly in a different order) as can be imported from the environment into the skin membrane of Π_i using the antiport rules that were chosen previously by M_i.

After completing this phase of the computation, $\mathcal{M}$ can start the simulation of the next computational step of Π in the same way as described above. Before continuing with the simulation, $\mathcal{M}$ can check whether the current configuration is final or not, and decide to proceed or to stop accordingly. (A configuration is final if it is halting, thus, if no rule can be applied in any of the regions.)

Note that the input reading operations do not violate the requirement that the sum of the numbers stored in the counters of a dSRCMA component M_i can only increase in a computational step as much as $c_i - 1$, where c_i is the number of symbols read in that step by M_i. This holds because if some objects enter a component Π_i of the simulated system Δ, then at least one object also leaves this component. Therefore, during the simulation at least one symbol left the simulated system, thus, at least once one of the output counters were decremented, and at the same time, one of the input assistant counters was incremented. This means that while decrementing the input assistant counter, it is possible to increment the $input_1$ and $input_2$ counters altogether by the value of $|v|$, where v is the multiset entering the component Π_i of the simulated system. This is sufficient, because we can store any value $c = 2 \cdot j + l$, $l \in \{0,1\}$ by storing j in the counter and keeping track of l in the state of the finite control, thus, by increasing the sum of the overall counter contents by $|v|$, we can store two numbers which are both less or equal to $|v|$.

We have seen that the words obtained by permuting the elements of the multisets in the multiset sequences accepted by the components of the dP automaton Π coincides with the words which can be accepted by the components of the dSRCMA system $\mathcal{M}$. This means that $\mathcal{L}_X(\text{dPA}, f_{perm}) \subseteq \mathcal{L}_X(\text{dSRCMA})$ for any $X \in \{concat, agree\}$. $\qquad\square$

Now we turn to the converse inclusion, we show how distributed counter machine acceptor systems can be simulated by distributed P automata.

Lemma 2. $\mathcal{L}_X(\text{dSRCMA}) \subseteq \mathcal{L}_X(\text{dPA}, f_{perm})$ *for any* $X \in \{concat, agree\}$.

Proof. We show how a dSRCMA system $\mathcal{M} = (\Sigma, M_1, \ldots, M_n, \delta_{\mathcal{M}})$ with $M_i = (Q_i, \Sigma, k, \delta_i, q_{i,0}, F_i)$, $1 \leq i \leq n$, can be simulated by a dP automaton. Let the transitions defined by $(\bigcup_{i=1}^{n} \delta_i) \cup \delta_{\mathcal{M}}$ be labeled in a one-to-one manner by the set $lab(\mathcal{M})$, and let the simulating dP automaton be defined as $\Delta = (V, \Pi_1, \ldots, \Pi_n, R)$. For any $M_i = (Q_i, \Sigma, k, \delta_i, q_{i,0}, F_i)$, $1 \leq i \leq n$, we define $\Pi_i = (V, \mu_i, w_{i,1}, \ldots, w_{i,k+2}, P_{i,1}, \ldots, P_{i,k+2})$ as follows.

The alphabet is $V = \Sigma \cup \{q_0, C, D, E, F\} \cup \{B_{i,t}, t_1, t_2, t_3, t_4 \mid 1 \leq i \leq 6, t \in lab(\mathcal{M})\} \cup \{A_i, A_i' \mid 3 \leq i \leq k + 2\}$, the membrane structure is $\mu_i = [\,[\,]_{i,2}\,[\,]_{i,3} \cdots [\,]_{i,k+2}\,]_{i,1}$, and the rule sets with the initial membrane contents are as follows. (For easier readability, instead of the string notation, we denote the initial multisets by enumerating their elements between curly brackets, as in the usual set notation.)

$w_{i,1} = \{q_0, C, D\}$,

$P_{i,1} = \{(a, out; u, in)|_{t_1} \mid a \in \Sigma, \ t \in lab(\delta_i)$ is a transition of M
   which reads a string representing u from the input tape$\}$

$w_{i,2} = \{a, E, B_{j,t}, t_1, (t_2)^k, (t_3)^k, (t_4)^k \mid 1 \leq j \leq 6, t \in lab(\delta_i)\}$ where a is
   some element of Σ and $(t_j)^k$ denotes k occurrences of the object t_j,

$P_{i,2} = \{(t_1 a, out; q_0 D, in) \mid a \in \Sigma, \ t \in lab(\delta_i)$ labels a transition
   from $q_{i,0} \in Q_i\} \cup$
   $\{(B_{1,t} D(t_2)^k, out; t_1, in) \mid t \in lab(\delta_i)\} \cup \{(a, out)|_D \mid a \in \Sigma\} \cup$
   $\{(B_{2,t}(t_3)^k, out; B_{1,t}, in), (B_{3,t}(t_4)^k, out; B_{2,t}, in),$
   $(B_{4,t}, out; B_{3,t}(t_2)^k, in), (B_{5,t}, out; (t_3)^k B_{4,t}, in),$
   $(B_{6,t}, out; (t_4)^k B_{5,t} Ca, in), (s_1 a, out; B_{6,t} D, in) \mid t, s \in lab(\delta_i)$ where
   s is a transition which can follow $t, \ a \in \Sigma\} \cup$
   $\{(E, out; B_{6,t}, in) \mid t \in lab(\delta_i)$ is a transition leading to a final
   state of $M_i\} \cup \{(a, in)|_C, (C, out) \mid a \in \Sigma\}$,

and for $3 \leq j \leq k + 2$, let

$$w_{i,j} = \{A_j, A'_j, F, F\},$$

$$P_{i,j} = \{(A_j, out; t_2, in), (A'_j, out)|_{t_2}, (A_j A'_j, in), (F, in; F, out)\} \cup$$

$\quad \{(t_2 a, out; t_3, in), (t_2 F, out), (t_3, out; t_4, in), (t_4, out) \mid t \in lab(\delta_i)$ is a

$\quad$ transition which decrements the value of counter $j - 2\} \cup$

$\quad \{(t_2, out; t_3, in), (t_3, out; t_4, in), (t_4, out; a, in) \mid t \in lab(\delta_i)$ is a

$\quad$ transition which increments the value of counter $j - 2\} \cup$

$\quad \{(F a, out)|_{t_2}, (t_2, out; t_3, in), (t_3, out; t_4, in), (t_4, out) \mid t \in lab(\delta_i)$ is a

$\quad$ transition which requires that the value of counter $j - 2$ is zero$\}$.

Let also

$$R = \{_{t_2 t_4}|((i,1), u/\lambda, (j,1))|_{t_2 t_4} \mid \text{ for all } u \text{ where } t \in \delta_{\mathcal{M}} \text{ labels a transition}$$

$\quad$ which results in the increase of the sum of the counter

$\quad$ contents of Π_j by $|u|\} \cup$

$\quad \{_{t_2 t_4}|((i,1), \lambda/v, (j,1))|_{t_2 t_4} \mid \text{ for all } v \text{ where } t \in \delta_{\mathcal{M}} \text{ labels a transition}$

$\quad$ which results in the increase of the sum of the counter

$\quad$ contents of Π_i by $|v|\}$.

Each of the components Π_i of the system defined above has a skin region (region $(i, 1)$), a region representing the finite control (region $(i, 2)$), and k regions corresponding to the k counters of M_i (regions (i, j), $3 \leq j \leq k + 2$, referred to as the counter regions). The counter regions represent the values stored in the counters of M_i with objects from Σ, region (i, j) contains as many such objects as the values stored in counter $j - 2$. The object q_0 present in the skin region in the initial configuration is exchanged for an indexed transition symbol t_1 where $t \in lab(\delta_i)$ denoting a transition from the initial state.

The simulation of a computational step of M_i starts by having one terminal object $a \in \Sigma$, and a transition symbol t_1 for some transition $t \in lab(\delta_i) \cup lab(\delta_{\mathcal{M}})$ in the skin membrane. (For the simulation of the initial step, these symbols arrive from region $(i, 2)$ in exchange to q_0 when Δ is started.) If $t \in lab(\delta_i)$, then the terminal object a is used by a rule $(a, out; u, in)|_{t_1}$ to import a multiset $u \in \Sigma^{\oplus}$ which is read by M_i during the transition t. Otherwise, if $t \in lab(\delta_{\mathcal{M}})$ no symbols are imported from the environment. Now the transition symbol is moved back to region $(i, 2)$, and k copies of t_2 (corresponding to the same transition, but indexed with 2) are exported to the skin region together with all the copies of objects from Σ which are not used inside the counter regions (these are stored in region $(i, 2)$ until they are needed). In the next six steps, the values stored in the k counter regions are modified as necessary while the symbol $B_{1,t}$ is changed to $B_{6,t}$, increasing its index by one in every step. If a counter needs to be decremented or checked for being zero, then the objects t_2 enter and take with them a terminal object to the skin region or perform the zero check as necessary. Meanwhile k copies of t_3 are released from region $(i, 2)$ which continue the process by changing to t_4 and then bringing in terminal objects to the counter regions when the counter in question needs to be incremented during transition t. If $t \in lab(\delta_{\mathcal{M}})$ is a communication transition, then the a number of objects which are necessary to maintain the values of the counters as required by t are also transferred between the components using the communication rules of R. Such a rule can be applied only in the step when both t_2 and t_4 are present in the skin region.

After the modification of the counter values, the remaining terminal objects are transported back to region $(i, 2)$, and the symbol $s_1 \in lab(\delta_i) \cup lab(\delta_{\mathcal{M}})$ for the next transition appears, together with exactly one terminal object $a \in \Sigma$, so the simulation of the next computational step of M_i can start in the same manner. The simulation finishes when, after executing a transition leading to a final state of M_i, the symbol E is exported from region $(i, 2)$ to the skin region and the component halts.

Note that the components of the SRCMA system read multisets in the sense that whenever $(q', \beta) \in \delta(w, q, \alpha)$ for some $w \in \Sigma^*$, then also $(q', \beta) \in \delta(\bar{w}, q, \alpha)$ where $\bar{w}$ is any permutation of w. This means that the components of the dP automaton described above accept the same words as the components of the dSR-CMA system, thus, they also accept the same concatenated or agreement languages.   □

Combining the two lemmas above, we obtain the following

Corollary 3. $\mathcal{L}_X(\text{dPA}, f_{perm}) = \mathcal{L}_X(\text{dSRCMA})$, for $X \in \{concat, agree\}$.

4 Conclusion

In this paper we have shown that dP automata with mapping f_{perm} are as powerful as the class of distributed systems of special restricted counter machine acceptors. Observing the proof and the concept of dSRCMA, the reader may easily notice that dSRCMA realize multi-head SRCMA in some sense, i.e., the (weak) agreement language of dP automata corresponds to the language of a multi-head SRCMA. We plan research in this direction, i.e., on the relation between one-way and two-way multi-head RCMA and SRCMA and languages of one-way and two-way dP automata in the future.

References

1. Csuhaj-Varjú, E., Ibarra, O.H., Vaszil, G.: On the computational complexity of P automata. In: Ferretti, C., Mauri, G., Zandron, C. (eds.) DNA10. LNCS, vol. 3384, pp. 76–89. Springer, Heidelberg (2005)
2. Csuhaj-Varjú, E., Oswald, M., Vaszil, G.: P automata. In: [13], ch. 6, pp. 144–167
3. Csuhaj-Varjú, E., Vaszil, G.: P automata. In: Păun, G., Zandron, C. (eds.) Pre-Proceedings of the Workshop on Membrane Computing WMC-CdeA 2002, Curtea de Argeş, Romania, August 19-23, pp. 177–192, Pub. No. 1 of MolCoNet-IST-2001-32008 (2002)

4. Csuhaj-Varjú, E., Vaszil, G.: P automata or purely communicating accepting P systems. In: Păun, G., Rozenberg, G., Salomaa, A., Zandron, C. (eds.) WMC 2002. LNCS, vol. 2597, pp. 219–233. Springer, Heidelberg (2003)
5. Csuhaj-Varjú, E., Vaszil, G.: Finite dP Automata versus multi-head Finite Automata. In: Gheorghe, M., Păun, G., Rozenberg, G., Salomaa, A., Verlan, S. (eds.) CMC 2011. LNCS, vol. 7184, pp. 120–138. Springer, Heidelberg (2012)
6. Csuhaj-Varjú, E., Vaszil, G.: On the power of P automata. In: Mauri, G., Dennunzio, A., Manzoni, L., Porreca, A.E. (eds.) UCNC 2013. LNCS, vol. 7956, pp. 55–66. Springer, Heidelberg (2013)
7. Freund, R., Oswald, M.: A short note on analysing P systems. Bulletin of the EATCS 78, 231–236 (2002)
8. Freund, R., Kogler, M., Păun, G., Pérez-Jiménez, M.J.: On the power of P and dP automata. Annals of Bucharest University Mathematics-Informatics Series LVIII, 5–22 (2009)
9. Ibarra, O.H.: Membrane hierarchy in P systems. Theoretical Computer Science 334(1-3), 115–129 (2005)
10. Monien, B.: Two-way multi-head automata over a one-letter alphabet. RAIRO - Informatique théorique/Theoretical Informatics 14(1), 67–82 (1980)
11. Păun, G.: Membrane Computing: An Introduction. Natural Computing Series. Springer, Berlin (2002)
12. Păun, G., Pérez-Jiménez, M.J.: Solving problems in a distributed way in membrane computing: dP systems. International Journal of Computers, Communication and Control V(2), 238–250 (2010)
13. Păun, G., Rozenberg, G., Salomaa, A. (eds.): The Oxford Handbook of Membrane Computing. Oxford University Press (2010)
14. Păun, G., Pérez-Jiménez, M.J.: P and dP automata: A survey. In: Calude, C.S., Rozenberg, G., Salomaa, A. (eds.) Maurer Festschrift. LNCS, vol. 6570, pp. 102–115. Springer, Heidelberg (2011)
15. Păun, G., Pérez-Jiménez, M.J.: An infinite hierarchy of languages defined by dP systems. Theoretical Computer Science 431, 4–12 (2012)
16. Păun, G., Pérez-Jiménez, M.J.: P automata revisited. Theoretical Computer Science 454, 222–230 (2012)
17. Pérez-Jiménez, M.J.: A computational complexity theory in membrane computing. In: Păun, G., Pérez-Jiménez, M.J., Riscos-Núñez, A., Rozenberg, G., Salomaa, A. (eds.) WMC 2009. LNCS, vol. 5957, pp. 125–148. Springer, Heidelberg (2010)
18. Rozenberg, G., Salomaa, A. (eds.): Handbook of Formal Languages. Springer, Berlin (1997)
19. Vaszil, G.: On the parallelizability of languages accepted by P automata. In: Kelemen, J., Kelemenová, A. (eds.) Păun Festschrift. LNCS, vol. 6610, pp. 170–178. Springer, Heidelberg (2011)

Model Checking Kernel P Systems

Ciprian Dragomir[1], Florentin Ipate[2,3], Savas Konur[1], Raluca Lefticaru[2,3],
and Laurentiu Mierla[3]

[1] Department of Computer Science, University of Sheffield
Regent Court, Portobello Street, Sheffield S1 4DP, UK
{c.dragomir,s.konur}@sheffield.ac.uk
[2] Department of Computer Science, University of Bucharest
Str. Academiei nr. 14, 010014, Bucharest, Romania
florentin.ipate@ifsoft.ro, raluca.lefticaru@fmi.unibuc.ro
[3] Department of Mathematics and Computer Science, University of Piteşti
Str. Târgu din Vale 1, 110040, Piteşti, Romania
laurentiu.mierla@gmail.com

Abstract. Recent research in membrane computing examines and con-
firms the anticipated modelling potential of kernel P systems in several
case studies. On the one hand, this computational model is destined to
be an abstract archetype which advocates the unity and integrity of P
systems onto a single formalism. On the other hand, this envisaged con-
vergence is conceived at the expense of a vast set of primitives and intricate semantics, an exigent context when considering the development
of simulation and verification methodologies and tools.

Encouraged and guided by the success and steady progress of similar
undertakings, in this paper we directly address the issue of formal verification of kernel P systems by means of model checking and unveil a
software framework, *kpWorkbench*, which integrates a set of related tools
in support of our approach.

A case study that centres around the well known *Subset Sum* problem progressively demonstrates each stage of the proposed methodology:
expressing a kP system model in recently introduced *kP-Lingua*; the automatic translation of this model into a Promela (Spin) specification;
the assisted, interactive construction of a set of LTL properties based on
natural language patterns; and finally, the formal verification of these
properties against the converted model, using the Spin model checker.

1 Introduction

Membrane computing, the research field introduced by Gheorghe Păun [21],
studies computational models, called P systems, inspired by the functioning
and structure of the living cell. In recent years, significant progress has been
made in using various types or classes of P systems to model and simulate
systems and problems from many different areas [5]. However, in many cases,
the specifications developed required the ad-hoc addition of new features, not
provided in the initial definition of the given P system class. While allowing more

A. Alhazov et al. (Eds.): CMC 2013, LNCS 8340, pp. 151–172, 2014.
© Springer-Verlag Berlin Heidelberg 2014

flexibility in modelling, this has led to a plethora of P system variants, with no coherent integrating view, and sometimes even confusion with regard to what variant or functioning strategy is actually used.

The concept of *kernel P system (kP system)* [7] has been introduced as a response to this situation. It integrates in a coherent and elegant manner many of the P system features most successfully used for modelling various applications and, thus, provides a framework for formally analyzing these models. The expressive power and efficiency of the newly introduced kP systems have been illustrated by a number of representative case studies [8,14]. Furthermore, the kP model is supported by a modelling language, called *kP-Lingua*, capable of mapping the kernel P system specification into a machine readable representation.

Naturally, formal modelling has to be accompanied by formal verification methods. In the membrane system context, formal verification has been approached, for example, using rewriting logic and the Maude tool [1] or PRISM and the associated probabilistic temporal logic [11] for stochastic systems [3]. Several, more recent, successful attempts to apply model checking techniques on transition P systems also exist [4,17,18,15]. However, to the best of our knowledge, there is no integrated formal verification approach to allow formal properties to be specified in a language easily accessible to the non-specialist user and to be automatically verified in a transparent way.

This paper proposes precisely such an integrated verification approach, which allows formal properties, expressed in a quasi-natural language using predefined patterns, to be verified against a kP-Lingua representation of the model using model checking techniques and tools (in this case the model checker Spin and the associated modelling language Promela). Naturally, this approach is supported by adequate tools, which automatically convert the supplied inputs (natural language queries and kP-Lingua representation) into their model checking specific counterparts (LTL queries and Promela representation, respectively). The approach is illustrated with a case study, involving a kP system solving a well-known NP-complete problem, the Subset Sum problem.

The paper is structured as follows: Section 2 recalls the definition of a kernel P system - the formal modelling framework central to our examination. We then review, in Section 3, some of the primary challenges of model checking applicable to kP system models and discuss the transformations such a model must undergo, in order to be exhaustively verified by Spin. We also present our implemented approach to achieve an automatic model conversion, targeting the process meta language, *Promela*. In Section 4, we address the complementary requirement of specifying system properties as temporal logic formulae. The section also includes an array of EBNF formal definitions which describe the construction of LTL properties that relate to kP system state constituents, a guided process which employs selected natural language query patterns. Section 5 applies our proposed methodology, exemplifies and demonstrates all stages of the process with a case study - an instance of the Subset Sum problem. Finally, we conclude our investigation and review our findings in Section 6.

2   Kernel P Systems

A kP system is made of compartments placed in a graph-like structure. A compartment C_i has a type $t_i = (R_i, \sigma_i)$, $t_i \in T$, where T represents the set of all types, describing the associated set of rules R_i and the execution strategy that the compartment may follow. Note that, unlike traditional P system models, in kP systems each compartment may have its own rule application strategy. The following definitions are largely from [7].

Definition 1. *A* kernel P (kP) system *of degree n is a tuple*

$$k\Pi = (A, \mu, C_1, \ldots, C_n, i_0),$$

where A is a finite set of elements called objects*; μ defines the* membrane structure*, which is a graph, (V, E), where V are vertices indicating components, and E edges; $C_i = (t_i, w_i)$, $1 \leq i \leq n$, is a* compartment *of the system consisting of a compartment type from T and an* initial multiset*, w_i over A; i_0 is the* output *compartment where the result is obtained.*

Each rule r may have a **guard** g denoted as $r \{g\}$. The rule r is applicable to a multiset w when its left hand side is contained into w and g holds for w. The guards are constructed using multisets over A and relational and Boolean operators. For example, rule $r : ac \to c \{\geq a^3 \land \geq b^2 \lor \neg > c\}$ can be applied iff the current multiset, w, includes the left hand side of r, i.e., ac and the guard holds for w - it has at least 3 a's and 2 b's or no more than a c. A formal definition may be found in [7].

Definition 2. *A rule associated with a compartment type l_i can have one of the following types:*

- *(a)* **rewriting and communication** *rule: $x \to y \{g\}$,*
  where $x \in A^+$ and y has the form $y = (a_1, t_1) \ldots (a_h, t_h)$, $h \geq 0$, $a_j \in A$ and t_j indicates a compartment type from T – see Definition 1 – with instance compartments linked to the current compartment; t_j might indicate the type of the current compartment, i.e., t_{l_i} – in this case it is ignored; if a link does not exist (the two compartments are not in E) then the rule is not applied; if a target, t_j, refers to a compartment type that has more than one instance connected to l_i, then one of them will be non-deterministically chosen;
- *(b)* **structure changing rules**; *the following types are considered:*
  - *(b1)* **membrane division** *rule: $[x]_{t_{l_i}} \to [y_1]_{t_{i_1}} \ldots [y_p]_{t_{i_p}} \{g\}$,*
    where $x \in A^+$ and y_j has the form $y_j = (a_{j,1}, t_{j,1}) \ldots (a_{j,h_j}, t_{j,h_j})$ like in rewriting and communication rules; the compartment l_i will be replaced by p compartments; the j-th compartment, instantiated from the compartment type t_{i_j} contains the same objects as l_i, but x, which will be replaced by y_j; all the links of l_i are inherited by each of the newly created compartments;

- *(b2)* **membrane dissolution** *rule:* $[x]_{t_{l_i}} \rightarrow \lambda \ \{g\}$;
  the compartment l_i and its entire contents is destroyed together with its links. This contrasts with the classical dissolution semantics where the inner multiset is passed to the parent membrane - in a tree-like membrane structure;
- *(b3)* **link creation** *rule:* $[x]_{t_{l_i}}; []_{t_{l_j}} \rightarrow [y]_{t_{l_i}} - []_{t_{l_j}} \ \{g\}$;
  the current compartment is linked to a compartment of type t_{l_j} and x is transformed into y; if more than one instance of the compartment type t_{l_j} exists then one of them will be non-deterministically picked up; g is a guard that refers to the compartment instantiated from the compartment type t_{l_i};
- *(b4)* **link destruction** *rule:* $[x]_{t_{l_i}} - []_{t_{l_j}} \rightarrow [y]_{t_{l_i}}; []_{t_{l_j}} \ \{g\}$;
  is the opposite of link creation and means that the compartments are disconnected.

Each compartment can be regarded as an instance of a particular *compartment type* and is therefore subject to its associated rules. One of the main distinctive features of kP systems is the execution strategy which is now statutory to types rather than unitary across the system. Thus, each membrane applies its type specific instruction set, as coordinated by the associated execution strategy.

An execution strategy can be defined as a sequence $\sigma = \sigma_1 \& \sigma_2 \& \ldots \& \sigma_n$, where σ_i denotes an atomic component of the form:

- ϵ, an analogue to the generic *skip* instruction; *epsilon* is generally used to denote an *empty* execution strategy;
- r, a rule from the set R_t (the set of rules associated with type t). If r is applicable, then it is executed, advancing towards the next rule in the succession; otherwise, the compartment terminates the execution thread for this particular computational step and thus, no further rule will be applied;
- $(r_1, \ldots, r_n)$, with $r_i \in R_t, 1 \leq i \leq n$ symbolizes a non-deterministic choice within a set of rules. One and only one applicable rule will be executed if such a rule exists, otherwise the atom is simply skipped. In other words the non-deterministic choice block is always applicable;
- $(r_1, \ldots, r_n)^*$, with $r_i \in R_t, 1 \leq i \leq n$ indicates the arbitrary execution of a set of rules in R_t. The group can execute zero or more times, arbitrarily but also depending on the applicability of the constituent rules;
- $(r_1, \ldots, r_n)^\top, r_i \in R_t, 1 \leq i \leq n$ represents the maximally parallel execution of a set of rules. If no rules are applicable, then execution proceeds to the subsequent atom in the chain.

The execution strategy itself is a notable asset in defining more complex behaviour at the compartment level. For instance, priorities can be easily expressed as sequences of maximally parallel execution blocks: $(r_1)^\top \& (r_2)^\top \& \ldots \& (r_3)^\top$ or non-deterministic choice groups if single execution is required. Together with composite guards, they provide an unprecedented modelling fluency and plasticity for membrane systems. Whether such macro-like concepts and structures are preferred over traditional modelling with simple but numerous compartments in complex arrangements is a debatable aspect.

3   kP System Models and the Spin Model Checker

Formal verification of P systems has become an increasingly investigated subject, owing to a series of multilateral developments which have broaden its application scope and solidified some domain specific methodologies. Although there have been several attempts that successfully demonstrated model checking techniques on P systems ([17], [18], [15]), the analysis is always bound to an array of constraints, such as specific P system variants with a limited feature set and a very basic set of properties. Nevertheless, there are notable advancements which have paved the path towards a more comprehensive, integrated and automated approach we endeavour to present in this paper.

The task of P system model checking is perhaps a most inviting and compelling one due to the many onerous challenges it poses. On the one hand we are confronted with the inherent shortcomings of the method itself, which have a decisive impact on the tractability of some models and, in the best case, the efficiency or precision of the result is severely undermined. Speaking generally, but not inaccurately, model checking entails an exhaustive, *strategic* exploration of a model's state space to assert the validity of a logically defined property. Hence, the state space is of primary concern and we can immediately acknowledge 1. the requirement for models to have a finite state space and 2. the proportionality between the state space *size* and the stipulated computational resources, which ultimately determines the feasibility of the verification process.

On the other hand, the complex behaviour of certain computational models translates to elaborate formal specifications, with intricate semantics and more often than not, a vast set of states. However, it is the tireless state explosion problem that diminishes the applicability of model checking to concurrent systems, a rather ironical fact, since such systems are now the primary target for exhaustive verification.

We shall not delve any further into general aspects since our focus is not the vivisection of a methodology, but rather the introduction of a robust, integrated and automated approach that constellates around kernel P systems and overtly addresses the predominant challenges of model checking emphasised so far.

The three most conspicuous features that typify membrane systems are 1. a structured, distributed computational environment; 2. multisets of objects as atomic terms in rewriting rules and 3. an *execution strategy* according to which the rules are applied. We recall that kP systems explicitly associate an instruction set to an array of compartments employing the *type - instance* paradigm. As it turns out, this distinction is highly relevant in mapping a formal state transition system, where a system state is conveyed compositionally, as the union of individual states attributed to instances (in our case), or disjoint volatile components in more generic terms. Thus, a kP system state S is an aggregate of S_C, the set of compartment states and μ which denotes the membrane structure as a set of interconnections between compartments. A compartment state is identified by its associated multiset configuration at a particular computational step, together with the membrane type the compartment it subject to. The following set like expression exemplifies a kernel P system state for three compartments c_1, c_2 and

c_3, of types t_1, t_2, t_2, having configurations $2a$ b, a $2c$ and *empty* respectively. The second fragment is a set of pairs which symbolize links between compartments: c_1 is connected to both c_2 and c_3, who do not share a link in-between.

$$(\{(c_1, t_1, \{2a, b\}), (c_2, t_2, \{a, 2c\}), (c_3, t_2, \{\})\}, \{(c_1, c_2), (c_1, c_3)\})$$

Since kP systems feature a dynamic structure by preserving structure changing rules such as membrane division, dissolution and link creation/destruction, a state defined in this expansive context is consequently variable in size. This is not unnatural for a computational model, however it does become an issue when conflicting with the requirement of a fixed sized pre-allocated data model imposed by most model checker tools. The instinctive solution is to bound the expansion of these collections to a certain maximum based on the algorithmic necessities. For instance, an initial analysis of the problem we are modelling can provide relevant details about the number of steps required for a successful execution, the number of divisions that may occur and the maximum number of links generated.

One of the most fruitful advantages of model checking is the fact it can be completely automated. The principal insight is that both the system's state space (commonly referred to as *global reachability graph*) and the correctness claim specified as a temporal logic formula can be converted to non-deterministic finite automata. The product of the two automata is another NDFA whose accepted language is either empty in which case the correctness claim is not satisfied, or non-empty if the system exhibits precisely the behaviour specified by the temporal logic statement. There are numerous implementations of this stratagem boasting various supplementary features, a survey of which is beyond the scope of this study. The model checker extensively adopted in formal verification research on membrane systems is Spin. Developed by Gerard J. Holzmann in the 1990s, Spin is now a leading verification tool used by professional software engineers and has an established authority amidst model checkers. Among plentiful qualities, Spin is particularly suited for modelling concurrent and distributed systems by means of interleaving atomic instructions. For a more comprehensive description of the tool, we refer the reader to [12].

A model checker requires an unambiguous representation of its input model, together with a set of correctness claims expressed as temporal logic formulae. Spin features a high level modelling language, called Promela, which specializes in concise descriptions of concurrent processes and inter-process communication supporting both rendezvous and buffered message passing. Another practical and convenient aspect of the language is the use of discrete primitive data types as in the C programming language. Additionally, custom data types and single dimensional arrays are also supported, although in restricted contexts only.

The kernel P systems specification is an embodiment of elementary components shared by most variants, complemented by innovative new features, promoting a versatile modelling framework without transgressing the *membrane computing* paradigm. Characterised by a rich set of primitives, kP systems offer many high level functional contexts and building blocks such as the exhaustive and arbitrary execution of a set of rules, complex guards and the popular concept of membrane division - powerful modelling instruments from a user centric perspective. An attempt, however, to equate such a complex synthesis of related abstractions to a mainstream specification is a daunting and challenging task. It is perhaps evident that users should be entirely relieved of this responsibility, and all model transformations should be handled automatically. It is precisely this goal which motivates the development of **kpWorkbench**, a basic framework which integrates a set of translation tools that bridge several target specifications we employ for kernel P system models. The pivotal representation medium is, however, the newly introduced kP-Lingua, a language designed to express a kP system coherently and intuitively. kP-Lingua is described in detail in [7], which includes an EBNF grammar of its syntax. We exemplify kP-Lingua in our dedicated case study, presented in section 5 of this paper.

One of the fundamental objectives in devising a conversion strategy is to establish a correspondence with respect to data and functional modules between the two specifications. In some cases, a direct mapping of entities can be identified:

- A **multiset of objects** is encoded as an integer array, where an index denotes the object and the value at that index represents the multiplicity of the object;
- A **compartment type** is translated into a data type definition, a structure consisting of native elements, the multiset of objects and links to other compartments, as well as auxiliary members such as a temporary storage variable, necessary in order to simulate the inherent parallelism of P systems.
- A **compartment** is an instance of a data type definition and a set of compartments is organised into an array of the respective type;
- A **set of rules** is organised according to an **execution strategy** is mapped by a Proctype definition - a Promela process;
- A **guard** is expressed as a composite conditional statement which is evaluated inside an *if* statement;
- A **rule** is generally converted into a pair of instructions which manage subtraction and addition on compartment multisets, but can also process structural elements such as compartments and links;
- **Exhaustive and arbitrary execution** are resolved with using the *do* block;
- **Single non-deterministic execution** is reflected by an *if* statement with multiple branches; we note that Promela evaluates *if* statements differently than most modern programming languages: if more than one branch evaluates to true, then one is non-deterministically chosen.

It is not, however, the simplicity and limpidity of these projections that prevail, especially when dealing with a computational model so often described as unconventional. Rather, concepts such as maximal parallelism and membrane division challenge the mainstream modelling approach of sequential processes and settle on contrived syntheses of clauses. These artificial substitutes operate as auxiliary functions and therefore require abstraction from the global state space generated by a model checker tool. Spin supports the hiding of mediator instruction sets by enveloping code into *atomic* or *d_step* blocks. Although this is a very effective optimisation, we are still faced with the problem of instruction interleaving, the de facto procedure which reconciles parallel and sequential computation. It is not this forced simulation of parallelism that obstructs a natural course for P system verification with Spin, but rather the inevitable inclusion of states generated by interleaved atomic instructions or ensembles of instructions.

In our approach we overcome this obstacle with a hybrid solution, involving both the model in question and the postulated properties. Firstly, we collapse individual instructions (to atomic blocks) to the highest degree permitted by Spin, minimizing the so-called *intermediate state space* which is irrelevant to a P system computation; and secondly, we appoint the states relevant to our model explicitly, using a global flag (i.e. a Boolean variable), raised when all processes have completed a computational step. Hence, we make a clear distinction between states that are pertinent to the formal investigation and the ones which should be discarded. This contrast is in turn reflected by the temporal logic formulae, which require adjustment to an orchestrated context where only a narrow subset of the global state space is pursued. The technique is demonstrated in our case study of section 5.

While the approach is a practical success, its efficacy is still a questionable matter. Although a substantial set of states is virtually *neglected* when asserting a correctness claim, the complete state space is nevertheless generated (i.e. including the superfluous states) and each state examined: if the state is flagged as a genuine P system state, then it is queried further, otherwise it is *skipped*. In terms of memory usage, the implications are significant and certainly not to be underestimated, particularly when the model exhibits massively parallel and non-deterministic behaviour.

We conclude this section with an informal synopsis of the *kP system - Promela* translation strategy and the rationale behind some of its noteworthy particularities:

- While each compartment type is represented by a Promela process definition, a *Scheduler* process is employed to launch and coordinate the asynchronous execution of procedures per compartment. The following pseudo-code illustrates the managerial role played by our scheduler:

```
process Scheduler {
    while system is not halted {
        for each type T_i {
            for each compartment C_j of type T_i {
                appoint process P(T_i) to compartment C_j;
            }
        }
```

```
        start all appointed processes;
        wait until all appointed processes finish;
        state = step_complete;
        print configuration;
        state = running;
    }
}
```

– Each compartment consists of two multisets of objects, one which rules operate on and *consume* objects from; and the second which temporarily stores the produced or communicated objects. Before the end of each computational step, the content of the auxiliary multiset is committed to the primary multiset, which also denotes the compartment's configuration. This interplay is required to simulate a parallel execution of the system.

Our software framework, kpWorkbench includes a faithful implementation of the hitherto described translation principles and supports the automatic conversion of a Kernel P system into a Promela specification. Relevant technical notes, downloads and installation instructions are available at http://www.muvet.ifsoft.ro/kpWorkbench.html. kpWorkbench is distributed under GPL license.

4   Queries on Kernel P Systems

A much debated aspect of model checking based formal verification is specifying and formulating a set of properties whose correctness is to be asserted. Since model checking is essentially an exhaustive state space search, there is a persistent and irreconcilable concern over the limitations of this method when investigating the behaviour of concurrent models, generative of an astronomical state spaces. More precisely, the complexity of the model itself has a great subversive impact on the property gamut which can be employed such that the procedure remains feasible given reasonable computational resources.

It is not just the inherent limitations of this technique which must be taken into consideration, but also the effort and tenacity required to formally express specific queries concisely and faithfully into prescribed logical frameworks. Amir Pnueli's seminal work on temporal logic [20] was a major advance in this direction, enabling the elegant representation of time dependent properties in deductive systems. Essential adverbial indicators such as *never* and *eventually* have a diametric correspondent in temporal logic, as operators which relate system states in terms of reachability, persistence and precedence, supporting more powerful queries in addition to simple state equivalence assertions and basic invariance. Exploiting the potential of these logics, as evident as it may seem, can still be problematic and laborious under certain circumstances.

Firstly, devising a temporal logic formula for a required property is a cumbersome and error-prone process even for the experienced. It is often the case that the yielded expressions, although logically valid, are counter-intuitive and abstruse, having little to tell about the significance of the property itself. As with any abstraction that is based on pure logical inference, it is devoid of meaning outside the logical context. To clearly emphasize our affirmations, consider the following example:

$$G \ (vm\_functional = true \ \wedge \ vm\_coin > 0 \rightarrow$$
$$F \ (vm\_dipsensed\_drink > 0 \ \wedge \ F \ (vm\_coin = 0)) \ \vee$$
$$F \ (vm\_functional = false))$$

is a faithful LTL (linear time temporal logic) representation of a property which can be phrased as *"a vending machine, if functional, will always dispense a drink after having accepted coins and will either become dysfunctional or its coin buffer will be depleted."* Although we have used intuitive variable names, it is not immediately apparent what this expression stands for, requiring a thorough understanding of the LTL specification together with effort and insight to accurately decipher its meaning.

The second notable issue we wish to evince is the correctness of the formula itself which can often be questionable even if the property is of moderate complexity and is syntactically accepted by a model checker tool. How can one prove that a temporal logic expression is indeed a valid representation of a property we wish to verify? Is this a genuine concern we should address, or is it acceptable to assume the faithfulness of temporal logic expressions to specific queries, as formulated by expert and non-expert users?

In response to these controversies, we propose a strategy that facilitates a *guided construction* of relevant LTL properties and automates the translation to their formal equivalent. It is the Natural Language Query (NLQ) builder that was developed to support this methodology. The tool features a rich set of *natural language patterns*, presented to users as sequences of GUI (graphical user interface) form elements: labels, text boxes and drop-down lists. Once the required values have been selected or directly specified and the template populated, NLQ automatically converts the natural language statement to its temporal logic correspondent. The translation from an informal to a formal representation is based on an interpreted grammar which accompanies each natural language pattern.

In Table 1, we illustrate a selection of patterns whose instantiation generates properties suitable for kP system models and their formal verification. Table 2 depicts the EBNF based grammar according to which, *state formulae* are derived, with reference to kernel P system components.

In order to verify kP systems modeled in kP-Lingua using Spin model checker, properties specified in LTL should be reformulated in Spin language for the corresponding Promela model. In Table 3, we give LTL formulae of the patterns shown in Table 1, and their corresponding translations in Spin language for the Promela specification. Each LTL formula described for P systems in general (and kP systems in our case) should be translated to Spin using a special predicate, pInS, showing that the current Spin state represents a P system configuration (the predicate is true when a computation step is completed) or represents an intermediate state (it is false if intermediary steps are executed) [15,18].

Table 1. Grammar for query patterns

Pattern	::= Occurrence | Order
Occurrence	::= Next | Existence | Absence | Universality | Recurrence | Steady-State
Order	::= Until | Precedence | Response
Next	::= stateFormula *'will hold in the next state'*
Existence	::= stateFormula *'will eventually hold'*
Absence	::= stateFormula *'never holds'*
Universality	::= stateFormula *'always holds'*
Recurrence	::= stateFormula *'holds infinitely often'*
Steady-State	::= stateFormula *'will hold in the long run (steady state)'*
Until	::= stateFormula *'will eventually hold, until then'* stateFormula *'holds continuously'*
Response	::= stateFormula *'is always followed by'* stateFormula
Precedence	::= stateFormula *'is always preceded by'* stateFormula

The idea of capturing recurring properties into categories of patterns was initiated by Dwyer et al. in their seminal paper of 1999 [6]. This study surveyed more than five hundred temporal properties and established a handful of pattern classes. In [9], this mapping was extended to include additional time related patterns and their associated observer automata. This was further supplemented with real-time specification patterns in [16].

A unified pattern system was introduced in [2], adding new real-time property classes. Probabilistic properties were similarly catalogued based on a survey of 200 properties [10], and provisioned with a corresponding structured grammar.

An analogous undertaking can also be observed in [19], where an array of query templates which target biological models was proposed.

Although the NLQ builder is based on an extensive set of patterns investigated in above mentioned literature, the templates relevant to our formal examination of kP system models represent a small subset of this collection; particularly we only employ patterns which generate temporal properties.

5   Case Study: The Subset Sum Problem

In this section we demonstrate the proposed methodology with a case study, the subject of which is the well known Subset Sum problem.

The Subset Sum problem is stated as follows:

Given a finite set $A = \{a_1, \ldots, a_n\}$, of n elements, where each element a_i has an associated weight, w_i, and a constant $k \in N$, it is requested to determine whether or not there exists a subset $B \subseteq A$ such that $w(B) = k$, where $w(B) = \sum_{a_i \in B} w_i$.

Table 2. EBNF based grammar for state formulae

stateFormula	::= statePredicate | statePredicate *'does not hold'* | stateFormula *'and'* stateFormula | stateFormula *'or'* stateFormula
statePredicate	::= numericExpression relationalOperator numericExpression
numericExpression	::= objectCount | localObjectCount | compartmentCount | linkCount | linkToCount | numericLiteral
linkCount	::= *'the number of links from'* compartmentQuery *'to'* compartmentQuery
linkToCount	::= *'the number of links to'* compartmentQuery
compartmentQuery	::= *'all compartments'* | *'compartments'* compartmentCondition
compartmentCondition	::= *'of type'* typeLabel | *'of type other than'* typeLabel | *'linked to'* compartmentQuery | *'not linked to'* compartmentQuery | localObjectCount relationalOperator numericExpression | linkToCount relationalOperator numericExpression
localObjectCount	::= *'the number of objects'* localObjectCondition
objectCount	::= *'the number of objects'* objectCondition
localObjectCondition	::= *'with label'* objectLabel | *'with label different than'* objectLabel | localObjectCondition *'and'* localObjectCondition | localObjectCondition *'or'* localObjectCondition
objectCondition	::= localObjectCondition | *'in'* compartmentQuery | *'not in'* compartmentQuery | objectCondition *'and'* objectCondition | objectCondition *'or'* objectCondition
relationalOperator	::= *'is equal to'* | *'is not equal to'* | *'is greater than'* | *'is less than'* | *'is greater than or equal to'* | *'is less than or equal to'*
numericLiteral	::= ? {0-9} ?

Table 3. LTL formulae and translated Spin specifications of the property patterns

Pattern	Informal Formula	LTL formula	Spin formula
Next	p will hold in the next state	$\mathrm{X}\,p$	`X(!pInS U (p && pInS))`
Existence	p will eventually hold	$\mathrm{F}\,p$	`<>(p && pInS)`
Absence	p never holds	$\neg(\mathrm{F}\,p)$	`!(<>(p && pInS))`
Universality	p always holds	$\mathrm{G}\,p$	`[] (p || !pInS)`
Recurrence	p holds infinitely often	$\mathrm{G}\,\mathrm{F}\,p$	`[](<>(p && pInS) || !pInS)`
Steady-State	p will hold in the steady state	$\mathrm{F}\,\mathrm{G}\,p$	`<>([](p || !pInS) && pInS)`
Until	p will eventually hold, until then q holds continuously	$p\,\mathrm{U}\,q$	`(p || !pInS) U (q && pInS)`
Response	p is always followed by q	$\mathrm{G}\,(p \to \mathrm{F}\,q)$	`[]((p -> <> (q && pInS)) || !pInS)`
Precedence	p is always preceded by q	$\neg(\neg p\,\mathrm{U}\,(\neg p \wedge q))$	`!((!p || !pInS) U (!p && q && pInS))`

The Subset Sum problem is representative for the NP complete class because it portrays the underlying necessity to consider *all combinations* of distinct elements of a finite set, in order to produce a result. Consequently, such a problem requires exponential computational resources (assuming $P \neq NP$), either in the temporal (number of computational steps) or spatial (memory) domain, or both. The Subset Sum problem explicitly denominates combinations of integers as subsets of the initial set A, or more accurately, the set of weights respective to A. It is therefore transparent that the number of all combinations which can be generated and evaluated is the cardinality of the power set of A, that is 2^n. Since our elements are in fact integers, optimisations have been considered, leveraging the intrinsic order relation between numbers, coupled with efficient sorting algorithms to avoid generating all possible subsets [13]. This did not, however, manage to reduce the complexity of the problem to a non-exponential order.

P system variants endowed with *membrane division* proved to be ideal computational frameworks for solving NP complete problems efficiently. The insightful strategy, often referred to as *trading space for time*, can be envisaged as the linear generation of an exponential computational space (compartments) together with the linear distribution (replication) of constituent data (multiset of objects). The topic is very popular in the community and was subject to extensive investigation; while the underlying principle is pertinent to our study, we shall illustrate it more sharply as applied, using a kernel P system model to solve the Subset Sum problem:

Consider the kP system

$$k\Pi = (\{a, x, step, yes, no, halt, r_1, \ldots, r_n\}, \mu, (Main, \{a\}), (Output, \{step\}))$$

with μ represented by a link between the two instances of type *Main* and *Output* respectively.

The rules for compartments of type *Main* are:

- R_i: $a \longrightarrow [a, r_i][w_i x, a, r_i]\{\neg r_i\}$, $1 \le i \le n$
- R_{n+1}: $a \longrightarrow (yes, halt)_{Output} \{= kx\}$
- R_{n+2}: $a \longrightarrow \lambda \{> kx\}$

where

- n is the number of elements in set A, that is the cardinal of A;
- r_i with $1 \leq i \leq n$ is an object which flags the execution of a membrane division rule, prohibiting multiple applications of the same addition;
- w_i is the weight of the ith element in the set A, with $1 \leq i \leq n$;
- k is the constant we refer to, when assessing the sum of the values in a subset; if $\sum w_i = k$, then a solution has been found;

The execution strategy $\sigma(Main)$ unfolds as follows:

$$\sigma(Main) = (R_{n+1}, R_{n+2})\&(R_{1..n})$$

Thus, each step a compartment of type $Main$ performs two preliminary evaluations: if the number of x objects is precisely k, then a yes and a $halt$ object are sent to the output membrane. We recall the specialised $halt$ object as a universal, model independent and convenient means of halting a computation for kernel P systems: when such an object is encountered in any of the system's compartments, the execution stops at the completion of the computational step. This is generally preferred to specifying halting conditions which relate to configurations or system states particular to the modelled problem.

If the multiplicity of x is greater than k, a condition assessed with the guard $> kx$, the compartment is dissolved, pruning a fruitless search path. Otherwise, a division rule is selected non-deterministically, splitting the compartment in two and adding $w_i x$s to the current multiplicity of x in one of the newly created regions, while preserving the weight of x in the other. Both compartments also receive a r_i object which marks the execution of the ith rule. This will be prevented from executing a second time by the guard $\neg r_i$. The object a is auxiliary and recurs in every compartment of type $Main$.

There is only one compartment of type $Output$ which persists throughout the execution, playing the role of an output membrane, as its name plainly indicates: either it receives a yes object if a solution is found, or it generates a no object if the computation does not halt after $n + 1$ steps. The two rules which correlate with this behaviour are:

- $R_1 :$ $step \longrightarrow 2step$
- $R_2 : (n + 2)step \longrightarrow no, halt$

The rules are executed sequentially:

$$\sigma(Output) = (R_1 \& R_2)$$

Remark 1. The illustrated algorithm is a faithful **linear time** solution to the Subset Sum problem: it computes an answer to the stipulated enquiry in **maximum** $n + 2$ **steps**, where n is the cardinality of the set A of elements.

Remark 2. The algorithm will generate the sums of all subsets of A in linear time using membrane division; the process is interrupted when a solution is found and computation halts at this stage. A notable difference to the skP (simple kernel P) system based solution presented in [14], is the use of non-deterministic choice in the selection of division rules. This rather unconventional approach facilitates the generation of subset sums that is irrespective of the order of elements in A. Evidently, the artifice owes its merit to the commutativity of integer addition.

Remark 3. The kP system model requires a total of: $n+6$ distinct objects, $n+4$ rules of which $n+1$ employ basic guards and a maximum of 2^n+1 compartments.

Remark 4. Although we have extensively referred to integer weights (of the elements in A) throughout this section, it is important to note that we can not directly represent negative numbers as object multiplicities alone (some encoding can be devised for this purpose). Since the only mathematical operation required is addition, which is a monotonically increasing function, a simple translation to the positive domain can be mapped on the set of weights $w(A)$, which in turn makes this issue irrelevant.

We next demonstrate the implementation of our kP system model in kP-Lingua, highlighting some of the most prominent features of its syntax. The illustrated model maps an instance of the Subset Sum problem with $n = 7$ elements: $w(A) = \{3, 25, 8, 23, 5, 14, 30\}$ and $k = 55$.

```
type Main {
    choice {
        = 55x: a -> {yes, halt} (Output) .
        > 55x: a -> # .
    }
    choice {
        !r1: a -> [a, r1][3x, a, r1] .
        !r2: a -> [a, r2][25x, a, r2] .
        !r3: a -> [a, r3][8x, a, r3] .
        !r4: a -> [a, r4][23x, a, r4] .
        !r5: a -> [a, r5][5x, a, r5] .
        !r6: a -> [a, r6][14x, a, r6] .
        !r7: a -> [a, r7][30x, a, r7] .
    }
}

type Output {
    step -> 2 step .
    9 step -> no, halt .
}

{a} (Main) - {step} (Output) .
```

The code comprises of two type definitions, *Main* and *Output*, together with the instantiation of two, linked, compartments of the respective types. The first two rules are guarded by $\{= 55x\}$ and $\{> 55x\}$ respectively, and organized in a *choice* block since they are mutually exclusive and each may execute once and only once. Indeed, enclosing these rules in a maximally parallel grouping would result in equivalent behaviour. A guard always relates to the multiset contained in the compartment it evaluates in and terminates with a colon; the $->$ symbol denotes the transition of a non-empty multiset on the left hand side to a rewrite-communication outcome (objects *yes*, *halt* into the compartment of type Output), or a *single* structure changing element (# which symbolises membrane dissolution). Next, the choice block is applied as a non-deterministic selection of *one* of the rules it envelopes: there are seven division rules, which resemble the addition of a value from $w(A)$. Each rule is prefixed by a guard $!r_i$, in order to prevent its subsequent application which would equate to multiple additions of the same number.

Type *Output* lists two rewriting rules which execute successively and non-repetitively. The first rule *increments* the number of *step* objects in the compartment, updating the step count as the computation unfolds. The second rule will only execute if we have reached the 9th step and no *halt* object was received from any of the *Main* compartments, effectively pronouncing a negative answer to the problem.

The kP-Lingua implementation is a compact and intuitive representation of the formally described model presented earlier. The specification is next translated into Spin's modelling language, Promela, a fully automated process accomplished by a *kP-Lingua parser* and *kP system - Promela* model converter, constituent tools of *kpWorkbench*. We document this stage of our approach with several fragments of the rather cryptic Promela encoding, as generated by our converter.

```
#define A0_SIZE 9
#define A1_SIZE 4

typedef C0 {
    int x[A0_SIZE] = 0;
    int xt[A0_SIZE] = 0;
    int c1Links[1];
    int c1LCount = 0;
    int c1LSize = 0;
    bit isComputing = 0;
    bit isDissolved = 0;
    bit isDivided = 0;
}

typedef C1 {
    int x[A1_SIZE] = 0;
    int xt[A1_SIZE] = 0;
    int c0Links[100];
    int c0LCount = 0;
    int c0LSize = 0;
    bit isComputing = 0;
```

```
}

int step = 0;
bit halt = 0;
C0 m0[20];
int m0Count = 0;
int m0Size = 0;
C1 m1[1];
int m1Count = 0;
int m1Size = 0;

int m0DissolvedCount = 0;
int stepsExp = 1;
```

In Table 4 we elucidate the constituent elements of the above printed data structures and variable declarations.

Table 4. Interpretation of variable expressions generated in Promela

A0_SIZE, A1_SIZE	The size of the alphabet for each type of compartment;
C0, C1	The compartment types *Main* and *Output* respectively;
x, xt	The arrays which store multiplicities of objects encoded as indices;
c1Links[1]	The array of links to compartments of type C1;
isComputing	A flag indicating whether a process is running on this instance or not;
isDissolved	A flag indicating whether the compartment is dissolved or not;
isDivided	Indicates if the compartment was divided (and henceforth considered non-existent);
m0, m1	The arrays which store compartments of type C0 (*Main*) and C1 (*Output*), respectively;
m0[0].x[2]	The object with index 2 in the 0th compartment of type C0;
m1[0].x[0]	Multiplicity of object *step* in compartment 0 of type *Output*;
m1[0].x[1]	Multiplicity of object *yes* in the output compartment;
m1[0].x[2]	Multiplicity of object *no* in the output compartment;
m1[0].x[3]	Multiplicity of object *halt* in the output compartment;
m0DissolvedCount	The number of dissolved compartments of type *Main*;
stepsExp	A number updated each step with the value of 2^{step}.

The second key requirement for the model checking methodology we exemplify in this section is the provision of LTL formulae the validity of which is to be asserted against the model. As methodically described in the previous section, a set of properties is generated by instantiating various natural language patterns. These are appointed as templates to be completed by the user with model variables or numeric constants, interactively, through a graphical user interface. Several screenshots which illustrate the Natural Language Query (NLQ) builder, integrated into kpWorkbench are supplied in the Appendix.

Table 5 lists an array of ten properties we have compiled and derived from natural language patterns for the Subset Sum example. These properties have

Table 5. List of properties derived from natural language patterns using NLQ and their generated LTL equivalent

Prop.	Pattern	Natural Language Statement and Spin formula

1	Until	The computation will eventually halt.
		`halt == 0 U halt > 0`
		`(m1[0].x[3] == 0 || !pInS) U (m1[0].x[3] > 0 && pInS)`

2	Until	The computation will halt within $n + 2$ steps.
		`(halt == 0 && steps < n + 2) U (halt > 0 && steps <= n + 2)`
		`(m1[0].x[3] == 0 && m1[0].x[0] < n+2 || !pInS) U`
		`(m1[0].x[3] >= 0 && m1[0].x[0] <= n+2 && pInS)`

3	Until	The computation will eventually halt with either a 'yes' or 'no' result.
		`halt == 0 U (halt > 0 && (yes > 0 || no > 0))`
		`(m1[0].x[3] == 0 || !pIns) U`
		`(m1[0].x[3] > 0 && (m1[0].x[1] > 0 || m1[0].x[2] > 0) && pInS)`

4	Until	At least one membrane division will eventually occur (before a result is obtained).
		`(yes == 0 && no == 0) U mOCount > 1`
		`(m1[0].x[1] == 0 && m1[0].x[2] == 0) || !pInS U mOCount > 1 && pInS`

5	Existence	A 'yes' result is eventually observed within no more than three steps.
		`F (yes > 0 && steps <= 3)`
		`<> (m1[0].x[1] > 0 && m1[0].x[0] <= 3 && pInS)`

6	Existence	A 'yes' result is eventually observed within more than three steps.
		`F (yes > 0 && steps > 3)`
		`<> (m1[0].x[1] > 0 && m1[0].x[0] > 3 && pInS)`

7	Existence	A result ('yes' or 'no') is eventually obtained without any membrane dissolutions.
		`F (yes > 0 || no > 0) && mODissolvedCount == 0`
		`<> ((m1[0].x[1] > 0 || m1[0].x[2] > 0) && mODissolvedCount == 0 && pInS)`

8	Existence	A 'yes' result is eventually obtained with membrane dissolution occuring.
		`F yes > 0 && mODissolvedCount > 0`
		`<> (m1[0].x[1] > 0 && mODissolvedCount > 0 && pInS)`

9	Universality	The number of compartments in use is always equal to $2^{stepcount}$.
		`G mOCount + 1 == TwoToTheNumberOfSteps`
		`[] (mOCount + 1 == TwoToTheNumberOfSteps || !pInS)`

10	Absence	There will never be a negative answer for this example.
		`!F no > 0`
		`!(<> (m1.x[2] > 0 && pInS ))`

been successfully verified with Spin on a Core i7 980X based machine, with 24GB RAM and running Windows 8 Professional Edition.

Devising a set of properties assisted by the NLQ tool becomes an intuitive, effortless and streamlined task, however, there may be cases when a generated natural language statement does not reflect the meaning of the property in its entirety, although it is logically equivalent. This may lead to shallow interpretations if the formal representation is not consulted and ultimately to oversights of relevant implications of the property. For example, in Table 5, the property *a 'yes' result is eventually observed within no more than three step* is as a fabricated form of *there exists a non-deterministic execution strategy that yields an affirmative result to the problem in no more than three steps*. The second expression is significantly more elevate and meaningful in comparison with its generated counterpart which clearly describes the underlying LTL formulae, but requires a deeper understanding of the model for an accurate interpretation.

6   Conclusions

The approach to kernel P system model checking presented in this paper is a power-ful synthesis of concepts and ideas, materialised into an aggregate of software tools and template data sets. The investigation permeates two innovative leaps, namely the kP system computational model in the context of membrane computing and the use of natural language patterns to generate temporal logic properties in the field of model checking. After establishing a model equivalence relation together with a procedural translation from a generic representation to a notation required by Spin, non-specialist users can benefit from the standard features offered by the model checker. The often intricate and abstruse process of constructing temporal logic formulae has also been abstracted to natural language statements and in-teractive visual representation through graphical user interface (GUI) elements. Another consequential advantage of significance is the correctness guarantee con-ferred by an automatic model conversion and formula generation.

Our case study illustrated in section 5, demonstrates the feasibility of this approach with its illustrious qualities, but also exposes the potential limitations of the method: on one hand, the notorious state space explosion problem is an inexorable fact that circumscribes the model checking of concurrent and non-deterministic systems; on the other hand, some generated properties, products of composite natural language patterns, are devoid of meaning and can possibly lead to shallow or inaccurate interpretations and even confusion.

Evidently, a more consistent qualitative evaluation of the methodology, involv-ing several other case studies is required to highlight its potential and limitations more generally. It would be interesting to see the outcome of future investigations in this newly established context.

Acknowledgements. The work of FI, RL and LM was supported by a grant of the Romanian National Authority for Scientific Research, CNCS-UEFISCDI (project number: PN-II-ID-PCE-2011-3-0688). SK acknowledges the support provided for synthetic biology research by EPSRC ROADBLOCK (project num-ber: EP/I031812/1). CD was sponsored by an EPSRC studentship.

References

1. Andrei, O., Ciobanu, G., Lucanu, D.: A rewriting logic framework for operational semantics of membrane systems. Theoretical Computer Science 373(3), 163–181 (2007)
2. Bellini, P., Nesi, P., Rogai, D.: Expressing and organizing real-time specification patterns via temporal logics. Journal of Systems and Software 82(2), 183–196 (2009)
3. Bernardini, F., Gheorghe, M., Romero-Campero, F.J., Walkinshaw, N.: A hybrid approach to modeling biological systems. In: Eleftherakis, G., Kefalas, P., Păun, G., Rozenberg, G., Salomaa, A. (eds.) WMCS 2007. LNCS, vol. 4860, pp. 138–159. Springer, Heidelberg (2007)

4. Blakes, J., Twycross, J., Konur, S., Romero-Campero, F.J., Krasnogor, N., Gheorghe, M.: Infobiotics workbench - A P systems based tool for systems and synthetic biology. Applications of Membrane Computing in Systems and Synthetic Biology (to appear, 2013)
5. Ciobanu, G., Pérez-Jiménez, M.J., Păun, G. (eds.): Applications of Membrane Computing. Natural Computing Series. Springer (2006)
6. Dwyer, M.B., Avrunin, G.S., Corbett, J.C.: Patterns in property specifications for finite-state verification. In: Proceedings of the 21st International Conference on Software Engineering, ICSE 1999, pp. 411–420. ACM (1999)
7. Gheorghe, M., Ipate, F., Dragomir, C., Mierla, L., Valencia-Cabrera, L., García-Quismondo, M., Pérez-Jiménez, M.J.: Kernel P systems. Eleventh Brainstorming Week on Membrane Computing, 97–124 (2013)
8. Gheorghe, M., Ipate, F., Lefticaru, R., Pérez-Jiménez, M.J., Turcanu, A., Valencia-Cabrera, L., García-Quismondo, M., Mierla, L.: 3-Col problem modelling using simple kernel P systems. International Journal of Computer Mathematics 90(4), 816–830 (2013)
9. Gruhn, V., Laue, R.: Patterns for timed property specifications. Electronic Notes Theoretical Computer Science 153(2), 117–133 (2006)
10. Grunske, L.: Specification patterns for probabilistic quality properties. In: Proceedings of the 30th International Conference on Software Engineering, ICSE 2008, pp. 31–40. ACM (2008)
11. Hinton, A., Kwiatkowska, M., Norman, G., Parker, D.: PRISM: A tool for automatic verification of probabilistic systems. In: Hermanns, H., Palsberg, J. (eds.) TACAS 2006. LNCS, vol. 3920, pp. 441–444. Springer, Heidelberg (2006)
12. Holzmann, G.J.: The model checker SPIN. IEEE Transactions on Software Engineering 23(5), 275–295 (1997)
13. Horowitz, E., Sahni, S.: Computing partitions with applications to the knapsack problem. Journal of the Association for Computing Machinery 21, 277–292 (1974)
14. Ipate, F., et al.: Kernel P systems: Applications and implementations. In: Proceedings of the Eighth International Conference on Bio-Inspired Computing: Theories and Applications (BIC-TA), 2013. AISC, vol. 212, pp. 1081–1089. Springer, Heidelberg (2013)
15. Ipate, F., Lefticaru, R., Tudose, C.: Formal verification of P systems using Spin. International Journal of Foundations of Computer Science 22(1), 133–142 (2011)
16. Konrad, S., Cheng, B.: Real-time specification patterns. In: Proceedings of 27th International Conference on Software Engineering, pp. 372–381 (2005)
17. Lefticaru, R., Ipate, F., Valencia-Cabrera, L., Turcanu, A., Tudose, C., Gheorghe, M., Pérez-Jiménez, M.J., Niculescu, I.M., Dragomir, C.: Towards an integrated approach for model simulation, property extraction and verification of P systems. Tenth Brainstorming Week on Membrane Computing I, 291–318 (2012)
18. Lefticaru, R., Tudose, C., Ipate, F.: Towards automated verification of P systems using Spin. International Journal of Natural Computing Research 2(3), 1–12 (2011)
19. Monteiro, P.T., Ropers, D., Mateescu, R., Freitas, A.T., de Jong, H.: Temporal logic patterns for querying dynamic models of cellular interaction networks. Bioinformatics 24(16), i227–i233 (2008)
20. Pnueli, A.: The temporal logic of programs. In: Proceedings of the 18th Annual IEEE Symposium on Foundations of Computer Science, pp. 46–57. IEEE Computer Society Press (1977)
21. Păun, G.: Computing with membranes. Journal of Computer and System Sciences 61(1), 108–143 (2000)

Appendix A: Screenshots Illustrating Our NLQ Tool

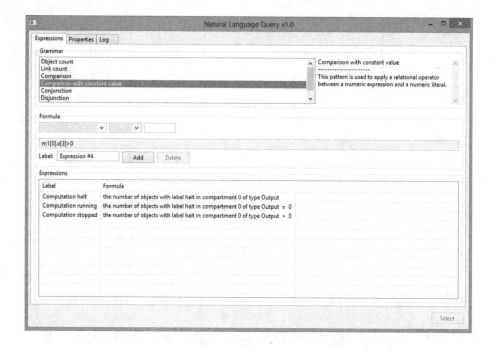

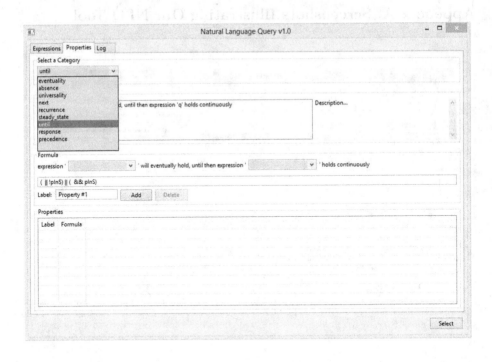

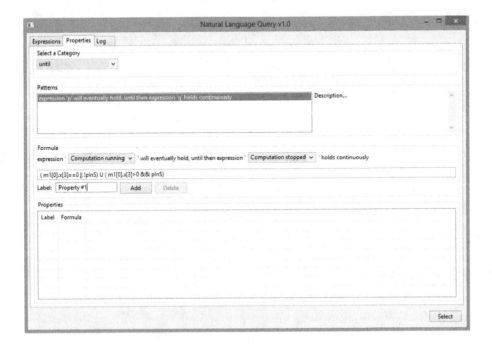

Flattening in (Tissue) P Systems

Rudolf Freund[1], Alberto Leporati[2], Giancarlo Mauri[2],
Antonio E. Porreca[2], Sergey Verlan[3], and Claudio Zandron[2]

[1] Faculty of Informatics, Vienna University of Technology
Favoritenstr. 9, 1040 Vienna, Austria
`rudi@emcc.at`
[2] Dipartimento di Informatica, Sistemistica e Comunicazione
Università degli Studi di Milano-Bicocca
Viale Sarca 336/14, 20126 Milano, Italy
`{alberto.leporati,giancarlo.mauri,porreca,claudio.zandron}@unimib.it`
[3] LACL, Département Informatique, Université Paris Est
61, av. Général de Gaulle, 94010 Créteil, France
`verlan@univ-paris12.fr`

Abstract. For many models of P systems and tissue P systems, the main behavior of a specific system can be simulated by a corresponding system with only one membrane or cell, respectively; this effective construction is called flattening. In this paper we describe the main procedure of flattening for specific variants of static (tissue) P systems as well as for classes of dynamic (tissue) P systems with a bounded number of possible membrane structures or a bounded number of cells during any computation.

1 Introduction

One of the main ideas of membrane systems as introduced by Gheorghe Păun in [10] is the distributed way of computation in the different membrane regions of a membrane system. On the other hand, even for the original variant of membrane systems using catalysts it has been shown that all computations can be carried out in only one single membrane for getting computational completeness (see [4]). Using the idea of flattening which we are going to discuss in this paper, i.e., constructing a (tissue) P system with only one membrane (cell) simulating the computations of a given (tissue) P system, especially for P systems working in the sequential or the maximally parallel derivation mode one often can show that the number of membranes does not matter. For example, as is well known, with transition P systems using only non-cooperative rules in the sequential derivation mode one can characterize the family of Parikh sets of regular languages, no matter how many membranes are used.

Whereas without any doubt for communication P systems, where computations are carried out by moving objects through membranes, the underlying membrane structure of a P system or the underlying graph structure of a tissue P system will always play an essential role, in the case of transition P systems or

A. Alhazov et al. (Eds.): CMC 2013, LNCS 8340, pp. 173–188, 2014.
© Springer-Verlag Berlin Heidelberg 2014

tissue P systems with evolution rules, a flattening procedure may allow for reducing the number of membranes or cells to one, i.e., to pure multiset rewriting, without changing the main concept for the computational power of such systems. Yet depending on the exact definitions of how these systems are supposed to use their rules and how to get the final results, specific issues have to be discussed carefully.

As this paper addresses to experts in the area of P systems, in general we only refer the reader to [11] and the P page [13] for specific notions and results used or stated afterwards. Formal definitions for a general model of static (tissue) P systems can be found in [6], a formal framework for dynamically evolving structures in [5]. Several other examples for flattening and flattening strategies, described in the formal framework of [6] and [5], can be found in [14].

2   Definitions

The set of non-negative integers is denoted by $\mathbb{N}$, the set of d-dimensional vectors of non-negative integers by $\mathbb{N}^d$. An *alphabet* V is a finite non-empty set of abstract *symbols*. Given V, the free monoid generated by V under the operation of concatenation is denoted by V^*; the elements of V^* are called strings, and the *empty string* is denoted by λ; $V^* \setminus \{\lambda\}$ is denoted by V^+. Let $\{a_1, \cdots, a_d\}$ be an arbitrary alphabet; the number of occurrences of a symbol a_i in a string x is denoted by $|x|_{a_i}$; the *Parikh vector* associated with x with respect to $a_1, \cdots, a_d$ is $\left(|x|_{a_1}, \cdots, |x|_{a_d}\right) \in \mathbb{N}^d$. The *Parikh image* of a language L over $\{a_1, \cdots, a_d\}$ is the set of all Parikh vectors of strings in L, and we denote it by $Ps(L)$. For a family of languages FL, the family of Parikh images of languages in FL is denoted by $PsFL$; for families of languages of a one-letter alphabet, the corresponding sets of non-negative integers are denoted by NFL. Moreover, by N^dFL we denote the family of Parikh images of languages over an alphabet of d letters in FL. Finally, we also use the convention that two sets of d-dimensional vectors in $\mathbb{N}^d$ are considered to be equal if they only differ at most by the zero-vector $(0, \cdots, 0)$.

A (finite) multiset over the (finite) alphabet V, $V = \{a_1, \cdots, a_d\}$, is a mapping $f : V \longrightarrow \mathbb{N}$ and is represented by $\langle f(a_1), a_1 \rangle \cdots \langle f(a_d), a_d \rangle$ or by any string x the Parikh vector of which with respect to $a_1, \cdots, a_d$ is $(f(a_1), \cdots, f(a_d))$. In the following we will not distinguish between a vector $(m_1, \cdots, m_d)$, its representation by a multiset $\langle a_1, m_1 \rangle \cdots \langle a_d, m_d \rangle$ or its representation by a string x having the Parikh vector $\left(|x|_{a_1}, \cdots, |x|_{a_d}\right) = (m_1, \cdots, m_d)$. Fixing the sequence of symbols $a_1, \cdots, a_d$ in the alphabet V in advance, the representation of the multiset $\langle m_1, a_1 \rangle \cdots \langle m_d, a_d \rangle$ by the string $a_1^{m_1} \cdots a_d^{m_d}$ is unique. The set of all finite multisets over an alphabet V is denoted by $\langle V, \mathbb{N} \rangle$. If we allow some objects to appear in an unbounded number, then we consider a (finite or infinite) multiset as a mapping $f : V \longrightarrow \mathbb{N}_\infty$, where $\mathbb{N}_\infty = \mathbb{N} \cup \{\infty\}$ with ∞ denoting infinity. The set of all (finite or infinite) multisets over an alphabet V is denoted by $\langle V, \mathbb{N}_\infty \rangle$.

The family of regular and recursively enumerable string languages is denoted by REG and RE, respectively. For more details of formal language theory the reader is referred to the monographs and handbooks in this area as [3] and [12].

As a formal model we consider a *network of cells of degree* $n \geq 1$ as a construct

$$\Pi = (V, T, Inf_0, \dots, Inf_n, w_0, \dots, w_n, R, f)$$

where

- V is a finite alphabet;
- $T \subseteq V$ is the terminal alphabet;
- $Inf_i \subseteq V$, for all $0 \leq i \leq n$, specifies the set of objects appearing in an unbounded number in cell i (the $n + 1$ cells are labeled by $0 \dots n$ or, in a more general way, uniquely labeled by labels from a set Lab);
- $w_i \in \langle V, \mathbb{N} \rangle$, for all $0 \leq i \leq n$, is the finite multiset from $V \backslash Inf_i$ initially associated with cell i; in total, the initial configuration of Π is described by the multisets $w_i \cup \bigcup_{a \in Inf_i} \langle a, \infty \rangle$, $0 \leq i \leq n$;
- R is a finite set of *rules* of the form $(X \to Y; E)$;
- f, $0 \leq f \leq n$, is the cell where the output is collected in the generating case and the input is put in in the accepting case.

In a rule $(X \to Y; E)$, X and Y are $(n+1)$-vectors of multisets over V, i.e., $X = (x_0, \dots, x_n)$, $Y = (y_0, \dots, y_n)$, $x_i, y_i \in \langle V, \mathbb{N} \rangle$, $0 \leq i \leq n$, and E, in the most general form, is a decidable condition on the contents of the $n+1$ cells; for example, we may take $E = (P, Q)$, where $P = (p_0, \dots, p_n)$ and $Q = (q_0, \dots, q_n)$ are *permitting* and *forbidden* contexts, with p_i, q_i being from $\langle V, \mathbb{N} \rangle$ or being finite subsets from $2^{\langle V, \mathbb{N} \rangle}$, $0 \leq i \leq n$ (for details see [6]). The application of such a rule means replacing the multiset x_i in cell i by the multiset y_i, $0 \leq i \leq n$, provided E is fulfilled; for example, for $E = (P, Q)$ this means that (every multiset from) p_i is contained in cell i whereas (any multiset from) q_i is not, for $1 \leq i \leq n$.

Transitions in a network of cells may be carried out in the *sequential mode* (exactly one rule is applied), in the *maximally parallel mode* (an applicable multiset which cannot be extended to an applicable multiset of rules is applied), etc.; usually, a computation ends when no rule can be applied any more, i.e., Π *halts*, but there are also other ways of halting (again see [6]), e.g., stopping when a specific symbol appears. During a computation, the *configurations* of the network of cells Π describe the finite multisets of objects from $V \backslash Inf_i$ contained in each cell i, $0 \leq i \leq n$.

A network of cells may be used to *generate* a (vector of) non-negative integer(s) in a specific output cell (membrane) or to *accept* a (vector of) non-negative integer(s) placed in a specific input cell at the beginning of a computation. Moreover, the goal can also be to *compute* an output from a given input or to output **yes** or **no** to *decide* a specific property of a given input.

For a network of cells Π, we consider the communication graph $CG(\Pi)$ built up from all rules in R as follows: the cells of Π are the nodes of $CG(\Pi)$; for each pair (k, m) with $k \neq m$, $x_k \neq \lambda$, and $y_m \neq \lambda$ we introduce an edge $\{k, m\}$ between the nodes k and m. If this communication graph $CG(\Pi)$ is a tree whose root has only one successor, then Π is called a *hierarchical P system*, with the root corresponding to the *environment* (usually then labeled by 0) and its single successor being the *skin membrane* (usuall labeled by 1), and the cells are called *membranes*. Usually, at least some objects occur infinitely often in the environment (but not in other membrane regions); these need not be taken into account within the rules with respect to the environment. If the communication graph $CG(\Pi)$ does not allow for the interpretation of Π as a hierarchical P system, then in this paper such a network of cells Π will also be called a *tissue P system*, although in the literature this notion is often used for – with respect to the communication structure – more restricted variants of networks of cells.

A *hierarchical P system* is (represented as) a construct

$$\Pi = (V, T, Env, \mu, w_0, w_1, \ldots, w_n, R, f)$$

where

- V is a finite alphabet;
- $T \subseteq V$ is the terminal alphabet;
- $Env \subseteq V$ is the set of elements appearing infinitely often in the environment (in all other membranes, all objects only appear in a finite number of copies), i.e., this corresponds to $Inf_0 = Env$ and $Inf_i = \emptyset$ for $1 \leq i \leq n$;
- μ describes the hierarchical membrane structure where 0 denotes the environment and 1 is the skin membrane;
- $w_i \in \langle V, \mathbb{N} \rangle$, for all $1 \leq i \leq n$, is the multiset initially associated with membrane i, w_0 specifies the finite multiset of objects from $V \backslash Env$ initially appearing in the environment;
- R is a finite set of *rules* of the form $(i : X \to Y; E)$ where $1 \leq i \leq n$, $X \in \langle V, \mathbb{N} \rangle$, $Y = (y_{\alpha_1}, \alpha_1) \ldots (y_{\alpha_k}, \alpha_k)$ with $\alpha_j \in TAR_\mu$, $y_{\alpha_j} \in \langle V, \mathbb{N} \rangle$, $1 \leq j \leq k$, $k \geq 0$, and with

$$TAR_\mu = \{here, in, out\} \cup \{in_j \mid 2 \leq j \leq n\}$$

being the set of targets; the target *here* means that the generated objects remain in membrane i, $1 \leq i \leq n$; the target *out* means that the generated objects are sent out to the membrane surrounding membrane i (i.e., the parent of i, $1 \leq i \leq n$, in the tree representing the membrane structure μ); the target *in* means that the generated objects are sent into one of the membranes directly inside membrane i (one of the children of i in the tree representing the membrane structure μ), and by in_j one can directly specify one of the inner membranes where the objects are sent to;
- $f, 0 \leq f \leq n$, is the membrane where the output is collected in the generating case and the input is put into in the accepting case.

Example 1. Consider the network of cells with four cells

$$\Pi = (\{a\}, \{a\}, \emptyset, \emptyset, \emptyset, \emptyset, \langle a, 0 \rangle, \langle a, 0 \rangle, \langle a, 0 \rangle, \langle a, 0 \rangle, R, 1)$$

with

$$R = \{(\lambda, aa, \lambda, \lambda) \to (\lambda, a, \lambda, \lambda), (\lambda, a, \lambda, \lambda) \to (\lambda, \lambda, a, \lambda)\}$$
$$\cup \{(\lambda, \lambda, aa, \lambda) \to (\lambda, \lambda, \lambda, aa), (\lambda, \lambda, \lambda, aa) \to (\lambda, \lambda, aa, \lambda)\}.$$

As we can see, cell 0 is not involved in any rule (so we can take it as the environment), and transitions only take place between cells 1, 2, and 3; hence, we can represent this network of cells in a more readable way as the corresponding hierarchical P system

$$\Pi'' = (\{a\}, \{a\}, \emptyset, [_1 [_2 [_3]_3]_2]_1, \lambda, \lambda, \lambda, \lambda, R'', 1).$$

with

$$R'' = \{1 : aa \to (a, here), 1 : a \to (a, in)\}$$
$$\cup \{2 : aa \to (aa, in), 3 : aa \to (aa, out)\}.$$

If we consider (Π and) Π'' as accepting P systems working in the maximally parallel mode, then the accepted set (of multisets) is $\{a^{2^n} \mid n \geq 0\}$, corresponding to the non-semilinear set of natural numbers $\{2^n \mid n \geq 0\}$: the rule $1 : aa \to (a, here)$ applied in parallel to the input of objects a in membrane 1 divides their number by 2; if (and only if) the original number of input objects is a power of 2, then the rule $1 : a \to (a, in)$ is only to be applied at the end of the computation; a single object a cannot be processed any more in membrane 2, whereas as soon as this rule is applied at least twice, the application of the rules $2 : aa \to (aa, in)$ and $3 : aa \to (aa, out)$ causes an infinite loop, hence, exactly the inputs a^{2^n}, $n \geq 0$, are accepted by halting computations.

3 The Basic Flattening Procedure for Static (Tissue) P Systems

Any element a in cell i of a network of cells

$$\Pi = (V, T, Inf_0, \ldots, Inf_n, w_0, \ldots, w_n, R, f)$$

can be represented as a symbol (a, i) in a network of cells (tissue P system)

$$\Pi' = (V', T', Inf_1, w, R', 1)$$

with only one cell where

- $V' = \{(a, i) \mid a \in V, 0 \leq i \leq n\}$;
- $T' = \{(a, f) \mid a \in T\}$; especially for the generating case, only the terminal symbols in the output cell/membrane count;
- $Inf_1 = \{h_i (a_i) \mid a_i \in Inf_i, 0 \leq i \leq n\}$ where the h_i, $0 \leq i \leq n$, are the renaming morphisms $h_i : V \to V \times \{i\}$ with $h_i (a) = (a, i)$ for all $a \in V$;
- $w = h_0 (w_0) \ldots h_n (w_n)$;

- for getting the rules in R', any $(n+1)$-vector of multisets $(z_0, \ldots, z_n)$ over V in the rules from R is replaced by the single multiset $h_0(z_0) \ldots h_n(z_n)$. Similar replacements have to be taken into account for every condition E in a rule $(X \to Y; E) \in R$. For example, if $X = (x_0, \ldots, x_n)$, $Y = (y_0, \ldots, y_n)$, $E = (P, Q)$, $P = (p_0, \ldots, p_n)$, $Q = (q_0, \ldots, q_n)$, we take the corresponding rule

$$(h_0(x_0) \ldots h_n(x_n) \to h_0(y_0) \ldots h_n(y_n);$$
$$((h_0(p_0), \ldots, h_n(p_n)), (h_0(q_0), \ldots, h_n(q_n))))$$

into R'.

It is quite obvious that each computation step in Π' corresponds to a computation step in Π and vice versa, no matter which of the basic derivation modes – sequential, asynchronous, maximally parallel – we use; Π' working in the sequential mode now corresponds to a pure multiset rewriting system $G = (V', T', w, R')$ with permitting and forbidden contexts (provided Inf_1 is empty).

In this static case, the flattened network of cells essentially is of the same kind as the original one, hence, we speak of *strong flattening*.

Example 2. Consider the accepting P system Π working in the maximally parallel mode from Example 1; then the corresponding flattened tissue P system (in the following, we omit Inf_1, as this set of objects being available infinitely often is empty) is

$$\Pi' = (\{(a, i) \mid i \in \{1, 2, 3\}\}, \{(a, 1)\}, \lambda, R', 1) \text{ with}$$
$$R = \{(a, 1)(a, 1) \to (a, 1), (a, 1) \to (a, 2)\}$$
$$\cup \{(a, 2)(a, 2) \to (a, 3)(a, 3), (a, 3)(a, 3) \to (a, 2)(a, 2)\}.$$

The accepted set (of multisets) is $\left\{(a, 1)^{2^n} \mid n \geq 0\right\}$, again corresponding to the non-semilinear set of natural numbers $\{2^n \mid n \geq 0\}$.

We would like to mention that Π' can also be seen as a hierarchical P system with only one membrane, thereby neglecting the environment outside the skin membrane, as there is no communication between these two regions. In that sense, the single cell in Π' has been assigned the label 1 (and not 0).

Even in the case of strong flattening, some specific small issues have to be taken into consideration carefully: as we have seen in Example 2, in the accepting case, the input vector has to be encoded by h_f, $0 \leq f \leq n$; in the generating case, in most cases we cannot avoid having to take the projection on the terminal alphabet (there are some simple exceptions, where all non-terminal objects have vanished whenever the computation halts, e.g., the semilinear sets, i.e., $NREG$, can be generated in that way).

Special care has to be taken for treating the environment: for tissue P systems, we may assume the environment to be one of the cells; for hierarchical P systems, the environment usually is considered to be an additional membrane with label 0; the necessary changes for Π' and especially R' are rather obvious, only the treatment of the symbols occurring infinitely often in the environment needs some special conventions (for details we refer to [6]).

4   Communication P Systems

The general model of networks of cells also captures a lot of variants of (pure) communication P systems, e.g., P systems using antiport and symport rules. Hence, in principle, the basic flattening procedure can be applied to such communication P systems, too. Yet in this case, flattening means a dramatic change in the underlying philosophy of these system: whereas in pure communication P systems objects just move between the cells/membranes and are never destroyed or generated, in the corresponding flattened system we have rewriting rules doing exactly this kind of operations. Thus, with flattening we lose the main idea of the underlying concept. Hence, the flattened (tissue) P system is not of the same kind as the original one, and we can only speak of *flattening*, but not of strong flattening any more. We would like to point out that communication P systems with only one membrane as often occurring in the literature in fact correspond to tissue P systems with two cells, as the environment plays an essential role as the additional second cell; therefore, P systems using antiport and symport rules always need at least two cells to be represented with still capturing the idea of communication instead of rewriting, hence, in this case strong flattening is not possible.

On the other hand, flattening may still be a useful tool when investigating specific features of special variants of communication P systems, e.g., see [1].

5   Flattening for (Tissue) P Systems with Polarizations

In a more general case, we may allow the membranes (cells) to carry so-called polarizations from a finite set *Pol*; depending on those polarizations, the set of transition rules available for the objects in a membrane (cell) may vary. The unique label $h \in Lab$ and the current polarization p of a membrane (cell) can be put together in a pair (h, p) which can be taken as the new unique label of this membrane (cell); hence, using a rule changing the polarization from p to p' then means changing the label from (h, p) to (h, p'). The current structure of a (tissue) P system with polarizations can be described by a function $\mu : Lab \to Pol$ assigning one polarization to each membrane (cell). Now let M be the (finite!) set of all such functions; for each $\mu \in M$, we introduce a variable $V(\mu)$, which in the flattened system will be used as an object representing μ, and we denote $V(M) = \{V(\mu) \mid \mu \in M\}$. In our general model of networks of cells, the rules in R in a network of cells Π now are of the extended form $(X \to Y; E; \mu \to \mu')$ with the rules $\mu \to \mu'$ including the changes of polarizations induced by the application of the rule $(X \to Y; E)$; we also assume that such a rule is only applicable if the current polarizations of the membranes (cells) are consistent with μ. Moreover, several such rules can only be applied in parallel if all of them together exactly yield the new structure μ'.

For a network of cells Π working in one of the basic derivation modes, i.e., in the sequential, the asynchronous, or the maximally parallel mode, we immediately get the flattened network of cells Π' by just adapting the basic flattening procedure with using the extended rules and their applicability constraints as described above; moreover, the function μ_0 representing the structure of the start configuration of Π has initially to be assigned to the single cell of Π'. In general, the flattened system will be of a different kind of (tissue) P systems as the original one, as we have used extended variants of rules and additional constraints for the applicability of a multiset of rules in the flattened system.

In the *sequential mode*, we can get even more: based on the construction of the flattened tissue P system Π' as given above, we construct a tissue P system

$$\Pi'' = (V'', T', wV(\mu_0), R'', 1)$$

with the basic type of rules of the form $(X \rightarrow Y; E)$: the structure information from Π is stored in an additional symbol; therefore, we take $V'' = V' \cup V(M)$ and start with the axiom $wV(\mu_0)$ with $V(\mu_0)$ representing the structure of the start configuration of Π. Moreover, we take

$$R'' = \{(uV(\mu) \rightarrow vV(\mu'); E) \mid (u \rightarrow v; E; \mu \rightarrow \mu') \in R'\}.$$

The change of the structure now is included in (the application of) the rule itself; the only drawback of this construction is that the rules $uV(\mu) \rightarrow vV(\mu')$ now are cooperative rules, while the original rules $u \rightarrow v$ might have been only non-cooperative rules. Yet in the best case, we even get strong flattening for (tissue) P systems with cooperative rules working in the sequential mode.

For P systems with active membranes working in the asynchronuous derivation mode, having polarizations on the membranes and even allowing for dissolution, but not for membrane division, a flattening procedure was described in [8].

There are several other ideas for how to obtain a flattened (tissue) P system in the case of the maximally parallel mode using permitting and/or forbidding contexts which will also be discussed in the next section together with membrane (cell) dissolution. Instead of one single symbol $V(\mu)$ describing the actual structure of the (tissue) P system we may also use a distinct symbol for describing the actual state of each membrane (cell); again, the number of these symbols is finite, as we only have a finite number of membranes (cells) and corresponding polarizations. If we assume that at most one rule in any computation step may affect the status of each membrane (cell), we can use the corresponding cooperative rules $(uV(\mu_i) \rightarrow vV(\mu_i'); E)$ as already discussed earlier for the sequential mode, where the index i now indicates that only the status of membrane (cell) i is affected. But this construction is not yet sufficient for the parallel case now, as all the other rules have to *know* which current status the related membrane (cell) has; the easiest way to capture this obviously is to use permitting contexts, i.e., we have to replace each rule $(u \rightarrow v; E)$ applicable under the condition of structure μ_i by the new rule $(u \rightarrow v; E \wedge (\{\mu_i\}, \emptyset))$.

Example 3. Consider the hierarchical P system

$\Pi = (\{a\}, \{a\}, \emptyset, [_{(1,0)}]_{(1,0)}, \lambda, a, R, 1)$ with
$R = \{(1,0) : a \rightarrow (aa, here), (1,0) : a \rightarrow (aa, here) \, \delta \, ((1,0) \rightarrow (1,1))\}.$

In the rule $(1,0) : a \to (aa, here)\, \delta\, ((1,0) \to (1,1))$, the part $\delta\, ((1,0) \to (1,1))$ indicates that with this rule the polarization of membrane 1 is changed from 0 to 1. With this new polarization, no rule is applicable any more. Therefore, if we consider Π as generating P system working in the maximally parallel mode, then the generated set (of multisets) is $\{a^{2^n} \mid n \geq 1\}$, corresponding to the non-semilinear set of natural numbers $\{2^n \mid n \geq 1\}$: the rule $(1,0) : a \to (aa, here)$ applied in parallel to objects a in membrane 1 duplicates their number; if (and only if) the rule $(1,0) : a \to (aa, here)\, \delta\, ((1,0) \to (1,1))$ is also applied once (at the end of the computation), the polarization of membrane 1 is changed from 0 to 1. With this new polarization, no rule is applicable any more, hence, the computation halts, with the result a^{2^n}, $n \geq 1$, with n being the number of computation steps.

In principle, this hierarchical system already has only one membrane (the environment plays no role in the evolution of the system), but we now want to construct a (tissue) P system with only one cell which does not change the polarization of its membrane: According to the construction described above, we obtain the following (tissue) P system

$$\Pi' = (\{(a,1), \mu_{(1,0)}, \mu_{(1,1)}\}, \{(a,1)\}, (a,1)\, \mu_{(1,0)}, R', 1) \text{ with}$$
$$R' = \{((a,1) \to (a,1)\,(a,1) ; (\{\mu_{(1,0)}\}, \emptyset)),$$
$$((a,1)\, \mu_{(1,0)} \to (a,1)\,(a,1)\, \mu_{(1,1)} ; (\{\mu_{(1,0)}\}, \emptyset))\}.$$

The objects $\mu_{(1,0)}$ and $\mu_{(1,1)}$ represent the polarizations 0 and 1 of membrane 1. Starting with the initial configuration $((a,1)\, \mu_{(1,0)})$, the rule $((a,1) \to (a,1)\,(a,1) ; (\{\mu_{(1,0)}\}, \emptyset))$ can only be applied in a maximally parallel way as long as the second rule $((a,1)\, \mu_{(1,0)} \to (a,1)\,(a,1)\, \mu_{(1,1)} ; (\{\mu_{(1,0)}\}, \emptyset))$ is not applied, too, whereafter the computation immediately halts.

6   Flattening for (Tissue) P Systems with Membrane (Cell) Dissolution

Already in the original model of membrane systems introduced in [10], the possibility of membrane dissolution was investigated. The objects from the dissolved membrane r are moved into the surrounding membrane region. In a more general context, the dissolution of a cell and the moving of its contents were discussed in [5] as the operation *Delete-and-Move(r)*. Such systems with membrane (cell) dissolution have a finite number of possible membrane structures, as the dissolution operation can only decrease the number of membranes (cells) already present at the beginning of the computation. Hence, it is possible to mimic the effect of the dissolution by assigning a marker to each membrane in order to indicate if the membrane is dissolved or not, and by using permitting and/or forbidding contexts in order to check these markers and by using a subset construction at the level of rules in order to capture all possible structure changes.

The main idea for the flattening procedure is that the objects from a deleted membrane (cell) i are moved to another membrane (cell) j and there are treated as objects from membrane (cell) j, i.e., every object (a, i) now has to be treated as an object (a, j). Hence, for any possible membrane (cell) structure μ we define a mapping I_μ interpreting the objects (a, i) with respect to the current membrane (cell) structure μ. In the flattened (tissue) P system even with polarizations as described before we then have the rules $(I_\mu (u) \to I_{\mu'} (v) ; I_\mu (E) ; \mu \to \mu')$ instead of the rules $(u \to v; E; \mu \to \mu')$ – obviously the condition E has to be interpreted in the sense of I_μ, too. For technical details concerning the formal interpretation of the structure changes caused by $\mu \to \mu'$ including the deletion of a membrane (cell) with moving its contents to the surrounding membrane region (to another cell) we refer the expert reader to [5].

For the sequential mode, according to the construction given in the preceding section, we get the (tissue) P system

$$\Pi'' = \left(V'', T', I_{\mu_0} (w) V (\mu_0), R'', 1\right) \text{ with}$$
$$R'' = \{(I_\mu (u) V (\mu) \to I_{\mu'} (v) V (\mu') ; I_\mu (E)) \mid (u \to v; E; \mu \to \mu') \in R'\}.$$

For hierarchical P systems working in the maximally parallel derivation mode, a flattening procedure was described in [2]. The main idea of such a proof is that, besides taking the additional rules $V (\mu) \to V (\mu')$ for all possible membrane structures μ, μ', the maximally parallel application of the original rules together with exactly one of these rules is controlled by taking $V (\mu)$ as (eventually additional) permitting context in a similar way as we have already discussed in the preceding section, e.g., see Example 3. With such a construction, even the dissolution of several membranes in one computation step can be captured.

In the following example, we now follow the idea already exhibited at the beginning of this section with describing the status (existing/not existing) of each membrane (cell) by a distinct symbol; moreover, each object in a rule, according to these symbols (characterizing the actual structure of the system) given as permitting contexts, may originate from different membranes (cells).

Example 4. Consider the hierarchical P system

$$\Pi = (\{a, b\}, \{b\}, \emptyset, [_1 [_2]_2 [_3]_3]_1, \lambda, \lambda, a, a, R, 1) \text{ with}$$
$$R = \{2 : a \to \left(a^2, here\right), 2 : a \to \left(a^2, here\right) \delta\}$$
$$\cup \{3 : a \to \left(a^4, here\right), 3 : a \to \left(a^4, here\right) \delta\}$$
$$\cup \{1 : aa \to \left(b^3, here\right)\}.$$

We consider Π as a generating P system working in the maximally parallel mode: in membranes 2 and 3, in each computation step, the actual number of objects is multiplied by 2 and 4 by the rules $2 : a \to \left(a^2, here\right)$ and $3 : a \to \left(a^4, here\right)$, respectively. By applying the rules with the membrane dissolution operator δ in one of these membranes, the corresponding membrane is dissolved and the objects a are sent to the skin membrane, where in the next step, from each couple of objects a three terminal objects b evolve. As soon as both membranes 2 and 3 have been dissolved, the system halts. In sum, the generated set (of multisets) corresponds to the non-semilinear set of natural numbers

$\left\{ 3.2^{n-1} \mid n \geq 1 \right\} \cup \left\{ 6.4^{m-1} \mid m \geq 1 \right\}$ where n and m are the numbers of computation steps in membranes 2 and 3 until the dissolution of the corresponding membrane.

As the environment is not involved in the P system Π, the corresponding flattened (tissue) P system can be constructed as follows:

$$\Pi' = (V', \{(b,1)\}, (a,2)(a,3), R', 1),$$
$$V' = \{(a,i), (b,i) \mid i \in \{1,2,3\}\} \cup \{s_i, \bar{s}_i \mid i \in \{1,2,3\}\},$$
$$R' = \{((a,2) \to (a,2)^2; (\{s_2\}, \emptyset)), ((a,2) s_2 \to (a,2)^2 \bar{s}_2; (\{s_2\}, \emptyset))\}$$
$$\cup \{((a,3) \to (a,3)^4; (\{s_3\}, \emptyset)), ((a,3) s_3 \to (a,3)^4 \bar{s}_3; (\{s_3\}, \emptyset))\}$$
$$\cup \{(a,1)(a,1) \to (b,1)^3; (\{s_1\}, \emptyset)), (a,1)(a,2) \to (b,1)^3; (\{s_1, \bar{s}_2\}, \emptyset)),$$
$$\quad (a,2)(a,2) \to (b,1)^3; (\{s_1, \bar{s}_2\}, \emptyset)), (a,1)(a,3) \to (b,1)^3; (\{s_1, \bar{s}_3\}, \emptyset)),$$
$$\quad (a,3)(a,3) \to (b,1)^3; (\{s_1, \bar{s}_3\}, \emptyset)),$$
$$\quad (a,2)(a,3) \to (b,1)^3; (\{s_1, \bar{s}_2, \bar{s}_3\}, \emptyset))\}.$$

The symbols s_i ($\bar{s}_i$) indicate that membrane i is (not) present. In membrane 1, the symbol a may originate from membranes 1, 2, and 3; hence, for the left-hand side of the original rule $1 : aa \to (b^3, here)$ each of the two symbols a may come from each of the three membranes depending on the underlying membrane structure which is visible from the permitting context. As the skin membrane (membrane 1) must not be deleted, each occurrence of s_1 in the permitting contexts could be omitted.

When the computation halts, the symbols $s_1, \bar{s}_2, \bar{s}_3$ are present. In order to eliminate these additional symbols (instead of having to make the projection on the terminal alphabet $\{(b,1)\}$), we would have to add the rule

$$(s_1 \bar{s}_2 \bar{s}_3 \to \lambda; (\emptyset, \{(a,1), (a,2), (a,3)\}))$$

with the forbidden context guaranteeing that no rule can be applied any more. This idea with such a forbidden context can be used in general, too.

7   Flattening for (Tissue) P Systems with Membrane (Cell) Creation, Division, and Dissolution

Whereas the deletion of membranes (cells) still allows for flattening using specific constructions, as soon as membrane (cell) division and/or creation are allowed, in general the number of membranes (cells) need not be bounded any more. Hence, a naive adaptation of the flattening procedure as described above would lead to potentially infinite numbers of objects and rules. On the other hand, if in any computation of the system the number of possible structures (membranes/cells) can be bounded by some constant max, then similar constructions as given for systems with membrane (cell) dissolution may yield a flattened system.

Example 5. Consider the P system (with active membranes)

$$\Pi = (\{a,b\}, \{a\}, \emptyset, [_1 \;]_1, \lambda, b, R, 1)$$
$$R = \{1 : b \to [_2 a]_2 [_2 a]_2\}$$
$$\cup \{2 : a \to (a^2, here), 2 : a \to (a^2, here) \delta\}.$$

We consider Π as a generating P system working in the maximally parallel mode: starting with the initial configuration $[_1 b]_1$, the rule $1 : b \to [_2 a]_2 [_2 a]_2$ creates two inner membranes with the same label 2, i.e., we obtain the configuration $[_1 [_2 a]_2 [_2 a]_2]_1$. In both membranes, in each computation step, the actual number of objects a is duplicated by the rules $2 : a \to (a^2, here)$ until the application of at least one rule $2 : a \to (a^2, here) \delta$ dissolves the membrane. As in membrane 1 no rule can be applied to objects a, at the end, we obtain k objects a with $k \in \{2^m + 2^n \mid m, n \geq 1\}$.

A specific problem of such P systems with active membranes is that we may generate new membranes having the same label. Yet the assumption that only a finite number of different membrane structures may arise allows us to assign different labels to copies of membranes having the same label, e.g., for the two membranes with label 2 in Π we may take the labels $(2, 1)$ and $(2, 2)$; in that way we obtain an equivalent P system Π'' where we have to duplicate the rules for membrane 2 for the two membranes now labeled by $(2, 1)$ and $(2, 2)$:

$$
\begin{aligned}
\Pi'' &= (\{a, b\}, \{a\}, \emptyset, [_1]_1, \lambda, b, R'', 1) \\
R'' &= \{1 : b \to [_{(2,1)} a]_{(2,1)} [_{(2,2)} a]_{(2,2)}\} \\
&\cup \{(2,1) : a \to (a^2, here), (2,1) : a \to (a^2, here) \delta\} \\
&\cup \{(2,2) : a \to (a^2, here), (2,2) : a \to (a^2, here) \delta\}.
\end{aligned}
$$

As the environment 0 is not involved in the P systems Π and Π'', for Π'' an equivalent flattened (tissue) P system can be constructed as follows using extended rules of the form $(I_\mu (u) \to I_{\mu'} (v); \mu \to \mu')$, i.e., the left-hand sides of the rules are interpreted according to the current membrane structure μ, whereas the evolving objects from the right-hand sides have to be interpreted already as objects in the new membrane structure μ':

$$
\begin{aligned}
\Pi' &= (V', \{(a, 1)\}, (b, 1), R', 1), \\
V' &= \{(a, i), (b, i) \mid i \in \{1, (2, 1), (2, 2)\}\}, \\
R' &= \{((b, 1) \to (a, (2, 1)) (a, (2, 2)); [_1]_1 \to [_1 [_{(2,1)}]_{(2,1)} [_{(2,2)}]_{(2,2)}]_1)\} \\
&\cup \{((a, (2, 1)) \to (a, (2, 1))^2; [_1 [_{(2,1)}]_{(2,1)} [_{(2,2)}]_{(2,2)}]_1 \to \mu'), \\
&\quad \mu' \in \{[_1 [_{(2,1)}]_{(2,1)} [_{(2,2)}]_{(2,2)}]_1, [_1 [_{(2,1)}]_{(2,1)}]_1\}\} \\
&\cup \{((a, (2, 2)) \to (a, (2, 2))^2; [_1 [_{(2,1)}]_{(2,1)} [_{(2,2)}]_{(2,2)}]_1 \to \mu'), \\
&\quad \mu' \in \{[_1 [_{(2,1)}]_{(2,1)} [_{(2,2)}]_{(2,2)}]_1, [_1 [_{(2,2)}]_{(2,2)}]_1\}\} \\
&\cup \{((a, (2, 1)) \to (a, 1)^2; [_1 [_{(2,1)}]_{(2,1)} [_{(2,2)}]_{(2,2)}]_1 \to \mu'), \\
&\quad \mu' \in \{[_1 [_{(2,2)}]_{(2,2)}]_1, [_1]_1\}\} \\
&\cup \{((a, (2, 2)) \to (a, 1)^2; [_1 [_{(2,1)}]_{(2,1)} [_{(2,2)}]_{(2,2)}]_1 \to \mu'), \\
&\quad \mu' \in \{[_1 [_{(2,1)}]_{(2,1)}]_1, [_1]_1\}\} \\
&\cup \{((a, (2, 1)) \to (a, 1)^2; [_1 [_{(2,1)}]_{(2,1)}]_1 \to [_1]_1)\} \\
&\cup \{((a, (2, 2)) \to (a, 1)^2; [_1 [_{(2,2)}]_{(2,2)}]_1 \to [_1]_1)\}.
\end{aligned}
$$

The condition that only rules starting from the same membrane structure μ and yielding the same new membrane structure μ' can be applied in parallel, guarantees that in each derivation step the correct symbols are evolving in the current membrane structure μ with respect to the next membrane structure μ'.

For any halting computation, the final configuration is of the form $\left[_1 \, (a, 1)^k \right]_1$ with $k \in \{2^m + 2^n \mid m, n \geq 1\}$.

We have to point out that a construction like that given above only works with the maximally parallel derivation mode, as with the change of the structure all symbols from a dissolved membrane have to be converted into symbols of the membrane they are sent to by the dissolution of the membrane. On the other hand, in the preceding example, after the first derivation step, each of the possible membrane structures evolves by dissolution only, hence, we could also apply each of the flattening techniques as described in the preceding section.

In the following example, the membrane structure may evolve from $[_1 \,]_1$ to $[_1 \, [_2 \,]_2 \,]_1$ and back an unbounded number of times, hence, the parallel rewriting of all symbols is a crucial point of the flattening procedure:

Example 6. Consider the P system (with active membranes)

$$\Pi = (\{a, b, c\}, \{c\}, \emptyset, [_1 \,]_1, \lambda, ba, R, 1) \text{ with}$$
$$R = \{1 : b \to [_2 \, c] _2, 1 : b \to \lambda,$$
$$1 : a \to (c^3, here), 1 : c \to (a^2, in)\}$$
$$\cup \{2 : c \to (b, here), 2 : b \to (b, out)\, \delta\}.$$

We consider Π as a generating P system working in the maximally parallel mode: starting with the initial configuration $[_1 \, ba]_1$, the rule $1 : b \to [_2 \, c]_2$ creates an inner membrane with label 2, whereas by the rule $1 : a \to (c^3, here)$ from each object a we get three symbols c, i.e., after the first derivation step we obtain the configuration $[_1 \, c^3 \, [_2 \, c]_2 \,]_1$. In the next computation step, from each object c we get two objects a which are sent into membrane 2 by the rules $1 : c \to (a^2, in)$, and at the same time, in membrane 2 the single object c evolves back to b by the rule $2 : c \to (b, here)$, i.e., after this derivation step we have got the configuration $[_1 \, [_2 \, a^6 b]_2 \,]_1$. With the dissolution of membrane 2 – using the rule $2 : b \to (b, out)\, \delta$ – all objects a and the single object b are back in membrane 1. This cycle continues as long as in membrane 1 the rule $1 : b \to [_2 \, c]_2$ is applied, whereas the derivation halts after the application of the rule $1 : b \to \lambda$. In that way, Π generates $\{c^{3 \cdot 6^n} \mid n \geq 0\}$.

As the environment 0 is not involved in the P system Π, an equivalent flattened (tissue) P system can be constructed as follows using extended rules of the form $(I_\mu (u) \to I_{\mu'} (v) ; \mu \to \mu')$:

$$\Pi' = (V', T', w, R', 1),$$
$$V' = \{(a, i), (b, i), (c, i) \mid i \in \{1, 2\}\},$$
$$T' = \{(c, 1)\},$$
$$w = (ab, 1),$$

$$R' = \{((b,1) \to (c,2) ; [_1 \ ]_1 \to [_1 \ [_2 \ ]_2]_1),$$
$$((b,1) \to \lambda ; [_1 \ ]_1 \to [_1 \ ]_1),$$
$$((a,1) \to (c,1)^3 ; [_1 \ ]_1 \to [_1 \ [_2 \ ]_2]_1),$$
$$((c,1) \to (a,2)^2 ; [_1 \ [_2 \ ]_2]_1 \to [_1 \ [_2 \ ]_2]_1)\}$$
$$\cup\{((c,2) \to (b,2) ; [_1 \ [_2 \ ]_2]_1 \to [_1 \ [_2 \ ]_2]_1),$$
$$((b,2) \to (b,1) ; [_1 \ [_2 \ ]_2]_1 \to [_1 \ ]_1)\}$$
$$\cup\{((a,2) \to (a,1) ; [_1 \ [_2 \ ]_2]_1 \to [_1 \ ]_1)\}.$$

As they would never be applicable, rules like $((a,1) \to (c,1)^3 ; [_1 \ ]_1 \to [_1 \ ]_1)$ and $((c,2) \to (b,1) ; [_1 \ [_2 \ ]_2]_1 \to [_1 \ ]_1)$ are omitted, whereas the rule $((a,2) \to (a,1) ; [_1 \ [_2 \ ]_2]_1 \to [_1 \ ]_1)$ has to be added to rename the symbols a appearing as objects $(a,2)$ in membrane 1 into objects $(a,1)$ when membrane 2 is dissolved. For any halting computation, the final configuration is of the form $[_1 (c,1)^{3.6^n}]_1$ for some $n \geq 0$, i.e., as Π also Π' generates the non-semilinear set $\{3.6^n \mid n \geq 0\}$.

Finally, we consider a simple hierarchical P system with non-elementary membrane division, where the contents of the original cell is duplicated into two new cells:

Example 7. Consider the P system (with active membranes)

$$\Pi = (\{a,b\}, \{a\}, \emptyset, [_1 \ [_2 \ ]_2]_1, \lambda, b, a, R, 1) \text{ with}$$
$$R = \{0 : [_1 b]_1 \to [_2]_2 [_3]_3, 2 : a \to b\delta, 2 : b \to \delta, 3 : b \to \delta\}.$$

We consider Π as a computing P system working in the maximally parallel mode, with the input a^n, $n \geq 0$, being given in membrane 1, and the output being collected in the environment (membrane 0): starting with the initial configuration $[_1 ba^n \ [_2 a]_2]_1$, the rule $[_1 b]_1 \to [_2]_2 [_3]_3$ divides the non-elementary membrane 1 and copies its contents into two new membranes 2 and 3; in the original inside membrane 2 the rule $2 : a \to b\delta$ causes the membrane to be dissolved and to release an object b into the surrounding membrane region; thus, we obtain the configuration $[_2 a^n b]_2 [_3 a^n b]_3$. In the second step, the single objects b in membranes 2 and 3 dissolve the membranes, thus releasing their contents to the environment: the objects a in membrane 3 are not affected by any rule, whereas each copy of the symbol a in membrane 2 is changed to b by the rule $2 : a \to b\delta$. Hence, the computation stops after two steps with $a^n b^n$ in the environment as the result of the computation.

An equivalent flattened (tissue) P system Π' can be constructed as follows using extended rules of the form $(I_\mu (u) \to I_{\mu'} (v) ; \mu \to \mu')$; again, we only include those rules which can be applied during a computation:

$\Pi' = (V', \{(a,1)\}, (b,1)(a,2), R', 1)$,

$V' = \{(a,i), (b,i) \mid i \in \{0,1,2,3\}\}$,

$R' = \{((b,1) \to \lambda; [_0 [_1 [_2]_2]_1]_0 \to [_0 [_2]_2 [_3]_3]_0)$,

$\quad ((a,1) \to (a,2)(a,3); [_0 [_1 [_2]_2]_1]_0 \to [_0 [_2]_2 [_3]_3]_0)$,

$\quad ((a,2) \to (b,2)(b,3); [_0 [_1 [_2]_2]_1]_0 \to [_0 [_2]_2 [_3]_3]_0)\}$

$\quad \cup \; \{((b,2) \to \lambda; [_0 [_2]_2 [_3]_3]_0 \to [_0]_0)$,

$\quad ((b,3) \to \lambda; [_0 [_2]_2 [_3]_3]_0 \to [_0]_0)$,

$\quad ((a,2) \to (b,0); [_0 [_2]_2 [_3]_3]_0 \to [_0]_0)$,

$\quad ((a,3) \to (a,0); [_0 [_2]_2 [_3]_3]_0 \to [_0]_0)\}$.

Π' starts with the axiom $(b,1)(a,2)$ and the (additional) input $(a,1)^n$ in its single cell; by applying the first three rules we obtain $(b,2)(a,2)^n (b,3)(a,3)^n$, whereas the remaining rules are used in the second computation step to obtain the result of the computation $(a,0)^n (b,0)^n$. Finally, we again have to point out that the computations in Π can only be simulated in Π' in real time because Π and Π' work in the maximally parallel derivation mode.

8 Flattening with Changing the Derivation Mode

Several models of tissue P systems work in such a way that in each cell one rule is applied (if possible), but in one computation step such a sequential derivation has to take place in all cells, i.e., such systems work sequentially on the level of the cells, but in a maximally parallel way on the level of the whole system. Examples for such models are spiking neural P systems or variants of enzymatic numerical P systems considered in several papers just recently (e.g., see [9] and the references therein).

The basic flattening procedure may be applied to the objects in such systems as usual, but in the single membrane of the flattened system Π' to these objects the original rules now have to be applied in the min_1 derivation mode (see [7]): the new rule set R' is the union of the original rule sets R_0 to R_n associated with the cells of the original system, but for the application of the min_1 derivation mode again divided into the sets R_0 to R_n, i.e., from each set R_i, $0 \leq i \leq n$, exactly one rule (if possible) is taken for any multiset to be applied in a computation step of Π'.

9 Final Remarks

In this paper we have discussed the flattening procedure for several of the most common models of (tissue) P systems in the general framework of networks of cells, even with membrane (cell) dissolution and polarizations. For (tissue) P systems with membrane (cell) generation or division, in general the number of membranes (cells) is not bounded. But if the number of cells during any computation is bounded, flattening even works for these cases of dynamically changing structures. In sum, several models of (tissue) P systems can be reduced to pure multiset rewriting by flattening these systems to one membrane (cell), but in general a lot of interesting features arising from the idea to distribute the objects and their evolution into different membranes (cells) still remains valid.

References

1. Alhazov, A., Antoniotti, M., Freund, R., Leporati, A., Mauri, G.: Self-stabilization in membrane systems. The Computer Science Journal of Moldova 20(2), 133–146 (2012)
2. Agrigoroaiei, O., Ciobanu, G.: Flattening the transition P systems with dissolution. In: Gheorghe, M., Hinze, T., Păun, G., Rozenberg, G., Salomaa, A. (eds.) CMC 2010. LNCS, vol. 6501, pp. 53–64. Springer, Heidelberg (2010)
3. Dassow, J., Păun, G.: Regulated Rewriting in Formal Language Theory. Springer (1989)
4. Freund, R., Kari, L., Oswald, M., Sosík, P.: Computationally universal P systems without priorities: two catalysts are sufficient. Theor. Comp. Sci. 330, 251–266 (2005)
5. Freund, R., Pérez-Hurtado, I., Riscos-Núñez, A., Verlan, S.: A formalization of membrane systems with dynamically evolving structures. Int. J. Comput. Math. 90(4), 801–815 (2013)
6. Freund, R., Verlan, S.: A formal framework for static (tissue) P systems. In: Eleftherakis, G., Kefalas, P., Păun, G., Rozenberg, G., Salomaa, A. (eds.) WMC 2007. LNCS, vol. 4860, pp. 271–284. Springer, Heidelberg (2007)
7. Freund, R., Verlan, S.: (Tissue) P systems working in the k-restricted minimally parallel derivation mode. In: Csuhaj-Varjú, E., Freund, R., Oswald, M., Salomaa, K. (eds.) International Workshop on Computing with Biomolecules, Wien, Austria, August 27, vol. 244, pp. 43–52 (2008), books@ocg.at, OCG
8. Leporati, A., Manzoni, L., Porreca, A.E.: Flattening and simulation of asynchronous divisionless P systems with active membranes. In: Alhazov, A., Cojocaru, S., Gheorghe, M., Rogozhin, Y., Rozenberg, G., Salomaa, A. (eds.) CMC 2013, vol. 8340, pp. 238–248. Springer, Heidelberg (2014)
9. Leporati, A., Mauri, G., Porreca, A.E., Zandron, C.: Improved universality results for parallel enzymatic numerical P systems. International Journal of Unconventional Computing 9(5-6), 385–404 (2013)
10. Păun, G.: Computing with membranes. J. Comput. Syst. Sci. 61, 108–143 (2000); see also TUCS Report 208 (November 1998), www.tucs.fi
11. Păun, G., Rozenberg, G., Salomaa, A. (eds.): The Oxford Handbook of Membrane Computing. Oxford University Press (2010)
12. Rozenberg, G., Salomaa, A. (eds.): Handbook of Formal Languages, 3 vols. Springer (1997)
13. The P Systems Website, http://ppage.psystems.eu
14. Verlan, S.: Using the formal framework for P systems. In: Alhazov, A., Cojocaru, S., Gheorghe, M., Rogozhin, Y., Rozenberg, G., Salomaa, A. (eds.) CMC 2013, vol. 8340, pp. 57–80. Springer, Heidelberg (2014)

Solving SAT by P Systems
with Active Membranes in Linear Time
in the Number of Variables

Zsolt Gazdag[*]

Department of Algorithms and their Applications
Faculty of Informatics
Eötvös Loránd University
gazdagzs@inf.elte.hu

Abstract. In this paper we solve the SAT problem (the satisfiability problem of propositional formulas in conjunctive normal form) by two polynomially uniform families of P systems with active membranes. The novelty of these solutions is that these P systems can solve the SAT problem in linear time in the number of propositional variables occurring in the input. This means that the number of computation steps is independent form the number of clauses of the input. To achieve this efficiency our systems employ only the standard rules of P systems with active membranes plus membrane creation rules. Moreover, in the first solution the P systems do not use the polarizations of the membranes but use such membrane division rules which can change the labels of the involved membranes. In the second solution the P systems do not employ membrane label changing but use the polarizations of the membranes instead.

Keywords: Membrane computing, P systems, SAT problem.

1 Introduction

P systems with active membranes [10] are widely investigated variants of P systems [9]. These systems have the possibility of dividing elementary membranes which combined with the massive parallelism that is present in these systems can yield exponential workspace in linear time. This feature is frequently used in P system based efficient solutions of well known NP-complete problems such as the SAT problem. The SAT problem (satisfiability problem of propositional formulas) is probably the best known NP-complete decision problem where the question is whether a given propositional formula in conjunctive normal form is satisfiable.

Solving the SAT problem efficiently by P systems with active membranes is a subject of many papers in the literature (see e.g. [1], [2], [3], [4], [8], [10], and

---

[*] This paper was finished during the author's visit at the Research Institute of Mathematics of the University of Sevilla (IMUS).

A. Alhazov et al. (Eds.): CMC 2013, LNCS 8340, pp. 189–205, 2014.

[13]). These solutions differ, for example, in the types of the rules employed, the possibility of changing the labels of the membranes, and the use of the polarizations of the membranes. On the other hand, these solutions commonly work in a way where all possible truth valuations of the input formula are created and then a satisfying one (if it exists) is chosen.

In the above mentioned papers the SAT problem is solved by polynomially (semi-)uniform families of P systems. This means that the P systems in these families can be constructed in polynomial time by a deterministic Turing machine from the size of the input formula (in the uniform case) or from the formula itself (in the semi-uniform case). (For more details on polynomially (semi-)uniform families of P systems we refer to [12] and [13]). The size of the input formula is usually described by the number of distinct variables and the number of clauses in the formula. The P systems introduced in the above works can decide SAT in polynomial time in the size of the input formula. This means that the number of the computation steps of these systems usually depends also on the number of clauses. The only exception is the solution of [4] where the SAT problem is solved in linear time in the number of variables. However, in [4] the presented P systems employ non-elementary membrane division rules, which are very powerful rules capable to duplicate such membranes also which contain further membranes. There is an interesting solution of the SAT problem where instead of membrane division rules membrane creation rules are used to create every possible truth valuations of the input formula [7]. The computation steps of the P systems in this solution is also linear in the number of variables. However, the semantics of the rules in this solution is slightly differs to the one that is commonly used in P systems with active membranes. A more detailed comparison of the solution of [7] and our solution will be given after presenting the main results of this paper.

In [6] two families of polarizationless P systems were given which use neither non-elementary membrane division nor membrane creation, but still can solve the SAT problem in linear time in the number of the variables in the input formula. These solutions implement a decision procedure which is strongly based on the well known resolution rule of propositional logic. However, the first solution is not polynomially uniform since its object alphabet is exponential in the number of the variables. The second solution, on the other hand, uses a polynomial time constructable family of P systems, but the P systems are constructed from the input formula, thus it is a semi-uniform solution.

In this paper we present two families of P systems that are based on these systems but do not have their drawbacks in the following sense. Our new solutions are polynomially uniform ones still capable to decide the satisfiability of a formula in linear time in the number of variables. In the first solution the P systems do not use the polarizations of the membranes but use such membrane division rules which can change the labels of the involved membranes. In the second solution the P systems do not employ membrane label changing but use the polarizations of the membranes instead. Moreover, in contrast to the solutions of [6], our new solutions employ membrane creation rules also.

This paper is based on the conference paper [5]. The first solution presented here is a slight variant of the one presented in [5]. The second solution is a variant of the first one, where we avoid to use rules with membrane label changing.

The paper is organised as follows. In Section 2 we clarify the used notations and notions and give the necessary definitions and preliminary results. Section 3 contains our families of P systems, and Section 4 presents some concluding remarks.

2   Definitions

Alphabets, Words, Multisets. An *alphabet* Σ is a non-empty and finite set of symbols. The elements of Σ are called *letters*. Σ^* denotes the set of all finite *words* (or *strings*) over Σ, including the *empty word* ε. We will use *multisets* of objects in the membranes of a P system. As usual, these multisets will be represented by strings over the object alphabet of the P system. The set of natural numbers is denoted by $\mathbb{N}$. For $i, j \in \mathbb{N}$, $[i, j]$ denotes the set $\{i, i+1, \ldots, j\}$ (notice that if $j < i$, then $[i, j] = \varnothing$). Moreover, for the shake of simplicity, for a number $n \in \mathbb{N}$, we denote the set $[1, n]$ by $[n]$.

The SAT Problem. Let $X = \{x_1, x_2, x_3, \ldots\}$ be a recursively enumerable set of *propositional variables* (*variables*, to be short), and, for every $n \in \mathbb{N}$, let $X_n := \{x_1, \ldots, x_n\}$. An *interpretation of the variables in X_n* (or just an *interpretation* if X_n is clear from the context) is a function $\mathcal{I} : X_n \to \{true, \ false\}$.

The variables and their negations are called *literals*. A *clause* C is a disjunction of finitely many pairwise different literals satisfying the condition that there is no $x \in X$ such that both x and $\bar{x}$ occur in C, where $\bar{x}$ denotes the negation of x. The set of all clauses over the variables in X_n is denoted by $\mathcal{C}_n$. A *formula in conjunctive normal form* (CNF) is a conjunction of finitely many clauses. We denote the conjunction and the disjunction operator by $\wedge$ and $\vee$, respectively. However, when it is more convenient, we will treat formulas in CNF as finite sets of clauses, where the clauses are finite sets of literals. A clause $C \in \mathcal{C}_n$ is called a *complete clause* if, for every $x \in X_n$, $x \in C$ or $\bar{x} \in C$. Let $Form$ be the set of all formulas in CNF over the variables in X and, for every $n \in \mathbb{N}$, let $Form_n$ be the set of those formulas in $Form$ that have variables in X_n. It is easy to see that $Form$ is a recursively enumerable set (notice that, for a given $n \in \mathbb{N}$, $Form_n$ is a finite set).

Let $\varphi \in Form_n$ $(n \in \mathbb{N})$ and let $\mathcal{I}$ be an interpretation for φ. We say that $\mathcal{I}$ *satisfies* φ, denoted by $\mathcal{I} \models \varphi$, if φ evaluates to *true* under the truth assignment defined by $\mathcal{I}$. Notice that $\mathcal{I} \models \varphi$ if and only if, for every $C \in \varphi$, $\mathcal{I} \models C$. We say that φ is satisfiable if there is an interpretation $\mathcal{I}$ such that $\mathcal{I} \models \varphi$. The SAT *problem* (boolean satisfiability problem of propositional formulas in CNF) can be defined as follows:

> Given a formula φ in CNF, decide whether or not there is an interpretation $\mathcal{I}$ such that $\mathcal{I} \models \varphi$.

Let $\varphi \in Form$. The set of variables occurring in φ, denoted by $var(\varphi)$, is defined by $var(\varphi) := \{x \in X \mid \exists C \in \varphi : x \in C \text{ or } \bar{x} \in C\}$. Next we define an operation on a clause in C_n. This operation is a key component in our method of solving the SAT problem by P systems. For a clause $C \in C_n$ and a set $Y \subseteq X_n$ $(n \in \mathbb{N})$ such that $var(C) \cap Y = \emptyset$, let C_Y be the following set of clauses. Assume that $Y = \{x_{i_1}, \ldots, x_{i_k}\}$ $(k \leq n, 1 \leq i_1 < \ldots < i_k \leq n)$. Then let $C_Y := \{C \cup \{l_1, \ldots, l_k\} \mid j \in [k] : l_j \in \{x_{i_j}, \bar{x}_{i_j}\}\}$. Intuitively, C_Y is the set of those clauses that can be created by adding, for every variable $x \in Y$, x or $\bar{x}$ to C. For example, if $C = \{x_1, \bar{x}_2\}$ and $Y = \{x_3\}$, then $C_Y = \{\{x_1, \bar{x}_2, x_3\}, \{x_1, \bar{x}_2, \bar{x}_3\}\}$. For a formula $\varphi = \{C_1, \ldots, C_m\} \in Form_n$ $(m, n \in \mathbb{N})$, let $\varphi^c := \bigcup_{C \in \varphi} C_Y$, where $Y := X_n - var(C)$.

The following statement claims that the satisfiability of a formula $\varphi \in Form_n$ can be reduced to the question whether φ^c contains every complete clause in C_n.

Proposition 1. For a formula $\varphi \in Form_n$ $(n \in \mathbb{N})$, φ is satisfiable if and only if $\mid \varphi^c \mid < 2^n$.

The formal proof of this statement can be found, for example, in [6]. We only note here that the correctness of this statement is based on the following observations. For a formula $\varphi \in Form_n$, $C \in \varphi$, and $x \in X_n - var(C)$, φ is satisfiable if and only if the formula $(\varphi - C) \cup C_{\{x\}}$ is satisfiable. Moreover, trivially, a set of complete clauses is satisfiable if and only if it contains every complete clause in C_n, for some $n \in \mathbb{N}$.

As an example consider the formula $\varphi = (x_1 \vee \bar{x}_2) \wedge \bar{x}_1 \wedge x_2 \in Form_2$. Let us denote the clauses of φ by C_1, C_2, and C_3, respectively. Clearly $var(C_1) = \{x_1, x_2\}$, $var(C_2) = \{x_1\}$, and $var(C_3) = \{x_2\}$. Thus, the clauses of φ^c are C_1, $C_2 \cup \{x_2\}$, $C_2 \cup \{\bar{x}_2\}$, $C_3 \cup \{x_1\}$, and $C_3 \cup \{\bar{x}_1\}$, i.e., $\varphi^c = (x_1 \vee \bar{x}_2) \wedge (\bar{x}_1 \vee x_2) \wedge (\bar{x}_1 \vee \bar{x}_2) \wedge (x_1 \vee x_2)$ (notice that the second clause of φ^c can be created from both C_2 and C_3). As φ^c contains every complete clause in C_2, using Proposition 1 we can derive that φ is unsatisfiable.

According to this, our P systems, roughly, will work in the following way. For an input formula φ with n variables the corresponding P system will

- create the clauses of φ^c,
- separate the clauses of φ^c into different cells, and
- decide if there is 2^n cells containing a complete clause of φ^c.

P Systems with Active Membranes. We will use P systems with active membranes to solve the SAT problem. In these P systems we will use such membrane division rules that can change the labels of the membranes involved. We will also use membrane creation and dissolution rules. The following is the formal definition of the P systems we will use (see also [11]). A *P system with active membranes* is a construct $\Pi = (O, H, \mu, w_1, \ldots, w_m, R)$, where:

- $m \geq 1$ (the *initial degree* of the system);
- O is the *alphabet of objects*;
- H is a finite set of *labels* for membranes;

- μ is a *membrane structure*, consisting of m membranes, labelled (not necessarily in a one-to-one manner) with elements of H;
- $w_1, \ldots, w_m$ are strings over O, describing the *multisets of objects* placed in the m regions of μ;
- R is a finite set of *developmental rules*, of the following forms:
  - (a) $[a \rightarrow v]_h^e$, for $e \in \{+, -, 0\}$, $h \in H, a \in O, v \in O^*$
    (object evolution rules, associated with membranes and depending on the label and the charge of the membranes, but not directly involving the membranes, in the sense that the membranes are neither taking part in the application of these rules nor are they modified by them);
  - (b) $a[\ ]_h^{e_1} \rightarrow [b]_h^{e_2}$, for $e_1, e_2 \in \{+, -, 0\}$, $h \in H$, $a, b \in O$
    (*in* communication rules, sending an object into a membrane, maybe modified during this process; also the polarization of the membrane can be modified, but not its label);
  - (c) $[a]_h^{e_1} \rightarrow [\ ]_h^{e_2} b$, for $e_1, e_2 \in \{+, -, 0\}$, $h \in H$, $a, b \in O$
    (*out* communication rules; an object is sent out of the membrane, maybe modified during this process; also the polarization of the membrane can be modified, but not its label);
  - (d) $[a]_h^e \rightarrow b$, for $e \in \{+, -, 0\}$, $h \in H$, $a, b \in O$
    (membrane dissolving rules; in reaction with an object, a membrane can be dissolved, while the object specified in the rule can be modified);
  - (e) $[a]_{h_1}^{e_1} \rightarrow [b]_{h_2}^{e_2}[c]_{h_3}^{e_3}$, for $e_1, e_2, e_3 \in \{+, -, 0\}$, $h_1, h_2, h_3 \in H$, $a, b, c \in O$
    (division rules for elementary membranes; in reaction with an object, the membrane is divided into two membranes with possibly different labels or polarizations; the object a specified in the rule is replaced in the two new membranes by (possibly new) objects b and c respectively, and the remaining objects are duplicated);
  - (f) $a \rightarrow [b]_h^e$, for $e \in \{+, -, 0\}$, $h \in H$, $a, b \in O$
    (membrane creation rules; in reaction with an object a new membrane with label h can be created; the object a specified in the rule is replaced in the new membrane by the object b);

As usual, Π works in a *maximal parallel* manner:

- In one step, any object of a membrane that can evolve must evolve, but one object can be used by only one rule in (a)-(f);
- when some rules in (b)-(f) can be applied to a certain membrane, then one of them must be applied, but a membrane can be the subject of only one rule of these rules during each step.

We say that Π is a *recognizing P system* if

- O has two designated objects *yes* and *no*; every computation of Π halts and sends out to the environment either *yes* or *no*, but not both, and this is done exactly in the last step of the computation;
- Π has a designated input membrane i_0;
- for a word w, called the *input of Π*, w can be added to the system by placing it into the region i_0 in the initial configuration.

A P system Π with active membranes is *deterministic* if it has only a single computation from its initial configuration to its unique halting configuration. Π is *confluent* if every computation of Π halts and sends out to the environment the same object. Notice that, by definition, recognizing P systems are confluent. A family $\mathbf{\Pi} := (\Pi(i))_{i \in \mathbb{N}}$ of recognizing P systems is called *polynomially uniform* if, for every $n \in \mathbb{N}$, $\Pi(n)$ can be constructed from n by a deterministic Turing machine in polynomial time in n.

We say that the *SAT problem can be solved by a family* $\mathbf{\Pi} := (\Pi(i))_{i \in \mathbb{N}}$ *of recognizing P systems* if, for a formula $\varphi \in Form$ with size n ($n \in \mathbb{N}$), starting $\Pi(n)$ with a polynomial time encoding of φ in its input membrane, $\Pi(n)$ sends out to the environment *yes* if and only if φ is satisfiable.

3   The Main Result

Here we present two polynomially uniform families of recognizing P systems that can solve the SAT problem in linear time in the number of distinct variables in the input formula. The first solution does not use the polarizations of the membranes but employs membrane division rules with membrane label changing. In case of this solution we use a formula encoding that is similar to the often used ones in the theory of P systems (see e.g. the definition of $cod(\varphi)$ on page 314 in [12]). The only difference here is that if a variable is not represented in a clause, then this fact is encoded in an object appropriately. Let $\varphi = C_1 \wedge \ldots \wedge C_m$ be a formula. Then

$$cod(\varphi) := \bigcup_{j=1}^{m} \left(\{x_{j,i} \mid x_i \in C_j\} \cup \{\bar{x}_{j,i} \mid \bar{x}_i \in C_j\} \cup \{\hat{x}_{j,i} \mid x_i \notin C_j \text{ and } \bar{x}_i \notin C_j\} \right).$$

Clearly, for every formula φ with m clauses and n variables, $cod(\varphi) \subseteq O_{m,n} \cup \widehat{O}_{m,n}$, where $O_{m,n} := \bigcup_{i \in [n], j \in [m]} \{x_{j,i}, \bar{x}_{j,i}\}$ and $\widehat{O}_{m,n} := \bigcup_{i \in [n], j \in [m]} \{\hat{x}_{j,i}\}$. We will also need the primed versions of the objects in $O_{m,n}$, thus let $O'_{m,n} := \bigcup_{i \in [n], j \in [m]} \{x'_{j,i}, \bar{x}'_{j,i}\}$. Finally, we will use the size function

$$\langle m, n \rangle := \frac{(n+m)(n+m+1)}{2} + n$$

also used e.g. in [3] to represent the size of φ.

Definition 1. For every $m, n \in \mathbb{N}$, let $\Pi(\langle m, n \rangle) := (O, H, \mu, w_{skin}, w_{aux}, w_1, R)$, where:

- $O := O_{m,n} \cup \widehat{O}_{m,n} \cup O'_{m,n} \cup \{yes, no, yes', e, c_1, c_2, d_1, d_2, \ldots, d_{2n+1}\}$;
- $H := \{skin, aux, aux', 1, 2 \ldots, 2n+1\} \cup \{(i,j) \mid j \in [m], i \in [n-1]\}$;
- $\mu := [[[\ ]_1]_{aux}]_{skin}$, where the input membrane is $[\ ]_1$;
- $w_{skin} := \varepsilon$, $w_{aux} := \varepsilon$ and $w_1 := d_1$;
- R is the set of the rules defined below. We note that, for the sake of simplicity, we define different set of rules in item (iii) according to that $n = 1$ or $n > 1$. Moreover, in some cases we give explanations of the presented rules.

(i) $[\hat{x}_{j,i}]_1 \rightarrow [x_{j,i}\bar{x}_{j,i}]_1 \ (i \in [n], j \in [m])$

(at the first step the system creates from every object $\hat{x}_{j,i}$ two new objects, $x_{j,i}$ and $\bar{x}_{j,i}$; this corresponds to the creation of the complete clauses of φ^c);

(ii) $[d_1]_1 \rightarrow [d_2]_2[d_3]_3$,
$[d_{2i+k}]_{2i+k} \rightarrow [d_{2i+2}]_{2i+2}[d_{2i+3}]_{2i+3} \ (i \in [n-1], k \in [0,1])$,
$[\bar{x}_{j,i} \rightarrow \varepsilon]_{2i}, [x_{j,i} \rightarrow \varepsilon]_{2i+1} \ (j \in [m], i \in [n])$

(by these membrane division rules the system divides the cells with label $2i$ or $2i+1$; during this division the objects representing the literals of φ^c are duplicated and distributed between the new cells; after this step the system should remove certain superfluous literals from the corresponding cells; this is done by the object evolution rules above);

(iii) **If $n = 1$:**
$[x_{j,1} \rightarrow x'_{j,1}]_2, [\bar{x}_{j,1} \rightarrow \bar{x}'_{j,1}]_3 \ (j \in [m])$.

If $n > 1$:
$[x_{j,1} \rightarrow x'_{j,1}]_{2n+k}, [\bar{x}_{j,1} \rightarrow \bar{x}'_{j,1}]_{2n+k} \ (j \in [m], k \in [0,1])$,
$[x'_{j,i} \rightarrow [c_1]_{j,i}]_{2n+k}, [\bar{x}_{j,i} \rightarrow [c_1]_{j,i}]_{2n+k} \ (j \in [m], i \in [n-1], k \in [0,1])$,
$[c_1 \rightarrow c_2]_{j,i}, [c_2]_{j,i} \rightarrow c_2 \ (j \in [m], i \in [n-1])$,
$x_{j,i}[\ ]_{j,i-1} \rightarrow [x'_{j,i}]_{j,i-1}, \bar{x}_{j,i}[\ ]_{j,i-1} \rightarrow [\bar{x}'_{j,i}]_{j,i-1}$,
$[x'_{j,i}]_{j,i-1} \rightarrow x'_{j,i}, [x'_{j,i}]_{j,i-1} \rightarrow x'_{j,i} \ (j \in [m], i \in [2,n], k \in [0,1])$

(after $n+1$ steps, each cell with label $2n$ or $2n+1$ can contain literals forming a complete clause of φ^c; with these rules the system can decide if such a cell contains a complete clause or not);

(iv) (a) $[x'_{j,n}]_{2n+k} \rightarrow e$ and $[\bar{x}'_{j,n}]_{2n+k} \rightarrow e \ (j \in [m], k \in [0,1])$
(those cells with label $2n+k$ which contain a primed literal involving the nth variable are dissolved by these rules introducing new objects e);

   (b) $e[\ ]_{2n+k} \rightarrow [yes']_{2n+k}, [yes']_{2n+k} \rightarrow [\ ]_{2n+k}yes' \ (k \in [0,1])$,
$[yes']_{aux} \rightarrow yes$,
$[yes]_{skin} \rightarrow [\ ]_{skin}yes$
(if there are cells with label $2n + k$ which are not dissolved by the rules in (a), then objects e go into these cells introducing objects yes'; the other rules are used to send objects yes' out to the cell aux; there one yes' introduces yes by dissolving the cell aux; then yes is sent out to the environment);

   (c) $[e]_{aux} \rightarrow [e]_{aux'}[no]_{aux'}$,
$[no]_{aux'} \rightarrow [\ ]_{aux'}no$,
$[no]_{skin} \rightarrow [\ ]_{skin}no$
(if every membrane with label $2n + k$ could be dissolved by the rules in (a), then an object e is used to duplicate the membrane with label aux and to introduce the object no; during the duplication of the cell its label is changed to aux'; the other rules are used to send no out to the environment).

Consider now a formula $\varphi \in Form_n$ with m clauses ($m, n \in \mathbb{N}$). The computation of $\Pi(\langle m, n \rangle)$ when the cell with label 1 contains $cod(\varphi)$ can be described as follows (from now on, by saying that *a complete clause C is contained in a cell*, we mean that the cell contains such objects that represent the literals of C).

In the first step, the system replaces every object $\hat{x}_{j,i}$ ($j \in [m], i \in [n]$) in cell 1 by two objects $x_{j,i}$ and $\bar{x}_{j,i}$ using the rules in (i). It is easy to see that after this replacement, the cell with label 1 contains a complete clause $C \in \mathcal{C}_n$ if and only if $C \in \varphi^c$. Thus, this step corresponds to the creation of φ^c.

Still in the first step, the system duplicates all literals of φ^c and distributes them between the two new cells created by the corresponding membrane division rule in (ii). Thus, after the first step, every clause of φ^c are contained in both of the new cells. However, for every $i \in [n]$, after the ith application of a membrane division rule in (ii), the system removes those objects from the cells with label $2i$ that represent literals which are negations of the ith variable. Likewise, the objects representing the ith variable without negation are removed from the cells with label $2i + 1$.

After n steps, the system contains 2^n cells with label $2n$ or $2n + 1$. We call in the sequel a cell with such a label a *final cell*. As described above, during the next step the system removes the corresponding objects from the final cells by the object evolution rules in (ii). We will prove later that after the first $n + 1$ steps, for every complete clause $C \in \varphi^c$, C occurs in exactly one final cell of the system (see Lemma 1). However, the system should decide if a final cell contains a complete clause or not. This is done by the rules in (iii). We only discuss here the case when $n > 1$.

In the $(n + 1)$th step, in every final cell, each object $x'_{j,1}$ or $\bar{x}'_{j,1}$ can create a new cell with label $(j, 1)$. A new object c_1 is also introduced in this cell. This object is used to dissolve the new cell in two steps. Another possibility to dissolve it if there is an object $x_{j,2}$ or $\bar{x}_{j,2}$ (notice that only one of them can occur in a final cell). These objects can get into this new cell. During this a primed version of them is introduced which can dissolve the new cell in the next step. The above described procedure is repeated until new primed objects are introduced in the final cell. It is easy to see that if the primed version of the objects $x_{j,n}$ or $\bar{x}_{j,n}$ occur in a final cell, than this cell should contain a complete clause after the $(n + 1)$th step. This part of the computation takes $3(n - 1)$ steps.

Then, using rules in (iv)(a), the system dissolves those final cells that contain primed versions of the objects $x_{j,n}$ or $\bar{x}_{j,n}$. During a dissolution of a final cell, an object e is introduced. At this point the computation can continue in two different cases.

If every finite cell is dissolved, then, using the first rule in (iv)(c), the system divides the membrane with label aux, changes its label to aux' and introduces the object no. In the last two steps the object no is sent out to the environment, and the computation halts (as the label of the cell is changed from aux to aux', symbols e can not introduce new no symbols).

If there is at least one final cell that is not dissolved, then only the first rule in (iv)(b) can be applied, introducing the object yes' (notice that the division rule in (iv)(c) cannot be applied as the membrane with label aux is not elementary in this case). Next yes' dissolves the cell aux introducing the object yes. In the last two steps of the system the object yes is sent out to the environment, and the computation halts (as the cell aux is dissolved, no new yes objects can be introduced).

It can be seen that after at most $4n + 2$ steps the system halts and sends out to the environment either yes or no. We demonstrate the above described work of these P systems by the following example.

Example 1. Let $\varphi = (\bar{x}_1 \vee x_2) \wedge (x_1 \vee x_2) \wedge \bar{x}_2$. Then $cod(\varphi) = \{\bar{x}_{1,1}, x_{1,2}, x_{2,1}, x_{2,2}, \hat{x}_{3,1}, \bar{x}_{3,2}\}$. Let $\Pi(\langle 3, 2 \rangle)$ be the P system constructed in Definition 1 with $cod(\varphi)$ in its input membrane. The initial configuration of $\Pi(\langle 3, 2 \rangle)$ and its configurations after the first three steps can be seen on Figure 1 (in the figure the underlined terms indicate the labels of the cells).

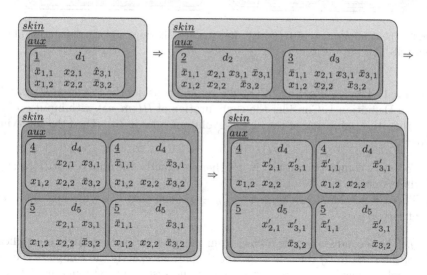

Fig. 1. The first three steps of $\Pi(\langle 3, 2 \rangle)$

Next consider the first membrane with label 4 in the last configuration of the system. We show the evaluation of the objects in this cell during the next four steps in Figure 2.

The first configuration in Figure 3 is the configuration of the system after the first six steps. The second configuration shows the state of the system after dissolving the cells with label 4 or 5. Then only rules in (iv)(c) can be applied which means that no is introduced and sent out to the environment. This answer of the system is correct as the input formula is clearly not satisfiable.

The correctness of our P systems will be shown using the following lemma.

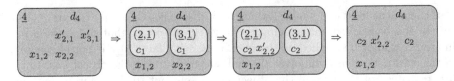

Fig. 2. The evolution of the first membrane with label 4 using rules in (c)

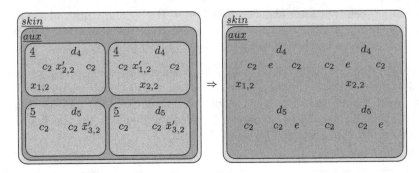

Fig. 3. The configuration of $\Pi(\langle 3,2 \rangle)$ after the first six steps and the dissolution of the inner cells

Lemma 1. Let $\varphi \in Form_n$ with m clauses and consider the P system $\Pi(\langle m,n \rangle)$ given in Definition 1. Consider the configuration of $\Pi(\langle m,n \rangle)$ with input $cod(\varphi)$ after the nth application of the object evolution rules in (ii). Then the following holds:

(1) For every complete clause C in φ^c, there is exactly one final cell of $\Pi(\langle m,n \rangle)$ that contains C.

(2) There is no complete clause $C \in C_n - \varphi^c$ such that C occurs in a final cell of $\Pi(\langle m,n \rangle)$.

Proof. The second statement follows from the observation that after the application of the rules in (i) the cell with label 1 contains exactly the complete clauses of φ^c and no new literals are introduced by the system in the remaining steps.

To see that the first statement also holds we prove a more general statement. Let us call in the sequel a cell of $\Pi(\langle m,n \rangle)$ with label $2i$ or $2i+1$ ($i \in [1,n]$) a *level i cell*. We show that, for every $i \in [1,n]$, after the ith application of the object evolution rules in (ii), for every complete clause C in φ^c, there is exactly one level i cell of $\Pi(\langle m,n \rangle)$ that contains C. We prove this statement by induction on i.

Let $C \in \varphi^c$. If $i = 1$, then C is contained in both level 1 cells (those with label 2 or 3) after the application of the first rule in (ii). Then objects of the form $\bar{x}_{j,1}$ are removed from the cell with label 2, while objects of the form $x_{j,1}$ are removed from cell with label 3 by applying the corresponding object evolution rules in (ii). But then, since C can not contain complement literal pairs, one of the two new cells contains C while the other one does not.

Now assume that the statement holds when $i = l$ for some $l \in [2, n-1]$. We prove that it also holds when $i = l + 1$. Consider the configuration of $\Pi(\langle m, n \rangle)$ after the lth application of object evolution rules (ii). By the induction hypothesis, there is exactly one level l cell that contains C. Let us denote this cell by c and consider the two level $l+1$ cells that are created from c by the corresponding membrane division rule in (ii). Clearly, each of these new cells also contains C, and exactly one of them will contain it after the application of the corresponding object evolution rules in (ii). Since the other level $l + 1$ cells can not contain C, this finishes the proof of the lemma. $\square$

Theorem 1. The SAT problem can be solved by a polynomially uniform family $\mathbf{\Pi} := (\Pi(\langle m, n \rangle))_{m,n \in \mathbb{N}}$ of recognizing P systems with the following properties:

(1) the elements of $\mathbf{\Pi}$ ...
   ... do not use polarizations of the membranes,
   ... use the standard rules of P systems with active membranes plus membrane creation rules,
   ... can change the labels of the involved membranes during membrane division;
(2) for a formula φ with n variables and m clauses, starting $\Pi(\langle m, n \rangle)$ with $cod(\varphi)$ in its input membrane, $\Pi(\langle m, n \rangle)$ stops in linear number of steps in n.

Proof. Let $\varphi \in Form_n$ with m clauses and consider the P system $\Pi(\langle m, n \rangle)$ defined in Definition 1. The fact that $\Pi(\langle m, n \rangle)$ decides correctly the satisfiability of φ can be seen using Proposition 1, Lemma 1, and the fact that the system sends out to the environment *no* if and only if its every final cell contains a complete clause. It also can be seen that $\Pi(\langle m, n \rangle)$ is a recognizing P system. In particular, the fact that it is confluent follows from the following observation. The non-determinism occurs in $\Pi(\langle m, n \rangle)$ only when the final cells are dissolved using rules in (iv)(a) and when the objects e chose a final cell (first rules in (iv)(b)). Clearly these non-deterministic choices do not affect the output of the system. This means that $\mathbf{\Pi}$ solves the SAT problem and the elements of $\mathbf{\Pi}$ are recognizing P systems. Moreover, since, for every $m, n \in \mathbb{N}$, $\Pi(\langle m, n \rangle)$ has polynomial size in $\langle m, n \rangle$, $\mathbf{\Pi}$ is polynomially uniform.

Properties in (1) follow from the definitions, while Property (2) was shown at the end of the discussion after Definition 1 about the computation steps of these systems. $\square$

Next we define a family of recognizing P systems that also can solve the SAT problem in linear time in the number of variables, but the rules of the P systems in this family do not employ membrane label changing. The P systems in this family will use instead the polarizations of the membranes and several copies of the objects.

In our previous solution the membrane label changing is used for the following reason. When $\Pi(\langle m, n \rangle)$ applies the object evolution rules in (ii), the label of the membranes is used to select the applicable rules: for $i \in [n]$, in a membrane with label $2i$, only the objects $\bar{x}_{j,i}$ can be subjects of rules, while in a membrane with label $2i + 1$, only the objects $x_{j,i}$ can be erased. If there is no possibility of membrane label changing, we can use polarizations of the membranes to select whether a variable or its negation can be erased. To ensure that after the ith membrane division only the ith variable or its negation can be erased we can do the following. We can use n copies of the objects in $O_{m,n}$ and add such rules that at every step when a membrane division happens, a new copy of every object in $O_{m,n}$ is introduced. Moreover, we can define the rules in (ii) such that when the ith copies of the objects are in the membrane then only the literals containing the ith variable can be subjects of rules.

First we define, for every $p \in [0, n+1]$, a copy of the objects in $O_{m,n}$. Let $O^{\mathbf{P}} := \bigcup_{j\in[m],i\in[n]} \{x_{j,i}^{\mathbf{P}}, \bar{x}_{j,i}^{\mathbf{P}}\}$. Here and in the sequel the superscript $^{\mathbf{P}}$ is written in boldface in order not to confuse it by the notation of the multiplicity of the objects in multisets. Moreover, we will employ a different formula encoding here. Let $\varphi = C_1 \wedge \ldots \wedge C_m$ be a formula. Then

$$
cod_p(\varphi) := \bigcup_{j=1}^{m} \left(\{x_{j,i}^0 \mid x_i \in C_j\} \cup \{\bar{x}_{j,i}^0 \mid \bar{x}_i \in C_j\} \cup \right.
$$

$$
\left. \{\hat{x}_{j,i}^0 \mid x_i \notin C_j \text{ and } \bar{x}_i \notin C_j\} \right).
$$

The following is the definition of the mentioned family of P systems.

Definition 2. For every $m, n \in \mathbb{N}$, let $\Pi_p(\langle m, n \rangle) := (O, H, \mu, w_{skin}, w_{aux}, w_1, R)$, where:

- $O := \bigcup_{p\in[0,n+1]} O^{\mathbf{P}}_{m,n} \cup \widehat{O}_{m,n} \cup \{yes, no, e, c_1, c_2, d_1, d_2, \ldots, d_{n+1}\}$;
- $H := \{skin, aux, 1\} \cup \{(i,j) \mid j \in [m], i \in [n-1]\}$;
- $\mu := [[[\ ]_1]_{aux}]_{skin}$, where the input membrane is $[\ ]_1$;
- $w_{skin} := \varepsilon, w_{aux} := \varepsilon$ and $w_1 := d_1$;
- R is the set of the rules defined below. We also give explanations about the roles of the presented rules.
  (i) $[\hat{x}_{j,i}]_1^0 \to [x_{j,i}^1 \bar{x}_{j,i}^1]_1^0$ $(i \in [n], j \in [m])$,
  $[x_{j,i}^{\mathbf{P}}]_1^0 \to [x_{j,i}^{\mathbf{P+1}}]_1^0$,
  $[\bar{x}_{j,i}^{\mathbf{P}}]_1^0 \to [\bar{x}_{j,i}^{\mathbf{P+1}}]_1^0$ $(p \in [0, n-1], i \in [n], j \in [m])$.

  At the first step, the system creates from every object $\hat{x}_{j,i}$ two new objects $x_{j,i}^1$ and $\bar{x}_{j,i}^1$. This corresponds to the creation of the complete clauses of φ^c. Moreover, when a cell with label 1 has neutral polarization, the superscript of the objects in this cell is incremented by one.

  (ii) $[d_i]_1^0 \to [d_{i+1}]_1^+[d_{i+1}]_1^-$,
  $[\bar{x}_{j,i}^{\mathbf{i}} \to \varepsilon]_1^+, [x_{j,i}^{\mathbf{i}} \to \varepsilon]_1^-$ $(j \in [m], i \in [n])$,
  $[d_i]_1^e \to [\ ]_1^e d_i, \ d_i[\ ]_1^e \to [d_i]_1^0$ $(i \in [n+1], e \in \{+, -\})$.

  Using these membrane division rules, the system divides the cells with label 1 if they have neutral polarization. The two new cells will have positive and negative polarizations, respectively. The clauses contained in the original cells are duplicated and distributed between the new cells.

In the next step, those objects that correspond to the ith copies of literals that involve the ith variable are removed from the cells with label 1 according to the following principles: those literals that involve negated variables are removed from the cells with positive polarization, while those literals that involve variables without negation are removed from cells with negative polarization.

Meanwhile, the objects d_i evolve to d_{i+1}. Then they are sent out of the cells with label 1. In the next step they go back into these cells and change the polarization of these cells to neutral.

(iii) $[x_{j,1}^n \to x_{j,1}^{n+1}]_1^0, [\bar{x}_{j,1}^n \to \bar{x}_{j,1}^{n+1}]_1^0 \ (j \in [m])$

$[x_{j,i}^{n+1} \to [c_1]_{j,i}^0]_1^0, [\bar{x}_{j,i}^{n+1} \to [c_1]_{j,i}^0]_1^0 \ (j \in [m], i \in [n-1]),$

$[c_1 \to c_2]_{j,i}^0, [c_2]_{j,i}^0 \to c_2 \ (j \in [m], i \in [n-1]),$

$x_{j,i}^n [\ ]_{j,i-1}^0 \to [x_{j,i}^{n+1}]_{j,i-1}^0, \bar{x}_{j,i}^n [\ ]_{j,i-1}^0 \to [\bar{x}_{j,i}^{n+1}]_{j,i-1}^0,$

$[x_{j,i}^{n+1}]_{j,i-1}^0 \to x_{j,i}^{n+1}, [\bar{x}_{j,i}^n]_{j,i-1}^0 \to \bar{x}_{j,i}^{n+1} \ (j \in [m], i \in [2,n]).$

After $3n$ steps, each cell with label 1 can contain a complete clause of φ^c. Using these rules, the system can decide if such a cell contains a complete clause or not. Notice that the role of the objects in $O_{m,n}^{n+1}$ here is the same as that of the objects in $O'_{m,n}$ in Definition 1.

(iv) (a) $[x_{j,n}^{n+1}]_1^0 \to e$ and $[\bar{x}_{j,n}^{n+1}]_1^0 \to e$.
      Those cells with label 1 which contain the $(n+1)$th copy of a literal involving the nth variable are dissolved by these rules introducing new objects e.

   (b) $e[\ ]_1^0 \to [yes]_1^0, [yes]_1^0 \to yes,$
      $[yes]_{aux}^0 \to [\ ]_{aux}^- yes,$
      $[yes]_{skin}^0 \to [\ ]_{skin}^0 yes.$
      If there is a membrane with label 1 which is not dissolved by the rules in (iv)(a), then objects e can introduce objects yes; the other rules are used to send an object yes out to the environment.

   (c) $[e]_{aux}^0 \to [e]_{aux}^-[no]_{aux}^-,$
      $[no]_{aux}^- \to [\ ]_{aux}^- no,$
      $[no]_{skin}^0 \to [\ ]_{skin}^0 no.$
      If every membrane with label 1 could be dissolved by the rules in (iv)(a), then one copy of e is used to duplicate the membrane with label aux and to introduce the object no; the other rules are used to send no out to the environment.

Consider a formula $\varphi \in Form_n$ with m clauses $(m, n \in \mathbb{N})$. The computation of $\Pi_p(\langle m, n \rangle)$ when the membrane with label 1 contains $cod_p(\varphi)$ can be described similarly as it is done after Definition 1 using the notes given after the definition of the rules in Definition 2. It also can be seen easily that the system halts after at most $6n + 2$ steps.

In the following example we show some computation steps of $\Pi_p(\langle 3, 2 \rangle)$ when its input is the encoding of the formula appearing in Example 1.

Example 2. Let $\varphi = (\bar{x}_1 \vee x_2) \wedge (x_1 \vee x_2) \wedge \bar{x}_2$. Then $cod_p(\varphi) = \{\bar{x}_{1,1}^0, x_{1,2}^0, x_{2,1}^0, x_{2,2}^0, \hat{x}_{3,1}, \bar{x}_{3,2}^0\}$. Let $\Pi_p(\langle 3, 2 \rangle)$ be the P system constructed in Definition 2 with $cod_p(\varphi)$ in its input membrane. The initial configuration of $\Pi_p(\langle 3, 2 \rangle)$, its configurations after the first four steps, and its configuration after the dissolution of cells with label 1 can be seen in Figure 4. We note that the polarizations of the membranes in this figure can be found in the upper-right corners of the cells.

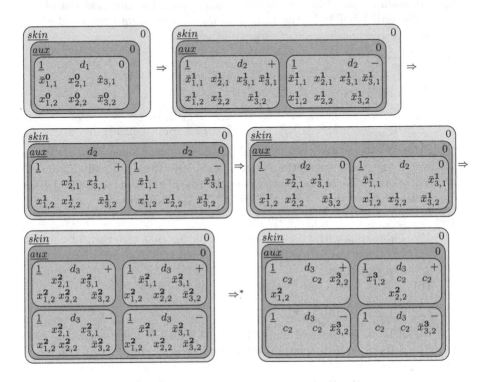

Fig. 4. Some computation steps of $\Pi_p(\langle 3, 2 \rangle)$

Theorem 2. The SAT problem can be solved by a polynomially uniform family $\mathbf{\Pi}_p := (\Pi_p(\langle m, n \rangle))_{m,n \in \mathbb{N}}$ of recognizing P systems with the following properties:

(1) the elements of $\mathbf{\Pi}_p$ ...

     ... use polarizations of the membranes,

     ... use the standard rules of P systems with active membranes plus membrane creation rules,

     ... do not change the labels of the membranes during membrane division;

(2) for a formula φ with n variables and m clauses, starting $\Pi_p(\langle m, n \rangle)$ with $cod_p(\varphi)$ in its input membrane, $\Pi_p(\langle m, n \rangle)$ stops in linear number of steps in n.

Proof. The correctness of the P systems in $\mathbf{\Pi}_p$ can be shown using the following observation. Consider a formula $\varphi \in Form_n$ with m clauses ($m, n \in \mathbb{N}$) and the P systems $\Pi(\langle m, n \rangle)$ and $\Pi_p(\langle m, n \rangle)$ defined in Definitions 1 and 2, respectively. Moreover, consider the configuration of $\Pi(\langle m, n \rangle)$ after $n + 1$ steps, and the configuration of $\Pi_p(\langle m, n \rangle)$ after $3n$ steps. Then it is not difficult to see that there is a one-to-one correspondence between the final cells of $\Pi(\langle m, n \rangle)$ and the cells with label 1 of $\Pi_p(\langle m, n \rangle)$. Furthermore, if we consider two corresponding cells in these configurations of $\Pi(\langle m, n \rangle)$ and $\Pi_p(\langle m, n \rangle)$, then there is a one-to-one correspondence between the objects in these cells (with the property that the primed objects of $\Pi(\langle m, n \rangle)$ correspond to the $(n + 1)th$ copies of objects in $\Pi_p(\langle m, n \rangle)$). The formal proof of the correctness is left to the reader.

The other properties of the elements of $\mathbf{\Pi}_p$ can be shown similarly as it is done in the proof of Theorem 1.   □

Although our P systems run in linear time in the number of variables of the input formula, the total time of the decision process might be more. Assume that we want to decide the satisfiability of a formula $\varphi \in Form_n$ that contains m clauses. Assume also that we want to use for this decision process the P system $\Pi(\langle m, n \rangle)$ given in Definition 1. If $\Pi(\langle m, n \rangle)$ is not constructed yet, then it should be constructed first. Since the family $\mathbf{\Pi}$ is polynomially uniform, there is a deterministic Turing machine T that can construct $\Pi(\langle m, n \rangle)$ in polynomial time in $\langle m, n \rangle$. Indeed, if the number $\langle m, n \rangle$ is on the input tape of T in unary encoded form, then T can compute m and n in quadratic time in M, where M is the maximum of m and n. Then, using m and n, T can construct $\Pi(\langle m, n \rangle)$ in linear time in mn. Thus, the construction of $\Pi(\langle m, n \rangle)$ takes $O(M^2)$ steps. Moreover, since every clause of φ can have at most n literals, $cod(\varphi)$ can be computed in $O(mn)$ steps. Thus, the total time of the decision process has $O(M^2)$ steps. Nevertheless, once $\Pi(\langle m, n \rangle)$ is constructed, it can be used for *every* formula in $Form_n$ having at most m clauses. Moreover, if we have an implementation of $\Pi(\langle m, n \rangle)$, then we may assume that φ is already presented using an appropriate data structure so that the implementation of $\Pi(\langle m, n \rangle)$ can be directly run on φ without computing $cod(\varphi)$.

Similar reasoning applies if we consider the family $\mathbf{\Pi}_p$ of P systems given in Definition 2. However, as in $\Pi_p(\langle m, n \rangle)$ we use $n + 1$ copies of the objects in $O_{m,n}$, here the total time of the construction of the P system is bounded by $O(nM^2)$. On the other hand, the time complexity of the computation of cod_p is the same as that in the case of cod. In fact, the time complexity of our formula encodings is not worse than that of the commonly used formula encodings (e.g. the one used on page 314 in [12]) in the following sense. For every $m, n \in \mathbb{N}$, there is a formula φ with n variables and m clauses such that the encoding of φ takes asymptotically the same time using any kind of formula encodings mentioned above.

As we have mentioned in the introduction, there is a solution of the SAT problem where the used P systems employ membrane creation and the number of computation steps of these systems is bounded by the number of variables of the input formula (see [7] or Section 12.6.1 in [12]). This solution, roughly, works in the following way. For a formula φ with n variables and m clauses, the P system first creates in $2n$ steps 2^n membranes, each of them corresponding to a possible evaluation of the variables in X_n. Meanwhile, the system stores in every membrane, by using new objects, those clauses of φ that are satisfied by the interpretation represented by the membrane. Finally, the system checks in constant steps, using again membrane creation, whether there is a membrane such that the objects in that membrane represent φ (i.e., the system decides if there is an interpretation that satisfies every clause in φ).

As it is stated in [7], the time complexity of this solution is $\theta(n)$. However, this result can not be directly compared to our results because of the following reason. Consider an *in* communication rule $a[\ ]_h^{e_1} \rightarrow [b]_h^{e_2}$ for some objects a, b, polarizations e_1, e_2, and label h. In our P systems, as it is usual in the framework of P systems with active membranes, during a derivation step at most one object a can go into each cell with label h by the application of this rule, even if there are more copies of a in the compartment than the number of the cells with label h. In [7] all objects a should go to a cell with label h during one derivation step. If we used in the solution of [7] the more strict derivation strategy used in our solution, then the time complexity of the solution in [7] would be $O(n + m)$. Nevertheless, the derivation strategy used in [7] is a common strategy used in P systems with membrane creation.

4   Conclusions

In this paper we presented two polynomially uniform families of P systems that can decide the satisfiability of a propositional formula in linear time in the number of variables in the formula. The given P systems use the classical rules of P systems with active membranes and, in addition, membrane creation rules. The first solution employs such elementary membrane division rules which can change the label of the involved membranes but not uses the polarizations of the membranes. The second solution does not employ membrane label changing but uses the polarizations of the membranes.

It is a challenging task however whether the SAT problem can be solved in linear time in the number of variables by such P systems with active membranes which employ only the standard rules (i.e., rules without membrane label changing and membrane creation). This might be a subject of a further research.

Acknowledgements. The author gratefully acknowledges the helpful suggestions and comments of the anonymous referees. The paper was finished during the author's visit at the Research Institute of Mathematics of the University of Sevilla (IMUS). The author would like to thank IMUS for supporting this visit and, in particular, Prof. Mario J. Pérez–Jiménez for his help and support concerning this visit.

References

1. Alhazov, A.: Minimal parallelism and number of membrane polarizations. The Computer Science Journal of Moldova 18(2), 149–170 (2010)
2. Alhazov, A., Pan, L., Paun, G.: Trading polarizations for labels in P systems with active membranes. Acta Inf. 41(2-3), 111–144 (2004)
3. Cecilia, J.M., García, J.M., Guerrero, G.D., Martínez-del-Amor, M.A., Pérez-Hurtado, I., Pérez-Jiménez, M.J.: Simulating a P system based efficient solution to SAT by using GPUs. J. Log. Algebr. Program. 79(6), 317–325 (2010)
4. Freund, R., Păun, G., Pérez-Jiménez, M.J.: Polarizationless P Systems with Active Membranes Working in the Minimally Parallel Mode. In: Akl, S.G., Calude, C.S., Dinneen, M.J., Rozenberg, G., Wareham, H.T. (eds.) UC 2007. LNCS, vol. 4618, pp. 62–76. Springer, Heidelberg (2007)
5. Gazdag, Z.: Solving SAT by P Systems with Active Membranes in Linear Time in the Number of Variables. In: Alhazov, A., Cojocaru, S., Gheorghe, M., Rogozhin, Y. (eds.) CMC 2013. LNCS, vol. 8340, pp. 189–205. Springer, Heidelberg (2013)
6. Gazdag, Z., Kolonits, G.: A new approach for solving SAT by P systems with active membranes. In: Csuhaj-Varjú, E., Gheorghe, M., Rozenberg, G., Salomaa, A., Vaszil, G. (eds.) CMC 2012. LNCS, vol. 7762, pp. 195–207. Springer, Heidelberg (2013)
7. Gutiérrez-Naranjo, M.A., Pérez-Jiménez, M.J., Romero-Campero, F.J.: A uniform solution to SAT using membrane creation. Theor. Comput. Sci. 371(1-2), 54–61 (2007)
8. Pan, L., Alhazov, A.: Solving HPP and SAT by P Systems with Active Membranes and Separation Rules. Acta Inf. 43(2), 131–145 (2006)
9. Paun, G.: Computing with membranes. J. Comput. Syst. Sci. 61(1), 108–143 (2000)
10. Paun, G.: P Systems with Active Membranes: Attacking NP-Complete Problems. Journal of Automata, Languages and Combinatorics 6(1), 75–90 (2001)
11. Paun, G.: Introduction to membrane computing. In: Applications of Membrane Computing, pp. 1–42 (2006)
12. Paun, G., Rozenberg, G., Salomaa, A.: The Oxford Handbook of Membrane Computing. Oxford University Press, Inc., New York (2010), http://portal.acm.org/citation.cfm?id=1738939
13. Pérez-Jiménez, M.J., Jiménez, Á.R., Sancho-Caparrini, F.: Complexity classes in models of cellular computing with membranes. Natural Computing 2(3), 265–285 (2003)

On Communication Complexity
of Some Hard Problems in ECPe Systems

Nestine Hope S. Hernandez, Richelle Ann B. Juayong, and Henry N. Adorna

Algorithms and Complexity Lab
Department of Computer Science
University of the Philippines Diliman
Diliman 1101 Quezon City, Philippines
{nshernandez,rbjuayong,hnadorna}@up.edu.ph

Abstract. In this paper, we present non-confluent solutions to some
NP-complete problems using recognizer Evolution-Communication P
systems with Energy (ECPe systems). We then evaluate the communication resources used in these systems using dynamical communication
measures proposed for computations in ECPe systems. Specifically, we
evaluate based on number of communication steps, communication rules
and energy required for all communication.

Keywords: Membrane computing, recognizer P systems, Evolution-
Communication P systems with Energy, communication complexity.

1 Introduction

With the goal of addressing the issue of communication complexity for P systems,
an initial approach in [1] involves investigating communication in a particular
P system cell-like variant called Evolution-Communication P systems [4]. The
main feature of these devices is the separation of evolution and communication
rules, i.e. a rule may be applied either to communicate or to evolve, but not both.
First, they introduced a measure of communication cost through so-called *energy*
objects. Based on this model, authors in [1] propose dynamical parameters for
communication complexity measure as well as ways of how such parameters can
be used for communication analysis.

It is worth mentioning that studies incorporating the concept of energy as a
model feature for membrane systems have already been investigated in several
literatures. However, these models are introduced for varying motivations. To
mention some, there are P system variants that focus on manipulating energy
assigned to objects (as in [9]) and assigned to membranes (as in [5] which ab-
stracts the behavior of energy carriers called conformons in biology). Another
model introduced in [2] assigns energy and rules to membranes. The novelty of
ECPe systems lies in how energy is utilized in the system's computations; in
ECPe systems, an energy parameter is assigned to each region. This parameter is only used to enable communication, i.e some energy must be used up to
enable passing of a certain object. When we treat energy as a catalyst in this

A. Alhazov et al. (Eds.): CMC 2013, LNCS 8340, pp. 206–224, 2014.

way such that an object is accompanied by some copies of 'energy' when passing through a membrane, we obtain a model similar to Proton Pumping P systems (introduced in [3]). However, while communication catalysts can pass through membranes, copies of energy cannot. In such scenario, [1] mentioned that energy is consumed during communication.

This study continues the works in [1] by examining the resources used in solving decision problems, specifically, Vertex Cover Problem (VCP), Independent Set problem (ISP) and 3-SAT Problem (3SP). We construct recognizer P systems (whose definitions are adapted from [11] and [12]) to non-confluently decide these problems. We use the dynamical communication measures in [1] to determine the amount of communication steps, rules, and energy employed in solving such problems.

The content of this paper is arranged as follows: Section 2 formally defines the NP-complete problems we investigated, Section 3 discusses the formal definition of ECPe systems and how we can decide on problems using the idea of non-confluence and recognizer P systems. The main contribution of our work is provided in Section 4. Finally, our conclusions are given in Section 5.

2   Definitions of Some NP-Complete Problems

We present formal definitions of the three NP-complete problems of interest for our study. Two of these problems use graphs as inputs while the remaining problem involves evaluation of boolean formula.

A graph is denoted by $G = (V, E)$ where V is a set of vertices and $E \subseteq V \times V$ is the set of edges. Note that in this paper, we only consider simple graphs, that is, graphs with no loops and parallel edges. Shown in Figure 1 is an example of a graph where $V = \{1, 2, \ldots, 5\}$ and $E = \{(1, 2), (1, 3), (1, 5), (2, 3), (3, 4), (4, 5)\}$. Without loss of generality, it is imposed that each edge in E is represented by a pair $(i, j), i < j$.

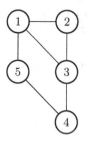

Fig. 1. An example of a graph

A vertex cover VC is a set of vertices in V where for all edge $(i, j) \in E$, either $i \in VC$ or $j \in VC$. We denote VC_k $(1 \leq k \leq |V|)$ as a vertex cover with size less than equal to k. It can be observed that in the graph given in Figure 1, there exists a vertex cover $VC_3 = \{1, 3, 4\}$.

Definition 1. Vertex Cover Problem (VCP) *Given a graph* $G = (V, E)$ *and a positive integer* k $(1 \leq k \leq |V|)$, *is there a vertex cover* VC_k?

An independent set IS is a set of vertices where for all pair $i, j \in IS$, there is no edge in E connecting i and j. We let IS_k be an independent set of size at least k. In Figure 1, $IS_2 = \{2, 5\}$ is an independent set of size 2. It can be observed that $IS_2 = V - VC_3$. This is a consequence of the lemma given in [6] stating that given a graph $G = (V, E)$ and subset $V' \subseteq V$, then V' is a vertex cover for G if and only if $V - V'$ is an independent set of G.

Definition 2. Independent Set Problem (ISP) *Given a graph* $G = (V, E)$ *and a positive integer* k $(1 \leq k \leq |V|)$, *is there an independent set* IS_k?

In boolean logic, a boolean formula in conjunctive normal form (CNF) involving a set of variables X is a conjunction of a set of propositional clauses where a propositional clause is defined as a disjunction of a set of variables in X that may take on values 1 (true) or 0 (false). Disjunction in a clause involves performing OR-operations on the variables involved while conjunction involves performing AND-operations on the result of the clause evaluations.

Formally, a formula ϕ_X in CNF over a set of variables $X = \{x_1, x_2, ..., x_p\}$ is a conjunction of a set of propositional clauses represented as:

$$\phi_X = C_1 \wedge C_2 \wedge \ldots \wedge C_m$$

where $m \in \mathbb{Z}^+$ and C_i's are propositional clauses such that

$$C_i = (y_{i1} \vee y_{i2} \vee \ldots \vee y_{in})$$

where $n \in \mathbb{Z}^+$ and $y_{ij} \in X \cup \{\bar{x} \mid x \in X\}$, $1 \leq j \leq n$. The notation $\bar{x}$ implies a negation so that $\bar{\bar{x}} = x$.

We define a k-CNF boolean formula as a boolean formula in CNF where each clause is a disjunction of exactly k variables. We say that a boolean formula is satisfiable if there exists an assignment for all variables such that the formula evaluates to true.

Definition 3. 3-SAT Problem (3SP) *Given a 3-CNF boolean formula* ϕ *over a set of variables* X, *is* ϕ *satisfiable?*

Let a 3-CNF boolean formula $\phi_x = (\bar{x}_1 \vee x_2 \vee x_3) \wedge (x_1 \vee \bar{x}_2 \vee x_3) \wedge (\bar{x}_1 \vee x_2 \vee x_4)$ where $X = \{x_1, x_2, x_3, x_4\}$. We say that ϕ is satisfiable since the formula evaluates to true when $x_1 = 0, x_2 = 0, x_3 = r, x_4 = r$, $r \in \{0, 1\}$.

3   ECPe Systems

Before we proceed, the readers are assumed to be familiar with the fundamentals of formal language theory and membrane computing [10].

A new variant of Evolution-Communication P systems [4] has been introduced in [1] to evaluate communication that is dependent on some energy produced from evolution rules. A special object e is introduced to the system to represent a quantum of energy. We use the definition for EC P system with energy (ECPe system) from [1].

Definition 4. *An EC P system with energy is a construct of the form*

$$\Pi = (O, e, \mu, w_1, \ldots, w_m, R_1, R'_1, \ldots, R_m, R'_m, i_{out})$$

where:

(i) m pertains to the total number of membranes;

(ii) O is the alphabet of objects;

(iii) e is a special object. Note that $e \notin O$.

(iv) μ is the membrane structure which can be denoted by a set of paired square brackets with labels. We say that membrane i is the *parent membrane* of a membrane j, denoted $parent(j)$, if the paired square brackets representing membrane j is located inside the paired square brackets representing membrane i, i.e. $[_i \ldots [_j]_j \ldots]_i$. Reversely, we say that membrane j is a *child membrane* of membrane i, denoted $j \in children(i)$ where $children(i)$ refers to the set of membranes contained in membrane i. The relation of parent and child membrane becomes more apparent when we represent the membrane structure as a tree.

(v) $w_1, \ldots, w_m$ are strings over O^* where w_i denotes the multiset of object present in the region bounded by membrane i.

(vi) $R_1, \ldots, R_m$ are sets of evolution rules, each associated with a region delimited by a membrane in μ;

 ○ An evolution rule is of the form $a \to v$ where $a \in O$, $v \in (O \cup \{e\})^*$. In the event that this type of rule is applied, the object a transforms into a multiset of objects v in the next time step. Through evolution rules, object e can be produced, but e should never be in the initial configuration and object e is not allowed to evolve.

(vii) $R'_1, \ldots, R'_m$ are sets of communication rules, each associated with a membrane in μ; A communication rule can either be a symport or an antiport rule:

 ○ A symport rule can be of the form (ae^i, in) or (ae^i, out), where $a \in O$, $i \geq 1$. By using this rule, i copies of object e are consumed to transport object a inside (denoted by in) or outside (denoted by out) the membrane where the rule is defined. To consume copies of object e means that upon completion of the transportation of object a, the occurrences of e are consumed, they do not pass from a region to another one.

 ○ An antiport rule is of the form $(ae^i, out; be^j, in)$ where $a, b \in O$ and $i, j \geq 1$. By using this rule, we know that there exists an object a in the region immediately outside the membrane where the rule is declared, and an object b inside the region bounded by the membrane. In the application of this rule, object a and object b are swapped using i and j copies of object e in the different regions, respectively. As in symport rules, the copies of object e are consumed during the application.

We say that a communication rule has a *sending* and *receiving* region. For a rule $r \in R'_i$ associated with an *in* label, its receiving region is region i and its sending region is the $parent(i)$. The sending and receiving regions are reversed for a rule $r \in R'_i$ associated with an *out* label. For an antiport rule $r \in R_i'$, region i and $parent(i)$ are both sending and receiving region. Also, note that no communication can be applied without the utilization of object e.

(viii) $i_{out} \in \{0, 1, \ldots, m\}$ is the output membrane. If $i_{out} = 0$, this means that the output will be in the environment.

Another way to look at the role of special object e is to treat energy as a property of each region; in which case, we monitor a non-negative integer value for each region's energy. The energy may increase when some evolution rules are applied and decrease whenever the region transfers objects through some communication rule.

Rules are applied in a nondeterministic, maximally parallel manner. Nondeterminism, in this case, has the following meaning: when there are more than two evolution rules that can be applied to an object, the system will randomly choose the rule to be applied for each copy of the object. The system assumes a universal clock for simultaneous processing of membranes; all applicable rules have to be applied to all possible objects at the same time. The behavior of maximally parallel application of rule requires that all object that can evolve (or be transferred) should evolve (or be transferred).

Note that there is a one-to-one mapping between region and membrane, however, strictly, region refers to the area delimited by a membrane. A configuration at any time i, denoted by C_i, is the state of the system; it consists of the membrane structure and the multiset of objects within each membrane. A transition from C_i to C_{i+1} through nondeterministic and maximally parallel manner of rule application can be denoted as $C_i \Rightarrow C_{i+1}$. A series of transition is said to be a computation and can be denoted as $C_i \Rightarrow^* C_j$ where $i < j$. Computation succeeds when the system halts; this occurs when the system reaches a configuration wherein none of the rules can be applied. This configuration is called a halting configuration. If there is no halting configuration—that is, if the system does not halt—computation fails, because the system did not produce any output. Output can either be in the form of objects sent outside the skin, the outermost membrane, or objects sent into the output membrane.

3.1 Dynamical Communication Complexity Measures for ECPe Systems

Based on [1], the dynamical communication complexity parameters associated with a given computation for ECPe systems are:

$$ComN(C_i \Longrightarrow C_{i+1}) = \begin{cases} 1 \text{ if at least a communication} \\ \quad \text{rule is used in this} \\ \quad \text{transition,} \\ 0 \text{ otherwise} \end{cases}$$

$$ComR(C_i \Longrightarrow C_{i+1}) = \text{the number of communi-}$$
$$\text{cation rules used in this}$$
$$\text{transition,}$$
$$ComW(C_i \Longrightarrow C_{i+1}) = \text{the total energy of the}$$
$$\text{communication rules used}$$
$$\text{in this transition.}$$

These parameters are related in that $ComN \leq ComR \leq ComW$. They can be extended in a natural way to results of computations, systems, and sets of numbers. Again, we adapt the next definition from [1].

Definition 5. *We let $N(\Pi)$ be the set of numbers computed by the system. For $ComX \in \{ComN, ComR, ComW\}$, the following is defined:*

$$ComX(\delta) = \sum_{i=0}^{h-1} ComX(C_i \Longrightarrow C_{i+1}),$$
$$\text{for } \delta : C_0 \Longrightarrow C_1 \Longrightarrow \ldots \Longrightarrow C_h$$
$$\text{is a halting computation,}$$
$$ComX(n, \Pi) = \min\{ComX(\delta) \mid$$
$$\delta : C_0 \Longrightarrow C_1 \Longrightarrow \ldots \Longrightarrow C_h$$
$$\text{in } \Pi \text{ with the result } n\},$$
$$ComX(\Pi) = \max\{ComX(n, \Pi) \mid n \in N(\Pi)\},$$
$$ComX(Q) = \min\{ComX(\Pi) \mid Q = N(\Pi)\}.$$

3.2 Solving Problems in ECPe Systems

When solving problems in P systems, [11] uses the notion of a recognizer P system. For our definition of recognizer ECPe systems, we use the definition from [12].

Definition 6. *Let Π be an ECPe system whose alphabet contains two distinct objects yes and no, such that every computation of Π is halting and during each computation, exactly one of the objects yes, no is sent out from the skin to signal acceptance or rejection. If all the computations of Π agree on the result, then Π is said to be confluent; if this is not necessarily the case, then it is said to be non-confluent and the global result is acceptance if and only if there exists an accepting computation.*

From [11], we can formally represent a decision problem as a pair $Y = (I_Y, \theta_Y)$ where I_Y is a language over a finite alphabet and θ_Y is a total boolean function over I_Y. A representation of an instance of a decision problem in P systems is given by a pair (cod, s) where $s \in \mathbb{N}$ and cod refers to an encoding of the instance which will be placed in an input membrane in the initial configuration.

Our notion of a P system solving a problem is adapted from definitions in both [11] and [12] where a problem is solved using a family of P systems. A family $\Pi(n)$, $n \in \mathbb{Z}^+$, of P systems (specifically ECPe systems in our context) is a set of P systems that takes a parameter n to construct each system.

Definition 7. *A family $\Pi(n)$, $n \in \mathbb{Z}^+$, of ECPe systems, solves a problem (I_Y, θ_Y) if there exists a pair (cod, s) over I_Y such that for each instance $u \in I_Y$:*

(i) $n = s(u) \in \mathbb{N}$ and $cod(u)$ is an input multiset of the system $\Pi(n)$;
(ii) there exists an accepting computation of $\Pi(n)$ with input $cod(u)$ if and only if $\theta_Y(u) = 1$.

The following definitions use dynamical communication measures given in Section 3.1 to analyze communication over ECPe systems solving problems.

Definition 8. *Let $Y = (I_Y, \theta_Y)$ be a decision problem, $\Pi(n)$, $n \in \mathbb{Z}^+$, be a family of recognizer ECPe systems solving Y with a pair (cod, s) over I_Y. For each instance $u \in I_Y$,*

$$ComX(u, \Pi(n)) = \min\{ComX(\delta) \mid \delta : C_0 \Longrightarrow C_1 \Longrightarrow \ldots \Longrightarrow C_h \text{ in } \Pi(n)$$
$$\text{with } n = s(u) \text{ and } cod(u) \text{ is an input multiset in } \Pi(n)\},$$

where $ComX \in \{ComN, ComR, ComW\}$. To analyze the communication resources used by $\Pi(n)$ in solving problem Y, $ComX(Y, \Pi(n))$ is defined as:

$$ComX(Y, \Pi(n)) = \max\{ComX(u, \Pi(n)) \mid u \in I_Y\}.$$

Definition 9. *Let $FComX \in \{FComN, FComR, FComW\}$. A decision problem $Y = (I_Y, \theta_Y) \in FComX(k)$ if and only if:*

(i) There exists a family $\Pi(n)$, $n \in \mathbb{Z}^+$, of confluent recognizer ECPe systems that decides Y.
(ii) $ComX(Y, \Pi(n)) = k$.

The analogous complexity classes for non-confluent recognizer ECPe systems are $NFComN$, $NFComR$, and $NFComW$.

We say that $Y \in FComNRW(p, q, r)$ if and only if $Y \in FComN(p)$, $Y \in FComR(q)$ and $Y \in FComW(r)$. We use $NFComNRW$ for non-confluent recognizer ECPe systems.

We note here that the definition of $FComX$ in the previous definition is slightly modified from its definition in [1].

4   ECPe System Solutions to NP-Hard Problems

In this section, we shall present solutions to three NP-hard problems, namely, the vertex cover problem, the independent set problem and the 3-SAT problem.

Let the Vertex Cover Problem (VCP) be represented by a pair $VCP = (I_{VCP}, \theta_{VCP})$ where $I_{VCP} = \{w_{(G,k)} | w_{(G,k)}$ is a string representing a graph G and a positive integer $k\}$. If the graph G contains a vertex cover of size at most k, $\theta_{VCP}(w_{(G,k)}) = 1$; otherwise, $\theta_{VCP}(w_{(G,k)}) = 0$.

Theorem 1. $VCP \in NFComNRW(6, |V_G| + 3k + 6, 3|E_G| + |V_G| + k + 5)$ where E_G is the edge set and V_G is the vertex set of the input graph G.

Proof. To prove our claim, we need to satisfy the requirements in Definition 9. To do this, we first introduce a family (denoted by $\Pi_{VCP}(n)$) of ECPe systems for $VCP = (I_{VCP}, \theta_{VCP})$. We then show that $ComN(VCP, \Pi_{VCP}(n)) = 6$, $ComR(VCP, \Pi_{VCP}(n)) = |V_G| + 3k + 6$, and $ComW(VCP, \Pi_{VCP}(n)) = 3|E_G| + |V_G| + k + 5$.

The first part of our proof provides a formal definition of $\Pi_{VCP}(n)$. We also define a pair (cod, s) over I_{VCP} and show that for each instance of I_{VCP}, the two conditions given in Definition 7 are satisfied. Our family of ECPe systems for VCP is defined as a tuple $\Pi_{VCP}(n)$:

$$\Pi_{VCP}(n) = (O, [_0[_1]_1[_2]_2[_3]_3]_0, w_0, \emptyset, \emptyset, R_0, R_0', R_1, R_1', R_2, R_2', R_3, R_3')$$

where:

- $O = \{A_{ij}, v_i, \widehat{v}_i, i, \widehat{i}, \underline{i} \mid 1 \leq i < j \leq n\} \cup \{c, c', d, d', \#_0, \#_1, \#_2, \#_3, \#_4, \#_5\}$
  $\cup \{\alpha_0, \alpha_1, \beta_0, \beta_1, \beta_2\}$
- $w_0 = v_1 v_2 \ldots v_n \; cod(w_{(G,k)}) \; \#_0$
- $R_0 = \{A_{ij} \to ie, A_{ij} \to je \mid 1 \leq i < j \leq n\} \cup \{v_i \to \widehat{v}_i e \mid 1 \leq i \leq n\}$
  $\cup \{\#_0 \to \#_1, \#_1 \to \#_2, \#_2 \to \#_3, \#_3 \to \#_4, \#_4 \to \#_5 \alpha_0 \beta_0 e^3\}$
  $\cup \{c \to c' e^2, d \to d' e\} \cup \beta_2 \to yese, \alpha_1 \to no\ e\}$
- $R_0' = \{(no\ e, out), (yes\ e, out)\}$

- $R_1 = \{\widehat{v}_i \to \widehat{i} \mid 1 \leq i \leq n\} \cup \{c' \to e\}$
- $R_1' = \{(\widehat{v}_i e, in), (ie, in; \widehat{i}e, out) \mid 1 \leq i \leq n\} \cup \{(c'e, in)\}$
- $R_2 = \{d' \to e\} \cup \{\widehat{i} \to \underline{i}^{n-2} \mid 1 \leq i < j \leq n\} \cup \{\alpha_0 \to \alpha_1\}$
- $R_2' = \{(\widehat{i}e, in), (ie, in; \underline{i}e, out) \mid 1 \leq i \leq n\} \cup \{(d'e, in), (\alpha_0 e, in)\}$
  $\cup \{(\#_5 e, in; \alpha_1 e, out)\}$
- $R_3 = \{\beta_0 \to \beta_1, \beta_1 \to \beta_2 e\}$
- $R_3' = \{(\beta_0 e, in), (\#_5 e, in; \beta_2 e, out)\}$

We associate a pair (cod, s) over I_{VCP} such that for a given instance $w_{(G,k)} \in I_{VCP}$ we have $n = s(w_{(G,k)}) = |V_G|$ and the encoding $cod(w_{(G,k)})$ is a multiset containing A_{ij} for every $(i, j) \in E_G$, k copies of object c and $|E_G| - k$ copies of object d. As shown in the construct $\Pi_{VCP}(n)$, the encoding is placed as part of the input in membrane 0. This guarantees that $s(u)$ is a natural number and $cod(u)$ is an input multiset for $\Pi_{VCP}(n)$, thus, satisfying condition (i) of Definition 7.

In order to show that condition (ii) of Definition 7 is satisfied, we discuss the system's computation:

Setup Phase. In this phase, for each edge in input region 0, an endpoint is nondeterministically chosen to cover that edge and represent that edge in the region. Also, representations of all the vertices are produced in region 1, along with an amount of energy equal to the maximum size of the vertex cover.

Initially, objects v_i ($1 \leq i \leq n$), c and d evolves to $\widehat{v}_i$, c', and d', respectively (through rules $v_i \rightarrow \widehat{v}_i e$, $c \rightarrow c'e^2$, $d \rightarrow d'e$). At the same time, objects A_{ij} nondeterministically evolves to one of i and j through any of rules $A_{ij} \rightarrow ie$ and $A_{ij} \rightarrow je$. The value i or j represents the vertex that is chosen to cover the edge $(i,j) \in E$.

In the next step, the single quantum of energy produced in the production of objects $\widehat{v}_i$ ($1 \leq i \leq n$), c', and d' will be used to communicate the $\widehat{v}_i$ and c' in region 1, and the d' in region 2. The third step involves evolution of communicated objects in region 1 and 2. Specifically, c' will evolve to object e and $\widehat{v}_i$ becomes $\widehat{i}$ (through rules $c' \rightarrow e$ and $\widehat{v}_i \rightarrow \widehat{i}$ ($1 \leq i \leq n$)) in region 1 while d' changes to e in region 2. Also, in region 0, $\#_{m-1}$ evolves to $\#_m$ in step m for $m = 1, 2, 3$.

Finding a Candidate Solution. In region 1, vertices to form a candidate vertex cover are selected and communicated to region 0.

The next step involves swapping the object $\widehat{i}$ in region 1 with its counterpart i in region 0 through rule $(ie, in; ie, out)$ in membrane 1. In this case, at most one copy of an object i will be placed in region 1. The set of all objects i that is transported in region 1 represents the *candidate vertex cover* chosen by a computation. Note that the size of the vertex cover is at most k. This size is assured by the limited number of e's in region 1 that will be used for the transportation. Also note that for each i representing a vertex in the candidate vertex cover, there is now a corresponding $\widehat{i}$ in region 0. Moreover, the second quantum of energy produced in region 0 in the production of c' is now utilized in the selection of a candidate vertex cover. During this selection, at most k of the edges are already verified to be covered by the vertices in the chosen set. Also, in region 0, $\#_3$ evolves to $\#_4$ in this step.

Validating Candidate Solution. Representation of the vertices in the candidate solution are produced in region 2. These objects are used to validate that all edges are covered by the selected vertex cover. This is true if no representation of the edges is retained in region 0.

In the next step, the $\widehat{i}$ in region 0 is transported to region 2 (through rule $(\widehat{i}e, in)$) to signal that the vertex represented by i is in the candidate vertex cover. At the same time, $\#_4$ evolves to $\#_5 \alpha_0 \beta_0 e^3$ in region 0. In the succeeding step, the objects α_0 and β_0 are communicated to regions 2 and 3, respectively, using up two of the quanta of energy, while the $\widehat{i}$ in region 2 will produce $|V|-2$ copies of $\underline{i}$. The $\underline{i}$ will then be used to determine if the vertices chosen to cover the remaining ($|E| - k$) unverified edges are present in the candidate. This ascertaining is done by applying the rule $(ie, in; \underline{i}e, out)$. Note that the maximum degree of simple graph is $|V| - 1$. Since one incident edge for each vertex in the candidate vertex cover has been verified in the previous phase, then a maximum of $(|V|-1)-1 =$

$|V| - 2$ edges that may be incident to a vertex still remain to be verified. Also, during this step, α_0 and β_0 evolve to α_1 and β_1 respectively.

Output Phase. In this phase, object yes is released to the environment if a valid vertex cover is selected. Otherwise, object no will be sent out.

Note that region 2 started with $|E| - k$ quanta of energy which equals the number of unverified edges at the start of the previous phase. Hence, in the case where not all of the vertices chosen (nondeterministically) to cover the edges in the setup phase belong to the candidate vertex cover, at least one e will be left in region 2. This case will allow the object α_1 to be sent out to region 0 and the object $\#_5$ to enter region 2 through the rule $(\#_5 e, in; \alpha_1 e, out)$. If the candidate solution is indeed a vertex cover, then no e is left in region 2 not allowing the rule $(\#_5 e, in; \alpha_1 e, out)$ to be used. Now, at this same step, object β_1 evolves to $\beta_2 e$. Hence, at the next step, the presence of object $\#_5$ in region 0 allows the rule $(\#_5 e, in; \beta_2 e, out)$ to be used and β_2 exits to region 0 while $\#_5$ enters region 3.

Finally, note that only one of the objects α_1 and β_2 will be communicated to region 0 by a computation. If α_1 is in region 0, it evolves to no e and no is then released to the environment. This case signals that the computation failed to produce the desired vertex cover. Whereas, if β_2 is in region 0, it evolves to yes e and yes is subsequently released to the environment. This case signals that the computation succeeded in finding a vertex cover with size at most k of the input graph G.

To complete our proof, we analyze the communication resources at each stage of the computation.

o The setup phase discussed previously takes three transitions. In this phase, the system communicates c', d' and $\widehat{v}_i$ ($1 \leq i \leq |V_G|$) from membrane 0 in exactly one communication step. Thus:
  - The number of communication steps to accomplish this phase is one.
  - The number of communication rules applied is $2 + |V_G|$
  - The number of communicated objects is $|E_G| + |V_G|$, i.e. $(|E_G| - k)$ number of d', k number of c' and $|V_G|$ number of $\widehat{v}_i$.
o Finding a candidate solution requires at least one communication step. In this phase, there will be one antiport rule for every member of the candidate solution. Thus:
  - The number of communication steps to accomplish this phase is one.
  - The maximum number of communication rules occurs when the size of the candidate solution is k. In this case, the number of communication rules applied is k.
  - Following the previous item, the maximum number of communicated objects is $2k$ since for every antiport rule, two objects are being communicated at the same time.
o For the validation and output phase:
  - The first communication step is used to initially place the $\widehat{i}$ representing the vertices of the candidate solution in membrane 2. This communication step is also necessary for the initial steps of the output phase. For

validating whether all remaining edges are covered, another communication step is needed. Finally, two additional communication steps will be used to produce a yes or a no and send to the environment.

- In the first communication step, a maximum of k rules of the form $(\widehat{ie}, in)$ $(1 \leq i \leq |V|)$ will be used. Simultaneously, rule $(\alpha_0 e, in) \in R'_2$ and $(\beta_0 e, in) \in R'_3$ will be used. In the succeeding communication step, a maximum of k rules of the form $(ie, in; \underline{i}e, out)$ will be used to validate the $|E_G| - k$ remaining edges. This case occurs when the size of the candidate solution is exactly k. The next communication steps involves the used of either (a) $(\#_5 e, in; \alpha_1 e, out)$ and $(no\ e; out)$, or (b) $(\#_5 e, in; \beta_2 e, out)$ and $(yes\ e; out)$. Thus, the maximum number of communication rules applied will be $k + k+2 + 2$.
- Following the previous item, the maximum number of communicated objects will be $k + 2 + 2(|E_G| - k) + 3$.

From our discussion above, it can be observed that the path with the most expensive communication resource (steps, rules and objects) is achieved when the candidate solution examined is of size equal to k and when this candidate is evaluated to be true. Summing the communication resources at each phase, we get $ComN(VCP, \Pi_{VCP}(n)) = 6$, $ComR(VCP, \Pi_{VCP}(n)) = |V_G| + 3k + 6$, and $ComW(VCP, \Pi_{VCP}(n)) = 3|E_G| + |V_G| + k + 5$.

An Example for VCP. Given an instance represented in Figure 1 with $k = 3$, an ECPe system solving VCP is a construct:

$$\Pi_{VCP}(5) = (O, [_0[_1]_1[_2]_2[_3]_3]_0, w_0, \emptyset, \emptyset, R_0, R'_0, R_1, R'_1, R_2, R'_2, R_3, R'_3)$$

where:

- $O = \{A_{ij}, v_i, \widehat{v}_i, i, \widehat{i}, \underline{i} \mid 1 \leq i < j \leq 5\} \cup \{c, c', d, d', \#_0, \#_1, \#_2, \#_3, \#_4, \#_5\}$
  $\cup \{\alpha_0, \alpha_1, \beta_0, \beta_1, \beta_2\}$
- $w_0 = v_1 v_2 v_3 v_4 v_5 A_{12} A_{13} A_{15} A_{23} A_{34} A_{45} c^3 d^3 \#_0$
- $R_0 = \{A_{ij} \rightarrow ie, A_{ij} \rightarrow je \mid 1 \leq i < j \leq 5\} \cup \{v_i \rightarrow \widehat{v}_i e \mid 1 \leq i \leq 5\}$
  $\cup \{\#_0 \rightarrow \#_1, \#_1 \rightarrow \#_2, \#_2 \rightarrow \#_3, \#_3 \rightarrow \#_4, \#_4 \rightarrow \#_5 \alpha_0 \beta_0 e^3$
  $\cup \{c \rightarrow c' e^2, d \rightarrow d'e\} \cup \beta_2 \rightarrow yes\ e, \alpha_1 \rightarrow no\ e\}$
- $R'_0 = \{(no\ e, out), (yes\ e, out)\}$

- $R_1 = \{\widehat{v}_i \rightarrow \widehat{i} \mid 1 \leq i \leq 5\} \cup \{c' \rightarrow e\}$
- $R'_1 = \{(\widehat{v}_i e, in), (ie, in; \widehat{i}e, out) \mid 1 \leq i \leq 5\} \cup \{(c'e, in)\}$
- $R_2 = \{d' \rightarrow e\} \cup \{\widehat{i} \rightarrow \underline{i}^3 \mid 1 \leq i < j \leq 5\} \cup \{\alpha_0 \rightarrow \alpha_1\}$
- $R'_2 = \{(ie, in), (ie, in; \underline{i}e, out) \mid 1 \leq i \leq 5\} \cup \{(d'e, in), (\alpha_0 e, in)\}$
  $\cup \{(\#_5 e, in; \alpha_1 e, out)\}$
- $R_3 = \{\beta_0 \rightarrow \beta_1, \beta_1 \rightarrow \beta_2 e\}$
- $R'_3 = \{\beta_0 e, in), (\#_5 e, in; \beta_2 e, out)\}$

Below is an example of a computation for $\Pi_{VCP}(5)$, represented as a series of configurations (C_i) $(0 \leq i \leq 11)$:

C_0: $[_0 \; v_1 v_2 v_3 v_4 v_5 \; A_{12} A_{13} A_{15} A_{23} A_{34} A_{45} \; c^3 \; d^3 \; \#_0 \; [_1 \;]_1 \; [_2 \;]_2 \; [_3 \;]_3 \;]_0$

C_1: $[_0 \; \hat{v}_1 e \; \hat{v}_2 e \; \hat{v}_3 e \; \hat{v}_4 e \; \hat{v}_5 e \; 1e \; 3e \; 1e \; 3e \; 3e \; 4e \; c'^3 e^6 \; d'^3 e^3 \; \#_1 \; [_1 \;]_1 \; [_2 \;]_2 \; [_3 \;]_3 \;]_0$

C_2: $[_0 \; 1\,3\,1\,3\,3\,4 \; e^9 \; \#_2 \; [_1 \; \hat{v}_1 \hat{v}_2 \hat{v}_3 \hat{v}_4 \hat{v}_5 \; c'^3 \;]_1 \; [_2 \; d'^3 \;]_2 \; [_3 \;]_3 \;]_0$

C_3: $[_0 \; 1\,3\,1\,3\,3\,4 \; e^9 \; \#_3 \; [_1 \; \hat{1}\,\hat{2}\,\hat{3}\,\hat{4}\,\hat{5} \; e^3 \;]_1 \; [_2 \; e^3 \;]_2 \; [_3 \;]_3 \;]_0$

C_4: $[_0 \; \hat{1}\,3\,\hat{1}\,3\,3\,\hat{4} \; e^6 \; \#_4 \; [_1 \; 1\,\hat{2}\,3\,4\,\hat{5} \,]_1 \; [_2 \; e^3 \;]_2 \; [_3 \;]_3 \;]_0$

C_5: $[_0 \; 1\,3\,3 \; e^3 \; \#_5 \alpha_0 \beta_0 e^3 \; [_1 \; 1\,\hat{2}\,3\,4\,5 \,]_1 \; [_2 \; \hat{1}\,\hat{3}\,\hat{4} \; e^3 \;]_2 \; [_3 \;]_3 \;]_0$

C_6: $[_0 \; 1\,3\,3 \; e^3 \; \#_5 e \; [_1 \; 1\,\hat{2}\,3\,4\,\hat{5} \,]_1 \; [_2 \; 1^3 \; 3^3 \; 4^3 \; e^3 \; \alpha_0]_2 \; [_3 \beta_0 \,]_3 \;]_0$

C_7: $[_0 \; \underline{1}\,\underline{3}\,\underline{3} \; \#_5 e \; [_1 \; 1\,\hat{2}\,3\,4\,\hat{5} \,]_1 \; [_2 \; 1\,3\,3\,1^2 \; \underline{3}\,4^3 \; \alpha_1 \,]_2 \; [_3 \; \beta_1 \,]_3 \;]_0$

C_8: $[_0 \; \underline{1}\,\underline{3}\,\underline{3} \; \#_5 e \; [_1 \; 1\,\hat{2}\,3\,4\,\hat{5} \,]_1 \; [_2 \; 1\,3\,3\,1^2 \; \underline{3}\,4^3 \; \alpha_1 \,]_2 \; [_3 \; \beta_2 e \,]_3 \;]_0$

C_9: $[_0 \; \underline{1}\,\underline{3}\,\underline{3} \; \beta_2 \; [_1 \; 1\,\hat{2}\,3\,4\,\hat{5} \,]_1 \; [_2 \; 1\,3\,3\,1^2 \; \underline{3}\,4^3 \; \alpha_1 \,]_2 \; [_3 \; \#_5 \,]_3 \;]_0$

C_{10}: $[_0 \; \underline{1}\,\underline{3}\,\underline{3} \; \text{yes} e \; [_1 \; 1\,\hat{2}\,3\,4\,\hat{5} \,]_1 \; [_2 \; 1\,3\,3\,1^2 \; \underline{3}\,4^3 \; \alpha_1 \,]_2 \; [_3 \; \#_5 \,]_3 \;]_0$

C_{11}: $\text{yes} \; [_0 \; \underline{1}\,\underline{3}\,\underline{3} \; [_1 \; 1\,\hat{2}\,3\,4\,\hat{5} \,]_1 \; [_2 \; 1\,3\,3\,1^2 \; \underline{3}\,4^3 \; \alpha_1 \,]_2 \; [_3 \; \#_5 \,]_3 \;]_0$

Configurations C_0 to C_3 represents the set-up phase where necessary objects are placed in their respective regions for the succeeding phases. At the same time, transition $C_0 \Rightarrow C_1$ makes use of rules in $\{A_{ij} \to ie, A_{ij} \to je \mid 1 \le i, j \le 5\}$ to choose the vertex that covers the edge represented by object $A_{i,j}$. Transition $C_3 \Rightarrow C_4$ represents the phase where a candidate vertex cover is chosen; in the example computation, the candidate vertex cover is $VC_3 = \{1, 3, 4\}$ as represented by objects 1, 3 and 4 in region 2. Computation $C_4 \Rightarrow^* C_7$ represents the verification phase to assure that selected vertex used to cover an edge belongs to the candidate vertex cover. Lastly, the computation $C_8 \Rightarrow^* C_{11}$ represents the output phase. Since all es in region 2 where used up, then α_1 will not exit the region and $\#5$ stays in region 0. This allows β_2 to exit region 3, resulting to the object yes to be communicated to the environment. This means that the computation succeeded in finding a vertex cover with size at most k of the input graph G.

If a different transition $C_0 \Rightarrow C_1'$ is introduced where

$$C_1': [_0 \; \hat{v}_1 e \; \hat{v}_2 e \; \hat{v}_3 e \; \hat{v}_4 e \; \hat{v}_5 e \; 1e \; 3e \; 1e \; 2e \; 4e \; 5e \; c'^3 e^6 \; d'^3 e^3 \; \#_1 \; [_1 \;]_1 \; [_2 \;]_2 \; [_3 \;]_3 \;]_0$$

then the set of vertices chosen to cover the edges of the input graph is $\{1, 2, 3, 4, 5\}$. Since only 3 quanta of energy is present in region 2, the use of rule $(ie, in; i'e, out)$ $(i \in \{1, 2, 3, 4, 5\})$ in region 1 is limited to 3 applications. This case implies that two of the objects 1, 2, 3, 4 and 5 will remain in region 0. Hence, the corresponding $\hat{i}$ for these remaining object will never exit region 1 and thus cannot be communicated to region 2 through rule $(\hat{i}e, in)$. This scenario implies that there will be two e's left in region 2. This case will allow α_1 to be communicated to region 0 in step 8 and subsequently, no is released to the environment in step 10. This means that not all of the vertices chosen to cover the edges in the setup phase belong to the candidate vertex cover.

The constructed family of ECPe systems used for VCP can also be used to solve ISP. This becomes apparent due to the lemma given in [6]. Note that the only difference will be the encoding of the instance for ISP where the initial copies of object c will be $|V_G| - k$ and d has $|E_G| - (|V_G| - k)$. Also, at the end of a successful computation, the elements of IS_k, $1 \le k \le |V|$ is represented by object $\hat{i}$ in region 1 (as illustrated by objects $\hat{2}, \hat{5}$ representing $IS_2 = \{2,5\}$ in the previous example).

Formally, let the Independent Set Problem (ISP) be represented by a pair $ISP = (I_{ISP}, \theta_{ISP})$ where $I_{ISP} = \{w_{(G,k)} | w_{(G,k)}$ is a string representing a graph G and a positive integer $k\}$. If the graph G contains an independent set of size at least k, $\theta_{ISP}(w_{(G,k)}) = 1$; otherwise, $\theta_{ISP}(w_{(G,k)}) = 0$.

Corollary 1. $ISP \in NFComNRW(6, 4|V_G| - 3k + 6, 3|E_G| + 2|V_G| - k + 5)$ where E_G is the edge set and V_G is the vertex set of the input graph G.

We now present a solution to the 3-SAT problem in ECPe systems. Let the 3-SAT problem ($3SP$) be represented by a pair (I_{3SP}, θ_{3SP}) where $I_{3SP} = \{w_{\phi x} | w_{\phi x}$ is a   string representing a 3-CNF boolean formula $\phi_x\}$. Boolean function $\theta_{3SP}(w_{\phi x})$ evaluates to 1 if ϕ is satisfiable, otherwise, $\theta_{3SP}(w_{\phi x}) = 0$.

Theorem 2. $3SP \in NFComNRW(5, 2n + 3, 4n + 3)$ where n is the number of clauses for the input 3-CNF boolean formula ϕ_X.

Proof. A family of ECPe systems that solves the 3-SAT problem is represented as a construct Π_{3SP}:

$$\Pi_{3SP}(n) = (O, [_0[_1]_1 \cdots [_n]_n[_{n+1}]_{n+1}]_0, w_0, \emptyset, \ldots, \emptyset, R_0, R_0', R_1, R_1', \ldots, R_n, R_n',$$
$$R_{n+1}, R_{n+1}')$$

where:

○ $O = \{x_d, d, \hat{d} \mid 1 \le d \le 3n\} \cup \{0_{dq}, 1_{dq} \mid 1 \le d \le 3n, 1 \le q \le n\}$

   $\cup \{A_{i_1 i_2 i_3, q}, B_{i_1 i_2 i_3, q} \mid 1 \le q \le n$ and $i_r \in \bigcup_{d=1}^{3n} \{d, \hat{d}\}, \forall r \in \{1,2,3\}\}$

   $\cup \{c, \#_0, \#_1, \#_2, \#_3, \#_4, \Omega, \beta_0, \beta_1, \text{no}, \text{yes}, e\}$

○ $w_0 = x_1 x_2 \ldots x_{3n} \#_0 \, cod(w_{\phi X})$

○ $R_0 = \{x_d \to 0_{d1} 0_{d2} 0_{d3}, x_d \to 1_{d1} 1_{d2} 1_{d3} \mid 1 \le d \le 3n\}$

   $\cup \{A_{i_1 i_2 i_3, q} \to B_{i_1 i_2 i_3, q} ce^2 \mid 1 \le q \le n$ and $i_r \in \bigcup_{d=1}^{3n} \{d, \hat{d}\}, \forall r \in \{1,2,3\}\}$

   $\cup \{\#_0 \to \#_1 \Omega e, \#_1 \to \#_2, \#_2 \to \#_3, \#_3 \to \#_4, \#_4 \to \text{yes } e^2\}$

   $\cup \{d \to e, \hat{d} \to e \mid 1 \le d \le 3n\}$

○ $R_0' = \{(\text{no } e, out), (\text{yes } e^{n+2}, out)\}$

○ For $1 \le q \le n$:

   • $R_q = \{B_{i_1 i_2 i_3, q} \to i_1 i_2 i_3 \beta_0 e \mid i_r \in \bigcup_{d=1}^{3n} \{d, \hat{d}\}, \forall r \in \{1,2,3\}\} \cup \{\beta_0 \to \beta_1\}$

   • $R_q' = \{(B_{i_1 i_2 i_3, q} e, in) \mid i_r \in \bigcup_{d=1}^{3n} \{d, \hat{d}\}, \forall r \in \{1,2,3\}\} \cup \{(ce, in; \beta_1 e, out)\}$

   $\cup \{(0_{dq} e, in; \hat{d} e, out), (1_{dq} e, in; de, out) \mid 1 \le d \le 3n\}$

○ $R_{n+1} = \{\Omega \to \text{no } e\}$

○ $R'_{n+1} = \{(\Omega e, in), (\beta_1 e, in; \text{no } e, out)\}$

We associate a pair $(cod(w_{\phi_X}), s(w_{\phi_X}))$ over I_{ϕ_X} where for each instance $w_{\phi_X} \in I_{\phi_X}$ we have $s(w_{\phi_X})$ being the number of clauses for the boolean formula ϕ_X, i.e. $s(w_{\phi_X}) = n$. The encoding $cod(w_{\phi_X})$ is a multiset containing $A_{i_1 i_2 i_3, q}$ for $1 \le q \le n$ where if $C_q = y_{i_1,q} \vee y_{i_2,q} \vee y_{i_3,q}$, then

$$i_l = \begin{cases} d & \text{if } y_{i_l,q} = x_d \\ \hat{d} & \text{if } y_{i_l,q} = \bar{x}_d \end{cases}$$

for $l = 1, 2, 3$, where $x_d \in \{x_1, x_2, \ldots, x_{3n}\}$. It can be noticed that we limit the cardinality of X to be at most $3n$ since the maximum number of variables that can simultaneously exist on a 3-CNF boolean formula is $3n$ (that is, when all variables in all clauses are distinct). If cardinality of the set X is more than the number of variables present in the boolean formula, then the extra variables can take any boolean value without affecting the satisfiability of the formula being evaluated. Our choice of $s(w_{\phi_X})$ for an instance $w_{\phi_X} \in I_{\phi_X}$ assures that $s(w_{\phi_X})$ is a natural number. Furthermore, our constructed Π_{3SP} includes the encoding $cod(w_{\phi_X})$ in region 1. This restriction guarantees that condition (i) of Definition 7 is satisfied.

To show that condition (ii) holds, we discuss how the computation proceeds as follows:

Setup and Finding a Candidate Solution Phase. In these steps, each variable is assigned a truth value. The input representation of each clause is also distributed to different regions.

The initial configuration requires object $A_{i_1 i_2 i_3, q}$ in region 0 as input to represent each clause in ϕ_X where q $(1 \le q \le n)$ symbolizes clause C_q and i_1, i_2 and i_3 corresponds to the variables contained in the clause C_q. In the next step, objects $A_{i_1 i_2 i_3, q}$ will evolve to object $B_{i_1 i_2 i_3, q}$ and c, producing two quanta of energy through rules $A_{i_1 i_2 i_3, q} \to B_{i_1 i_2 i_3, q} c \, e^2$ $(1 \le q \le n, i_l \in \bigcup\limits_{d=1}^{3n} \{d, \hat{d}\})$. Objects x_d will be consumed through one of rules $x_d \to 0_{d1} 0_{d2} 0_{d3}$ and $x_d \to 1_{d1} 1_{d2} 1_{d3}$ $(1 \le d \le 3n)$ simultaneously. This choice represents the possible truth assignment for all variable x_d such that if the latter rule is used, this means $x_d = 1$, otherwise, $x_d = 0$. Also, during this step, $\#_0$ evolves to $\#_1 \Omega e$. Upon completion of this step, the system determines a *candidate assignment* for variables in X.

Validating Candidate Solution and Output Phase. Simultaneously, each clause is checked whether it evaluates to true. If all clauses evaluate to true, the object yes is sent to the environment, otherwise, object no is sent out.

The next step involves validating the current candidate assignment. In this time step, object $B_{i_1 i_2 i_3, q}$ is communicated to region q through rule $(B_{i_1 i_2 i_3, q} e, in)$. At the same time, $\#_1$ in region 0 evolves to $\#_2$ while Ω enters region $n + 1$. While $\#_2$ in region 0 evolves to $\#_3$ and Ω in region $n + 1$ evolves to no e, the $B_{i_1 i_2 i_3, q}$'s evolve through rule $B_{i_1 i_2 i_3, q} \to i_1 i_2 i_3 \beta_0 e$. The objects i_1, i_2 and i_3 produced by this rule may take on values d (interpreted as x_d is contained in clause C_q) or $\hat{d}$ (interpreted as clause C_q contains $\bar{x}_d$), $x_d \in X$. Also, $\#_2$ in region 0 evolves to $\#_3$ while Ω in region $n + 1$ evolves to no e.

The quanta of energy left in region 0, as well as the object e produced in the aforementioned rule can be utilized to apply the antiport rules $(0_{dq}e, in; \hat{d}e, out)$ and $(1_{dq}e, in; de, out)$ in any one of the objects i_1, i_2 and i_3 present in a region q $(1 \leq q \leq n)$. Meanwhile, $\#_3$ evolves to $\#_4$ in region 0 and β_0 evolves to β_1 in regions 1 to n. Note that only a single application of any one of the antiport rules can be applied per region, which represents that for a clause $C_q = (y_{i_1,q} \vee y_{i_2,q} \vee y_{i_3,q})$, at least one of the $y_{i_l,q}$'s $(1 \leq q \leq 3)$ evaluates to 1. If all C_q's are satisfied, all the quanta of energy in regions 0 to n will be consumed. Henceforth, communication rules will no longer be applicable in membranes 1 to $n+1$. Afterwhich, $\#_4$ evolves to yes e then yes is communicated to the environment. If at least one of the C_q's is not satisfied, then at least one of regions 1 to n will have an e left, enabling at least one β_1 to be communicated to region 0. The presence of a β_1 in region 0 will allow the rule $(\beta_1 e, in; no\ e, out)$ to be used. This scenario results to the presence of no in region 0 and subsequently, the release of no to the environment.

We now evaluate the communication resources used as final requirement to satisfy Definition 9.

○ In the *setup and finding a candidate phase*, only one communication step is needed to communicate each B object (representing a particular clause) from membrane 0 using one symport rule for each clause. This communication step also involves transporting an object Ω in membrane $n + 1$.
  • number of communication step is one.
  • number of communication rules is n+1.
  • number of communication steps is n+1.
○ In the *validation and output phase*,
  • the maximum number of communication step occurs when some clauses are satisfied and other clauses are not satisfied. This scenario will require two communication steps for the validation phase. Another two communication steps will be dedicated to communication a no to the skin, and outside the system. Thus, maximum number of communication step is four.
  • the maximum number of communication rules occurs when the chosen variable assignment of the system evaluates to false. In such a case, each of the n clauses will use any one of antiport rules $(0_{dq}e, in; \hat{d}e, out)$ or $(1_{dq}e, in; de, out)$ where d refers to a variable and q refers to a clause (for satisfied clauses) and $(ce, in; \beta_1 e, out)$ (for unsatisfied clauses). Note that since our rules are local to membranes/regions, the $(ce, in; \beta_1 e, out)$ in a membrane i is different from $(ce, in; \beta_1 e, out)$ in a membrane j. The output phase will be using two communication rules, $(\beta_1 e, in; no\ e, out)$ and $(no\ e, out)$. Therefore, the maximum number of communication rules will be $n + 2$.
  • the maximum number of communication rules occurs when the chosen variable assignment of the system evaluates to true. In such a case, there

will be $2n$ quanta of energy needed for executing antiport rules for satisfied clause (as shown in previous item) and another n quanta of energy for executing (yes e^{n+2}, out). This occurrence means the maximum number of quanta of energy used is $3n + 2$.

It can be observed that the computations to compute the maximum number of communication steps, rules and objects are not necessarily the same. In fact, while the maximum number of communication rules occurs when the chosen variable assignments evaluates to false, the maximum number of energy for communication occurs when the chosen variable assignment evaluates to true. In summary, $ComN(3SP, \Pi_{3SP}(n)) = 5$, $ComR(3SP, \Pi_{3SP}(n)) = 2n + 3$, and $ComW(3SP, \Pi_{3SP}(n)) = 4n + 3$.

An Example for 3SP. Given an instance of a 3-CNF boolean formula $\phi_x = (\bar{x}_1 \vee x_2 \vee x_3) \wedge (x_1 \vee \bar{x}_2 \vee x_3) \wedge (\bar{x}_1 \vee x_2 \vee x_4)$ where $X = \{x_1, x_2, x_3, x_4\}$, an ECPe system solving 3SP is a construct:

$$\Pi_{3SP}(3) = (O, [_0[_1]_1[_2]_2[_3]_3[_4]_4]_0, w_0, \emptyset, \ldots, \emptyset, R_0, R_0', R_1, R_1', R_2, R_2', R_3, R_3', R_4, R_4')$$

where:

- $O = \{x_d, d, \hat{d} \mid 1 \leq d \leq 9\} \cup \{0_{dq}, 1_{dq} \mid 1 \leq d \leq 9, 1 \leq q \leq 3\}$
  $\cup \{A_{i_1 i_2 i_3, q}, B_{i_1 i_2 i_3, q} \mid 1 \leq q \leq 3 \text{ and } i_r \in \bigcup_{d=1}^{9} \{d, \hat{d}\}, \forall r \in \{1, 2, 3\}\}$
  $\cup \{c, \#_0, \#_1, \#_2, \#_3, \#_4, \Omega, \beta_0, \beta_1, \text{no}, \text{yes}, e\}$

- $w_0 = x_1 x_2 \ldots x_9 \#_0 \, cod(w_{\phi X})$

- $R_0 = \{x_d \to 0_{d1} 0_{d2} 0_{d3}, x_d \to 1_{d1} 1_{d2} 1_{d3} \mid 1 \leq d \leq 9\}$
  $\cup \{A_{i_1 i_2 i_3, q} \to B_{i_1 i_2 i_3, q} ce^2 \mid 1 \leq q \leq 3 \text{ and } i_r \in \bigcup_{d=1}^{9} \{d, \hat{d}\}, \forall r \in \{1, 2, 3\}\}$
  $\cup \{\#_0 \to \#_1 \Omega e, \#_1 \to \#_2, \#_2 \to \#_3, \#_3 \to \#_4, \#_4 \to \text{yes} e^2\}$
  $\cup \{d \to e, \hat{d} \to e \mid 1 \leq d \leq 9\}$

- $R_0' = \{(\text{no } e, out), (\text{yes } e^5, out)\}$

- For $1 \leq q \leq 3$:

  - $R_q = \{B_{i_1 i_2 i_3, q} \to i_1 i_2 i_3 \beta_0 e \mid i_r \in \bigcup_{d=1}^{9} \{d, \hat{d}\}, \forall r \in \{1, 2, 3\}\} \cup \{\beta_0 \to \beta_1\}$

  - $R_q' = \{(B_{i_1 i_2 i_3, q} e, in) \mid i_r \in \bigcup_{d=1}^{9} \{d, \hat{d}\}, \forall r \in \{1, 2, 3\}\} \cup \{(ce, in; \beta_1 e, out)\}$
    $\cup \{(0_{dq} e, in; \hat{d} e, out), (1_{dq} e, in; de, out) \mid 1 \leq d \leq 9\}$

- $R_4 = \{\Omega \to \text{no } e\}$
- $R_4' = \{(\Omega e, in), (\beta_1 e, in; \text{no } e, out)\}$

Below is an example of a computation for $\Pi_{3SP}(3)$, represented as a series of configurations (C_i) $(0 \leq i \leq 6)$:

C_0: $[_0 \ x_1x_2x_3x_4x_5x_6x_7x_8x_9 \ \#_0 \ A_{\hat{1}23,1}A_{1\hat{2}3,2}A_{\hat{1}24,3} \ [_1]_1 \ [_2]_2 \ [_3]_3 \ [_4]_4 \ ]_0$

C_1: $[_0 \ 0_{11}0_{12}0_{13} \ 0_{21}0_{22}0_{23} \ 0_{31}0_{32}0_{33} \ 1_{41}1_{42}1_{43} \ 0_{51}0_{52}0_{53} \ 0_{61}0_{62}0_{63} \ 0_{71}0_{72}0_{73}$
$0_{81}0_{82}0_{83}0_{91}0_{92}0_{93} \ \#_1\Omega e \ B_{\hat{1}23,1}ce^2 \ B_{1\hat{2}3,2}ce^2 \ B_{\hat{1}24,3}ce^2 \ [_1]_1 \ [_2]_2 \ [_3]_3 \ [_4]_4 \ ]_0$

C_2: $[_0 \ 0_{11}0_{12}0_{13} \ 0_{21}0_{22}0_{23} \ 0_{31}0_{32}0_{33} \ 1_{41}1_{42}1_{43} \ 0_{51}0_{52}0_{53} \ 0_{61}0_{62}0_{63} \ 0_{71}0_{72}0_{73}$
$0_{81}0_{82}0_{83} \ 0_{91}0_{92}0_{93} \ \#_2 \ c^3e^3[_1 \ B_{\hat{1}23,1} \ ]_1 \ [_2 \ B_{1\hat{2}3,2} \ ]_2 \ [_3 \ B_{\hat{1}24,3} \ ]_3 \ [_4 \ \Omega \ ]_4 \ ]_0$

C_3: $[_0 \ 0_{11}0_{12}0_{13} \ 0_{21}0_{22}0_{23} \ 0_{31}0_{32}0_{33} \ 1_{41}1_{42}1_{43} \ 0_{51}0_{52}0_{53} \ 0_{61}0_{62}0_{63} \ 0_{71}0_{72}0_{73}$
$0_{81}0_{82}0_{83} \ 0_{91}0_{92}0_{93} \ \#_3 \ c^3e^3[_1 \ \hat{1}23\beta_0e \ ]_1 \ [_2 \ 1\hat{2}3\beta_0e \ ]_2 \ [_3 \ \hat{1}24\beta_0e \ ]_3 \ [_4 \ \text{no } e \ ]_4 \ ]_0$

C_4: $[_0 \ \hat{1} \ 0_{12}0_{13} \ 0_{21} \ \hat{2} \ 0_{23} \ 0_{31}0_{32}0_{33} \ 1_{41}1_{42} \ 4 \ 0_{51}0_{52}0_{53} \ 0_{61}0_{62}0_{63} \ 0_{71}0_{72}0_{73}$
$0_{81}0_{82}0_{83} \ 0_{91}0_{92}0_{93} \ \#_4 \ c^3 \ [_1 \ 0_{11} \ 23 \ \beta_1 \ ]_1 \ [_2 \ 1 \ 0_{22} \ 3 \ \beta_1 \ ]_2 \ [_3 \ \hat{1}2 \ 1_{43} \ \beta_1 \ ]_3 \ [_4 \ \text{no } e \ ]_4 \ ]_0$

C_5: $[_0 \ e \ 0_{12}0_{13} \ 0_{21} \ e \ 0_{23} \ 0_{31}0_{32}0_{33} \ 1_{41}1_{42} \ e \ 0_{51}0_{52}0_{53} \ 0_{61}0_{62}0_{63} \ 0_{71}0_{72}0_{73}$
$0_{81}0_{82}0_{83} \ 0_{91}0_{92}0_{93} \ \text{yes } e^2 \ c^3 \ [_1 \ 0_{11} \ 23 \ \beta_1 \ ]_1 \ [_2 \ 1 \ 0_{22} \ 3 \ \beta_1 \ ]_2 \ [_3 \ \hat{1}2 \ 1_{43} \ \beta_1 \ ]_3 \ [_4 \ \text{no } e \ ]_4 \ ]_0$

C_6: $\text{yes } [_0 \ 0_{12}0_{13} \ 0_{21}0_{23} \ 0_{31}0_{32}0_{33} \ 1_{41}1_{42} \ 0_{51}0_{52}0_{53} \ 0_{61}0_{62}0_{63} \ 0_{71}0_{72}0_{73}$
$0_{81}0_{82}0_{83} \ 0_{91}0_{92}0_{93} \ c^3 \ [_1 \ 0_{11} \ 23 \ \beta_1 \ ]_1 \ [_2 \ 1 \ 0_{22} \ 3 \ \beta_1 \ ]_2 \ [_3 \ \hat{1}2 \ 1_{43} \ \beta_1 \ ]_3 \ [_4 \ \text{no } e \ ]_4 \ ]_0$

Configurations C_0 to C_3 represent the set-up phase where necessary objects are placed in their respective regions for the succeeding phases. At the same time, transition $C_0 \Rightarrow C_1$ makes use of rules in $\{x_d \to 0_{d1}0_{d2}0_{d3}, x_d \to 1_{d1}1_{d2}1_{d3} \mid 1 \leq d \leq 9\}$ to choose assignment for each variable $x_d \in X$.

Transition $C_3 \Rightarrow C_4$ represents the validation phase where the antiport rules $\{(0_{dq}e, in; \hat{d}e, out), (1_{dq}e, in; de, out) \mid 1 \leq d \leq 9\}$ are used to check if the candidate assignments satisfies all clauses.

Note that in C_4 all the quanta of energy in regions 0 to 3 were consumed. Henceforth, communication rules will no longer be applicable in membranes 1 to 4. Finally, transition $C_4 \Rightarrow^* C_6$, represents the output phase where the object yes is released to the environment to mean that a satisfying assignment was found for the given 3-CNF formula.

If we introduce a different transition $C_0 \Rightarrow C_1'$ where configuration C_1' is represented as:

C_1': $[_0 \ 1_{11}1_{12}1_{13} \ 0_{21}0_{22}0_{23} \ 1_{31}1_{32}1_{33} \ 0_{41}0_{42}0_{43} \ 0_{51}0_{52}0_{53} \ 0_{61}0_{62}0_{63} \ 0_{71}0_{72}0_{73}$

$0_{81}0_{82}0_{83}0_{91}0_{92}0_{93} \ \#_1\Omega e \ B_{\hat{1}23,1}ce^2 \ B_{1\hat{2}3,2}ce^2 \ B_{\hat{1}24,3}ce^2 \ [_1]_1 \ [_2]_2 \ [_3]_3 \ [_4]_4 \ ]_0$

representing the assignment $x_1 = 1$, $x_2 = 0$, $x_3 = 1$, $x_4 = 0$. Note that in step 4, a quantum of energy is left in each of the regions 0 and 3. Hence, in the next step, we can apply the communication rule $(ce, in; \beta_1 e, out)$ in membrane 3. The presence of β_1 in region 0 allows the application of $(\beta_1 e, in; \text{no } e, out)$ in membrane 4. Finally, in step 7, the object no is released to the environment to mean that the candidate solution does not satisfy the given 3-CNF formula.

5   Conclusion

In this paper, we studied the communication resources needed to non-confluently decide NP-complete problems namely, Vertex Cover Problem (VCP), consequently Independent Set Problem (ISP), and 3-SAT problem (3SP) using recognizer Evolution-Communication P systems with energy (ECPe systems). The following results were obtained : $VCP \in NFComNRW(6, |V_G| + 3k + 6, 3|E_G| + |V_G| + k + 5)$ and $ISP \in NFComNRW(6, 4|V_G| - 3k + 6, 3|E_G| + 2|V_G| - k + 5)$ where E_G is the edge set and V_G is the vertex set of the input graph G while $3SP \in NFComNRW(5, 2n + 3, 4n + 3)$ where n is the number of clauses in the input 3-CNF boolean formula.

In the solutions presented, it can be observed that while the number of membranes needed to solve VCP is constant (exactly four membranes), the number of membranes needed to solve 3SP is dependent on the number of clauses. However, in the results presented in both solutions, the number of communication steps are constant whereas the number of communication rules and energy for communication is dependent on the number of vertices and edges (for VCP), and clauses (for 3SP).

It remains an open problem whether we can reduce the number of communication steps, rules and energy; for example, can we construct recognizer ECPe systems using constant amount of rules or energy for communication? Also, from our results, it can be observed that the amount of communication steps needed to solve VCP is greater than the amount needed to solve 3SP, can we achieve a better result? Otherwise, can we characterize the class of problems that can be decided using five communication steps? six communication steps? or lower number of communication steps? It is also worth mentioning that the constructed ECPe systems used in this paper decides non-confluently. Evaluating communication resources on ECPe systems that decide on problems confluently also remains to be explored.

As final remarks, part of our future work includes exploring the use of carpets in understanding communication over the recognizer ECPe systems defined for solving VCP and 3SP. It is worth noting that Sevilla carpets can be used to provide a visualization of communication on ECPe systems as explored in [8].

Acknowledgments. N.H. S. Hernandez would like to thank the UP Diliman College of Engineering through the Jose P. Dans Jr. professorial chair for the financial support. R.A. B. Juayong is supported by the Engineering Research and Development for Technology (ERDT) Scholarship Program. H.N. Adorna is funded by a DOST-ERDT research grant and the Semirara Mining Corporation professorial chair of the UP Diliman, College of Engineering.

References

1. Adorna, H., Păun, G., Pérez-Jiménez, M.: On Communication Complexity in Evolution-Communication P systems. Romanian Journal of Information Science and Technology 13(2), 113–130 (2010)
2. Alhazov, A., Freund, R., Leporati, A., Oswald, M., Zandron, C. (Tissue) P systems with unit rules and energy assigned to membranes. Fundamenta Informaticae 74, 391–408 (2006)
3. Alhazov, A., Cavaliere, M.: Proton Pumping P systems. In: Martín-Vide, C., Mauri, G., Păun, G., Rozenberg, G., Salomaa, A. (eds.) WMC 2003. LNCS, vol. 2933, pp. 1–18. Springer, Heidelberg (2004)

4. Cavaliere, M.: Evolution-Communication P systems. In: Păun, G., Rozenberg, G., Salomaa, A., Zandron, C. (eds.) WMC-CdeA 2002. LNCS, vol. 2597, pp. 134–145. Springer, Heidelberg (2003)

5. Frisco, P.: The conformon-P system: a molecular and cell biology-inspired computability model. Theoretical Computer Science 312, 295–319 (2004)

6. Garey, M.R., Johnson, D.S.: Computers and Intractability, A Guide to the Theory of NP-Completeness. W. H. Freeman (1979) ISBN 0-7167-1044-7

7. Gutiérrez-Naranjo, M.A., Pérez-Jiménez, M.J.: Computing Backwards with P systems. WMC10, Curtea de Argeş, Romania, 282–295 (2009)

8. Juayong, R.A.B., Adorna, H.N.: Communication Complexity of Evolution-Communication P systems with Energy and Sevilla Carpet. Philippine Computing Journal 6(1), 34–40 (2010)

9. Mauri, G., Leporati, A., Zandron, C.: Energy-Based Models of P systems. In: Păun, G., Pérez-Jiménez, M.J., Riscos-Núñez, A., Rozenberg, G., Salomaa, A. (eds.) WMC 2009. LNCS, vol. 5957, pp. 104–124. Springer, Heidelberg (2010)

10. Păun, G.: Introduction to Membrane Computing. In: Ciobanu, G., Pérez-Jiménez, M.J., Păun, G. (eds.) Applications of Membrane Computing. Natural Computing Series, pp. 1–42. Springer (2006)

11. Pérez–Jiménez, M.J.: A Computational Complexity Theory in Membrane Computing. In: Păun, G., Pérez-Jiménez, M.J., Riscos-Núñez, A., Rozenberg, G., Salomaa, A. (eds.) WMC 2009. LNCS, vol. 5957, pp. 125–148. Springer, Heidelberg (2010)

12. Porreca, A.E., Mauri, G., Zandron, C.: Non-confluence in divisionless P systems with active membranes. Theoretical Computer Science 411(6), 878–887 (2010)

13. Zeng, X., Adorna, H., Martínez-del-Amor, M.Á., Pan, L., Pérez-Jiménez, M.J.: Matrix Representation of Spiking Neural P Systems. In: Gheorghe, M., Hinze, T., Păun, G., Rozenberg, G., Salomaa, A. (eds.) CMC 2010. LNCS, vol. 6501, pp. 377–391. Springer, Heidelberg (2010)

About One-Sided One-Symbol Insertion-Deletion P Systems

Sergiu Ivanov[1] and Sergey Verlan[1,2]

[1] Laboratoire d'Algorithmique, Complexité et Logique,
Université Paris Est – Créteil Val de Marne,
61, av. gén. de Gaulle, 94010 Créteil, France
{sergiu.ivanov,verlan}@u-pec.fr
[2] Institute of Mathematics and Computer Science,
Academy of Sciences of Moldova,
Academiei 5, Chisinau, MD-2028, Moldova

Abstract. In this article we consider insertion-deletion P systems inserting or deleting one symbol in one or two symbol(s) left context (more precisely of size $(1, 2, 0; 1, 1, 0)$ and $(1, 1, 0; 1, 2, 0)$). We show that computational completeness can be achieved by using only 3 membranes in a tree-like structure. Hence we obtain a trade-off between the sizes of contexts of insertion and deletion rules and the number of membranes sufficient for computational completeness.

1 Introduction

The operations of insertion and deletion were first considered with a linguistic motivation [19, 8, 22]. Another inspiration for these operations comes from the fact that the insertion operation and its iterated variants are generalized versions of Kleene's operations of concatenation and closure [14], while the deletion operation generalizes the quotient operation. A study of properties of the corresponding operations may be found in [10–12]. However, insertion and deletion also have interesting biological motivations, e.g., they correspond to a mismatched annealing of DNA sequences; these operations are also present in the evolution processes in the form of point mutations as well as in RNA editing, see the discussions in [3, 4, 26] and [24]. These biological motivations of insertion-deletion operations led to their study in the framework of molecular computing, see, for example, [6, 13, 24, 27].

In general, an insertion operation means adding a substring to a given string in a specified (left and right) context, while a deletion operation means removing a substring of a given string from a specified (left and right) context. A finite set of insertion-deletion rules, together with a set of axioms provide a language generating device: starting from the set of initial strings and iterating insertion-deletion operations as defined by the given rules, one gets a language.

Even in their basic variants, insertion-deletion systems are able to characterize the recursively enumerable languages. Moreover, as it was shown in [20], the context dependency may be replaced by insertion and deletion of strings of

A. Alhazov et al. (Eds.): CMC 2013, LNCS 8340, pp. 225–237, 2014.
© Springer-Verlag Berlin Heidelberg 2014

sufficient length, in a context-free manner. If the length is not sufficient (less or equal to two) then such systems are decidable and a characterization of them was shown in [28].

Similar investigations were continued in [21, 16, 17] on insertion-deletion systems with one-sided contexts, i.e., where the context dependency is present only from the left or only from the right side of all insertion and deletion rules. The papers cited above give several computational completeness results depending on the size of parameters of insertion and deletion rules. We recall the interesting fact that some combinations are not leading to computational completeness, i.e., there are recursively enumerable languages that cannot be generated by such devices, in particular, by systems of size $(1, 1, 0; 1, 1, 0)$, where the first three numbers represent the maximal size of the inserted string and the maximal size of the left and right contexts, respectively, while the last three numbers provide the same information about deletion rules.

In order to increase the computational power of the corresponding variants they were considered in the framework of P systems [18] and it was shown that computational completeness can be achieved if 5 membranes are used. In [7] tissue P systems are considered and computational completeness is achieved with 4 membranes. In [2] computational completeness is achieved by simpler insertion-deletion rules, but instead using priorities. A summary of related results can be found in [1, 29].

In this article we would like to consider the trade-offs between the sizes of the contexts and the number of membranes. We consider insertion-deletion P systems of size $(1, 2, 0; 1, 1, 0)$ and $(1, 1, 0; 1, 2, 0)$, and show that computational completeness can be achieved with only 3 membranes. We remind that previously it was shown that 4 membranes are enough to achieve computational completeness with insertion and deletion rules of size $(1, 1, 0)$.

2   Preliminaries

In this paper, the empty string is denoted by λ, the family of recursively enumerable, context-sensitive, and context-free languages by RE, CS and CF, respectively. We will use the notation $|w|$ for the length of a string w, while the number of occurrences of the symbol a in the string w will be referred to by the notation $|w|_a$. We do not define the standard concepts of the theory of formal languages in this section; the reader is invited to consider [25] for further details.

A type-0 grammar $G = (N, T, S, P)$ is said to be in *Geffert normal form* [9] if the set of non-terminals N is defined as $N = \{S, A, B, C, D\}$, T is an alphabet and P only contains context-free rules of the forms $S \to uSv$ with $u \in \{A, C\}^+$ and $v \in (T \cup \{B, D\})^+$ as well as $S \to \lambda$ and two (non-context-free) erasing rules $AB \to \lambda$ and $CD \to \lambda$.

We remark that according to [9] the generation of a string using a grammar in this normal form is done in two stages. During the first stage only context-free rules $S \to uSv$ can be applied (this follows from the fact that $u \in \{A, C\}^+$ and $v \in (\{B, D\} \cup T)^+$). During the second stage only non-context-free rules can be applied (because there is no more symbol S in the string). The transition between the stages is done by the rule $S \to \lambda$ (note that in [9] a set of rules of the form $S \to uv$ is used instead leading to an equivalent result). Note that the symbols A, B, C, D are treated like terminals during the first stage and so, each rule $S \to uSv$ is in some sense "linear".

Throughout this paper we will use the special Geffert normal form. Let $G = (N, T, S, P)$ be a grammar with $N = N' \cup N''$, $N' \cap N'' = \emptyset$, where $N'' = \{A, B, C, D\}$ and N' is a set of non-terminals containing S, S' and some other auxiliary non-terminals (that are introduced by the translation from the Geffert normal form to the special variant). We say that G is in the *special Geffert normal form* if it only has two (non-context-free) erasing rules $AB \to \lambda$ and $CD \to \lambda$ and several context-free rules of one of the following forms:

$$X \to bY, \quad \text{where } X, Y \in N', b \in N'', X \neq Y$$
$$X \to Yb, \quad \text{where } X, Y \in N', b \in T \cup N'', X \neq Y$$
$$S' \to \lambda.$$

Moreover, it may be assumed without loss of generality that for any two rules $X \to w$ and $U \to w$ in P with the first symbol of w different from S, S', we have $U = X$.

Any grammar G in the Geffert normal form can be transformed into a grammar G' in the special Geffert normal form generating the same language by replacing the "linear" rules by right- and left-linear ones. Let S' be a new non-terminal that will be used to mark the transition from the first stage to the second. The rule $S \to uSv$ of G, where $u = a_1 \ldots a_n$ and $v = b_1 \ldots b_m$ is replaced in G' by the following rules: $S \to a_1 X_1$, $X_1 \to a_2 X_2$, $\ldots$, $X_{n-1} \to a_n X_n$, $X_n \to X_{n+1} b_m$, $\ldots$, $X_{n+m} \to S b_1$, where $X_1, \ldots, X_{n+m}$ are new non-terminals different from each other as well as from the corresponding non-terminals introduced by the translation of other rules. We also add rules $X_{n+m} \to S' b_m$ and $S' \to \lambda$ to G' in order to mark the transition to the second stage. Note that the rule $S \to \lambda$ is not preserved in G'.

We also note that during the first stage of the derivation of a grammar in the special Geffert normal form there is exactly one non-terminal from N' present in the string and during the second stage the string does not contain any symbol from N'.

An *insertion-deletion system* is a construct $\Gamma = (V, T, A, I, D)$, where V is an alphabet, $T \subseteq V$ is the *terminal* alphabet (the symbols from $V \setminus T$ are called *non-terminal* symbols), $A \subseteq V^*$ is the set of *axioms*, and I and D are finite sets of triples of the form (u, α, v), where u, α, and v are strings over V, with $\alpha \neq \lambda$. The triples in I are called *insertion rules*, and those in D are called *deletion rules*.

An insertion rule $(u, \alpha, v) \in I$ indicates that the string α can be inserted between u and v, while a deletion rule $(u, \alpha, v) \in D$ indicates that α can be removed from between the contexts u and v. In other words, $(u, \alpha, v) \in I$ corresponds to the rewriting rule $uv \to u\alpha v$, while $(u, \alpha, v) \in D$ corresponds to the rewriting rule $u\alpha v \to uv$.

We denote the "derives by insertion" relation induced by insertion rules by $\Longrightarrow_{ins}$. Formally, $x \Longrightarrow_{ins} y$ ("x derives y by insertion") if and only if $x = x_1 u v x_2$ and $y = x_1 u \alpha v x_2$, $x_1, x_2 \in V^*$, and there exists $(u, \alpha, v) \in I$. By the notation $\Longrightarrow_{del}$ we refer to the "derives by deletion" relation defined by deletion rules. Formally, $x \Longrightarrow_{del} y$ ("x derives y by deletion") if and only if $x = x_1 u \alpha v x_2$ and $y = x_1 u v x_2$, $x_1, x_2 \in V^*$, and there exists $(u, \alpha, v) \in D$. By $\Longrightarrow$ we refer to the union of the relations $\Longrightarrow_{ins}$ and $\Longrightarrow_{del}$, and by $\overset{*}{\Longrightarrow}$ we denote the reflexive and transitive closure of $\Longrightarrow$.

Instead of relying on separate sets I and D, we will often consider their union $R = I \cup D$ and distinguish between insertion and deletion rules by the subscripts $_{ins}$ and $_{del}$. Thus instead of $(u, \alpha, v) \in I$, we will write $(u, \alpha, v)_{ins}$, and instead of $(u, \alpha, v) \in D$, we will write $(u, \alpha, v)_{del}$.

The language generated by the insertion-deletion system $\Gamma = (V, T, A, I, D)$ is defined as follows:

$$L(\Gamma) = \{w \in T^* \mid x \overset{*}{\Longrightarrow} w, x \in A\}.$$

The complexity of an insertion-deletion system $\Gamma = (V, T, A, I, D)$ is described by the vector $(n, m, m'; p, q, q')$ called *size*, where

$$
\begin{aligned}
n &= \max\{|\alpha| \mid (u, \alpha, v) \in I\}, & p &= \max\{|\alpha| \mid (u, \alpha, v) \in D\}, \\
m &= \max\{|u| \mid (u, \alpha, v) \in I\}, & q &= \max\{|u| \mid (u, \alpha, v) \in D\}, \\
m' &= \max\{|v| \mid (u, \alpha, v) \in I\}, & q' &= \max\{|v| \mid (u, \alpha, v) \in D\}.
\end{aligned}
$$

The *total size* of an insertion-deletion system Γ of size $(n, m, m'; p, q, q')$ is defined as the sum of all the numbers from the vector: $\Sigma(\Gamma) = n+m+m'+p+q+q'$.

By $INS_n^{m,m'} DEL_p^{q,q'}$ we denote the families of languages generated by insertion-deletion systems of size $(n, m, m'; p, q, q')$.

If $*$ is specified instead of one of the parameters n, m, m', p, q, or q', then there are no restrictions on the length of the corresponding component. In particular, $INS_*^{0,0} DEL_*^{0,0}$ denotes the family of languages generated by context-free insertion-deletion systems.

If one of the numbers from the pairs m, m' or q, q' is equal to zero, while the other one is not, we say that the family is with one-sided context.

An *insertion-deletion P system* of degree n is the following construct:

$$\Pi = (V, T, \mu, M_1, \ldots, M_n, R_1, \ldots, R_n)$$

where

- V is a finite alphabet,
- $T \subseteq V$ is the terminal alphabet,
- μ is the membrane (tree) structure of the system which has n membranes (nodes). This structure will be represented by a word containing correctly nested marked parentheses.
- M_i, for each $1 \le i \le n$ is a finite language associated with the membrane i.

- R_i, for each $1 \leq i \leq n$ is a set of insertion and deletion rules with target indicators associated with membrane i and having the following forms: $(u, x, v; tar)_{ins}$, where (u, x, v) is an insertion rule, and $(u, x, v; tar)_{del}$, where (u, x, v) is an deletion rule, and tar, called the *target indicator*, is from the set $\{here, in, out\}$.

Any n-tuple $(N_1, \ldots, N_n)$ of languages over V is called a configuration of Π. For two configurations $(N_1, \ldots, N_n)$ and $(N'_1, \ldots, N'_n)$ of Π we write $(N_1, \ldots, N_n) \implies (N'_1, \ldots, N'_n)$ if one can pass from $(N_1, \ldots, N_n)$ to $(N'_1, \ldots, N'_n)$ by applying the insertion and deletion rules from each region of μ, in the maximally parallel way, i.e., in parallel to all possible strings from the corresponding regions, and following the target indications associated with the rules. We assume that every string represented in a membrane has arbitrary many copies. Hence, by applying a rule to a string we get both arbitrary many copies of resulting string as well as old copies of the same string.

More specifically, if $w \in N_i$ and $r = (u, x, v; tar)_{ins} \in R_i$, respectively $r = (u, x, v; tar)_{del} \in R_i$, such that $w \implies_{ins}^r w'$, respectively $w \implies_{del}^r w'$, then w' will go to the region indicated by tar. If $tar = here$, then the string remains in N_i, if $tar = out$, then the string is moved to the region immediately outside the membrane i (maybe, in this way the string leaves the system), if $tar = in$, then the string is moved to one of the regions immediately below region i.

A sequence of transitions between configurations of a given insertion-deletion P system Π, starting from the initial configuration $(M_1, \ldots, M_n)$, is called a computation with respect to Π. The result of a computation consists of all strings over T which are sent out of the system at any time during the computation. We denote by $L(\Pi)$ the language of all strings of this type. We say that $L(\Pi)$ is generated by Π.

As in [23] we denote by $ELSP_k(ins_n^{m,m'}, del_p^{q,q'})$ the family of languages generated by insertion-deletion P systems of degree at most $k \geq 1$ having the size $(n, m, m'; p, q, q')$.

3   Computational Power of One-Sided Insertion-Deletion Systems of Small Size

In this section we consider insertion-deletion P systems of size $(1, 2, 0; 1, 1, 0)$ and $(1, 1, 0; 1, 2, 0)$. While the computational power of normal insertion-deletion systems with these parameters is not yet known, based on observations from [15] we conjecture that the corresponding models are not computationally complete. We also recall that most combinations of parameters involving left and right contexts as well as the insertion or deletion of more than one symbol are known to produce computationally complete insertion-deletion systems, see [29] for a complete list.

Theorem 1. $ELSP_3(ins_1^{2,0}, del_1^{1,0}) = RE$.

Proof. Consider a type-0 grammar $G = (N, T, P, S)$ in the special Geffert normal form and let $N'' = \{A, B, C, D\} \subseteq N$. We construct an insertion-deletion P system

$$\Pi = (V, T, [_1[_2[_3]_3]_2]_1, \{\{\mathcal{X}S\}\}, \emptyset, \emptyset, R_1 \cup R_1', R_2, R_3)$$

that simulates G as follows. The rules from P are supposed to be labeled in a one-to-one manner with labels from the set $[1..|P|]$. The alphabet of Π is $V = N \cup T \cup \{M_i \mid i : X \to \alpha \in P\} \cup \{K, K', \mathcal{X}\}$. The sets of rules R_1, R_2, R_3 of Π are defined as follows.

For any rule $i : X \to bY \in P$ we consider following sets of rules:

$R_1^i = \{i.1 : (X, M_i, \lambda; in)_{ins}\}$,

$R_2^i = \{i.2 : (XM_i, Y, \lambda; in)_{ins}\} \cup \{i.3 : (\mathbf{a}, M_i, \lambda; out)_{del} \mid \mathbf{a} \in N''\}$,

$R_3^i = \{i.4 : (\mathbf{a}, X, \lambda; here)_{del} \mid \mathbf{a} \in N''\} \cup \{i.5 : (\mathbf{a}M_i, b, \lambda; out)_{ins} \mid \mathbf{a} \in N''\}$.

For any rule $i : X \to Yb$ we consider following sets of rules:

$R_1^i = \{i.1 : (X, M_i, \lambda; in)_{ins}\}$,

$R_2^i = \{i.2 : (XM_i, b, \lambda; in)_{ins}\} \cup \{i.3 : (\mathbf{a}, M_i, \lambda; out)_{del} \mid \mathbf{a} \in N''\}$,

$R_3^i = \{i.4 : (\mathbf{a}, X, \lambda; here)_{del} \mid \mathbf{a} \in N''\} \cup \{i.5 : (\mathbf{a}M_i, Y, \lambda; out)_{ins} \mid \mathbf{a} \in N''\}$.

For the rules $i_1 : AB \to \lambda$ and $i_2 : CD \to \lambda$ and $i_3 : S' \to \lambda$ we consider following sets of rules:

$$R_1^{i_1} = \{i_1.1 : (\lambda, K, \lambda; in)_{ins}\},$$
$$R_2^{i_1} = \{i_1.2 : (K, A, \lambda; in)_{del}\} \cup \{i_1.3 : (\lambda, K, \lambda; out)_{del}\},$$
$$R_3^{i_1} = \{i_1.4 : (K, B, \lambda; out)_{del}\},$$
$$R_1^{i_2} = \{i_2.1 : (\lambda, K', \lambda; in)_{ins}\},$$
$$R_2^{i_2} = \{i_2.2 : (K', C, \lambda; in)_{del}\} \cup \{i_2.3 : (\lambda, K, \lambda; out)_{del}\},$$
$$R_3^{i_2} = \{i_2.4 : (K', D, \lambda; out)_{del}\},$$
$$R_1^{i_3} = \{i_3.1 : (\lambda, S', \lambda; here)_{del}\}.$$

Now for $j = 1, 2, 3$ we define $R_j = \cup_{1 \le i \le |P|} R_j^i$ and we define $R_1' = \{\mathcal{X} : (\lambda, \mathcal{X}, \lambda; out)_{del}\}$.

We state that $L(\Pi) = L(G)$. For this we show how each rule of G can be simulated in Π. Consider a string wXw' in membrane 1 and suppose that there is a rule $i : X \to bY$ in P. Then the following unique evolution can happen:

$$(wXw', 1) \Longrightarrow_{i.1} (wXM_iw', 2) \Longrightarrow_{i.2} (wXM_iYw', 3) \Longrightarrow_{i.4}$$
$$\Longrightarrow_{i.4} (wM_iYw', 3) \Longrightarrow_{i.5} (wM_ibYw', 2) \Longrightarrow_{i.3} (wbYw', 1).$$

In the second step it was possible to apply the rule $i.3$, yielding string wXw' in membrane 1, but this just returns to the previous configuration.

The rule $X \to Yb$ is simulated in a similar manner:

$$(wXw', 1) \Longrightarrow_{i.1} (wXM_iw', 2) \Longrightarrow_{i.2} (wXM_ibw', 3) \Longrightarrow_{i.4}$$
$$\Longrightarrow_{i.4} (wM_ibw', 3) \Longrightarrow_{i.5} (wM_iYbw', 2) \Longrightarrow_{i.3} (wYbw', 1).$$

The rule $i_1 : AB \to \lambda$ is simulated as follows (the case of rule $i_2 : CD \to \lambda$ is treated in an analogous way). First a symbol K is inserted in a context-free manner into the string ww' by using the rule $i_1.1$, yielding wKw'. If the symbol to the right of K is not an A, then the only possibility is to apply rule $i_1.3$ which deletes K and returns the string ww' to membrane 1. If K is inserted in front of a symbol A ($w' = Aw''$) then rule $i_1.2$ can be applied and string wKw'' goes to membrane 3. Now if w'' does not start with B, then the computation of this word is stopped and it does not yield a result. Otherwise ($w'' = Bw'''$), rule $i_1.4$ is applied yielding wKw''' in membrane 2. Now the computation may be continued in the same manner and K either eliminates another couple of symbols AB if this is possible, or the string appears in the skin membrane without K and then is ready for new evolutions.

When the system Π reaches the configuration $\mathcal{X}w$ with $w \in T^*$, rule $\mathcal{X}$ from R_1' can be applied yielding a terminal string w in the environment as a result of the computation.

Now in order to complete the proof, we observe that the only sequences of rules leading to a terminal derivation in Π correspond to the groups of rules as defined above. Hence, a derivation in G can be reconstructed from a derivation in Π. $\qquad\square$

Theorem 2. $ELSP_3(ins_1^{1,0}del_1^{2,0}) = RE$.

Proof. Consider the type-0 grammar $G = (N, T, S, P)$ in the special Geffert normal form and denote $N'' = \{A, B, C, D\} \subseteq N$. Consider as well that the rules from P are bijectively labelled with the numbers from the set $[1..|P|]$. We will now construct the following insertion-deletion P system Π which simulates G:

$$\Pi = (V, T, [_1[_2[_3]_3]_2]_1, \{\{\mathcal{X}S\}\}, \emptyset, \emptyset, R_1 \cup R_1', R_2 \cup R_2', R_3 \cup R_3').$$

The set of objects of Π will contain new special symbols per each rule of G and is constructed in the following way:

$$\begin{aligned} V = &\{M_i, \bar{Y}_i, M_i' && | \, i : X \to bY \in P\} \\ \cup &\{M_i, N_i, \bar{Y}_i, M_i' && | \, i : X \to Yb \in P\} \\ \cup &\{K, K', \mathcal{X}\} \cup N \cup T. \end{aligned}$$

For each $i : X \to bY \in R$, we construct the following three sets of rules:

$$\begin{aligned} R_1^i &= \{i.1 : (\lambda, M_i, \lambda; in)_{ins}\}, \\ R_2^i &= \{i.2 : (M_i, \bar{Y}_i, \lambda; here)_{ins}\} \cup \{i.3 : (M_i, b, \lambda; in)_{ins}\} \\ &\quad \cup \{i.4 : (b\bar{Y}_i, X, \lambda; out)_{del}\}, \\ R_3^i &= \{i.5 : (\lambda, M_i, \lambda; out)_{del}\}. \end{aligned}$$

For each $i : X \to Yb \in R$, we construct the following three sets of rules:

$$R_1^i = \{i.1 : (\lambda, M_i, \lambda; in)_{ins}\},$$
$$R_2^i = \{i.2 : (M_i, N_i, \lambda; here)_{ins}\} \cup \{i.3 : (N_i, b, \lambda; in)_{ins}\}$$
$$\cup \{i.4 : (\bar{Y}_i b, X, \lambda; out)_{del}\},$$
$$R_3^i = \{i.5 : (M_i, \bar{Y}_i, \lambda; here)_{ins}\} \cup \{i.6 : (\lambda, M_i, \lambda; here)_{del}\}$$
$$\cup \{i.7 : (a\bar{Y}_i, N_i, \lambda; out)_{del} \mid \mathbf{a} \in N''\}.$$

Moreover, we also build the following three sets:

$$R_1' = \{i_1' : (\lambda, M_i', \lambda; in)_{ins} \quad \mid i : X \to bY \in P \text{ or } i : X \to Yb \in P\},$$
$$R_2^i = \{i_2' : (M_i', Y, \lambda; in)_{ins} \quad \mid i : X \to bY \in P \text{ or } i : X \to Yb \in P\}$$
$$\cup \{i_3' : (\lambda, M_i', \lambda; in)_{del} \quad \mid i : X \to bY \in P \text{ or } i : X \to Yb \in P\},$$
$$R_3^i = \{i_4' : (M_i'Y, \bar{Y}_i, \lambda; out)_{del} \mid i : X \to bY \in P \text{ or } i : X \to Yb \in P\}.$$

Finally, for the rules $i_1 : AB \to \lambda$, $i_2 : CD \to \lambda$, and $i_3 : S' \to \lambda$ we consider the following sets of rules:

$$R_1^{i_1} = \{i_1.1 : (\lambda, K, \lambda; in)_{ins}\},$$
$$R_2^{i_1} = \{i_1.2 : (K, A, \lambda; in)_{del}\} \cup \{i_1.3 : (\lambda, K, \lambda; out)_{del}\},$$
$$R_3^{i_1} = \{i_1.4 : (K, B, \lambda; out)_{del}\},$$
$$R_1^{i_2} = \{i_2.1 : (\lambda, K', \lambda; in)_{ins}\},$$
$$R_2^{i_2} = \{i_2.2 : (K', C, \lambda; in)_{del}\} \cup \{i_2.3 : (\lambda, K, \lambda; out)_{del}\},$$
$$R_3^{i_2} = \{i_2.4 : (K', D, \lambda; out)_{del}\},$$
$$R_1^{i_3} = \{i_3.1 : (\lambda, S', \lambda; here)_{del}\}.$$

Now for $j = 1, 2, 3$ we define the sets $R_j = \cup_{1 \leq i \leq |P|} R_j^i$ and also $R_1' = \{\mathcal{X} : (\lambda, \mathcal{X}, \lambda; out)_{del}\}$.

We state that $L(\Pi) = L(G)$. For this we show how each rule of G can be simulated in Π. Consider a string wXw' in membrane 1 and suppose that there is a rule $i : X \to bY$ in P. The simulation of this rule occurs in two phases: in the first phase we rewrite X to $b\bar{Y}_i$, while in the second one we substitute $\bar{Y}_i$ with Y. The following is the valid first-phase simulation sequence in Π:

$$(wXw', 1) \Longrightarrow_{i.1} (wM_iXw', 2) \Longrightarrow_{i.2} (wM_i\bar{Y}_iXw', 2) \Longrightarrow_{i.3} (wM_ib\bar{Y}_iXw', 3)$$
$$\Longrightarrow_{i.5} (wb\bar{Y}_iXw, 2) \Longrightarrow_{i.4} (wb\bar{Y}_iw', 1).$$

The second phase happens due to the rules in the sets R_i', $i = 1, 2, 3$, and consists of the following steps:

$$(w\bar{Y}_ibw', 1) \Longrightarrow_{i'.1} (wM_i'\bar{Y}_ibw', 2) \Longrightarrow_{i'.2} (wM_i'Y\bar{Y}_ibw', 3)$$
$$\Longrightarrow_{i'.4} (wM_i'Ybw', 2) \Longrightarrow_{i'.3} (wYbw', 1).$$

We claim the both the first phase and the second phase simulation sequences are the only ones which can happen in valid derivations of Π. Indeed, consider the wXw' into which $i.1$ has inserted an instance of M_i. By inspecting the symbol requirements of the rules associated with membrane 2, we conclude that only the rules $i.2$ and $i.3$ may become applicable. Suppose that rule $i.3$ is applied directly. If, for example, M_i has been inserted to the right of X, this will produce the string $\gamma M_i b\gamma'' Xw'$, which will be moved into membrane 3. The case when $i.1$ inserts M_i to the right of X is treated in a similar way. Now, the only way to further move the computation out of membrane 3 is by applying the rule $i.5$ which will remove the instance of M_i and move the string into the second membrane. However, no more rules will be applicable from now on, because the string contains no service symbols at all, but is in the second membrane.

Suppose now that, after the application of $i.1$, the rule $i.2$ is applied $k > 1$ times. The subsequent application of the rule $i.3$ will insert an instance of b after M_i, thus yielding the substring $M_i b(\bar{Y}_i)^k$. Again, the only way to move the string out of membrane 3 is to erase the symbol M_i which produces a string with a substring of k instances of $\bar{Y}_i$. It is clear that, if X is situated to the left of this $(\bar{Y}_i)^k$, the string cannot contain $\bar{Y}_i X$, which is required by $i.3$. On the other hand, if X is to the right of $(\bar{Y}_i)^k$, it will not be possible to apply $i.3$ again, because the string does not contain the substring $\bar{Y}_i X$ preceded by a symbol from N''.

Finally, it is rather clear that, if $i.1$ does not insert the M_i just to the left of X, Π will not be able to move the string containing a $\bar{Y}_i$ and an X out of membrane 2, thus blocking without producing any meaningful result.

We will focus on the second-phase simulation sequence now. The application of the rule $i'.1$ inserts an instance of M_i' somewhere and moves the string into membrane 2. There are only two rules that may become applicable: $i'.2$ and $i'.3$. Suppose that $i'.3$ is applied directly after $i'.1$. In this case the system will come back into the configuration it has been in before the application of $i'.1$ without doing any changes to the string whatsoever. Therefore, to actually modify the string, the rule $i'.2$ must be applied.

An application of the rule $i'.2$ inserts exactly one instance of Y after M_i' and puts the string into the innermost membrane 3. Now, the only way to exit this membrane is by applying the rule $i'.4$, which means that, if the application of the rule $i'.1$ has not inserted M_i' to the left of $\bar{Y}_i$, the system Π will unproductively block in the third membrane. Consequently, after the application of $i'.4$, the string in the second membrane must be of the form $wM_i'Ybw'$. At this point, two rules are still applicable, $i'.2$ and $i'.3$. Suppose indeed that the rule $i'.2$ is applied a second time and inserts another instance of Y after M_i', thus yielding the string $wM_i'YYbw'$ and moving it into membrane 3. Now, however, the rule $i'.4$ is not applicable because the string lacks $\bar{Y}_i$ and Π will thus block. Therefore, the only productive way to move the string $wM_i'Ybw'$ out of the second membrane is to apply $i'.3$.

Now consider a rule $i : X \to Yb$. Again, the simulation of i happens in two phases: in the first phase we rewrite X to $\bar{Y}_i b$, while in the second phase we substitute $\bar{Y}_i$ with Y. Since the second phase of the simulation happens in exactly the same way as in the case of the rule $X \to bY$, we will only focus on the first-stage simulation sequence:

$$(wXw', 1) \Longrightarrow_{i.1} (wM_iXw', 2) \Longrightarrow_{i.2} (wM_iN_iXw', 2) \Longrightarrow_{i.3} (wM_iN_ibXw', 3)$$
$$\Longrightarrow_{i.5} (wM_i\bar{Y}_iN_ibXw', 3) \Longrightarrow_{i.6} (w\bar{Y}_iN_ibXw', 3)$$
$$\Longrightarrow_{i.7} (w\bar{Y}_ibXw', 2) \Longrightarrow_{i.4} (w\bar{Y}_ibw', 1).$$

We claim that the first-phase simulation sequence we have just shown is the only possible valid derivation of Π. We will now consider the variations that can interfere with this subderivation and show that none of them can influence the result of a computation of Π.

Consider the application of $i.1$ which inserts M_i into the original string wXw' and moves the new string, say $\gamma M_i \gamma' Xw'$, into membrane 2. The case when M_i is inserted to the right of X is treated in a similar way. In the current situation, the only applicable rule is $i.3$, which may insert k instances of N_i, thus yielding the string $\gamma M_i(N_i)^k \gamma' Xw'$. If one discards the possibility to produce yet more instances of N_i, the only other way to evolve is the application of the rule $i.3$ to insert a b after one of the N_i's and thereby to move the string into membrane 3.

In the new configuration, membrane 3 will contain $\gamma M_i(N_i)^{k_1}b(N_i)^{k_2}\gamma' Xw'$, where $k_1 \geq 1$ and $k_1 + k_2 = k$. We immediately remark that the only way for Π to move out of this membrane is to apply the rule $i.7$. This rule requires that there is a substring of $\bar{Y}_iN_i$ preceded by a symbol from N''. The string $\gamma M_i(N_i)^{k_1}b(N_i)^{k_2}\gamma' Xw'$, with which the system Π has just arrived in membrane 3, does not contain any instances of $\bar{Y}_i$, but the rule $i.5$ can introduce them. Suppose this latter rule is applied t times, $t \geq 0$, thus yielding the following result:

$$\gamma M_i(\bar{Y}_i)^t(N_i)^{k_1}b(N_i)^{k_2}\gamma' Xw'.$$

Clearly, the rule $i.7$ is not yet applicable, because there are no instances of $\bar{Y}_i$ preceded by symbols from N''. The only way to reach this situation is to apply the rule $i.6$ to obtain the string

$$\gamma(\bar{Y}_i)^t(N_i)^{k_1}b(N_i)^{k_2}\gamma' Xw'.$$

The rule $i.7$ imposes an even stronger requirement: the instance of $\bar{Y}_i$ which is preceded by a symbol from N'' must be immediately followed by N_i. Since instances of $\bar{Y}_i$ can only be inserted to the right of M_i, and since the process of inserting N_i's has already been completed in membrane 2, applying $i.7$ actually requires that exactly one instance of $\bar{Y}_i$ has been inserted by $i.5$ (i.e., it requires that $t = 1$), giving

$$\gamma\bar{Y}_i(N_i)^{k_1}b(N_i)^{k_2}\gamma' Xw'.$$

An application of the rule $i.7$ will erase the leftmost instance of N_i and will put the following string into membrane 2:

$$\gamma\bar{Y}_i(N_i)^{k_1-1}b(N_i)^{k_2}\gamma' Xw'.$$

The rule $i.3$ will still be applicable at this moment. Remark, however, that the string which will be moved into membrane 3 by this application will contain no instances of M_i, so the rule which may be applicable is $i.7$, which will remove yet another instance of N_i following $\bar{Y}_i$. Applications of the rules $i.3$ and $i.7$ in a loop will only be possible as long as there are instances of N_i just to the right of $\bar{Y}_i$ and then Π will either block in membrane 3 or move the string into membrane 1 with an application of $i.4$.

Based on the observations we have made in the previous paragraph, we can assert that the general form of the strings which may appear in membrane 2 after at least one traversal of membrane 3 is $\gamma \bar{Y}_i (N_i^* (N_i b)^*)^* \gamma' X w'$. If we discard the possibility of yet again re-tracing the loop formed by the rules $i.3$ and $i.7$, the only other way for Π to proceed is to apply $i.4$ and move the string into membrane 1. However, the rule $i.4$ imposes a strong condition on the form of the string it can be applied to: there has to exist a substring $\bar{Y}_i b X$. Clearly, the only way to have exactly one b between $\bar{Y}_i$ and X is, firstly, to have $i.1$ insert M_i exactly to the left of X (that is, γ' should be zero) and, secondly, to only apply $i.3$ once during the whole simulation process, thus obtaining the string $\gamma \bar{Y}_i b X w'$ in membrane 2. The application of $i.4$ will thus erase the X and successfully finish the rewriting of X into $\bar{Y}_i b$.

We conclude the proof by stating the simulation of the rules $AB \rightarrow \lambda$ and $CD \rightarrow \lambda$ is done in exactly the same way as in the case of the systems from the class $ELSP_3(ins_1^{2,0} del_1^{1,0})$. $\qquad\qquad\square$

4   Conclusion

In this article we considered insertion-deletion P systems of size $(1, 2, 0; 1, 1, 0)$ and $(1, 1, 0; 1, 2, 0)$ and showed that computational completeness can be achieved with 3 membranes. Compared to [7] this result shows an interesting trade-off between the size of contexts in insertion-deletion rules and the number of membranes: with 4 membranes, computational completeness is obtained already with insertion and deletion rules of size $(1, 1, 0)$. Now it remains an open question if the number of membranes can be further decreased for the investigated systems or for systems having bigger contexts for the insertion or deletion rules.

References

1. Alhazov, A., Krassovitskiy, A., Rogozhin, Y., Verlan, S.: Small size insertion and deletion systems. In: Martin-Vide, C. (ed.) Scientific Applications of Language Methods. Mathematics, Computing, Language, and Life: Frontiers in Mathematical Linguistics and Language Theory, vol. 2, ch. 9, pp. 459–524. World Sci. (2010)
2. Alhazov, A., Krassovitskiy, A., Rogozhin, Y., Verlan, S.: P Systems with Minimal Insertion and Deletion. Theoretical Computer Science 412(1-2), 136–144 (2011)
3. Benne, R.: RNA Editing: The Alteration of Protein Coding Sequences of RNA. Ellis Horwood, Chichester, West Sussex (1993)
4. Biegler, F., Burrell, M.J., Daley, M.: Regulated RNA rewriting: Modelling RNA editing with guided insertion. Theor. Comput. Sci. 387(2), 103–112 (2007)
5. Csuhaj-Varjú, E., Salomaa, A.: Networks of Parallel Language Processors. In: Păun, G., Salomaa, A. (eds.) NTFL. LNCS, vol. 1218, pp. 299–318. Springer, Heidelberg (1997)

6. Daley, M., Kari, L., Gloor, G., Siromoney, R.: Circular contextual insertions/deletions with applications to biomolecular computation. In: SPIRE/CRIWG, pp. 47–54 (1999)

7. Freund, R., Kogler, M., Rogozhin, Y., Verlan, S.: Graph-controlled insertion-deletion systems. In: McQuillan, I., Pighizzini, G. (eds.) Proc. of 12th Workshop on Descriptional Complexity of Formal Systems. EPTCS, vol. 31, pp. 88–98 (2010)

8. Galiukschov, B.: Semicontextual grammars. Matem. Logica i Matem. Lingvistika, 38–50, Tallin University (1981) (in Russian)

9. Geffert, V.: Normal forms for phrase-structure grammars. ITA 25, 473–498 (1991)

10. Haussler, D.: Insertion and Iterated Insertion as Operations on Formal Languages. PhD thesis, Univ. of Colorado at Boulder (1982)

11. Haussler, D.: Insertion languages. Information Sciences 31(1), 77–89 (1983)

12. Kari, L.: On Insertion and Deletion in Formal Languages. PhD thesis, University of Turku (1991)

13. Kari, L., Păun, G., Thierrin, G., Yu, S.: At the crossroads of DNA computing and formal languages: Characterizing RE using insertion-deletion systems. In: Proc. of 3rd DIMACS Workshop on DNA Based Computing, Philadelphia, pp. 318–333 (1997)

14. Kleene, S.C.: Representation of events in nerve nets and finite automata. In: Shannon, C., McCarthy, J. (eds.) Automata Studies, pp. 3–41. Princeton University Press, Princeton (1956)

15. Krassovitskiy, A.: Complexity and Modeling Power of Insertion-Deletion Systems. PhD thesis, Universitat Rovira i Virgili, Tarragona, Spain (2011)

16. Krassovitskiy, A., Rogozhin, Y., Verlan, S.: Further results on insertion-deletion systems with one-sided contexts. In: Martín-Vide, C., Otto, F., Fernau, H. (eds.) LATA 2008. LNCS, vol. 5196, pp. 333–344. Springer, Heidelberg (2008)

17. Krassovitskiy, A., Rogozhin, Y., Verlan, S.: Computational power of P systems with small size insertion and deletion rules. In: Neary, T., Woods, D., Seda, A.K., Murphy, N. (eds.) Proc. International Workshop on The Complexity of Simple Programs, Cork, Ireland, December 6-7. EPTCS, vol. 1, pp. 108–117 (2009)

18. Krassovitskiy, A., Rogozhin, Y., Verlan, S.: Computational power of insertion-deletion (P) systems with rules of size two. Natural Computing 10(2), 835–852 (2011)

19. Marcus, S.: Contextual grammars. Rev. Roum. Math. Pures Appl. 14, 1525–1534 (1969)

20. Margenstern, M., Păun, G., Rogozhin, Y., Verlan, S.: Context-free insertion-deletion systems. Theor. Comput. Sci. 330(2), 339–348 (2005)

21. Matveevici, A., Rogozhin, Y., Verlan, S.: Insertion-deletion systems with one-sided contexts. In: Durand-Lose, J., Margenstern, M. (eds.) MCU 2007. LNCS, vol. 4664, pp. 205–217. Springer, Heidelberg (2007)

22. Păun, G.: Marcus Contextual Grammars. Kluwer Academic Publishers, Norwell (1997)

23. Păun, G.: Membrane Computing. An Introduction. Springer (2002)

24. Păun, G., Rozenberg, G., Salomaa, A.: DNA Computing: New Computing Paradigms. Springer (1998)

25. Rozenberg, G., Salomaa, A. (eds.): Handbook of Formal Languages. Springer, Berlin (1997)

26. Smith, W.D.: DNA computers in vitro and in vivo. In: Lipton, R., Baum, E. (eds.) Proceedings of DIMACS Workshop on DNA Based Computers. DIMACS Series in Discrete Math. and Theoretical Computer Science, pp. 121–185. Amer. Math. Society (1996)

27. Takahara, A., Yokomori, T.: On the computational power of insertion-deletion systems. In: Hagiya, M., Ohuchi, A. (eds.) DNA8. LNCS, vol. 2568, pp. 269–280. Springer, Heidelberg (2003)

28. Verlan, S.: On minimal context-free insertion-deletion systems. Journal of Automata, Languages and Combinatorics 12(1-2), 317–328 (2007)

29. Verlan, S.: Study of language-theoretic computational paradigms inspired by biology. Habilitation thesis, University of Paris Est (2010)

Flattening and Simulation of Asynchronous Divisionless P Systems with Active Membranes

Alberto Leporati[1], Luca Manzoni[2], and Antonio E. Porreca[1]

[1] Dipartimento di Informatica, Sistemistica e Comunicazione
Università degli Studi di Milano-Bicocca
Viale Sarca 336/14, 20126 Milano, Italy
{leporati,porreca}@disco.unimib.it
[2] Laboratoire i3S, Université Nice Sophia Antipolis,
CS 40121 – 06903 Sophia Antipolis CEDEX, France
luca.manzoni@i3s.unice.fr

Abstract. We prove that asynchronous P systems with active membranes without division rules can be simulated by single-membrane transition P systems using cooperative rules, even if the synchronisation mechanisms provided by electrical charges and membrane dissolution are exploited. In turn, the latter systems can be simulated by means of place/transition Petri nets, and hence all these models are computationally weaker than Turing machines.

1 Introduction

P systems with active membranes [10] are parallel computation devices inspired by the structure and functioning of biological cells. A tree-like hierarchical structure of membranes divides the space into regions, where *multisets* of objects (representing chemical substances) are located. The systems evolve by means of rules rewriting or moving objects, and possibly changing the membrane structure itself (by dissolving or dividing membranes) or the state of the membranes (by changing their electrical charge).

Under the *maximally parallel* updating policy, whereby all components of the system that can evolve concurrently during a given computation step are required to do so, these devices are known to be computationally universal. Alternative updating policies have also been investigated. In particular, *asynchronous* P systems with active membranes [7], where any, not necessarily maximal, number of non-conflicting rules may be applied in each computation step, have been proved able to simulate partially blind register machines [8], computation devices equivalent under certain acceptance conditions to place/transition Petri nets and vector addition systems [11]. This simulation only requires object evolution (rewriting) rules and communication rules (moving objects between regions).

In an effort to further characterise the effect of asynchronicity on the computational power of P systems, we prove that asynchronous P systems with active membranes without dissolution can be flattened if we allow the use of cooperative rules, obtaining a system that can be easily simulated by place/transition Petri

A. Alhazov et al. (Eds.): CMC 2013, LNCS 8340, pp. 238–248, 2014.

nets, and as such they are not computationally equivalent to Turing machines: indeed, the reachability of configurations and the deadlock-freeness (i.e., the halting problem) of Petri nets are decidable [2]. This holds even when membrane dissolution, which provides an additional synchronisation mechanism (besides electrical charges) whereby all objects are released simultaneously from the dissolving membrane, is employed by the P system being simulated. Unfortunately, this result does not seem to immediately imply the equivalence with partially blind register machines, as the notion of acceptance for Petri nets employed here is by halting and not by placing a token into a "final" place [8].

The paper is organised as follows: in Section 2 we recall the relevant definitions of (divisionless) P systems with active membranes and place/transition Petri nets; in Section 3 we prove that asynchronous P systems with active membranes are computationally equivalent to their *sequential* version, where a single rule is applied during each computation step; in Section 4 we show that sequential P systems with dissolution rules can be simulated by sequential transition P systems with cooperative rules having only one membrane; finally, in Section 5 we show how sequential single-membrane transition P systems using cooperative rules can be simulated by Petri nets. Section 6 contains our conclusions and some open problems.

2   Definitions

We first recall the definition of P systems with active membranes and its various operating modes.

Definition 1. *A P system with active membranes of initial degree $d \geq 1$ is a tuple $\Pi = (\Gamma, \Lambda, \mu, w_{h_1}, \ldots, w_{h_d}, R)$, where:*

- *Γ is an alphabet, i.e., a finite nonempty set of objects;*
- *Λ is a finite set of labels for the membranes;*
- *μ is a membrane structure (i.e., a rooted unordered tree) consisting of d membranes injectively labelled by elements of Λ;*
- *$w_{h_1}, \ldots, w_{h_d}$, with $h_1, \ldots, h_d \in \Lambda$, are strings over Γ, describing the initial multisets of objects located in the d regions of μ;*
- *R is a finite set of rules.*

Each membrane possesses, besides its label and position in μ, another attribute called *electrical charge*, which can be either neutral (0), positive (+) or negative (−) and is always neutral before the beginning of the computation.

The following four kinds of rules are employed in this paper.

- *Object evolution rules*, of the form $[a \rightarrow w]_h^\alpha$
  They can be applied inside a membrane labeled by h, having charge α and containing an occurrence of the object a; the object a is rewritten into the multiset w (i.e., a is removed from the multiset in h and replaced by every object in w).

- *Send-in communication rules*, of the form $a\,[\,]_h^\alpha \to [b]_h^\beta$

  They can be applied to a membrane labeled by h, having charge α and such that the external region contains an occurrence of the object a; the object a is sent into h becoming b and, simultaneously, the charge of h is changed to β.

- *Send-out communication rules*, of the form $[a]_h^\alpha \to [\,]_h^\beta\,b$

  They can be applied to a membrane labeled by h, having charge α and containing an occurrence of the object a; the object a is sent out from h to the outside region becoming b and, simultaneously, the charge of h is changed to β.

- *Dissolution rules*, of the form $[a]_h^\alpha \to b$

  They can be applied to a membrane labeled by h, having charge α and containing an occurrence of the object a; the membrane h is dissolved and its contents are released in the surrounding region unaltered, except that an occurrence of a becomes b.

We recall that the most general form of P systems with active membranes [10] also includes *membrane division rules*, which duplicate a membrane and its contents; however, these rules are not used in this paper.

Each instantaneous configuration of a P system with active membranes is described by the current membrane structure, including the electrical charges, together with the multisets located in the corresponding regions. A computation step changes the current configuration according to the following set of principles:

- Each object and membrane can be subject to at most one rule per step, except for object evolution rules (inside each membrane several evolution rules having the same left-hand side, or the same evolution rule can be applied simultaneously; this includes the application of the same rule with multiplicity).
- When several conflicting rules can be applied at the same time, a nondeterministic choice is performed; this implies that, in general, multiple possible configurations can be reached after a computation step.
- In each computation step, all the chosen rules are applied simultaneously (in an atomic way). However, in order to clarify the operational semantics, each computation step is conventionally described as a sequence of microsteps as follows. First, all evolution rules are applied inside the elementary membranes, followed by all communication and dissolution rules involving the membranes themselves; this process is then repeated to the membranes containing them, and so on towards the root (outermost membrane). In other words, the membranes evolve only after their internal configuration has been updated. For instance, before a membrane dissolution occurs, all chosen object evolution rules must be applied inside it; this way, the objects that are released outside during the dissolution are already the final ones.
- The outermost membrane cannot be dissolved, and any object sent out from it cannot re-enter the system again.

In the *maximally parallel* mode, the multiset of rules to be applied at each step must be maximal, in the sense that no further rule can be added without creating conflicts. In the *asynchronous* mode, any nonempty multiset of applicable rules can be chosen. Finally, in the *sequential* mode, exactly one rule per computation step is applied. In the following, only the latter two modes will be considered.

A *halting computation* of the P system Π is a finite sequence of configurations $\mathcal{C} = (\mathcal{C}_0, \dots, \mathcal{C}_n)$, where $\mathcal{C}_0$ is the initial configuration, every $\mathcal{C}_{i+1}$ is reachable from $\mathcal{C}_i$ via a single computation step, and no rule can be applied in $\mathcal{C}_n$. A *non-halting* computation $\mathcal{C} = (\mathcal{C}_i : i \in \mathbb{N})$ consists of infinitely many configurations, again starting from the initial one and generated by successive computation steps, where the applicable rules are never exhausted.

The other model of computation we will employ is Petri nets. In particular, with this term we denote place/transition Petri nets with weighted arcs, self-loops and places of unbounded capacity [4]. A Petri net N is a triple (P, T, F) where P is the set of *places*, T the set of *transitions* (disjoint from P) and $F \subseteq (P \times T) \cup (T \times P)$ is the *flow relation*. The arcs are weighted by a function $w \colon F \to (\mathbb{N} - \{0\})$. A *marking* (i.e., a configuration) is a function $M \colon P \to \mathbb{N}$. Given two markings M, M' of N and a transition $t \in T$ we say that M' is reachable from M via the firing of t, in symbols $M \to_t M'$, if and only if:

- for all places $p \in P$, if $(p, t) \in F$ and $(t, p) \notin F$ then $M(p) \geq w(p, t)$ and $M'(p) = M(p) - w(p, t)$;
- for all $p \in P$, if $(t, p) \in F$ and $(p, t) \notin F$ then $M'(p) = M(p) + w(t, p)$;
- for all $p \in P$, if both $(p, t) \in F$ and $(t, p) \in F$ then $M(p) \geq w(p, t)$ and $M'(p) = M(p) - w(p, t) + w(t, p)$.

Petri nets are nondeterministic devices, hence multiple markings may be reachable from a given configuration. We call *halting computation* a sequence of markings $(M_0, \dots M_n)$ where $M_0 \to_{t_1} M_1 \to_{t_2} \cdots \to_{t_n} M_n$ for some $t_1, \dots, t_n$, and no transition may fire in M_n. Several problems related to the reachability of markings and halting configurations (or *deadlocks*) are decidable [2].

3   Asynchronicity and Sequentiality

In this section we show how it is possible to construct, for every asynchronous P system with active membranes, a *sequential* version that is equivalent to the original one, in the sense that each asynchronous step where more than one rule is applied can be substituted by a sequence of asynchronous steps where the rules are reordered and applied one at a time.

Proposition 1. *Let Π be a P system with active membranes using object evolution, communication, and dissolution rules. Then, the asynchronous and the sequential updating policies of Π are equivalent in the following sense: for each asynchronous (resp., sequential) computation step $\mathcal{C} \to \mathcal{D}$ there exists a series of sequential (resp., asynchronous) steps $\mathcal{C} = \mathcal{C}_0 \to \cdots \to \mathcal{C}_n = \mathcal{D}$ for some $n \in \mathbb{N}$.*

Proof. Every asynchronous computation step $\mathcal{C} \to \mathcal{D}$ consists in the application of a finite multiset of rules $\{e_1, \dots, e_p, c_1, \dots, c_q, d_1, \dots, d_r\}$, where $e_1, \dots, e_p$

are object evolution rules, $c_1, \ldots, c_q$ are communication rules (either send-in or send-out), and $d_1, \ldots, d_r$ are dissolution rules.

Since evolution rules do not change any charge nor the membrane structure itself, the computation step $\mathcal{C} \to \mathcal{D}$ can be decomposed into two asynchronous computation steps $\mathcal{C} \to \mathcal{E} \to \mathcal{D}$, where the step $\mathcal{C} \to \mathcal{E}$ consists in the application of the evolution rules $\{e_1, \ldots, e_p\}$, and the step $\mathcal{E} \to \mathcal{D}$ in the application of the remaining rules $\{c_1, \ldots, c_q, d_1, \ldots, d_r\}$. Notice that in $\mathcal{E}$ there still exist enough objects to apply these communication and dissolution rules, since by hypothesis $\mathcal{C} \to \mathcal{D}$ is a valid computation step.

Furthermore, notice how there is no conflict between object evolution rules (once they have been assigned to the objects they transform). Therefore, the application of the rules $\{e_1, \ldots, e_p\}$ can be implemented as a series of sequential steps $\mathcal{C} = \mathcal{C}_0 \to \cdots \to \mathcal{C}_p = \mathcal{E}$.

Each membrane can be subject to at most a single rule of communication or dissolution type in the computation step $\mathcal{C} \to \mathcal{D}$; hence, applying one of these rules does not interfere with any other. Thus, these rules can also be serialised into sequential computation steps $\mathcal{E} \to \mathcal{C}_{p+1} \to \cdots \to \mathcal{C}_{p+q+r} = \mathcal{D}$. Once again, all rules remain applicable since they were in the original computation step.

By letting $n = p + q + r$, the first half of the proposition follows. The second part is due to the fact that every sequential computation step is already an asynchronous computation step.   □

4   Single-Membrane Transition P Systems

In this section we recall the notion of *transition P system*, imposing as an additional constraint that the system has only one membrane. For a description of a general framework in which these systems can be described see [6]. As proved in [5], these systems are not universal; indeed, a simple simulation by means of Petri nets, inspired by [3], is provided in the next section. Our simulation involves a flattening of the membrane structure and the use of cooperative rules; the first simulation of this type was presented in [1] and, in fact, our construction is similar. Unlike that construction, however, the semantics that we use is sequential and we do not include promoters and inhibitors.

Definition 2. *A single-membrane transition P system is a structure*

$$\Pi = (\Gamma, w, R)$$

where Γ is a finite alphabet, w is a multiset of elements representing the initial state of the system, and R is a set of cooperative rules in the form $v \to w$ where v and w are multisets of objects of Γ.

Notice that the definition is a simplified version of the original definition of transition P systems [9], since specifying the membrane structure is not needed. We can now show that single-membrane transition P systems are equivalent to divisionless P systems with active membranes when operating under the sequential semantics.

Let $\Pi = (\Gamma, \Lambda, \mu, w_{h_1}, \ldots, w_{h_d}, R)$ be a P system with active membranes and $\mathcal{C}$ a configuration of Π. The *flattened encoding* of $\mathcal{C}$ is the multiset $E(\mathcal{C})$ over $(\Gamma \cup \{-, 0, +\}) \times \Lambda$ defined as follows:

1. If there are n copies of the object a contained in a membrane h in $\mathcal{C}$, then $E(\mathcal{C})$ contains n copies of the element (a, h).
2. If a membrane h has charge c, then the object (c, h) is in $E(\mathcal{C})$.

It is easy to see that, for a fixed Π, the encoding function is a bijection between the configurations of Π and its image, that is, the function E is invertible. Hence, for any multiset A that is the encoding of some configuration, the decoding is uniquely identified, i.e., for any configuration $\mathcal{C}$, $E^{-1}(E(\mathcal{C})) = \mathcal{C}$.

Proposition 2. *Let $\Pi = (\Gamma, \Lambda, \mu, w_{h_1}, \ldots, w_{h_d}, R)$ be a P system with active membranes working in the sequential mode and using object evolution, communication, and dissolution rules, with initial configuration $\mathcal{C}_0$. Then, there exists a single-membrane transition P system $\Pi' = ((\Gamma \cup \{-, 0, +\} \cup \{\bullet\}) \times \Lambda, v, R')$, for some initial multiset v, working in the sequential mode, such that:*

(i) If $\mathcal{C} = (\mathcal{C}_0, \mathcal{C}_1, \ldots, \mathcal{C}_m)$ is a halting computation of Π, then there exists a halting computation $\mathcal{D} = (E(\mathcal{C}_0), \mathcal{D}_1, \ldots, \mathcal{D}_n)$ of Π' such that $\mathcal{D}_n$ is the union of $E(\mathcal{C}_m)$ and the set of all the elements in the form $(\bullet, h)$ where h is a membrane that has been dissolved in $\mathcal{C}$.

(ii) If $\mathcal{D} = (E(\mathcal{C}_0), \mathcal{D}_1, \ldots, \mathcal{D}_n)$ is a halting computation of Π', then there exists a halting computation $\mathcal{C} = (\mathcal{C}_0, \mathcal{C}_1, \ldots, \mathcal{C}_m)$ of Π such that $\mathcal{D}_n$ can be written as the union of the set of elements in the form $(\bullet, h)$, where h is a membrane that was dissolved in $\mathcal{C}$, and the set $E(\mathcal{C}_m)$.

(iii) Π admits a non-halting computation $(\mathcal{C}_0, \mathcal{C}_1, \ldots)$ if and only if Π' admits a non-halting computation $(E(\mathcal{C}_0), \mathcal{D}_1, \ldots)$.

Proof. The main idea is to replace every dissolution rule of a membrane h in R with a cooperative rule such that an object in the form $(\bullet, h)$ is generated and all the objects in the form (a, h) are rewritten to (a, h'), where h' is the lowest ancestor of h in μ that has not been dissolved.

Let $[a]_{h_1}^\alpha \to b$ be a dissolution rule in R. Then, R' contains the following cooperative rules:

$$(a, h_1)(\alpha, h_1) \to (b, h_1)(\bullet, h_1). \tag{1}$$

The objects that have h_1 as the second component are then rewritten by means of the following rules:

$$(a, h_1)(\bullet, h_1) \to (a, h_2)(\bullet, h_1) \tag{2}$$

where h_2 is the parent membrane of h_1 in μ. Notice that, if $(\bullet, h_2)$ exists, then membrane h_2 has been dissolved during a previous computation step; this means that there exists another rule of type (2) rewriting all the objects having h_2 as the second component. This process continues as long as there are objects with the label of a dissolved membrane as their second component (excluding the ones having $\bullet$ as the first component).

An object evolution rule $[a \to w]_h^\alpha$ is simulated by the following cooperative rule:

$$(a, h)(\alpha, h) \to (w_1, h) \dots (w_n, h)(\alpha, h). \tag{3}$$

A send-out communication rule $[a]_{h_1}^\alpha \to [\,]_{h_1}^\beta b$ is replaced by the following rules:

$$(a, h_1)(\alpha, h_1) \to (b, h_2)(\beta, h_1) \tag{4}$$

where h_2 is the parent membrane of h_1 in μ. As mentioned before, if $(\bullet, h_2)$ exists, then a rule of type (2) will subsequently rewrite (b, h_2).

Finally, a send-in communication rule $a\,[\,]_{h_1}^\alpha \to [b]_{h_1}^\beta$ is simulated as follows. Let $(h_n, h_{n-1}, \dots, h_2, h_1)$ be a sequence of nested membranes surrounding h_1, i.e., a descending path in the membrane tree μ. For every such sequence, we add the following rules to R':

$$(\bullet, h_{n-1}) \cdots (\bullet, h_2)(\alpha, h_1)(a, h_n) \to (\bullet, h_{n-1}) \cdots (\bullet, h_2)(\beta, h_1)(b, h_1). \tag{5}$$

These rules rewrite the object (a, h_n) into (b, h_1) if in Π all the membranes between h_n and h_1 have been dissolved. Observe that the number of descending paths leading to h_1 is bounded above by the depth of μ.

Notice how every rule of R' is exactly of one type among (1)–(5); in particular, given a rule in R' of type (1), (3), (4), or (5), it is always possible to reconstruct the original rule in R.

Each computation step of Π consisting in the application of an evolution or send-in communication rule is simulated by a single computation step of Π' by means of a rule of type (3) or (5), respectively.

The dissolution of a membrane h_1 in Π requires a variable number of steps of Π': first, a rule of type (1) is applied, then each object in the form (a, h_1) must be rewritten, by using rules of type (2), in order to obtain an object in the form (a, h_n), where h_n is the lowest ancestor membrane of h_1 that has not been dissolved in the original system. The exact number of steps depends on the number of objects located inside h_1 and the number of membranes that have been dissolved. The reasoning is analogous for send-out communication rules, simulated by means of rules of type (4) and (2).

Part (i) of the proposition directly follows from the semantics of the above cooperative rules.

Now let $\boldsymbol{D} = (\mathcal{D}_0 = E(\mathcal{C}_0), \mathcal{D}_1, \dots, \mathcal{D}_n)$ be a halting computation of Π'. Then there exists a sequence of rules $\boldsymbol{r} = (r_1, \dots, r_n)$ in R' such that

$$\mathcal{D}_0 \to_{r_1} \mathcal{D}_1 \to_{r_2} \cdots \to_{r_{n-1}} \mathcal{D}_{n-1} \to_{r_n} \mathcal{D}_n$$

where the notation $\mathcal{X} \to_r \mathcal{Y}$ indicates that configuration $\mathcal{Y}$ is reached from $\mathcal{X}$ by applying the rule r. Let $f \colon \mathbb{N} \to \mathbb{N}$ be defined as

$$f(t) = \big|\{r_i : 1 \leq i \leq t \text{ and } r_i \text{ is not of type (2)}\}\big|.$$

We claim that there exists a sequence of rules $s = (s_1, \ldots, s_m)$ such that the computation $\mathcal{C} = (\mathcal{C}_0, \ldots, \mathcal{C}_m)$ of Π generated by applying the rules of s, i.e.,

$$\mathcal{C}_0 \to_{s_1} \mathcal{C}_1 \to_{s_2} \cdots \to_{s_{m-1}} \mathcal{C}_{m-1} \to_{s_m} \mathcal{C}_m$$

has the following property $P(t)$ for each $t \in \{0, \ldots, n\}$:

> For all $h \in \Lambda$ and $a \in \Gamma$, if (γ, h) with $\gamma \in \{+, 0, -\}$ is in configuration $\mathcal{D}_t$ of Π', then the number of copies of the objects of the form (a, h') with h' any descendant of h in μ, or h itself, is equal to the number of copies of a contained in the membrane substructure rooted in h in $\mathcal{C}_{f(t)}$, and h has the charge γ. If $(\bullet, h)$ is in $\mathcal{D}_t$, then h does not appear in $\mathcal{C}_{f(t)}$ (having been dissolved before).

We prove this property by induction on t. The case $t = 0$ clearly holds, by the definition of the encoding function: $E(\mathcal{C}_{f(0)}) = E(\mathcal{C}_0) = \mathcal{D}_0$, as $f(0) = |\varnothing|$.

Now suppose $P(t)$ holds for some $t < n$. If r_{t+1} is a rule of type (2) then for each object $a \in \Gamma$, the only change in the objects with a as the first component is when the second component h is the label of a membrane that has been dissolved in Π and the objects retain a as the first component while the second one became the label of the parent membrane of h in μ. Furthermore, no symbol in the form (γ, h), where γ is a charge, is rewritten to a different symbol. Since r_{t+1} is of type (2), we have $f(t+1) = f(t)$ hence $\mathcal{C}_{f(t+1)} = \mathcal{C}_{f(t)}$, and property $P(t+1)$ holds.

On the other hand, if r_{t+1} is not of type (2), then $f(t+1) = f(t) + 1$ by definition. Let $s_{f(t)+1} = s_{f(t+1)}$ be the rule corresponding to the cooperative rule r_{t+1} as described above (an object evolution rule if r_{t+1} is of type (3), a dissolution rule if r_{t+1} is of type (1), and so on). Observe that if r_{t+1} is applicable in $\mathcal{D}_t$, then $s_{f(t)+1}$ is applicable in $\mathcal{C}_{f(t)}$ by induction hypothesis:

- if (γ, h) is in $\mathcal{D}_t$ then the membrane h has charge γ in $\mathcal{C}_{f(t)}$;
- if r_{t+1} is of type (1), (3), or (4) and uses an object (a, h) in $\mathcal{D}_t$, then a copy of a appears in membrane h in $\mathcal{C}_{f(t)}$;
- if r_{t+1} is of type (5) and uses an object (a, h) and $(\bullet, h)$ is in $\mathcal{D}_t$, then the object a appears in $\mathcal{C}_{f(t)}$ inside the membrane having the same label as the lowest ancestor of h in the original membrane structure such that (γ, h) with $\gamma \neq \bullet$ is in $\mathcal{D}_t$.

The configuration $\mathcal{C}_{f(t)+1}$ such that $\mathcal{C}_{f(t)} \to_{s_{f(t)+1}} \mathcal{C}_{f(t)+1}$, due to the semantics of the corresponding rules applied by Π and Π', is such that the property $P(t+1)$ holds.

In particular, $P(n)$ holds: configurations $\mathcal{D}_n$ and $\mathcal{C}_{f(n)}$ have the following properties: the encoding $E(\mathcal{C}_{f(n)})$ is contained in $\mathcal{D}_n$ and all other objects not contained in $E(\mathcal{C}_{f(n)})$ are in the form $(\bullet, h)$, where h is the label of a membrane that has been dissolved during the computation. Notice that $\mathcal{C}_{f(n)}$ is a halting configuration, since otherwise any rule applicable from it could be simulated from $\mathcal{D}_n$ as in statement (i). Furthermore, if an object $(\bullet, h)$ is in $\mathcal{D}_n$ then no object in form (a, h) with $a \in \Gamma$ exists, otherwise further rules of type (2) could be applied, contradicting the hypothesis that $\mathcal{D}_n$ is a halting configuration. For all membranes h in $\mathcal{C}_{f(n)}$ and for all objects $a \in \Gamma$, the number of copies of a that are inside the membrane h in $\mathcal{C}_{f(n)}$ is equal to the number of objects in the form (a, h) in $\mathcal{D}_n$, and statement (ii) follows.

Finally, let us consider a non-halting computation of Π. Each time a computation of Π can be extended by one step by applying a rule, that rule can be simulated by Π' using the same argument employed to prove statement (i), thus yielding a non-halting computation of Π'. Vice versa, in a non-halting computation of Π' it is never the case that infinitely many rules of type (2) are applied sequentially, as only finitely many objects exist at any given time, and eventually they are rewritten to have the form (a, h) without also having the object $(\bullet, h)$. As soon as a rule of type (1), (3), (4), or (5) is applied, the corresponding rule can also be applied by Π, thus yielding a non-halting computation.   □

5   Simulation with Petri Nets

The single-membrane transition P systems described in the last section can be simulated by Petri nets in a straightforward way. The idea of using Petri nets as a device for the simulation is originally due to [3].

Proposition 3. *Let $\Pi = (\Gamma, w, R)$ be a single-membrane sequential transition P system. Then, there exists a Petri net N, having Γ among its places, such that $\mathcal{C} \to \mathcal{C}'$ is a computation step of Π if and only if $M \to M'$ is a computation step of N, where $M(a)$ is the number of instances of a in $\mathcal{C}$.*

Proof. The set of places of N is defined as $\Gamma \cup \{\text{lock}\}$, where lock is a place always containing a single token that is employed in order to ensure the firing of at most one transition per step. For each cooperative rule $v_1 \cdots v_n \to u_1 \cdots u_m$ the net has a transition defined as follows:

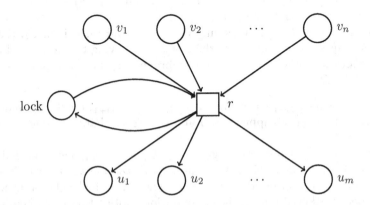

Notice that the output places need not be distinct, as the multiset in the left hand side may contain multiple occurrences of the same symbol; in that case, a weighted arc is used. The output places need not be distinct from the input places either; in that case, the net contains a corresponding loop.

The initial marking M_0 of N is given by $M_0(a) = |w|_a$, for all $a \in \Gamma$, where $|w|_a$ is the multiplicity of a in w.

Notice that a transition r in N is enabled exactly when the corresponding rule $r \in R$ is applicable, producing a transition $M \rightarrow_r M'$ corresponding to a computation step $\mathcal{C} \rightarrow_r \mathcal{C}'$ of Π as required. In every moment the number of tokens in a place is equal to the multiplicity of the corresponding object in the configuration of Π. □

By combining Propositions 1, 2, and 3, we can finally prove the following theorem.

Theorem 1. *For every asynchronous P system with active membranes Π using evolution, communication, and dissolution rules, there exists a Petri net N such that (i) every halting configuration of Π corresponds to a halting configuration of N and vice versa (under the encoding of Propositions 2 and 3), and (ii) every non-halting computation of Π corresponds to a non-halting computation of N and vice versa.* □

Notice that, given the strict correspondence of computations and their halting configurations (if any) between the two devices, this result holds both for P systems computing functions over multisets/Parikh vectors and those recognising or generating families of multisets/Parikh vectors, since the only difference between these computing modes is the initial configuration and the acceptance condition; these are translated directly into the simulating Petri net.

6   Conclusions

We have proved that asynchronous P systems with active membranes (without division rules) can be flattened and simulated by single-membrane transition P systems using cooperative rules. These systems can, in turn, be easily simulated by place/transition Petri nets, and hence are not computationally universal. In order to achieve this result, we exploited the equivalence between the asynchronous and the sequential parallelism policies for divisionless P systems with active membranes.

The conjectured equivalence of asynchronous P systems with active membranes and Petri nets does not seem to follow immediately from our result and the previous simulation of partially blind register machines by means of asynchronous P systems with active membranes [7]. Indeed, an explicit signalling (putting a token into a specified place) instead of accepting by halting seems to be required in order to simulate Petri nets with partially blind register machines [8]. Directly simulating Petri nets with asynchronous P systems with active membranes is also nontrivial, since transitions provide a stronger synchronisation mechanism than the limited context-sensitivity of the rules of a P system with active membranes. This equivalence is thus left as an open problem.

Acknowledgements. We would like to thank Luca Bernardinello for his advice on the theory of Petri nets. We would also like to thank the anonymous reviewers for pointing out relevant literature that allowed a simplification of the original construction.

This research was partially funded by Lombardy Region under project NEDD and by the French National Research Agency project EMC (ANR-09-BLAN-0164).

References

1. Agrigoroaiei, O., Ciobanu, G.: Flattening the transition P systems with dissolution. In: Gheorghe, M., Hinze, T., Păun, G., Rozenberg, G., Salomaa, A. (eds.) CMC 2010. LNCS, vol. 6501, pp. 53–64. Springer, Heidelberg (2010)
2. Cheng, A., Esparza, J., Palsberg, J.: Complexity results for 1-safe nets. Theoretical Computer Science 147, 117–136 (1995)
3. Dal Zilio, S., Formenti, E.: On the dynamics of PB systems: A Petri net view. In: Martín-Vide, C., Mauri, G., Păun, G., Rozenberg, G., Salomaa, A. (eds.) WMC 2003. LNCS, vol. 2933, pp. 153–167. Springer, Heidelberg (2004)
4. Desel, J., Reisig, W.: Place/transition Petri nets. In: Reisig, W., Rozenberg, G. (eds.) APN 1998. LNCS, vol. 1491, pp. 122–173. Springer, Heidelberg (1998)
5. Freund, R.: Asynchronous P systems and P systems working in the sequential mode. In: Mauri, G., Păun, G., Pérez-Jiménez, M.J., Rozenberg, G., Salomaa, A. (eds.) WMC5 2004. LNCS, vol. 3365, pp. 36–62. Springer, Heidelberg (2005)
6. Freund, R., Verlan, S.: A formal framework for static (tissue) P systems. In: Eleftherakis, G., Kefalas, P., Păun, G., Rozenberg, G., Salomaa, A. (eds.) WMC8 2007. LNCS, vol. 4860, pp. 271–284. Springer, Heidelberg (2007)
7. Frisco, P., Govan, G., Leporati, A.: Asynchronous P systems with active membranes. Theoretical Computer Science 429, 74–86 (2012)
8. Greibach, S.A.: Remarks on blind and partially blind one-way multicounter machines. Theoretical Computer Science 7, 311–324 (1978)
9. Păun, G.: Computing with membranes. Journal of Computer and System Sciences 61(1), 108–143 (2000)
10. Păun, G.: P systems with active membranes: Attacking NP-complete problems. Journal of Automata, Languages and Combinatorics 6(1), 75–90 (2001)
11. Peterson, J.L.: Petri net theory and the modeling of systems. Prentice-Hall (1981)

Enzymatic Numerical P Systems
Using Elementary Arithmetic Operations

Alberto Leporati, Giancarlo Mauri, Antonio E. Porreca, and Claudio Zandron

Dipartimento di Informatica, Sistemistica e Comunicazione
Università degli Studi di Milano-Bicocca
Viale Sarca 336/14, 20126 Milano, Italy
{leporati,mauri,porreca,zandron}@disco.unimib.it

Abstract. We prove that all-parallel enzymatic numerical P systems whose production functions can be expressed as a combination of sums, differences, products and integer divisions characterise **PSPACE** when working in polynomial time. We also show that, when only sums and differences are available, exactly the problems in **P** can be solved in polynomial time. These results are proved by showing how EN P systems and random access machines, running in polynomial time and using the same basic operations, can simulate each other efficiently.

1 Introduction

Numerical P systems have been introduced in [8] as a model of membrane systems inspired both from the structure of living cells and from economics. Each region of a numerical P system contains some numerical variables, that evolve from initial values by means of *programs*. Each program consists of a *production function* and a *repartition protocol*; the production function computes an output value from the values of some variables occurring in the same region in which the function is located, while the repartition protocol distributes this output value among the variables in the same region as well as in the neighbouring (parent and children) ones.

In [8], and also in Chapter 23.6 of [9], some results concerning the computational power of numerical P systems are reported. In particular, it is proved that nondeterministic numerical P systems with polynomial production functions characterize the recursively enumerable sets of natural numbers, while deterministic numerical P systems, with polynomial production functions having non-negative coefficients, compute strictly more than semilinear sets of natural numbers.

Enzymatic Numerical P systems (EN P systems, for short) have been introduced in [10] as an extension of numerical P systems in which some variables, named the *enzymes*, control the application of the rules, similarly to what happens in P systems with promoters and inhibitors [2]. As shown in [11,3] and references therein, the most promising application of EN P systems seems to be the simulation of control mechanisms of mobile and autonomous robots.

A. Alhazov et al. (Eds.): CMC 2013, LNCS 8340, pp. 249–264, 2014.
© Springer-Verlag Berlin Heidelberg 2014

The computational power of EN P systems has also been thoroughly investigated. In [6] a short review of previously known universality results is presented, together with an improvement on some of them: linear production functions involving only one variable suffice to obtain universality in the one-parallel and all-parallel modes.

In this paper we deal with computational complexity issues, and show how the choice of arithmetical operations allowed in the production functions influences the efficiency of computation of all-parallel EN P systems, exactly as it happens for random access machines [5]. Indeed, we prove that these two computation devices can simulate each other efficiently in some relevant cases. As a consequence, we show the limitations of linear production functions, and how these are overcome by allowing multiplication and integer division, leading to polynomial time solutions to **PSPACE**-complete problems.

The paper is organised as follows. In Section 2 we recall the definitions of EN P systems and random access machines, together with the relevant results from the literature. In Section 3 we show, as a technical result, how indirect addressing can be eliminated when RAMs operate in polynomial time, thus simplifying the simulation by means of all-parallel EN P systems that is presented in Section 4. The converse simulation is illustrated in Section 5, leading to our main result about the computational complexity of all-parallel EN P systems. Finally, conclusions and open problems are described in Section 6.

2   Definitions and Previous Results

An *enzymatic numerical P system* (EN P system, for short) is a construct of the form:

$$\Pi = \big(m, H, \mu, (Var_1, Pr_1, Var_1(0)), \ldots, (Var_m, Pr_m, Var_m(0))\big)$$

where $m \geq 1$ is the degree of the system (the number of membranes), H is an alphabet of labels, μ is a tree-like membrane structure with m membranes injectively labeled with elements of H, Var_i and Pr_i are respectively the set of variables and the set of programs that reside in region i, and $Var_i(0)$ is the vector of initial values for the variables of Var_i. All sets Var_i and Pr_i are finite. In the original definition of EN P systems [10] the values assumed by the variables may be real, rational or integer numbers; in what follows we will allow instead only integer numbers. The variables from Var_i are written in the form $x_{j,i}$, for j running from 1 to $|Var_i|$, the cardinality of Var_i; the value assumed by $x_{j,i}$ at time $t \in \mathbb{N}$ is denoted by $x_{j,i}(t)$. Similarly, the programs from Pr_i are written in the form $P_{l,i}$, for l running from 1 to $|Pr_i|$.

The *programs* allow the system to evolve the values of variables during computations. Each program is composed of two parts: a *production function* and a *repartition protocol*. The former can be any function using variables from the region that contains the program. Using the production function, the system computes a *production value*, from the values of its variables at that time. This value is distributed to variables from the region where the program resides, and to variables in its upper (parent) and lower (children) compartments, as specified by the repartition protocol. Formally, for a given region i, let $v_1, \ldots, v_{n_i}$ be all these variables; let $x_{1,i}, \ldots, x_{k_i,i}$ be some variables from Var_i, let $F_{l,i}(x_{1,i}, \ldots, x_{k_i,i})$ be the production function of a given program $P_{l,i} \in Pr_i$, and let $c_{l,1}, \ldots, c_{l,n_i}$ be natural numbers. The program $P_{l,i}$ is written in the following form:

$$F_{l,i}(x_{1,i}, \ldots, x_{k_i,i}) \to c_{l,1}|v_1 + c_{l,2}|v_2 + \cdots + c_{l,n_i}|v_{n_i} \tag{1}$$

where the arrow separates the production function from the repartition protocol. Let $C_{l,i} = \sum_{s=1}^{n_i} c_{l,s}$ be the sum of all the coefficients that occur in the repartition protocol. If the system applies program $P_{l,i}$ at time $t \geq 0$, it computes the value

$$q = \frac{F_{l,i}(x_{1,i}(t), \ldots, x_{k_i,i}(t))}{C_{l,i}}$$

that represents the "unitary portion" to be distributed to variables $v_1, \ldots, v_{n_i}$ proportionally with coefficients $c_{l,1}, \ldots, c_{l,n_i}$. So each of the variables v_s, for $1 \leq s \leq n_i$, will receive the amount $q \cdot c_{l,s}$. An important observation is that variables $x_{1,i}, \ldots, x_{k_i,i}$ involved in the production function are reset to zero after computing the production value, while the other variables from Var_i retain their value. The quantities assigned to each variable from the repartition protocol are added to the current value of these variables, starting with 0 for the variables which were reset by a production function. As pointed out in [12], a delicate problem concerns the issue whether the production value is divisible by the total sum of coefficients $C_{l,i}$. As it is done in [12], in this paper we assume that this is the case, and we deal only with such systems; see [8] for other possible approaches.

Besides programs (1), EN P systems may also have programs of the form

$$F_{l,i}(x_{1,i}, \ldots, x_{k_i,i})|_{e_{j,i}} \to c_{l,1}|v_1 + c_{l,2}|v_2 + \cdots + c_{l,n_i}|v_{n_i}$$

where $e_{j,i}$ is a variable from Var_i different from $x_{1,i}, \ldots, x_{k_i,i}$ and $v_1, \ldots, v_{n_i}$. Such a program can be applied at time t only if $e_{j,i}(t) > \min(x_{1,i}(t), \ldots, x_{k_i,i}(t))$. Stated otherwise, variable $e_{j,i}$ operates like an *enzyme*, that enables the execution of the program but, as happens with catalysts, it is neither consumed nor modified by the execution of the program. However, in EN P systems enzymes can evolve by means of other programs, that is, enzymes can receive "contributions" from other programs and regions.

A *configuration* of Π at time $t \in \mathbb{N}$ is given by the values of all the variables of Π at that time; in a compact notation, we can write it as the sequence $(Var_1(t), \ldots, Var_m(t))$, where m is the degree of Π. The *initial configuration* can thus be described as the sequence $(Var_1(0), \ldots, Var_m(0))$. The system Π evolves from an initial configuration to other configurations by means of *computation steps*, in which one or more programs of Π (depending upon the *mode* of computation) are executed. In [12], at each computation step the programs to be executed are chosen in the so called *sequential* mode: one program is nondeterministically chosen in each region, among the programs that can be executed at that time. Another possibility is to select the programs in the so called *all-parallel* mode: in each region, all the programs that can be executed are selected, with each variable participating in all programs where it appears. Note that in this case EN P systems become *deterministic*, since nondeterministic choices between programs never occur. A variant of parallelism, analogous to the maximal one which is often used in membrane computing, is the so called *one-parallel* mode: in each region, all the programs which can be executed can be selected, but the actual selection is made in such a way that each variable participates in only one of the chosen programs. We say that the system reaches a *final configuration* if and when it happens that no applicable set of programs produces a change in the current configuration.

EN P systems may be used as (polynomial) time-bounded recognising devices as follows. Notice that we use two variables (instead of just one of them), named *accept* and *reject*, to signal the end of computations. This is done because some programs of the system may be applied forever, causing the system to never halt even if the configuration does not change any more. By using two variables, the event of reaching a final configuration is made visible and distinguishable from the outside.

Definition 1. *Let $L \subseteq \{0,1\}^\star$ be a language, and let Π be a deterministic EN P system with two distinguished variables accept and reject. We say that Π decides L in polynomial time iff, for all $x \in \{0,1\}^\star$, when the integer having binary representation $1x$ is initially assigned to a specified input variable[1] the P system Π reaches a final configuration such that*

- *if $x \in L$, then accept $= 1$ and reject $= 0$*
- *if $x \notin L$, then accept $= 0$ and reject $= 1$*

within a number of steps bounded by $O(|x|^k)$ for some $k \in \mathbb{N}$.

As proved in [6], every all-parallel and one-parallel EN P system can be "flattened" into an equivalent (both in terms of output and number of computation steps) system having only one membrane. For simplicity, in the following sections we shall always deal with flattened EN P systems.

The proofs in this paper will be based on random access machines [7,5]. We define the specific variant we will employ:

Definition 2 (RAM). *A random access machine consists of an infinite number of registers $(r_i : i \in \mathbb{N})$ having values in $\mathbb{N}$, initially set to zero, and a finite sequence of instructions injectively labelled by elements $\ell \in \mathbb{N}$. The instructions are of the following types:*

- *assignment of a constant $k \in \mathbb{N}$: "$\ell \colon r_i := k$" (r_i is assigned a constant value)*
- *copying a register: "$\ell \colon r_i := r_j$" (r_i is assigned the content of a fixed register)*
- *indirect addressing: "$\ell \colon r_i := r_{r_j}$" ($r_i$ is assigned the content of a register whose number is given by a fixed register)*

---

[1] The "1" is prefixed to the input string x in order to keep the leading zeroes.

- *arithmetic operations, with $\bullet \in \{+, -, \times, \div\}$:* "$\ell: r_i := r_j \bullet r_k$"
- *conditional jump, with $\ell_1, \ell_2 \in \mathbb{N}$:* "$\ell$: if $r_i \neq 0$ then ℓ_1 else ℓ_2"
- *halt and accept:* "ℓ: accept"
- *halt and reject:* "ℓ: reject".

The labels of the instructions will sometimes be left implicit.

We assume, without loss of generality, that it is never the case that a register or a label are mentioned multiple times in the same instruction (e.g., in "$\ell : r_i := r_j \bullet r_k$" we assume $i \neq j$, $j \neq k$, and $i \neq k$).

Since RAMs operate on natural numbers, we only allow *non-negative* subtraction, i.e., $x - y = 0$ when $y > x$.

Definition 3. *Let $L \subseteq \{0,1\}^\star$ be a language, and let M be a RAM. We say that M decides L in polynomial time iff, for all $x \in \{0,1\}^\star$, when the integer having binary representation $1x$ is loaded into a specified input register, the machine M behaves as follows:*

- *if $x \in L$, then M reaches an "accept" instruction*
- *if $x \notin L$, then M reaches a "reject" instruction*

within a number of steps bounded by $O(|x|^k)$ for some $k \in \mathbb{N}$.

In the rest of this paper we will denote the class of random access machines using the set of basic operations $X \subseteq \{+, -, \times, \div\}$ by RAM(X), and the class of all-parallel EN P systems whose production functions can be expressed in terms of X by ENP(X). In particular, we are interested in all-parallel EN P systems having linear production functions, ENP($+, -$), and those with production functions consisting of polynomials augmented by integer division, ENP($+, -, \times, \div$).

We shall also employ the following notation for complexity classes:

Definition 4. *Let D be one of the classes of computing devices described above. Then, by **P**-D we denote the class of decision problems solvable in polynomial time by devices of type D.*

The computational power of polynomial-time RAMs is strictly dependent on the set of basic operations that can be computed in a single time step. When only addition and subtraction are available, then polynomial-time RAMs are equivalent to polynomial-time Turing machines [4].

Proposition 1. P-RAM($+, -$) = **P**.   □

On the other hand, multiplication and division considerably increase the efficiency of polynomial-time RAMs [1]:

Proposition 2. P-RAM($+, -, \times, \div$) = **PSPACE**.   □

```
1  e := y
2  z := 1
3  while e > 0 do
4        {x^e × z = x^y}
5        p := 1
6        p' := 2
7        a := x
8        a' := x × x
9        while p' ≤ e do
10             p := p'
11             p' := p' + p'
12             a := a'
13             a' := a' × a'
14       end
15       {e - p ≤ e/2}
16       e := e - p
17       z := z × a
18 end
```

$O(\log y)$ iterations (inner)

$O(\log y)$ iterations (outer)

Fig. 1. Polynomial-time exponentiation algorithm by repeated squaring

3 Avoiding Indirect Addressing

In this section we recall how indirect addressing may be eliminated from random access machines by encoding any number of registers as a single large integer. The resulting machine only needs a constant number of registers and, when the original machine runs in polynomial time, the slowdown is only polynomial.

In order to eliminate indirect addressing we employ multiplication, integer division and exponentiation. The first two operations, which are built-in on a RAM$(+, -, \times, \div)$, can be computed in quadratic time by a RAM$(+, -)$ using repeated doubling.

Proposition 3. *The product $x \times y$ and the quotient $x \div y$ can be computed in $O\big((\log y)^2\big)$ time and $O\big((\log x)^2\big)$ time respectively by a RAM$(+, -)$ using a constant number of auxiliary registers.*   □

Exponentiation can be also computed in polynomial time, using a repeated squaring algorithm, both by a RAM$(+, -)$ and a RAM$(+, -, \times, \div)$.

Proposition 4. *The exponential x^y can be computed in $O\big((\log y)^2\big)$ time by a RAM$(+, -, \times)$ and in $O\big((y \log y \log x)^2\big)$ time by a RAM$(+, -)$ using a constant number of auxiliary registers.*

Proof. The algorithm of Fig. 1 computes $z := x^y$ by repeated squaring.

The outermost loop maintains the invariant $x^e \times z = x^y$, and the innermost loop computes the largest power 2^i less than or equal to e, which is then subtracted from e, thus reducing the value of this register by half or more (hence, eventually, to 0); the product of the values x^{2^i} is accumulated into z. In other words, the algorithm computes the value x^y as

$$x^y = x^{y_m 2^m} \times x^{y_{m-1} 2^{m-1}} \times \cdots \times x^{y_1 2^1} \times x^{y_0 2^0}$$
$$= x^{y_m 2^m + y_{m-1} 2^{m-1} + \cdots + y_1 2^1 + y_0 2^0}$$

where $y_m y_{m-1} \cdots y_1 y_0$ is the binary expansion of y.

Each line of the algorithm is performed by a $\mathrm{RAM}(+, -, \times)$ in constant time, for a total of $O((\log y)^2)$ time. On a $\mathrm{RAM}(+, -)$, the product of line 8 is computed in $O((\log x)^2)$ time, and the products of lines 13 and 17 in $O((\log x^y)^2) = O((y \log x)^2)$ time, since a reaches the value x^y in the worst case (i.e., when y is a power of 2). The total time is thus $O((y \log y \log x)^2)$. $\quad\square$

An arbitrary random access machine never uses more registers than time steps; however, in principle, the largest register index employed can be exponential on a $\mathrm{RAM}(+, -)$, or even doubly exponential on a $\mathrm{RAM}(+, -, \times, \div)$. The following proposition [5] obviates the problem.

Proposition 5. *Let M be a RAM with addition, subtraction and possibly multiplication and division, working in time $t(n)$. Then there exists a RAM with the same basic operations working in time $O(t(n)^2)$, having the same output as M, and using only its first $O(t(n))$ registers.* $\quad\square$

The three Propositions 3, 4, and 5 allow us to simulate indirect addressing from polynomial-time RAMs with a polynomial slowdown.

Proposition 6. *Let M_1 be a $\mathrm{RAM}(+, -)$ (respectively, a $\mathrm{RAM}(+, -, \times, \div)$) working in polynomial time $O(n^k)$. Then, there exists a $\mathrm{RAM}(+, -)$ (resp., a $\mathrm{RAM}(+, -, \times, \div)$) M_2 working in $O(n^{8k} (\log n)^2)$ time (resp., $O(n^{2k} (\log n)^2)$) and computing the same result as M_1 without using indirect addressing.*

Proof. Since M_1 works in polynomial time, by Proposition 5 there exists another RAM M_1' with the same output as M_1, working in polynomial time $t = c_1 n^{2k} + c_0$ and using at most the first $m = d_1 n^k + d_0$ registers (for some $c_0, c_1, d_0, d_1 \in \mathbb{N}$).

The machine M_2 simulates M_1' as follows. All the registers $(r_0, \ldots, r_{m-1})$ of M_1' are stored in a single register r of M_2 as a base-b number:

$$r = b^{m-1} r_{m-1} + b^{m-2} r_{m-2} + \cdots + b^1 r_1 + b^0 r_0.$$

The base b is one more than the largest number that can ever be stored in a register by M_1', which can be computed as follows:

- If M_1' is a $\mathrm{RAM}(+, -)$, the most expensive instruction (in terms of magnitude of the values of the registers) is "$x := x + x$", where x is the input register. After t steps, the value of any register is thus bounded by $2^t x$, and we choose $b = 2^t x + 1$.
- If M_1' is a $\mathrm{RAM}(+, -, \times, \div)$, then the most expensive instruction is squaring, i.e., "$x := x \times x$", leading to an upper bound of x^{2^t} after t steps. In this case, we choose $b = x^{2^t} + 1$.

Notice that r has an upper bound of b^{m+1}.

The machine M_2 first computes the length $n = O(\log x)$ of the input (contained in the register x) as follows:

```
1 y := x
2 n := 0
3 while y ≠ 0 do
4     y := y ÷ 2
5     n := n + 1
6 end
```

This requires $O(\log x)$ steps on a RAM$(+, -, \times, \div)$, and $O((\log x)^3)$ steps on a RAM$(+, -)$, due to the cost of the division of line 4.

M_2 then computes the number of steps t of M_1' to be simulated:

```
7 t := c_1 n^{2k} + c_0
```

Line 7 can be executed in $O(1)$ time by a RAM$(+, -, \times, \div)$, since k, c_0, and c_1 are constants; on a RAM$(+, -)$ the time is $O((\log n)^2) = O((\log \log x)^2)$. Notice that evaluating such complex expressions only requires a constant number of auxiliary registers.

The base b described above is then computed. For a RAM$(+, -)$ the calculation is

```
8 b := 2^t x + 1
```

which executes in $O((t \log t)^2 + (\log x)^2) = O((n^{2k} \log n)^2)$ time.

For a RAM$(+, -, \times, \div)$ the calculation is

```
8 b := x^{2^t} + 1
```

which executes in $O(t^2) = O(n^{4k})$ time.

The last phase of the initialisation of M_2 sets up register r, which initially contains only x in its 0-th position:

```
9 r := x
```

Every time a register of M_1', say r_i (with i a constant), has to be read, its value can be extracted from the register r of M_2 and stored in an auxiliary register, say y, as follows:

$$y := (r \div b^i) \bmod b$$

where $a \bmod b = a - (a \div b \times b)$. This requires

$$O\left((\log b)^2 + (\log r)^2\right) = O\left((\log b)^2 + (\log b^{m+1})^2\right) = O\left((\log b^{m+1})^2\right)$$
$$= O\left((m \log b)^2\right) = O\left(((d_1 n^k + d_0) \log(2^t x + 1))^2\right)$$
$$= O\left((n^k(t + \log x))^2\right) = O(n^{6k})$$

time on a RAM$(+,-)$, and $O(1)$ time on a RAM$(+,-,\times,\div)$.

If indirect access is needed, that is, we read r_i where $i < m$ is *not* a constant, then the computation time becomes

$$
\begin{aligned}
O\big((i \log i \log b)^2 + (\log r)^2\big) &= O\big((m \log m \log b)^2 + (m \log b)^2\big) \\
&= O\big((m \log m \log b)^2\big) = O\big((n^k \log n \log b)^2\big) \\
&= O\big((n^k \log n \cdot (t + \log x))^2\big) \\
&= O\big((n^k \log n \cdot n^{2k})^2\big) = O\big((n^{3k} \log n)^2\big) \\
&= O\big(n^{6k} (\log n)^2\big)
\end{aligned}
$$

on a RAM$(+,-)$, and

$$
O\big((\log i)^2\big) = O\big((\log m)^2\big) = O\big((\log n)^2\big)
$$

on a RAM$(+,-,\times,\div)$. Hence, reading a register of M_1' (and, in particular, indirect addressing) can be simulated in polynomial time both on a RAM$(+,-)$ and on a RAM$(+,-,\times,\div)$.

The operation of writing the value of a register y of M_2 into a simulated register r_i of M_1' is similar:

```
1  z := (r ÷ b^i) mod b
2  r := r - (z × b^i) + (y × b^i)
```

and has the same asymptotical time complexity as above (keeping in mind that i is a constant in this case).

We can now finally describe how the instructions of M_1' are simulated by M_2.

- Assignment of a constant "$r_i := c$"
$$
\begin{aligned}
z &:= (r \div b^i) \bmod b \\
r &:= r - (z \times b^i) + (c \times b^i)
\end{aligned}
$$
- Copying the value of a register "$r_i := r_j$"
$$
\begin{aligned}
y &:= (r \div b^j) \bmod b \\
z &:= (r \div b^i) \bmod b \\
r &:= r - (z \times b^i) + (y \times b^i)
\end{aligned}
$$
- Copying the value of a register through indirect addressing "$r_i := r_{r_j}$"
$$
\begin{aligned}
y &:= (r \div b^j) \bmod b \\
y' &:= (r \div b^y) \bmod b \\
z &:= (r \div b^i) \bmod b \\
r &:= r - (z \times b^i) + (y' \times b^i)
\end{aligned}
$$
- Arithmetical operations "$r_i := r_j \bullet r_k$" with $\bullet \in \{+,-\}$ (for a RAM$(+,-)$) or $\bullet \in \{+,-,\times,\div\}$ (for a RAM$(+,-,\times,\div)$)
$$
\begin{aligned}
y_1 &:= (r \div b^j) \bmod b \\
y_2 &:= (r \div b^k) \bmod b \\
y &:= y_1 \bullet y_2 \\
z &:= (r \div b^i) \bmod b \\
r &:= r - (z \times b^i) + (y \times b^i)
\end{aligned}
$$

– Conditional jump "if $r_i \neq 0$ then ℓ_1 else ℓ_2"

$$y := (r \div b^i) \bmod b$$
$$\text{if } y \neq 0 \text{ then } \ell'_1 \text{ else } \ell'_2$$

where ℓ'_1 (resp., ℓ'_2) is the label of the first of the instructions of M_2 simulating the instruction ℓ_1 (resp., ℓ_2) of M'_1.

The discussion above implies that simulating each instruction of M'_1 requires at most $O\big(n^{6k}(\log n)^2\big)$ for a RAM$(+,-)$, and $O\big((\log n)^2\big)$ for a RAM$(+,-,\times,\div)$. Hence, the total number of steps to complete the simulation is $O\big(n^{8k}(\log n)^2\big)$ and $O\big(n^{2k}(\log n)^2\big)$ respectively. □

4   Simulating RAMs without Indirect Addressing

We now prove that each RAM, whose instructions satisfy the mild constraints we have imposed in the definition, and do not use indirect addressing, can be simulated by an appropriate EN P system working in the all-parallel mode. The simulation is efficient, in the sense that each RAM instruction is simulated in just one step.

Theorem 1. *Let M be a RAM that does not use indirect addressing. Then, for each instruction of M there exists a set of programs for an all-parallel EN P system Π that simulates it in one computation step.*

Proof. We proceed by examining all possible cases. In what follows, z is a variable whose value is always zero, variables r_i, r_j, r_k represent registers of M (containing non negative integer values), and variables p_ℓ assume values in $\{0,1\}$ to indicate the next instruction of M to be simulated.

RAM instructions of type "$\ell: r_i := k$" can be simulated by the following set of all-parallel programs:

$$0r_i + k + z|_{p_\ell} \rightarrow 1|r_i$$
$$p_\ell \rightarrow 1|p_{\ell+1}$$

When $p_\ell = 0$ the first program is not executed, while the second program zeroes p_ℓ (thus leaving its value unaltered) and gives a contribution of zero to variable $p_{\ell+1}$, thus behaving as a NOP (No OPeration). Hence no interference is produced in the variables involved in the RAM instruction currently simulated. On the other hand, if $p_\ell = 1$ then the first program first zeroes r_i and then assigns the value k to it, while the second program zeroes p_ℓ and sets $p_{\ell+1}$ to 1, thus pointing to the next instruction of M to be simulated.

Assignment instructions of type "$\ell: r_i := r_j$", with $j \neq i$, can be simulated using the following programs:

$$0r_i + 2r_j + z|_{p_\ell} \rightarrow 1|r_i + 1|r_j$$
$$p_\ell \rightarrow 1|p_{\ell+1}$$

As in the previous case, when $p_\ell = 0$ the first program is not active while the second one operates like a NOP. When $p_\ell = 1$, instead, the first program first zeroes both r_i and r_j and then assigns to them the old value of r_j; the second program, as before, passes the control to instruction $\ell+1$. Albeit in our definition of RAMs we have avoided the case when $j = i$, here we just observe that we can also easily deal with it: we simply remove the first program, since in this case it always operates like a NOP.

Arithmetic instructions of type "ℓ: $r_i := r_j \bullet r_k$", with $\bullet \in \{+, -, \times, \div\}$ and $i \neq j$, $j \neq k$, and $i \neq k$, can be simulated as follows:

$$0r_i + r_j \bullet r_k + z|_{p_\ell} \to 1|r_i$$

$$r_j + z|_{p_\ell} \to 1|r_j \tag{2}$$

$$r_k + z|_{p_\ell} \to 1|r_k \tag{3}$$

$$p_\ell \to 1|p_{\ell+1}$$

When $p_\ell = 0$ the first three programs are not executed, while the last program behaves as a NOP. On the other hand, if $p_\ell = 1$ then the first program first zeroes variables r_i, r_j and r_k, and then it assigns to r_i the result of the operation $r_j \bullet r_k$, using the old values of r_j and r_k. Programs (2) and (3) are used to preserve the old values of variables r_j and r_k, whereas the last program passes the control to instruction $\ell + 1$.

Finally, instructions of type "ℓ: if $r_i \neq 0$ then ℓ_1 else ℓ_2", with $\ell \neq \ell_1$, $\ell \neq \ell_2$, and $\ell_1 \neq \ell_2$, can be simulated by the following programs:

$$p_\ell \to 1|p_{\ell_1}$$

$$r_i - 1|_{p_\ell} \to 1|p_{\ell_1} \tag{4}$$

$$r_i + 1|_{p_\ell} \to 1|p_{\ell_2} \tag{5}$$

in which we assume $r_i \neq 0$ and correct if this is not the case. Note, in particular, that programs (4) and (5) are active if and only if $p_\ell = 1$ and $r_i = 0$. So, when $p_\ell = 0$ only the first program is executed, behaving as a NOP. When $p_\ell = 1$ and $r_i > 0$, the first program passes the control to instruction ℓ_1 whereas the other two programs are not executed. Finally, when $p_\ell = 1$ and $r_i = 0$ the first program zeroes p_ℓ and (incorrectly) sets p_{ℓ_1} to 1. This time, however, also the other two programs are executed: after resetting once again the value of r_i to 0, program (4) gives a contribution of -1 to p_{ℓ_1}, so that its final value will be zero, whereas program (5) sets p_{ℓ_2} to 1, indicating the next instruction of M to be simulated. □

5   Simulating All-Parallel EN P Systems with RAMs

Having proved that all-parallel EN P systems are able to simulate efficiently random access machines using the same arithmetic operations, we now turn our attention to the converse simulation. Without loss of generality, we assume that the all-parallel EN P systems being simulated have a single membrane [6].

Since the production functions of EN P systems may evaluate to negative numbers, even if the variables themselves are always non-negative, it is convenient to employ RAMs with registers holding values in $\mathbb{Z}$. This poses no restriction, since signed integers may be simulated with a constant-time slowdown by RAMs using non-negative numbers, for instance by storing them with a sign-and-modulus representation.

Proposition 7. *Let Π be an $\mathrm{ENP}(+,-)$ (respectively, an $\mathrm{ENP}(+,-,\times,\div)$) working in all-parallel mode and polynomial time $t(n) \leq c_1 n^k + c_0$. Then, there exists a $\mathrm{RAM}(+,-)$ (respectively, a $\mathrm{RAM}(+,-,\times,\div)$) M computing the same output as Π in time $O(t(n)^3)$ (respectively, $O(t(n))$).*

Proof. Let $x_1, \ldots, x_m$ be the variables of Π. The machine M stores the values of these variables in registers that we will denote with the same names, and will have the same values in the initial configuration, including the input variable of Π. Let $p_1, \ldots, p_h$ be the programs of Π.

Before describing the simulation proper, let us compute the maximum value of a variable of Π. If Π is an $\mathrm{ENP}(+,-)$, then the rules have one of the following forms:

$$a_{i_1} x_{i_1} \pm \cdots \pm a_{i_k} x_{i_k} \pm a \rightarrow b_1 | x_1 + \cdots + b_m | x_m$$
$$a_{i_1} x_{i_1} \pm \cdots \pm a_{i_k} x_{i_k} \pm a|_e \rightarrow b_1 | x_1 + \cdots + b_m | x_m$$

for some constants $a, a_{i_1}, \ldots, a_{i_k}, b_1, \ldots, b_m \in \mathbb{N}$. The following program, with some constant $a \in \mathbb{N}$, produces the maximum increase in the variable x, which we assume to be the input variable:

$$ax \rightarrow 1|x \tag{6}$$

After $t = c_1 n^k + c_0$ computation steps, the value of x reaches its maximum $a^t x$. (Naturally, a program such as (6) is not admissible in a halting EN P system; that program is considered here only in order to provide an upper bound to the value of the variables of Π.)

On the other hand, if Π is an $\mathrm{ENP}(+,-,\times,\div)$, the program that maximises the value of x is

$$x^a \rightarrow 1|x$$

for some $a \in \mathbb{N}$. In this case, after t steps the value of x reaches x^{a^t}. These upper bounds to the values of the variables of Π will be used later in order to determine the time required by M in order to simulate the EN P system.

The following is an overview of the simulation of Π:

> **repeat**
>> *save the current values of the variables*
>> *compute the variations due to p_1 (if applicable)*
>> $\vdots$
>> *compute the variations due to p_h (if applicable)*
>> *compute the new values of the variables*
> **until** *a final configuration is reached*
> **if** Π *accepted* **then**
>> **accept**
> **else**
>> **reject**
> **end**

At the beginning of each simulated step, the current values of the variables are copied:

$$x'_1 := x_1$$
$$\vdots$$
$$x'_m := x_m$$

In the variables $\Delta_1, \ldots, \Delta_m$, initially zero, we accumulate the contributions to $x_1, \ldots, x_m$ given by the programs of Π during the current step:

$$\Delta_1 := 0$$
$$\vdots$$
$$\Delta_m := 0$$

Each program p_i of the form $f(x_{i_1}, \ldots, x_{i_k}) \to a_1|x_1 + \cdots + a_m|x_m$ is simulated as follows:

$$f := f(x_{i_1}, \ldots, x_{i_k})$$
$$x'_{i_1} := 0$$
$$\vdots$$
$$x'_{i_k} := 0$$
$$u := f \div (a_1 + \cdots + a_m)$$
$$\Delta_1 := \Delta_1 + a_1 u$$
$$\vdots$$
$$\Delta_m := \Delta_m + a_m u$$

First, the value of the production function is computed. This requires $O(1)$ time, since by construction Π and M admit the same basic arithmetic operations.

Then, the copies of the variables occurring on the left-hand side of the program are zeroed.

The unit u to be distributed according to the repartition protocol is then computed. Here the division is performed in $O(1)$ time if M is a RAM$(+, -, \times, \div)$, but $O\big((\log f)^2\big) = O\big((\log(a^t x))^2\big) = O(t^2) = O(n^{2k})$ if it is a RAM$(+, -)$.

Finally, the contributions to the variables of Π are updated according to the repartition protocol. This only requires $O(1)$ time, as $a_1, \ldots, a_m$ are constants.

Programs p_i of the form $f(x_{i_1}, \ldots, x_{i_k})|_e \to a_1|x_1 + \cdots + a_m|x_m$ are simulated analogously, only with an extra test in order to ensure that the value of the enzyme is larger than the minimum of the variables.

> **if** $e > x_{i_1}$ **or** $e > x_{i_1}$ **or** $\cdots$ **or** $e > x_{i_k}$ **then**
> $\quad f := f(x_{i_1}, \ldots, x_{i_k})$
> $\quad x'_{i_1} := 0$
>
> $\qquad \vdots$
>
> $\quad x'_{i_k} := 0$
> $\quad u := f \div (a_1 + \cdots + a_m)$
> $\quad \Delta_1 := \Delta_1 + a_1 u$
>
> $\qquad \vdots$
>
> $\quad \Delta_m := \Delta_m + a_m u$
> **end**

The time required is again $O(1)$ if Π is an ENP$(+, -, \times, \div)$ and $O(n^{2k})$ if it is an ENP$(+, -)$.

After all programs have been examined (and applied, when possible), we can check whether a final configuration is reached: this occurs when, for each variable x_i, we have $x_i = x'_i + \Delta_i$, i.e., when the old value x_i equals the (possibly zeroed) value increased by the sum of the contributions it received in the current simulated step. If this is *not* the case, then the values of the variables are updated:

$$x_1 := x'_1 + \Delta_1$$
$$\vdots$$
$$x_m := x'_m + \Delta_m$$

and the next step of Π is simulated.

When a final configuration is actually reached, the machine M checks the value of the *accept* variable of Π and provides the same result:

> **if** *accept* $= 1$ **then**
> $\quad$ **accept**
> **else**
> $\quad$ **reject**
> **end**

The total time required in order to perform the simulation of Π is $O(n^{3k})$ for an ENP$(+, -)$, and $O(n^k)$ for an ENP$(+, -, \times, \div)$.   □

We can now state our main result, summarising the computational efficiency of EN P systems using arithmetic operations.

Theorem 2. *The following complexity classes coincide:*

$$\textbf{P-ENP}(+, -) = \textbf{P-RAM}(+, -) = \textbf{P}$$
$$\textbf{P-ENP}(+, -, \times, \div) = \textbf{P-RAM}(+, -, \times, \div) = \textbf{PSPACE}$$

Furthermore, the inclusion $\textbf{P-ENP}(+, -, \times) \subseteq \textbf{P-RAM}(+, -, \times)$ *holds.*   □

6   Conclusions

We have analysed the computational efficiency of all-parallel EN P systems and their relationships with more traditional computing devices such as RAMs and Turing machines. We have showed some efficient simulations of all-parallel EN P systems by RAMs and vice versa, when the same basic arithmetic operations are used.

Hence we found that, by using only addition and subtraction, EN P systems working in polynomial time and all-parallel mode characterise the complexity class **P**, whereas by also allowing multiplication and integer division we obtain a characterisation of **PSPACE**.

Establishing the precise efficiency of all-parallel EN P systems (as well as random access machines) with addition, subtraction and multiplication is still an open problem. The possibility to extend the results exposed in this paper to EN P systems working in the sequential or in the one-parallel mode, as well as to numerical P systems not using the enzyme control, is also open.

References

1. Bertoni, A., Mauri, G., Sabadini, N.: A characterization of the class of functions computable in polynomial time on random access machines. In: STOC 1981 Proceedings of the Thirteenth Annual ACM Symposium on Theory of Computing, pp. 168–176 (1981), http://dx.doi.org/10.1145/800076.802470
2. Bottoni, P., Martin-Vide, C., Păun, G., Rozenberg, G.: Membrane systems with promoters/inhibitors. Acta Informatica 38(10), 695–720 (2002), http://dx.doi.org/10.1007/s00236-002-0090-7
3. Buiu, C., Vasile, C., Arsene, O.: Development of membrane controllers for mobile robots. Information Sciences 187, 33–51 (2012), http://dx.doi.org/10.1016/j.ins.2011.10.007
4. Cook, S.A., Reckhow, R.A.: Time bounded random access machines. Journal of Computer and System Sciences 7, 354–375 (1973), http://dx.doi.org/10.1016/S0022-0000(73)80029-7
5. Hartmanis, J., Simon, J.: On the power of multiplication in random access machines. In: IEEE Conference Record of 15th Annual Symposium on Switching and Automata Theory, pp. 13–23 (1974), http://dx.doi.org/10.1109/SWAT.1974.20

6. Leporati, A., Porreca, A.E., Zandron, C., Mauri, G.: Improved universality results for parallel enzymatic numerical P systems. International Journal of Unconventional Computing 9, 385–404 (2013), http://www.oldcitypublishing.com/IJUC/IJUCcontents/IJUCv9n5-6contents.html

7. Papadimitriou, C.H.: Computational Complexity. Addison-Wesley (1993)

8. Păun, G., Păun, R.: Membrane computing and economics: Numerical P systems. Fundamenta Informaticae 73(1-2), 213–227 (2006), http://iospress.metapress.com/content/7xyefwrwy7mkg46a/

9. Păun, G., Rozenberg, G., Salomaa, A. (eds.): The Oxford Handbook of Membrane Computing. Oxford University Press (2010)

10. Pavel, A.B., Arsene, O., Buiu, C.: Enzymatic numerical P systems – A new class of membrane computing systems. In: Li, K., Tang, Z., Li, R., Nagar, A.K., Thamburaj, R. (eds.) Proceedings 2010 IEEE Fifth International Conference on Bio-Inspired Computing: Theories and Applications (BIC-TA 2010), pp. 1331–1336 (2010), http://dx.doi.org/10.1109/BICTA.2010.5645071

11. Pavel, A.B., Buiu, C.: Using enymatic numerical P systems for modeling mobile robot controllers. Natural Computing 11(3), 387–393 (2012), http://dx.doi.org/10.1007/s11047-011-9286-5

12. Vasile, C.I., Pavel, A.B., Dumitrache, I., Păun, G.: On the power of enzymatic numerical P systems. Acta Informatica 49, 395–412 (2012), http://dx.doi.org/10.1007/s00236-012-0166-y

Communication Rules Controlled
by Generated Membrane Boundaries

Tamás Mihálydeák[1], Zoltán Ernő Csajbók[2], and Péter Takács[2]

[1] Department of Computer Science, Faculty of Informatics,
University of Debrecen Kassai út 26, 4028 Debrecen, Hungary
`mihalydeak.tamas@inf.unideb.hu`
[2] Department of Health Informatics, Faculty of Health, University of Debrecen,
Sóstói út 2-4, 4400 Nyíregyháza, Hungary
`{csajbok.zoltan,takacs.peter}@foh.unideb.hu`

Abstract. In natural processes, the events represented by communication rules in membrane computing are taken place in the vicinity of membranes. Looking at regions as multisets, partial approximation spaces generalized for multisets give a plausible opportunity to model membrane boundaries in an abstract way. Thus, motivated by natural phenomena, the abstract notion of "to be close enough to a membrane" can be built in membrane computing. Restricting communication rules to these boundaries, the interactions along the membranes can be controlled locally during the membrane computations.

Keywords: Membrane computing, multiset theory, partial approximation of multisets.

1 Introduction

Membrane computing invented by Păun [14,15,17] is motivated by biological and chemical processes. Membranes delimit regions for which a set of rules is given. Evolution rules model reactions inside regions, whereas communication rules model movements of objects through membranes.

In natural processes, the events represented by communication rules are taken place in the vicinity of the membranes. There are some attempts to interpret membrane boundaries relying on space perception [1,2]. In regions, however, there is no precise information about the nature of the space of objects or their positions in general [3].

An abstract, not necessarily space–like, notion of membrane boundary was proposed in [10]. Accordingly, looking at regions as multisets, partial approximation spaces generalized for multisets give a plausible model of the abstract concept of "to be close enough to a membrane". Restricting communication rules to these boundaries and keeping the maximal parallelism of membrane computations, the interactions along the membranes can be controlled locally. Moreover, it has a special influence on the nondeterministic nature of membrane computations, and so nondeterminism may change.

A. Alhazov et al. (Eds.): CMC 2013, LNCS 8340, pp. 265–279, 2014.
© Springer-Verlag Berlin Heidelberg 2014

The paper, with the help of examples, undertakes to show what happens when the executions of communication rules are restricted to membrane boundaries defined in an abstract way. Having outlined the fundamental notions of partial multiset approximation spaces in Section 2, Section 3 and 4 present its application to membrane computing and the examples indicated before.

2   General Multiset Approximation Spaces

Set approximations were invented by Pawlak [12,13]. There are many different generalizations of Pawlakian rough set theory, among others, for multisets relying on equivalence or general multirelations [5,7]. Partial nature of real–life problems, however, requires working out partial approximation schemes. Such a scheme for multiset first was proposed in [9,10] in connection with membrane computing. In this section, the most important features of partial multiset approximation spaces are summarized (based on [10]).

2.1   Set-Theoretical Relations and Operations for Multisets

Let U be a finite nonempty set. A *multiset* M, or mset M for short, over U is a mapping $M : U \to \mathbb{N} \cup \{\infty\}$, where $\mathbb{N}$ is the set of natural numbers. The set $M^* = \{a \in U \mid M(a) \neq 0\}$ is called the *support* of M. M is *finite* if $M(a) < \infty$ for all $a \in M^*$. The mset M over U is the *empty mset*, denoted by $\emptyset$, if $M^* = \emptyset$.

Let $\mathcal{MS}(U)$ denote the set of all msets over U.

A set $\mathcal{M}$ of finite msets over U is called a *macroset* $\mathcal{M}$ over U [8]. We define the following two fundamental macrosets: $\mathcal{MS}^n(U)$ ($n \in \mathbb{N}$), the set of all msets M over U such that $M(a) \leq n$ for all $a \in U$, and $\mathcal{MS}^{<\infty}(U) = \bigcup_{n=0}^{\infty} \mathcal{MS}^n(U)$.

The basic set–theoretical relations can be generalized for msets as follows.

Definition 1 ([10]). *Let M, M_1, M_2 be msets over U.*

1. *Multiplicity relation for an mset M over U is: $a \in M$ ($a \in U$) if $M(a) \geq 1$.*
2. *Let $n \in \mathbb{N}^+$ be a positive integer. n–times multiplicity relation for an mset M over U is: $a \in^n M$ ($a \in U$) if $M(a) = n$.*
3. *$M_1 = M_2$ if $M_1(a) = M_2(a)$ for all $a \in U$ (mset equality relation).*
4. *$M_1 \sqsubseteq M_2$ if $M_1(a) \leq M_2(a)$ for all $a \in U$ (mset inclusion relation).*

The next definitions give the generalizations for msets of the basic set–theoretical operations.

Definition 2 ([10]). *Let $M, M_1, M_2 \in \mathcal{MS}(U)$ be msets over U and $\mathcal{M} \subseteq \mathcal{MS}(U)$ be a set of msets over U.*

1. *$(M_1 \sqcap M_2)(a) = \min\{M_1(a), M_2(a)\}$ for all $a \in U$ (intersection).*
2. *$(\sqcap \mathcal{M})(a) = \min\{M(a) \mid M \in \mathcal{M}\}$ for all $a \in U$.*
3. *$(M_1 \sqcup M_2)(a) = \max\{M_1(a), M_2(a)\}$ for all $a \in U$ (set–type union).*

4. $(\bigsqcup \mathcal{M})(a) = \mathsf{sup}\{M(a) \mid M \in \mathcal{M}\}$ for all $a \in U$. By definition, $\bigsqcup \emptyset = \emptyset$.
5. $(M_1 \oplus M_2)(a) = M_1(a) + M_2(a)$ for all $a \in U$ (mset addition).
6. For any $n \in \mathbb{N}$, n-times addition of M, denoted by $\oplus_n(M)$ or simply $\oplus_n M$, is given by the following inductive definition:
   (a) $\oplus_0 M = \emptyset$;
   (b) $\oplus_1 M = M$;
   (c) $\oplus_{n+1} M = \oplus_n M \oplus M$.
7. $(M_1 \ominus M_2)(a) = \mathsf{max}\{M_1(a) - M_2(a), 0\}$ for all $a \in U$ (mset subtraction).

By the n-times addition, the *n-times inclusion* relation ($\sqsubseteq^n$) can be defined.

Definition 3. *Let $M_1 \neq \emptyset, M_2$ be two msets over U.*
For any $n \in \mathbb{N}$, $M_1 \sqsubseteq^n M_2$ if $\oplus_n M_1 \sqsubseteq M_2$ but $\oplus_{n+1} M_1 \not\sqsubseteq M_2$.

Corollary 1. *Let $M_1 \neq \emptyset, M_2$ be two msets over U.*
Then for all $n \in \mathbb{N}$, $M_1 \sqsubseteq^n M_2$ if and only if $nM_1(a) \leq M_2(a)$ for all $a \in U$ but there is an $a' \in U$ such that $(n+1)M_1(a') > M_2(a')$.

Note that U $\langle \mathcal{MS}(U), \sqcup, \sqcap \rangle$ is a complete lattice [4,6], and $\langle \mathcal{MS}(U), \sqsubseteq \rangle$ is a partially ordered set in which $M_1 \sqsubseteq M_2$ if and only if $M_1 \sqcup M_2 = M_2$, or equivalently, $M_1 \sqcap M_2 = M_1$ $(M_1, M_2 \in \mathcal{MS}(U))$.
In addition, $\langle \mathcal{MS}^{<\infty}(U), \sqcup, \sqcap \rangle$ is the sublattice of $\langle \mathcal{MS}(U), \sqcup, \sqcap \rangle$. However, $\langle \mathcal{MS}^{<\infty}(U), \sqcup, \sqcap \rangle$ is not a complete lattice because of it lacks a top element. For more details, see [11].

2.2   General Multiset Approximation Spaces

A general mset approximation space has four basic components:

- a set of msets as the *domain* of the space whose members are approximated;
- some distinguished msets of the domain as the *basis* of approximations;
- *definable msets* which are derived from base msets in some way and marked as possible approximations of members of the domain;
- an *approximation pair* determining the lower and upper approximations of members of the domain based on definable msets.

Definition 4 ([10]). *The ordered 5–tuple* $\mathsf{MAS}(U) = \langle \mathcal{MS}^{<\infty}(U), \mathfrak{B}, \mathfrak{D}_{\mathfrak{B}}, \mathsf{l}, \mathsf{u} \rangle$ *is a (general) mset approximation space over U with the domain $\mathcal{MS}^{<\infty}(U)$ if*

1. $\mathfrak{B} \subseteq \mathcal{MS}^{<\infty}(U)$ *and if $B \in \mathfrak{B}$, then $B \neq \emptyset$ (in notation $\mathfrak{B} = \{B_\gamma \mid \gamma \in \Gamma\}$ where Γ is an arbitrary non–empty set of indexes);*
   $\mathfrak{B}$ *is called the* base system, *its members are called the* base msets;
2. $\mathfrak{D}_{\mathfrak{B}} \subseteq \mathcal{MS}^{<\infty}(U)$ *is an extension of $\mathfrak{B}$ satisfying the following minimal requirement: if $B \in \mathfrak{B}$, then $\oplus_n B \in \mathfrak{D}_{\mathfrak{B}}$ for all $n \in \mathbb{N}$; members in $\mathfrak{D}_{\mathfrak{B}}$ are called* definable msets;

3. *the functions* $\mathsf{l}, \mathsf{u} : \mathcal{MS}^{<\infty}(U) \to \mathcal{MS}^{<\infty}(U)$ *(called* lower *and* upper *approximations) form a* weak approximation pair $\langle \mathsf{l}, \mathsf{u} \rangle$ *if*

(C0) $\mathsf{l}(\mathcal{MS}^{<\infty}(U)), \mathsf{u}(\mathcal{MS}^{<\infty}(U)) \subseteq \mathfrak{D}_\mathfrak{B}$ *(definability of* l, u*);*[1]

(C1) the functions l *and* u *are monotone, i.e., for all* $M_1, M_2 \in \mathcal{MS}^{<\infty}(U)$ *if* $M_1 \sqsubseteq M_2$, *then* $\mathsf{l}(M_1) \sqsubseteq \mathsf{l}(M_2)$, $\mathsf{u}(M_1) \sqsubseteq \mathsf{u}(M_2)$ *(monotonicity of* l, u*);*

(C2) $\mathsf{u}(\emptyset) = \emptyset$ *(normality of* u*);*

(C3) if $M \in \mathcal{MS}^{<\infty}(U)$, *then* $\mathsf{l}(M) \sqsubseteq \mathsf{u}(M)$ *(weak approximation property).*

Corollary 2. $\mathsf{l}(\emptyset) = \emptyset$ *(normality of* l*).*

$\mathsf{MAS}(U)$ is *total*, if for any $M \in \mathcal{MS}^{<\infty}(U)$ there is a definable mset $D \in \mathfrak{D}_\mathfrak{B}$ such that $M \sqsubseteq D$, it is *partial* otherwise.

It is reasonable to assume that the base msets and their n-times additions are exactly approximated from "lower side". In certain cases, it is also required of definable msets.

Definition 5. *A weak approximation pair* $\langle \mathsf{l}, \mathsf{u} \rangle$ *is*

(C4) granular if $B \in \mathfrak{B}$, *then* $\mathsf{l}(\oplus_n B) = \oplus_n B$ *($n \in \mathbb{N}$) (in other words,* l *is granular);*

(C5) standard if $D \in \mathfrak{D}_\mathfrak{B}$, *then* $\mathsf{l}(D) = D$ *(in other words,* l *is standard).*

An important question is how lower and upper approximations relate to the approximated mset.

Definition 6. *A weak approximation pair* $\langle \mathsf{l}, \mathsf{u} \rangle$ *is*

(C6) lower semi–strong *if* $\mathsf{l}(M) \sqsubseteq M$ *($M \in \mathcal{MS}^{<\infty}(U)$) (*$\mathsf{l}$ *is* contractive*);*

(C7) upper semi–strong *if* $M \sqsubseteq \mathsf{u}(M)$ *($M \in \mathcal{MS}^{<\infty}(U)$) (*$\mathsf{u}$ *is* extensive*);*

(C8) strong *if it is lower and upper semi–strong simultaneously, i.e., each subset* $M \in \mathcal{MS}^{<\infty}(U)$ *is bounded by* $\mathsf{l}(M)$ *and* $\mathsf{u}(M)$*:* $\mathsf{l}(M) \sqsubseteq M \sqsubseteq \mathsf{u}(M)$.

Definition 7. *The general mset approximation space* $\mathsf{MAS}(U)$ *is a weak/granular/standard/lower semi-strong/upper semi-strong/strong mset approximation space, if the approximation pair* $\langle \mathsf{l}, \mathsf{u} \rangle$ *is weak/granular/standard/lower semi-strong/upper semi-strong/strong, respectively.*

2.3   Generalized Pawlakian Multiset Approximation Spaces

It is a natural assumption that $\mathfrak{D}_\mathfrak{B}$ is obtained (derived) from $\mathfrak{B}$ by some sorts of transformations, for the most important cases, see [10].

In order to build a generalized Pawlakian mset approximation space, first, we define $\mathfrak{D}_\mathfrak{B}$ as follows.

Definition 8 ([10]). $\mathsf{MAS}(U)$ *is a strictly set–union type mset approximation space if* $\mathfrak{D}_\mathfrak{B}$ *is given by the following inductive definition:*

---

[1] $\mathsf{l}(\mathcal{MS}^{<\infty}(U))$, $\mathsf{u}(\mathcal{MS}^{<\infty}(U))$ denote the ranges of the functions l and u, respectively.

1. $\emptyset \in \mathfrak{D}_{\mathfrak{B}}$;
2. $\mathfrak{B} \subseteq \mathfrak{D}_{\mathfrak{B}}$;
3. if $\mathfrak{B}^{\oplus} = \{\oplus_n B \mid B \in \mathfrak{B}, \ n = 1, 2, \dots\}$ and $\mathfrak{B}' \subseteq \mathfrak{B}^{\oplus}$, then $\bigsqcup \mathfrak{B}' \in \mathfrak{D}_{\mathfrak{B}}$.

The next proposition summarizes the most important features of strictly set–union type mset approximation spaces.

Proposition 1 ([11]). *Let* $\mathsf{MAS}(U) = \langle \mathcal{MS}^{<\infty}(U), \mathfrak{B}, \mathfrak{D}_{\mathfrak{B}}, \mathsf{l}, \mathsf{u} \rangle$ *be a strictly set–union type mset approximation space over* U.

1. *For any definable set* $D \in \mathfrak{D}_{\mathfrak{B}}$,

$$D = \bigsqcup \{\oplus_n B \in \mathfrak{B}^{\oplus} \mid n \in \mathbb{N}^+, B \in \mathfrak{B}, B \sqsubseteq^n D\}.$$

2. *If* $\mathsf{MAS}(U)$ *is granular and lower semi–strong as well, for any* $M \in \mathcal{MS}^{<\infty}(U)$,

$$\mathsf{l}(M) = \bigsqcup \{\oplus_n B \in \mathfrak{B}^{\oplus} \mid n \in \mathbb{N}^+, B \in \mathfrak{B}, B \sqsubseteq^n M\}.$$

Next, the Pawlakian approximation pair for msets is generalized in strictly set–union type mset approximation spaces.

Definition 9 ([10]). *Let* $\mathsf{MAS}(U) = \langle \mathcal{MS}^{<\infty}(U), \mathfrak{B}, \mathfrak{D}_{\mathfrak{B}}, \mathsf{l}, \mathsf{u} \rangle$ *be a strictly set–union type mset approximation space.*
The functions $\mathsf{l}, \mathsf{u} : \mathcal{MS}^{<\infty}(U) \to \mathcal{MS}^{<\infty}(U)$ *are a (generalized) Pawlakian mset approximation pair* $\langle \mathsf{l}, \mathsf{u} \rangle$ *if for any mset* $M \in \mathcal{MS}^{<\infty}(U)$

1. $\mathsf{l}(M) = \bigsqcup \{\oplus_n B \mid n \in \mathbb{N}^+, B \in \mathfrak{B} \text{ and } B \sqsubseteq^n M\}$,
2. $\mathsf{b}(M) = \bigsqcup \{\oplus_n B \mid B \in \mathfrak{B}, B \not\sqsubseteq M, \ B \sqcap M \neq \emptyset \text{ and } B \sqcap M \sqsubseteq^n M\}$,
3. $\mathsf{u}(M) = \mathsf{l}(M) \sqcup \mathsf{b}(M)$,

where the function b *gives the Pawlakian boundary of the mset* M.

It is easy to check by Definition 9 that when $\mathsf{MAS}(U)$ is a strictly set–union type mset approximation space with a Pawlakian mset approximation pair, $\mathsf{MAS}(U)$ is a lower semi–strong mset approximation space, and l is granular. In other words, $\mathsf{MAS}(U)$ fulfills the conditions *(C0)–(C3)*, *(C4)*, *(C6)*.

Definition 10. *A strictly set–union type approximation space with a Pawlakian mset approximation pair is called a Pawlakian mset approximation space.*

3   Applications in Membrane Computing

Definition 11. *A membrane structure* μ *of degree* m *(*$m \geq 1$*) is a rooted tree with* m *nodes identified with the integers* $1, \dots, m$.

A membrane structure μ of degree m ($m \geq 1$) can be represented by the set $R_\mu \subseteq \{1, \dots, m\} \times \{1, \dots, m\}$. $\langle i, j \rangle \in R_\mu$ means that there is an edge from i (parent) to j (child) of the tree μ which is formulated by $\mathsf{parent}(j) = i$.

Definition 12. *Let μ be a membrane structure with m nodes and V be a finite alphabet. The tuple*

$$\Pi = \langle V, \mu, w_1, w_2, \ldots, w_m, R_1, R_2, \ldots, R_m \rangle$$

is a P system if

1. $w_i \in \mathcal{MS}^{<\infty}(V)$ *for $i = 1, 2, \ldots, m$;*
2. R_i *is a finite set of rules for $i = 1, 2, \ldots, m$ such that if $r \in R_i$, its form is one of the following:*
   (a) *symport rules:* $\langle u, in \rangle$, $\langle u, out \rangle$, *where $u \neq \lambda$ and there is an mset $M \in \mathcal{MS}^{<\infty}(V)$ such that u represents M;*
   (b) *antiport rule:* $\langle u, in; v, out \rangle$, *where $u \neq \lambda, v \neq \lambda$ and there are msets $M_1, M_2 \in \mathcal{MS}^{<\infty}(V)$ such that u, v represent M_1, M_2, respectively.*

If the P system $\Pi = \langle V, \mu, w_1, w_2, \ldots, w_m, R_1, R_2, \ldots, R_m \rangle$ is given, let $\mathsf{MAS}(\Pi) = \langle \mathcal{MS}^{<\infty}(V), \mathfrak{B}, \mathfrak{D}_{\mathfrak{B}}, \mathsf{l}, \mathsf{u} \rangle$ be a strictly set–union type mset approximation space with a generalized Pawlakian approximation pair $\langle \mathsf{l}, \mathsf{u} \rangle$. $\mathsf{MAS}(\Pi)$ is called a *joint membrane approximation space*.

Having given a membrane system Π and its joint membrane approximation space $\mathsf{MAS}(\Pi)$, we can define the boundaries of the regions $w_1, w_2, \ldots, w_m$ as msets with the help of approximative functions $\mathsf{l}, \mathsf{u}, \mathsf{b}$ specified in Definition 9.[2]

Definition 13 ([10]). *Let $\Pi = \langle V, \mu, w_1, w_2, \ldots, w_m, R_1, R_2, \ldots, R_m \rangle$ be a P system and $\mathsf{MAS}(\Pi) = \langle \mathcal{MS}^{<\infty}(V), \mathfrak{B}, \mathfrak{D}_{\mathfrak{B}}, \mathsf{l}, \mathsf{u} \rangle$ be its joint membrane approximation space. If $B \in \mathfrak{B}$ and $i = 1, 2, \ldots, m$, let*

$$N(B, i) = \begin{cases} 0, & \text{if } B \sqsubseteq w_i \text{ or } B \sqcap w_i = \emptyset; \\ n, & \text{if } i = 1 \text{ and } B \sqcap w_1 \sqsubseteq^n w_1; \\ \min\{k, n \mid B \sqcap w_i \sqsubseteq^k w_i, \text{ and } B \ominus w_i \sqsubseteq^n w_{\mathsf{parent}(i)}\}, & \text{otherwise.} \end{cases}$$

Then, for $i = 1, \ldots, m$,

$$\mathsf{bnd}(w_i) = \bigsqcup \{\oplus_{N(B,i)} B \mid B \in \mathfrak{B}\};$$
$$\mathsf{bnd}^{\mathsf{out}}(w_i) = \mathsf{bnd}(w_i) \ominus w_i;$$
$$\mathsf{bnd}^{\mathsf{in}}(w_i) = \mathsf{bnd}(w_i) \ominus \mathsf{bnd}^{\mathsf{out}}(w_i).$$

The functions bnd, $\mathsf{bnd}^{\mathsf{out}}$ and $\mathsf{bnd}^{\mathsf{in}}$ give *membrane boundaries, outside* and *inside membrane boundaries*, respectively.

Note that $\mathsf{bnd}(w_i)$ is definable in $\mathsf{MAS}(\Pi)$, but $\mathsf{bnd}^{\mathsf{in}}(w_i)$ and $\mathsf{bnd}^{\mathsf{out}}(w_i)$ are not in general ($i = 1, \ldots, m$). However, we focus on needs of membrane computations and so it is not a real restriction to our proposal.

The general notion of boundaries given in Definition 9 cannot be used here, because membrane boundaries have to follow the given membrane structure μ. The lower approximations $\mathsf{l}(w_i)$ ($i = 1, \ldots, m$) obey the membrane structure. The upper approximation $\mathsf{u}(w_1)$ and the Pawlakian boundaries $\mathsf{b}(w_1)$ are completely within the environment of the membrane structure. However, the upper approximation $\mathsf{u}(w_i)$, therefore the Pawlakian boundary $\mathsf{b}(w_i)$ ($i = 2, \ldots, m$) do

---

[2] We are speaking about the boundaries of regions but, to tell the truth, these boundaries are the boundaries of msets of different regions.

not obey the membrane structure necessarily. Thus, the Pawlakian boundaries have to be adjusted to the membrane structure by the function bnd. Of course, $b(w_1) = \mathsf{bnd}(w_1)$, but $b(w_i) \neq \mathsf{bnd}(w_i)$ $(i = 2, \ldots, m)$ in general. Moreover, membrane boundaries $\mathsf{bnd}(w_i)$ $(i = 1, \ldots, m)$ are split into two parts, inside and outside membrane boundaries.

Using membrane boundaries, the following constraints for rule executions are prescribed: a rule $r \in R_i$ of a membrane i $(i = 1, \ldots, m)$ has to work only in the membrane boundary of its region. More precisely,

- a symport rule of the form $\langle u, in \rangle$ is executed only in the case when $u \sqsubseteq \mathsf{bnd}^{out}(w_i)$;
- a symport rule of the form $\langle u, out \rangle$ is executed only in the case when $u \sqsubseteq \mathsf{bnd}^{in}(w_i)$;
- an antiport rule of the form $\langle u, in; v, out \rangle$ is executed only in the case when $u \sqsubseteq \mathsf{bnd}^{out}(w_i)$ and $v \sqsubseteq \mathsf{bnd}^{in}(w_i)$.

It can be shown that the membrane computation actually works in the membrane boundaries, see [10], Theorem 1.

4   An Illustrative Example

In this section, we follow the customary representations of msets. Accordingly, if an mset M is finite, it is represented by all permutations of the string w:

$$w = \begin{cases} a_{k_1}^{M(a_{k_1})} a_{k_2}^{M(a_{k_2})} \ldots a_{k_l}^{M(a_{k_l})}, & \text{if } M \text{ is nonempty;} \\ \lambda, & \text{otherwise;} \end{cases}$$

where $M^* = \{a_{k_1}, a_{k_2}, \ldots, a_{k_l}\} \subseteq U$ and λ is the empty string.

As usual, with a slight abuse of terminology, simply "the mset w" is said instead of "the mset M represented by the string w and all of its permutations". Moreover, any permutation of the string w can also represent M.

4.1   Giving the P System and Its Joint Membrane Approximation Space

Let the P system be $\Pi = \langle U, \mu, w_1, R \rangle$, where

- $U = \{a, b, c, d, e, f\}$ is a finite alphabet;
- μ is a membrane structure of degree 1;
- the region w_1 is represented by the multiset $w_1 = a^2 b^{11} c^3 d^9 e$;
- $R = \{r_1, r_2, r_3\}$ is the set of communication rules with

$$r_1 = \langle ac; out \rangle, r_2 = \langle b^6 d^6; out \rangle, r_3 = \langle d^3 e; out \rangle.$$

Let the joint membrane approximation space $\mathsf{MAS}(\Pi)$ of the P system Π be a strictly set–union type mset approximation space with a generalized Pawlakian approximation pair, where $\mathsf{MAS}(\Pi) = \langle \mathcal{MS}^{<\infty}(U), \mathfrak{B}, \mathfrak{D}_{\mathfrak{B}}, \mathsf{l}, \mathsf{u} \rangle$ with

- $\mathcal{MS}^{<\infty}(U)$ is the domain of $\mathsf{MAS}(\Pi)$;
- $\mathfrak{B} = \{a^2 b, abcdef, ac, b^3 cd^2, b^3 d^2, b^3 d^2 f, c, e^3, f^2, f^4\}$ is the base system;

- $\mathfrak{D}_\mathfrak{B}$ is the set of definable sets such that
  - $\emptyset \in \mathfrak{D}_\mathfrak{B}$;
  - $\mathfrak{B}^\oplus = \{a^2b, a^4b^2, a^6b^3, \ldots, abcdef, a^2b^2c^2d^2e^2f^2, a^3b^3c^3d^2e^3f^3, \ldots,$
    $ac, a^2c^2, a^3c^3, \ldots, b^3cd^2, b^6c^2d^4, b^9c^3d^6, \ldots, b^3d^2, b^6d^4, b^9d^6, \ldots,$
    $b^3d^2f, b^6d^4f^2, b^9d^6f^3, \ldots, c, c^2, c^3 \ldots, e^3, e^6, e^9, \ldots,$
    $f^2, f^4, f^6, \ldots, f^8, f^{12}\}$, and for any $\mathfrak{B}' \subseteq \mathfrak{B}^\oplus$, $\bigsqcup \mathfrak{B}' \in \mathfrak{D}_\mathfrak{B}$;
  - $\mathfrak{D}_\mathfrak{B}$ does not have any other member;
- $\langle \mathsf{l}, \mathsf{u} \rangle$ is a Pawlakian mset approximation pair.

Throughout the computation processes, we utilize the fact that $M_1 \sqsubseteq^n M_2$ if and only if $\oplus_n M_1 \sqsubseteq^1 M_2$ $(M_1, M_2 \in \mathcal{MS}^{<\infty}(U), n \in \mathbb{N}^+)$.

4.2   Computing the Pawlakian Lower- and Upper Approximations and the Boundary

Computation of $\mathsf{l}(w_1)$ By Definition 9,

$$\mathsf{l}(w_1) = \mathsf{l}(a^2b^{11}c^3d^9e) = \bigsqcup\{\oplus_n B \mid n \in \mathbb{N}^+, B \in \mathfrak{B} \text{ and } B \sqsubseteq^n a^2b^{11}c^3d^9e\}.$$

The computation process of $\mathsf{l}(w_1)$ can be tracked by Table 1. The result is:

$$\begin{aligned}
\mathsf{l}(w_1) &= \oplus_1 a^2b \sqcup \oplus_2 ac \sqcup \oplus_3 b^3cd^2 \sqcup \oplus_3 b^3d^2 \sqcup \oplus_3 c \\
&= a^2b \sqcup a^2c^2 \sqcup b^9c^3d^6 \sqcup b^9d^6 \sqcup c^3 \\
&= a^2b^9c^3d^6
\end{aligned}$$

Computation of $\mathsf{b}(w_1)$ By Definition 9,

$$\mathsf{b}(w_1) = \mathsf{b}(a^2b^{11}c^3d^9e) = \bigsqcup\{\oplus_n B \mid B \in \mathfrak{B}, B \not\sqsubseteq a^2b^{11}c^3d^9e, B \sqcap a^2b^{11}c^3d^9e \neq \emptyset$$
$$\text{and } B \sqcap a^2b^{11}c^3d^9e \sqsubseteq^n a^2b^{11}c^3d^9e\}.$$

The computation process of $\mathsf{b}(w_1)$ can be tracked by Table 2. The result is:

$$\begin{aligned}
\mathsf{b}(w_1) &= \oplus_1 abcdef \sqcup \oplus_3 b^3d^2f \sqcup \oplus_1 e^3 \\
&= abcdef \sqcup b^9d^6f^3 \sqcup e^3 \\
&= ab^9cd^6e^3f^3
\end{aligned}$$

Computation of $\mathsf{u}(w_1)$ By Definition 9, $\mathsf{u}(w_1) = \mathsf{l}(w_1) \sqcup \mathsf{b}(w_1)$, and so

$$\begin{aligned}
\mathsf{u}(w_1) &= \mathsf{u}(a^2b^{11}c^3d^9e) = \mathsf{l}(a^2b^{11}c^3d^9e) \sqcup \mathsf{b}(a^2b^{11}c^3d^9e) \\
&= a^2b^9c^3d^6 \sqcup ab^9cd^6e^3f^3 \\
&= a^2b^9c^3d^6e^3f^3.
\end{aligned}$$

Table 1. Computation of $l(w_1) = l(a^2b^{11}c^3d^9e)$

$\mathfrak{B}$	$\oplus_1 B \sqsubseteq^1 w_1$	$\oplus_2 B \sqsubseteq^1 w_1$	$\oplus_3 B \sqsubseteq^1 w_1$	$\oplus_4 B \sqsubseteq^1 w_1$
a^2b	$(a^2b) \sqsubseteq^1$	$a^4b^2 \not\sqsubseteq^1$	-	-
$abcdef$	$abcdef \not\sqsubseteq^1$	-	-	-
ac	$ac \sqsubseteq^1$	$(a^2c^2) \sqsubseteq^1$	$a^3c^3 \not\sqsubseteq^1$	-
b^3cd^2	$b^3cd^2 \sqsubseteq^1$	$b^6c^2d^4 \sqsubseteq^1$	$(b^9c^3d^6) \sqsubseteq^1$	$b^{12}c^4d^8 \not\sqsubseteq^1$
b^3d^2	$b^3d^2 \sqsubseteq^1$	$b^6d^4 \sqsubseteq^1$	$(b^9d^6) \sqsubseteq^1$	$b^{12}d^8 \not\sqsubseteq^1$
b^3d^2f	$b^3d^2f \not\sqsubseteq^1$	-	-	-
c	$c \sqsubseteq^1$	$c^2 \sqsubseteq^1$	$(c^3) \sqsubseteq^1$	$c^4 \not\sqsubseteq^1$
e^3	$e^3 \not\sqsubseteq^1$	-	-	-
f^2	$f^2 \not\sqsubseteq^1$	-	-	-
f^4	$f^4 \not\sqsubseteq^1$	-	-	-

Table 2. Computation of $b(w_1) = b(a^2b^{11}c^3d^9e)$

$\mathfrak{B}$	$B \not\sqsubseteq w_1$	Let $B' = B \sqcap w_1$				
		$B' \neq \emptyset$	$\oplus_1 B' \sqsubseteq^1 w_1$	$\oplus_2 B' \sqsubseteq^1 w_1$	$\oplus_3 B' \sqsubseteq^1 w_1$	$\oplus_4 B' \sqsubseteq^1 w_1$
a^2b	$\sqsubseteq$	-	-	-	-	-
$abcdef$	$\not\sqsubseteq$	$abcde \neq \lambda$	$(abcde \sqsubseteq^1)$	$a^2b^2c^2d^2e^2 \not\sqsubseteq^1$	-	-
ac	$\sqsubseteq$	-	-	-	-	-
b^3cd^2	$\sqsubseteq$	-	-	-	-	-
b^3d^2	$\sqsubseteq$	-	-	-	-	-
b^3d^2f	$\not\sqsubseteq$	$b^3d^2 \neq \lambda$	$b^3d^2 \sqsubseteq^1$	$b^6d^4 \sqsubseteq^1$	$(b^9d^6 \sqsubseteq^1)$	$b^{12}d^8 \not\sqsubseteq^1$
c	$\sqsubseteq$	-	-	-	-	-
e^3	$\not\sqsubseteq$	$e \neq \lambda$	$(e \sqsubseteq^1)$	$e^2 \not\sqsubseteq^1$	-	-
f^2	$\not\sqsubseteq$	$= \lambda$	-	-	-	-
f^4	$\not\sqsubseteq$	$= \lambda$	-	-	-	-

Since $u(w_1) \in \mathfrak{D}_\mathfrak{B}$, by Proposition 1(1), $u(w_1)$ is decomposable, i.e., $u(w_1)$ can be formed as a set–type unions of base msets. Its computation can be tracked by Table 3. The result is:

$$u(w_1) = u(ab^{11}c^3d^9e) = a^2b^9c^3d^6e^3f^3$$
$$= a^2b \sqcup a^2b^2c^2d^2e^2f^2 \sqcup a^2c^2 \sqcup b^9c^3d^6 \sqcup b^9d^6 \sqcup b^9d^6f^3 \sqcup e^3 \sqcup f^2$$
$$= \oplus_1 a^2b \sqcup \oplus_2 abcdef \sqcup \oplus_2 ac \sqcup \oplus_3 b^3cd^2 \sqcup \oplus_3 b^3d^2 \sqcup \oplus_3 b^3d^2f \sqcup \oplus_3 c$$
$$\sqcup \oplus_1 e^3 \sqcup \oplus_1 f^2$$

4.3   Computing (Inside/Outside) Membrane Boundaries

Computation of $\mathsf{bnd}(w_1)$ The membrane boundary and the Pawlakian boundary are equal for the skin membrane, i.e., $\mathsf{bnd}(w_1) = \mathsf{b}(w_1)$. Therefore,

$$\mathsf{bnd}(w_1) = \mathsf{b}(w_1) = ab^9cd^6e^3f^3.$$

The Pawlakian boundary $\mathsf{b}(w_1) = ab^9cd^6e^3f^3$ was computed by Definition 9 with the help of Table 2. In order to check the equality $\mathsf{bnd}(w_1) = \mathsf{b}(w_1)$, let us compute $\mathsf{bnd}(w_1)$ by Definition 13, too.

The numbers $N(B,1)$ $(B \in \mathfrak{B})$ (see Definition 13) can be determined as follows:

$N(a^2b,1) = 0$, because $a^2b \sqsubseteq a^2b^{11}c^3d^9e$;

$N(abcdef,1) = 1$, because $abcdef \not\sqsubseteq a^2b^{11}c^3d^9e$, $abcdef \sqcap a^2b^{11}c^3d^9e = abcde \neq \emptyset$,

$\qquad\qquad$ and $abcdef \sqcap a^2b^{11}c^3d^9e = abcde \sqsubseteq^1 a^2b^{11}c^3d^9e$;

$N(ac,1) = 0$, because $ac \sqsubseteq a^2b^{11}c^3d^9e$;

$N(b^3cd^2,1) = 0$, because $b^3cd^2 \sqsubseteq a^2b^{11}c^3d^9e$;

$N(b^3d^2,1) = 0$, because $b^3d^2 \sqsubseteq a^2b^{11}c^3d^9e$;

$N(b^3d^2f,1) = 3$, because $b^3d^2f \sqcap a^2b^{11}c^3d^9e = b^3d^2 \sqsubseteq^3 a^2b^{11}c^3d^9e$;

$N(c,1) = 0$, because $c \sqsubseteq a^2b^{11}c^3d^9e$;

$N(e^3,1) = 1$, because $e^3 \not\sqsubseteq a^2b^{11}c^3d^9e$, $e^3 \sqcap a^2b^{11}c^3d^9e = e \neq \emptyset$,

$\qquad\qquad$ and $e^3 \sqcap a^2b^{11}c^3d^9e = e \sqsubseteq^1 a^2b^{11}c^3d^9e$;

$N(f^2,1) = 0$, because $f^2 \not\sqsubseteq a^2b^{11}c^3d^9e$, $f^2 \sqcap a^2b^{11}c^3d^9e = \emptyset$;

$N(f^4,1) = 0$, because $f^4 \not\sqsubseteq a^2b^{11}c^3d^9e$, $f^4 \sqcap a^2b^{11}c^3d^9e = \emptyset$.

Hence, by Definition 13,

$$\mathsf{bnd}(w_1) = \bigsqcup\{\oplus_{N(B,1)}B \mid B \in \{a^2b, abcdef, ac, b^3cd^2, b^3d^2, b^3d^2f, c, e^3, f^2, f^4\}\}$$
$$= \oplus_0 a^2b \sqcup \oplus_1 abcdef \sqcup \oplus_0 ac \sqcup \oplus_0 b^3cd^2 \sqcup \oplus_0 b^3d^2 \sqcup \oplus_3 b^3d^2f \sqcup \oplus_0 c$$
$$\sqcup \oplus_1 e^3 \sqcup \oplus_0 f^2 \sqcup \oplus_0 f^4$$
$$= \emptyset \sqcup abcdef \sqcup \emptyset \sqcup \emptyset \sqcup \emptyset \sqcup b^9d^6f^3 \sqcup \emptyset \sqcup e^3 \sqcup \emptyset \sqcup \emptyset$$
$$= ab^9cd^6e^3f^3.$$

Computation of $\mathsf{bnd}^{\mathsf{out}}(w_1)$ By Definition 13,

$$\mathsf{bnd}^{\mathsf{out}}(w_1) = \mathsf{bnd}(w_1) \ominus w_1 = \mathsf{bnd}^{\mathsf{out}}(a^2b^{11}c^3d^9e)$$
$$= ab^9cd^6e^3f^3 \ominus a^2b^{11}c^3d^9e = e^2f^3.$$

Computation of $\mathsf{bnd}^{\mathsf{in}}(w_1)$ By Definition 13,

$$\mathsf{bnd}^{\mathsf{in}}(w_1) = \mathsf{bnd}(w_1) \ominus \mathsf{bnd}^{\mathsf{out}}(w_1) = \mathsf{bnd}^{\mathsf{in}}(a^2b^{11}c^3d^9e)$$
$$= ab^9cd^6e^3f^3 \ominus e^2f^3 = ab^9cd^6e.$$

The computation of inside/outside membrane boundaries can easily be carried out when the msets are represented in Parikh vector form:

1. in Table 4, the rows 2, 3, 5 contain Parikh representations of $bnd(w_1)$, w_1 and $bnd^{out}(w_1)$, respectively;
2. in Table 5, the rows 2, 3, 5 contain Parikh representations of $bnd(w_1)$, $bnd^{out}(w_1)$ and $bnd^{in}(w_1)$, respectively.

4.4   Executions of Communication Rules without Membrane Boundary

In the present and the next subsections, the communication rules are executed without and with membrane boundaries.

In this subsection, the communication rules are executed without membrane boundary, i.e., in the multiset $a^2b^{11}c^3d^9e$ of the region w_1.

Let us recall that the set of communication rules residing in w_1 is

$$R = \{r_1, r_2, r_3\} \text{ with } r_1 = \langle ac; out \rangle, r_2 = \langle b^6d^6; out \rangle, r_3 = \langle d^3e; out \rangle.$$

A multiset of rules $r_1^{n_1} r_2^{n_2} r_3^{n_3}$ $(n_1, n_2, n_3 \in \mathbb{N})$ over R is applicable to w_1 if

$$\oplus_{n_1} ac \oplus \oplus_{n_2} b^6d^6 \oplus \oplus_{n_3} d^3e \sqsubseteq a^2b^{11}c^3d^9e.$$

Following [16], let us denote the set of all multisets of rules over R which are applicable to w_1 by $Appl(R, w_1)$. Then, relying on $Appl(R, w_1)$, the set of multisets of rules applicable to w_1 in the *maximally parallel* mode can formally be defined as follows:

$$Appl_{max}(R, w_1) = \{r \mid r \in Appl(R, w_1) \text{ and there is no}$$
$$r' \in Appl(R, w_1) \text{ with } r' \underset{\neq}{\sqsubseteq} r\}$$

Scanning the communication rules residing in w_1, we obtain that

$$Appl(R, w_1) = \{r_1, r_2, r_3, r_1r_2, r_1r_3, r_2r_3, r_1r_2r_3, r_1^2, r_1^2r_2, r_1^2r_3, r_1^2r_2r_3\}$$

and

$$Appl_{max}(R, w_1) = \{r_1^2r_2r_3\}.$$

Hence, we can "choose" from only one maximal multiset of rules over R in order to perform a maximally parallel transition step. Consequently, the evolution of the P system Π ends after one transition step in a deterministic manner:

$$a^2b^{11}c^3d^9e \overset{r_1^2r_2r_3}{\Longrightarrow} b^5c.$$

Indeed, the maximal multiset $r_1^2r_2r_3$ of rules is applicable to w_1 because

$$\oplus_2 ac \oplus \oplus_1 b^6d^6 \oplus \oplus_1 d^3e = a^2c^2 \oplus b^6d^6 \oplus d^3e = a^2b^6c^2d^9e \sqsubseteq a^2b^{11}c^3d^9e.$$

In this case, therefore, the mset $a^2b^6c^2d^9e$ leaves the region w_1 and enters the environment, and the computation of the P system Π halts after one transition step in a deterministic manner with the mset b^5c in the region w_1.

Table 3. Computation of the base mset decomposition of $u(w_1) = a^2b^9c^3d^6e^3f^3$

$\mathfrak{B}$	$\oplus_1 B \sqsubseteq^1 u(w_1)$?	$\oplus_2 B \sqsubseteq^1 u(w_1)$?	$\oplus_3 B \sqsubseteq^1 u(w_1)$?	$\oplus_4 B \sqsubseteq^1 u(w_1)$?
a^2b	$\boxed{a^2b}\ \sqsubseteq^1$	$a^4b^2\ \not\sqsubseteq^1$	-	-
$abcdef$	$abcdef \sqsubseteq^1$	$\boxed{a^2b^2c^2d^2e^2f^2}\ \sqsubseteq^1$	$a^3b^3c^3d^3e^3f^3\ \not\sqsubseteq^1$	-
ac	$ac \sqsubseteq^1$	$\boxed{a^2c^2}\ \sqsubseteq^1$	$a^4c^4\ \not\sqsubseteq^1$	-
b^3cd^2	$b^3cd^2\ \sqsubseteq^1$	$b^6c^2d^4\ \sqsubseteq^1$	$\boxed{b^9c^3d^6}\ \sqsubseteq^1$	$b^{12}c^4d^8\ \not\sqsubseteq^1$
b^3d^2	$b^3d^2\ \sqsubseteq^1$	$b^6d^4\ \sqsubseteq^1$	$\boxed{b^9d^6}\ \sqsubseteq^1$	$b^{12}d^8\ \not\sqsubseteq^1$
b^3d^2f	$b^3d^2f\ \sqsubseteq^1$	$b^6d^4f^2\ \sqsubseteq^1$	$\boxed{b^9d^6f^3}\ \sqsubseteq^1$	$b^{12}d^8f^4\ \not\sqsubseteq^1$
c	$c \sqsubseteq^1$	$c^2 \sqsubseteq^1$	$\boxed{c^3}\ \sqsubseteq^1$	$c^3\ \not\sqsubseteq^1$
e^3	$\boxed{e^3}\ \sqsubseteq^1$	$e^6\ \not\sqsubseteq^1$	-	-
f^2	$\boxed{f^2}\ \sqsubseteq^1$	$f^4\ \not\sqsubseteq^1$	-	-
f^4	$f^4\ \not\sqsubseteq^1$	-	-	-

Table 4. Computation of $\mathsf{bnd}^{\mathsf{out}}(w_1)$

	a	b	c	d	e	f
$\mathsf{bnd}(w_1) = \mathsf{b}(w_1) = ab^9cd^6e^3f^3$	1	9	1	6	3	3
$w_1 = a^2b^{11}c^3d^9e$	2	11	3	9	1	0
row 2 − row 3	-1	-2	-2	-3	2	3
$\mathsf{bnd}^{\mathsf{out}}(w_1) = \mathsf{bnd}(w_1) \ominus w_1 = e^2f^3$	0	0	0	0	2	3

Table 5. Computation of $\mathsf{bnd}^{\mathsf{in}}(w_1)$

	a	b	c	d	e	f
$\mathsf{bnd}(w_1) = \mathsf{b}(w_1) = ab^9cd^6e^3f^3$	1	9	1	6	3	3
$\mathsf{bnd}^{\mathsf{out}}(w_1) = e^2f^3$	0	0	0	0	2	3
row 2 − row 3	1	9	1	6	1	0
$\mathsf{bnd}^{\mathsf{in}}(w_1) = \mathsf{bnd}(w_1) \ominus \mathsf{bnd}^{\mathsf{out}}w_1 = ab^9cd^6e$	1	9	1	6	1	0

4.5 Executions of Communication Rules with Membrane Boundary

In this subsection, the executions of communication rules $R = \{r_1, r_2, r_3\}$ residing in w_1 are restricted to the membrane boundary

$$\mathsf{bnd}(w_1) = ab^9cd^6e^3f^3 = \oplus_1 abcdef \sqcup \oplus_3 b^3d^2f \sqcup \oplus_1 e^3.$$

A symport rule of the form $\langle u, out \rangle$ can be executed in $\mathsf{bnd}(w_1)$ only in the case when $u \sqsubseteq \mathsf{bnd}^{\mathsf{in}}(w_1)$. If this condition satisfies, the mset u leaves the inside membrane boundary $\mathsf{bnd}^{\mathsf{in}}(w_1) = ab^9cd^6e$ and enters the outside membrane boundary $\mathsf{bnd}^{\mathsf{out}}(w_1) = e^2f^3$. Moreover, these movements work within the base msets solely which ensures that the joint membrane approximation space will not change during the executions of communication rules R.

In this particular case, a multiset of rules $r_1^{n_1} r_2^{n_2} r_3^{n_3}$ $(n_1, n_2, n_3 \in \mathbb{N})$ over R is applicable to $\mathsf{bnd}(w_1)$ if

$$\oplus_{n_1} ac \oplus \oplus_{n_2} b^6 d^6 \oplus \oplus_{n_3} d^3 e \sqsubseteq \mathsf{bnd}^{in}(w_1) = ab^9 cd^6 e.$$

As before, let us form the set of all multisets of rules applicable to $\mathsf{bnd}^{in}(w_1)$ and the set of multisets of rules applicable to $\mathsf{bnd}^{in}(w_1)$ in the *maximally parallel* mode:

$$Appl(R, \mathsf{bnd}^{in}(w_1)) = \{r_1, r_2, r_3, r_1 r_2, r_1 r_3\}$$

and

$$Appl_{max}(R, \mathsf{bnd}^{in}(w_1)) = \{r_1 r_2, r_1 r_3\}.$$

Hence, we can choose from two maximal multisets of rules over R in order to perform maximally parallel transition steps. Consequently, the evolution of the P system Π ramifies and has two branchings chosen in a non–deterministic manner.

Transition Step 1. The maximal multiset $r_1 r_2$ of rules is applicable to $\mathsf{bnd}^{in}(w_1)$ because

$$\oplus_1 ac \oplus \oplus_2 b^6 d^6 = ab^6 cd^6 \sqsubseteq \mathsf{bnd}^{in}(w_1) = ab^9 cd^6 e.$$

If so, $r_1 r_2$ indicates that the mset $ab^6 cd^6$ leaves the inside membrane boundary $\mathsf{bnd}^{in}(w_1)$ and enters the outside membrane boundary $\mathsf{bnd}^{out}(w_1)$:

$$(\mathsf{bnd}^{in}(w_1), \mathsf{bnd}^{out}(w_1)) = (ab^9 cd^6 e, \ e^2 f^3) \overset{r_1 r_2}{\Longrightarrow} (b^3 e, \ ab^6 cd^6 e^2 f^3).$$

The movements of ac and $b^6 d^6$ take place within the base msets $abcdef$ and $\oplus_3 b^3 d^2 f$, respectively. Therefore, in this transition step, the computation of the P system Π halts with the mset $ab^5 c^2 d^3 e$ in the region w_1.

Transition Step 2. The maximal multiset $r_1 r_3$ of rules is applicable to $\mathsf{bnd}^{in}(w_1)$ because

$$\oplus_1 ac \oplus \oplus_1 d^3 e = acd^3 e \sqsubseteq \mathsf{bnd}^{in}(w_1) = ab^9 cd^6 e.$$

If so, $r_1 r_3$ indicates that the mset $acd^3 e$ leaves the inside membrane boundary $\mathsf{bnd}^{in}(w_1)$ and enters the outside membrane boundary $\mathsf{bnd}^{out}(w_1)$:

$$(\mathsf{bnd}^{in}(w_1), \mathsf{bnd}^{out}(w_1)) = (ab^9 cd^6 e, \ e^2 f^3) \overset{r_1 r_3}{\Longrightarrow} (b^9 d^3, \ acd^3 e^3 f^3).$$

The movement of ac takes place within the base mset $abcdef$, and the members of $d^3 e$ move within the base msets $\oplus_1 abcdef, \oplus_3 b^3 d^2 f, \oplus_1 e^3$. Therefore, in this transition step, the computation of the P system Π halts with the mset $ab^{11} c^2 d^6$ in the region w_1.

5   Conclusion

In this paper, the boundaries of membranes in P systems relying on multiset approximation spaces have been investigated. Restricting the communication rules to these boundaries, the interactions along the membranes can be controlled locally during the membrane computations. It has been shown that keeping the maximal parallel mode of membrane computations without as well as with membrane boundaries, the nondeterministic nature of computations may change.

One of the next possible steps is to investigate the complexity of P systems with boundaries. Is there any connection between the nature of approximation spaces and the complexity of membrane computation? The other task is to show the role of approximation algorithms in membrane computation.

Acknowledgments. The publication was supported by the TÁMOP–4.2.2.C–11/1/KONV–2012–0001 project. The project has been supported by the European Union, co–financed by the European Social Fund.

The authors are thankful to the anonymous referees of the conference CMC14 (Chisinau, Republic of Moldova, 2013) for their valuable suggestions for the earlier version of this paper. Many thanks to the participants of the conference CMC14 for their incisive comments to improve this article.

The authors are also thankful to György Vaszil for his insightful comments and suggestions.

References

1. Barbuti, R., Maggiolo-Schettini, A., Milazzo, P., Pardini, G., Tesei, L.: Spatial P systems. Natural Computing 10(1), 3–16 (2011)
2. Cardelli, L., Gardner, P.: Processes in space. In: Ferreira, F., Löwe, B., Mayordomo, E., Mendes Gomes, L. (eds.) CiE 2010. LNCS, vol. 6158, pp. 78–87. Springer, Heidelberg (2010)
3. Csuhaj-Varjú, E., Gheorghe, M., Stannett, M.: P systems controlled by general topologies. In: Durand-Lose, J., Jonoska, N. (eds.) UCNC 2012. LNCS, vol. 7445, pp. 70–81. Springer, Heidelberg (2012)
4. Davey, B.A., Priestley, H.A.: Introduction to Lattices and Order, 2nd edn. Cambridge University Press, Cambridge (2002)
5. Girish, K.P., John, S.J.: Relations and functions in multiset context. Information Sciences 179(6), 758–768 (2009)
6. Grätzer, G.: General Lattice Theory. Birkhäuser Verlag, Basel und Stuttgart (1978)
7. Grzymala-Busse, J.: Learning from examples based on rough multisets. In: Proceedings of the Second International Symposium on Methodologies for Intelligent Systems, pp. 325–332. North-Holland Publishing Co., Amsterdam (1987)
8. Kudlek, M., Martín-Vide, C., Păun, G.: Toward a formal macroset theory. In: Calude, C.S., Pun, G., Rozenberg, G., Salomaa, A. (eds.) WMC 2000. LNCS, vol. 2235, pp. 123–134. Springer, Heidelberg (2001)

9. Mihálydeák, T., Csajbók, Z.: Membranes with local environments. In: Csuhaj-Varjú, E., Gheorghe, M., Vaszil, G.Y. (eds.) Proceedings of 13th International Conference on Membrane Computing, CMC13, Budapest, Hungary, August 28 - 31, pp. 311–322. MTA SZTAKI, the Computer and Automation Research Institute of the Hungarian Academy of Sciences, Budapest, Hungary (2012)

10. Mihálydeák, T., Csajbók, Z.E.: Membranes with boundaries. In: Csuhaj-Varjú, E., Gheorghe, M., Rozenberg, G., Salomaa, A., Vaszil, G. (eds.) CMC 2012. LNCS, vol. 7762, pp. 277–294. Springer, Heidelberg (2013)

11. Mihálydeák, T., Csajbók, Z.E.: Partial approximation of multisets and its applications in membrane computing. In: Lingras, P., Wolski, M., Cornelis, C., Mitra, S., Wasilewski, P. (eds.) RSKT 2013. LNCS (LNAI), vol. 8171, pp. 99–108. Springer, Heidelberg (2013)

12. Pawlak, Z.: Rough sets. International Journal of Computer and Information Sciences 11(5), 341–356 (1982)

13. Pawlak, Z.: Rough Sets: Theoretical Aspects of Reasoning about Data. Kluwer Academic Publishers, Dordrecht (1991)

14. Păun, G.: Computing with membranes. Journal of Computer and System Sciences 61(1), 108–143 (2000)

15. Păun, G.: Membrane Computing. An Introduction. Springer, Berlin (2002)

16. Păun, G., Rozenberg, G.: An introduction to and an overview of membrane computing. In: Păun, et al. (eds.) [17], pp. 1–27

17. Păun, G., Rozenberg, G., Salomaa, A. (eds.): The Oxford Handbook of Membrane Computing. Oxford Handbooks, Oxford University Press, Inc., New York (2010)

Programming P Systems with Complex Objects

Radu Nicolescu[1], Florentin Ipate[2,3], and Huiling Wu[1]

[1] Department of Computer Science, University of Auckland,
Private Bag 92019, Auckland, New Zealand
r.nicolescu@auckland.ac.nz, hwu065@aucklanduni.ac.nz
[2] Department of Computer Science, University of Bucharest,
Bucharest, Romania
[3] Department of Computer Science, University of Piteşti,
Piteşti, Romania
florentin.ipate@ifsoft.ro

Abstract. We develop and formalise our earlier complex objects proposal and show that it enables an efficient high-level programming of P systems.

Keywords: P systems, complex objects, generic rules, data structures, control flow, parallel composition, function calls, recursion, numerical P systems, NP-complete, applications.

1   Introduction

A P system is a formal parallel and distributed computational model inspired by the structure and interactions of living cells, introduced by Păun [16]; for a recent overview of the domain, see Păun et al.'s recent monograph [18]. Essentially, a P system is specified by its membrane structure, symbols and rules. The underlying structure is a *network* such as a digraph, a directed acyclic graph (dag) or a tree (which seems the most studied case). Each node, here better known as *cell*, transforms its content symbols and sends messages to its neighbours using formal rules inspired by rewriting systems. Rules of the same cell can be applied in parallel (where possible) and all cells work in parallel.

P modules can be *asynchronous*, in the sense used in distributed algorithms and in Nicolescu [13], admitting the more traditional *synchronous* definitions as a special case. Sometimes we also make a fine distinction between (i) generated objects that can be thought, as traditionally in P systems, as being messaged back to the current cell, via a sort of *loopback* channel, and (ii) generated objects which become *immediately* available for the *following* rules, a matrix grammars inspired approach, used by ElGindy et al. [6]. However, here we strictly focus on *single cell* systems, so all these fine distinctions can be safely ignored.

In P systems, the practically very important *modularity* can be achieved by two distinct complementary ways: (i) an *external* modularity, for recursively aggregating groups of cells into higher order P modules, as described in Dinneen et al. [4], an approach which is not further discussed here, and (ii) an *internal*

A. Alhazov et al. (Eds.): CMC 2013, LNCS 8340, pp. 280–300, 2014.

modularity, possible inside each cell, where we recursively aggregate objects and rules to form higher-order components, a more recent approach which is more systematically discussed and assessed in this paper.

This article presents evidence that *complex objects* can enable a *high-level* programming style, with *data structures, control flow*, and several useful *functional programming* elements. We have previously used complex objects to successfully model and even improve large practical applications, ranging from computer vision [9,10,8] to complex graph theoretical problems [15,6] and to well-known critical distributed algorithms [19]. Here we attempt to generalise our field-proven methods and sketch how to apply similar techniques to other, more theoretical, domains: numerical P systems and NP-complete problems.

Because of space constraints, for the rest of the paper we assume that the reader is already familiar with basic definitions used in tissue-like transition P systems, including state based rules, weak priority, promoters and inhibitors. Section 2 presents a formal definition for complex objects, slightly beyond what we have earlier proposed [13,6]. Section 3 shows how fundamental data structures, such as stacks, trees and dictionaries, can be built and processed using our proposals. Section 4 sketches the basic ideas behind an integer arithmetic package, which can be extended to a rational package. Section 5 covers control flow techniques which can be used to implement higher level operations such as branching statements, parallel compositions, sequential functions definitions and invocations. Section 6 proposes a high-level linguistic support for developing P system models in a simple functional style. Section 7 illustrates a couple of more theoretical applications, not attempted in our earlier modelling projects: numerical P systems and NP-complete problems. Note that the ideas of integer arithmetic, compositional properties and high-level programming, although in different settings, recall similar ideas also presented to carry out arithmetic and register-machine computation, for example, in [1,11].

2 P Systems with Complex Objects

2.1 Complex Objects

We consider the following formal definition for *complex objects*, which are Prolog-like ground terms, which can include either lists of complex objects or dot-separated strings (here interpreted as sequences) of complex objects:

```
<complex-object> ::= <term-object>

<term-object> ::= <atom> | <functor-object> '(' <object-arguments> ')'

<functor-object> ::= <atom> | <complex-object>

<object-arguments> ::= λ | <object-list> | <object-sequence>

<object-list> ::= <complex-object> (',' <complex-object>)*

<object-sequence> ::= <complex-object> ('.' <complex-object>)*
```

Atoms (simple objects) are typically denoted by lower case letters, such as a, b, c, possibly with indices. Example ground complex objects: a, $a()$, $a(b, c)$, $a(b(c))$, $a.b().c$, $a(b.c)$, $a(b(c))(d(e))$, $a(b(c), d(e))$, $a(b(c), d.e)$, $a(b(c).d(e))$.

We typically reserve sequences to represent natural numbers. For example, considering that l represents the unary digit, then the following complex objects can be used to describe the contents of a virtual integer variable a: $a()$ — the value of a is 0; $a(l^3)$ — the value of a is 3.

We are considering to extend our string objects to mean *bags* (i.e. *multisets*), instead of sequences. This could be useful in some scenarios, but we are not following these ideas here.

2.2   Variables and Pattern Matching

Variables are used for *pattern matching* on object arguments and are typically denoted by uppercase letters, such as X, Y, Z, possibly with overbars, e.g. $\overline{X}$, and with indices, e.g. X_1, $\overline{X}_2$. Variable '_' (underscore) is a wild-card and is used when pattern matching is required but its value is not further used. Using variables require the following redefinitions:

```
<object-list> ::= <var-or-object> (',' <var-or-object>)*

<var-or-object> ::= <variable_1> | <complex-object>

<object-sequence> ::= <var-or-object-subsequence>
        (':' <var-or-object-subsequence>)*

<var-or-object-subsequence> ::= <variable_2>
        | λ | <var-or-object> ('.' <var-or-object>)*
```

With these definitions, a variable can match either:

1. a complex object in a list of arguments or in a string, or
2. any substring of a complex objects sequence, including λ.

Variables of the type 1 will be denoted by symbols without overbars and variables of type 2 will have overbars. For example:

- matching $a(b(c), d.e.f) = a(X, d.\overline{Y})$ creates the bindings $X, \overline{Y} = b(c), e.f$
- matching $a.b().c = X.\overline{Y}$ creates the binding $X, \overline{Y} = a, b().c$
- matching $a.b().c = \overline{X}.Y$ creates the binding $\overline{X}, Y = a.b(), c$
- matching $a.b().c = \overline{X}.\overline{Y}$ nondeterministically creates one of the following bindings $\overline{X}, \overline{Y} = \lambda, a.b().c$, $\overline{X}, \overline{Y} = a, b().c$, $\overline{X}, \overline{Y} = a.b(), c$, $\overline{X}, \overline{Y} = a.b().c, \lambda$

With the exception of subsequence matchings, our pattern matching rules are a simplified version of term unification in Prolog-like languages, so they can be implemented with reasonable efficiency. As we will later see, arithmetic operations are based on particular subsequence matchings on unary sequences: these matchings can also be efficiently implemented. However, general subsequence matchings could be expensive, so these should be prudently used, e.g. for proof-of-concept prototyping.

Type 2 (overbarred) variables and much of the pattern matching complexities have been mainly introduced to support efficient arithmetic operations (on unary sequences); the complex objects construction would look much simpler if we would accept natural numbers as primitives in our P modules.

2.3 Generic Rules

By default, rules are applied top-down, in the so-called *weak priority* order. As we are here exclusively focusing on *single cell* systems, we only consider a simplified generic rule format (with no messaging), of the following type:

current-state objects $\rightarrow_\alpha$ *target-state objects'* | *promoters* $\neg$ *inhibitors*,

where

- left-side objects, right-side objects', promoters and inhibitors are *bags of complex objects*, possibly containing (which makes rules *generic*) *variables*, which are *matched* (unified) as described in the previous section;
- $\alpha \in \{\text{min.min, min.max, max.min, max.max}\}$, is a combined instantiation and rewriting mode, as discussed in Nicolescu et al. [13,6] (discussion further adapted below).

To explain generics, consider a cell, σ, containing three counter-like complex objects, $c(c(a))$, $c(c(a))$, $c(c(c(a)))$, and all four possible instantiation.rewriting modes of the following "decrementing" rule:

$$(\rho_\alpha)\ S_1\ c(c(X)) \rightarrow_\alpha S_2\ c(X).$$

where $\alpha \in \{\text{min.min, min.max, max.min, max.max}\}$.

1. If $\alpha = \text{min.min}$, rule $\rho_{\text{min.min}}$ nondeterministically generates *one* of the following rule instances:

$$(\rho'_1)\ S_1\ c(c(a)) \rightarrow_{\text{min}} S_2\ c(a)\quad\text{or}$$
$$(\rho''_1)\ S_1\ c(c(c(a))) \rightarrow_{\text{min}} S_2\ c(c(a)).$$

In the first case, using (ρ'_1), cell σ ends with counters $c(a)$, $c(c(a))$, $c(c(c(a)))$. In the second case, using (ρ''_1), cell σ ends with counters $c(c(a))$, $c(c(a))$, $c(c(a))$.

2. If $\alpha = \text{max.min}$, rule $\rho_{\text{max.min}}$ generates *both* following rule instances:

$$(\rho'_2)\ S_1\ c(c(a)) \rightarrow_{\text{min}} S_2\ c(a)\quad\text{and}$$
$$(\rho''_2)\ S_1\ c(c(c(a))) \rightarrow_{\text{min}} S_2\ c(c(a)).$$

In this case, using (ρ'_2) and (ρ''_2), cell σ ends with counters $c(a)$, $c(c(a))$, $c(c(a))$.

3. If $\alpha = \mathtt{min.max}$, rule $\rho_{\mathtt{min.max}}$ nondeterministically generates *one* of the following rule instances:

$$(\rho_3')\ \ S_1\ c(c(a)) \to_{\mathtt{max}} S_2\ c(a)\quad \text{or}$$
$$(\rho_3'')\ \ S_1\ c(c(c(a))) \to_{\mathtt{max}} S_2\ c(c(a)).$$

In the first case, using (ρ_3'), cell σ ends with counters $c(a)$, $c(a)$, $c(c(c(a)))$. In the second case, using (ρ_3''), cell σ ends with counters $c(c(a))$, $c(c(a))$, $c(c(a))$.

4. If $\alpha = \mathtt{max.max}$, rule $\rho_{\mathtt{min.max}}$ generates *both* following rule instances:

$$(\rho_4')\ \ S_1\ c(c(a)) \to_{\mathtt{max}} S_2\ c(a)\quad \text{and}$$
$$(\rho_4'')\ \ S_1\ c(c(c(a))) \to_{\mathtt{max}} S_2\ c(c(a)).$$

In this case, using (ρ_4') and (ρ_4''), cell σ ends with counters $c(a)$, $c(a)$, $c(c(a))$.

The interpretation of $\mathtt{min.min}$, $\mathtt{min.max}$ and $\mathtt{max.max}$ modes is straightforward. While other interpretations could be considered, the mode $\mathtt{max.min}$ indicates that the generic rule is instantiated as *many* times as possible, without *superfluous* instances (i.e. without duplicates or instances which are not applicable) and each one of the instantiated rules is applied *once*, if possible.

For all modes, the instantiations are *conceptually* created when rules are tested for applicability and are also *ephemeral*, i.e. they disappear at the end of the step. P system implementations are encouraged to directly apply high-level generic rules, if this is more efficient (it usually is); they may, but need not, start by transforming high-level rules into low-level rules, by way of instantiations.

This type of generic rules allow (i) a reasonably fast parsing and processing of subcomponents, and (ii) algorithm descriptions with *fixed size alphabets* and *fixed sized rulesets*, independent of the size of the problem and number of cells in the system (sometimes impossible with only atomic symbols).

3   Data Structures

3.1   Stacks

A n-size *stack* s, with contents $a_1, a_2 \ldots a_{n-1}, a_n$ (top), can be represented by a complex object $s(a_n(a_{n-1}(\ldots a_2(a_1())\ldots)))$. Essentially, this is a *simple linked list* where the list head is the stack top. Examples: $s()$ — an empty stack, s; $s(a(b(c())))$ — a stack, s, with contents a, b, c.

Fundamental operations on stacks include:

– *construct* an empty stack

$$S_1 \to_{\mathtt{min.min}} S_2\ s()$$

- replace a by b, if s is *empty*

$$S_1\ a \to_{\texttt{min.min}} S_2\ b \mid s()$$

- *clear* a stack

$$S_1\ s(X) \to_{\texttt{min.min}} S_2\ s()$$

- *push* a, if a is in the current contents

$$S_1\ a\ s(X) \to_{\texttt{min.min}} S_2\ s(a(X))$$

- *push* the content of c, if this exists and is a term (not sequence)

$$S_1\ c(T)\ s(X) \to_{\texttt{min.min}} S_2\ s(T(X))$$

- conditional *pop* a, if a is on top

$$S_1\ s(a(X)) \to_{\texttt{min.min}} S_2\ a\ s(X)$$

- unconditional *pop*, if s is not empty

$$S_1\ s(T(X)) \to_{\texttt{min.min}} S_2\ T\ s(X)$$

- conditional *peek* a, if a is on top

$$S_1\ s(a(X)) \to_{\texttt{min.min}} S_2\ a\ s(a(X))$$

- unconditional *peek*, if s is not empty

$$S_1\ s(T(X)) \to_{\texttt{min.min}} S_2\ T\ s(T(X))$$

- *reverse* stack s on stack t

$$S_1\ s(T(X))\ t(Y) \to_{\texttt{max.min}} S_2\ s(X)\ t(T(Y))$$

Complexity. Each of the above stack operations can be accomplished in a single P step, $O(1)$, except the stack reversal, which may take longer (in this case the number of steps required equals the length of the stack).

Extensions. All preceding *stack* operations can be formally redefined to work on strings, instead of nested terms. *Queues* can also be implemented as strings, essentially by renaming pop as dequeue, and replacing push by an enqueue operation (adding to the other end):

- unconditional *dequeue*, if q is not empty

$$S_1\ q(T.\overline{X}) \to_{\texttt{min.min}} S_2\ T\ q(\overline{X})$$

- *enqueue* the content of c, if this exists and assuming is a term (not sequence)

$$S_1\ c(T)\ q(\overline{X}) \to_{\texttt{min.min}} S_2\ q(\overline{X}.T)$$

Alternatively, *queues* can be also be implemented as pairs of stacks, using stack reversals when needed. This can be reasonably efficient, as reversal costs will normally amortize in the long run.

3.2 Trees

Trees can be represented as nested terms, in a straightforward manner. For example: (1) a leaf node with contents X can be represented as $f(X)$; (2) an intermediary node, with contents X and two subnodes, can be represented as $n(X, Y, Z)$, where Y and Z can be leaves or other intermediary nodes. For example, the following term describes a binary tree consisting of 2 intermediary nodes and 3 leaves, all with integer contents:

$$n(l^{10}, n(l^{20}, f(l^{30}), f(l^{40})), f(l^{50}))$$

Most tree operations are either recursive or have rather elaborate descriptions (needed to simulate recursion). As recursion is discussed later in the article, here we only show a simple operation which, in P systems, does not really need recursion: a destructive summation of all values in a binary tree, n, with integer contents. The first rule creates placeholder for the total sum, s, and stores a copy of the original tree in a backup store, b:

$$
\begin{aligned}
&r_1 : S_0\, n(X, Y, Z) && \to_{\text{min.min}} S_1\, n(X, Y, Z)\, s()\, b(n(X, Y, Z)) \\
&r_2 : S_1\, s(T)\, v(X) && \to_{\text{min.min}} S_1\, s(T.X) \\
&r_3 : S_1\, v(X)\, v(Y) && \to_{\text{max.min}} S_1\, v(X.Y) \\
&r_4 : S_1\, f(X) && \to_{\text{max.min}} S_1\, v(X) \\
&r_5 : S_1\, n(X, f(Y), f(Z)) && \to_{\text{max.min}} S_1\, v(X)\, v(Y)\, v(Z) \\
&r_6 : S_1\, n(X, f(Y), n(Z, Z_1, Z_2)) && \to_{\text{max.min}} S_1\, v(X)\, v(Y)\, n(Z, Z_1, Z_2) \\
&r_7 : S_1\, n(X, n(Y, Y_1, Y_2), f(Z)) && \to_{\text{max.min}} S_1\, v(X)\, n(Y, Y_1, Y_2)\, v(Z) \\
&r_8 : S_1\, n(X, n(Y, Y_1, Y_2), n(Z, Z_1, Z_2)) && \to_{\text{max.min}} S_1\, v(X)\, n(Y, Y_1, Y_2)\, n(Z, Z_1, Z_2)
\end{aligned}
$$

For the above sample tree, the result is $s(l^{150})$, as indicated by the following traces, where $b(\dots)$ represents the backed up tree, $b(n(l^{10}, n(l^{20}, f(l^{30}), f(l^{40})), f(l^{50})))$:

$$
\begin{aligned}
& n(l^{10}, n(l^{20}, f(l^{30}), f(l^{40})), f(l^{50})) \\
& \xRightarrow{r_1} s()\, n(l^{10}, n(l^{20}, f(l^{30}), f(l^{40})), f(l^{50}))\, b(\dots) \\
& \xRightarrow{r_7} s()\, v(l^{10})\, n(l^{20}, f(l^{30}), f(l^{40}))\, v(l^{50})\, b(\dots) \\
& \xRightarrow{r_2} s(l^{10})\, n(l^{20}, f(l^{30}), f(l^{40}))\, v(l^{50})\, b(\dots) \\
& \xRightarrow{r_5} s(l^{10})\, v(l^{20})\, v(l^{30})\, v(l^{40})\, v(l^{50})\, b(\dots) \\
& \xRightarrow{r_2} s(l^{30})\, v(l^{30})\, v(l^{40})\, v(l^{50})\, b(\dots) \\
& \xRightarrow{r_3} s(l^{30})\, v(l^{120})\, b(\dots) \\
& \xRightarrow{r_2} s(l^{150})\, b(\dots)
\end{aligned}
$$

The complexity of this snippet is $O(h)$ P steps, where h is the height of the tree.

3.3 Dictionaries

Dictionaries are key/value mappings. Typical dictionaries have unique keys; their efficient implementations use hash tables or balanced trees (e.g. red-black trees).

A dictionary, d, can be represented by a string of complex objects of the form $m(k, v)$, where k is the key and v is the value. Examples: $d()$ — an empty dictionary, d; $d(m(a, b).m(c, d))$ — a dictionary, d, with two mappings, $a \rightarrow b$ and $c \rightarrow d$.

Fundamental operations on dictionaries include:

- *construct* an empty dictionary

$$S_1 \rightarrow_{\text{min.min}} S_2 \, d()$$

- *clear* a dictionary

$$S_1 \, d(\overline{X}) \rightarrow_{\text{min.min}} S_2 \, d()$$

- *add* $a \rightarrow b$, if key a is not already present (to preserve key uniqueness)

$$S_1 \, m(a, b) \, d(\overline{X}) \rightarrow_{\text{min.min}} S_2 \, d(m(a, b).\overline{X}) \, \neg \, d(\overline{Y}.m(a, V).\overline{Z})$$

- non-destructive *query* of the mapping for key a, if it exists

$$S_1 \, a \, d(\overline{X}.m(a, V).\overline{Y}) \rightarrow_{\text{min.min}} S_2 \, m(a, V) \, d(\overline{X}.m(a, V).\overline{Y})$$

- *reset* the mapping for key a to a new value, if a has a mapping (and also return the old value for this key)

$$S_1 \, m(a, b) \, d(\overline{X}.m(a, V).\overline{Y}) \rightarrow_{\text{min.min}} S_2 \, m(a, V) \, d(\overline{X}.m(a, b).\overline{Y})$$

- *remove* the mapping for key a, if it exists

$$S_1 \, a \, d(\overline{X}.m(a, V).\overline{Y}) \rightarrow_{\text{min.min}} S_2 \, d(\overline{X}.\overline{Y})$$

Complexity. Apparently, each of the above dictionary operations can be accomplished in a single P step, $O(1)$. However, these rules use a generalized string unification which probably is not efficient for practical purposes. Thus, this dictionary structure should be reserved for theoretical proofs-of-concept or prototype implementations.

Assuming a natural order on atoms, we can define a more efficient dictionary implementation based on balanced trees; however, we are not following this idea here.

4   Arithmetic

Recall that we use complex objects with sequence contents to represent natural numbers. For example, considering that l represents the unary digit, then the following complex objects can indicate that: $a()$ — the value of a is 0; $a(l^3)$ — the value of a is 3.

Fundamental arithmetic operations on natural numbers include:

– $c := a + b$, destructive *addition*:

$$S_1\, a(\overline{X})\, b(\overline{Y}) \to_{\texttt{min.min}} S_2\, c(\overline{X.Y})$$

– $c := a - b$, destructive *subtraction*:

$$S_1\, a(\overline{X.Y})\, b(\overline{Y}) \to_{\texttt{min.min}} S_2\, c(\overline{X})$$

– $c := a * b$, *multiplication*, which destroys a:

$$S_1 \qquad\qquad\qquad \to_{\texttt{min.min}} S_2\, c()$$
$$S_2\, a(l.\overline{X})\, b(\overline{Y})\, c(\overline{Z}) \to_{\texttt{max.min}} S_2\, a(\overline{X})\, b(\overline{Y})\, c(\overline{Y.Z})$$

– $c, d := a \,/\, b,\ a \,\%\, b$, *division*, which destroys a:

$$S_1 \qquad\qquad\qquad \to_{\texttt{min.min}} S_2\, c()$$
$$S_2\, a(\overline{X.Y})\, b(\overline{Y})\, c(\overline{Z}) \to_{\texttt{max.min}} S_2\, a(\overline{X})\, b(\overline{Y})\, c(l\,\overline{Z})$$
$$S_2\, a(\overline{X}) \qquad\qquad\qquad \to_{\texttt{max.min}} S_3\, d(\overline{X})$$

Complexity. Additions and subtractions can be performed in single P steps, $O(1)$, but multiplications and divisions may take longer. For multiplication, the number of steps equals the value of a plus one, whereas for division this is the value of the quotient c plus two.

If desired, non destructive operations can be implemented in a straightforward manner. Alternatively, we can define arithmetic operations using counter stacks, but this is much slower.

These ideas can be extended to define more complete arithmetic packages for integer numbers and for rational numbers.

5   Control Flow

Composing bigger chunks out of smaller rule snippets can require careful object relabelling, to ensure continuity and avoid clashes. This is probably best done automatically, using a well designed composition model. However, we do not follow this here; we just present a proof of concept where all required relabeling has been manually done.

5.1   Basic Composition

Basic composition includes sequencing and conditional transfers, which can be further used to define higher-level structured constructs, such as if-then-else conditionals and while loops (not detailed here).

- $BR(S')$, *branch*, unconditional branch to state S':

$$S \to_{\texttt{min.min}} S'$$

- $BP(S'; p_1, p_2, \dots)$, *branch on promoters*, branch to state S', given promoters $p_1, p_2, \dots$:

$$S \to_{\texttt{min.min}} S' \mid p_1\, p_2\, \dots$$

- $BI(S'; i_1, i_2, \dots)$, *branch on inhibitors*, branch to state S', given inhibitors $i_1, i_2, \dots$:

$$S \to_{\texttt{min.min}} S' \neg\, i_1\, i_2\, \dots$$

- $BPI(S'; p_1, p_2, \dots; i_1, i_2, \dots)$, *branch on promoters and inhibitors*, branch to state S', given promoters $p_1, p_2, \dots$ and inhibitors $i_1, i_2, \dots$:

$$S \to_{\texttt{min.min}} S' \mid p_1\, p_2\, \dots \neg\, i_1\, i_2\, \dots$$

Other branching primitives are described in the sections for function calls.

5.2 Parallel Composition

Consider running in parallel two rule fragments, Π_1, with M states, and Π_2, with N states. In general, the composed system, $\Pi_1 \times \Pi_2$, will need $M \cdot N$ states, thus it will need $O(M \cdot N)$ rules.

However, using complex state objects, we can define an equivalent parallel system, $\Pi_1 \parallel \Pi_2$, with just $O(M+N)$ rules — essentially the same rules initially used for describing Π_1 and Π_2. Additional semantics is required for matching variables on components of state objects.

We illustrate this on a simple ad-hoc example, not doing any meaningful work, except that Π_1 loops over three states and Π_2 loops over two states.

- Π_1, a fragment with 3 states and 3 rules:

$$S_1\, a \to_{\texttt{min}} S_2\, b$$
$$S_2\, b \to_{\texttt{min}} S_3\, c$$
$$S_3\, c \to_{\texttt{min}} S_1\, a$$

- Π_2, a fragment with 2 states and 2 rules:

$$S_1\, d \to_{\texttt{min}} S_2\, e$$
$$S_2\, e \to_{\texttt{min}} S_1\, d$$

- $\Pi_1 \times \Pi_2$, has 6 (= 3 · 2) states and 18 (= 3 · 2 · 3) rules:

$S_{11}\, a\, d \to_{\texttt{min}} S_{22}\, b\, e$	$S_{22}\, b\, e \to_{\texttt{min}} S_{31}\, c\, d$
$S_{11}\, a \to_{\texttt{min}} S_{21}\, b$	$S_{22}\, b \to_{\texttt{min}} S_{32}\, c$
$S_{11}\, d \to_{\texttt{min}} S_{12}\, e$	$S_{22}\, e \to_{\texttt{min}} S_{21}\, d$
$S_{12}\, a\, e \to_{\texttt{min}} S_{21}\, b\, d$	$S_{31}\, c\, d \to_{\texttt{min}} S_{12}\, a\, e$
$S_{12}\, a \to_{\texttt{min}} S_{22}\, b$	$S_{31}\, c \to_{\texttt{min}} S_{11}\, a$
$S_{12}\, e \to_{\texttt{min}} S_{11}\, d$	$S_{31}\, d \to_{\texttt{min}} S_{32}\, e$
$S_{21}\, b\, d \to_{\texttt{min}} S_{32}\, c\, e$	$S_{32}\, c\, e \to_{\texttt{min}} S_{11}\, a\, d$
$S_{21}\, b \to_{\texttt{min}} S_{31}\, c$	$S_{32}\, c \to_{\texttt{min}} S_{12}\, a$
$S_{21}\, d \to_{\texttt{min}} S_{22}\, e$	$S_{32}\, e \to_{\texttt{min}} S_{31}\, d$

- $\Pi_1 \parallel \Pi_2$, also has 6 (= 3 · 2) states, but only 5 (= 3 + 2) rules:

$$\Theta(S_1, Y) \, a \rightarrow_{\min} \Theta(S_2, Y) \, b$$
$$\Theta(S_2, Y) \, b \rightarrow_{\min} \Theta(S_3, Y) \, c$$
$$\Theta(S_3, Y) \, c \rightarrow_{\min} \Theta(S_1, Y) \, a$$
$$\Theta(X, S_1) \, d \rightarrow_{\min} \Theta(X, S_2) \, e$$
$$\Theta(X, S_2) \, e \rightarrow_{\min} \Theta(X, S_1) \, d$$

Note that, although $\Pi_1 \parallel \Pi_2$ has, in general, an order of magnitude fewer user-written rules than $\Pi_1 \times \Pi_2$, as $O(M+N) \ll O(M \cdot N)$, their state sets are isomorphic. Figure 1 shows state charts for Π_1, Π_2 and $\Pi_1 \times \Pi_2 \overset{states}{\simeq} \Pi_1 \parallel \Pi_2$.

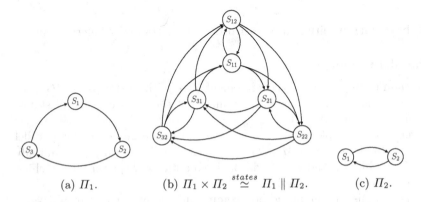

(a) Π_1.   (b) $\Pi_1 \times \Pi_2 \overset{states}{\simeq} \Pi_1 \parallel \Pi_2$.   (c) Π_2.

Fig. 1. State charts of Π_1, Π_2 and $\Pi_1 \times \Pi_2 \overset{states}{\simeq} \Pi_1 \parallel \Pi_2$

5.3   Parameterless Sequential Functions

We need states and a global stack for return states, let it be $\rho()$. Consider that: S_f is the entry state of function f's ruleset, S_c is the current state and S_r is the return state (to be entered after function f completes). We define the following high-level boiler-plate P macros:

- BAL(S_f, S_r), *branch and link* to state S_f, i.e. to function f, and request return to state S_r:

$$S_c \, \rho(X) \rightarrow_{\min.\min} S_f \, \rho(S_r(X))$$

- RET, *return* from function f (assuming that its last state is S_g):

$$S_g \, \rho(Z(X)) \rightarrow_{\min.\min} Z \, \rho(X)$$

5.4   Sequential Functions with Parameters

We need one more stack for each parameter. Alternatively, we can combine all parameters in a single complex object, so just one additional stack would suffice. We can even combine this with the return stack, to mimic a typical runtime stack frame.

Here we consider a single global stack for all parameters, π, and a global placeholder for function results, ϕ. If needed, but not shown here, global stack π could also be used to create slots for local variables. Additional high-level boiler-plate P macros:

- PUSHP$(p_1, p_2, \dots)$, *push parameters*, push contents of objects with functors $p_1, p_1, \dots$ on π, and create an empty $\phi()$, as a placeholder for the expected results (we assume that this does not yet exist):

$$S_c \, p_1(X_1) \, p_2(X_2) \dots \pi(X) \to_{\texttt{min.min}} S_c \, \pi(p(X_1, X_2, \dots)(X)) \, \phi()$$

- PEEKP$(p_1, p_2, \dots)$, *peek parameters*, peek top of π into contents of objects with functors $p_1, p_1, \dots$:

$$S_c \to_{\texttt{min.min}} S_c \, p_1(X_1) \, p_2(X_2) \dots \mid \pi(p(X_1, X_2, \dots)(X))$$

- POPP$()$, *pop parameters*, pop top of π:

$$S_c \, \pi(T(X)) \to_{\texttt{min.min}} S_c \, \pi(X)$$

- POPP$(p_1, p_2, \dots)$, *pop parameters*, pop top of π into contents of objects with functors $p_1, p_1, \dots$:

$$S_c \, \pi(p(X_1, X_2, \dots)(X)) \to_{\texttt{min.min}} S_c \, p_1(X_1) \, p_2(X_2) \dots \pi(X)$$

- RESULT$(r_1, r_2, \dots)$, *set result*, set ϕ using contents of objects with functors $r_1, r_2, \dots$:

$$S_c \, r_1(X_1) \, r_2(X_2) \dots \phi() \to_{\texttt{min.min}} S_c \, \phi(X_1, X_2, \dots)$$

- POPR$(q_1, q_2, \dots)$, *pop results*, extract ϕ's contents into objects with functors $q_1, q_2, \dots$:

$$S_c \, \phi(X_1, X_2, \dots) \to_{\texttt{min.min}} S_c \, q_1(X_1) \, q_2(X_2) \dots$$

For convenience, the following P macro combinations are also defined:

- CALL$(S_f; p_1, p_2, \dots; S_r; q)$ = PUSHP$(p_1, p_2, \dots)$; BAL(S_f, S_r); POPR(q)
- FUNC$(p_1, p_2, \dots)$ = PEEKP$(p_1, p_2, \dots)$
- RETURN$(r_1, r_2, \dots)$ = RESULT$(r_1, r_2, \dots)$; POPP; RET

5.5   A First Example

Consider a snippet calling an arithmetic multiply function, to compute $z = x * y$.

- Pseudo P code, using our high-level P macros (its essential two lines are exactly as given in Section 4):

% calling program	% inputs: $x(\overline{X})\ y(\overline{Y})$
$S_c\ \texttt{CALL}(S_m; x, y; S_r; z)$	% $\texttt{PUSHP}(x, y)$; $\texttt{BAL}(S_m, S_r)$; $\texttt{POPR}(z)$
$S_r...$	% output: $z(\overline{Z})$

% function mult S_m	
$S_m\ \texttt{FUNC}(a, b)$	% creates: $a(\overline{X})\ b(\overline{Y})$
S_m	$\to_{\texttt{min.min}} S_n\ c()$
$S_n\ a(l.\overline{X})\ b(\overline{Y})\ c(\overline{Z})$	$\to_{\texttt{max.min}} S_n\ a(\overline{X})\ b(\overline{Y})\ c(\overline{Y}.\overline{Z})$
$S_n\ a(\_)\ b(\_)$	$\to_{\texttt{min.min}} S_o$
$S_o\ \texttt{RETURN}(c)$	% $\texttt{RESULT}(c)$; $\texttt{POPP}$; $\texttt{RET}$

- Direct translation to P rules:

% calling program:	$x(\overline{X})\ y(\overline{Y})$	
$S_c\ x(\overline{X})\ y(\overline{Y})\ \pi(P)$	$\to_{\texttt{min.min}}$	$S_m\ \pi(p(\overline{X}, \overline{Y})(P)\ \phi()$
$S_c\ \rho(R)$	$\to_{\texttt{min.min}}$	$S_m\ \rho(S_r(R))$
$S_r\ \phi(\overline{Z})$	$\to_{\texttt{min.min}}$	$S_r\ z(\overline{Z})$

...

% function mult S_m		
S_m	$\to_{\texttt{min.min}}$	$S_n\ a(\overline{X})\ b(\overline{Y})\ \mid \pi(p(\overline{X}, \overline{Y})(P))$
S_m	$\to_{\texttt{min.min}}$	$S_n\ c()$
$S_n\ a(l.\overline{X})\ b(\overline{Y})\ c(\overline{Z})$	$\to_{\texttt{max.min}}$	$S_n\ a(\overline{X})\ b(\overline{Y})\ c(\overline{Y}.\overline{Z})$
$S_n\ a(\_)\ b(\_)$	$\to_{\texttt{min.min}}$	S_o
$S_o\ c(\overline{Z})\ \phi()$	$\to_{\texttt{min.min}}$	$S_o\ \phi(\overline{Z})$
$S_o\ \pi(T(P))$	$\to_{\texttt{min.min}}$	$S_o\ \pi(P)$
$S_o\ \rho(Z(R))$	$\to_{\texttt{min.min}}$	$Z\ \rho(R)$

5.6   A Recursive Example

As a more elaborated example, consider the classical naive definition of factorial:

```
fact n = if n = 0 then 1 else (fact (n-1)) * n
```

The following versions show the call y = fact x.

– Pseudo P code, using our high-level P macros:

% calling program   —   % input: $x(\overline{X})$
S_c CALL($S_f; x; S_r; y$)   % PUSHP(x); BAL(S_f, S_r); POPR(y)
S_r ...   —   % output: $y(\overline{Y})$

% function fact S_f —   defined with macros
S_f FUNC(n)   % creates: $n(\overline{N})$
S_f $n()$ $\rightarrow_{\texttt{min.min}}$ S_h $f(l)$
S_f $n(l.\overline{N})$ $\rightarrow_{\texttt{min.min}}$ S_f $n(\overline{N})$
S_f CALL($S_f; n; S_g; f$)   % creates: $f(\_)$
S_g PEEKP(n)   % recreates: $n(\overline{N})$
S_g CALL($S_m; f, n; S_h; f$)   % call mult
S_h RETURN(f)   % RESULT(f); POPP; RET

– The above function definition can be more efficiently (but less readably) implemented by the following rules, which peek parameter values directly from the stack, inline the mult call and use two temporary objects, σ and τ, to evaluate the product.

% calling program   —   % input: $x(\overline{X})$
S_c $x(\overline{X})$ $\pi(Y)$ $\rho(R)$ $\rightarrow_{\texttt{min.min}}$ S_f $\phi()$ $\pi(n(\overline{X})(Y))$ $\rho(S_r(R))$
S_r ...   —   % output: $\phi(\overline{Y})$
...
% function fact S_f —   manually optimised code
S_f $\phi()$ $\pi(n()(Y))$ $\rho(Z(X))$ $\rightarrow_{\texttt{min.min}}$ Z $\phi(l)$ $\pi(Y)$ $\rho(X)$
S_f $\phi()$ $\pi(n(l.\overline{N})(Y))$ $\rho(Z(X))$ $\rightarrow_{\texttt{min.min}}$ S_f $\phi()$ $\pi(n(\overline{N})(n(l.\overline{N})(Y)))$ $\rho(S_f(Z(X)))$
S_f $\phi(\overline{F})$ $\pi(n(\overline{N})(Y))$ $\rho(Z(X))$ $\rightarrow_{\texttt{min.min}}$ S_g $\phi()$ $\sigma(\overline{N})$ $\tau(\overline{F})$ $\pi(Y)$ $\rho(Z(X))$
S_g $\phi(\overline{P})$ $\sigma(l.\overline{N})$ $\tau(\overline{F})$ $\rightarrow_{\texttt{max.min}}$ S_g $\phi(\overline{F}.\overline{P})$ $\sigma(\overline{N})$ $\tau(\overline{F})$
S_g $\sigma()$ $\tau(\overline{F})$ $\rho(Z(X))$ $\rightarrow_{\texttt{min.min}}$ Z $\rho(X)$

– In the particular case $x = 5$: $X = l^5$, $Y = l^{120}$, $y = 120$.

6 Linguistic Support

With proper linguistic support, the factorial sample can be rewritten at a more user-friendly high level, where the user needs only develop application's specific "business" P rules and the system completes the required boiler-plate templates required by function invocations.

As shown in Figure 2, our proposed high-level language includes the following elements:

– Except hidden system objects, such as a parameter stack and a return stack, *no global* objects should be used (but the system does *not* enforce this recommendation).

```
1    function main =
2        state Sc =
3            →min.min x(l³)
4            set y = fact x continue Sr
5        state Sr =
6            . . .
7
8    function fact n =
9        state Sf =
10           n() →min.min Sh f(l)        % explicit target, Sh
11           →min.min n₁(N̄) | n(l.N̄)  % implicit target, Sf
12           set f₁ = fact n₁ continue Sg
13       state Sg =
14           set f = mult f₁ n continue Sh
15       state Sh =
16           return f
17
18   function mult a b =
19       state Sm =
20           →min.min c()
21       state Sn =
22           a(l.X̄) b(Ȳ) c(Z̄) →max.min a(X̄) b(Ȳ) c(Ȳ.Z̄)
23           return c
```

Fig. 2. High-level factorial sample. There are only 5 user defined "business" specific P rules (lines 3, 10, 11, 20, 22); the other P rules are automatically generated.

- States, parameters and variables are *local* (not visible outside the enclosing function).
- Statement **function** introduces a function, followed by an optional (space separated) list of parameters.
- A function invocation consists of (i) the keyword **set**, (ii) a parameter or variable name (which will receive the result), (iii) the function name, (iv) a (space separated) list of arguments, (v) the keyword **continue**, and (vi) the state to which the function must return.
- Each function argument is either (a) the name of a parameter or variable, or (b) the functor of a complex object.
- Each parameter or variable is implemented by a complex object with the same functor name, which contains its value.
- Complex objects which implement parameters and variables are automatically managed, but are also fully accessible within P system rules.
- We propose that function invocations use call-by-reference evaluations, followed by a copy-on-write, for parameters that are subsequently changed.

- Statement **state** starts a group of rules sharing the same start state (which is now omitted in individual rules). By default, if not explicit, the target state of each rule remains the current state.
- Inside a group, statements and rules are executed top-down, using a weak priority order.
- There is no implicit fall-through from one state to the textually following state.

The traces shown in Table 1 highlight critical steps which occur in the invocation of (fact 3).

We are still considering a default convention for the implicit return-to state after a function invocation, and, more important, extensions for parallel function invocations (which need parallel stacks). However, we are not further developing these ideas here.

Table 1. Traces for fact of 3. This table asserts the contents of (i) global hidden stacks and (ii) local parameters and variables, *before* a line starts. The small intervals between lines 14–16 indicate calls to mult, which are not detailed here.

Frame	Line	$\rho()$	$\pi()$	$n()$	$n_1()$	$f_1()$	$f()$
fact 3							
"	10	S_r	$p(l^3)$	l^3			
"	11	S_r	$p(l^3)$	l^3			
"	12	S_r	$p(l^3)$	l^3	l^2		◂
fact 2							
"	10	$S_g(S_r)$	$p(l^2)(p(l^3))$	l^2			
"	11	$S_g(S_r)$	$p(l^2)(p(l^3))$	l^2			
"	12	$S_g(S_r)$	$p(l^2)(p(l^3))$	l^2	l		
fact 1							
"	10	$S_g(S_g(S_r))$	$p(l)(p(l^2)(p(l^3)))$	l			
"	11	$S_g(S_g(S_r))$	$p(l)(p(l^2)(p(l^3)))$	l			
"	12	$S_g(S_g(S_r))$	$p(l)(p(l^2)(p(l^3)))$	l	λ		
fact 0							
"	10	$S_g(S_g(S_g(S_r)))$	$p(\lambda)(p(l)(p(l^2)(p(l^3))))$	λ			
"	16	$S_g(S_g(S_g(S_r)))$	$p(\lambda)(p(l)(p(l^2)(p(l^3))))$	λ			l
fact 1							
"	14	$S_g(S_g(S_r)))$	$p(l)(p(l^2)(p(l^3)))$	l		l	
"	16	$S_g(S_g(S_r)))$	$p(l)(p(l^2)(p(l^3)))$	l			l
fact 2							
"	14	$S_g(S_r)$	$p(l^2)(p(l^3))$	l^2		l	
"	16	$S_g(S_r)$	$p(l^2)(p(l^3))$	l^2			l^2
fact 3							
"	14	S_r	$p(l^3)$	l^3		l^2	
"	16	S_r	$p(l^3)$	l^3			l^6

7   Applications

7.1   Numerical P Systems

Consider first the numerical P system sample Π_1, given in Păun [17], which sequentially generates numbers in $\{n^2|n \geq 0\}$. Π_1 is equivalent to a P module, Π_1', with one single cell and a single generic rule involving three complex objects, a, b, c:

$$S_1 \, a(\overline{X}) \, b(\overline{Y}) \, c(\overline{Z}) \;\rightarrow_{\texttt{min.min}} S_1 \, a(\overline{XYYl}) \, b(\overline{Zl}) \, c(\overline{Zl})$$

Assuming that initially all three objects are empty, $a() \, b() \, c()$, after n steps, a contains $a(l^{n^2})$, which represents the number n^2.

Considering the arithmetic operations that can be efficiently modelled in P modules, we emit the following conjecture:

Conjecture 1. All numerical P systems with arithmetic functions on integers and rational numbers can be simulated in real-time by single cell P modules with complex objects.

Note that, if we are not interested in a faithful simulation, the above system can be straightforwardly implemented by the following single rule, which directly maps the algebraic rule $(n + 1)^2 = n^2 + 2n + 1$:

$$S_1 \, a(\overline{X}) \, b(\overline{Y}) \;\rightarrow_{\texttt{min.min}} S_1 \, a(\overline{XYYl}) \, b(\overline{Yl})$$

7.2   NP-Complete Problems

With complex objects, we can solve NP-complete problems using a single cell, a fixed-sized alphabet and a fixed-sized set of generic rules.

Consider, for example, the SAT problem; see Nagy [12] for a comprehensive overview of this problem and current state-of-art P solutions.

We start with an example. Consider the following formula, with $n = 3$ boolean variables:

$$f = (x_1 \vee \bar{x_2}) \wedge (x_1 \vee \bar{x_3}).$$

This formula can be expressed as a complex object, in fact a list of disjunctions, where each item is a list of conjunctions:

$$f = \wedge(\vee(x_1(\neg(x_2)))(\vee(x_1(\neg x_3)))).$$

As such formulas can quickly become unwieldy, we use a simplified notation for list structures, inspired from list structures in System F based functional programming languages:

$$a(d)(b(e)(c(f))) = [a(d); b(e); c(f)] = [a(d) : [b(e); c(f)]] = [a(d) : [b(e) : [c(f)]]]$$

With this notation, our formula f can be represented as:

$$f = \wedge[\vee[x_1; \neg(x_2)]; \vee[x_1; \neg(x_3)]].$$

To map our formula to a fixed vocabulary, we represent x_n by the complex object $x(l^n)$. Finally, our formula f can be represented as:

$$f = \wedge[\vee[x(l); \neg(x(ll))]; \vee[x(l); \neg(x(lll))]].$$

To check its satisfiability, we use a naive brute force approach: we create $2^n = 2^3 = 8$ dictionary complex objects, all named v, corresponding to all possible truth $(0/1)$ assignments of our $n = 3$ variables:

$$v(m(x(l), 0).m(x(ll), 0).m(x(lll), 0))$$
$$v(m(x(l), 0).m(x(ll), 0).m(x(lll), 1))$$
$$v(m(x(l), 0).m(x(ll), 1).m(x(lll), 0))$$
$$v(m(x(l), 0).m(x(ll), 1).m(x(lll), 1))$$
$$v(m(x(l), 1).m(x(ll), 0).m(x(lll), 0))$$
$$v(m(x(l), 1).m(x(ll), 0).m(x(lll), 1))$$
$$v(m(x(l), 1).m(x(ll), 1).m(x(lll), 0))$$
$$v(m(x(l), 1).m(x(ll), 1).m(x(lll), 1))$$

All these dictionaries can be built in parallel by the following rules, starting from an empty dictionary, $v()$, and a variable $n(\overline{N})$, which indicates the number of boolean variables; if this number is not given, it can be easily computed by scanning the given formula (this step is not detailed here):

$$S_1\ n(l\overline{N})\ v(\overline{M}) \rightarrow_{\text{max.min}} S_1\ n(\overline{N})\ v(m(x(l\overline{N}), 0).\overline{M})\ v(m(x(l\overline{N}), 1).\overline{M})$$
$$S_1\ n()\ v(\overline{M}) \quad \rightarrow_{\text{max.min}} S_2\ w(t(1), s(0), v(\overline{M}))$$

Next, we evaluate the given formula, f, in parallel over all existing dictionaries, v, which are now enclosed in larger complex objects, w. The partial results are stored in variables s, for the current disjunction, initially $s(0)$, and t, for the whole formula (a conjunction), initially $t(1)$. These variables start with default values for their corresponding boolean operations and are updated while the formula is evaluated left-to-right. The evaluation looks at the top variable in the top conjunction and picks its value from the associated dictionary. When the top conjunction becomes empty, the value of s is and-ed to the value of t, and then variable s is reset to 0, $s(0)$, to start the next disjunction. When there is no other disjunction, the evaluation has ended and t contains the correct evaluation value according to the current dictionary.

For clarity, we use the convenience *abbreviations* (abbreviations are *not* objects) $v_{ijk} = v(m(x(l), i).m(x(ll), j).m(x(lll), k))$, i.e. $x_1 = i$, $x_2 = j$, $x_3 = k$. The following two derivations illustrate the step-by-step evaluation of our formula, f, using the dictionaries v_{000} and v_{001}:

$$\wedge[\vee[\mathbf{x(1)}; \neg(x(ll))]; \vee[x(l); \neg(x(lll))]]\ w(t(1), s(0), v_{000}) \Rightarrow$$
$$\wedge[\vee[\neg(\mathbf{x(ll)})]; \vee[x(l); \neg(x(lll))]]\ w(t(1), s(0), v_{000}) \Rightarrow$$
$$\wedge[\vee[]; \vee[x(l); \neg(x(lll))]]\ w(t(1), s(1), v_{000}) \Rightarrow$$
$$\wedge[\vee[\mathbf{x(1)}; \neg(x(lll))]]\ w(t(1), s(0), v_{000}) \Rightarrow$$
$$\wedge[\vee[\neg(\mathbf{x(lll)})]]\ w(t(1), s(0), v_{000}) \Rightarrow$$
$$\wedge[\vee[]]\ w(t(1), s(1), v_{000}) \Rightarrow$$
$$\wedge[]\ w(t(1), s(0), v_{000}) \Rightarrow$$
$$t(1)$$

and

$$\land[\lor[\mathbf{x(1)};\neg(x(ll))];\lor[x(l);\neg(x(lll))]]\ w(t(1),s(0),v_{001}) \Rightarrow$$
$$\land[\lor[\neg(\mathbf{x(11)})];\lor[x(l);\neg(x(lll))]]\ w(t(1),s(0),v_{001}) \Rightarrow$$
$$\land[\lor[];\lor[x(l);\neg(x(lll))]]\ w(t(1),s(1),v_{001}) \Rightarrow$$
$$\land[\lor[\mathbf{x(1)};\neg(x(lll))]]\ w(t(1),s(0),v_{001}) \Rightarrow$$
$$\land[\lor[\neg(\mathbf{x(111)})]]\ w(t(1),s(0),v_{001}) \Rightarrow$$
$$\land[\lor[]]\ w(t(1),s(0),v_{001}) \Rightarrow$$
$$\land[]\ w(t(0),s(0),v_{001}) \Rightarrow$$
$$t(0)$$

Without using usual boolean shortcuts, these evaluations can be completed by following rules (using the simplified list notation, for clarity):

$$S_2 \land [\lor[\neg(\mathbf{x(\overline{X})}):D]:C]\ w(t(T),s(S),v(\overline{P}.m(\mathbf{x(\overline{X})},V).\overline{Q}))$$
$$\rightarrow_{\mathtt{max.min}} S_2 \land [\lor[D]:C]\ w(t(T),s(Z),v(\overline{P}.m(\mathbf{x(\overline{X})},V).\overline{Q}))\ |\ e(S,V,Z)$$
$$S_2 \land [\lor[\mathbf{x(\overline{X})}:D]:C]\ w(t(T),s(S),v(\overline{P}.m(\mathbf{x(\overline{X})},V).\overline{Q}))$$
$$\rightarrow_{\mathtt{max.min}} S_2 \land [\lor[D]:C]\ w(t(T),s(Z),v(\overline{P}.m(\mathbf{x(\overline{X})},V).\overline{Q}))\ |\ d(S,V,Z)$$
$$S_2 \land [\lor[]:C]\ w(t(T),s(S),v(\overline{M}))$$
$$\rightarrow_{\mathtt{max.min}} S_2 \land [C]\ w(t(Z),s(0),v(\overline{M}))\ |\ c(T,S,Z)$$
$$S_2 \land []\ w(t(T),s(S),v(\overline{M}))$$
$$\rightarrow_{\mathtt{max.min}} S_3\ t(T)$$

where $c()$, $d()$ and e are "read-only" internal tables for required boolean operations, given as complex objects (intuitively, these represent tables for $x \land y$, $x \lor y$, $x \lor \bar{y}$, respectively):

$$c(0,0,0)\ c(0,1,0)\ c(1,0,0)\ c(1,1,1)$$
$$d(0,0,0)\ d(0,1,1)\ d(1,0,1)\ d(1,1,1)$$
$$e(0,0,1)\ e(0,1,0)\ e(1,0,1)\ e(1,1,1)$$

The final rules collect and reduce the individual results, $t()$. In our case, the formula f is satisfiable, for example for $x_1 = 0$, $x_2 = 0$, $x_3 = 0$.

We have used a single cell, a fixed alphabet, $\{0, 1, x, l, \lor, \land, \neg, c, d, e, v, m, w, s, t\}$, and essentially just 6 generic rules and 3 states. In this example, we used only the most basic brute force approach; however, better variants are possible.

A similar approach seems to work well for other NP-complete problems, for example, the graph colouring problem; see Gheorghe et al. [7] for state-of-art P solutions of this problem. We emit the following conjecture:

Conjecture 2. Any NP-complete problems can be solved by a single cell P module with a fixed sized atomic alphabet and a fixed sized set of generic rules.

8   Conclusions

Despite their exceptional theoretical and modelling power, P systems seem to remain difficult to use for large practical applications, apparently requiring large varying size unstructured rulesets that can be difficult to verify. We want to show that this need not be the case, that there are ways to increase their usability.

This paper presents evidence that complex objects can enable a high-level programming style, with fixed sized alphabets and rulesets, adequate data structures and useful functional programming elements. We have previously used complex objects to successfully model and even improve large practical applications, ranging from computer vision to complex graph theoretical problems and to well-known critical distributed algorithms. Here we attempt to generalise our field-proven methods and sketch how to apply similar techniques to other, more theoretical, domains: numerical P systems and NP-complete problems.

The presented evidence suggests that complex objects could enable a more advanced high-level functional programming style, including: local functions (functions inside functions), closures, memoizations (i.e. top-down dynamic programming), combinators (e.g. the Y combinator), monads and meta-programming. A follow-up paper will address these topics.

Many of our extensions can be directly mapped on modern computing platforms, bypassing a possible translation to traditional simpler objects and rules, which opens the way towards more efficient general purpose simulators.

Acknowledgments. The work of RN and FI was partially supported by a grant of the Romanian National Authority for Scientific Research, CNCS–UEFISCDI, project number PN-II-ID-PCE-2011-3-0688. We are indebted to the anonymous reviewers for their valuable comments and suggestions.

References

1. Alhazov, A., Bonchis, C., Ciobanu, G., Izbasa, G.: Encodings and arithmetic operations in P systems. In: Gutierrez-Naranjo, M., Păun, G., Riscos-Nunez, A., Romero-Campero, F.J. (eds.) Brainstorming Week on Membrane Computing, vol. 2, pp. 1–28. Universidad de Sevilla (2006)
2. Alhazov, A., Ivanov, S., Rogozhin, Y.: Polymorphic P systems. In: Gheorghe, M., Hinze, T., Păun, G., Rozenberg, G., Salomaa, A. (eds.) CMC 2010. LNCS, vol. 6501, pp. 81–94. Springer, Heidelberg (2010)
3. Bălănescu, T., Nicolescu, R., Wu, H.: Asynchronous P systems. International Journal of Natural Computing Research 2(2), 1–18 (2011)
4. Dinneen, M.J., Kim, Y.-B., Nicolescu, R.: A faster P solution for the Byzantine agreement problem. In: Gheorghe, M., Hinze, T., Păun, G., Rozenberg, G., Salomaa, A. (eds.) CMC 2010. LNCS, vol. 6501, pp. 175–197. Springer, Heidelberg (2010)
5. Dinneen, M.J., Kim, Y.B., Nicolescu, R.: P systems and the Byzantine agreement. Journal of Logic and Algebraic Programming 79(6), 334–349 (2010)
6. ElGindy, H., Nicolescu, R., Wu, H.: Fast distributed DFS solutions for edge-disjoint paths in digraphs. In: Csuhaj-Varjú, E., Gheorghe, M., Rozenberg, G., Salomaa, A., Vaszil, G. (eds.) CMC 2012. LNCS, vol. 7762, pp. 173–194. Springer, Heidelberg (2013)

7. Gheorghe, M., Ipate, F., Lefticaru, R., Pérez-Jiménez, M., Turcanu, A., Valencia Cabrera, L., Garcia-Quismondo, M., Mierla, L.: 3-col problem modelling using simple kernel P systems. Int. J. Comput. Math. 90(4), 816–830 (2013)

8. Gimel'farb, G., Gong, R., Nicolescu, R., Delmas, P.: Concurrent propagation for solving ill-posed problems of global discrete optimisation. In: 2012 21st International Conference on Pattern Recognition Pattern Recognition (ICPR), pp. 1864–1867 (2012)

9. Gimel'farb, G., Nicolescu, R., Ragavan, S.: P systems in stereo matching. In: Real, P., Diaz-Pernil, D., Molina-Abril, H., Berciano, A., Kropatsch, W. (eds.) CAIP 2011, Part II. LNCS, vol. 6855, pp. 285–292. Springer, Heidelberg (2011)

10. Gimel'farb, G., Nicolescu, R., Ragavan, S.: P system implementation of dynamic programming stereo. Journal of Mathematical Imaging and Vision, 1–14 (2012)

11. Manca, V., Lombardo, R.: Computing with multi-membranes. In: Gheorghe, M., Păun, G., Rozenberg, G., Salomaa, A., Verlan, S. (eds.) CMC 2011. LNCS, vol. 7184, pp. 282–299. Springer, Heidelberg (2012)

12. Nagy, B.: On efficient algorithms for SAT. In: Csuhaj-Varjú, E., Gheorghe, M., Rozenberg, G., Salomaa, A., Vaszil, G. (eds.) CMC 2012. LNCS, vol. 7762, pp. 295–310. Springer, Heidelberg (2013)

13. Nicolescu, R.: Parallel and distributed algorithms in P systems. In: Gheorghe, M., Păun, G., Rozenberg, G., Salomaa, A., Verlan, S. (eds.) CMC 2011. LNCS, vol. 7184, pp. 35–50. Springer, Heidelberg (2012)

14. Nicolescu, R., Wu, H.: BFS solution for disjoint paths in P systems. In: Calude, C.S., Kari, J., Petre, I., Rozenberg, G. (eds.) UC 2011. LNCS, vol. 6714, pp. 164–176. Springer, Heidelberg (2011)

15. Nicolescu, R., Wu, H.: New solutions for disjoint paths in P systems. Natural Computing 11, 637–651 (2012)

16. Păun, G.: Computing with membranes. Journal of Computer and System Sciences 61(1), 108–143 (2000)

17. Păun, G., Păun, R.: Membrane computing and economics: Numerical P systems. Fundam. Inf. 73(1,2), 213–227 (2006)

18. Păun, G., Rozenberg, G., Salomaa, A.: The Oxford Handbook of Membrane Computing. Oxford University Press, Inc., New York (2010)

19. Wu, H.: Minimum spanning tree in P systems. In: Proceedings of the Asian Conference on Membrane Computing (ACMC 2012), Wuhan, China, October 15-18, pp. 88–104 (2012)

In Search of a Structure of Fractals
by Using Membranes as Hyperedges

Adam Obtułowicz

Institute of Mathematics, Polish Academy of Sciences
Śniadeckich 8, P.O.B. 21, 00-956 Warsaw, Poland
A.Obtulowicz@impan.pl

Abstract. The internal structure of the iterations of Koch curve and
Sierpiński gasket—the known fractals [4]—is described in terms of multi-
hypergraphical membrane systems related to membrane structures [13]
and whose membranes are hyperedges of multi-hypergraphs used to define gluing patterns for the components of the iterations of the considered
fractals.

1 Introduction

One finds in [10] a more or less explicit conclusion that the birth of functional
analysis was accompanied by the emergence of various mathematical structures
(from vector space, abstract metric spaces and topological spaces to Hilbert
spaces, including spaces of functions) which were an antidotum against 'capri-
cious' intuitiveness of symbolic 'calculations' of early calculus.

This conclusion inspired the author of the present paper to search for structures of fractals and self-similarity against their intuitive explanations[1] proposed
e.g. in [9]:

*'Local' statements of self-similarity say something like 'almost any small pat-
tern observed in one part of the object can be observed throughout the object,
at all scales'. Global statements say something like 'the whole object consists of
several smaller copies of itself glued together'; more generally, there may be a
whole family of objects, each of which can be described as several objects in the
family glued together.*

*Viewed from another angle, a theory of global self-similarity is a theory of
recursive decomposition.*

One should point out here that in a large extent the concepts of fractals and
self-similarity have been already described precisely in terms of iterated function
systems with their attractors constructed by using the tools of functional analysis (Hahn–Banach fix point theorem) [4] and domain theory (Tarski fix point
theorem) [3]. But a translation from the language of the above intuitive explanation to the language of some derived concepts from the precise description of

---

[1] The explanations suggested by the visual presentations of the iterations of some
fractals seen in the books and many articles about fractals.

A. Alhazov et al. (Eds.): CMC 2013, LNCS 8340, pp. 301–307, 2014.

fractals and self-similarity (e.g. the trees induced by iterated function systems, cf. [3]) is not effortless and not yet ready.

Thus searching for structure of fractals and self-similarity is approached by various mathematicians, cf. [7], [9], not necessarily motivated explicitly by a need of the above translation.

The goal of the paper is to propose an approach to searching for structure of fractals which could provide the above translation. We describe in Section 3 the internal structure of the iterations of Koch curve and Sierpiński gasket—the known fractals [4]—in terms of multi-hypergraphical membrane systems related to membrane structures [13] and whose membranes are hyperedges of multi-hypergraphs used to define gluing patterns for the components of the iterations of the considered fractals.

2   Multi-hypergraphical Membrane Systems

We introduce the following new concepts.

By a *directed multi-hypergraph* we mean a structure $\mathcal{G}$ given by its *set* $E(\mathcal{G})$ *of hyperedges*, its *set* $V(\mathcal{G})$ *of vertices* and the *source* and *target* mappings

$$s_{\mathcal{G}} : E(\mathcal{G}) \to \mathcal{P}(V(\mathcal{G})), \quad t_{\mathcal{G}} : E(\mathcal{G}) \to \mathcal{P}(V(\mathcal{G}))$$

such that $V(\mathcal{G})$ together with

$$\{(\mathcal{V}_1, \mathcal{V}_2) \,|\, s_{\mathcal{G}}(e) = \mathcal{V}_1 \text{ and } t_{\mathcal{G}}(e) = \mathcal{V}_2 \text{ for some } e \in E(\mathcal{G})\}$$

form a directed hypergraph as in [5], where $\mathcal{P}(X)$ denotes the set of all subsets of a set X.

We say that two directed multi-hypergraphs $\mathcal{G}, \mathcal{G}'$ are *isomorphic* if there exist two bijections $h : V(\mathcal{G}) \to V(\mathcal{G}')$, $h' : E(\mathcal{G}) \to E(\mathcal{G}')$ such that

$$s_{\mathcal{G}'}(h'(e)) = \{h(v) \,|\, v \in s_{\mathcal{G}}(e)\} \text{ and } t_{\mathcal{G}'}(h'(e)) = \{h(v) \,|\, v \in t_{\mathcal{G}}(e)\}$$

for all $e \in E(\mathcal{G})$.

Membrane structures in [13] are simply finite trees with nodes labelled by multisets, where the finite trees have a natural visual presentation by Venn diagrams and the tree nodes are called *membranes*.

We introduce (*directed*) *multi-hypergraphical membrane systems* to be finite trees with nodes labelled by (directed) multi-hypergraphs.

We consider directed multi-hypergraphical membrane systems of a special feature described formally in the following way.

A *multi-hyperedge membrane system* $\mathcal{S}$ is given by:

– the *underlying tree* $\mathbb{T}_{\mathcal{S}}$ of $\mathcal{S}$ which is a finite graph given by its set $V(\mathbb{T}_{\mathcal{S}})$ of *vertices*, its set $E(\mathbb{T}_{\mathcal{S}}) \subseteq V(\mathbb{T}_{\mathcal{S}}) \times V(\mathbb{T}_{\mathcal{S}})$ of *edges*, and its *root* r which is a distinguished vertex such that for every vertex v different from r there exists a unique path from v into r in $\mathbb{T}_{\mathcal{S}}$, where for every vertex v we define $\mathrm{rel}(v) = \{v' \,|\, (v', v) \in E(\mathbb{T}_{\mathcal{S}})\}$ and in trivial case $V(\mathbb{T}_{\mathcal{S}}) = \{r\}$ we assume $E(\mathbb{T}_{\mathcal{S}}) = \varnothing$;

- a family $(G_v \mid v \in V(\mathbb{T}_S))$ of finite directed multi-hypergraphs for G_v given by its set $V(G_v)$ of *vertices*, its set $E(G_v)$ of *edges*, its *source function* $s_v : E(G_v) \to \mathcal{P}(V(G_v))$, and its *target function* $t_v : E(G_v) \to \mathcal{P}(V(G_v))$ such that the following conditions hold:
  1) $E(G_v) = \mathrm{rel}(v)$,
  2) $V(G_v)$ is empty for every *elementary* vertex v, i.e. such that $\mathrm{rel}(v)$ is empty.

The above multi-hypergraphical membrane systems can be drawn by using Venn diagrams with discs or boxes d_v corresponding to vertices v of $\mathbb{T}_S$.

One can expect the applications of multi-hypergraphical membrane systems for modelling various hierarchically organized systems of nested modules (hyperedges) interconnected by many input and output lines (vertices), where the module interactions are described by source and target functions. These systems of modules appear in computer science, where the modules are complex actions, instructions, transitions (e.g. of structured Petri nets [2]), etc., from state charts [6], models of systemC components [17], the systems discussed in [1], to the semantics of some extensions of formal systems in [12], [17], and hierarchical specifications [15].

3   Koch Curve and Sierpiński Gasket

We describe in this section the iterations of Koch curve and Sierpiński gasket [8], [4], [14] in terms of multi-hypergraphical membrane systems.

For natural numbers $n > 0$ and $i \in \{\text{Koch}, \text{Sierp}\}$ we define multi-hyperedge membrane systems $\mathcal{S}_n^i$ in the following way:

- the underlying tree $\mathbb{T}_n^i$ of $\mathcal{S}_n^i$ is such that
  - the set $V(\mathbb{T}_n^i)$ of vertices is the set of all strings (sequences) of length not greater than n of digits in $D^{\text{Sierp}} = \{1, 2, 3\}$ for $i = \text{Sierp}$, and in $D^{\text{Koch}} = \{1, 2, 3, 4\}$ for $i = \text{Koch}$,
  - the set $E(\mathbb{T}_n^i)$ of edges of $\mathbb{T}_n^i$ is such that $E(\mathbb{T}_n^i) = \{(\Gamma j, \Gamma) \mid \{\Gamma j, \Gamma\} \subset V(\mathbb{T}_n^i)$ and $j \in D^i\}$ with source and target functions being the projections on the first and the second component, respectively, where Γj is the string obtained by juxtaposition a new digit j on the right end of Γ,
- the family $(G_\Gamma^i \mid \Gamma \in V(\mathbb{T}_n^i))$ of directed multi-hypergraphs of $\mathcal{S}_n^i$ is such that for every non-elementary vertex $\Gamma \in V(\mathbb{T}_n^i)$, i.e. with $\mathrm{rel}(\Gamma) \neq \varnothing$, G_Γ^i is determined in the following way:
  - for $i = \text{Koch}$ if Γ is the empty string, then the directed multi-hypergraph G_Γ^i is such that $V(G_\Gamma^i)$ is a five element set $\{v_0, \ldots, v_4\}$, $E(G_\Gamma^i) = \{\Gamma j \mid j \in D^i\}$, and the source and target functions of G_Γ^i are given by

$$s_{G_\Gamma^i}(\Gamma j) = \{v_{j-1}\}, \quad t_{G_\Gamma^i}(\Gamma j) = \{v_j\} \text{ for all } j \in \{1, \ldots, 4\},$$

where

$$v_0 = (0, 0), \ v_1 = (\tfrac{1}{3}, 0), \ v_2 = (\tfrac{1}{2}, \tfrac{2}{2\sqrt{3}}), \ v_3 = (\tfrac{2}{3}, 0), \ v_4 = (1, 0),$$

- for $i = $ Sierp if Γ is the empty string, then the directed multi-hypergraph G_Γ^i is such that $V(G_\Gamma^i)$ is a six element set $\{v_0, \ldots, v_5\}$, $E(G_\Gamma^i) = \{\Gamma j \mid j \in D^i\}$, and the source and target functions of G_Γ^i are given by

$$s_{G_\Gamma^i}(\Gamma 3) = \{v_1, v_2\}, \qquad t_{G_\Gamma^i}(\Gamma 3) = \{v_0\},$$
$$s_{G_\Gamma^i}(\Gamma j) = \{v_{j+2}, v_{j+3}\}, \qquad t_{G_\Gamma^i}(\Gamma j) = \{v_j\} \text{ for } j \in \{1, 2\},$$

where

$$v_0 = (\tfrac{1}{2}, \tfrac{\sqrt{3}}{2}),$$
$$v_1 = (\tfrac{1}{4}, \tfrac{\sqrt{3}}{4}), \quad v_2 = (\tfrac{3}{4}, \tfrac{\sqrt{3}}{4}),$$
$$v_3 = (0, 0), \quad v_4 = (\tfrac{1}{2}, 0), \quad v_5 = (1, 0),$$

- if a non-elementary vertex Γ of $\mathbb{T}_n^i$ is of the form[2] $k\Omega$ for $k \in D^i$ and a string Ω of digits in D^i, then

$$V(G_\Gamma^i) = \{f_k^i(v) \mid v \in V(G_\Omega^i)\}, \quad E(G_\Gamma^i) = \{\Gamma j \mid j \in D^i\},$$

and

$$\delta_{G_\Gamma^i}(\Gamma j) = \{f_k^i(v) \mid v \in \delta_{G_\Omega^i}(\Omega j)\} \quad \text{for all } j \in D^i \text{ and } \delta \in \{s, t\}$$

where f_k^i is the k-th function of the iterated function system given in Appendix for Koch curve in the case $i = $ Koch and for Sierpiński gasket in the case $i = $ Sierp, respectively.

Lemma. *For all natural numbers $n > 0$ and $i \in \{\text{Koch, Sierp}\}$ the multi-hyperedge membrane system $\mathcal{S}_n^i$ is such that for every non-elementary vertex Γ of $\mathbb{T}_n^i$ the directed multi-hypergraph G_Γ^i is isomorphic to G_Λ^i for empty string Λ—the root of $\mathbb{T}_n^i$.*

Proof. We prove the lemma by induction on n and by using the property of the functions of the iterated function systems for Koch curve and Sierpiński gasket that they are injections.

For all natural numbers $n > 0$ and $i \in \{\text{Koch, Sierp}\}$ we define a *geometrical realization* of $\mathcal{S}_n^i$, denoted by $\text{space}(\mathcal{S}_n^i)$, to be a subset of $\mathbb{R}^2$ ($\mathbb{R}^2$ is a Cartesian product of two copies of the set $\mathbb{R}$ of real numbers) which is the n-th iteration of Koch curve for $i = $ Koch and the n-th iteration of Sierpiński gasket for $i = $ Sierp, i.e.

$$\text{space}(\mathcal{S}_1^{\text{Koch}}) = \bigcup_{j \in D^{\text{Koch}}} f_j^{\text{Koch}}(\text{interval}),$$

$$\text{space}(\mathcal{S}_1^{\text{Sierp}}) = \bigcup_{j \in D^{\text{Sierp}}} f_j^{\text{Sierp}}(\text{equitriang}),$$

$$\text{space}(\mathcal{S}_{n+1}^i) = \bigcup_{j \in D^i} f_j^i(\text{space}(\mathcal{S}_n^i)) \text{ for } i \in \{\text{Koch, Sierp}\}$$

---

[2] The form $k\Omega$ of Γ is understood that the first element of Γ is k followed by the string Ω.

where $f_j^i(X)$ is the image of a set X for f_j^i, interval $= \{(t,0) \,|\, t \in \mathbb{R},\ 0 \leq t \leq 1\}$, and equitriang is the union of the interior and the frontier of the equilateral triangle in $\mathbb{R}^2$ whose vertices are $(0,0)$, $(\frac{1}{2}, \frac{\sqrt{3}}{2})$, $(1,0)$.

Theorem. *For all natural numbers $n > 0$ and $i \in \{\mathrm{Koch, Sierp}\}$ the set space $(\mathcal{S}_n^i)$ is not an amorphous set of points of $\mathbb{R}^2$ but it is a structured set by its hierarchically organized decomposition into subsets according to the underlying tree $\mathbb{T}_n^i$ of $\mathcal{S}_n^i$, where the components of the decomposition form a family $C_\Gamma^{i,n}$ ($\Gamma \in V(\mathbb{T}_n^i)$, Γ is non-empty and is not an elementary vertex of $\mathbb{T}_n^i$) such that:*

- *if Γ is of the form $j\Omega$ for $j \in D^i$ and a string Ω of digits in D^i, then*
  - *for the empty string Ω the component $C_{j\Omega}^{i,n}$ is $f_j^i(\mathrm{space}(\mathcal{S}_{n-1}^i))$,*
  - *for a non-empty string Ω the component $C_{j\Omega}^{i,n}$ is $f_j^i(C_\Omega^{i,n-1})$ for the Ω-th component $C_\Omega^{i,n-1}$ of space$(\mathcal{S}_{n-1}^i)$,*
- *for $m_i = \max D^i$ the m_i components $C_{\Gamma 1}^{i,n}, \ldots, C_{\Gamma m_i}^{i,n}$ are glued according to the pattern given by G_Γ^i understood that*

$$\delta(\Gamma j') \cap \gamma(\Gamma j'') = C_{\Gamma j'}^{i,n} \cap C_{\Gamma j''}^{i,n}$$

for all δ, γ, j', j'' with $\{\delta, \gamma\} \subseteq \{s_{G_\Gamma^i}^i, t_{G_\Gamma^i}^i\}$, $\{j', j''\} \subseteq D^i$, and $j' \neq j''$.

Proof. The theorem is an immediate consequence of the adopted definitions.

The above multi-hypergraphical membrane systems can be drawn by using Venn diagrams with discs or boxes d_Γ corresponding to vertices Γ of $\mathbb{T}_n^i$ such that d_{Γ_j} is an immediate subset of d_Γ.

Conclusion

The above lemma and theorem provide the translation claimed in the introduction of the paper for iterations of fractals in the cases of Koch curve and Sierpiński gasket. In this translation the main feature of self-similarity described in its 'local' statement corresponds to the isomorphisms of hypergraphs 'giving' the gluing patterns (see the above theorem) for every level of hierarchical organization of the decomposition, where the levels of hierarchical organization coincide with scale layers.

The iterations of jD-Cantor set ($j \in \{1,2,3\}$) require another approach which is proposed in [11], where multigraphical membrane systems are used with vertices as membranes. Thus one may say that the approach proposed in the present paper is a '*hyperedges as membranes*' approach.

Appendix

Basing on [14] we present the iterated function systems whose attractors are Koch curve and Sierpiński gasket, respectively. These iterated function systems consist of the bijections from $\mathbb{R}^2$ onto $\mathbb{R}^2$ described in terms of matrices as follows:

- for Koch curve

$$f_1^{\text{Koch}}(\mathbf{x}) = \begin{bmatrix} 1/3 & 0 \\ 0 & 1/3 \end{bmatrix} \mathbf{x} \qquad \text{scale by } 1/3$$

$$f_2^{\text{Koch}}(\mathbf{x}) = \begin{bmatrix} 1/6 & -\sqrt{3}/6 \\ \sqrt{3}/6 & 1/6 \end{bmatrix} \mathbf{x} + \begin{bmatrix} 1/3 \\ 0 \end{bmatrix} \qquad \text{scale by } 1/3, \text{ rotate by } 60°$$

$$f_3^{\text{Koch}}(\mathbf{x}) = \begin{bmatrix} 1/6 & \sqrt{3}/6 \\ -\sqrt{3}/6 & 1/6 \end{bmatrix} \mathbf{x} + \begin{bmatrix} 1/2 \\ \sqrt{3}/6 \end{bmatrix} \qquad \text{scale by } 1/3, \text{ rotate by } -60°$$

$$f_4^{\text{Koch}}(\mathbf{x}) = \begin{bmatrix} 1/3 & 0 \\ 0 & 1/3 \end{bmatrix} \mathbf{x} + \begin{bmatrix} 2/3 \\ 0 \end{bmatrix} \qquad \text{scale by } 1/3$$

- for Sierpiński gasket

$$f_1^{\text{Sierp}}(\mathbf{x}) = \begin{bmatrix} 1/2 & 0 \\ 0 & 1/2 \end{bmatrix} \mathbf{x} \qquad \text{scale by } 1/2$$

$$f_2^{\text{Sierp}}(\mathbf{x}) = \begin{bmatrix} 1/2 & 0 \\ 0 & 1/2 \end{bmatrix} \mathbf{x} + \begin{bmatrix} 1/2 \\ 0 \end{bmatrix} \qquad \text{scale by } 1/2$$

$$f_3^{\text{Sierp}}(\mathbf{x}) = \begin{bmatrix} 1/2 & 0 \\ 0 & 1/2 \end{bmatrix} \mathbf{x} + \begin{bmatrix} 1/4 \\ \sqrt{3}/4 \end{bmatrix} \qquad \text{scale by } 1/2$$

References

1. Bruni, R., Gadducci, F., Lluch Lafuente, A.: An algebra of hierarchical graphs. In: Wirsing, M., Hofmann, M., Rauschmayer, A. (eds.) TGC 2010, LNCS, vol. 6084, pp. 205–221. Springer, Heidelberg (2010)
2. Cherkasova, L.A., Kotov, V.E.: Structured nets. In: Gruska, J., Chytil, M. (eds.) Mathematical Foundations of Computer Science. LNCS, vol. 118, pp. 242–251. Springer, Heidelberg (1981)
3. Edalat, A.: Domains for computation in mathematics, physics and exact real arithmetic. The Bulletin of Symbolic Logic 3, 401–452 (1997)
4. Falconer, K.: Fractal Geometry. Mathematical Foundations and Applications. Wiley, Hoboken (2003)
5. Gallo, G., Longo, G., Pallottino, S., Nguyen, S.: Directed hypergraphs and applications. Discrete Appl. Math. 42, 177–201 (1993)
6. Harel, D.: On Visual Formalisms. Comm. ACM 31, 514–530 (1988)
7. Hasuo, I., Jacobs, B., Niqui, M.: Coalgebraic representation theory of fractals. Electron. Notes Theor. Comput. Sci. 265, 351–368 (2010)
8. Hutchinson, J.E.: Fractals and self-similarity. Indiana Univ. Math. J. 30, 713–747 (1981)

9. Leinster, T.: A general theory of self-similarity. Adv. Math. 226, 2935–3017 (2011)
10. Narici, L., Beckenstein, E.: The Hahn–Banach theorem: the life and times. Topology Appl. 77, 193–211 (1997)
11. Obtułowicz, A.: Multigraphical membrane systems revisited. In: Csuhaj-Varjú, E., Gheorghe, M., Rozenberg, G., Salomaa, A., Vaszil, G. (eds.) CMC 2012. LNCS, vol. 7762, pp. 311–322. Springer, Heidelberg (2013)
12. Orlarey, Y., Fober, D., Letz, S., Bilton, M.: Lambda calculus and music calculi. In: International Computer Music Conference ICMA 1994 (1994)
13. Păun, G.: Membrane Computing. An Introduction. Springer, Berlin (2002)
14. Riddle, L.: Classic iterated function systems, Koch curve, Sierpiński gasket, http://ecademy.agnesscott.edu/~lriddle/ifs/kcurve/kcurve.htm, http://ecademy.agnesscott.edu/~lriddle/ifs/siertri/siertri.htm
15. Rozenkrantz, D.J., Hunt III, H.B.: The complexity of processing hierarchical specifications. SIAM J. Comput. 22, 627–649 (1993)
16. Stefanescu, G.: The algebra of flownomials, Report, Technical University Munich (1994)
17. Vallée, N., Monsuez, B.: A formal model of system components using fractal hypergraphs. In: Proc. of the Int. Multiconference of Engineers and Computer Scientists, IMECS 2010, Hong Kong, vol. II (2010)

The Relevance of the Environment on the Efficiency of Tissue P Systems

Mario J. Pérez-Jiménez[1], Agustín Riscos-Núñez[1], Miquel Rius-Font[2], and Luis Valencia-Cabrera[1]

[1] Research Group on Natural Computing
Department of Computer Science and Artificial Intelligence
University of Sevilla
Avda. Reina Mercedes s/n, 41012 Sevilla, Spain
{marper,ariscosn,lvalencia}@us.es
[2] Department of Applied Mathematics IV
Universitat Politécnica de Catalunya, Spain
mrius@ma4.upc.edu

Abstract. The efficiency of computational devices is usually expressed in terms of their capability to solve computationally hard problems in polynomial time. This paper focuses on tissue P systems, whose efficiency has been shown for several scenarios where the number of cells in the system can grow exponentially, e.g. by using cell division rules or cell separation rules. Moreover, in the first case it suffices to consider very short communication rules with length bounded by two, and in the second one it is enough to consider communication rules with length at most three. This kind of systems have an environment with the property that objects initially located in it appear in an arbitrarily large number of copies, which is a somewhat unfair condition from a computational complexity point of view. In this context, we study the role played by the environment and its ability to handle infinitely many objects, in particular we consider tissue P systems whose environment is initially empty.

1 Introduction

Several different models of cell-like P systems have been successfully used to efficiently solve computationally hard problems by trading space for time. An exponential workspace is created in polynomial time by using some kind of rules, and then massive parallelism is used to simultaneously check all the candidate solutions. Inspired by living cells, several ways for obtaining exponential workspace in polynomial time were proposed: membrane division (*mitosis*) [12], membrane creation (*autopoiesis*) [5], and membrane separation (*membrane fission*) [8][1]. These three ways have given rise to the following models: *P systems with active*

---

[1] The name *separation rule* appeared earlier in [1], but with a slightly different definition.

A. Alhazov et al. (Eds.): CMC 2013, LNCS 8340, pp. 308–321, 2014.
© Springer-Verlag Berlin Heidelberg 2014

membranes, P systems with membrane creation, and *P systems with membrane separation,* respectively.

A new type of P systems, the so-called *tissue P systems,* was introduced in [7]. The hierarchical membrane structure that was commonly used in the first models, inspired on the way vesicles and compartments are arranged within a cell, is discarded. Instead, an arbitrary graph of connections among elementary membranes (now called *cells*) is considered. That is, the inspiration comes now not from a single cell but from a collection of cooperating cells within a multicellular organism, e.g. in a tissue. Moreover, the functioning of tissue P systems heavily relies on the intercellular communication, since objects can move under symport/antiport rules, but cannot be rewritten.

This paper addresses two models of tissue P systems which are of a great interest from a computational complexity point of view. The first one was presented in [14], where the definition of tissue P systems is combined with aspects of the definition of P systems with active membranes, yielding *tissue P systems with cell division.* In these models, cells may replicate, that is, the two new cells generated by a division rule have exactly the same objects except for at most one differing pair of objects. The second model that will be considered is *tissue P systems with cell separation* [9]. In this case, an alternative method for generating an exponential number of cells in linear time is used. When a cell divides, its contents are not replicated, but distributed, according to a fixed partition of the alphabet.

The paper is organized as follows. First, we recall the basic mathematical and theoretical background underlying the definitions of the two tissue P systems models mentioned above, together with the definition of complexity class in the membrane computing framework. Then, Section 3 compares the computational power achieved by cell division and by cell separation, evaluating in both cases the role of the environment. Some concluding remarks summarizing the borderlines of efficiency discussed in the paper are given in Section 4.

2   Tissue P Systems

Let us recall that an *alphabet* Γ is a non–empty set whose elements are called *symbols.* A *multiset* m over an alphabet Γ is a pair $m = (\Gamma, f)$ where $f : \Gamma \to \mathbb{N}$ is a mapping. If $m = (\Gamma, f)$ is a multiset then its *support* is defined as $supp(m) = \{x \in \Gamma \mid f(x) > 0\}$. A multiset is finite if its support is a finite set. Let $supp(m) = \{a_1, \ldots, a_k\}$ be the support of a finite multiset, m, then we will denote $m = a_1^{f(a_1)} \ldots a_k^{f(a_k)}$ (here the order is irrelevant), and we say that $f(a_1) + \ldots + f(a_k)$ is the cardinal of m, denoted by $|m|$. The empty multiset is denoted by λ. We also denote by $M_f(\Gamma)$ the set of all finite multisets over Γ.

Let $m_1 = (\Gamma, f_1)$ and $m_2 = (\Gamma, f_2)$ multisets over Γ. The *union* of m_1 and m_2, denoted by $m_1 + m_2$ is the multiset (Γ, g), where $g = f_1 + f_2$, that is, $g(x) = f_1(x) + f_2(x)$ for each $x \in \Gamma$. The *relative complement* of m_2 in m_1, denoted by $m_1 \setminus m_2$ is the multiset (Γ, g), where $g(x) = f_1(x) - f_2(x)$ if $f_1(x) \geq f_2(x)$ and $g(x) = 0$ otherwise.

Definition 1. *A basic tissue P system of degree $q \geq 1$ is a tuple*
$$\Pi = (\Gamma, \Sigma, \mathcal{E}, \mathcal{M}_1, \ldots, \mathcal{M}_q, \mathcal{R}, i_{in}, i_{out}), \text{ where:}$$

1. Γ *is a finite alphabet and $\mathcal{E}$ is a subset of Γ.*
2. Σ *is an (input) alphabet strictly contained in Γ such that $\mathcal{E} \cap \Sigma = \emptyset$.*
3. $\mathcal{M}_1, \ldots, \mathcal{M}_q$ *are finite multisets over $\Gamma \setminus \Sigma$.*
4. $\mathcal{R}$ *is a finite set of communication rules of the form $(i, u/v, j)$,*
   for $i, j \in \{0, 1, 2, \ldots, q\}, i \neq j$, $u, v \in M_f(\Gamma)$, and $|u + v| \neq 0$;
5. $i_{in} \in \{1, 2, \ldots, q\}$, *and $i_{out} \in \{0, 1, \ldots, q\}$.*

A *basic tissue P system* $\Pi = (\Gamma, \Sigma, \mathcal{E}, \mathcal{M}_1, \ldots, \mathcal{M}_q, \mathcal{R}, i_{in}, i_{out})$ of degree $q \geq 1$ can be viewed as a set of q cells, labelled by $1, \ldots, q$, with an environment labelled by 0 such that: (a) $\mathcal{M}_1, \ldots, \mathcal{M}_q$ are finite multisets over Γ representing the objects (elements in Γ) initially placed in the q cells of the system; (b) Σ is the input alphabet and $\mathcal{E}$ is the set of objects located initially in the environment of the system, all of them appearing in an *arbitrary number of copies*; and (c) i_{in} represents the input cell, and $i_{out} \in \{0, 1, \ldots, q\}$ indicates the *region* that stores the output of the system (which can be either a distinguished cell when $i_{out} \in \{1, \ldots, q\}$, or the environment when $i_{out} = 0$). If $\mathcal{E} = \emptyset$ then we say that the tissue P system is *without environment*.

A communication rule $(i, u/v, j)$ is *applicable* to regions i, j if the multiset u is contained in region i and multiset v is contained in region j. When applying a communication rule $(i, u/v, j)$, the objects of multiset u are sent from region i to region j and, simultaneously, the objects of multiset v are sent from region j to region i. The *length* of communication rule $(i, u/v, j)$ is defined as $|u| + |v|$.

The rules are used in a non-deterministic maximally parallel manner as customary in membrane computing. At each step, we apply a multiset of rules which is *maximal*: no further applicable rule can be added.

A *configuration* at any instant of a basic tissue P system is described by all multisets of objects over Γ associated with all the cells present in the system, and the multiset of objects over $\Gamma \setminus \mathcal{E}$ associated with the environment at that moment. Recall that there are infinitely many copies of objects from $\mathcal{E}$ in the environment, and hence this set is not properly changed along the computation. For each multiset m over the input alphabet Σ, the *initial configuration* with input m is $\mathcal{C}_0 = (\mathcal{M}_1, \cdots, \mathcal{M}_{i_{in}} + m, \cdots, \mathcal{M}_q; \emptyset)$. Therefore, we have an initial configuration associated with each input multiset m (over the input alphabet Σ) in this kind of systems. We will use the notation $(\Pi + m)$ to refer to a P system Π such that its initial configuration is the one associated with m. A configuration is a *halting configuration* if no rule of the system is applicable to it. We say that configuration $\mathcal{C}_1$ yields configuration $\mathcal{C}_2$ in one *transition step*, denoted by $\mathcal{C}_1 \Rightarrow_\Pi \mathcal{C}_2$, if we can pass from $\mathcal{C}_1$ to $\mathcal{C}_2$ by applying the rules from $\mathcal{R}$ following the previous remarks.

A *computation* of Π is a (finite or infinite) sequence of configurations such that: (a) the first term of the sequence is the initial configuration $\mathcal{C}_0$ of the system associated with a given input; (b) for each $n \geq 2$ the n–th configuration of the sequence is obtained from the previous configuration by applying a maximal multiset of rules of the system as described above; and (c) if the sequence is finite (called *halting computation*) then the last term of the sequence must be a halting configuration. Only halting computations give a result, which is encoded by the objects present in the output region i_{out} in the halting configuration. The result of a computation can be defined in various ways, just like in the cell-like case. Obviously, when the output is collected in the environment, symbols from $\mathcal{E}$ must be ignored.

If $\mathcal{C} = \{C_t\}_{0 \leq t \leq r}$ of Π ($r \in \mathbb{N}$) is a halting computation, then the *length of* $\mathcal{C}$, denoted by $|\mathcal{C}|$, is r.

2.1 Cell Division and Cell Separation

Reproduction is doubtlessly one of the fundamental mechanisms on every living being. Thus, there is a clear motivation to try to get inspiration from the various processes that generate new cells (or new membranes, in general) and to adapt them into the tissue P systems framework. Moreover, as mentioned in the Introduction, division rules (*mitosis*), and separation rules (*membrane fission*) have been already introduced for cell-like P systems [12,8].

Definition 2. *A tissue P system with cell division of degree $q \geq 1$ is a tuple $\Pi = (\Gamma, \Sigma, \mathcal{E}, \mathcal{M}_1, \ldots, \mathcal{M}_q, \mathcal{R}, i_{in}, i_{out})$, where:*

1. *$\Pi = (\Gamma, \Sigma, \mathcal{E}, \mathcal{M}_1, \ldots, \mathcal{M}_q, \mathcal{R}_c, i_{in}, i_{out})$ is a basic tissue P system, where $\mathcal{R}_c$ is the set of communication rules in $\mathcal{R}$.*
2. *$\mathcal{R}$ may also contain cell division rules of the form $[a]_i \rightarrow [b]_i[c]_i$, where $i \in \{1, 2, \ldots, q\}$, $i \neq i_{out}$ and $a, b, c \in \Gamma$.*

Definition 3. *A tissue P system with cell separation of degree $q \geq 1$ is a tuple $\Pi = (\Gamma, \Gamma_1, \Gamma_2, \Sigma, \mathcal{E}, \mathcal{M}_1, \ldots, \mathcal{M}_q, \mathcal{R}, i_{out})$, where:*

1. *$\Pi = (\Gamma, \Sigma, \mathcal{E}, \mathcal{M}_1, \ldots, \mathcal{M}_q, \mathcal{R}_c, i_{in}, i_{out})$ is a basic tissue P system, where $\mathcal{R}_c$ is the set of communication rules in $\mathcal{R}$.*
2. *$\{\Gamma_1, \Gamma_2\}$ is a partition of Γ, that is, $\Gamma = \Gamma_1 \cup \Gamma_2$, $\Gamma_1, \Gamma_2 \neq \emptyset$, $\Gamma_1 \cap \Gamma_2 = \emptyset$.*
3. *$\mathcal{R}$ may also contain cell separation rules of the form $[a]_i \rightarrow [\Gamma_1]_i[\Gamma_2]_i$, where $i \in \{1, \ldots, q\}$, $a \in \Gamma$ and $i \neq i_{out}$.*

A *tissue P system with cell division* is a basic tissue P system that allows cell division rules. When applying a division rule $[a]_i \rightarrow [b]_i[c]_i$, under the influence of object a, the cell with label i is divided into two cells with the same label; in the first copy, object a is replaced by object b, in the second one, object a is replaced by object c; all the other objects are replicated and copies of them are placed in the two new cells.

A *tissue P system with cell separation* is a basic tissue P system that allows cell separation rules. When applying a separation rule $[a]_i \rightarrow [\Gamma_1]_i[\Gamma_2]_i$, in reaction with an object a, the cell i is separated into two cells with the same label; at the same time, object a is consumed; all the other objects in the cell are distributed (not replicated): those from Γ_1 are placed in the first cell, while those from Γ_2 are placed in the second cell. The output cell i_{out} cannot be divided nor separated.

The label of a cell precisely identifies the rules which can be applied to it. Note that in the previous definitions $\{1, \ldots, q\}$ is used as the set of labels, but without loss of generality any finite set can be considered instead. The rules are used in a non-deterministic maximally parallel manner with the following restriction: when a cell is divided (or separated), the objects inside that cell do not get involved in any communication rule during this step. The two new resulting cells could participate in the interaction with other cells or the environment by means of communication rules at the next step – provided that they are not divided (or separated) again.

2.2   Recognizer Tissue P Systems

A *decision problem* is a pair (I_X, θ_X) where I_X is a language over a finite alphabet (whose elements are called *instances*) and θ_X is a total Boolean function over I_X. There are many different ways to describe instances of a decision problem, but we assume that each problem has associated with it a fixed *reasonable encoding scheme* (in the sense of [3], page 10) which provides a string associated with each problem instance. The *size* of an instance $u \in I_X$ is the length of the string associated with it by means of a reasonable encoding scheme.

A correspondence between decision problems and languages over a finite alphabet, can be established as follows. Given a decision problem $X = (I_X, \theta_X)$, its associated language is $L_X = \{w \in I_X : \theta_X(w) = 1\}$. Conversely, given a language L over an alphabet Σ, its associated decision problem is $X_L = (I_{X_L}, \theta_{X_L})$, where $I_{X_L} = \Sigma^*$, and $\theta_{X_L} = \{(x, 1) \mid x \in L\} \cup \{(x, 0) \mid x \notin L\}$. The solvability of decision problems is defined through the recognition of the languages associated with them by means of language recognizer devices.

Definition 4. *A* tissue P system *of degree* $q \geq 1$ *is a* recognizer *system if:*

1. *The working alphabet* Γ *has two distinguished objects* yes *and* no *being, at least, one copy of them present in some initial multisets, but none of them are present in the alphabet of the environment.*
2. *All computations halt.*
3. *If* C *is a computation of* Π, *then either object* yes *or object* no *(but not both) must have been released into the environment, and only at the last step of the computation.*

Note that, because of the first condition, the presence or absence of objects yes and no in the environment can be accounted for in any configuration. Note also that all computations are finite as a consequence of the second condition, and thus it is possible to refer to their "last step".

Given a recognizer tissue P system Π and a computation C of Π, we say that C is an *accepting computation* (respectively, *rejecting computation*) if object yes (respectively, object no) appears in the environment associated with the corresponding halting configuration of C. Note that, since Π is a recognizer system, neither object yes nor no appears in the environment associated with any non–halting configuration of C.

For each natural number $k \geq 1$, we denote by $\mathbf{TDC}(k)$ (respectively, $\mathbf{TSC}(k)$) the class of recognizer tissue P systems with cell division (respectively, with cell separation) and communication rules with length at most k. We denote by $\widehat{\mathbf{TDC}}(k)$ (respectively, $\widehat{\mathbf{TSC}}(k)$) the class of recognizer tissue P systems with cell division (respectively, with cell separation), with communication rules with length at most k, and without environment.

Now, we define what it means to solve a decision problem in the framework of tissue P systems efficiently and in a uniform way. Since we define each tissue P system to work on a finite number of inputs, to solve a decision problem we define a numerable family of tissue P systems.

Definition 5. *We say that a decision problem $X = (I_X, \theta_X)$ is solvable in a uniform way and polynomial time by a family $\mathbf{\Pi} = \{\Pi(n) \mid n \in \mathbb{N}\}$ of recognizer P systems if the following holds:*

1. *The family $\mathbf{\Pi}$ is polynomially uniform by Turing machines, that is, there exists a deterministic Turing machine working in polynomial time which constructs the system $\Pi(n)$ from $n \in \mathbb{N}$.*
2. *There exists a pair (cod, s) of polynomial-time computable functions over I_X such that:*
   (a) *for each instance $u \in I_X$, $s(u)$ is a natural number and $cod(u)$ is an input multiset of the system $\Pi(s(u))$;*
   (b) *for each $n \in \mathbb{N}$, $s^{-1}(n)$ is a finite set;*
   (c) *the family $\mathbf{\Pi}$ is polynomially bounded with regard to (X, cod, s), that is, there exists a polynomial function p, such that for each $u \in I_X$ every computation of $\Pi(s(u))$ with input $cod(u)$ is halting and it performs at most $p(|u|)$ steps;*
   (d) *the family $\mathbf{\Pi}$ is sound with regard to (X, cod, s), that is, for each $u \in I_X$, if there exists an accepting computation of $\Pi(s(u))$ with input $cod(u)$, then $\theta_X(u) = 1$;*
   (e) *the family $\mathbf{\Pi}$ is complete with regard to (X, cod, s), that is, for each $u \in I_X$, if $\theta_X(u) = 1$, then every computation of $\Pi(s(u))$ with input $cod(u)$ is an accepting one.*

From the soundness and completeness conditions above we deduce that every P system $\Pi(n)$ is *confluent*, in the following sense: every computation of a system with the *same* input multiset must always give the *same* answer.

Let $\mathbf{R}$ be a class of recognizer P systems. We denote by $\mathbf{PMC_R}$ the set of all decision problems which can be solved in a uniform way and polynomial time by means of families of systems from $\mathbf{R}$. The class $\mathbf{PMC_R}$ is closed under complement and polynomial–time reductions [16].

3 Computational Efficiency of Tissue P Systems without Environment

It is well known that tissue P systems with cell division and tissue P systems with cell separation are able to solve computationally hard problems efficiently.

Specifically, **NP**–complete problems have been solved in polynomial time in [19] by using families of tissue P systems with cell division and communication rules of length at most 2, and by using families of tissue P systems with cell separation and communication rules of length at most 3. Thus,

$$\mathbf{NP} \cup \mathbf{co} - \mathbf{NP} \subseteq \mathbf{PMC_{TDC(2)}} \cap \mathbf{PMC_{TSC(3)}}$$

In [4,9,10] it has been proved that only tractable problems can be efficiently solved by using families of tissue P systems with cell division and communication rules of length 1 (or with cell separation and communication rules of length bounded by 2). That is, $\mathbf{P} = \mathbf{PMC_{TDC(1)}} = \mathbf{PMC_{TSC(1)}} = \mathbf{PMC_{TSC(2)}}$. Therefore, in the framework of tissue P systems with cell division (respectively, cell separation), passing the maximum length of communication rules of the systems from 1 to 2 (respectively, from 2 to 3) amounts to passing from non–efficiency to efficiency, assuming that $\mathbf{P} \neq \mathbf{NP}$. That is, the cooperation of 2 objects (respectively, 3 objects) in the communication rules is a key feature that allows efficient solutions of **NP**–complete problems.

3.1 Efficiency of Tissue P Systems with Cell Division and without Environment

In this section, we give a family of tissue P systems with cell division, communication rules of length at most 2, and without environment which solves the HAM-CYCLE problem, a well known **NP**–complete problem [3], in polynomial time, according to Definition 5.

Let us recall that the HAM-CYCLE problem is the following: *given a directed graph, to determine whether or not there exists a Hamiltonian cycle in the graph.*

Our starting point will be the family $\mathbf{\Pi} = \{\Pi(n) \mid n \in \mathbb{N}\}$ of tissue P systems from **TDC(2)** provided in [19]. We will not recall in detail the definition of this solution, but let us provide an informal overview of the design. The authors follow a brute force approach, generating all possible combination of arcs from the graph, and then checking whether they represent a Hamiltonian cycle or not. Let us consider an arbitrary instance $G = (V, E)$ of the HAM-CYCLE problem, where $|V| = n$. In order to represent the generated paths, there are n special obects $(u, v)_1, \ldots (u, v)_n$ in the input multiset of the system for each arc $(u, v) \in E$. Having the object $(u, v)_i$ in the multiset of a cell after the generation stage is completed will mean "the arc (u, v) is the $i-th$ component of the path associated with this cell". All possible subsets of the input multiset are generated in the first stage of the computation, and then there is a checking stage that filters all invalid paths, as well as those which are not Hamiltonian cycles (a collection of auxiliary cells and symbols are used, but we will skip the details here). Finally, the computation ends with a final stage that sends the appropriate answer to the environment, depending on the results of all those checkings.

The idea of the solution presented here is the following: starting from the above mentioned family $\mathbf{\Pi}$, we construct a family $\mathbf{\Pi'} = \{\Pi'(n) \mid n \in \mathbb{N}\}$ of tissue P systems from $\widehat{\mathbf{TDC}}(2)$ such that $\Pi'(n)$ processes all instances G of HAM-CYCLE with n nodes. The construction is implemented according to Definition 6.2 in [15], in such a way that each $\Pi'(n)$ *simulates* its counterpart $\Pi(n)$ in an efficient way. We refer to [15] for details, but informally speaking, each computation from $\Pi'(n)$ matches (or "simulates") an equivalent one from $\Pi(n)$, except for a polynomial amount of additional auxiliary steps.

Let us recall that for each $n \in \mathbb{N}$, $\Pi(n)$ is the following tissue P system:

$$\Pi(n) = (\Gamma, \Sigma, \mathcal{E}, \mathcal{M}_{in}, \mathcal{M}_h, \mathcal{M}_y, \mathcal{M}_{yes}, \mathcal{M}_{no}, \mathcal{M}_{out},$$
$$\mathcal{M}_{e_{i,j,k}}(1 \leq i, j, k \leq n), \mathcal{M}_{c_i}(1 \leq i \leq n), \mathcal{R}, i_{in}, i_{out})$$

- The input alphabet is $\Sigma = \{(i,j)_k \mid 1 \leq i, j, k \leq n\}$.
- The working alphabet is

$$\Gamma = \{(i,j)_k, (i,j)'_k, (i,j)''_k \mid 1 \leq i, j, k \leq n\} \cup$$
$$\{(i,j)_{k,r}, (i,j)'_{k,r}, (i,j)''_{k,r} \mid 1 \leq i, j, k \leq n \wedge 1 \leq r \leq n^3\} \cup$$
$$\{w_i \mid 1 \leq i \leq n^3 + 6\} \cup \{c_r, h_r, y_r \mid 1 \leq r \leq n^3\} \cup$$
$$\{w, c, c', c'', h, h', h'', h''', y, y', y'', y''', y'''', x, yes, no, \#\}$$

- The alphabet of the environment is

$$\mathcal{E} = \{w_i \mid 1 \leq i \leq n^3 + 5\} \cup \{w, c'', y'', h'', y''', h''', y''''\}$$

- The initial multisets are

$$\begin{cases} \mathcal{M}_{in} = c^n\, y\, h \\ \mathcal{M}_{e_{i,j,k}} = (i,j)''_{k,n^3},\ 1 \leq i, j, k \leq n \\ \mathcal{M}_{c_i} = c_{n^3},\ 1 \leq i \leq n \\ \mathcal{M}_h = h_{n^3} \\ \mathcal{M}_y = y_{n^3} \\ \mathcal{M}_{yes} = yes \\ \mathcal{M}_{no} = w_{n^3+6}\, no \\ \mathcal{M}_{out} = x \end{cases}$$

- The set $\mathcal{R}$ consists of the following rules:

(1) $(no\,,\, w_r\,/\,w_{r-1}\,,\, 0)$, for $2 \leq r \leq n^3 + 6$.

(2) $(no\,,\, w_1\,/\,w\,,\, 0)$.

(3) $[\,(i,j)_k\,]_{in} \rightarrow [\,(i,j)'_k\,]_{in}\ [\,\#\,]_{in}$, for $1 \leq i, j, k \leq n$.

(4) $[\,(i,j)''_{k,r}\,]_{e_{i,j,k}} \rightarrow [\,(i,j)''_{k,r-1}\,]_{e_{i,j,k}}\ [\,(i,j)''_{k,r-1}\,]_{e_{i,j,k}}$,
   for $1 \leq i, j, k \leq n$ and $2 \leq r \leq n^3$.

(5) $[\,(i,j)''_{k,1}\,]_{e_{i,j,k}} \rightarrow [\,(i,j)''_k\,]_{e_{i,j,k}}\ [\,(i,j)''_k\,]_{e_{i,j,k}}$, for $1 \leq i, j, k \leq n$.

(6) $[\,c_r\,]_{c_i} \rightarrow [\,c_{r-1}\,]_{c_i}\ [\,c_{r-1}\,]_{c_i}$, for $1 \leq i \leq n \wedge 1 \leq r \leq n^3$.

(7) $[\,y_r\,]_y \rightarrow [\,y_{r-1}\,]_y\ [\,y_{r-1}\,]_y$, for $1 \leq r \leq n^3$.

(8) $[\,h_r\,]_h \rightarrow [\,h_{r-1}\,]_h\ [\,a_{r-1}\,]_h$, for $1 \leq r \leq n^3$.

(9) $(in\,,\, (i,j)'_k\,/\,(i,j)''_k\,,\, e_{i,j,k})$, for $1 \leq i, j, k \leq n$.

(10) $(in\,,\, c\,/\,c'\,,\, c_i)$, for $1 \leq i \leq n$.

(11) $(in\,,\, y\,/\,y'\,,\, y)$.

(12) $(in\,,\, h\,/\,h'\,,\, h)$.

(13) $(in, (i,j)''_k (i,j')''_{k'} / \lambda, 0)$, for $1 \le i, j, j', k, k' \le n$.

(14) $(in, (i,j)''_k (i',j)''_{k'} / \lambda, 0)$, for $1 \le i, i', j, k, k' \le n$.

(15) $(in, (i,j)''_k (i',j')''_{k+1} / \lambda, 0)$, for $1 \le i, i', j, j', k \le n$, and $j \ne i'$.

(16) $(in, (i,j)''_k (i',j')''_k / \lambda, 0)$, for $1 \le i, i', j, j', k \le n$.

(17) $(in, c' / c'', 0)$.

(18) $(in, y' / y'', 0)$.

(19) $(in, h' / h'', 0)$.

(20) $(in, (i,j)''_k c'' / \lambda, 0)$ for $1 \le i, j, k \le n$.

(21) $(in, y'' / y''', 0)$.

(22) $(in, h'' / h''', 0)$.

(23) $(in, c'' h''' / \lambda, 0)$.

(24) $(in, y''' / y'''', 0)$.

(25) $(in, h''' y'''' / \lambda, yes)$.

(26) $(yes, y'''' yes / \lambda, out)$.

(27) $(out, x\, yes / \lambda, 0)$.

(28) $(no, w\, no / \lambda, out)$.

(29) $(out, x\, no / \lambda, 0)$.

- The input cell is $i_{in} = in$.
- The output region is the environment, $i_{out} = 0$.

Let us notice that $|\Gamma| = 3n^4 + 7n^3 + 23$, $|\mathcal{E}| = n^3 + 12$ and the degree of $\Pi(n)$ is $q = n^3 + n + 6$. Let Lab_n denote the set of labels of cells in $\Pi(n)$. Besides, the execution-time is $n^3 + 7$ if the answer is affirmative and it is $n^3 + 8$ if the answer is negative. We thus consider $p(n) = n^3 + 8$ as the polynomial function needed for the construction of $\Pi'(n)$, according to Definition 6.2 in [15].

Now, for each $n \in \mathbb{N}$, let us construct, using $\Pi(n)$ as a starting point, a tissue P system from $\widehat{\mathbf{TDC}}(2)$ of degree $q_1 = 1 + (n^3 + n + 6) \cdot (n^3 + 10) + (n^3 + 12)$,

$$\Pi'(n) = (\Gamma', \Sigma', \mathcal{E}', \mathcal{M}'_0, \mathcal{M}'_1, \ldots, \mathcal{M}'_{q_1-1}, \mathcal{R}', i'_{in}, i'_{out})$$

defined as follows:

- $\Gamma' = \Gamma \cup \{\alpha_j \mid 0 \le j \le n^3 + 7\}$.
- $\Sigma' = \Sigma$ and $\mathcal{E}' = \emptyset$.
- Each one of the q cells of $\Pi(n)$ provides a cell of $\Pi'(n)$ with the same label. In addition, $\Pi'(n)$ has:
  - For each one of the q cells of $\Pi(n)$, $n^3 + 9$ new cells, labelled by $(i,0), \ldots, (i, n^3+8)$, respectively, where i stands for the original label of the cell in $\Pi(n)$.
  - A distinguished cell labelled by 0.
  - A new cell, labelled by l_b, for each $b \in \mathcal{E}$.
- $\mathcal{M}'_{l_b} = \{\alpha_0\}$, for each $b \in \mathcal{E}$, $\mathcal{M}'_{(i,0)} = \mathcal{M}_i$, for each $i \in Lab_n$, and every other multiset of $\Pi'(n)$ is initially empty.

- $\mathcal{R}' = \mathcal{R} \cup \{[\alpha_j]_{l_b} \to [\alpha_{j+1}]_{l_b}\ [\alpha_{j+1}]_{l_b} \mid b \in \mathcal{E} \wedge 0 \le j \le n^3 + 6\}$
  $\cup \{[\alpha_{n^3+7}]_{l_b} \to [b]_{l_b}\ [b]_{l_b} \mid b \in \mathcal{E}\}$
  $\cup \{(l_b,\ b/\lambda\ ,0) \mid b \in \mathcal{E}\}$
  $\cup \{((i,j),\ a/\lambda\ ,(i,j+1)) \mid a \in \Gamma \wedge i \in Lab_n \wedge 0 \le j \le n^3 + 7\}$
  $\cup \{((i,n^3+8),\ a/\lambda\ ,i) \mid a \in \Gamma \wedge i \in Lab_n\}$
- $i'_{in} = (i_{in},0)$, and $i'_{out} = 0$.

Let us notice that $\Pi'(n)$ can be considered as an *extension* of $\Pi(n)$ *without environment*, in the following sense:

- $\star$ $\Gamma \subseteq \Gamma', \Sigma \subseteq \Sigma'$ and $\mathcal{E}' = \emptyset$.
- $\star$ Each cell in $\Pi(n)$ is also a cell in $\Pi'(n)$.
- $\star$ There is a distinguished cell in $\Pi'(n)$ labelled by 0 which plays the role of environment of $\Pi(n)$.
- $\star$ $\mathcal{R} \subseteq \mathcal{R}'$, and now 0 is the label of a "normal cell" in $\Pi'(n)$.

Note also that this construction does not affect the maximum length of the communication rules, since the communication rules in $\mathcal{R}' \setminus \mathcal{R}$ are of type symport and length 1.

An Overview of the Computations

Let $G = (V, E)$, with $V = \{1, \dots, n\}$ and $E = \{(u_1, v_1), \dots, (u_p, v_p)\}$, be an arbitrary instance of the HAM-CYCLE problem.

The *size* mapping on the set of instances is defined as $s(G) = n$, and the encoding of the instance is the multiset

$$cod(G) = \{(u_i, v_i)_k \mid 1 \le i \le p \wedge 1 \le k \le n \wedge (u_i, v_i) \in E\}$$

Each object $(u_i, v_i)_k$ can be interpreted as considering arc (u_i, v_i) being "placed" in the "k-th position" in a sequence of n arcs that could be a Hamiltonian cycle.

This way of encoding arcs by means of objects is one of the keys to understand the design of the solution. A brute force approach is followed, generating all possible combinations by division and subsequently checking for each subset of n objects from $cod(G)$ whether it represents a Hamiltonian cycle or not.

Let us now informally describe how system $\Pi'(s(G))$ with input multiset $cod(G)$, denoted by $\Pi'(s(G)) + cod(G)$, works, in order to process the instance G of the HAM-CYCLE problem.

At the initial configuration of $\Pi'(s(G)) + cod(G)$ we have the following:

- Cell labelled by 0 is empty.
- For each $i \in Lab_n$, the contents of cell i is empty and the contents of cell $(i,0)$ is $\mathcal{M}_i$ (except for the case $i = i_{in}$, where $\mathcal{M}'_{(in,0)} = \mathcal{M}_{in} + cod(G)$).
- For each i, j ($i \in Lab_n$ and $1 \le j \le n^3 + 8$), the contents of cell (i,j) is empty.
- For each $b \in \mathcal{E}$, cell labelled by l_b contains only object α_0.

It is easy to check that the rules of a system $\Pi(n)$ of the family are recursively defined from n and the amount of resources needed to build an element of the family is of a polynomial order in n. Therefore, there exists a deterministic Turing machine that builds the system $\Pi(n)$ in time polynomial with respect to n. The same holds for $\Pi'(n)$, since only a polynomial number of cells, objects and rules have been added to the definition.

At the first $n^3 + 9$ steps of any computation $\mathcal{C}'$ of $\Pi'(n)$, only the following rules can be applied:

- $\{[\alpha_j]_{l_b} \to [\alpha_{j+1}]_{l_b} \ [\alpha_{j+1}]_{l_b} \mid b \in \mathcal{E} \ \wedge \ 0 \le j \le n^3 + 6\}$
- $\{[\alpha_{n^3+7}]_{l_b} \to [b]_{l_b} \ [b]_{l_b} \mid b \in \mathcal{E}\}$
- $\{(l_b, \ b/\lambda , 0) \mid b \in \mathcal{E}\}$
- $\{((i,j), \ a/\lambda , (i,j+1)) \mid a \in \Gamma \ \wedge \ i \in Lab_n \ \wedge \ 0 \le j \le n^3 + 7\}$
- $\{((i, n^3 + 8), \ a/\lambda , i) \mid a \in \Gamma \ \wedge \ i \in Lab_n\}$

The purpose of the division rules is to generate an exponential amount of copies of each element of the environment alphabet. After the division process is completed, all copies of these objects are transferred to cell 0 by symport rules. In the meantime, the rest of the objects initially present in the system are "delayed", by being forced to travel through a sequence of auxiliary cells. More precisely, the initial multiset of cell i starts from cell $(i, 0)$, then goes through every intermediate cell (i, j) until reaching cell $(i, n^3 + 8)$. After that, the multiset can finally be transferred to cell i.

Besides, the above mentioned rules are applied in a deterministic manner. Then, the configuration $\mathcal{C}'_{n^3+9}$ of any computation $\mathcal{C}'$ of $\Pi'(s(G)) + cod(G)$ is characterized by the following:

(1) The contents of cell 0 is $b_1^{2^{n^3+8}} \dots b_\alpha^{2^{n^3+8}}$, where $\mathcal{E} = \{b_1, \dots, b_\alpha\}$.
(2) For each $i \in Lab_n$, the contents of cell i is $\mathcal{M}_i$ (except for the case $i = i_{in}$, that contains $\mathcal{M}_{in} + cod(G)$).
(3) For i, j ($i \in Lab_n$ and $0 \le j \le n^3 + 8$) the contents of cell (i, j) is empty.
(4) For each $b \in \mathcal{E}$, there exist 2^{n^3+8} cells labelled by l_b whose content is empty.

Basically, this is the "initial" configuration of the system $\Pi(s(G)) + cod(G)$, with a standard cell labelled by 0 that will play the role of the environment, and with a large number of spare empty cells. Therefore, from step $n^3 + 9$ any computation of $\Pi'(s(G)) + cod(G)$ "reproduces" a computation of the system $\Pi(s(G)) + cod(G)$ with a delay.

Bearing in mind that the family $\mathbf{\Pi} = \{\Pi(n) \mid n \in \mathbb{N}\}$ solves HAM-CYCLE problem in polynomial time, we deduce that the family $\mathbf{\Pi'} = \{\Pi'(n) \mid n \in \mathbb{N}\}$ also solves HAM-CYCLE problem in polynomial time. Hence, we have the following result:

Theorem 1. HAM-CYCLE $\in \mathbf{PMC}_{\widehat{TDC}(2)}$.

That is, a uniform solution working in polynomial time has been found for an **NP**–complete problem using an empty environment alphabet. Hence, the environment does not play a relevant role in recognizer tissue P systems with cell division with respect to the efficiency of these models.

3.2   Non-efficiency of Tissue P Systems with Cell Separation and without Environment

In [6] it has been proved that only tractable problems can be efficiently solved by using tissue P systems with cell separation where there is no environment having infinitely many copies of some objects. Thus, tissue P systems with cell separation and without environment are non-efficient in the sense that they are not capable to solve **NP**–complete problems in polynomial time, according to Definition 5, assuming that $\mathbf{P} \neq \mathbf{NP}$.

Theorem 2. *For each* $k \in \mathbb{N}, k \geq 1$ *we have* $\mathbf{P} = \mathbf{PMC}_{\widehat{\mathrm{TSC}}(k)}$.

Hence, the environment plays a relevant role in recognizer tissue P systems with cell separation with respect to the efficiency of these models. That is, by using the environment, **NP**–complete problems can be solved in polynomial time, but this is not possible when the initial environment is empty.

Another interesting consequence of the previous result is the following. In the framework of recognizer tissue P systems without environment, the kind of rules provides a frontier for the efficiency, that is, passing from division rules to separation rules amounts to passing from efficiency to non-efficiency, assuming that $\mathbf{P} \neq \mathbf{NP}$.

4   Conclusions

In this paper we have discussed how allowing an infinite supply of objects in the environment determines (or not) that the model of tissue P systems considered will be efficient or not.

More precisely, we have highlighted the key role that the environment plays in the case of tissue P systems with cell separation. It does actually constitute a borderline between efficiency and non-efficiency for the classes $\mathbf{TSC}(k)$ and $\widehat{\mathbf{TSC}}(k)$, for every $k \geq 3$. However, it is important to note that cooperation (of at least 3 objects) in the communication rules is another important ingredient, since we cannot get efficient solutions with tissue P systems with cell separation and communication rules of length bounded by 2, irrespectively of using the environment or not [10].

On the other hand, the environment has been shown to be an irrelevant ingredient in the case of tissue P systems with cell division. Indeed, a uniform polynomial solution has been described for HAM-CYCLE using a family of tissue P systems with cell division and without environment from $\widehat{\mathbf{TDC}}(2)$. Note that the borderline of efficiency concerning the length of communication rules remains the same as what was already known when the environment is exploited: symport of length 1 versus cooperation of 2 objects.

Acknowledgements. The work was supported by TIN2012-37434 Project of the Ministerio de Ciencia e Innovación of Spain and Project of Excellence with *Investigador de Reconocida Valía*, from Junta de Andalucía, grant P08 – TIC 04200, both cofinanced by FEDER funds.

References

1. Alhazov, A., Ishdorj, T.O.: Membrane operations in P systems with active membranes. In: Păun, G., et al. (eds.) Proceedings of the Second Brainstorming Week on Membrane Computing, Seville, Spain, February 2-7, Technical Report 01/2004, University of Seville, pp. 37-44 (2004)
2. Díaz-Pernil, D., Gutiérrez-Naranjo, M.A., Pérez-Jiménez, M.J., Riscos-Núñez, A., Romero–Campero, F.J.: Computational efficiency of cellular division in tissue-like P systems. Romanian Journal of Information Science and Technology 11(3), 229–241 (2008)
3. Garey, M.R., Johnson, D.S.: Computers and Intractability A Guide to the Theory of NP-Completeness. W.H. Freeman and Company (1979)
4. Gutiérrez–Escudero, R., Pérez–Jiménez, M.J., Rius–Font, M.: Characterizing tractability by tissue-like P systems. In: Păun, G., Pérez-Jiménez, M.J., Riscos-Núñez, A., Rozenberg, G., Salomaa, A. (eds.) WMC 2009. LNCS, vol. 5957, pp. 289–300. Springer, Heidelberg (2010)
5. Ito, M., Martín Vide, C., Păun, G.: A characterization of Parikh sets of ET0L laguages in terms of P systems. In: Ito, M., Păun, G., Yu, S. (eds.) Words, Semigroups and Transducers, pp. 239–254. World Scientific, Singapore (2001)
6. Macías-Ramos, L.F., Pérez-Jiménez, M.J., Riscos-Núñez, A., Rius-Font, M., Valencia-Cabrera, L.: The efficiency of tissue P systems with cell separation relies on the environment. In: Csuhaj-Varjú, E., Gheorghe, M., Rozenberg, G., Salomaa, A., Vaszil, G. (eds.) CMC 2012. LNCS, vol. 7762, pp. 243–256. Springer, Heidelberg (2013)
7. Martín-Vide, C., Pazos, J., Păun, G., Rodríguez-Patón, A.: A New Class of Symbolic Abstract Neural Nets: Tissue P Systems. In: Ibarra, O.H., Zhang, L. (eds.) COCOON 2002. LNCS, vol. 2387, pp. 290–299. Springer, Heidelberg (2002)
8. Pan, L., Ishdorj, T.-O.: P systems with active membranes and separation rules. Journal of Universal Computer Science 10(5), 630–649 (2004)
9. Pan, L., Pérez-Jiménez, M.J.: Computational complexity of tissue–like P systems. Journal of Complexity 26(3), 296–315 (2010)
10. Pan, L., Pérez-Jiménez, M.J., Riscos-Núñez, A., Rius-Font, M.: New frontiers of the efficiency in tissue P systems. In: Pan, L., Păun, G., Song, T. (eds.) Preproceedings of Asian Conference on Membrane Computing, October 15-18, pp. 61–73. Huazhong University of Science and Technology, Wuhan (2012)
11. Păun, A., Păun, G.: The power of communication: P systems with symport/antiport. New Generation Computing 20(3), 295–305 (2002)
12. Păun, G.: Attacking **NP**-complete problems. In: Antoniou, I., Calude, C., Dinneen, M.J. (eds.) Unconventional Models of Computation, UMC'2K, pp. 94–115. Springer (2000)
13. Păun, G.: Membrane Computing. An Introduction. Springer, Berlin (2002)
14. Păun, G., Pérez-Jiménez, M.J., Riscos-Núñez, A.: Tissue P systems with cell division. Int. J. of Computers, Communications and Control 3(3), 295–303 (2008)
15. Pérez-Jiménez, M.J., Riscos-Núñez, A., Rius-Font, M., Romero-Campero, F.J.: The role of the environment in tissue P systems with cell division. In: García-Quismondo, M., et al. (eds.) Proceedings of the Tenth Brainstorming Week on Membrane Computing, Seville, Spain, January 30-February 3, Report RGNC 02/2012, Fénix Editora, vol. II, pp. 89–104 (2012); A revised and improved version can be found in: Pérez-Jiménez, M.J., Riscos-Núñez, A., Rius-Font, M., Romero-Campero, F.J.: A polynomial alternative to unbounded environment for tissue P systems with cell division. Int. J. Comput. Math. 90(4), 760–775 (2013)

16. Pérez-Jiménez, M.J., Romero-Jiménez, A., Sancho-Caparrini, F.: Complexity classes in models of cellular computing with membranes. Natural Computing 2(3), 265–285 (2003)
17. Pérez-Jiménez, M.J., Romero-Jiménez, A., Sancho-Caparrini, F.: A polynomial complexity class in P systems using membrane division. Journal of Automata, Languages and Combinatorics 11(4), 423–434 (2006)
18. Pérez-Jiménez, M.J., Sosík, P.: Improving the efficiency of tissue P systems with cell separation. In: García-Quismondo, M., et al. (eds.) Proceedings of the Tenth Brainstorming Week on Membrane Computing, Seville, Spain, January 30-February 3, Report RGNC 02/2012, Fénix Editora, vol. II, pp. 105–140 (2012)
19. Porreca, A.E., Murphy, N., Pérez-Jiménez, M.J.: An optimal frontier of the efficiency of tissue P systems with cell division. In: García-Quismondo, M., et al. (eds.) Proceedings of the Tenth Brainstorming Week on Membrane Computing, Seville, Spain, January 30-February 3, Report RGNC 02/2012, Fénix Editora, vol. II, pp. 141–166 (2012)

Author Index